The War Lawyers

The War Lawyers

The United States, Israel, and Juridical Warfare

CRAIG JONES

OXFORD
UNIVERSITY PRESS

OXFORD
UNIVERSITY PRESS

Great Clarendon Street, Oxford, OX2 6DP,
United Kingdom

Oxford University Press is a department of the University of Oxford.
It furthers the University's objective of excellence in research, scholarship,
and education by publishing worldwide. Oxford is a registered trade mark of
Oxford University Press in the UK and in certain other countries

First Edition published in 2020

Impression: 5

Published in the United States of America by Oxford University Press
198 Madison Avenue, New York, NY 10016, United States of America

British Library Cataloguing in Publication Data
Data available

Library of Congress Control Number: 2020937006

ISBN 978–0–19–884292–7

Printed and bound by
CPI Group (UK) Ltd, Croydon, CR0 4YY

For mum and dad

Praise

The War Lawyers makes a major contribution to understanding the role lawyers play in the 'legalization' of military operations, particularly aerial bombing in asymmetric wars. Craig Jones literally writes the book on 'operational law' and he does so by drawing on extensive ethnographic research among the US and Israeli lawyers who have contributed to the reshaping of war itself as a juridical project. This book should be on the reading list of every warmaker, every anti-war critic, and every scholar of violence.

Lisa Hajjar, Professor of Sociology at the University of California —Santa Barbara, author of *Courting Conflict and Torture: A Sociology of Violence*

Craig Jones's *The War Lawyers* is an absolutely essential book that goes right to the heart of the contemporary reality of war. How the American military legalized itself after its Vietnam catastrophe, out of a combination of ethics and optics, has marked our time deeply, along with the parallels and relationship America established with Israeli practices (especially in target selection under law). No study has illuminated these developments more carefully and insightfully—or held out an alternative to our brutal and legalized present.

Samuel Moyn, Yale University

This deeply researched and absorbing book cuts through tired bromides about and unthinking adulation of military law, to show how deeply entangled with the very process of war-making military lawyers are. War Lawyers trenchantly reveals that law, instead of constraining the violence of war, often facilitates and alibis it.

Laleh Khalili, Professor of international politics at Queen Mary University of London and author of *Time in the Shadows: Confinement in Counterinsurgencies*

This magnificent book is the first to comprehensively analyze what war lawyers do in war to justify, defend, or reject killing, injury and destruction on the battlefield today. Ethnographically rich, theoretically sophisticated, and historically detailed, *The War Lawyers* illuminates the role of U.S. military lawyers in Iraq and Afghanistan and Israeli lawyers in Gaza in conceptualizing and enabling aerial targeting in war. Jones brilliantly demonstrates how war lawyers are active participants in creating the definition, implementation, and assessment of violence in war, and how they shape the law which both governs and facilitates it. As a treatise on war, law, and suffering this book is a deeply inspiring ethical call to reimagine collective responsibility and responsiveness to the violence of war.

Helen M. Kinsella, Associate Professor of Political Science at University of Minnesota and author of *The Image Before the Weapon: A Critical History of the Distinction between Combatants and Civilians*

We tend to think of international humanitarian law as helping to limit violence during war. In this gripping and counterintuitive book, Craig Jones traces the increasing role military lawyers have played in wars over the past fifty years, particularly in aerial strikes where lawyers have become part of the 'kill chain'. He shows how those trained in the laws of armed conflict are actively involved in shaping military objectives and creating the rules of engagement, and how they use technical and procedural legality to eclipse ethical considerations. Jones reveals how legal experts can use the law as a force multiplier, providing commanders justification to unleash lethal violence in instances where civilians are at risk of being killed. *The War Lawyers* is a great achievement, an incredibly insightful book.

Neve Gordon, Professor of International Law at Queen Mary University of London and co-author of *Human Shields: A History of People in the Line of Fire*

The War Lawyers is a remarkably interesting book. It offers a look at an underappreciated aspect of war making, namely the work that lawyers do in guiding lethal decision making. Craig Jones provides a lucid and readable account of the way lawyers use the indeterminacy of the laws of war to make law themselves. War without law is unimaginable. Jones helps us see that war without lawyers is just as unimaginable. I know of no other book that so intelligently illuminates law's complex interconnections with violence.

Austin Sarat, Associate Provost and Associate Dean of the Faculty, William Nelson Cromwell Professor Jurisprudence & Political Science Amherst College

Contents

List of Figures

the Malik invasion. From [illegible] Kunduz [illegible] Afghanistan [illegible] attacked by the US military on 3 October 2015.

Source: Médecins [illegible] Frontières, reproduced with permission.

[illegible]

[illegible] Engineering [illegible] DRC [illegible] Washington [illegible]

[illegible] 2 June 2020.

(b) [illegible] Air [illegible] the [illegible]

Source: United States [illegible]

[illegible]

[illegible] August [illegible] 2019 [illegible]

List of Abbreviations

AAR	After Action Report
AFCENT	Air Force Central Command
ANSF	Afghan National Security Forces
AOC	Air Operations Center
ATO	Air Tasking Order
BAE	British Aerospace Engineering
BDA	Battle Damage Assessment
CAAT	Campaign Against Arms Trade
CAOC	Combined Air Operations Centre
CAS	Close Air Support
CCARs	Credibility Assessment Reports
CDE	Collateral Damage Estimate
CDEM	Collateral Damage Estimation Methodology
CEP	Circular Error Probable
CENTAF	Central Command Air Force
CENTCOM	Central Command
CFACC	Combined Forces Air Component Commander
CIA	Central Intelligence Agency
CIAC	Coalition Incident Assessment Committee
CIVCAS	Civilian Casualties
CJSOAC	Combined Joint Special Operations Air Component
CJTF	Combined Joint Task Force
CLAMO	Center for Law and Military Operations
COAC	Combined Air Operations Center
CONUS	Continental United States
CPD	Combat Plans Division
CSIS	Center for Strategic and International Studies
CSOTF	Combined Special Operations Task Force
DOD	Department of Defense
DPH	Direct Participation in Hostilities
EKIA	Enemy Killed In Action
EU	European Union
FMV	Full Motion Video
FOB	Forward Operating Base
GATT	General Agreements on Tariff and Trade
GPW	Third Geneva Convention of 1949 Relative to the Treatment of Prisoners of War

HVIs	High-Value Individuals
ICC	International Criminal Court
ICRC	International Committee of the Red Cross
ICTY	International Criminal Tribunal for the Former Yugoslavia
ICTR	International Criminal Tribunal for Rwanda
IDF	Israel Defense Force
IED	Improvised Explosive Device
ICL	International Criminal Law
IHL	International Humanitarian Law
IHRL	International Human Rights Law
IMFA	Israel Ministry of Foreign Affairs
ISAF	International Security Assistance Force
ISC	Israel Supreme Court
ISIS	Islamic State
ISR	Intelligence, Surveillance and Reconnaissance
JAGs	Judge advocates
JAOP	Joint Air Operations Plan
JCCS	Joint Civilian Casualty Study
JCS	Joint Chiefs of Staff
JFACC	Joint Forces Air Component Command
JIPTL	Joint Integrated Prioritized Targeting List
JPEL	Joint Prioritized Effects List
JSOTF	Joint Special Operations Task Force
JTAC	Joint Terminal Attack Controller
JTCB	Joint Targeting Coordination Board
LOAC	Laws of Armed Conflict
MAAG	Military Assistance Advisory Group
MACV	Military Assistance Command, Vietnam
MAG	Military Advocate General Corps
MAM	military aged male
MISREPS	Mission Reports
MNF-I	Multi National Force-Iraq
MSF	Médicines Sans Frontièrs
NATO	North Atlantic Treaty Organization
NCV	Non-Combatant cut-off Value
MOD	Ministry of Defence
MOOTW	Military Operation Other Than War
NGO	Non-Governmental Organization
NLF/VC	National Liberation Front/Viet Cong
NSL	No-Strike List
OEF	Operation Enduring Freedom
OIF	Operation Iraqi Freedom
OIR	Operation Inherent Resolve

OLC	Office of Legal Council
OPLAW	Operational Law
PCATI	Public Committee Against Torture in Israel
PID	Positive Identification (of the target)
PGMs	Precision-Guided Munitions
POL	Pattern of Life
POW	Prisoners of War
ROE	Rules of Engagement
RTL	Restricted Target List
SAM	Surface-to-Air-Missile
SOFA	Status of Forces Agreements
SROE	Standing Rules of Engagement
STAR	Sensitive Target Approval and Review Process
TACCS	Tactical Air Control Center
TST	Time-Sensitive Targeting
UAV	Unmanned Aerial Vehicle
UN	United Nations
UNAMA	United Nations Assistance Mission to Afghanistan
UNICEF	United Nations Children's Fund
USMJ	Uniform Code of Military Justice
USAF	United States Air Force
USARV	United States Army Republic of Vietnam
USSOUTHCOM	United States Southern Command
VBIED	Vehicle-Borne Improvised Explosive Device
VCI	Viet Cong infrastructure
WTO	World Trade Organization

Acknowledgements

From initial research to publication, this book took the best part of a decade to complete. Without the extraordinary support of a wide range of people and institutions, *The War Lawyers* would have been simply impossible. I owe great thanks to so many.

The Department of Geography at The University of British Columbia (UBC) provided a welcoming environment and a supportive intellectual home for thinking and writing about a topic that in many ways could not be further from the tranquil life I came to know in Vancouver. First and foremost I want to thank Derek Gregory, my dear friend and supervisor, who introduced me to later modern war and its many juridical spaces and who taught me so much about military violence. His guidance and support over the last decade have been tremendous sources of inspiration for this work and I will remain ever-grateful for our many conversations at Cardero's and far beyond. I am extremely grateful to the wonderful and supportive community in the Department of Geography and to all those at UBC who taught and helped me in so many ways in the early stages of this project, including Jim Glassman, Trevor Barnes, Geraldine Pratt, Juanita Sundberg, Daniel Hiebert, Jamie Peck, Merje Kuus, Marwan Hassan, Phillipe LeBillon, and Gaston Gordillo. I owe special thanks to James Stewart and Michael Smith for their immense intellectual generosity and time over many years. Jacquie Brinkman provided invaluable feedback and encouraging support when they were needed most.

The School of Geography, Politics and Sociology at Newcastle University has supported this project ever since I first arrived in Newcastle. The Department and the School have been a sanctuary for thinking and writing and I count myself extremely lucky to be part of such a supportive and intellectually engaging group. Special thanks to Stephen Graham, who read the whole manuscript and pushed me to think more carefully about infrastructural violence and urban warfare, who also showed me the roads of Northumberland on much needed breaks between writing, and who became a dear friend and neighbour. Rachel Woodward has been an incredible mentor and guided me through the first years on the job, providing encouragement, support, and laughs on the way. Nick Megoran gave me the opportunity to present my ideas to wide and various activist audiences and has shown great interest in my work—his energy is contagious and I hope *The War Lawyers* lives up to his vision for a less violent world. Stuart Dawley, Anoop Nayak, Matt Benwell, Olivia Mason, Alison Williams, Caleb Johnson, Al James, Alex Huges, and Michael Richardson, especially, have all been such supportive and welcoming colleagues while I worked to complete this book and I appreciate their thoughts and friendships greatly.

Several people have read chapters and have engaged closely with the various iterations of this project. Their feedback and insights helped greatly to clarify my arguments and writing and encouraged me to push myself more than I otherwise would have been able. Andrew Robertson read the manuscript from start to finish more than once and provided invaluable feedback on countless drafts; his careful editorial hand helped improve the manuscript in innumerable ways and I am ever grateful for his outstanding input and commentary. Helen M. Kinsella read several chapters and provided incisive feedback that helped me to develop my conceptual framework, and she did so in especially difficult times; she is a brilliant critical thinker and her scholarship on the laws of war has been absolutely foundational to my thinking. Jim Glassman, Trevor Barnes, James Stewart, Michael Byers, Emily Gilbert, Neve Gordon, Brian Cuddy, Mark Griffiths, John Morrissey, Lisa Hajjar, Chris Jones, Caitrin Innis, Olivia Mason, Mike Thomason, Jessi Lehman, and Carrie Rosenthal all read draft chapters and provided crucial insights that, in one way or another, made their way into this text.

I am very grateful to the war lawyers and military operators who agreed to be interviewed for this work, many of whom requested not to be named. A special thanks to Nicholas Lancaster and the Center for Law and Military Operations (CLAMO) for hosting me and giving me access to your soldiers and lawyers.

I owe thanks to the many individuals and organizations who answered my questions, met with me and provided rich perspectives on complex and contentious issues: Bassim Razzo, Jennifer Gibson at Reprieve, Chris Cole at Drone Wars UK, Chris Woods at Airwars, Emily Schaeffer and Michael Sfard, Yotam Feldman, Uri Blau, Noura Erekat, Eyal Benvenisti, Amichai Cohen, William Boothby, Philip Alston, Ron Smith, Charles Garraway, Ian Henderson, Duncan Blake, Brian Cavanaugh, Yuval Shany, Orna Ben-Naftali, Steven Myrow, Laura Dickenson, and many more—thank you.

The research for this book was generously supported by a UBC Four-Year Fellowship and a Harry Frank Guggenheim Foundation Dissertation Fellowship. These provided much needed support and financial assistance and gave me the most precious of things: time and space to research, think, and write.

I am very grateful to the team at Oxford University Press for helping me navigate through the publishing process. I thank John Louth for initially reaching out to me, and his interest in publishing this work. I am also grateful to my patient editors Merel Alstein and Jordan Burke. Fiona Tatham provided diligent copy-editing and encouraging words. I would also like to thank the four anonymous reviewers and OUP delegates who provided valuable feedback on the initial draft.

Finally, and above all, my love and gratitude go to Caitrin and my family for their enduring love and support.

Any errors and mistakes are, of course, my own.

Preface: Lawyers in the War Room

> [A]ny theory of law must locate violence at the center of its concerns. It must examine law's devices for transforming and concealing its violence, for covering its tracks, and for turning lifeless words into bloody acts of violence.
>
> Austin Sarat and Thomas Kearns, The Fate of Law.[1]

Permission to Kill

It is 2003 and a meeting is taking place inside the Kirya, the Israeli military's main headquarters in central Tel Aviv. A 'terrorist group' in Gaza has reportedly kidnapped an undercover Palestinian agent who is working for the Israeli military. He is currently being interrogated and tortured inside a building in Gaza City. The Israeli military recognizes the dangerousness of the situation and the risk of the agent relinquishing classified material to the enemy. Those present at the meeting in the Kirya have received intelligence suggesting that the group is planning to kill him in about twenty minutes.[2] Assembled around the table are senior personnel who make up the Israeli military's 'focused prevention team';[3] they are discussing whether a missile should be used against the target, effectively ending the interrogation. But they have come up against an operational problem. The mathematical analysis of the missile trajectory and blast radius shows that no matter how they fire, the neighbouring apartment is likely to be 80 per cent destroyed in the explosion.[4] Unable to decide

[1] Austin Sarat and Thomas Kearns, 'A Journey Through Forgetting: Toward a Jurisprudence of Violence', in *The Fate of Law*, ed. Austin Sarat and Thomas Kearns, *The Amherst Series in Law, Jurisprudence, and Social Thought* (Ann Arbor, MI: University of Michigan Press, 1991), 212–13.

[2] What kind of intelligence, or how reliable, was not discussed with the author.

[3] סיכול ממוקד (*sikul memukad*) translates as 'focused prevention' or 'focused foiling'. It is an official euphemism for the policy and practice of targeted killing.

[4] Like the United States and other technologically advanced militaries, the Israeli military routinely conducts collateral damage assessments of potential targets *where time permits*. According to the Israel Ministry of Foreign Affairs: 'The IDF devotes significant resources to assessing and minimising the collateral damage that is expected as a direct or indirect result of attacks': Israel Ministry of Foreign Affairs, 'The 2014 Gaza Conflict: Factual and Legal Aspects' (Tel Aviv: Israel Ministry of Foreign Affairs, May

how to proceed—to fire the missile or not—they send an aide upstairs to request the assistance of Colonel Daniel Reisner.[5]

From 1995 to 2004 Colonel Daniel Reisner held the prestigious position of Head of the International Law Department of the Israeli military. When I meet the Colonel in 2013 he is working for a large private legal firm in Tel Aviv. Colonel Reisner exudes a certain charisma and likes to tell stories about himself and his deft legal opinions. He seems very comfortable when it comes to talking about the life and death decisions he has been involved in. I have read almost all there is to read about (and by) Reisner in preparation for my interview with him, and some of it is highly critical. At one extreme he and his legal department are accused of committing war crimes against Palestinians, an accusation that has fuelled claims that they should be tried in the International Criminal Court (ICC).[6] At the other extreme, he is celebrated as the legal conscience of the Israeli military, the man who created a new legal paradigm to deal with an especially turbulent time in the occupation of Palestine, the Second Intifada.[7]

I am here, sitting on a comfortable leather chair in this rather plush meeting room of a corporate legal office several stories high, to ask Reisner about his involvement in making and interpreting laws that both protect and kill, and the seriousness of the subject makes me slightly queasy (the important question, of course, is *who* do they protect and *who* do they kill?). As though able to sense my unease, Reisner asks his assistant to make me a cappuccino. He no longer drinks coffee because the caffeine is not good for his weak heart; he recently had a heart attack. When my drink arrives Reisner smiles and, relaxing back into his chair, begins his story: 'This will take a long time.' We are just a few blocks away from the events in the Kirya that Reisner recounts.

2015), 183, http://mfa.gov.il/ProtectiveEdge/Pages/default.aspx, accessed 15 September 2016. The same document also concedes, 'collateral damage is often unavoidable [. . .]' (182).

[5] This section draws on an interview with Colonel Reisner who retired from active military service in 2004 but continues to be involved in military initiatives in other capacities. It reports Reisner's re-telling of a targeting operation he was involved in in 2003.

[6] Yotam Feldman and Uri Blau, 'Consent and Advise', *Haaretz.Com*, 29 January 2009, http://www.haaretz.com/cmlink/consent-and-advise-1.269127, accessed 26 May 2013; Maryam Monalisa Gharavi and Anat Matar, 'Israeli Officer Promotes War Crimes at Harvard', *The Electronic Intifada*, 22 July 2009, https://electronicintifada.net/content/israeli-officer-promotes-war-crimes-harvard/8357, accessed 15 September 2016. Israel does not recognize the jurisdiction of the ICC.

[7] Israel Ministry of Foreign Affairs, 'Press Briefing by Colonel Daniel Reisner', 15 November 2000, https://mfa.gov.il/MFA/PressRoom/2000/Pages/Press%20Briefing%20by%20Colonel%20Daniel%20Reisner-%20Head%20of.aspx, accessed 12 June 2020. Intifada is an Arabic word derived from the Arabic term *nafada*, meaning to 'shake off', and the year 2000 marked the birth of the second major popular uprising against the colonial occupation of Palestine (the First Intifada took place between 1987 and 1993).

Colonel Reisner has now joined the meeting of the targeting team, who are scratching their heads because they cannot decide whether to order the missile to destroy the target. The problem is that they have absolutely no intelligence about whether the next-door apartment is inhabited or not. They think it lawful to kill the kidnappers (they are terrorists, Reisner keeps assuring me)—and even lawful to kill their own agent—but they are not sure whether they are also allowed to destroy the adjacent apartment and injure or kill anybody who may be inside. There may be innocent men, women, and children present, some or all of whom could be killed or injured if the strike goes ahead. The legal question boils down to this: is the risk of causing incidental loss of civilian life in the building next door *excessive* in relation to the concrete and direct military advantage anticipated by carrying out the strike (i.e. killing the 'terrorists')?

If the risk of killing civilians were excessive then the attack would be illegal because it would violate the principle of proportionality in the laws of war. Proportionality requires the attacking party to weigh military advantage against potential negative secondary effects of carrying out any attack, and to strike a balance between the two. If the incidental effects clearly outweigh the anticipated military advantage, then the attack would be considered excessive. In this instance, the risk that civilians might be killed is to be weighed against at least two military advantages: (a) ending the interrogation and thereby preventing the agent from giving up potentially classified information; and (b) killing the 'terrorists'. But given that the targeting team have no way of knowing if (and how many) civilians are near the target, there is no objective, balanced, or fair way to make a judgement. They must do the best with what they have. This is the proverbial 'fog of war'; even with all their human and technological expertise—drones in the sky and eyes and ears on the ground—the targeting team cannot see through it.[8]

All the time, the clock is ticking, and it is tense in the war room. These targeted killing meetings have a man in charge, a commander of senior rank whose ultimate responsibility it is to make the final call on a potential killing. This commander (who Reisner cannot identify by name) has grown impatient with the conversation. He interrupts, points directly to Reisner, and asks the rest of the team:

[8] Lucy Suchman argues that the fog thickens and intensifies as technologies of surveillance expand. Lucy Suchman, 'Situational Awareness: Deadly Bioconvergence at the Boundaries of Bodies and Machines', *MediaTropes* 5, no. 1 (2015): 20.

'*Has he* [Reisner] *approved* [the strike] *yet?*'.

'*Not yet*', the others say, clearly under the impression that Reisner has been called into the meeting to make the final call.

'*Hurry up! We don't have much time!*', exclaims the commander before leaving the room.

Those remaining at the table turn to Reisner: '*So can we fire the missile?*', they ask, now with less than fifteen minutes to act.

At this point Reisner becomes frustrated because it seems like everyone is asking *him* to make the decision. Technically—*legally*—this is not his decision to make. The commander must make the decision, not Reisner. Reisner's job is to *advise* the commander and make him aware of the relevant law and what his legal options are. It is the commander who must make the final decision. As the adage goes, 'military lawyers advise, commanders decide'.[9] His frustration evident, Reisner launches into an impassioned speech to correct the misunderstanding:

> *I am not the Chief of Staff [the head of the Israeli military], I am a lawyer and I don't decide for you who you kill. I advise you on the risks of any decision you make and what you are doing right now is trying to throw the responsibility on me because you don't know what to do. And that can't happen. Not because I'm afraid of the responsibility, but because it's not my job. Your job is to make the difficult decisions and I'll tell you what are the legal risks you are going to take, and don't get mixed up because I think you've lost command responsibility here.*

His words are met with silence. Then, with his advisory hat on, he changes his tune and renders his legal bottom line:

> *I will tell you that I don't think it's a war crime to attack the house. I'll tell you why not: because you have a military reason to attack, you've got the target, you don't have any indications of any civilians, you haven't seen any civilians in the house and the blinds are shut, there is no laundry, let's say 60% that the house is currently uninhabited and 40% that maybe there is someone [in] there. But given the balance of things and the time here it doesn't look like a war crime even*

[9] Geoffrey Corn, James Dapper, and Winston Williams, 'Targeting and the Law of Armed Conflict', in *U.S. Military Operations: Law, Policy, and Practice*, ed. Geoffrey S. Corn, Rachel E. VanLandingham, and Shane R. Reeves (Oxford; New York, NY: Oxford University Press, 2015), 171.

if you get it wrong. However, if it's a local orphanage and we get it wrong, and we are going to kill them, then we are all in shit.

The commander, who has re-entered the room to hear the legal advice, thanks Reisner for his opinion. He interprets it as giving him a green light. From a legal point of view the attack can go ahead, but in line with Reisner's advice the commander must also seek political approval from the Minister of Defense. Reisner's job is done.

The War Lawyers

My encounter with Reisner and his story go to the heart of what this book is about. Between 2013 and 2017 I interviewed over fifty war lawyers in order to learn about their role in the conduct of lethal targeting operations. I use the term 'war lawyer' to describe a uniformed person who serves a military in an official legal capacity.[10] I first learned about war lawyers several years earlier—on a cold January morning in 2009. Missiles were raining down on Gaza in what the Israeli military called 'Operation Cast Lead'. The military operation was designed to prevent rockets being fired on Israel from Gaza, but it also caused widespread civilian casualties and destroyed much of Gaza's vital infrastructure. I stumbled across an article in *Haaretz*, an Israeli liberal newspaper. Journalists Yotam Feldman and Uri Blau detailed how:

> Prior to the Gaza operation, IDF [Israel Defense Force] officers were receiving legal advice that allowed for large numbers of civilian casualties and the targeting of government buildings. Some legal experts, among them the former head of the army's international law division, maintain that the IDF harnessed the law in the service of the war effort.[11]

[10] This narrow definition allows me to attend to the particularities of the military-legal profession, to understand its cultures, and say something specific about its powers and effects in shaping targeting in particular and war in general. The role that war lawyers play in targeting (and other areas of military operations) is so particular that it demands its own analytical and empirical attention. This is not to say that their legal world is hermetically sealed from that of civilians; in the account that follows I bring attention to the areas where they intersect. For purposes other than this book, a broader range of legal actors and experts (and even non-experts) might be equally in focus, including civilians, governmental and non-governmental lawyers, legal scholars, activists, judges, juries, and witnesses, or indeed anyone who has a legal stake in war—for war is far too important to be left to uniformed lawyers alone.

[11] Feldman and Blau, 'Consent and Advise'. The Hebrew name for the Israeli military is צְבָא הַהֲגָנָה לְיִשְׂרָאֵל (Tzva Hahagana LeYisra'el, lit. 'The Army of Defense for Israel'), more commonly referred to by its Hebrew acronym *tzhal*. This is commonly translated into English as the Israel Defense Force (IDF). These self-descriptions normalize the Israeli military's own ideological preferences as a defence force. I therefore use the more neutral term 'Israeli military'.

Who were these legal experts? Exactly what role were they playing in the war on Gaza? I began with an interest in these questions, and the answers prompted more. It was not until the early 1990s, during the First Gulf War, that the United States would employ and deploy war lawyers in lethal aerial targeting operations (Chapter 3). Israel began to emulate US practice following the breakout of the Second Intifada a decade later (Chapter 4). Inspired by US practice, it was Colonel Reisner who led the initiative to get war lawyers involved in Israeli targeting operations, and he managed to do so against significant opposition from others in the military establishment.[12]

From matters of military justice to legal reviews of nuclear arsenals, and almost everything in between, war lawyers currently perform a mind-boggling array of tasks for their military masters. As militaries like the US and Israel have blurred the boundaries between war and peace, and as military operations have become fought over an increasingly vast spatio-temporal and socio-legal terrain—humanitarian intervention, counter-insurgency, cyberwarfare, and so-called 'military operations other than war'—war lawyers have had to expand their remit and skills, to include the rendering of life and death legal advice in the operational war room. Indeed, war lawyers are increasingly incorporated into the various stages of lethal targeting operations not only in Israel but also among members of NATO and especially in the United States, the United Kingdom, Australia, and Canada.[13]

War lawyers have thus become a key intermediary in the categorization of lives and acts on the contemporary battlefield. Reisner may have refused to answer the commander in black and white terms, but what is striking is how his assurance ('it is not a war crime even if you get it wrong') amounts to a legal answer, and does so in-part from what is operationally *unknown*. While the commander must make a judgement based on a number of variables, of which the law is one among many, having positive legal reinforcement from a legal adviser strengthens his case. He has been provided with the legal authority to carry out the attack—but who or what exactly *constructs* that authority? War-making and law-making processes are deeply intertwined.[14] As Sir General

[12] Reisner, interview.

[13] See generally: Military Law and Law of War Review, 'Agora: The Role and Responsibilities of Legal Advisors in the Armed Forces—Evolution and Present Trends (Celebration of the Military Law and the Law of War Review's 50th Anniversary)', *Military Law and Law of War Review*, 50, nos. 1–2 (2011): 5–617; The North Atlantic Treaty Organization (NATO), 'Legal Gazette: Special Issue for Nato School, Oberammergau, Germany', *Nato Legal Gazette* 36 (2016): 1–167; Ian Henderson, 'Legal Officers in the Australian Defence Force: Functions by Rank and Competency Level, along with a Case-Study on Operations', *Military Law and Law of War Review* 50, nos. 1–2 (2011): 37; Kenneth W. Watkin, 'Coaltion Operations: A Canadian Perspective', *International Law Studies* 84, no. 1 (2008): 251–62.

[14] Neve Gordon and Nicola Perugini, *Human Shields: A History of People in the Line of Fire* (Oakland, CA: University of California Press, 2020).

David Richards put it: '[m]odern Generals need to have in their back pockets not the sapper and gunner of tradition, but a media man and a *lawyer*. If you haven't got those cards in your deck, you're lost'.[15]

Looking back, Reisner's account of the involvement of war lawyers in lethal targeting operations demonstrates the three sub-arguments that I wish to advance in this book. First, *the law is indeterminate*, hence why questions over the legality of the Gaza strike can be raised to begin with. Second, *law is productive of violence*, hence the ever present possibility that others may die not only in spite of the law but also because of it (the death of the informant and the 'terrorists' are legally sanctioned; any people inside the could-be-orphanage become regrettable, though not legally prohibited, 'civilian casualties'). And finally, *war lawyers are engaged in a law-making enterprise* when they render legal advice on targeting. Reisner's legal advice that shut blinds and the absence of laundry are taken as signifiers for the absence of 'civilians' (a legally constitutive category), which in turn is interpreted as a reason not to halt the strike.

In this, the Kirya scenario reminds me of the seminal work of Robert Cover on the institutionalized relationship between law and violence and particularly his observation: 'The judicial word is a mandate for the deeds of others'.[16] Cover was interested, among other things, in the violence of juridical interpretation and the dispersal of responsibility in the context of US criminal justice. Think, for example, of the chain of violence enabled by a judge who dispenses the death penalty, and the multiple actors required to carry out the sentence. We witness a particularly acute and radically dispersed version of the juridical mandate in the contemporary targeting process—what the US military aptly calls the 'kill chain'. Along with other areas of military operations, the kill chain has become a juridical field, 'the site of a competition for the monopoly of the right to determine the law'.[17] Targeting has not always been a juridical field and it has taken much political work since the mid twentieth century to make it so.

In my research on the involvement of war lawyers in aerial targeting operations I learned of several instances in which commanders looked to lawyers for something approximating a permission. But these were the exceptions, rather than the norm. The 'norm' is rather more banal, an ongoing rapport between commander and lawyer that serves to enable targeting operations on a routine, everyday basis. Nevertheless, these are routines on which larger

[15] David Richards, *Taking Command* (London: Headline, 2014), 110 (emphasis added).

[16] Robert M. Cover, 'Violence and the Word', *Yale Law Journal* 95, no. 8 (1986): 1611.

[17] Pierre Bourdieu, 'The Force of Law: Toward a Sociology of the Juridical Field', *Hastings Law Journal* 38, no. 5 (1987): 817. See also David Kennedy, *Of War and Law* (Princeton, NJ: Princeton University Press, 2006).

strategy depends. As one Israeli war lawyer said, the purpose of legal advice is 'not to fetter the army, but to give it the tools to win in a lawful manner'.[18] If commanders look to war lawyers for anything it is to enable them to do whatever it is their job to do, and to do it under the assurance that their action is within the bounds of what has been legally enabled.[19] This book does not claim that militaries employ war lawyers only as apologists for military violence, neither is it about dressing up decisions and policies to give them an outward appearance of legality. Such arguments would unduly simplify the complex and messy realities of targeting and would unfairly represent the work that war lawyers do. To follow Pierre Bourdieu, that work is 'not simply a cat's paw of State power' (though neither is it independent of state power).[20]

It is precisely the banal, repetitive, and everyday work that war lawyers do that makes them so effective (and they are effective). Working often in the background, far away from the front pages but often close to the literal and virtual front lines, war lawyers have woven a complex web of institutional arrangements in recent decades that now *require* legal input not only throughout the entire targeting process, but across the full spectrum of military operations.[21] In other words, life and death decisions in the war room are the tip of the iceberg. This book is my attempt to get a critical measure of the structuring role that law and war lawyers have come to play in aerial targeting operations and, more widely, our very understandings of war.

* * *

[18] Quoted in: Yotam Feldman and Uri Blau, 'Consent and Advise', *Haaretz*, http://www.haaretz.com/cmlink/consent-and-advise-1.269127, accessed 26 May 2013.

[19] A US war lawyer claimed that the basic responsibility of his profession is to 'keep military personnel from going to jail for doing the right thing': W. A. Stafford, 'How to Keep Military Personnel from Going to Jail for Doing the Right Thing: Jurisdiction, ROE & the Rules of Deadly Force', *The Army Lawyer*, November (2000): 1, quoted in John Morrissey, 'Liberal Lawfare and Biopolitics: US Juridical Warfare in the War on Terror', *Geopolitics* 16, no. 2 (2011): 294. I depart from accounts which suggest that commanders look to war lawyers only as a way of avoiding criminal prosecution because my research and interviews show that military commanders are principally concerned with executing their mission and not with avoiding jail. Instead, I suggest that the pre-empting of criminal behaviour (and thus criminal prosecution and, ultimately, the possibility of jail) enhances mission success because it provides some minimal legal assurances that allow commanders to do their job without worrying unduly about whether their actions will be subject to criminal investigation. Seen thus, the principal job of both war lawyers and commanders remains mission success; avoiding criminality in both fact and perception is nevertheless an important component in the realization of the mission.

[20] Richard Terdiman, trans., 'Translator's Introduction. The Force of Law: Toward a Sociology of the Juridical Field, Pierre Bourdieu', *Hastings Law Journal* 38, no. 5 (1987): 807.

[21] John Morrissey, *The Long War: CENTCOM, Grand Strategy, and Global Security* (Athens, GA: University of Georgia Press, 2017).

The literature about war lawyers is for the most part written *by* war lawyers *for* war lawyers and is published in relatively obscure military law journals.[22] Relatedly, the accounts of what war lawyers do tend to be descriptive rather than analytical and tend to adopt a relatively uncritical and unreflexive stance toward the profession in general and its role in targeting specifically. There are some exceptions, and a small handful of accounts have been written by non-war lawyers.[23] These are all valuable sources that I rely on extensively. However, I realized very early on in the research for this book that if I wanted to understand not only what war lawyers do, but also how they became so important to the conduct of aerial targeting operations, I would have to both talk to them and do some digging in the archives. In conversations with friends and colleagues interested in questions of war, I also realized that outside a few specialist circles, the world of war lawyers is largely unheard of.

There are signs that this may be beginning to change. The 2015 film *Eye in the Sky* examines the complex legal issues of drone warfare and features scenes where Katherine, a British colonel (played by Helen Mirren) consults with her war lawyer Harold (Jeff Heffernan). In a final scene Katherine turns to Harold, much like the Israeli commander turned to Reisner, and asks for permission to kill: 'Are we clear to engage, yes or no? Come on, make a decision.' Virtually all other lawyers have had their Hollywood moment, but the war lawyer, it seems, is finally becoming visible in popular culture. Jason McCue has even predicted that:

> [F]uture Hollywood movies will not focus on the likes of Patton or Private Ryan but on the lawyers: a band of fearless demigod decision makers that patrol the wasteland of the modern world. The red carpets of the Cannes Film

[22] e.g. Frederic L. Borch, Judge Advocates in Combat: Army Lawyers in Military Operations from Vietnam to Haiti (Washington, DC: Government Printing Office, 2001); Geoffrey S. Corn and Gary P. Corn, 'The Law of Operational Targeting: Viewing the LOAC through an Operational Lens', *Texas International Law Journal* 47, no. 2 (2011): 337–80; Henderson, 'Legal Officers in the Australian Defence Force'; Liron A. Libman, 'Legal Advice in the Conduct of Operations in the Israel Defense Forces', *Military Law and Law of War Review* 50 nos. 1–2 (2011): 67–97.

[23] Laura Dickinson, 'Military Lawyers on the Battlefield: An Empirical Account of International Law Compliance', *American Journal of International Law* 104, no. 1 (2010): 1–28; Janina Dill, *Legitimate Targets?: Social Construction, International Law and US Bombing* (Cambridge: Cambridge University Press, 2014); Stephen A. Myrow, 'Waging War on the Advice of Counsel: The Role of Operational Law in the Gulf War', United States Air Force Academy Journal of Legal Studies 7 (1996): 131; Amichai Cohen, 'Legal Operational Advice in the Israeli Defense Forces: The International Law Department and the Changing Nature of International Humanitarian Law', *Connecticut Journal of International Law* 26, no. 2 (2011): 367–413; Alan Craig, 'The Struggle For Legitimacy: A Study Of Military Lawyers In Israel', PhD thesis, University of Leeds, 2011, White Rose eTheses Online, http://etheses.whiterose.ac.uk/2702/, accessed 12 June 2020.

> festival will abound with fictional legal characters that defeated Isil [Islamic State of Iraq and the Levant] with their quills.[24]

This is perhaps a little overzealous, but it rightly highlights the increasing importance of lawyers in the conduct of war. In 2015, the US Air Force alone had around 1,250 war lawyers (or 'JAGs'—judge advocates), of which 100–200 are deployed around the globe at any one time, depending on operational requirements.[25] By comparison, the Israeli Military Advocate General (MAG) Corps has around 300 war lawyers, and of these around 30 work in the branch that is responsible for providing targeting advice.[26] Not being a war lawyer myself, my own account is more distanced than those writing about their own field, and what is novel about my approach is its comparative and historical focus. While there are a small handful of accounts that consider the work of Israeli or US war lawyers, even fewer consider their role in targeting specifically, and no work has yet considered them together. Similarly, while there are some historical accounts of how war lawyers were involved in war in the twentieth century, there are no detailed histories of how the role of war lawyers has evolved from the twentieth century to the present day. My hope is to bring a fresh and critical perspective to existing works, but also to acquaint non-specialists with a sense of how contemporary military violence is governed by law—and this means attending to the ways in which such violence is not only moderated by law but is also *enabled, legitimized, and extended* by it.

[24] Jason McCue, 'Today's Wars Are Fought by Lawyers, Not Soldiers', *The Telegraph*, 25 May 2016, http://www.telegraph.co.uk/news/2016/05/25/todays-wars-are-fought-by-lawyers-not-soldiers/, accessed 14 June 2016.

[25] Telephone conversation with Air Force Judge Advocate General's Office, 15 May 2015.

[26] Mandelblit, interview.

Introduction. The War Lawyers and the Self-Legalization of the Military

> [W]e defended all the magic formulas for dealing with terrorism. [. . .] What we are seeing now is a revision of international law [. . .] If you do something for long enough, the world will accept it. The whole of international law is now based on the notion that an act that is forbidden today becomes permissible if executed by enough countries.
>
> Colonel Daniel Reisner, head of the International Law Department of the Israeli military 1995–2004[1]

Indeterminacy, Violence, Legal Advice

In this book I examine the role of the laws of war and war lawyers in aerial targeting operations carried out by the US military in Iraq and Afghanistan, and the Israeli military in Gaza. I focus on how and why war lawyers became kill chain lawyers and explore two governing questions. I ask first, *what material and discursive effects do the laws of war and war lawyers have on aerial targeting specifically, and the way we understand war more generally*? This is a tricky question to answer because war and law are not separate entities; rather, they co-constitute and animate each other in all kinds of ways.[2] War lawyers are no exception; they do not stand outside or above the technical targeting matters on which they advise—they are a constitutive and entangled part of the targeting apparatus.[3] Because war and law are not independent variables, rather than posit counter-factual questions about the relationship between

[1] Quoted in Yotam Feldman and Uri Blau, 'Consent and Advise', *Haaretz*, 29 January 2009, http://www.haaretz.com/cmlink/consent-and-advise-1.269127, accessed 26 May 2013.

[2] Craig Jones, 'Lawfare and the Juridification of Late Modern War', *Progress in Human Geography* 40, no. 2 (2016): 221–39; Craig Jones and Michael D. Smith, 'War/Law/Space Notes toward a Legal Geography of War', *Environment and Planning D: Society and Space* 33, no. 4 (2015): 581–91.

[3] On the co-constitution of legal expertise and the field of international security, see: Anna Leander and Tanja Aalberts, 'Introduction: The Co-Constitution of Legal Expertise and International Security', *Leiden Journal of International Law* 26, no. 4 (December 2013): 783–92.

The War Lawyers. Craig Jones, Oxford University Press (2020). © Craig Jones.
DOI: 10.1093/oso/9780198842927.001.0001.

the two, I propose that we give due attention to what the laws of war and war lawyers *do*.[4] My core argument is that war lawyers have come to play an increasingly vital though as-yet under-appreciated role in lethal aerial targeting operations, and this is transforming the way that war is fought and understood.

The laws of war and legal advice do not fall under categories (e.g. war/peace, civilian/combatant) so much as *create* and *police* them.[5] Another way of saying this is that the laws of war are socially constructed: they are the product not of natural order but of a fraught and still unfolding history. If the laws of war are indeterminate, it is because they concern ever-expanding rather than static (military) *capabilities* involving negotiated rather than fixed ethico-legal *practices*. Actors who speak in its vernacular and work with its materials do so strategically, at least in part.[6] It is my contention, then, that what war lawyers say and do, and how, matters not only to military conduct and outcomes but also for our very understanding of what it means to kill, injure, and destroy in the twenty-first century. Their work is crucial to understanding how the laws of war are interpreted, made, and worlded.[7]

Attending to the material and discursive practices of law and war lawyers gives rise to a historical question: *when and why did war lawyers become involved in the provision of legal advice in aerial targeting operations?* How, in the late twentieth century, did war lawyers come to be seen as a solution to a host of military anxieties that were on the one hand about killing the 'right' number of the 'right' people in the 'right' way, and on the other, about doing—and being seen to do—the 'right' and legal thing? Paradoxically, those anxieties were heightened by the techo-cultural apparatus of so-called 'precision warfare' that made it *technically* possible to distinguish between civilians and combatants from the air, and even to hunt particular individuals in near-live time, but which simultaneously necessitated adjudication upon new patterns of violence, and the calibration of their acceptable thresholds.[8]

[4] For a counter-factual account of US bombing and international law see: Janina Dill, *Legitimate Targets?: Social Construction, International Law and US Bombing* (Cambridge: Cambridge University Press, 2014).

[5] Helen M. Kinsella, *The Image Before the Weapon: A Critical History of the Distinction Between Combatant and Civilian* (Ithaca, NY: Cornell University Press, 2011).

[6] David Kennedy, *Of War and Law* (Princeton, NJ: Princeton University Press, 2006).

[7] I borrow the idea of 'worlded' law from the interdisciplinary intellectual project of legal geography: '[N]early every aspect of law is located, takes place, is in motion, or has some spatial frame of reference. In other words, law is always 'worlded' in some way [. . .] Distinctively legal forms of meaning are projected onto every segment of the physical world': Irus Braverman et al., *The Expanding Spaces of Law: A Timely Legal Geography* (Stanford, CA: Stanford Law Books, 2014), 1.

[8] I borrow the language of a techo-cultural targeting apparatus from Derek Gregory: Derek Gregory, 'From a View to a Kill Drones and Late Modern War', *Theory, Culture & Society* 28, no. 7–8 (2011): 188–215.

In answering these governing questions, I advance three central and related claims. First, I argue that the laws of war are *indeterminate*. Second, I argue that the laws of war are *productive* of violence. Third, I argue that when they render legal advice on targeting, war lawyers are engaged in a law-*making* enterprise. War lawyers work to determine the law in an ongoing process of bounded interpretation: they provide answers and options for harried decision makers, but in negotiation with the broader indeterminacy and permissibility of the law.

The laws of war have traditionally been framed as either exerting some form of constraint or compliance-based behavioural change in service of a norm (in the liberal version); or as being a convenient fig leaf that provides state power with an appearance of legitimacy (in the strict realist version).[9] Throughout this book my findings problematize not only the dichotomy between liberal and realist explanations but also the categories on which they depend. They confirm that the laws of war and state power are not—and have never been—discrete entities: state power gives shape to the laws of war (through treaty negotiation and customary practice) and the laws of war in turn give flavour to state power by constraining *and* enabling it. In short, the laws of war and state power are co-constitutive.

The indeterminacy of the laws of war is by no means a new phenomenon and has long haunted the principle categories and central questions of the laws of war.[10] But in recent decades, issues of indeterminacy and pragmatism have taken on new salience as the US and Israeli militaries and their allies, bolstered by the work of legal scholars and practitioners, have boldly and openly declared their intentions of annexing the laws of war for the pursuit of military strategy. As Israel's Justice Ministry recently announced, Israel has been involved in 'in depth discussions' with NATO regarding 'how the law can be used to promote a military and political campaign [. . .].'[11] The US and Israeli militaries increasingly insist that warfare has become what they call 'lawfare'. Major General Charles Dunlap (ret.), a two-star US Air Force lawyer who formerly held a central position in the US Judge Advocate General Corps, was one of the earliest

[9] This schematic has become more nuanced in recent years. See: Jennifer M. Dixon, 'Rhetorical Adaptation and Resistance to International Norms', *Perspectives on Politics* 15, no. 1 (2017): 83–99; Ian Hurd, *How to Do Things with International Law* (Princeton, NJ: Princeton University Press, 2017); Rebecca Sanders, *Plausible Legality: Legal Culture and Political Imperative in the Global War on Terror* (Oxford; New York, NY: Oxford University Press, 2018).

[10] Kinsella, *The Image Before the Weapon*.

[11] Ministry of Justice statement quoted in: Yonah Jeremy Bob, 'Israel Gov't Lawyers Help NATO Fight Lawfare, Receive Awards', *The Jerusalem Post*, 2 September 2019, https://www.jpost.com/Israel-News/Israel-govt-lawyers-help-NATO-fight-lawfare-receive-awards-600346, accessed 27 November 2019.

proponents of lawfare, and he popularized the term in 2001 to denote 'the use of law as a weapon of war'.[12]

War's legal power

Targeting requires a special paradigm in order to be activated, legitimized, and normalized. More often than not, that paradigm is war. But like a target, war is not a pre-existing category; it must be *produced*. As David Kennedy has argued, 'the boundary between war and peace has become something we argue about, as much or more than something we cross. [. . .] War today is both a fact and an argument.'[13] Making war requires all sorts of work, including legal work. Arguments must be made, justifications provided, actions defended; but once established, the legal benefits (and costs) can be significant.

I discuss the making of several wars including the Vietnam War (Chapter 1), the First Gulf War (Chapter 3), Israel's ongoing war on Gaza (Chapter 4) and the US wars in Iraq and Afghanistan (Chapters 5 and 6). Each of these wars were established through legal work—legal work that is a *prerequisite* to targeting. By this, I mean that it is difficult to have a sustained targeting campaign without relying in one way or another on the language and law of war. This legal work is ordinarily identified as trafficking in *jus ad bellum* (the international law regulating the resort to force) and is seen as separate from the questions of *jus in bello* (the international law regulating behaviour in war).[14] Recent scholarship has suggested that the two overlap and intersect more than has previously been thought.[15] While I do not wish to weigh-in on these

[12] Charles Dunlap, 'Law and Military Interventions: Preserving Humanitarian Values in 21st Century Conflicts', in *Conference on Humanitarian Challenges in Military Intervention [Online]. Washington, DC: Carr Center for Human Rights Policy, Kennedy School of Government, Harvard University. November*, vol. 29 (Humanitarian Challenges in Military Intervention, Washington, DC, 2001), 5. The term 'lawfare' was purportedly first used by two Chinese People's Liberation Army officers in 1999 to describe one of several ways of waging unconventional war: Qiao Liang and Wang Xiangsui, *Unrestricted Warfare* (Beijing: PLA Literature and Arts Publishing House, 1999). The concept is not well defined in this work but the authors suggest lawfare is about proactively seizing opportunities to set up regulations in order to gain a strategic advantage in the international sphere. Wouter G. Werner, 'The Curious Career of Lawfare', *Case Western Reserve Journal of International Law* 43, no. 1 (2010): 61–72.

[13] Kennedy, *Of War and Law*, 4–5.

[14] This book is principally concerned with the *jus in bello*. I employ the term 'laws of war' to refer to the *jus in bello* legal regime commonly referred to as International Humanitarian Law (IHL) or the Laws of Armed Conflict (LOAC). On the politics of naming the laws of war in military and humanitarian cultures see: Eyal Benvenisti, 'The Legal Battle to Define the Law on Transnational Asymmetric Warfare', *Duke Journal of Comparative & International Law* 20, no. 3 (2010): 339–59; David Luban, 'Military Necessity and the Cultures of Military Law', *Leiden Journal of International Law* 26, no. 2 (2013): 315–49.

[15] Eyal Benvenisti, 'Rethinking the Divide between Jus Ad Bellum and Jus in Bello in Warfare against Nonstate Actors Essays in Honor of W. Michael Reisman: Use of Force', *Yale Journal of International Law* 34, no. 2 (2009): 541–8.

debates, it is important to underscore the extent to which targeting and other tasks that war lawyers undertake depend in crucial ways on *jus ad bellum*, the making and establishment of a sphere of activity we call 'war'.

In the years following the outbreak of the Second Intifada in 2000, and the 9/11 terror attacks of 2001, the United States and Israel developed a coordinated interpretive project designed to justify the use of force and radically expand and redraw the legal geographies of war. The project involved a series of legal manoeuvres designed to give the United States and Israel maximum military flexibility in 'prosecuting' what they would come to call the 'war on terror'. One of the first and most important legal manoeuvres by the United States and Israel was to create a paradigm of war within and through which military action could subsequently take place. As Lisa Hajjar has cogently argued of the United States:

> Over the years since 9/11, we have witnessed the development of a counter-terrorism war paradigm built to advance claims about the scope and discretion of US executive power and to articulate specific national security interests, strategic objectives, and operational practices in this long-running unconventional war. What makes this a paradigm [. . .] is the cohesiveness and mutual reinforcement of its underlying rationales about the rights of the US government to pursue national security through violent means against an evolving cast of enemies.[16]

Israel has pursued a similar and parallel strategy. These strategies feed into and depend upon one another. Israel created a paradigm of war by inventing and advancing a new legal category and interpreting the events of the Second Intifada as 'an armed conflict short of war', as I show in Chapter 4.[17] Attesting to the flexibility of legal regimes of war, this was an act of what Bourdieu calls 'juridical creation', designed to construe Palestinians' actions as having crossed a threshold demanding a war or war-like response.[18] Essential to such a framing was Israel's attendant assertion of a legal right to employ lethal violence against Palestinians.

[16] Lisa Hajjar, 'The Counterterrorism War Paradigm versus International Humanitarian Law: The Legal Contradictions and Global Consequences of the US "War on Terror"', *Law & Social Inquiry* 44, no. 4 (2019): 922.

[17] George Mitchell et al., 'Sharm El-Sheikh Fact-Finding Committee' (Washington, DC: US Department of State, April 30, 2001), http://2001-2009.state.gov/p/nea/rls/rpt/3060.htm, accessed 29 September 2015.

[18] Pierre Bourdieu, 'The Force of Law: Toward a Sociology of the Juridical Field', *Hastings Law Journal* 38, no. 5 (1987): 842.

The United States was at first sceptical of Israel's approach. But using similar arguments to Israel, the United States chose to frame the 9/11 attacks as an act of war, rather than a crime, partly to make a military response possible.[19] The contention was that the attacks triggered an 'armed conflict'—the term for war in international law—and thus the laws of war now applied. The United States could have instead responded with diplomatic or police initiatives but as Simon Dalby argued, these would 'have required a different series of assumptions concerning the nature of world order and the appropriate political responses under international law'.[20] By triggering a war and making a legal appeal to the laws of war the United States privileged a combat paradigm over a human rights paradigm. Françoise Hampson explains the profound significance of the distinction:

> The starting point of human rights law is the right of the individual, including the right not to be arbitrarily killed. The international law of armed conflict, which is very much older in its origins than human rights law, starts from totally different premises. The soldier has the right to kill another soldier.[21]

In recent decades human rights law has increasingly been incorporated into the laws of war so the distinction is not as pronounced as Hampson suggests.[22] Nevertheless, a paradigm of war asserts a legal right to kill which, although not unlimited, is largely permissive of violence. In this sense a paradigm of war sanctions aerial targeting specifically, and military violence more generally, in a way that that few other paradigms can.

It is important not to think of the laws of war only or even primarily as 'humanizing' war but as legally *constructing* war. Nathanial Berman captures exactly what is at stake when we conceptualize war as a legal *construction*:

> [I]t is misleading to see law's relationship to war as primarily one of the limitation of organized violence, and even more misleading to see the laws of war as historically progressing toward an ever-greater limitation of violence.

[19] Derek Gregory, *The Colonial Present: Afghanistan, Palestine, Iraq* (Malden, MA; Oxford: Wiley-Blackwell, 2004).

[20] Simon Dalby, 'Calling 911: Geopolitics, Security and America's New War', *Geopolitics* 8, no. 3 (2003): 61–86.

[21] Françoise Hampson, 'Human Rights Law and International Humanitarian Law: Two Coins or Two Sides of the Same Coin?', *Bulletin of Human Rights* 911 (1992): 50. Quoted in: Nathaniel Berman, 'Privileging Combat—Contemporary Conflict and the Legal Construction of War', *Columbia Journal of Transnational Law* 43, no. 1 (2004): 3.

[22] Amanda Alexander, 'A Short History of International Humanitarian Law', *European Journal of International Law* 26, no. 1 (2015): 109–38.

> [. . .] Rather than *opposing violence*, the legal construction of war serves to *channel violence* into certain forms of activity engaged in by certain kinds of people, while excluding other forms engaged in by other people.[23]

In a hugely influential article published in 2000 Theodor Meron celebrated what he called 'The Humanization of Humanitarian Law' and one of its key features was the import of International Human Rights Law (IHRL) into the laws of war.[24] IRHL seeks to protect the sanctity of the right to life above all else. The principle of humanity in the laws of war is much more provisional as it is always balanced against military necessity.[25] Historically, IHRL and International Humanitarian Law (IHL) have been two distinct disciplines with very different histories, but they merged to a considerable degree in the late twentieth and early twenty-first centuries.[26] As Meron argued:

> [H]uman rights have exercised vast influence on instruments of international humanitarian law, producing a large measure of parallelism between norms, and a growing measure of convergence in their personal and territorial applicability. The fact that the law of war and human rights law stem from different historical and doctrinal roots has not prevented the principle of humanity from becoming the common denominator of both systems.[27]

The laws of war might be about humanisation for *some* people *sometimes* but the clash of fundamental priorities is inescapable: very simply put, targets (including people) are those things that are militarily 'necessary' to target. Eyal Benvenisit argues that there are two epistemic communities at loggerheads over the very foundation and purpose of the laws of war, one referring to 'International Humanitarian Law' (or 'IHL') and the other referring to the 'Laws of Armed Conflict' (or 'LOAC'). In principle, both IHL and LOAC refer

[23] Berman, 'Privileging Combat—Contemporary Conflict and the Legal Construction of War', 4–5.

[24] Theodor Meron, 'The Humanization of Humanitarian Law', *American Journal of International Law* 94, no. 2 (2000): 239–78.

[25] In his assessment of IHRL and IHL Christian Tomuschat concludes that IHL 'is still predominantly under the influence of the concept of military necessity' as opposed to the principle of humanity: Christian Tomuschat, 'Human Rights and International Humanitarian Law', *European Journal of International Law* 21, no. 1 (2010): 15.

[26] Meron, 'The Humanization of Humanitarian Law'; Dietrich Schindler, 'Human Rights and Humanitarian Law', *American University Law Review* 31, no. 4 (1981): 935–43; Hans-Joachim Heintze, 'On the Relationship between Human Rights Law Protection and International Humanitarian Law', *International Review of the Red Cross* 86, no. 856 (2004): 789–814; Louise Doswald-Beck, 'Implementation of International Humanitarian Law in Future Wars', *Naval War College Review* 52, no. 1 (1999): 24.

[27] Meron, 'The Humanization of Humanitarian Law', 245.

to the same body of law (i.e. the laws of war), but the 'IHL camp' emphasize its humanitarian and restrictive principles, whereas those in the 'LOAC camp' instead focus on its more military and permissive aspects and especially on the idea of necessity.[28]

Even Hersch Lauterpacht, one of the most respected international lawyers of the twentieth century and a principled believer in the laws of war and their capacity to bring reason and restraint to the hell of war realized the limits of what he once called the 'almost entirely humanitarian' vision of the laws of war.[29] During his lifetime (1897–1960) not only had the laws of war resolutely failed to prevent the outbreak of two world wars and countless colonial (and de-colonial) wars, but they also had failed to prevent the death and suffering of countless millions once those wars were underway. These signal failures led Lauterpacht to famously conclude: '[. . .] if international law is, in some ways, at the vanishing point of law, the law of war is, perhaps even more conspicuously, at the vanishing point of international law.'[30] The fact that he wrote these surrendering words only a few years after the most significant codification of the laws of war ever to be achieved—the signing of the Geneva Conventions of 1949—demonstrates the precarity of any argument that views the laws of war as 'truly' humanitarian.[31]

Scope and Method

The laws of war both enable and constrain violence—this is a key component of their indeterminacy—and I show how war lawyers helped their fellow commanders to harvest the force-multiplying potential of the laws of war. In Israel, war lawyers have long been useful in creating and administering the occupation of the Palestinian Territories (Chapter 4) but it was the United States, and specifically US war lawyers, who in the 1970s and 1980s formalized the enabling aspects of the laws of war into military doctrine (Chapter 2). They called it 'operational law', a deliberate domestication of the laws of war that would emphasize military *rights* (and de-emphasize constraints). In so doing, operational

[28] Benvenisti, 'The Legal Battle to Define the Law on Transnational Asymmetric Warfare'. See also: Luban, 'Military Necessity and the Cultures of Military Law'.

[29] Hersch Lauterpacht, 'The Problem of the Revision of the Law of War', *British Year Book of International Law* 29 (1952): 363–4.

[30] Ibid., 382.

[31] Cf. Alexander, 'A Short History of International Humanitarian Law'. Claiming: '[T]he correct understanding of the *ius in bello* by the end of the 20th century was that it was a truly international humanitarian law, a law in which considerations of humanity trumped military necessity.' Ibid., 135.

law made the laws of war ever more pragmatic, practitioner-orientated, and military-friendly.

More recently, much attention, with good reason, has been paid to the coterie of US lawyers working for the Department of Justice and the Office of Legal Counsel who bent the law beyond recognition in order to attempt to legalize and justify torture in the early days of the so-called 'war on terror'.[32] (The US war lawyer community fought vociferously against their civilian counterparts but were ultimately over-ruled.[33]) But beneath these extraordinary attempts to justify the unjustifiable, war lawyers in the United States and Israel have, in their own different ways and in very different contexts, been instrumental in the *everyday operationalization* of military violence.

This book is concerned primarily with aerial targeting operations and the involvement of war lawyers in the conduct of air warfare. It does not focus on ground operations except for some instances where ground operations rely on or intersect closely with air operations, such as when troops on the ground call for aerial support (commonly known as a 'troops in contact' or 'TIC' strike). This book also does not deal with sea or marine targeting operations, nor with the increasingly important area of cyber operations and cyber warfare.[34] Legal advisers in both the United States and Israel are involved in the full spectrum of military operations—air, ground, sea, marine, and cyber—but these are beyond the scope of the present work (and aside from some fairly specific examples in Chapter 6, I make no claims about these other kinds of targeting operations, where decision-making and the advising process may be quite different).[35]

[32] Jens David Ohlin, *The Assault on International Law* (New York, NY: Oxford University Press, 2015); David Luban, *Torture, Power, and Law* (Cambridge: Cambridge University Press, 2014); Lisa Hajjar, *Torture: A Sociology of Violence and Human Rights* (New York, NY: Routledge, 2013).

[33] Laura Dickinson, 'Military Lawyers on the Battlefield: An Empirical Account of International Law Compliance', *American Journal of International Law* 104, no. 1 (2010): 1–28.

[34] See: Michael N. Schmitt, ed., *Tallinn Manual 2.0 on the International Law Applicable to Cyber Operations*, 2nd edition (Cambridge; New York, NY: Cambridge University Press, 2017).

[35] See generally: The Judge Advocate General's Legal Center & School, Center for Law and Military Operations (CLAMO), United States Army, 'Legal Lessons Learned From Afghanistan and Iraq Volume I Major Combat Operations (11 September 2001–1 May 2003)', 1 August 2004 (Charlottesville, VA: United States Army), https://fas.org/irp/doddir/army/clamo-v1.pdf, accessed 15 December 2016; The Judge Advocate General's Legal Center & School, Center for Law and Military Operations (CLAMO), United States Army, 'Legal Lessons Learned From Afghanistan and Iraq Volume II Full Spectrum Operations (2 May 2003–30 June 2004)', 1 August 2004 (Charlottesville, VA: United States Army) https://fas.org/irp/doddir/army/clamo-v2.pdf, accessed 22 March 2017; Dickinson, 'Military Lawyers on the Battlefield'; Richard P. DiMeglio, 'Training Army Judge Advocates to Advise Commanders as Operational Law Attorneys', *Boston College Law Review* 54, no. 3 (2013): 1185; Israel Ministry of Foreign Affairs (IMFA), 'The Operation in Gaza-Factual and Legal Aspects', 29 July 2009 (https://www.mfa.gov.il), http://www.mfa.gov.il/MFA/ForeignPolicy/Terrorism/Pages/Operation_in_Gaza-Factual_and_Legal_Aspects.aspx, accessed 5 November 2013; Israel Ministry of Foreign Affairs, 'The 2014 Gaza Conflict: Factual and Legal Aspects'; The Judge Advocate General's Legal Center & School, International & Operational Law Department, United States Army, 'Operational Law

I focus on the United States and Israel first, because these two states pioneered the use of war lawyers in targeting operations along with the United Kingdom. However, the UK military's refusal to participate in my research (citing 'national security considerations') meant that the United Kingdom is excluded from my analysis—something I reflect further on in the Conclusion. It was the United States, in the First Gulf War in 1990–1991, that first employed war lawyers in targeting operations and it was Israel that began to emulate the policy in 2000.[36] While other militaries (mainly those in NATO) also use war lawyers in targeting operations, their role is not as extensive or as well developed as it is in the United States, Israel, or the United Kingdom.[37] The International Security Assistance Force (ISAF) in Afghanistan and the Multi National Force—Iraq (MNF-I) coalitions saw war lawyers from many nations working closely together on complex multinational targeting operations.[38] But it is the US military (and, to a lesser extent, the UK military) that has led establishing and expanding the role of war lawyers in the operational environment and on matters of targeting in particular.[39] This is perhaps not surprising

Handbook 2017' 2017 (Charlottesville, VA: United States Army) http://www.loc.gov/rr/frd/Military_Law/operational-law-handbooks.html, accessed 8 November 2019; United States Joint Chiefs of Staff, 'Legal Support to Military Operations' (Washington, DC: Joint Chiefs of Staff, 2 August 2016), https://www.jcs.mil/Portals/36/Documents/Doctrine/pubs/jp1_04.pdf, accessed 28 January 2016.

[36] The First Gulf War was the first major war in which military lawyers provided legal advice on targeting, but military lawyers were also employed in a similar capacity during the US military campaign in Panama in 1989.

[37] For example, an Australian report into allegations of civilian casualties from a 2009 NATO strike criticizes the lack of training in targeting operations received by Australian Defence Force military lawyers. The report cites (redacted) directives requiring the involvement of legal officers 'in all stages of the targeting process' but found that 'there is no formal training [. . .] in the complex Afghanistan context' and goes on to note that for certain Australian Defence Force legal officers '*Their testing in kinetic targeting essentially began once they began conducting targeting operations for real*': Department of Defence Australia, 'Report of an Inquiry Officer: Possible Civilian Casualties from Close Air Support Strike at [Redacted] Afghanistan on 28 Apr 09' (Government of Australia, online: Defence Publications Commission of Inquiry, 2009), http://www.defence.gov.au/publications/coi/reports/28APR09%20CIVCAS%20report%20-%20redacted.pdf, accessed 9 January 2017. Australian military lawyers informed me that the Australian Defence Force has addressed the issue of training raised in this report. Interviews: Blake, Cavanagh, Henderson.

[38] Richard C. Gross and Ian Henderson, 'Multinational Operations', in *U.S. Military Operations: Law, Policy, and Practice*, ed. Geoffrey S. Corn, Rachel E. VanLandingham, and Shane R. Reeves (Oxford: Oxford University Press, 2015), 341–70; Jody Prescott, 'Tactical Implementation of Rules of Engagement in a Multinational Force Reality', in *U.S. Military Operations: Law, Policy, and Practice*, ed. Geoffrey S. Corn, Rachel E. VanLandingham, and Shane R. Reeves (Oxford: Oxford University Press, 2015), 249–74; Ian Henderson, 'Legal Officers in the Australian Defence Force: Functions by Rank and Competency Level, along with a Case-Study on Operations', *Military Law and Law of War Review* 50, nos. 1–2 (2011); Kenneth W. Watkin. 'Coalition Operations: A Canadian Perspective'. *International Law Studies* 84, no. 1 (2008): 251–62.

[39] Stefano (pseudonym), interview; Blake, interview.

given the central role that the United States has come to play in leading large multinational coalitions in the post-Cold War era.[40]

The assault through international law

The second reason I focus on the United States and Israel is that they have been at the forefront of efforts to shape the international law on targeting. In close cooperation and exchange, both states have adopted targeting tactics and policies that have proved controversial and which push at the boundaries of international law. A substantial part of this book is devoted to showing how the United States and Israel have gone to great efforts to legally rationalize targeting policies and decisions. Chapter 3 shows how the United States pursued particularly aggressive interpretations of the laws of war in order to justify and legitimize the large-scale infrastructural destruction of Baghdad and other parts of Iraq in the First Gulf War. The destruction turned in part on the legal interpretation of significant parts of Iraq's life-sustaining infrastructures as 'dual use' (having military as well as civilian purposes). Chapter 4 shows how Israel was instrumental in the early legal rationalization of what has become known as 'targeted killing'—a mainstay of US and Israeli counterterrorism policy and a cornerstone of drone warfare today. In the early days of the 'war on terror' the United States sought Israel's counsel on 'creating a legal justification for the assassination of terrorism suspects'[41] and emulated some aspects of Israel's targeted killing program. There is therefore real value in attending to the US and Israel together.[42] I argue that the United States and Israel have actively and deliberately sought to widen the scope and space of what constitutes a permissible target and this has been achieved not by ignoring or circumventing international law but through diligent and creative interpretive legal work.

In his book *The Assault on International Law* Jens David Ohlin argues that: 'International law is under attack in the United States'.[43] Ohlin is concerned in particular with a 'small group of legal scholars' he calls the New Realists who, in the wake of 9/11, set about undermining international law and

[40] Patricia Weitsman, 'With a Little Help from Our Friends?: The Costs of Coalition Warfare', Origins: Current Events in Historical Perspective, January 2009, https://origins.osu.edu/article/little-help-our-friends-costs-coalition-warfare/page/0/0, accessed 4 November 2019.

[41] Ori Nir, 'Bush Seeks Israeli Advice on "Targeted Killings"', *The Electronic Intifada/The Forward*, 7 February 2003, http://electronicintifada.net/content/bush-seeks-israeli-advice-targeted-killings/4391, accessed 5 November 2013.

[42] Craig Jones, 'Travelling Law: Targeted Killing, Lawfare and the Deconstruction of the Battlefield', in *American Studies Encounters the Middle East* (Chapel Hill: University of North Carolina Press, 2016).

[43] Ohlin, *The Assault on International Law*, 8.

asserting the supremacy of Presidential power and US sovereignty.[44] The assault was based on an assumption that international law *impinges* on US sovereignty and would thus *hamper* the ability of the United States to fight its enemies in the 'war on terror'. Ohlin argues that this portrait of international law is misleading, and the assault thus advanced on a mistaken premise. As a corrective he proffers:

> In the war on terror, international law is our best friend, not our worst enemy [. . .] In reality, the laws of war provide the United States with all the tools it needs to aggressively fight al-Qaeda [. . .] and other jihadist organizations [. . .][45]

The language of assault is appropriate, but my contention is that this is not so much an assault 'on' international law as it is an assault *through* international law. First, an assault on international law assumes an essentialist conception of law—and especially the liberal idea that international law is ultimately a force for good—whereas an assault *through* international law refuses such a conception in favour of indeterminacy (i.e. international law is whatever states *do* with it). Second, an assault on international law implores us to identify with international law as a victim rather than a *vector* of violence. International law has a long history of violence and has been implicated in the pursuit of colonial conquests, imperialism, slavery, and the imposition of capitalist and (neo) liberal orders the world over, so it makes more sense to think of the ways in which violence operates *through* rather than 'on' it.[46] The assault through international law does not dispense with international law; instead, it strategically employs and deploys its vocabulary and content in order to *wage and win wars*.

[44] Ibid.

[45] Ibid., 155. One of Ohlin's key arguments is that this small list of legal scholars have had a disproportionate influence among Washington elites: 'these professors do more than just write articles; they also serve as lawyers working for the State Department, and the CIA. [. . .] The assault on international law [. . .] influences how the president fights the War on Terror, whether federal judges can 'interfere' with the detention or killing of suspected terrorists, and whether victims of human rights abuses can file lawsuits in federal courts. It determines whether international treaties can be enforced in US courts and whether foreigners on death row should have access to consular assistance [. . .] In short, arguments about international law implicate every corner of our foreign relations, and it is hard to imagine an area of the law with more practical consequences': Ibid., 11.

[46] Antony Anghie, *Imperialism, Sovereignty and the Making of International Law* (Cambridge: Cambridge University Press, 2007); Lauren A. Benton, *Law and Colonial Cultures: Legal Regimes in World History, 1400-1900*, Studies in Comparative World History (Cambridge; New York, NY: Cambridge University Press, 2002); Lauren A. Benton, *A Search for Sovereignty: Law and Geography in European Empires, 1400--1900* (Cambridge; New York, NY: Cambridge University Press, 2010); Laleh Khalili, *Time in the Shadows: Confinement in Counterinsurgencies* (Stanford, CA: Stanford University Press, 2012); Kinsella, *The Image Before the Weapon*; China Mieville, *Between Equal Rights: A Marxist Theory of International Law* (Chicago: Historical Materialism, 2006).

International law is not just a medium of assault; it is the assailant par excellence because it comes dressed in the emperor's new clothes, simultaneously disguised as a victim—that which has been breached and violated—and that which must prevail if we, 'humanity', are to realize a kinder, gentler, and more humane vision of war.[47]

Recent critical scholarship is increasingly showing that states like the United States and Israel do not simply ignore, violate, or blindly comply with international law.[48] These states, powerful military and legal actors that they are, are increasingly redrawing the boundaries between these categories and transforming the very meaning of what it means to comply with or violate international law. For example, Rebecca Sanders has persuasively argued that in the 'war on terror', international law functions not as constraint *or* permission but, paradoxically, as 'permissive constraint'—'a force that can be marshaled to serve cynical state interests, but that also deeply structures the boundaries of legitimacy'.[49] In a parallel series of arguments Jennifer Dixon shows how states regularly employ something like what she calls 'rhetorical adaptation' in their dealings with international law. For Dixon, 'rhetorical adaptation involves drawing on a norm's *content* in order to craft arguments that could diffuse pressures to comply with a norm or minimize perceptions that certain actions are in violation of a norm'.[50] Throughout this work I will show how the US and Israeli approach to targeting contains all of these key ingredients: an assault through the very architectures and vocabulary of international law,

[47] For critiques of the concept of humanity, and in particular the ways in which international law makes appeals to the 'human' in order to secure its legitimacy, see: Ayca Cubukcu, *For the Love of Humanity: The World Tribunal on Iraq* (Philadelphia: University of Pennsylvania Press, Inc., 2018); Costas Douzinas, *Human Rights and Empire: The Political Philosophy of Cosmopolitanism* (Abingdon; New York, NY: Routledge-Cavendish, 2007); Samera Esmeir, *Juridical Humanity: A Colonial History* (Stanford, CA: Stanford University Press, 2012); Samuel Moyn, *The Last Utopia: Human Rights in History* (Cambridge, MA: Belknap Press of Harvard University Press, 2010); Nicola Perugini and Neve Gordon, *The Human Right to Dominate* (New York, NY: Oxford University Press, 2015).

[48] Neve Gordon and Nicola Perugini, 'The Politics of Human Shielding: On the Resignification of Space and the Constitution of Civilians as Shields in Liberal Wars', *Environment and Planning D: Society and Space* 34, no. 1 (2016): 168–87; Derek Gregory, 'The Black Flag: Guantánamo Bay and the Space of Exception', *Geografiska Annaler: Series B, Human Geography* 88, no. 4 (2006): 405–27; Lisa Hajjar, *Courting Conflict: The Israeli Military Court System in the West Bank and Gaza*, 1st edition (University of California Press, 2005); Lisa Hajjar, 'The Counterterrorism War Paradigm versus International Humanitarian Law: The Legal Contradictions and Global Consequences of the US "War on Terror"', *Law & Social Inquiry* 4, no. 4 (2019): 922–56; Fleur Johns, 'Guantanamo Bay and the Annihilation of the Exception', *European Journal of International Law* 16, no. 4 (2005): 613–35; Rebecca Sanders, 'Legal Frontiers: Targeted Killing at the Borders of War', *Journal of Human Rights* 13, no. 4 (2014): 512–36; E. Weizman, *The Least of All Possible Evils: Humanitarian Violence from Arendt to Gaza* (London: Verso, 2012).

[49] Sanders, *Plausible Legality*, 3.

[50] Dixon, 'Rhetorical Adaptation and Resistance to International Norms', 85.

permissively constraining targeting policy and practice, and using an array of legal rhetorical adaptation techniques to do so.

These controversial interpretations and attempts to shape the laws of war vis-à-vis targeting should be seen in a broader context of US and Israeli strategic investment in international law. Highlighting a distinct overlap between US and Israeli preferences for flexible juridical forms of warfare, Laleh Khalili argues: 'The two powers converge on their use of overwhelming force alongside a discourse of legality. In both cases, the law has been innovatively interpreted and deployed to allow a fairly unfettered freedom of action for the military.'[51] The United States and Israel are major military powers who have been engaged in multiple and long-standing wars in recent decades, and they have a disproportionately large impact in shaping public perceptions of the laws of war and setting international legal agendas. These specific forms of law-making power might usefully be thought of in terms of what Martti Koskenniemi has called 'hegemonic contestation', which he defines as:

> [T]he process by which international actors routinely challenge each other by invoking legal rules and principles on which they have projected meanings that support their preferences and counteract those of their opponents. [. . .] To think of this struggle as *hegemonic* is to understand that the objective of the contestants is to make their partial view of that meaning appear as the total view, their preference seem like the *universal preference*.[52]

The United States is often singled out as chief candidate for global hegemon but when it comes to shaping the law of targeting, I suggest we accord Israel a similar or perhaps joint status.[53] Consider, for example, Daniel Reisner's view on Israel's role in developing customary international law through acts of violation:

> After we bombed the [nuclear] reactor in Iraq [in 1981], the Security Council condemned Israel and claimed the attack was a violation of international law.

[51] Khalili, *Time in the Shadows*, 64.

[52] Martti Koskenniemi, 'International Law and Hegemony: A Reconfiguration', *Cambridge Review of International Affairs* 17, no. 2 (2004): 199 (emphasis in original), quoted in: Hajjar, 'The Counterterrorism War Paradigm versus International Humanitarian Law', 2019, 924.

[53] Christian Henderson has argued that since the end of the Cold War the United States has been a '"persistent objector" to the development of international law on many contemporary issues', citing US opposition to the International Criminal Court as one example. He further argues that in the post Cold-War period the United States has been what he calls a 'persistent advocate' for the use of force. Christian Henderson, *The Persistent Advocate and the Use of Force: The Impact of the United States upon the Jus Ad Bellum in the Post-Cold War Era* (Farnham, Surrey; Burlington, VT: Routledge, 2010), 1–2.

> The atmosphere was that Israel had committed a crime. Today everyone says it was preventive self-defense. *International law progresses through violations.* We invented the targeted assassination thesis [in 2000–2001] and we had to push it. At first there were protrusions that made it hard to insert easily into the legal moulds. Eight years later it is in the center of the bounds of legitimacy.[54]

Lubricating the policy transfers between the US and Israel is a new way of forging customary law, one that departs from the democratic model of sovereign equality and consent in favour of a trail-blazing custom forged by the hegemonic few and largely unopposed by asymmetrically 'weaker' and legally unequipped states.[55] The implications of such aggressive attempts to forge customary law through violation are profound. To begin with, they demonstrate just how flexible and indeterminate the laws of war can be, but perhaps more worryingly they highlight the legislative force of violence and violation; to borrow from Eyal Weizman, violence *legislates*.[56] Such legislative violence may begin as an 'exception' to the 'rule' but as Lisa Hajjar has argued, if 'underlying justifications were to become accepted as legal by significant sectors of the international community, they could "ripen" into custom and thus become legal for all.'[57] The 'exception', if practiced and unopposed by the powerful, becomes the norm and the 'rule' is rewritten.

Afghanistan, Iraq, Gaza

I focus on Afghanistan, Iraq, and Gaza because it is in these places that US and Israeli aerial targeting operations have largely, though not exclusively, been concentrated over the last approximately two decades (and longer in the case of Iraq).

The United States has been bombing Afghanistan since 7 October 2001 when the US military launched 'Operation Enduring Freedom' against al Qaeda and the Taliban in response to the terror attacks of 9/11. Over thirteen years later, in late 2014, President Obama officially announced the end of Operation

[54] Quoted in: Feldman and Blau, 'Consent and Advice' (emphasis added).

[55] On the distinction between consensus and hegemonic based approaches to customary international law see: Victor Kattan, 'Furthering the "War on Terrorism" through International Law: How the United States and the United Kingdom Resurrected the Bush Doctrine on Using Preventive Military Force to Combat Terrorism', *Journal on the Use of Force and International Law* 5, no. 1 (2017): 97–144.

[56] E. Weizman, 'Legislative Attack', *Theory, Culture & Society* 27, no. 6 (2010): 11–32.

[57] Hajjar, 'The Counterterrorism War Paradigm versus International Humanitarian Law', 924.

Enduring Freedom, but US military operations continue in Afghanistan today under the rebranded banner of 'Operation Freedom's Sentinel and Resolute Support Mission'. The aerial attacks in Afghanistan began with around sixty-three combat sorties a day, focusing mainly on fixed Taliban targets, but as the United States changed tactics to provide air support to ground troops, the number of airstrikes rose dramatically.[58] Data on the air war is patchy at best, but according to figures published by Air Force Central Command, by 2006 the US Air Force was dropping nearly 2,000 weapons a year on Afghanistan, a number that rose to over 5,000 in both 2007 and 2008.[59] Between January 2010 and October 2019, the US Air Force fired 39,932 aerial weapons in Afghanistan, a rate of over 4,000 per year.[60] This amounts to more than an average of eleven bombs a day dropped on Afghanistan every day for a decade—or a bomb approximately every two hours (Chapter 5).

US bombing in Iraq predates 9/11 by over a decade. The United States launched a short but massively destructive aerial assault on Iraq in 1991 in what has since become known as the First Gulf War. As I detail in Chapter 3, in one of the most intensive air bombardments in military history the United States laid waste to large parts of Iraq and in just forty-two days the US Air Force imposed modes of infrastructural destruction that are still felt by Iraqis today. Once the bombs had stopped falling, the United States and United Nations Security Council imposed a series of crippling sanctions on Iraq that remained in place until the US-led coalition launched 'Operation Iraqi Freedom' in March 2003.[61] Saddam Hussein's government was quickly toppled, and Hussein was captured and executed, but US troops faced a growing insurgency, and the military strategy thus switched to counterinsurgency and 'winning the hearts and minds' of Iraqis.[62] In the first month of Operation Iraqi

[58] Benjamin S. Lambeth, *Air Power Against Terror: America's Conduct of Operation Enduring Freedom*, 2nd edition (Santa Monica, CA: RAND Corporation, 2006), 106. According to Air Force Central Command there is no data for 2001 to 2003 for Afghanistan. U.S. Air Forces Central Command Public Affairs, '2004-2011 Combined Forces Air Component Commander Airpower Statistics' (archived by Alexa O'Brian, n.d., https://alexaobrien.com/afcent-cfacc-airpower-summaries-and-statistics, accessed 16 June 2020).

[59] US Air Forces Central Command Public Affairs, '2004-2011 Combined Forces Air Component Commander Airpower Statistics'.

[60] The Bureau of Investigative Journalism, 'Afghanistan: US Air and Drone Strikes', November 2019, https://www.thebureauinvestigates.com/projects/drone-war/afghanistan, accessed 18 November 2019.

[61] Anthony Arnove, ed., *Iraq Under Siege, Updated Edition: The Deadly Impact of Sanctions and War*, 2nd revised edition (Cambridge, MA: South End Press, 2003); Joy Gordon, *Invisible War: The United States and the Iraq Sanctions* (Cambridge, MA: Harvard University Press, 2010). Gordon notes, 'The United States exercised a singular influence in determining these policies [sanctions], and often did so in the face of vehement opposition from the majority of the Security Council, UN agencies, and the UN General Assembly' Ibid., ix.

[62] Derek Gregory, 'Seeing Red: Baghdad and the Event-Ful City', *Political Geography* 29, no. 5 (2010): 266–79.

Freedom the US-led coalition flew 41,404 sorties, over 24,000 of which were flown by the US Air Force.[63] Again, data is sparse but from 2004 to 2010 the US Air Force dropped 3,678 weapons, though importantly this figure excludes data from 2003, when the major aerial bombing campaign took place.[64]

Operation Iraqi Freedom officially ended in 2011 but the United States became re-involved in 2014 at the head of a new coalition called the Combined Joint Task Force—Operation Inherent Resolve. Operation Inherent Resolve is the name of the military campaign against the Islamic State and involves a US-led coalition in Iraq and Syria.[65] The aggregated strike data for Iraq and Syria is staggering even when compared to Operation Enduring Freedom and Operation Iraqi Freedom: just under 100,000 weapons released between 2015 and 2017 and a further 13,600 in 2018 and 2019 (Chapter 5, Figure 5.4).[66] According to Airwars, a UK-based independent organization that monitors and assesses civilian harm from airpower-dominated international military actions, the US-led coalition conducted well over 14,000 aerial strikes in Iraq between August 2014 and November 2019 with a further 19,786 strikes in Syria since September 2014.[67] Airwars estimates that these strikes have killed between 8,214 and 13,125 civilians, and although the number of airstrikes decreased significantly in 2018, at the time of writing (December 2019) Operation Inherent Resolve shows little sign of abating.[68]

Afghanistan and Iraq are, of course, not the only places that the United States has bombed in the last two decades. From the beginning, these 'core fronts' were conjoined with—and made possible by—forms of irregular warfare launched in what Maria Ryan calls 'peripheral or smaller, secondary theaters of the war on terror—weak states that lacked full control over their borders and territory, that policymakers feared terrorists might exploit as operational

[63] T. Michael Moseley, 'Operation Iraqi Freedom: By the Numbers' (Assessment and Analysis Division, US Air Force Central Command (AFCENT), 30 April 2003), 7 (on file with author).

[64] US Air Forces Central Command Public Affairs, '2004-2011 Combined Forces Air Component Commander Airpower Statistics'.

[65] Events over the last few years demonstrate the proliferation of US targeting operations around the globe. In 2014 the United States began bombing targets in Syria and the line between military operations in Iraq and Syria became blurred under the banner of Operation Inherent Resolve. The blurring of these lines can be seen in Chapter 5, Figure 5.4, where the US Air Force does not make any distinction between Iraq and Syria but rather reports them together in its 'airpower statistics'. I analyse parts of Operation Inherent Resolve in Chapters 5 and 6 but I have been unable to devote specific attention to the US air war in Syria.

[66] United States Air Force, 'Airpower Summaries: 31 December 2019', https://www.afcent.af.mil/About/Airpower-Summaries/, accessed 16 June 2020.

[67] Airwars, 'US-Led Coalition in Iraq & Syria', 18 November 2019, https://airwars.org/conflict/coalition-in-iraq-and-syria/, accessed 18 November 2019.

[68] Ibid.

bases'.[69] The cartographies of aerial violence include other conventional wars like Libya in 2011 but also bleed into a series of long-standing, semi-covert aerial wars in a number of territories outside of conventional battlefields. This includes Yemen, Pakistan, and Somalia.[70] The US aerial assaults in those countries have attracted significant media and scholarly attention.[71] But these air wars are semi-covert, and are run jointly and separately by both the Central Intelligence Agency (CIA) and the US military; in the first decade of the 'war on terror' at least, information about drone strikes in places like Yemen, Pakistan, and Somalia was hard to obtain. Far away from conventional battlefields like Afghanistan and Iraq, these 'drone wars' have enabled the United States to geographically expand the war on terror, so that commentators now speak of an 'everywhere war' or insist that the 'world is a battlefield'.[72] As important as these other theatres of war are, I focus on Iraq and Afghanistan partly because they dwarf these drone wars in scope and scale, and also because there is significantly more publicly available information about them.[73]

* * *

[69] Maria Ryan, *Full Spectrum Dominance: Irregular Warfare and the War on Terror* (Stanford, CA: Stanford University Press, 2019), Kindle version, location 244. Ryan details how the often-overlooked US military operations in the Philippines, Sub-Saharan Africa, and Georgia and the Casbian Basin were key testing grounds for the utilization of irregular tactics of warfare that were later adopted in Afghanistan and Iraq.

[70] The United States began airstrikes in Yemen in 2002 when the Central Intelligence Agency (CIA) targeted and killed Qaed Salim Sinan al-Harethi using a drone. For an account of the killing and its significance in setting a precedent for drone strikes outside of conventional battlefields see: Christopher Woods, *Sudden Justice: America's Secret Drone Wars* (New York, NY: Oxford University Press, 2015), 55–61. For US airstrikes statistics in Yemen, Pakistan, and Somalia see: The Bureau of Investigative Journalism, 'Drone Warfare', The Bureau of Investigative Journalism, n.d. https://www.thebureauinvestigates.com/projects/drone-war, accessed 22 January 2020.

[71] e.g. Derek Gregory, 'Drone Geographies', *Radical Philosophy* 183 (2014): 7–19; Markus Gunneflo, *Targeted Killing: A Legal and Political History* (Cambridge: Cambridge University Press, 2016); Jameel Jaffer, ed., *The Drone Memos: Targeted Killing, Secrecy, and the Law* (New York, NY: The New Press, 2016); Woods, *Sudden Justice*, 2015.

[72] Derek Gregory, 'The Everywhere War', *The Geographical Journal* 177, no. 3 (2011): 238–50; Jeremy Scahill, *Dirty Wars: The World Is a Battlefield* (London: Serpent's Tail, 2013).

[73] The focus on Iraq and Afghanistan has the added advantage that I was able to conduct the overwhelming majority of my interviews and research 'on the record', something I could not guarantee if I were to expand the research to include covert wars. Works on these covert wars include: James Cavallaro, Stephan Sonnenberg, and Sarah Knuckey, 'Living Under Drones: Death, Injury and Trauma to Civilians from US Drone Practices in Pakistan' (International Human Rights and Conflict Resolution Clinic, Stanford Law School, Stanford and NYU School of Law, Global Justice Clinic, New York, 2012), https://law.stanford.edu/publications/living-under-drones-death-injury-and-trauma-to-civilians-from-us-drone-practices-in-pakistan/, accessed 19 November 2019; Andrew Cockburn, *Kill Chain: The Rise of the High-Tech Assassins* (New York, NY: Henry Holt and Co., 2015); Derek Gregory, 'Dirty Dancing and Spaces of Exception in Pakistan', in *Life in the Age of Drone Warfare*, ed. Lisa Parks and Caren Kaplan (Durham, NC: Duke University Press Books, 2017); Open Society Justice Initiative and Amrit Singh, 'Death by Drone: Civilian Harm Caused by U.S. Targeted Killings in Yemen' (New York, NY: Open Society Justice Initiative, April 2015), http://www.opensocietyfoundations.org/reports/death-drone, accessed 15 April 2015; Charlie Savage, *Power Wars: Inside Obama's Post-9/11 Presidency* (New York, NY: Little, Brown and Company, 2015); Scahill, *Dirty Wars*; Woods, *Sudden Justice*.

Israel has been involved in several wars over the last two decades and notably launched a major aerial bombing campaign in Lebanon in 2006, but if one place has borne the brunt of enduring Israeli aerial violence in recent years it is Gaza.[74] In order to understand why Gaza has been repeatedly attacked in recent years, we must first understand something about the long-standing and ongoing Israeli occupation of the Palestinian Territories (Chapter 4).

The Palestinian Territories—the West Bank, Gaza, and East Jerusalem—have been subject to a variety of military measures for over seventy years and have been occupied by Israel since 1967. Since the start of the Second Intifada in 2000 Israel has increasingly defined its relationship with the Territories as one of war and has launched a series of air and ground wars in the West Bank and Gaza over the last two decades. One of the effects of the Israeli 'withdrawal' from Gaza in 2005 and the concomitant political ostracism of Gaza (classified by Israel's security cabinet as a 'hostile entity' in 2007,[75] Hamas having been listed as a terrorist organisation by the United States and the European Union since 1997 and 2001 respectively) is that Israel has increasingly relied on a massive use of air power in Gaza over the last decade.

Major recent military operations include 'Operation Cast-Lead' (Gaza, 2008–2009); 'Operation Pillar of Defense' (Gaza, 2012); and 'Operation Protective Edge' (Gaza, 2014), each of which began with aerial bombardments of Gaza, only later followed by ground invasions (in 2009 and 2014). During the three-week war of 2008–2009 Israeli forces killed 1,398 Palestinians. Of these, 764, or 55 per cent, were civilians, including 345, or 25 per cent, children. Eight Israelis were killed.[76] The one-week war in November 2012 saw Israeli military violence kill a further 168 Palestinians, of whom 101, or 60 per cent, are believed to be civilians, including 33 children.[77] Four Israeli civilians and

[74] In 2006 Israel launched a major air war against Hezbollah in Southern Beirut and South Lebanon. I was able to glean only basic information about the involvement of Israeli war lawyers in this war, so while the bombing of Lebanon in 2006, and also in 1982, are crucial examples of Israel's military aerial targeting, they do not form a significant part of my analysis. On the 2006 bombing see: William M. Arkin, *Divining Victory: Airpower in the 2006 Israel-Hezbollah War* (Maxwell Air Force Base, AL: Air University Press, 2007); Alan Craig, 'Lebanon 2006 and the Front of Legitimacy', *Israel Affairs* 15, no. 4 (2009): 427–44; Patrick Porter, 'The Divine Victory: Hizballa, Israel and the 2006 "July War"', in *Military Orientalism: Eastern War Through Western Eyes* (New York, NY: Columbia University Press, 2009), 171–90.

[75] Lisa Bhungalia, 'A Liminal Territory: Gaza, Executive Discretion, and Sanctions Turned Humanitarian', *GeoJournal* 75, no. 4 (2010): 347–57.

[76] B'Tselem, 'Fatalities during Operation Cast Lead', B'Tselem, n.d., https://www.btselem.org/statistics/fatalities/during-cast-lead/by-date-of-event, accessed 19 November 2019.

[77] United Nations Human Rights Council, 'Concerns Related to Adherence to International Human Rights and International Humanitarian Law in the Context of the Escalation between the State of

two soldiers were killed.[78] The most recent round of war in July and August 2014 was the most destructive yet (Chapter 4, Figure 4.1): 2,251 Palestinians were killed and 18,000 homes destroyed or damaged. Of these, 1,462, or 65 per cent, were civilians, including 551 children.[79] 68 Israelis were killed, 5 of whom were civilians.[80] The United Nations Human Rights Council noted that in the wake of the 2014 war, 'the scale of the devastation was unprecedented'.[81]

Israel has conducted targeting operations in Syria, Iraq, and Lebanon in recent years but these have tended to be ad hoc and piecemeal and, much like US strikes outside of recognized battlefields, these targeting operations have tended to be covert.[82] For these reasons, and because Gaza has become the principle theatre of Israeli air warfare over the last decade, I focus my attention principally on the thin piece of land sandwiched between the Mediterranean and Israel.

Method

I adopt a primarily empirical approach towards war lawyers, legal advice, and the laws of war. I do so partly because empirical accounts of these areas and how they work in practice are relatively rare, but also because, as Ian Hurd points out, an empirical approach allows us to examine 'law's normative

Israel, the de Facto Authorities in Gaza and Palestinian Armed Groups in Gaza That Occurred from 14 to 21 November 2012', Report of the United Nations High Commissioner for Human Rights on the Implementation of Human Rights Council Resolutions S-9/1 and S-12/1 (United Nations, 6 March 2013), 4, https://www.ohchr.org/Documents/HRBodies/HRCouncil/RegularSession/Session22/A.HRC.22.35.Add.1_AV.pdf, accessed 30 December 2019.

[78] B'Tselem, 'Human Rights Violations during Operation Pillar of Defense' (Jerusalem, May 2013), http://www.btselem.org/download/201305_pillar_of_defense_operation_eng.pdf, accessed 30 September 2014.

[79] United Nations Human Rights Commission, 'Report of the Detailed Findings of the Independent Commission of Inquiry Established Pursuant to Human Rights Council Resolution S-21/1' (United Nations Human Rights Council, 24 June 2015), 153, https://www.ohchr.org/en/hrbodies/hrc/coigazaconflict/pages/reportcoigaza.aspx, accessed 30 December 2019.

[80] B'Tselem, '50 Days: More than 500 Children—Facts and Figures on Fatalities in Gaza, Summer 2014', n.d., https://www.btselem.org/2014_gaza_conflict/en/il/, accessed 27 June 2017.

[81] United Nations Human Rights Commission, 'Report of the Detailed Findings of the Independent Commission of Inquiry Established Pursuant to Human Rights Council Resolution S-21/1', 153.

[82] Agence France-Presse, 'Second Round of Deadly Israeli Strikes Hit Syria', France 24, 3 June 2019, 24, https://www.france24.com/en/20190603-syria-israel-second-deadly-strikes-hit, accessed 29 November 2019; Oliver Holmes, 'UN Calls for "maximum Restraint" after Alleged Israeli Strike in Lebanon', *The Guardian*, 26 August 2019, sec. World, https://www.theguardian.com/world/2019/aug/26/israel-accused-of-targeting-iran-allies-in-lebanon-bombing, accessed 19 November 2019; Stratfor, 'For Israel, It's Open Skies Over Syria and Iraq', Stratfor, 14 October 2019, https://worldview.stratfor.com/article/israel-its-open-skies-over-syria-and-iraq-iran-hezbollah-airstrike, accessed 19 November 2019.

valence' as 'a question for investigation' rather than something that is known or assumed in advance.[83] My approach, inspired by Bourdieu's sociology of law, is important because it provides a way of working through and moving beyond what have become very entrenched positions between formalism (law as an independent variable) and instrumentalism (law as a reflection or tool in the service of dominant groups).[84] Thinking empirically and reflexively may also help us to make sense of the apparent contradictions that run through the laws of war and legal advice, and the juridical field as 'the site of competition for monopoly of the right to determine law',[85] that is, a space of contestation. The laws of war and legal advice have many generative functions: they both limit and unleash violence, permit and prohibit, legitimize and de-legitimize certain forms of action, and they simultaneously protect and expose populations—and not always in bifurcated ways. In what follows I bring these tensions to the fore and pay special attention to the legal interpretive projects of war advanced by the United States and Israel and made possible, in part, by war lawyers and their expertise.

This book is informed by seven years of research which has included three months of fieldwork,[86] over sixty interviews, archival research,[87] and extensive analysis of military documents and targeting doctrine. Interviews are a crucial part of this book and provide new insights into the world of war lawyers and their involvement in lethal targeting operations. I conducted a total of thirty-three interviews with US military personnel either retired or in active service, including twenty-five interviews with war lawyers and eight 'operators'.[88] Many of the interviews with war lawyers were conducted at The Judge Advocate General's Legal Center and School in Charlottesville (Virginia) during a five-day visit in July 2013.[89] I also conducted telephone, Skype, and Facetime interviews with war lawyers and operators based at various locations in the United States and military bases in the Middle East. I interviewed a further twelve

[83] Hurd, *How to Do Things with International Law*, 3.
[84] Bourdieu, 'The Force of Law'.
[85] Ibid., 817.
[86] Fieldwork was conducted in Tel Aviv, Jerusalem, and Charlottesville (Virginia) between 2013 and 2015.
[87] Archival research was conducted at three locations: (a) the Centre for Legal and Military Operations (CLAMO) library at the US Judge Advocate General's Legal Centre & School (Charlottesville, Virginia); (b) The US Air Force Library Information Program (Washington, DC); and (c) the National Archives and Records Administration at College Park, Maryland.
[88] For my purposes an operator is anyone who works on targeting in any capacity other than as a legal adviser.
[89] The US JAG Corps has five branches: Army; Marine; Navy; Air Force; and Coast Guard. Most of my interviews were with members of the US Air Force JAG Corps but I interviewed members from across the five branches.

Israeli war lawyers from the Military Advocate General Corps (MAG), most of whom were retired from active duties—these interviews were mostly conducted in Tel Aviv and Jerusalem in 2013 and 2014. I also interviewed three active-service Australian Defence Force war lawyers and three retired Royal Air Force and UK Army war lawyers. In addition to interviews with war lawyers and operators, I also conducted a total of ten interviews with human rights lawyers, non-governmental organizations (NGOs) involved in litigating targeting decisions, and selected legal scholars engaged with issues of targeting and the laws of war.

Militaries carve out areas, divide up jobs, and distribute and disperse responsibilities over an unimaginably large and complex geography. This meant that finding the right war lawyers and operators with the relevant experience was not a straightforward task. The kill chain is an especially dispersed part of the military apparatus and so my approach in a sense had to mimic the geographies of the kill chain. This meant going through but also beyond the offices of public affairs; it meant contacting specific Air Force components and departments, different judge advocate (JAG) departments, and individuals across many different units and departments in several different locations in the United States and the Middle East.

The United States and Israeli militaries have designated offices responsible for targeting, but they are multiple and decentralized over many locations. Each 'targeting cell', as they are called, tends to have rotational staff, meaning that every six to twelve months there is a changeover in personnel. This makes it difficult to know who and how many people are involved in targeting at any one time, and to identify the right people to interview. Complicating matters further is the fact that the US Air Force and, to a lesser degree, the Israeli military do not have designated permanent 'targeting lawyers'. Instead, they have a select group of lawyers who are *sometimes* involved in targeting. In Israel there is a greater degree of specialization in areas relating to targeting than in the United States. For example, war lawyers in the Israeli military's International Law Department specialize in 'international law (particularly the Law of Armed Conflict) and have expertise on a range of issues, including targeting, weapons, and detention'.[90] This means that targeting law is one of several areas of expertise for the select group of war lawyers—who number around thirty—who work in the International Law Department.[91] The US Air Force prefer their war lawyers to be generalists rather than specialists, which means that a

[90] Israel Ministry of Foreign Affairs, 'The 2014 Gaza Conflict: Factual and Legal Aspects', 140.
[91] Libman, interview.

typical Air Force lawyer will work across a much broader range of areas than their Israeli counterparts.[92] One year US Air Force lawyers might be responsible for conducting the legal overview of the US nuclear war plan. The next year they may find themselves in a targeting cell.[93] A select few US Air Force lawyers who gain targeting experience may remain involved in targeting for a number of years, and some even remain in this position to help teach targeting law to lawyers who have recently been given a targeting assignment, but this is very much the exception.[94] In order to negotiate these difficulties I worked to build trust with those who I met and interviewed and relied on the goodwill of interviewees who would refer me to relevant colleagues.

In order to keep pace with the rapidly evolving world of aerial warfare and legal advice I developed, organized, and analysed a 'living archive' of primary and secondary source publications and reports from a host of state and non-state organizations. This 'archive' consists of: (a) official government and military speeches, statements, and transcripts; (b) court decisions and legislation; (c) military doctrine, including doctrine on targeting and legal operational support; (d) jurisprudence and other legal statements and publications by legal practitioners and legal scholars; (e) reports published by think-tank, non-governmental, and human rights groups; (f) journalistic accounts, including media coverage of military and security leaks; and (g) book and journal length scholarship. These materials quickly became vital resources for developing my thinking around the laws of war and the role of war lawyers in aerial targeting operations.

When it comes to aerial targeting and ongoing military operations, access to material and personnel is uneven at best. Drawing on multiple methods enabled access to different kinds of knowledge and perspectives on targeting but crucially it also allowed me to navigate the gaps in information that inevitably reveal themselves when researching such sensitive matters. Using different methods has also made space for an analysis which is both historical and contemporary. Archival research, for example, was necessary to document the role of war lawyers in the Vietnam War, while interviews combined with online archival research was utilized for investigating the role of war lawyers from the First Gulf War (1990–1991) onwards. A flexible methodological approach permitted me to react to the specificities and constraints of each context. For example, in places where travel is restricted (e.g. Gaza, Afghanistan, and Iraq)

[92] Stefano (pseudonym), interview; Hopkins, interview.
[93] Solis, interview.
[94] Stefano (pseudonym), interview; Richards, interview.

I relied on publicly available reports from militaries and non-governmental organizations and on journalists and others on the ground. Where information was protected and unavailable because of security and classification issues, I turned to declassified or leaked documents. Where active-duty military personnel were not able or were unwilling to be interviewed, I sought interviews with higher authorities or retired personnel (who are often not under the same constraints as active-duty personnel).

At various points throughout this book I reflect on issues of method, access, and positionality because these are inseparable from my analysis of the role of war lawyers and the laws of war in aerial targeting operations.

Targeting Typologies and Targeting Law

There are two main types of aerial targeting operations: deliberate and dynamic.[95] Deliberate targeting operations (sometimes called planned targeting) are those that have been planned or pre-authorized. Dynamic targeting operations (sometimes called time-sensitive targeting—or TST) are not planned but rather emerge during 'live' battle. If a pilot has been briefed on a target *before* she or he steps into the aircraft, then it is a deliberate target. If a target appears *after* the aircraft has taken off and the pilot receives her or his orders while flying, then it is a dynamic target. In a dynamic targeting operation, the time between the identification of the target and the use of weapons against it—what is called the 'Find, Fix, Finish' phase—is typically much shorter than deliberate targeting operations: hours and minutes, rather than days, weeks, or months.

There are two main types of dynamic targeting. The first type is where a strike is required to support troops who have encountered the enemy. This is called 'troops in contact' (or 'TIC'), which in turn requires 'close air support' ('CAS').[96] The second, a 'time-sensitive target' (also called 'target of opportunity' or 'fleeting target'), is a target that emerges during battle which is either deemed to be of 'high value' (hence the phrase 'high value target' or 'high value individual') or because it is thought to pose—or may soon pose—a threat to friendly forces. These distinctions are made by the Joint Forces of

[95] These are ideal types of targeting. In the fast pace of military practice, the distinction between deliberate and dynamic targeting is often blurred.

[96] Human Rights Watch, '"Troops in Contact": Airstrikes and Civilian Deaths in Afghanistan', September 2008, http://www.hrw.org/sites/default/files/reports/afghanistan0908webwcover_0.pdf, accessed 9 November 2014.

Categories of Targeting and Targets

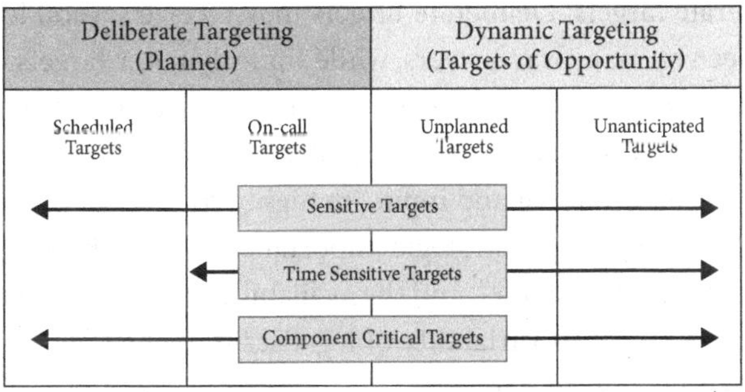

Figure 0.1 Categories of targeting and targets.
Source: United States Joint Chiefs of Staff, 'Joint Targeting', Joint Publication 3-60 (Washington, DC, 31 January 2013), II–1.

the US military—which, unlike Israel, publishes vast amounts of doctrine on targeting—but Israel reportedly uses similar distinctions.[97] The relationships between the four types of targeting (and three further, cross-cutting distinctions) are summarized in Figure 0.1.

The distinction between deliberate and dynamic targeting operations is important for several reasons, but three are especially significant to the involvement of war lawyers and the juridification of the kill chain. First, as I show in Chapter 6, and drawing on important analysis by Human Rights Watch, dynamic targeting operations have been linked to an especially high number of civilian casualties.[98] Second, certain forms of dynamic targeting—including close air support—raise the risk of fratricide. The US Air Force refer to the increasing rapidity of dynamic targeting operations as the 'compression of the kill chain' but speed can come with a significant cost.[99] In a dynamic targeting, time is short, intelligence is rushed, and everyone in the process is under additional pressure; if something goes wrong the best case scenario is that they may miss an 'opportunity' but in the worst case their comrades on the ground may be killed.[100] Third (and relatedly), while war lawyers are involved in both types

[97] Laurie R. Blank and Amos Guiora, 'Updating the Commander's Toolbox: New Tools for Operationalizing the Laws of Armed Conflict', *PRISM* 1, no. 3 (2010): 64; Israel Ministry of Foreign Affairs, 'The Operation in Gaza-Factual and Legal Aspects', 81.

[98] Human Rights Watch, '"Troops in Contact": Airstrikes and Civilian Deaths in Afghanistan'.

[99] Adam J. Hebert, 'Compressing the Kill Chain', *Air Force Magazine* 86, no. 3 (2003): 50–5.

[100] Nancy Benac and Associated Press, 'The Long, Unfortunate History of Friendly Fire Accidents in U.S. Conflicts', *PBS NewsHour*, 11 June 2014, https://www.pbs.org/newshour/nation/long-unfortunate-history-friendly-fire-accidents-u-s-conflicts, accessed 30 January 2020; CBS News, 'The Afghan War's Deadliest Friendly Fire Incident for U.S. Soldiers', *CBS News*, 9 November 2017, https://www.cbsnews.com/news/the-afghan-wars-deadliest-friendly-fire-incident-involving-u-s-soldiers/, accessed 30 January 2020.

of operations, dynamic targets often do not receive the same level of legal scrutiny as deliberate targets. Deliberate targets may receive several legal reviews and may be seen by many war lawyers, while some dynamic targets may receive no legal review at all or may be reviewed only very quickly (Chapters 5 and 6). Thus, while war lawyers are deeply involved in all kinds of aerial targeting operations their involvement and input are highly contingent and provisional, even today. The intensity and strategic importance of the fighting, the political and legal sensitivity of the target, and the availability of qualified personnel, are some of the factors in this variability of legal scrutiny. War lawyers are not—and will never be—omnipresent.

I must make one further distinction to address what has become known as 'targeted killing'. Targeted killing focuses exclusively on the *killing of individuals* (as distinct from both objects and the more generalized form of the 'enemy', who constitute a collective). Legal Adviser for the International Committee of the Red Cross Nils Melzer defines targeted killing as 'the use of lethal force attributable to a subject of international law with the intent, premeditation and deliberation to kill *individually selected persons* who are not in the physical custody of those targeting them.'[101] Targeted killing has become an increasingly important part of war over the last two decades and has been a key driver and outcome of the individuation of war, which I discuss later in this chapter. Yet, as important as the targeting of individuals has become, it remains one targeting strategy among a much broader range of lethal targeting options in the US and Israeli repertoire.

The laws of war

The laws of war are not the only legal regime that governs aerial targeting operations; they are also governed by rules of engagement (ROE) and operational law. War lawyers play an increasingly important role in shaping these legal regimes into *facts on the ground*. The three regimes exist in dialectical relation both to one another and to the practice of targeting itself, each producing and animating the other in a reciprocal ongoing exchange.

The laws of war have two central functions. First, they *regulate* conduct, setting out permissible and prohibited behaviour and proscribing the latter. Helen

[101] Nils Melzer, *Targeted Killing in International Law* (Oxford; New York, NY: Oxford University Press, 2009), 5 (emphasis added). Melzer provides an overview of definitions of targeted killing by several authors and all of them focus on killing individuals.

M. Kinsella has argued that this function of the laws of war implies not only that wars are regulated in the usual sense of the word but also that wars are '*made regular*; that is, they must unfold as a predictable sequence of events, conforming to a particular pattern as practiced by professionals'.[102] Second, the laws of war seek to limit the effects of armed conflict and provide a series of protections for certain groups of people (such as civilians, prisoners of war, and those who are *hors du combat*). These two functions are not necessarily complementary, and actors put different amounts of emphasis on them depending on their identity and normative alliances.

The laws of war consist of two main sources: treaty law, which is law between states; and customary law, which is based on the practice (custom) of states. Treaty law, also sometimes called conventional international law, binds states that sign and ratify treaties, whereas customary international law's jurisdiction is universal.[103] Until as late as the mid-nineteenth century the laws of war were based more on custom, religion, and morality than on any kind of formal codified law.[104] This changed in the 1860s as President Lincoln had a legal code drawn up for his Union forces. The Lieber Code, or General Orders 100 as it became known, became the definitive law of war manual for the American Civil War but it also subsequently informed one of the first formal statements on the laws of war, the Hague Conventions of 1899 and 1907. As Gordon and Perugini argue, military manuals like the Lieber Code interpret what the legal norms convey in a way that is compatible with military objectives, and this interpretation often becomes the dominant way the laws of war are construed more generally. They argue, 'the code was conceived as both an operational manual and an international instrument for defining the legitimate and illegitimate use of violence for "civilized nations" well beyond the borders of the country where it had been drafted.'[105] This shows the law-making power of military manuals, which war lawyers today are extensively involved in writing, but it also highlights the disproportionate power some states can have in defining and shaping the laws of war. It also reveals part of the dialectical relationship between military instructions made by and for militaries (or what would become known as rules of engagement) and the laws of war that regulate military conduct.

[102] Kinsella, *The Image Before the Weapon*, 105 (emphasis added).

[103] Lisa Hajjar, 'International Humanitarian Law and "Wars on Terror": A Comparative Analysis of Israeli and American Doctrines and Policies', *Journal of Palestine Studies* 36, no. 1 (2006): 38, fn. 21.

[104] Kinsella, *The Image Before the Weapon*.

[105] Neve Gordon and Nicola Perugini. *Human Shields: A History of People in the Line of Fire* (Oakland: University of California Press, 2020), 130.

The Hague Convention begins with a famous preamble written by Frederic de Martens, a Russian lawyer and diplomat and a delegate at the Hague Peace Conference in 1899. The 'Martens clause', as it became known, asserts:

> [T]hese provisions, the wording of which has been inspired by the desire to diminish the evils of war so far as military necessities permit, are destined to serve as general rules of conduct for belligerents in their relations with each other and with populations.[106]

The Martens clause embodies a central tension of the laws of war; namely, the balance between limiting the effects of war while also permitting what is militarily 'necessary'. One of the key arguments that runs through this book is that the United States and Israel often take an especially broad and flexible view of 'military necessity' and this systematically muddies any 'humanitarian' vision of the laws of war (see '*War's legal power*').[107] The other principal set of treaties underpinning the laws of war are the Geneva Conventions, which date back to 1864 and prominently include the Four Geneva Conventions:

1. The Geneva Convention for the Amelioration of the Condition of the Wounded and Sick in Armed Forces in the Field (1864);
2. The Geneva Convention for the Amelioration of the Condition of Wounded, Sick and Shipwrecked Members of Armed Forces at Sea (1906);
3. The Geneva Convention relative to the Treatment of Prisoners of War (1929);
4. The Geneva Convention relative to the Protection of Civilian Persons in Times of War (1949).

The modern law of targeting is enshrined in the 1977 Protocols Additional to the Geneva Conventions of 1949 (henceforth: Additional Protocols) and in customary international law. Additional Protocol I—the Protection of Victims of International Armed Conflicts—'provides that armed conflicts in which

[106] International Committee of the Red Cross, 'Preamble to Convention (IV) Respecting the Laws and Customs of War on Land and Its Annex: Regulations Concerning the Laws and Customs of War on Land.' (The Hague, 18 October 1907), https://ihl-databases.icrc.org/applic/ihl/ihl.nsf/Article.xsp?action=openDocument&documentId=BD48EA8AD56596A3C12563CD0051653F, accessed 29 December 2016.

[107] cf. Alexander, 'A Short History of International Humanitarian Law'.

peoples are fighting against colonial domination, alien occupation or racist regimes are to be considered international conflicts.'[108] Additional Protocol II—the Protection of Victims of Non-International Armed Conflicts—sought to extend existing protections in the Geneva Conventions (so called 'Common Article 3' protections) to *internal* armed conflicts. Although the United States and Israel never became state parties to Additional Protocol I (Chapter 2) the Additional Protocols constitute customary, and therefore binding, international law.

The law of targeting is based upon four interrelated fundamental principles:

1. *Necessity*: Attacks shall be limited strictly to military objectives. In so far as objects are concerned, military objectives are limited to those objects which by their nature, location, purpose or use make an effective contribution to military action and whose total or partial destruction, capture or neutralization, in the circumstances ruling at the time, offers a definite military advantage.[109]
2. *Distinction*: In order to ensure respect for and protection of the civilian population and civilian objects, the Parties to the conflict shall at all times distinguish between the civilian population and combatants and between civilian objects and military objectives and accordingly shall direct their operations only against military objectives.[110]
3. *Proportionality*: Launching an attack which may be expected to cause incidental loss of civilian life, injury to civilians, damage to civilian objects, or a combination thereof, which would be excessive in relation to the concrete and direct military advantage anticipated, is prohibited.[111]
4. *Humanity*: The principle of humanity forbids the infliction of all suffering, injury or destruction not necessary for achieving the legitimate purpose of a conflict.[112]

[108] International Committee of the Red Cross, 'Protocol Additional to the Geneva Conventions of 12 August 1949, and Relating to the Protection of Victims of International Armed Conflicts (Protocol I)' (Bern, Switzerland, 8 June 1977), Art. 1, ¶4, https://ihl-databases.icrc.org/ihl/INTRO/470, accessed 29 December 2016.

[109] Additional Protocol I, Art 52.2.
[110] Additional Protocol I, Art. 48
[111] International Committee of the Red Cross, Customary Rules of International Humanitarian Law, Rule 14.
[112] International Committee of the Red Cross, 'What Is IHL?', *International Committee of the Red Cross*, 18 September 2015, https://www.icrc.org/en/document/what-ihl?language=en, accessed 11 January 2017.

Rules of engagement

In addition to the laws of war, targeting is also governed by rules of engagement (ROE). ROE are rules that set out 'when, where, against whom, and how force can be used'.[113] A military will commonly have standard rules of engagement (SROE) that establish fundamental policies and procedures governing the actions to be taken by commanders during all military operations but these are augmented by additional ROE that are specific to particular: (a) military components (e.g. Air, Land, Sea); (b) command levels (e.g. command headquarters, brigade, battalion); (c) military operations (e.g. 'Operation Inherent Resolve'—the war against the Islamic State in Iraq and Syria); and (d) designated geographical areas (e.g. Baghdad, North or South Afghanistan). ROE are fluid documents; their content and applicability vary in both time and space and they are constantly reissued, rescinded, and updated. The plural and fluid nature of ROE mean that soldiers of the same military can be subject to different rules depending on what their particular mission is and when, where, and for which section (and level) of the military they are fighting.

ROE are informed by the laws of war (and, in turn, the ROE dialectically inform the laws of war) but they tend to be more detailed and specific. Where the laws of war are made up of (often vague) principles, ROE are more like a set of instructions or a list of dos and don'ts. As former US military lawyer Gary Solis explains:

> Rules of engagement are not law of armed conflict or international humanitarian law. They are not mentioned in the Geneva Conventions or Additional Protocols, and they are not the subject of a multinational treaty bearing on armed conflict. Nor are they domestic law. *They are military directives, heavy with acronyms.*[114]

ROE have three well-mixed ingredients: law, politics, and military exigencies. As a legal construct, ROE provide constraints and permissions on a force's actions based on both domestic and international law.[115] ROE

[113] Kristin Bergtora Sandvik, 'Regulating War in the Shadow of Law: Toward a Re-Articulation of ROE', *Journal of Military Ethics* 13, no. 2 (2014): 118.

[114] Gary D. Solis, *The Law of Armed Conflict: International Humanitarian Law in War*, 1st edition (Cambridge: Cambridge University Press, 2010), 490 (emphasis added, acronyms removed).

[115] United States Air Force Judge Advocate General's School, 'Air Force Operations and the Law' (Maxwell Air Force Base, AL: US Air Force, 2014), 255–56, http://www.afjag.af.mil/Portals/77/documents/AFD-100510-059.pdf, accessed 13 February 2014.

maximize military flexibility by strategically moving between domestic and international law.[116] As a political construct, ROE reflect national policies (and, to some extent, the public national appetite for any given war effort) and push these forward into the theatre of combat. If the policy objective is decisive aerial firepower (as it was during the initial weeks of the invasion of Afghanistan and Iraq in 2001 and 2003), the ROE will ideally reflect this. But if the goal then becomes the winning of 'hearts and minds' (as it did in Iraq shortly after the destruction wrought by 'shock and awe' bombing in 2003), this will require not only a rewriting of the ROE but also a vast political-cultural shift in the way that war is fought and understood. Finally, as a military construct, ROE assist commanders to accomplish missions and hence must be compatible with military objectives. The cornerstone of all ROE is a clear articulation of the rights of self-defence, including individual, unit, and national self-defence.

ROE do not recite vast extracts from the laws of war. Instead, and with assistance from war lawyers, they actively interpret and redeploy key legal principles such as necessity, distinction, proportionality, and humanity. This helps to make war fighting rules understandable to commanders and soldiers who could be as young as 18 years old. Mission- or component-specific ROE also help clarify to respective troops exactly which rules they are operating under at any given time and place. The laws of war stipulate that civilian casualties resulting from an attack must be *proportional* to the military advantage gained by carrying out the attack, but it does not provide an exact threshold or number to determine proportionality—another example of the law's indeterminacy. ROE, however, *may* go as far as to dictate such a number: it could be zero or it could be thirty, depending on military and political considerations (Chapter 5). This degree of specificity makes ROE easier to understand for those who ultimately use them. This process is referred to as 'operationalizing' the law, a process that, as I show in Chapter 2, involves a mixing of law, military exigencies, and strategic considerations in the 'worlding' of rules.

[116] A prominent example is the US assertion, under President George W. Bush, that the Geneva Conventions do not apply to detainees captured and imprisoned in the liminal spaces of the 'war on terror'. As Khalili details: '[F]lexibility in legal categories is created through both the creation of categories themselves and a strategic vacillation between different regimes of law that facilitate the process of categorisation. [. . .] the Geneva Conventions and the Conventions against Torture had to be set aside to allow domestic laws to provide such flexibility.' Khalili, *Time in the Shadows*, 78.

Operational law and the 'military gaze'

The third legal regime relevant to targeting is operational law (also sometimes known as 'operations law'). Operational law was invented and developed by US war lawyers in the 1970s and 1980s in order to communicate the importance of the laws of war and attendant rights and responsibilities in the execution of war. Commanders tend not to think in terms of the laws of war, partly because its principles are so indeterminate and require significant levels of interpretation. Ambiguous legal categories are one thing to debate in a classroom setting, but quite another to implement during the heat of battle, which is why commanders increasingly demand well-defined ROE and require ever more operational legal advice. In terms of understanding the practical edge of how law has come to matter to the 'prosecution' of war, the question of how law is 'operationalized' is therefore paramount. Indeed, as one Israeli war lawyer confided to me in an interview:

> The biggest challenge for lawyers in the military is to take this huge body of international law which is really complicated and very grey and very obfuscated, and basically reduce it to a one-liner or a paragraph which gives the military commander the right kind of tools to make the right kind of decision . . . Our clients need to get something distilled.[117]

But, as I show in Chapter 2, simplification (or 'distillation') is not the only thing that operational law achieves. By simplifying the laws of war, operational law also *produces* law; in doing so it clears the ground for what has been termed the 'military gaze'—a military way of seeing and knowing the world that normalizes, indeed necessitates, violence.[118] Military targets can be thought of as representational and performative spaces where people, places, infrastructures (digital and analogue), and objects are interpreted as possessing or displaying threatening markers of enmity that must be incapacitated or rendered inoperable by various means (injury, death, damage, destruction, or hacking).

A military target encourages and entrains a directionality of violence. Once designated as such, a military target suggests and even recommends its own immolation, sacrifices itself to the violent abstractions and representations that

[117] Benjamin, interview.

[118] Derek Gregory, 'Dis/Ordering the Orient: Scopic Regimes and Modern War', in *Orientalism and War*, ed. Tarak Barkawi and Keith Stanski (New York, NY: Columbia University Press, 2013), 151–76.

have produced it. As Rey Chow has succinctly put it, 'seeing is destroying.'[119] She quotes W. J. Perry, a former United States Under Secretary of State for Defense, who claimed: 'If I had to sum up current thinking on precision missiles and saturation weaponry in a single sentence, I'd put it like this: once you can see the target, you can expect to destroy it.'[120] This militarized way of seeing is inseparable from the construction of targets, for as Derek Gregory has argued: 'The politico-cultural construction of a wider 'landscape of threat' is crucial to the production and performance of a specific 'space of the target'.'[121] But our world is not made of military targets and as tempting as it may be to think about certain places, objects, or groups of people as 'natural' targets—'terrorist training camps', 'bomb making facilities', 'the Islamic State'—we should resist the tendency to naturalize that which has been established through sedimented political, linguistic, and increasingly *legal* work.

No amount or type of law can eliminate the violence of targeting because violence is *intrinsic* to targeting. This is not to say that law cannot change the way that targeting is carried out, or its quantity, and so lead to less violent outcomes. It can and does. But law can also have the opposite effect, enabling, legitimizing, and extending violence. Violence is *mediated* by and through law. The intrinsic violence of targeting can be easy to forget or deny, especially when it has become routine—routine for both those who *do* targeting (Chapter 5) and also for the publics who have become accustomed to air and drone strikes as an inevitable and unproblematic part of the modern geopolitical landscape.[122]

Amidst talk of 'precision' warfare and 'surgical' strikes, it is worth reminding ourselves that technologically advanced warfare is not nearly as clean and bloodless as many of its proponents claim. The violence of targeting and the military gaze is felt on a daily basis by what Lisa Parks has memorably called a disenfranchised 'targeted class'.[123] Inhabitants of the places and spaces that the United States and Israel target—Afghanistan, Iraq, and Gaza, but also *inter*

[119] Rey Chow, *The Age of the World Target: Self-Referentiality in War, Theory, and Comparative Work* (Durham, NC: Duke University Press, 2006), 27. See also: Derek Gregory, '"Doors into Nowhere": Dead Cities and the Natural History of Destruction', in *Cultural Memories: The Geographical Point of View*, ed. Peter Meusburger, Michael Heffernan, and Edgar Wunder (Dordrecht; Heidelberg; London; New York, NY: Springer, 2011), 249–83.

[120] Chow, *The Age of the World Target*, 35.

[121] Derek Gregory, 'Kunduz and "Seeing like a Military"', *Geographical Imaginations* (blog), 2 January 2014, https://geographicalimaginations.com/2014/01/02/kunduz-and-seeing-like-a-military/, accessed 24 January 2017.

[122] For critical accounts of which, see: Grégoire Chamayou, *Drone Theory* (London: Penguin, 2015); Gregory, 'From a View to a Kill Drones and Late Modern War'; Gregory, 'Drone Geographies'; Ian G. R. Shaw, *Predator Empire: Drone Warfare and Full Spectrum Dominance* (Minneapolis: University of Minnesota Press, 2016); Woods, *Sudden Justice*, 2015.

[123] Lisa Parks, 'Drones, Vertical Mediation, and the Targeted Class', *Feminist Studies* 42, no. 1 (2016): 227–35.

alia, Yemen, Pakistan, Somalia, and Lebanon—have 'become part of a targeted class simply because they live and move in areas in which terror suspects *may* operate. In such areas, anyone and everyone is at risk, and daily life is haunted by the specter of aerial monitoring and bombardment.'[124]

* * *

On the other side of the fence, war lawyers' involvement in aerial targeting operations has become routine, normal, and even unremarkable. War lawyers who work on the 'operational floor' of the Combined Air Operations Center (CAOC) in Al Udeid, Qatar—the command and control centre for US air wars in Iraq, Afghanistan, and Syria—speak about the mundane nature of their work.[125] An Israeli war lawyer told me that many of the younger generation of kill chain lawyers are not aware that there was an era in which war lawyers were *not* involved in targeting: 'today [. . .] no one even knows there was a revolution, that's how good it was!'[126] Every institution has its own way of normalizing particular practices and divisions of labour, especially when the product of that labour is explicitly violent;[127] the military kill chain is an accelerated mode of bureaucratic death.[128] As Diddier Fassin's cautionary observation reminds us: 'Where the self-evidence of the social world imposes itself through current affairs and everyday life, a capacity for surprise needs to be maintained.'[129] There is value in problematizing and interrogating the means by which war lawyers have become *kill chain* lawyers.

Later Modern War and the Rise of the Kill Chain Lawyer

In answering the question, *why did war lawyers become involved in the provision of legal advice in aerial targeting operations?*—the historical answer of this book rests in large part on how the US military interpreted the successes and failures of its actions in the Vietnam War (1955–1975). In particular, veterans who came to be in leadership positions after the Vietnam War took a different

[124] Ibid., 231.

[125] In fact, the CAOC at Al Udeid Air Base provides command and control of air power throughout Iraq, Syria, Afghanistan, and seventeen other nations (see Chapter 5).

[126] Reisner, Interview.

[127] Robert M. Cover, 'Violence and the Word', *Yale Law Journal* 95, no. 8 (1986); Zygmunt Bauman, *Modernity and the Holocaust* (Ithaca, NY: Cornell University Press, 2001).

[128] Gregory, 'From a View to a Kill Drones and Late Modern War'; Shaw, *Predator Empire*.

[129] Didier Fassin, *Humanitarian Reason: A Moral History of the Present* (Berkeley and Los Angeles, CA; London: University of California Press, 2012), 244.

view to their predecessors of how the laws of war and ROE could and should operate. In Chapter 2 I trace the origins of operational law and show how, through careful interpretive work, it put the laws of war to work for the US military—certainly not for the first time, but to a then unprecedented degree—and paved the way for the involvement of war lawyers in aerial targeting operations in the early 1990s. War lawyers were deployed to provide direct legal advice on aerial targeting operations for the first time in the First Gulf War (1990–1991—Chapter 3). The Israeli military looked to and borrowed from the US approach in incorporating war lawyers into its kill chain but as I show in Chapter 4, Israeli war lawyers gained their experience from their extensive involvement in administering the occupation of the Palestinian Territories from 1967, and they continue to sharpen it to the present day. The year 2000 was something of catalyst for the incorporation of Israeli war lawyers into the kill chain and the Israeli military used the Second Intifada as an opportunity to legally rationalize a new 'targeted killing' policy.

By the invasions of Afghanistan in 2001 and Iraq in 2003 US war lawyers were already well integrated into the kill chain but these inauspicious conflicts have seen an extension and deepening of the expectations placed on war lawyers as their centrality to mission success has become more fully appreciated (Chapters 5 and 6). The rise of the kill chain lawyer, then, did not take place overnight; it took time and was forged in the crucibles of several wars. More than this; warfare itself has changed over the period covered by this book. Transformations in the way that war is fought and understood have generated particular ways of killing and specific representational regimes that came to require input from war lawyers and webs of legal advice.

Later modern war

In recent years there has been much said and written on the topic of so-called 'new wars'.[130] Mary Kaldor used the term to denote a series of differences between what she called 'new' and 'old' wars, and although scholars have pointed out that Kaldor may have overstated the distinctiveness of these categories the new wars thesis has generated useful debates and new concepts for grappling

[130] Mats Berdal, 'How "New" Are "New Wars"? Global Economic Change and the Study of Civil War', *Global Governance* 9, no. 4 (2003): 477–502; Mary Kaldor, 'In Defence of New Wars', *Stability: International Journal of Security and Development* 2, no. 1 (2013): Art. 4, 1–16; Mary Kaldor, *New and Old Wars: Organized Violence in a Global Era*, 2nd edition (Stanford, CA: Stanford University Press, 2007).

with the changing character of war.[131] Derek Gregory has written of what he calls the 'everywhere war', where military, paramilitary, and terrorist violence 'can, in principle, occur anywhere'.[132] Stephen Graham has argued that the 'battlefield' has become a '*battlespace*', a concept that prefigures 'a boundless and unending process of militarization where everything becomes a permanent site of war'.[133] Jolle Demmers and Lauren Gould spell out what is at stake in the contemporary moment of what they call 'liquid warfare':

> [C]onventional ties between war, space and time have become undone. Liquid warfare is about flexible, open-ended, 'pop-up' military interventions, supported by remote technology and reliant on local partnerships and private contractors, through which (coalitions of) parties aim to promote and protect interests. Liquid warfare is thus temporally open-ended and event-ful, as well as spatially dispersed and mobile.[134]

My own preference is to think about recent changes in warfare in terms of modern and later modern war. Derek Gregory uses the latter to denote a series of transformations that have taken place in the conduct and representation of war, especially in the second half of the twentieth century and early twenty-first century.[135] This includes a move away from the industrial standing armies and set-piece battles of the late nineteenth and early twentieth centuries,[136] towards more flexible and responsive modes of (para)military organization. It also denotes a move away from total war and area bombing—where whole cities are the target—to more focused targeting, which increasingly (though by no means exclusively) focuses on mobile—as opposed to fixed—targets and individuals. As Gregory has argued, there is a crucial sense in which war has always been fought 'among the people' (i.e. among civilians) but in later modern

[131] Mats Berdal's critique is particularly pointed: 'As an analytical category, the notion of "new wars" does more, in the end, to obscure than to illuminate': Mats Berdal, 'The "new Wars" Thesis Revisited', in *The Changing Character of War*, ed. Sibylle Scheipers and Hew Strachan (New York, NY: Oxford University Press, 2011), 110. See generally: Hew Strachan and Sibylle Scheipers, *The Changing Character of War* (Oxford; New York, NY: Oxford University Press, 2011).

[132] Gregory, 'The Everywhere War', 238.

[133] Stephen Graham, 'Cities as Battlespace: The New Military Urbanism', *City* 13, no. 4 (2009): 383–402, 389.

[134] Jolle Demmers and Lauren Gould, 'An Assemblage Approach to Liquid Warfare: AFRICOM and the "Hunt" for Joseph Kony', *Security Dialogue* 49, no. 5 (2018): 364–81, 364.

[135] 'From a View to a Kill Drones and Late Modern War', 188–215; Gregory, 'The Everywhere War', 238–50.

[136] Derek Gregory, 'Gabriel's Map: Cartography and Corpography in Modern War', in *Geographies of Knowledge and Power*, ed. Peter Meusburger, Derek Gregory, and Laura Suarsana, 2015 edition (New York, NY: Springer, 2015), 89–121; Derek Gregory, 'The Natures of War', *Antipode* 48, no. 1 (2016): 3–56.

war it is 'formidably, constitutively difficult to distinguish between combatants and civilians'.[137] Similarly, wars have always been fought between enemies of different strengths, but late modern war takes asymmetries to the extreme.[138]

As the divide between those who have the destructive technologies of war and those who do not has become more pronounced, war increasingly resembles colonial massacres,[139] and like colonial modes of warfare where the fighting was outsourced to the colony, today the killing is often done remotely but with even less risk to 'our' side.[140] The line between modern and *late modern* war is not always distinct and in many ways 'modern' wars and the maximum destruction they sow are very much still with us, as aerial assaults on Baghdad (1991, 2003), Beirut (2006), Gaza (2009, 2012, 2014), Homs (2012), Aleppo (2016), Mosul (2017), Raqqa (2017), Ghouta (2012–2018), and elsewhere so painfully demonstrate. *Later modern war* does not dispose of modern war; it emerges from, and often *with* it. Notwithstanding that other militaries vary widely in how far they reference law, it is in the context of later modern war that US and Israeli war lawyers became kill chain lawyers.

The juridification of later modern war—or what I call juridical warfare—is not about rendering this war or that method of combat legal; it is not about—or is not only about—how war and methods of combat have become more lawful in the sense of compliance with a legal rule. Rather, it is about how war has become more *law-full*—full of law—in the sense that it is increasingly conducted and understood in relation to law, legal discourse, and legal debates—issues we shall return to in the Conclusion.

Civilians and civilian casualties

Three broad and related features of later modern war have been particularly important in the drive to incorporate war lawyers into the kill chain. The first concerns the changing role of civilians and the increasingly complex values ascribed to them in later modern war. The concern for civilian casualties emerged partly out of the US experience in Vietnam (Chapter 1), but I go on to show how it was not until the First Gulf War (Chapter 3) and especially wars of the post-9/11 era that the United States (and later Israel)

137 Gregory, 'From a View to a Kill Drones and Late Modern War', 200.
138 Chamayou, *Drone Theory*.
139 Achille Mbembe, 'Necropolitics', *Public Culture* 15, no. 1 (2003): 11–40.
140 Paul W. Kahn, 'Imagining Warfare', *European Journal of International Law* 24, no. 1 (2013): 199–226; Khalili, *Time in the Shadows*.

began institutionalizing policies of civilian casualty mitigation (Chapters 4–6). Legal questions around military necessity and proportionality are critical to civilian causality mitigation policy and, where the rubber meets the road, war lawyers became a crucial component in helping commanders decide who can be legally targeted and what constitutes an acceptable level of civilian and infrastructural harm.

Deciding who is a civilian and who is a combatant is not a question of 'finding' some innate differences between these categories because the categories themselves are constantly being reconfigured.[141] Practically speaking it is difficult—often impossible—to distinguish between civilians and combatants, especially in the deep residential and urban spaces through which later modern war is increasingly fought (see Chapter 6).[142] Law and war lawyers have not settled and will not settle the answers to these questions once and for all because the distinction between civilians and combatants is an interpretive and changeable artefact. Nevertheless, the anxieties engendered by the simultaneous ethico-legal imperative of distinguishing between civilians and combatants and the relative difficulty of doing so have nevertheless driven militaries towards legal process and procedure and the legal-technical fix promised by the incorporation of war lawyers into the kill chain.

Just as it was constitutively difficult to distinguish between civilians and combatants in the Second World War—and no such distinction was made when it came to strategies like 'morale bombing'—it remains constitutively difficult when bombing (in) cities today. The key change is that by the end of the twentieth century, advanced militaries had the technologies that enable them to *try*—an important caveat—to distinguish between civilians and combatants and between those civilians who participate in hostilities and those who do not. With this change has come an adjudicative apparatus, one that is no doubt imperfect, but which nevertheless entrains military subjects to think and to act according to their ability to target the 'right' people.

The participation of civilians in hostilities (often referred to as Direct Participation in Hostilities—or DPH) and the problems it engenders for the principle of distinction has become a central feature of US and Israeli targeting. Consider what one war lawyer with extensive experience working on US and coalition targeting operations in Afghanistan told me:

[141] Kinsella, *The Image Before the Weapon.*

[142] Stephen Graham, *Cities Under Siege: The New Military Urbanism* (London; New York, NY: Verso, 2011); David Kilcullen, *Out of the Mountains: The Coming Age of the Urban Guerrilla* (London: Hurst Publishers, 2013).

> In Afghanistan, everybody's a fricking civilian. There are no opposing military forces that are wearing uniforms. It's not the Nazis' over there. Everybody in Afghanistan is either a combatant or non-combatant because they're all civilians. And when you're talking [about the] global war on terror generally, that's where the distinction needs to be made, between combatant and non-combatant, not civilian vs military because a terrorist is a civilian.[143]

The claim here is that all targeting in Afghanistan is directed against participants in hostilities, that is, against civilians who lose their protected status because they are thought to be directly participating in hostilities. It is perhaps counter-intuitive to hear from a member of the US military that 'everyone in Afghanistan is a civilian' because at first glance this would seem to imply that everyone in Afghanistan is entitled to protections that civilians should enjoy in war. The effect, however, is the opposite: by making everyone a civilian, the very category of civilian is watered-down; everyone—or nearly everyone—becomes suspicious because nearly everyone *could* directly participate in hostilities.[144] Indeed, according to Israeli sociologist Amitai Etzioni there is a growing class of what he calls 'abusive civilians' who do not deserve the protections afforded to 'truly innocent civilians'.[145] He argues that because these so-called 'abusive civilians' do not abide by the laws of war, it is *their* fault when people on their side—'innocent' and 'guilty'—are killed by US and Israeli forces:

[143] Stefano (pseudonym), interview.

[144] I use the word 'nearly' advisedly: babies in no way have the capacity to directly participate in hostilities, despite claims that babies represent what US member of the House of Representatives (R-TX) Louie Gohmert called 'future terrorists': Heath Lander, 'The Latency Phase—of "Terrorist Babies" and "Dead Children Strategies"', *Daily Kos* (blog), https://www.dailykos.com/story/2010/8/12/892586/-, accessed 6 July 2017. Alan Dershowitz has similarly implied that children are indivertibly contributing to hostilities as part of Hezbollah and Hamas's 'dead children strategy' in which images of dead Palestinian children are paraded in front of the media in order to delegitimize Israel. Dershowitz explained that one of the strongest visual objects in the media is a mother holding a dead baby in her hand, which is similar to the picture of Mary holding baby Jesus: Anat Shalev, 'Dershowitz: Jews Initiate Legal Terror against Israel', *Ynetnews*, 5 November 2010, http://www.ynetnews.com/articles/0,7340,L-3888025,00.html, accessed 6 July 2017. For a more balanced reading of direct child participation in hostilities see: International Criminal Court, *The Prosecutor v. Thomas Lubanga Dyilo* (ICC-01/04-01/06) International Criminal Court, 14 March 2012. Lubanga was found guilty, on 14 March 2012, of the war crimes of enlisting and conscripting children under the age of 15 years and using them to participate actively in hostilities (child soldiers). For a discussion see: Joshua Yuvaraj, 'When Does a Child "Participate Actively in Hostilities" under the Rome Statute? Protecting Children from Use in Hostilities after Lubanga', *Utrecht Journal of International and European Law* 32, no. 83 (2016): 69–93; Nicole Urban, 'Direct and Active Participation in Hostilities: The Unintended Consequences of the ICC's Decision in Lubanga', *EJIL: Talk!* (blog), 11 April 2012, https://www.ejiltalk.org/direct-and-active-participation-in-hostilities-the-unintended-consequences-of-the-iccs-decision-in-lubanga/, accessed 7 July 2017.

[145] Amitai Etzioni, 'Unmanned Aircraft Systems: The Moral and Legal Case', *Joint Forces Quarterly* 57, no. 2 (2010): 66–7.

> [I]nstead of apologizing each time the wrong individual is targeted or collateral damage is caused, we should stress that the issue would be largely resolved in short order if the abusive civilians would stop their abusive practices and fight—if they must—according to established rules of war.[146]

The expansion of the increasingly grey zone of direct participation in hostilities targeting, as I discuss in detail in Chapter 4, requires an extensive adjudicative apparatus. Who is participating? What does *direct* participation mean? How long must the civilian cease activities before s/he is no longer 'participating' and is therefore entitled to protection under the laws of war? These questions have been answered by the International Committee of the Red Cross, legal scholars, and militaries alike.[147] There is very little consensus on the meaning and utility of direct participation in hostilities—in fact there are radically divergent opinions on the matter—but the various attempts to address the operational and legal questions it raises points, again, to the increasing role that law and war lawyers have come to play in lethal targeting operations and debates about how war should be conducted. In several ways then, the instability of the category of the civilian and the indeterminacy of when s/he may or may not be participating in hostilities necessitate war lawyers and their legal expertise (although they also co-produce the indeterminacy).

[146] Ibid., 67. See also: Amitai Etzioni, 'Terrorists, Neither Soldiers Nor Criminals', *Military Review* (July–August 2009): 108–18.

[147] See *inter alia*: International Committee of the Red Cross and Nils Melzer, 'Interpretive Guidance on the Notion of Direct Participation In Hostilities Under International Humanitarian Law' (Geneva: International Committee of the Red Cross, 2009); Bill Boothby, 'And for Such Time as: The Time Dimension to Direct Participation in Hostilities', *New York University Journal of International Law and Politics* 42, no. 3 (2010): 741–68; Michael N Schmitt, 'Deconstructing Direct Participation in Hostilities: The Constitutive Elements', *New York University Journal of International Law and Politics* 42, no. 3 (2010): 697–739; Hilly Moodrick-Even Khen, 'Can We Now Tell What "Direct Participation in Hostilities" Is? HCJ 769/02 the Public Committee Against Torture in Israel v. The Government of Israel', *Israel Law Review* 40, no. 1 (2007): 213–44; Dapo Akande, 'Clearing the Fog of War? The ICRC's Interpretive Guidance on Direct Participation in Hostilities', *EJIL: Talk!* (blog), 4 June 2009, https://www.ejiltalk.org/clearing-the-fog-of-war-the-icrcs-interpretive-guidance-on-direct-participation-in-hostilities/, accessed 7 July 2017; W. Hays Parks, 'Part IX of the ICRC "Direct Participation in Hostilities" Study: No Mandate, No Expertise, and Legally Incorrect', *New York University Journal of International Law and Politics* 42, no. 3 (2010): 769–830; Ryan Goodman and Derek Jinks, 'The ICRC Interpretive Guidance on the Notion of Direct Participation in Hostilities under International Humanitarian Law: An Introduction to the Forum: Direct Participation In Hostilities: Perspectives on the ICRC Interpretive Guidance', *New York University Journal of International Law and Politics* 42, no. 3 (2010): 637–40; Nils Melzer, 'Keeping the Balance between Military Necessity and Humanity: A Response to Four Critiques of the ICRC's Interpretive Guidance on the Notion of Direct Participation in Hostilities Forum: Direct Participation In Hostilities: Perspectives on the ICRC Interpretive Guidance', *New York University Journal of International Law and Politics* 42, no. 3 (2010): 831–916.

The individuation of warfare

The second thematic explanation as to why war lawyers were incorporated into the kill chain has to do with the fact that targeting increasingly—though not exclusively—focuses on individuals as opposed to collectives. This drive towards what Samuel Issacharoff and Richard Pildes have called 'the individuation of warfare' (and which is more colloquially referred to as 'targeted killing') has in turn precipitated the need to constantly adjudicate on questions with profound legal implications: who can be targeted? Under what conditions is it legal to target a particular individual?—like Iranian Major General Qassem Soleimani who was killed in a US drone strike in Baghdad in January 2020.[148] When and where can someone like Soleimani be struck? These questions put law at the front and centre of targeting operations and the demand to provide answers drives the juridification of later modern war and the need for war lawyers to be 'in the loop'.

Twentieth-century war and laws of war for the most part focused on the *status* of the enemy rather than on the *conduct* of individuals. Being a member of a state or non-state armed group was sufficient reason to be targeted; membership of an armed group confers the status of combatant and combatancy is targetable. This *status-based* targeting still occurs, of course, but it is increasingly supplemented by *conduct*-based targeting whereby individuals (not enemy collectives) are targeted because of their behaviour—because they exhibit what the US military refers to as threatening 'patterns of life'. As Issacharrof and Pildes explain:

> [W]hereas the traditional practices and laws of war defined 'the enemy' in terms of categorical, group-based judgments that turned on status—a person was an enemy not because of any specific actions he himself engaged in, but

[148] For a discussion of the Trump administration's legal rationale for the killing of Qassem Soleimani, see: Ryan Goodman, 'White House "1264 Notice" and Novel Legal Claims for Military Strikes Against Iran', *Just Security* (blog), 14 February 2020, https://www.justsecurity.org/68594/white-house-1264-notice-and-novel-legal-claims-for-military-action-against-iran/, accessed 23 February 2020; Adil Ahmad Haque, 'U.S. Legal Defense of the Soleimani Strike at the United Nations: A Critical Assessment', *Just Security*, 10 January 2020, https://www.justsecurity.org/68008/u-s-legal-defense-of-the-soleimani-strike-at-the-united-nations-a-critical-assessment/, accessed 23 February 2020. Antony Dworkin has argued: 'The drone strike against Qassem Soleimani marks a significant escalation in the United States' use of force against external security threats as it has evolved in the years since September 11, 2001. [It] brings the signature technique of the so-called "war on terror"—the targeted killing of individuals outside any wider conventional military engagement—into the context of inter-state relations. Antony Dworkin, 'Soleimani Strike Marks a Novel Shift in Targeted Killing, Dangerous to the Global Order', *Just Security* (blog), 7 January 2020, https://www.justsecurity.org/67937/soleimani-strike-marks-a-novel-shift-in-targeted-killing-dangerous-to-the-global-order/, accessed 23 February 2020.

> because he was a member of an opposing army—we are instead now moving to a world which implicitly or explicitly requires the individuation of personal responsibility of specific 'enemy' persons before the use of military force is considered justified, at least as a moral and political matter.[149]

This transformation—which is far from universal and complete—has been enabled by technological advances in warfare and especially by advances in Intelligence, Surveillance and Reconnaissance (ISR). While proponents of these technologies frequently overstate their powers of precision, it is undeniable that the kill chain was radically transformed in the twentieth and early twenty-first century as radio and visual technologies enabled advanced militaries—predominantly the US and later Israel—to track and target *mobile* (as opposed to fixed) targets in near-real time (Chapter 6).[150] These new techno-cultural assemblages enable advanced militaries to move away from an exclusively object-ontology of fixed and static targets to an event-ontology characterized by emergence and events as they unravel in near-real time.[151] The ontology of the event has entrained technologically advanced militaries to 'prosecute' war in an ever-unfolding 'instantaneous present' where targets could, in principle, emerge anywhere at any time.[152]

Individuation has made targeting into something that increasingly resembles pursuit of a criminal on the run—a particularly dramatic form of law enforcement, but also one with cultural overtones of hunting non-human animals—which in turn requires an adjudicative apparatus. Grégoire Chamayou gives expression to this by referring to what he calls the 'manhunt doctrine' in which 'small flexible units' are deployed 'in a logic of targeted attacks'.[153] The manhunt, Chamayou notes 'does not involve two fighters facing off, but something

[149] Samuel Issacharoff and Richard H. Pildes, 'Drones and the Dilemma of Modern Warfare', *NYU School of Law, Public Law Research Paper No. 13-34*, 1 June 2013, 2, http://papers.ssrn.com/abstract=2268596, accessed 4 November 2013.

[150] Derek Gregory, 'Lines of Descent', in *From Above: War, Violence, and Verticality*, ed. Peter Adey, Mark Whitehead, and Alison Williams (New York, NY: Oxford University Press, 2014), 41–70; Cockburn, *Kill Chain*; John Fyfe, 'Evolution of Time Sensitive Targeting: Operation Iraqi Freedom Results and Lessons' (Maxwell Air Force Base, Alabama: Air University, College of Aerospace Doctrine, Research and Education, 2005).

[151] Following Judith Butler, I understand ontology 'not as a foundation, but a normative injunction that operates insidiously by installing itself into political discourse': Judith Butler, *Gender Trouble*, tenth anniversary edition (London; New York, NY: Routledge, 2014), 189. For a discussion of event-ontologies see: Gregory, 'Seeing Red'.

[152] Astrid H. M. Nordin and Dan Öberg, 'Targeting the Ontology of War: From Clausewitz to Baudrillard', *Millennium*, 43, no. 2 (2014): 392–310, 405.

[153] Grégoire Chamayou, 'The Manhunt Doctrine', *Radical Philosophy* (blog), October 2011, 2, https://www.radicalphilosophy.com/commentary/the-manhunt-doctrine, accessed 6 July 2017. See also: Grégoire Chamayou, *Manhunts: A Philosophical History*, trans. Steven Rendall (Princeton, NJ: Princeton University Press, 2012); Ryan Devereaux, 'Manhunting in the Hindu Kush', *The Intercept*,

else: a hunter who advances and a prey who flees or who hides'.[154] This is precisely what President George W. Bush had in mind when in 2003 he declared that the United States had launched a new kind of war, a 'war that requires us to be on an international manhunt',[155] and as things would transpire, the hunt was not just for the perpetrators of 9/11.[156]

As Gabriella Blum has argued, 'wartime regulation is increasingly aspiring to make war look more like a policing operation, in which people are expected to be treated according to their individual actions rather than as representatives of a collective'.[157] This adjudicative apparatus requires new forms of intelligence and analysis, it requires up-to-date information and a series of expertise capable—theoretically—of making informed decisions about *individual* targets as they move from place to place, in and out of urban and residential areas. It is not difficult to see how war lawyers quickly became a crucial part of this adjudicative apparatus and perhaps it is not surprising that late modern militaries increasingly refer to the 'prosecution' of the target (and the 'prosecution' of war more generally).[158] The language of prosecution implies that the target is always and already 'guilty' (why would anyone want to chase or prosecute an 'innocent' target?). The law and war lawyers help deliver to targets what the same George Bush memorably called 'sudden justice'.[159]

Proliferation, complexity, and human rights

The third set of anxieties that have led later modern militaries like the United States and Israel towards war lawyers concerns the proliferation of international

18 October 2015, https://theintercept.com/drone-papers/manhunting-in-the-hindu-kush/, accessed 13 December 2016.

154 Chamayou, 'The Manhunt Doctrine', 2.

155 Quoted in: Ibid.

156 'Although the Bush administration did not explicitly define which regions of the world would be core and which would be peripheral in its new [war on terror] schema, the war was defined in expansive terms. From its inception policymakers discussed the possibility of multiple fronts [. . .]: Ryan, *Full Spectrum Dominance: Irregular Warfare and the War on Terror*, Kindle edition, location 565.

157 Gabriella Blum, 'The Individualization of War', in *Law and War*, ed. Austin Sarat, Lawrence Douglas, and Martha Merrill Umphrey, *The Amherst Series in Law, Jurisprudence, and Social Thought* (Stanford, CA, Stanford University Press, 2014), 49; Kahn, 'Imagining Warfare'.

158 A recent NATO targeting doctrine publication uses the words 'prosecute' or 'prosecution' thirty-nine times in relation to targets and targeting: North Atlantic Treaty Organisation (NATO), 'Allied Joint Doctrine for Joint Targeting' (NATO Standardisation Office, April 2016), https://assets.publishing.service.gov.uk/government/uploads/system/uploads/attachment_data/file/628215/20160505-nato_targeting_ajp_3_9.pdf, accessed 24 October 2019.

159 Chris Woods, former BBC journalist and founder of Airwars, borrowed Bush's dark phrase for the title of his book: Woods, *Sudden Justice*, 2015, 8.

law treaties and, especially, the import of human rights norms into the laws of war.

Since their initial codification in the mid-nineteenth century, the laws of war have become vastly more numerous and infinitely more complex. Political scientist Tanisha Fazal has written of what she calls a 'proliferation' of the laws of war, arguing that they have changed dramatically in both quantity and quality over the last two centuries. Fazal puts the laws of war of today in a comparative historical context, usefully pointing out: 'At the close of the Napoleonic Wars in the early nineteenth century there were no multilateral treaties on the laws of war. The customary law of the day was such that prisoners taken in were routinely shot, and brutality against civilian populations was common both inside and outside western Europe'.[160] Today, by contrast, there are over seventy law of war treaties and conventions listed in the treaty database of the International Committee of the Red Cross.[161] As the laws became more complex, detailed, and extensive, so militaries and military commanders required legal expertise in order to help them navigate war's juridical terrain. On this point it is worth noting that proliferation and protection are not exact correlates. The expansion of the laws of war has not always gone hand in hand with increased protections, neither for soldiers nor civilians, and often increased protections for one group have resulted in heightened risk for others.[162]

For better or worse, the human rights agenda is now a central part of warfare. Conventional accounts of the convergences between the human rights agenda and the war paradigm, and between military and humanitarian worlds more generally, suggest that these are positive developments that ultimately

[160] Tanisha M. Fazal, *Wars of Law: Unintended Consequences in the Regulation of Armed Conflict* (Ithaca, NY: Cornell University Press, 2018), 11.

[161] Ibid.

[162] The extent to which the laws of war protect combatants and civilians, and finding the balance between the two, is one of the great chasms in debates about the laws of war. Discussions are often partisan. Just war theorist Michael Walzer refers to the tension between protecting civilians and protecting combatants as the 'risk dilemma', which he formulates as two questions. First, 'how should we fight against insurgents/terrorists who hide among, and attack from the midst of, the civilian population? And answering that question leads immediately to another, which is also the core issue, the issue that makes everyone nervous: how much risk must our soldiers take to reduce the risks they impose on civilians when they respond to those attacks?' Michael Walzer, 'The Risk Dilemma', *Philosophia* 44, no. 2 (2016): 289–93. Martin Shaw has argued that risk-averse Western militaries transfer risk from their soldiers to civilians on the battlefield: M. Shaw, *The New Western Way of War: Risk-Transfer War and Its Crisis in Iraq* (Cambridge; Malden, MA: Polity, 2005). For a counter view see: Gabriella Blum, 'The Dispensable Lives of Soldiers', *Journal of Legal Analysis* 2, no. 1 (2010): 69–124; Asa Kasher and Amos Yadlin, 'Human Life in the War on Terrorism: A Response to "the Risk Dilemma" by Michael Walzer', *Philosophia* 44, no. 2 (1 June 2016): 295–308. For a rare account that attempts to reconcile the protections afforded to civilians *and* combatants and a discussion of how lives are weighted in war see: Jens David Ohlin, Larry May, and Claire Finkelstein, eds, *Weighing Lives in War* (Oxford; New York, NY: Oxford University Press, 2017).

protect lives and help realize evermore human rights.[163] By this telling the human rights agenda has made militaries more accountable, while also making them more vulnerable to criticism that they are not doing enough to protect human rights. For example, Palestinians have used the language of human rights to gain international recognition as subjects whose human rights are being violated on a daily basis.[164] This may have had insufficient impact in terms of Israel's policies but the language of human rights has been central to fostering a growing solidarity movement that may one day put real pressure on Israel to respect the human rights of those who it occupies. The human rights agenda has made the US military more aware of the potential negative effects of, for example, killing civilians. Several US war lawyers I interviewed spoke about how human rights abuses (such as those in Guantanamo Bay) have disastrous consequences for the military, not just on the 'PR front' but also from a war-fighting point of view: it strengthens and fosters opposition.[165] If we put this together with what war lawyers refer to as the 'CNN effect', whereby images of atrocity can be broadcast worldwide almost instantaneously, and add the social-media component, it is not difficult to see why militaries like the US have become sensitive about how their actions are perceived. This has not—and likely will not—stop them from killing civilians but it is undeniable that the human rights agenda has been internalized by advanced militaries like the US and Israel, even if it is often for strategic purposes.[166]

But as human rights discourses and practices have been internalized by militaries like (but not limited to) the United States and Israel, they have also—simultaneously—been *weaponized*. We will hear more about the weaponization of human rights in the Conclusion, but its basic contours are worth sketching here. Costas Douzinas and Noam Chomsky have written of what they call a 'military humanism' in which Western military powers co-opt the language of human rights in order to further belligerent ends and legitimize wars on several fronts in the 'war on terror'.[167] Central to their argument is the

[163] Alexander, 'A Short History of International Humanitarian Law'; Kennedy, *Of War and Law*; Meron, 'The Humanization of Humanitarian Law'.

[164] Lori A. Allen, 'Martyr Bodies in the Media: Human Rights, Aesthetics, and the Politics of Immediation in the Palestinian Intifada', *American Ethnologist* 36, no. 1 (2009): 161–80; Lori Allen, *The Rise and Fall of Human Rights Cynicism and Politics in Occupied Palestine* (Stanford: Stanford University Press, 2013).

[165] Dunlap, interview; Brown, interview; Stefano (pseudonym), interview.

[166] Neta C. Crawford, *Accountability for Killing: Moral Responsibility for Collateral Damage in America's Post-9/11 Wars* (New York, NY: Oxford University Press, 2013).

[167] Noam Chomsky, *The New Military Humanism: Lessons from Kosovo*, Pages Bent edition (London: Pluto Press, 1999); Costas Douzinas, 'Humanity, Military Humanism and the New Moral Order', *Economy and Society* 32, no. 2 (2003): 159–83; Costas Douzinas, 'The Many Faces of Humanitarianism', *Monthly Review Online*, 29 May 2009, https://mronline.org/2009/05/29/the-many-faces-of-humanitarianism/, accessed 24 February 2020.

fact that violence and human rights are not necessarily antithetical. In practice, as Nicola Perugini and Neve Gordon have argued, 'human rights, which most people assume to be progressive and liberating, can just as easily be connected with domination'.[168] By this telling, the import of human rights norms into military practices has a wide spectrum of consequences, and can just as easily enhance military violence as it can limit it. This helps to explain why the US and Israeli militaries have been so forthcoming in adopting and invoking the language of human rights—it has become a key means of ensuring compliance with regulations including (military) codes of ethics.[169] This is a vast and slippery juridical terrain; it encompasses both the internalization of human rights norms for *offensive* military purposes as well as the *defence* of military commanders and personnel who may find themselves accused of human rights violations. War lawyers prepare and navigate the full breadth of this terrain, which is why, as Major General Charles Dunlap (ret.) put it, 'knowing the legal challenges they will face, savvy American commanders seldom go to war without their attorneys'.[170]

Having provided an overview of the conceptual and historical argument: that legal advice within militaries—or this scope of aerial targeting operations, at the very least—is *indeterminate, productive of violence, and productive of law*—we are left with the sense of a self-reinforcing process. In the hands of militaries that enjoy technical and political superiority on the global or regional level, international law and its spin-off, lawfare, seem to be 'the gifts that keep on giving'. But before tracing that argument in full, it is perhaps appropriate to keep in sight those who make up the targeted—whether as a class (Lisa Parks, see '*Operational law and the "military gaze"*') or as individuals.

* * *

Basim Razzo and his family lived in eastern Mosul in a bucolic neighbourhood on the banks of the river Tigris. Late in the evening on 20 September 2015 Basim was clicking through car reviews on Youtube while his wife, Mayada, and daughter, Tuqa, slept upstairs. Basim's brother Mohannad lived next door in an almost identical house with his wife, Azza, and son, Najib, and they

[168] Perugini and Gordon, *The Human Right to Dominate*, 8.
[169] James Eastwood, *Ethics as a Weapon of War: Militarism and Morality in Israel* (Cambridge: Cambridge University Press, 2017); Khalili, *Time in the Shadows*.
[170] Dunlap, 'Law and Military Interventions', 15.

were almost certainly asleep when Basim finally shut down the computer and headed to bed at 1 a.m. He settled next to Mayada, but as the *New York Times* reported:[171]

> Some time later, he snapped awake. His shirt was drenched, and there was a strange taste—blood?—on his tongue. The air was thick and acrid. He looked up. He was in the bedroom, but the roof was nearly gone. He could see the night sky, the stars over Mosul. Basim reached out and found his legs pressed just inches from his face by what remained of his bed. He began to panic. He turned to his left, and there was a heap of rubble.
>
> '*Mayada!*' he screamed. '*Mayada!*'
>
> It was then that he noticed the silence. '*Mayada*' he shouted. '*Tuqa!*'
>
> The bedroom walls were missing, leaving only the bare supports. He could see the dark outlines of treetops. He began to hear the faraway, unmistakable sound of a woman's voice. He cried out, and the voice shouted back, '*Where are you?*' It was Azza, his sister-in-law, somewhere outside.
>
> '*Mayada's gone!*' he shouted.
>
> '*No, no, I'll find her!*'
>
> '*No, no, no, she's gone,*' he cried back. '*They're all gone!*'

The account continues:

> Later that same day, the American-led coalition fighting the Islamic State in Iraq and Syria uploaded a video to its YouTube channel. The clip, titled 'Coalition Airstrike Destroys Daesh VBIED [vehicle-borne improvised explosive device] Facility Near Mosul, Iraq 20 Sept 2015' shows spectral black-and-white night-vision footage of two sprawling compounds, filmed by an aircraft slowly rotating above. There is no sound. Within seconds, the structures disappear in bursts of black smoke. The target, according to the caption, was a car-bomb factory, a hub in a network of 'multiple facilities spread across Mosul used to produce VBIEDs for ISIL's [Islamic State of Iraq and the Levant] terrorist activities,' posing 'a direct threat to both civilians and Iraqi security forces.' Later, when he found the video, Basim could watch only the first few frames.

[171] The following testimony is adapted and condensed from: Azmat Khan and Anand Gopal, 'The Uncounted—The New York Times', *The New York Times*, 16 November 2017, https://www.nytimes.com/interactive/2017/11/16/magazine/uncounted-civilian-casualties-iraq-airstrikes.html, accessed 28 November 2019.

Seventeen months later Basim told the *New York Times* of an email he received from the coalition:

> We deeply regret this unintentional loss of life in an attempt to defeat Da'esh [another term for the Islamic State]. We are prepared to offer you a monetary expression of our sympathy and regret for this unfortunate incident.

Basim was invited to Erbil to discuss the matter with the coalition. He was greeted by Captain Jaclyn Feeney, an Army war lawyer, who introduced herself and invited Basim to be seated. In the course of the conversation Feeney offered Basim an apology and a condolence payment:[172]

> It's not meant to recompensate you for what you've lost, or for rebuilding or anything like that. It's just meant to be an expression of our sympathy, our apologies for your loss.

Basim had spent hours calculating the actual damages: $500,000 for his and Mohannad's homes, furnishings, and belongings; $22,000 for two cars; and $13,000 in medical bills from Turkey. The US military had done its own—very different—calculations:

> *'[T]he amount in U.S. dollars is $15,000 [. . .] And so, if you're willing to accept that—'*
>
> Basim looked at her in disbelief. *'No.'*
>
> *'You're not willing to accept that?'*
>
> *'This is—this is an insult to me. No, I will not accept it. I'm sorry.'*

Basim Razzo was placed in the targeted class and experienced its violence first-hand. Law has played a crucial and as-yet under-appreciated role in the normalization and routinization of targeting and aerial violence like that which was visited upon Basim and his family.[173] According to the coalition's

[172] On condolence payments paid to victims of US military violence see: Emily Gilbert, 'The Gift of War: Cash, Counterinsurgency and "Collateral Damage"', *Security Dialogue* 46, no. 5 (2015): 403–21.

[173] The most authoritative scholarly accounts of civilian harm caused by US military violence are: Crawford, *Accountability for Killing*; Sahr Conway-Lanz, *Collateral Damage: Americans, Noncombatant Immunity, and Atrocity after World War II* (New York, NY: Routledge, 2006). An independent and reliable database on civilian harm in contemporary air wars, including US and coalition operations in Iraq and Syria, is maintained by Airwars at https://airwars.org, accessed 18 June 2020. The Costs of War at Brown University maintains a similarly independent and reliable database on the human costs of war in US (air and ground) wars at: https://watson.brown.edu/costsofwar/costs/human, accessed 18 June 2020.

interpretation of the laws of war: the Islamic State 'VBIED Facility' was a *valid military objective*: at the time of the attack,[174] they did not know that they were targeting Bassim and his brothers' homes—so while regrettable, the strike was not in violation of the laws of war. This is not an especially controversial reading of the laws of war among military powers; in fact, it captures a long-standing and prevailing deference to the concept of military necessity. What is important in this example, as with the Gaza targeting episode I outlined in the Preface, is that the laws of war are sufficiently flexible to allow for such violent interpretations.

I spoke to Basim in April 2019, over three and a half years later, and he told me how difficult day-to-day life still was. He suffers from chronic pain and has had several surgeries; he has been unable to work and earn a living because of his ongoing injuries, and he grieves the loss of his family. As Basim put it, 'there are no words to describe what happened to me'.[175]

[174] The 'Rendulic' rule, named after German General Lothar Rendulic holds that the lawfulness of a commander's actions should be judged on what the commander knew and expected at the time he or she made his or her decision, rather than on the facts that became available after the action was taken. Brian J. Bill, 'The Rendulic "Rule": Military Necessity, Commander's Knowledge and Methods of Warfare', *Yearbook of International Humanitarian Law* 12 (2009): 119–55, .

[175] Razzo, interview.

1

Targeting Without Lawyers

The Vietnam War

1.1 Vietnam Matters

This chapter is about the roles that military lawyers did and did not play in the US-led war in Vietnam (1955–1975). The Vietnam War is an important place to begin the historical analysis because military lawyers emerged from it both better equipped and with a formal mandate to advise military commanders on the legality of targeting operations. Military lawyers performed a wide range of duties in the Vietnam War and were deployed in what at the time were unprecedented numbers. While military lawyers were not involved in targeting, despite what one prominent US commentator and former military lawyer has argued, the Vietnam War helped to create the conditions for their involvement in subsequent wars (Chapters 3–6).[1] The conflict was also a turning point in that it precipitated the emergence of a new doctrinal approach to the laws of war called 'operational law' (Chapter 2). This new doctrine emerged in the 1970s and 1980s and would help the US military realize the force-multiplying potential latent in the laws of war.

The migration of military lawyers into the realm of targeting was gradual, messy, and non-linear; it was the result of several intersecting factors, many of which—but certainly not all—originated in the crucible of Vietnam. My argument rests on an examination of three key areas. First, the work that military lawyers performed on the ground in Vietnam, especially around Prisoner of War (POW) issues (section 1.2). Second, the two major US air wars in Vietnam, Operation Rolling Thunder and Operation Linebacker (section 1.3). And finally, the infamous My Lai massacre of 1968 and the subsequent creation of the US Law of War Program (section 1.4). Together, these three areas were crucial in creating the conditions for the involvement of military lawyers in

[1] W. Hays Parks, 'The Law of War Adviser', *JAG Journal* 31, no. 1 (1980): 1–52; W. Hays Parks, 'Linebacker and the Law of War', *Air University Review* 34, no. 2 (1983): 2–30.

The War Lawyers. Craig Jones, Oxford University Press (2020). © Craig Jones.
DOI: 10.1093/oso/9780198842927.001.0001.

targeting decisions, albeit a decade and a half after the fall of Saigon (as US missiles began falling on Iraq in 1991, not for the last time).

Two caveats are crucial. By arguing that military lawyers were not involved in targeting decisions I am not claiming that the Vietnam War was conducted without reference to, or with disregard for, international law and the laws of war. Nor am I implying that targeting decisions, specifically, were taken without legal consideration. My claim is a more limited one about the nature of involvement, or more precisely the *non*-involvement, of military lawyers in matters of targeting—in stark contrast from the ways in which military lawyers are involved in targeting today. As historian Brian Cuddy has argued, 'law was not so much flagrantly violated in Vietnam as it was interpreted and applied'.[2] Cuddy shows that law played an important role in structuring the Vietnam War in general and in targeting policy in particular. While these observations might at first glance appear to contradict my findings about the non-involvement of military lawyers in targeting operations, the two are in fact complementary. Cuddy shows that legal considerations drove policy debates in the United States at the very highest levels, as successive administrations from Johnson to Nixon sought legal justification for everything from the decision to go to war, to the expansion of the bombing campaign ever further into North Vietnam.[3] Military lawyers were not involved in these high-level strategic and policy-level articulations of law, but they would soon become part of the juridical backdrop to US warfare. Such legal articulations were in fact a key catalyst for requiring robust legal structures *throughout* the kill chain in the decades that followed.

The second caveat is that the central foci of this chapter—the work of military lawyers in Vietnam, the major aerial campaigns of the war, and the My Lai massacre—are not the only factors that explain why military lawyers became involved in targeting operations subsequently. Two other factors, which I explore in section 1.3, were particularly important: (a) the increasing attention that the US military began to pay to civilian casualties—and civilian casualty mitigation in particular; and (b) the shift in US targeting logic from military necessity to proportionality, or, more accurately, the increasing emphasis placed on the latter.[4]

***

[2] Brian Cuddy, 'Wider War: American Force in Vietnam, International Law, and the Transformation of Armed Conflict, 1961-1977', PhD thesis, Cornell University Ithaca, NY, 2016, 212 (on file with author; cited with permission).

[3] Ibid.

[4] Ibid.

The Vietnam War matters for my argument about the rise of military lawyers but I also hope to show that it matters in a more general and perhaps more profound sense: the same dynamic of military policy as a force actively shaping the development of international law is observable in all the wars the United States has fought since, and had a long US vintage dating back to at least the US Civil War.[5] The historian Marilyn Young has powerfully suggested: 'Vietnam still matters because the central issues it raised about the United States in the world over four decades ago remain central issues today. Unresolved, they come back not as ghosts but as the still living.'[6] Young lists a series of examples to animate her argument (many of which I discuss in this chapter):

> The Phoenix Program of targeted assassination, torture, and wholesale detention; the indiscriminate bombing of densely populated areas; the credibility of the United States as an explanation for an indefinite commitment to misguided military policies; the unchecked expansion of presidential power; the corruption and demoralization of the military; illegal domestic spying; dissent defined as treason; the insistence that fighting 'them' over there protects 'us' over 'here'—all continue in daily practice.[7]

In places, Young over stresses continuity (the United States does not indiscriminately bomb densely populated areas and has not done so since the Second World War) and in the pages that follow I also examine the key *changes* that the Vietnam War set in motion.[8]

1.2 JAGs on the Ground in Vietnam

Military lawyers served a variety of functions in Vietnam. The role they played depended very much on when and where they were deployed, what level of

[5] John Fabian Witt, *Lincoln's Code: The Laws of War in American History* (New York, NY: Free Press, 2013).

[6] Marilyn Young, 'Introduction: Why Vietnam Still Matters', in *The War That Never Ends: New Perspectives on the Vietnam War*, ed. David L. Anderson and John Ernst, reprint edition (Lexington, KY: University Press of Kentucky, 2014), 9. The first part of this quote is quoted in: Cuddy, 'Wider War: American Force in Vietnam, International Law, and the Transformation of Armed Conflict, 1961-1977', 5.

[7] Young, 'Introduction: Why Vietnam Still Matters', 9.

[8] The United States continues to bomb densely populated areas but does not do so indiscriminately.

command they served, and in which service (e.g. Army or Air Force).[9] The Army deployed by far the greatest number of military lawyers. At the peak of the US military build-up in 1969 there were 135 Army judge advocate (JAG) officers in Vietnam,[10] serving in at least fourteen different locations.[11] Between 1962 and 1973, 207 Air Force JAGs were deployed to Vietnam, rising to around 20 in theatre at any one time at the peak of the build-up, plus additional military lawyers serving across the border in Thailand.[12]

There was no such thing as a 'typical' deployment for military lawyers in Vietnam.[13] When Colonel Paul Durbin of the US Army, and the first military lawyer deployed to Vietnam was asked to go in late 1958 he is said to have responded, 'Where is that? And what will I do?' Durbin would not find out the answer to the second question until after he arrived in Vietnam, and even then, he found himself 'on his own', without much guidance from the JAG Office in Washington or the Pentagon. Durbin and the Army lawyers who immediately followed him 'provided a full range of traditional judge advocate legal services' to the Military Assistance Advisory Group (MAAG) in Vietnam.[14] The services that the early deployed military lawyers provided ranged 'from wills, powers of attorney, and tax assistance to advice on domestic relations, civil suits, and the filing of claims for damaged property'.[15]

Some of these were typical peacetime JAG roles, not so different to what they might have been doing in 'CONUS'—Continental United States—but in Vietnam even the familiar was infused with the foreign, posing new tasks and challenges for JAGs. Take claims law, for example, the area of military law that compensates 'local residents, host nation governments, allied forces, and even U.S. service members' for 'damage, loss and injuries' that occur as a result of

[9] Military lawyers serve at various levels in the US military chain of command. The command hierarchy runs from the President and the Secretary of Defense, through the Joint Chief of Staff to several levels of command in each of the services (i.e. Army, Navy, Air Force, and Marines) all the way down to field commanders, soldiers, and pilots engaged in combat.

[10] George Shipley Prugh, *Law at War, Vietnam: 1964-1973* (Washington, DC: Department of the Army, 1975), 100.

[11] Frederic L. Borch, *Judge Advocates in Combat: Army Lawyers in Military Operations from Vietnam to Haiti* (Washington, DC, Government Printing Office, 2001), 17.

[12] Rodriguez, interview.

[13] For example, compare: Irvin M. Kent et al., 'A Lawyer's Day in Vietnam', *American Bar Association Journal* 54, no. 12 (1968): 1177–82; David Morehouse, 'A Year in Vietnam', *The Reporter* 26, Special History edition (1999): 126–9. Denise Burke, 'Changing Times and New Challenges: The Vietnam War', *The Reporter* 26, Special History edition (1999): 120–5.

[14] The MAAG was a team of military advisers sent to assist the French with aid and weapons in the First Indochina War, but following French defeat it became an early harbinger of the US war in Vietnam and was later folded into the central command institute of the war, the Military Assistance Command Vietnam—or MACV.

[15] Borch, *Judge Advocates in Combat*, 6.

military operations.[16] One Air Force lawyer who served at Bien Hoa Air Base recalled that the dominant workload was: 'Not the usual pots and pans household goods claims, but battle damage claims' and the administration of solatia payments to 'friendly civilian casualties', some of which was done in field by JAGs wielding suitcases 'full of Vietnamese piasters [sic]'.[17] Solatia payments (also known as condolence payments) are a form of compensation given to some families after one (or more) of their members have been killed or injured by US forces. These payments became popular in Iraq and Afghanistan in the mid-2000s but date back to the Korean and Vietnam wars.[18] In the Vietnam War, the 'going rate for adult lives was $33. Children merited just half that'.[19]

Historian and investigative journalist Nick Turse provides an example of how absurdly low and arbitrary the payments could be: 'In one instance, after two members of Huynh Van Thanh's family were crushed to death by cargo dropped by a U.S. helicopter, the American military paid him about sixty dollars and gave him some surplus food, a bottle of liquid soap, two coloring books, and a box of crayons.'[20] For comparison, Emily Gilbert's work on solatia payments issued to Iraqi and Afghani civilians has revealed that the typical amount awarded for death is $2,500. Gilbert further explains how today 'a sliding scale is used to determine the extent of injury or property damage: for example, $600–$1,500 for loss of a limb or other injuries, up to $500 for property damage, and $500–$2,500 for a destroyed vehicle'.[21] Today, military lawyers are heavily involved in the administration of US military condolence payments.[22] Indeed, as one author notes: 'One of the most pressing legal issues facing troops on overseas deployments is the adjudication of claims by civilians against U.S. military forces.'[23]

[16] The Judge Advocate General's Legal Center & School, International & Operational Law Department, United States Army, 'Operational Law Handbook 2017' 2017 (Charlottesville, VA: United States Army) http://www.loc.gov/rr/frd/Military_Law/operational-law-handbooks.html, accessed 8 November 2019, 319.

[17] Morehouse, 'A Year in Vietnam', 127–8.

[18] Emily Gilbert, 'The Gift of War: Cash, Counterinsurgency and "Collateral Damage"', *Security Dialogue* 46, no. 5 (2015).

[19] Ibid., 407, quoting Nick Turse, *Kill Anything That Moves: The Real American War in Vietnam* (New York, NY: Metropolitan Books/Henry Holt and Co., 2013), 155.

[20] Turse, *Kill Anything That Moves*, 155.

[21] Gilbert, 'The Gift of War', 407.

[22] Jonathan Tracy, 'Compensating Civilian Casualties: "I Am Sorry for Your Loss and I Wish You Well in a Free Iraq"' (Center for Civilians in Conflict, 30 May 2008), https://civiliansinconflict.org/publications/policy/compensating-civilian-casualties-sorry-loss-wish-well-free-iraq/, accessed 13 July 2019; John Fabian Witt, 'Form and Substance in the Law of Counterinsurgency Damages', *Loyola of Los Angeles Law Review* 41, no. 4 (2007): 1455–81.

[23] Jordan Walerstein, 'Coping with Combat Claims: An Analysis of the Foreign Claims Act's Combat Exclusion', *Cardozo Journal Conflict Resolution* 11, no. 1 (2009): 319–51.

As troop deployments to Vietnam increased, so too did JAG deployments. When Military Assistance Command Vietnam (MACV)—the major US joint service military command in Vietnam—was established in 1962 it had a permanent, albeit small, legal staff.[24] To assist with the build-up, JAGs were assigned to the US Army Support Group and deployed forward to the field. Each major combat and support unit had its own legal staff, commonly consisting of five lawyers per division, and from 1965 to 1969 more than 350 JAGs served in the field outside MACV and US Army Vietnam (USARV, the Army component of MACV).[25] Conditions were far from ideal and in the early years organization was especially ad hoc and austere. Judge Advocate General Corps Historian Frederic Borch describes the working conditions of Captain Arthur H. Taylor, who was assigned to the US Army Support Group in 1962:

> His office was a tent open to the local weather, in which desktops were quickly covered with insects, paper clips rusted so quickly that they could be used only once, and the frayed electrical wire strung about the makeshift office caused the canvas cloth to catch fire. Security was also a concern. Shortly after arriving, Taylor learned that a Viet Cong attack was imminent, but could find no spare personal weapons for his use. He had his brother in the United States quickly send him a .45-caliber semiautomatic pistol.[26]

Other JAGs set up mobile 'offices', which for some recalled the heroics of the frontier:

> Dressed in fatigues, combat boots, and helmet rather than chaps, cowboy boots, and ten gallon hat, Capt. John F. Rudy II is out riding the trails of South Vietnam, bringing legal aid to those who desire it with the same spirit and dedication as the Old West's fabled circuit riding judges. [. . .] they might

[24] 'The staff judge advocate's operation at the MACV was so small that there was minimal formal organization.' It consisted of Colonel George Prugh and a staff of three: Borch, *Judge Advocates in Combat*, 10.

[25] Ibid., 31.

[26] Ibid., 9. Taylor wasn't the only JAG to carry a gun; in fact, JAGs were commonly issued a .45 calibre pistol, a source of frustration for some JAGs who found themselves in combat situations facing enemy fire: Ibid., 67. The danger to forward deployed JAGs was real. A former Air Force lawyer recalled: 'Those of us who were in Vietnam were of the position that [the] guys in Thailand were safe; you're over there in your big bases, there's no VC [Viet Cong] around you, there's no large Vietnamese divisions around you, Goddamn it; you get the combat pay too but we're the ones here that, you know, you go to a restaurant and you know, they throw a grenade on your table. [. . .] They were like on a big aircraft carrier called Thailand.' Rodriguez, interview. Another JAG recalls how close rocket fire often came even to JAG living quarters: 'Launched rockets, trailing behind them a fiery rooster tail, were easily spotted [. . .] we typically had twenty seconds to get from poker game, dart board, bar, latrine, shower, or bed to bunker.' Morehouse, 'A Year in Vietnam', 128.

> have to blaze their own trail and do so in temperatures which sometimes ranged as high as 140 degrees and in torrential downpours which mark the rainy season, [but] Captain Rudy and Rice fired up their cycle and headed out into the boondocks, taking the legal office to the troops.[27]

Conditions such as these would be recognizable to many Army JAGs deployed to Iraq and Afghanistan in recent years, though of course the terrain was vastly different—sand and desert, not jungle and swamp. Here, for example, is a reflection on how Army military lawyers faced punishing physical conditions in Iraq and Afghanistan to perform some of their duties in the early 2000s:

> Deployments to Afghanistan and Iraq presented a climate that many of our troops were not used to— extreme heat. Soldiers and Marines worked exceedingly long hours in the heat for seven days a week. Some days were eighteen hour work days. Legal personnel also wore chemical suits and flak vests for extended periods of time; some personnel found it impossible to conduct physical training. Limited physical training, the stress of a combat deployment, irregular eating habits, and close quarters often resulted in minor ailments sweeping through offices. Moreover, those deployed to Afghanistan sometimes had to hike difficult mountain trails to investigate and pay claims [. . .] dust-like sand and the large swarms of biting insects made mission accomplishment even more challenging.[28]

The office environment may have been unconventional, but for the most part lawyers assigned to MACV provided regular peacetime legal assistance to commanders, just as they had done in the Second World War. As the war went on, however, a number of JAGs took on non-traditional roles, first innovating and later institutionalizing a series of new activities that would fall under the military lawyer's mandate. Colonel George S. Prugh is celebrated as one such pioneering figure. Prugh was assigned as General William Westmoreland's Staff Judge Advocate (i.e. top of the JAG command at MACV) from 1964 to 1966 and after the war he wrote a history of military lawyer involvement in Vietnam.[29] Prugh is an important figure because he helped drive changes in US

[27] Anon, 'Travelin' Judge', *The Reporter* (originally published in *LOADSTAR*, an American University magazine 20, Winter 1967) 26, Special History edition (1999): 130–1.

[28] The Judge Advocate General's Legal Center & School, Center for Law and Military Operations (CLAMO), United States Army, 'Legal Lessons Learned From Afghanistan and Iraq Volume I Major Combat Operations (11 September 2001–1 May 2003)', 1 August 2004 (Charlottesville, VA: United States Army), https://fas.org/irp/doddir/army/clamo-v1.pdf, accessed 15 December 2016, 264 (footnotes removed).

[29] Prugh, *Law at War, Vietnam*.

policy towards POW, and in 1974 he helped to extend and formalize new roles for military lawyers in a major new Department of Defense (DOD) Directive (section 1.4).[30]

Shortly after his arrival in Vietnam, Prugh identified three areas that at that time were deemed beyond the scope of traditional JAG responsibilities. These were: 'the status and treatment of captured enemy personnel [. . .], the investigation and reporting of war crimes, and [. . .] assisting the South Vietnamese with resource control'.[31] The last of these was a sort of vast hoarding enterprise designed to block supplies from reaching the enemy, complementing the 'interdiction' strikes that were a major part of the US aerial campaign in Vietnam. Critical material—'food, medicine, transport and other items'—was strictly controlled and surplus stored in government-controlled facilities. The role of the JAG was to advise commanders on how to implement this complex system, a job that required 'collecting, translating, interpreting, mimeographing, and distributing governmental decrees and directives'.[32] The skill-set of the JAG was expanding, but did not yet include the provision of legal advice about matters of direct combat.

The issues of POWs and military justice gained in significance as the Vietnam War intensified. According to Prugh, he and his staff became 'deeply involved' in these twin issues.[33]

Prisoners of war and 'detainees'

The Third Geneva Convention of 1949 Relative to the Treatment of Prisoners of War (GPW) set out a number of conditions concerning the protection of enemy prisoners of war. The United States ratified the treaty in 1955 and generally understood it to apply to its efforts in Vietnam.[34] There was, however, some disagreement over the applicability and scope of the Geneva Conventions as they related to 'captives' in the Vietnam War. Traditionally, POW status is afforded only to regular forces (generally those who wear a uniform and belong to an organized armed group) and not to irregular forces, which include

[30] See: Ibid.; Borch, *Judge Advocates in Combat*, 10–13.

[31] Borch, *Judge Advocates in Combat*, 11.

[32] Ibid., 13.

[33] Prugh, *Law at War, Vietnam*, 61.

[34] 'Because the US had justified its use of force in Vietnam under the UN Charter's right to respond to an international armed attack, Washington felt compelled to accept the stronger Geneva Convention regime relating to international armed conflicts rather than the weaker (Common Article 3) regime relating to non-international armed conflicts.' Cuddy, 'Wider War: American Force in Vietnam, International Law, and the Transformation of Armed Conflict, 1961-1977', 138.

'political prisoners', 'saboteurs', 'terrorists', and 'subversives'. As US combat units became heavily engaged in the war in 1965, the question was raised as to who should be treated as a POW and who should not.

It seemed obvious to accord POW status to the regular forces of North Vietnam; irregulars who fought for the National Liberation Front (NLF, also called the Viet Cong, or VC) as part of the insurgency in South Vietnam were another matter. But it was not only—or even principally—a US call to make, because the government of South Vietnam regarded NLF fighters as 'criminals who violated the security laws of South Vietnam and who consequently were subject to trial for their crimes'.[35] The implication was that such detainees were criminals, not prisoners of war, and should be dealt with in the domestic courts of South Vietnam (and thus away from any international oversight, for example from the International Committee of the Red Cross (ICRC)). After much debate, the United States resolved to treat not only captured North Vietnamese regular soldiers but also captured NLF fighters as POW, a move that effectively made the latter 'lawful enemy combatants rather than domestic criminals'.[36] The United States eventually also persuaded the South Vietnamese government to do the same, which they agreed to in principle. This was important because the United States would turn over to the South Vietnamese armed forces all individuals captured by US forces, a process that was 'beset by serious legal and practical difficulties' according to Prugh (and he would know because resolving these difficulties became one of his core duties).[37] This was the first time that JAGs had been involved in processing and calibrating the conditions of enemy detention, but it would not be the last.[38]

The United States extended POW status to this wider group—which it was not legally obliged to do—for several not-straightforward reasons. Foremost among them, according to Cuddy, was the logic of reciprocity. The hope was that if the United States and South Vietnam treated those who they captured with dignity and respect, North Vietnam might start to do the same.[39] Whether the logic worked in practice is subject to much dispute, yet Cuddy notes several

[35] Prugh, *Law at War, Vietnam*, 62.

[36] Cuddy, 'Wider War: American Force in Vietnam, International Law, and the Transformation of Armed Conflict, 1961-1977', 13.

[37] Prugh, *Law at War, Vietnam*, 62.

[38] Richard Nisa, 'Capturing Humanitarian War: The Collusion of Violence and Care in US-Managed Military Detention', *Environment and Planning A* 47 (2015): 2276–91.

[39] Alongside its strategic bargaining vis-à-vis North Vietnam and the NLF, the US 'was also reciprocally committed, by way of a multilateral treaty regime that centered on the UN Charter and the Geneva Conventions, to the international community more generally': Cuddy, 'Wider War: American Force in Vietnam, International Law, and the Transformation of Armed Conflict, 1961-1977', 138. See also: Prugh, *Law at War, Vietnam*, 62.

examples where the humanitarian gesture seems to have had some reciprocal effect on the treatment of US prisoners by the NLF and North Vietnam.[40] But as Cuddy also notes, the detention system 'worked' in other, not nearly so positive, ways as well.

Captured persons were not automatically given POW status (and the attendant rights and assumptions that go with it). In September 1966 MACV issued a directive pertaining to the determination of POW status. Under the directive identifiable North Vietnamese Army and NLF fighters were accorded POW status upon capture but all others were henceforth required to go through screening procedures, or so-called 'Article 5 tribunals', at 'Combined Tactical Screening Centers'.[41] This was no insignificant number because the legal status of a detained person was, as historian Frederic Borch points out, 'often' in doubt in Vietnam: 'rarely did the Viet Cong wear a recognizable uniform, and only occasionally did the guerillas carry their arms openly'.[42] The MACV staff Judge Advocate reviewed 'all tribunal decisions' to 'insure [sic] there were no irregularities in the proceedings' but, according to Borch, the serious issue of 'the treatment of those regarded as political prisoners by these tribunals remained unaddressed'.[43] This is a major understatement; what happened to those not deemed POWs laid the foundations for a parallel, covert programme of detention, torture, and assassination.

The Central Intelligence Agency (CIA), in conjunction with US Special Forces and the Republic of Vietnam, had its own system that ran alongside the 'regular' detention system in Vietnam. This system was known as the Phoenix Program. The historian Douglas Valentine has done much to bring its workings to light.[44] He and Jennifer Van Bergen have persuasively argued that 'where you find administrative detention', whether in Vietnam or the various prisons of the 9/11 era, 'you are likely to find torture'.[45] They characterize Phoenix as follows:

> In June 1967, the CIA launched a screening, detention, and interrogation program in Vietnam that was a major building block of what eventually became known as 'the Phoenix Program'. By the end of the Vietnam War, Phoenix

[40] Cuddy, 'Wider War: American Force in Vietnam, International Law, and the Transformation of Armed Conflict, 1961-1977', 143.

[41] Jennifer Van Bergen and Douglas Valentine, 'Dangerous World of Indefinite Detentions: Vietnam to Abu Ghraib, The', *Case Western Reserve Journal of International Law* 37, no. 2 (2006): 479.

[42] Borch, *Judge Advocates in Combat*, 21.

[43] Ibid.

[44] Douglas Valentine, *The Phoenix Program* (New York, NY: Morrow, 1990).

[45] Van Bergen and Valentine, 'Dangerous World of Indefinite Detentions', 449.

> had become notorious for its paramilitary death squads, which claimed between 20,000 (according to the CIA) and 40,000 (according to the South Vietnamese) lives. Seldom, however, has Phoenix been recognized for the huge detention and interrogation facet that enabled the CIA to compile computerized blacklists of suspected terrorists.[46]

Explaining its principal functions, they describe how:

> [T]he Phoenix Program coordinated the paramilitary and intelligence components of some two-dozen counterinsurgency programs in an attempt to 'neutralize' the 'Vietcong infrastructure' ('VCI'). The euphemism 'neutralize' meant to kill, capture, make to defect, or turn members of the 'infrastructure' into double agents. The word 'infrastructure' referred to civilian members of the 'shadow government' that was managing the insurgency in South Vietnam. In other words, the Vietcong or VCI.[47]

Phoenix was highly classified and so does not feature in most accounts of the Vietnam War; it is entirely absent from the JAG records I have been able to review. Lawyers were, however, involved: five captains—all trained lawyers—from Military Intelligence assisted with the day-to-day business of the Program, but these were likely civilian lawyers, not military JAGs. William Colby, the Director of the Phoenix Program had his own (civilian) lawyer, Gage McAfee from the State Department. I tracked down McAfee for an interview (he was living in Hong Kong when we spoke) and he was understandably reticent about what he and the five other lawyers actually contributed. Mcafee did, however, provide one example of his involvement in reviewing targeting dossiers (in this instance targeting refers to both capture and potential kill missions):

> Essentially the goal was that the right people were being targeted, which is pretty fundamental [. . .] I made sure these dossiers were good. For example, before they targeted anybody they had to have three corroborating pieces of evidence and the one rule I made, which made a difference later, was that the dossier would be thrown out—it would be dead—if they didn't have information which was within a year—within the calendar year.[48]

[46] Ibid., 459.
[47] Ibid., 463. For more on the Phoenix Program, see: Valentine, *The Phoenix Program*; Dale Andrade, *Ashes to Ashes: The Phoenix Program and the Vietnam War* (Lexington, MA: Lexington Books, 1990).
[48] McAfee, interview.

Valentine and Bergen paint a rather different picture of the procedural realities:

> [D]ue process was totally non-existent for suspected members of the VCI.[65] People whose names appeared on Phoenix blacklists were subject to midnight arrest, kidnapping, torture, indefinite detention, or assassination, simply on the word of an anonymous informer. After capture and interrogation, if they were still alive, they were tried by 'special courts' or military tribunals not unlike those proposed by [President G.W.] Bush that were not staffed by legally trained judges.[49]

That is not all:

> The hearings were clearly one-sided, weighted in favor of detention, and assumed accuracy of intelligence and the detaining unit's documentation. No provision appears to have been made at these screening hearings for the detainee to present evidence in his favor, for legal representation, proper standards of proof, or other traditional due process protections.[50]

Conditions fell short of any kind of defendable moral or legal standard:

> [T]he interrogation and detention centers there had substandard living conditions and indiscriminate crowding of POWs, common criminals, and VCI suspects. There was no way of knowing who should be interrogated, jailed, or released.[51]

It is worth underscoring that the historical record shows no evidence that JAGs were involved in the Phoenix Program. Not only that, having interviewed, reviewed the writings, and listened to oral testimonies of several JAGs who served in Vietnam, my sense is that JAGs would have opposed both the legal rationales given for the (criminal) mistreatment of non-POWs as well as their conditions of treatment. Among JAGs who served in Vietnam, and especially among those who dealt with POW issues, there was a palpable normative sense of wanting to honour US commitments to the Third Geneva Convention.

Between the experiences of recognized POWs on the one hand and those who ended up languishing in administrative detention or the depths of the

[49] Van Bergen and Valentine, 'Dangerous World of Indefinite Detentions', 464.
[50] Ibid., 481.
[51] Ibid., 466.

Phoenix Program on the other, there was an unbridgeable gulf. This was to re-open nearly forty years later with the release of the infamous 'torture memos', detailing US policy on what was euphemistically referred to as 'enhanced interrogation methods'. Once again the United States was involved with the ugly business of torture and once again the Geneva Conventions seem to have been circumvented. When it came to Guantanamo, Abu-Ghraib, and other sites in the global network of US war prisons, Donald Rumsfeld claimed that the Geneva Conventions did not apply to what he and a coterie of lawyers had started calling 'unlawful combatants'.[52] Likewise, in Vietnam Valentine and Bergen write of an 'official intent to evade Geneva's requirements'.[53]

Almost without exception every military lawyer I interviewed was quick to distance their cadre from the torture memos and the Guantanamo torture debacle, and credibly so: military lawyers forcefully and vocally resisted the legal arguments made by the Office of Legal Counsel (OLC) that attempted to justify torture. For example, the Deputy Judge Advocate General of the Air Force, Major General Jack Rives, advised that many of the 'more extreme interrogation techniques, on their face, amount to violations of domestic criminal law, as well as military law'.[54] Major General Thomas J. Romig, the Army's top-ranking uniformed lawyer, wrote in 2003 that the approach recommended by the OLC 'will open us up to criticism that the U.S. is a law unto itself'.[55] But military lawyers were shut out and not listened to: the OCL continued with its defective legal reasoning regardless, which led to practices of torture. Much the same happened in Vietnam, albeit with different offices and individuals involved. In both cases military lawyers may not have been part of the apparatus which justified and ultimately led to torture, but at best, they appear to have been powerless to stop it.

1.3 Violent Skies and 'Restrained' Bombing

There were two major aerial bombing campaigns in the Vietnam War, as well as intermittent bombing operations that were carried out between them.[56] The

[52] Derek Gregory, 'The Black Flag: Guantánamo Bay and the Space of Exception', *Geografiska Annaler: Series B, Human Geography* 88, no. 4 (2006); Lisa Hajjar, *Torture: A Sociology of Violence and Human Rights* (New York, NY: Routledge, 2013); Jens David Ohlin, *The Assault on International Law* (New York, NY: Oxford University Press, 2015).

[53] Van Bergen and Valentine, 'Dangerous World of Indefinite Detentions', 479.

[54] Quoted in: Laura Dickinson, 'Military Lawyers on the Battlefield: An Empirical Account of International Law Compliance'. *American Journal of International Law* 104, no. 1 (2010): 14.

[55] Quoted in: Ibid.

[56] Operation Rolling Thunder and Operation Linebacker were not the only aerial campaigns the United States conducted, and while there may have been a 'break' in the bombing of Vietnam between

first campaign, Operation Rolling Thunder, began in March 1965 and ended in November 1968. Its main military objective was to interdict the flow of material supplies and troops from North to South Vietnam by targeting both the source of the supplies in North Vietnam and the supply routes themselves, while its political objective was to pressure North Vietnam into peace talks by 'steadily ratcheting up civilian pain'.[57] In March 1972 negotiations between the North and South stalled and almost immediately North Vietnamese forces launched another major offensive on South Vietnam (the so-called 'Easter Offensive'). In an attempt to halt the offensive and get North Vietnam back to the negotiating table, the United States launched what would become the most intensive bombing campaign of the war—Operation Linebacker (9 May 1972–23 October 1972)—and a subsequent and final campaign—Operation Linebacker II (18–29 December 1972).

Conventional understandings of the two campaigns go something like this: Operation Rolling Thunder was a gradualist campaign controlled largely by civilian leaders in Washington with many—and some argue *too many*—political restrictions on what could be targeted.[58] This is contrasted with the 'gloves coming off' in Operation Linebacker, which was executed by military men in Vietnam with less political interference from civilian leaders in Washington. Linebacker was a 'proper' air war but one nonetheless conducted with some restrictions and in full accordance with the laws of war.[59]

Such accounts tend to overstate the law/politics dichotomy and are overly concerned with whether restraints are political or legal in origin (issues I will return to later in this section). Nevertheless, there is little doubt that restraint played a role in both campaigns. Taking the historical view, Neta Crawford points out that the air war against Vietnam 'was from the outset more restrained than bombing in World War II and Korea' (though it must be said that these wars set the bar historically low).[60] Restrictions on targeting in Vietnam were many—more in Rolling Thunder, less in Linebacker—and frequently frustrated the US Air Force.[61] President Johnson, who initiated Rolling

1968 and 1972, the United States relentlessly continued to bomb Laos and Cambodia because ammunition and supplies were being moved through these states on the Ho Chi Mihn trail. These campaigns were particularly brutal and are usefully summarized by Neta Crawford. Neta C. Crawford, 'Targeting Civilians and U.S. Strategic Bombing Norms', in *The American Way of Bombing: Changing Ethical and Legal Norms, from Flying Fortresses to Drones*, ed. Matthew Evangelista (Ithaca, NY; London: Cornell University Press, 2014), 71.

[57] Ibid., 69.
[58] W. Hays Parks, 'Rolling Thunder and the Law of War', *Air University Review* 33, no. 2 (1982): 2–23.
[59] Parks, 'Linebacker and the Law of War'.
[60] Crawford, 'Targeting Civilians and U.S. Strategic Bombing Norms' 68.
[61] Parks, 'Linebacker and the Law of War'.

Thunder, contended with an international political climate that was against a total and expansive war in Southeast Asia, so he set strategic restrictions that reflected a limited bombing campaign. As General Maxwell Taylor wrote at the time: 'The overall purpose was to apply limited force with limited means to gain limited results.'[62]

Nixon, who came into office shortly after the cessation of Rolling Thunder and the year after the My Lai massacre, faced growing domestic opposition to the Vietnam War.[63] Although he placed far fewer restrictions on what targets could be struck he allegedly took all 'reasonable precautions' to 'minimize collateral civilian casualties'.[64] Whether or not such precautions and restrictions had their origins in politics or law (for what the distinction is worth), and whether they went too far or not far enough, remain matters of great dispute. But whatever we make of these debates, one thing is certain: civilians continued to be injured and killed in Operation Rolling Thunder and Operation Linebacker. Rolling Thunder killed an estimated 52,000 North Vietnamese—or about 0.3 per cent of the population of North Vietnam, while Linebacker killed a further 13,000 civilians.[65]

Rolling Thunder

In March 1964 the White House directed the Joint Chiefs of Staff (JCS) to prepare options for increasing military pressure on Hanoi. The resulting plan called for the rapid destruction of three principal sets of targets: the major enemy command posts and headquarters; lines of supply and communication (including airfields, bridges, and supply and ammunition depots); and industrial targets (including petroleum, oil, and lubricants ('POL') targets).[66] By August 1964, Air Force planners had developed a list of ninety-four targets for a sixteen-day bombing campaign. The list was sent to the Secretary of Defense, Robert McNamara, who in turn referred it to his General Counsel for legal review. The General Counsel approved the list—military lawyers were not involved—but McNamara and President Johnson rejected both the stages of

[62] Quoted in: George J. Eade, 'Reflections on Air Power in the Vietnam War', *Air University Review* 25, no. 1 (1973): 2–9.
[63] See: David Delaney, 'What is Law (Good) For? Tactical Maneuvers of the Legal War at Home', *Law, Culture and the Humanities* 5, no. 3 (2009): 337–52.
[64] Parks, 'Linebacker and the Law of War'.
[65] Crawford, 'Targeting Civilians and U.S. Strategic Bombing Norms', 70, 72.
[66] Charles T. Kamps, 'The JCS 94-Target List: A Vietnam Myth That Still Distorts Military Thought', *Aerospace Power Journal* 15, no. 1 (2001): 67; Benjamin S. Lambeth, *The Transformation of American Air Power* (Ithaca, NY: Cornell University Press, 2000), 14.

the bombing program and the list itself.[67] President Johnson had his own ideas about what should be struck, when, and how, and wanted tight control of the targeting process, including approving which targets could be struck.[68] 'The procedure', according to Derek Gregory, 'was convoluted' and micromanaged by those back in Washington:

> The Air Force and the Navy submitted lists of targets to the Commander-in-Chief Pacific Command (CINCPAC), whose office reviewed and forwarded a revised list to the Joint Chiefs of Staff, who in turn reviewed and forwarded a revised list to the Pentagon. After officials had calculated the probable impact of a strike and the likelihood of civilian casualties, the Secretary of Defense produced a modified list in consultation with the Secretary of State. By this stage the folders for each numbered target had been reduced to a single sheet of paper with just four columns: military advantage; risk to aircraft and crew; estimated civilian casualties; and danger to third-country nationals (Russian and Chinese advisers). The final target list was decided during the President's Tuesday luncheon at the White House. [. . .] it followed a meeting of the National Security Council, and those attending were briefed before grading each target. The President reviewed the grades and made his decision, which was delivered to the NSC [National Security Council] in the evening and transmitted to CINCPAC through the Joint Chiefs for immediate execution. The instructions included not only the number of sorties to be conducted against each target but also in the early stages of the campaign the timing of the attacks and the ordnance to be used.[69]

Gregory has noted the parallels between Johnson's Tuesday lunch and what Jo Becker and Scott Shane of the *New York Times* called President Obama's 'Terror Tuesdays', the Obama administration's weekly counterterrorism meetings

[67] Parks, 'Rolling Thunder and the Law of War'. Janina Dill claims that most of the targets initially selected were nevertheless eventually attacked.Janina Dill, *Legitimate Targets?: Social Construction, International Law and US Bombing* (Cambridge: Cambridge University Press, 2014), 164.

[68] See: Jonathan D. Caverley, 'The Myth of Military Myopia: Democracy, Small Wars, and Vietnam', *International Security* 34, no. 3 (2010): 119–57; c.f. James McAllister, 'Who Lost Vietnam?: Soldiers, Civilians, and U.S. Military Strategy', *International Security* 35, no. 3 (2010): 95–123.

[69] Gregory, 'Lines of Descent'. See also: David M. Barrett, 'Doing "Tuesday Lunch" at Lyndon Johnson's White House: New Archival Evidence on Vietnam Decision Making', *PS: Political Science and Politics* 24, no. 4 (1991): 676–79; David C. Humphrey, 'Tuesday Lunch at the Johnson White House: A Preliminary Assessment', *Diplomatic History* 8, no. 1 (1984): 81–102,; Kevin V. Mulcahy, 'Rethinking Groupthink: Walt Rostow and the National Security Advisory Process in the Johnson Administration', *Presidential Studies Quarterly* 25, no. 2 (1995): 237–50; Stuart Schrader, 'Lyndon Johnson's Tuesday Lunch, Hold the Counterinsurgency', 31 October 2012, http://stuartschrader.com/lyndon-johnsons-tuesday-lunch-hold-counterinsurgency, accessed 2 June 2015.

held in the White House where targets were nominated for 'kill or capture' (it was normally the former).[70] One key difference was the absence of lawyers at Johnson's lunch meetings and throughout the Vietnam kill chain. In fact, no military officers—let alone military lawyers—were present at the Tuesday lunches until as late as October 1967 and Johnson relied solely on non-legal, civilian advisers.[71] This is radically different to the US kill chain today, which involves military lawyers from the very outset of the targeting process all the way through to the firing of munitions and the post-strike assessment (Chapters 5 and 6).

During both the targeting nomination and target execution process, Johnson set strict rules of engagement (ROE); insisted on a lengthy no-strike list (buildings, structures, or places that were prohibited from attack); and imposed other limitations on the bombing campaign.[72] For example, the ROE in Rolling Thunder stipulated that American aircraft could only attack surface-to-air missile (SAM) sites that were actually firing at them (rather than striking them before they fired). Further restraints meant that US radar-equipped aircraft were not able to 'hunt' for these sites even when it was known that they were being used to fire on US aircraft. Meanwhile, the US military was also prevented from targeting the main operating bases of the North Vietnamese Air Force.[73] Other restrictions included a ban on nuclear weapons and the restricted employment of B-52 bombers. Geographic restrictions were also set: targets within a thirty-mile radius from the centre of Hanoi; a ten-mile radius from the centre of Haipong; and within thirty miles of China could not be struck.[74]

Conventional accounts suggest that the air wars in Vietnam in general, and Rolling Thunder in particular, were restrained by political rather than legal considerations. W. Hays Parks, who served as a Marine infantry officer and JAG in Vietnam, repeatedly refers to law and politics as if the two are entirely separable and have nothing to do with each other. He variously disparages the 'political shackles' and 'predominantly political character' of 'stringent strike

[70] Derek Gregory, 'I Don't like Tuesdays . . .', *Geographical Imaginations* (blog), 26 October 2012, http://geographicalimaginations.com/2012/10/26/i-dont-like-tuesdays/, accessed 28 May 2015; Jo Becker and Scott Shane, 'Secret "Kill List" Tests Obama's Principles', *The New York Times*, 29 May 2012, http://www.nytimes.com/2012/05/29/world/obamas-leadership-in-war-on-al-qaeda.html, accessed 2 June 2012; Christopher Woods, *Sudden Justice: America's Secret Drone Wars* (New York, NY: Oxford University Press, 2015).

[71] Lambeth, *The Transformation of American Air Power*, 31.

[72] Mark Clodfelter, *The Limits of Air Power: The American Bombing of North Vietnam* (New York, NY: The Free Press, 2006), 117–46.

[73] Lambeth, *The Transformation of American Air Power*, 17–19.

[74] Clodfelter, *The Limits of Air Power*, 119.

restrictions' that were 'imposed on strike forces by the White House' in the conduct of Rolling Thunder. '[T]o what degree did the White House base its decisions on the law of war?', he asks before answering:

> [V]ery little, and then more by coincidence than choice. Except for the prohibition against attack of coastal fishing boats, the [. . .] White House criteria and prohibitions/restrictions have little basis in the law of war. With the exception of the General Counsel's approval of the JCS 94-target list, the record is rather clear that Secretary McNamara and the White House never sought advice with regard to U.S. responsibilities and rights under the law of war with respect to the conduct of Rolling Thunder.[75]

Janina Dill similarly distinguishes between law and politics in reference to the restraints on targeting in Vietnam: 'While navigating complicated *political* restrictions that were widely perceived as cumbersome, the military personnel involved in the US air wars against the Democratic Republic of Vietnam do not seem to have been guided by a sense of *legal* obligation.'[76]

My own sense is that the law/politics distinction is not always helpful because it overstates the differences between law and politics and minimizes the multiple ways that they overlap. Law and politics inform and flow into one another, but such fluid interpretations were frequently denied in the wake of Vietnam because they proved politically expedient to those making claims about what constitutes law and politics. One of the effects of Parks' invocation of the law/politics distinction is that it enables him to blame 'politics' (Washington, the White House, President Johnson, etc.) for imposing excessive and unnecessary restrictions on the Rolling Thunder bombing campaign. In turn, he is able to suggest that 'law' should have been the benchmark and reference point for targeting, not least because it would have allowed the United States to pursue a more aggressive aerial strategy. According to Parks, political constraints went *beyond* the requirements set by the laws of war, inflicting an unnecessary burden on the US military by depriving it of its 'right' to attack legitimate military targets.[77] These political constraints, he argues, were based largely and erroneously on what he called a 'paranoiac fixation' with minimizing civilian casualties, 'based in part on apparent ignorance of belligerent rights under the

[75] Parks, 'Rolling Thunder and the Law of War'.
[76] Dill, *Legitimate Targets?*, 158 (emphasis added).
[77] See e.g.: W. Hays Parks, 'Deadly Force Is Authorized', *U.S. Naval Institute Proceedings* 127, no. 1 (2001): 32.

laws of war'.[78] In an extraordinary passage he goes on to argue that although the laws of war prohibit *excessive* collateral civilian casualties:

> Historically, this standard has enjoyed a high threshold—requiring collateral civilian casualties that shock the conscience of the world because of their vast number— condemning only acts so blatant as to be tantamount to a total disregard for the safety of the civilian population, or to amount to the indiscriminate use of means and methods of warfare.[79]

Here, Parks is advocating this historically high threshold, and recommends that the 'minimum standards of conduct' should also represent the 'maximum limitation acceptable to belligerents', that is, no more than the absolute minimum protections for civilians in the laws of war should be adhered to.[80] For Parks then, politics and political intervention imply excessive constraints—excessive because they are not *required* by the laws of war. Separating law and politics enables Parks to rail against political constraints on targeting while simultaneously excusing high civilian casualties through the language of law. It also enables him to present what is ultimately an extremely controversial legal interpretation as a legal 'fact'. The presentation of legal interpretation as fact matters greatly to Parks as he turns to consider what might have been if only 'politics' had not got in the way and 'law' instead had had the final say in Rolling Thunder. Had the US Air Force been able to conduct the bombing campaign according to their 'rights' under the laws of war, Parks determines, 'Rolling Thunder undoubtedly would have concluded in a manner favorable to the United States and at a substantially lower cost'.[81]

Notwithstanding his counter-factual conjecture (the supposed results of more 'law', less 'politics'), it is worth noting that Parks relies on legal argument and reference to the laws of war even as he attempts to argue that Rolling Thunder was not conducted with the law in mind. For example, he claims: 'The restrictions imposed by this nation's civilian leaders were not based on the law of war but on an obvious ignorance of the law'; but this claim relies on knowing—or claiming to know—both the content of the laws of war and the boundary between the laws of war and politics. Here, Parks offers a *retroactive*

[78] Parks, 'Linebacker and the Law of War'.

[79] Parks, 'Rolling Thunder and the Law of War' (emphasis added).

[80] This threshold is highly controversial and has been disputed by the Canadian Judge Advocate General J. P. Wolfe, who complained: 'Parks has set the standard much too high'. Major General J. P. Wolfe, 'More "Rolling Thunder"', *Air University Review* 33, no. 6 (1982): 82.

[81] Parks, 'Rolling Thunder and the Law of War'.

legal assessment that is at the same time profoundly political. By claiming that the laws of war should have guided Rolling Thunder, and should have done so in part because of its high tolerance for civilian casualties, Parks is also making a normative claim about what *future* bombing campaigns should look like. But Parks' assessment of Rolling Thunder is also interesting for another reason: it shows the indeterminate, open, and contested nature of law and is a strong example of a military lawyer exploiting this indeterminacy in order to make a judgement and present a legal 'fact'. In this complex bombing operation, Parks, the military lawyer, does not simply 'find' the law; instead, he constitutes it in a series of powerful interpretive acts. In this way, the legal debates opened up by questions about targeting in Rolling Thunder prefigure military lawyers' interpretive work—and its practical payoffs—in the years after the Vietnam War.

Operation Linebacker

Linebacker shared some of the same goals as Rolling Thunder but was markedly different in its execution.[82] The main difference was that, unlike Rolling Thunder under Johnson, the military—and especially the Air Force and Navy—were given day-to-day control:

> President Nixon gave the Seventh Air Force Commander considerably more latitude and flexibility in directing the aerial operation than previously permitted [. . .] Now, the Seventh Air Force Commander usually set his own priorities, selected targets, and determined the strike. This allowed him to consider such important factors as military priorities, weather, enemy defences, and operational status of the target. The theatre air commander also had the authority to restrike or divert strikes based on his assessment of post-strike reconnaissance. This fundamental change in management returned a portion of the process of prosecuting the war to the professional military commander in the field.[83]

Alongside this greater relative military autonomy from civilian leaders in Washington, Linebacker forces also enjoyed fewer constraints and more relaxed targeting guidance.[84] Bombing was no longer a piecemeal affair and

[82] Clodfelter, *The Limits of Air Power*, 158.
[83] Paul Burbage et al., *The Battle for the Skies Over North Vietnam: 1964–1972*, reprint of the 1976 edition (Washington, DC: Office of Air Force History, 1985), 150.
[84] Parks, 'Linebacker and the Law of War'.

authority was given to strike categories of targets as opposed to vetting targets individually. An Air Force report at the time noted that, 'the prevailing authority to strike almost any valid military target during Linebacker was in sharp contrast to the extensive and vacillating restrictions in existence during Rolling Thunder'.[85]

But Linebacker was not without its restraints. Initially, Nixon maintained the restrictions on bombing raids within thirty miles of the Chinese border and within ten miles of Hanoi and Haipong, though these restrictions were later reduced to ten and five miles respectively. In Linebacker II the geographical restraints 'vanished' and military targets near Hanoi and Haiphong were attacked.[86] In parallel with the Rolling Thunder procedures, a master target list still had to be reviewed by the Joint Chiefs of Staff and approved by Nixon and the Secretary of Defense who instructed the Pacific and Strategic Commands to 'minimize risk of civilian casualties'.[87] In particular, the Seventh Air Force directed its pilots to use only laser-guided bombs in areas of high population density. Additionally, operational commanders in theatre were required to inform the Joint Chiefs of Staff 'of target selections 24 hours prior to their strike'.[88]

Parks maintains that there was a further distinction between Rolling Thunder and Linebacker. According to him, unlike Rolling Thunder, Linebacker was 'planned and executed with a conscious consideration of the law of war'.[89] Specifically, he claims that targeting guidance 'for the first time reflected accurate application of the law of war'.[90] Parks claims that the contrast between the application of the laws of war in Linebacker and its absence in Rolling Thunder 'appears to have been the result of the presence on the staff of the Chairman of the Joint Chiefs of Staff of a judge advocate with a knowledge of the law of war'.[91] Elsewhere, Parks claims: 'judge advocates serving as counsel to the Chairman of the Joint Chiefs of Staff participated in the decision-making process regarding target selection and mission parameters for the attack of military targets'.[92] In short, Parks suggests that the reason that Linebacker was conducted with the laws of war in mind was because a military lawyer was involved in the target selection process. Parks' source for this

[85] Clodfelter, *The Limits of Air Power*, 163.
[86] Ibid.
[87] Crawford, 'Targeting Civilians and U.S. Strategic Bombing Norms', 72. For the full procedure see: Derek Gregory, 'Lines of Descent', *OpenDemocracy.Net*, 8 November 2011, 14–15, http://www.opendemocracy.net/derek-gregory/lines-of-descent, accessed 27 April 2020.
[88] Parks, 'Linebacker and the Law of War'.
[89] Ibid.
[90] Ibid.
[91] Ibid.
[92] Parks, 'The Law of War Adviser', 12.

claim is an interview that he conducted with Colonel (ret.) Robert M. Lucy, US Marine Corps, the senior legal adviser to the Chairman of the Joint Chiefs of Staff from 1971 to 1974.

I contacted Colonel (ret.) Lucy to gain a fuller understanding of JAG involvement in targeting operations in the Vietnam air wars and Linebacker in particular. What he told me, however, directly contradicts Parks' account:

> Hays [Parks] is a good friend, but I wish that he had called me before saying that 'judge advocates serving as counsel to the Chairman of the Joint Chiefs of Staff participated in the decision-making process regarding target selection' in Vietnam. *I was the chief counsel for the Chairman during that time and the statement is not correct.* I was aware of some of the targets, of course, because I prepared the Chairman's written statements that he had to submit to Congressional Committees in the hearing we had on Vietnam at this time. My discussions with the Chairman on Vietnam were usually related to legislative matters, but not on targeting. I attended briefings on operational matters, *but was not asked for legal advice on targets.*[93]

Again, Parks' argument appears to be based on a retroactive legal assessment—or at least it is not based on the actual involvement of military lawyers in the targeting process. In my extensive investigation of whether military lawyers were involved in targeting in Vietnam I was able to find only one mention of a single JAG who is said to have been assigned as an exchange officer to the embassy in Thailand from 1967 to 1969. As far as I have been able to verify, this was not a central location in the targeting apparatus, but this single JAG reportedly gave a limited form of operations law advice to 'some of the airmen operating in North Vietnam and Thailand'.[94]

[93] Email correspondence with Colonel (ret.) Robert Lucy, USMC. July 10, 2015 (emphasis added).

[94] His name was Walter Reed. Reed was a Major at the time but he would later go on to take the highest position as a lawyer in the Air Force and was regarded as one of the Air Force's premier experts in the field of international law, a rare specialization at the time: Patricia A. Kerns, *The First 50 Years* (Washington, DC: US Air Force Judge Advocate General's Department, 2003), 54, 109. His job included a review of the target lists to ensure compliance both with the laws of war and restrictions set by the National Command Authority (NCA). An agreement between the United States, the Government of South Vietnam, and Thailand at the time stated that no bombing mission could be launched from Thailand without approval from an 'authority located in Thailand' and it was likely for this reason, and to protect US basing interests in Thailand, that the USAF took extra precautions when operating from Thailand. For more details see: T. M. Gent, 'The Role of Judge Advocates in a Joint Air Operations Center', *Airpower Journal* 13 (1999, Spring): 40–55. Gent interviewed Reed twenty years after the fact and so Reed's account is one reconstructed from his memory. When I reached out to Walter Reed he was 91 years old and was not able to speak about his deployment to Southeast Asia.

Many of the Air Force JAGs who served in Vietnam have since died or are unable to talk about their experience because of infirmity. Fortunately, however, in the late 1990s former US Air Force lawyer Lieutenant Colonel Terrie M. Gent interviewed several JAGs about their role in Vietnam. Targeting was executed in what were called Tactical Air Control Centers (TACCs) located in South Vietnam. Gent's interviews confirm that JAGs had 'almost no contact with the people who planned or executed air operations.'[95] In fact, JAGs faced a significant bureaucratic barrier that prevented them from having such contact: they did not have security clearance to enter the TACCs, let alone provide legal advice on the targeting operations being orchestrated inside. Michael R. Emerson, a captain assigned to the 377th Combat Support Group Office of the Staff Judge Advocate at Tan Son Nhut Air Base during 1970 and 1971, recalled: 'no one in our office gave briefings to the guys in the TACC. I remember it was in the Seventh Air Force Headquarters building, a gray-green building surrounded by concertina wire and guarded by lots of cops. You had to have a [high-level] clearance to get in there, and none of us had one.'[96]

The image of military lawyers being literally locked out of the building where targeting decisions were being made further contradicts Parks' claim about their involvement in the air wars. It also serves as an illustration of how things have changed. Today, the majority of US air campaigns are executed in what is now called a Combined Air Operations Center (CAOC) located at Al Udeid Air Base in Qatar—the modern equivalent of Vietnam's TACCs. As I show in Chapter 5, far from being locked out of the CAOC military lawyers have a 24/7 presence on the 'operations floor' (the place where all the important decisions are made) and a security clearance to view—and review—even the most sensitive and classified information about targets.

Civilian casualty mitigation and proportionality

In the introduction to this chapter I noted that an absence of military lawyers in targeting did not mean an absence of law in the conduct of the US war in Vietnam. In this section I flesh out two related developments that originated, partially, in the US air wars in Vietnam: the increasing emphasis that the US placed on civilian casualty mitigation and the principle of proportionality. These developments are important for two reasons. First, the move towards

95 Gent, 'The Role of Judge Advocates in a Joint Air Operations Center'.
96 Ibid.

weighing the proportionality of attacks and calculating possible civilian casualties created a logic of targeting that would come to require the involvement of legal experts. As civilians became part of such casualty calculations, so military lawyers would be required to adjudicate on the legality and proportionality of attacks. Second, civilian casualty mitigation and the language and practice of proportionality have since become mainstays of both US and Israeli logics of warfare (Chapters 4–6). This matters for the debates I discussed earlier in this section about whether restraints on US bombing in Vietnam were political or/and legal in nature (see *Rolling Thunder* and *Operation Linebacker*). Even if such restraints were predominantly 'political' in origin, as some have argued, this would miss the arguably more important point that certain forms of restraint, including civilian casualty mitigation, have *become* law and are widely practiced (however imperfectly) by states like, and certainly not limited to, the United States and Israel.

Vietnam marked the beginning of a shift in US policy towards civilian casualty mitigation. This is not to say that civilians stopped being killed by the end of the Vietnam War—or indeed since—but the killing of civilians as the conflict wore on exacted a growing political, moral, and legal cost. Neta C. Crawford, a world-leading expert and scholar of US civilian casualty policy, has persuasively argued that during the long Vietnam War, 'it became less acceptable among military professionals and the public to deliberately target civilians or to strike in ways that could lead to foreseeable harm.'[97] She offers three explanations for the shift: (a) there was a change in the normative beliefs (i.e. beliefs about what is right and wrong) among elites and the general public about targeting civilians, spurred by the human rights movement, that (slowly) caused the United States to alter its bombing practices; (b) elite understandings of military necessity changed such that leaders no longer saw the targeting of civilians as militarily productive (as they had done in the Second World War), and instead began to see the killing of civilians as 'unnecessary, ineffective, or counterproductive' to their military objectives;[98] and (c) in order to conform to public understandings of what counts as legitimate warfare, and to try to win over public support for the war, the US military began to avoid civilian casualties.

The attempts by the US military to mitigate civilian casualties do not easily square with the incontestable fact of dead and injured civilians in Vietnam, even though mitigation did not and does not mean the absolute prevention

[97] Crawford, 'Targeting Civilians and U.S. Strategic Bombing Norms', 64.
[98] Ibid., 66.

of civilian casualties (killing civilians is perfectly legal so long as they are not the object of attack and provided their deaths are proportional to the expected military gain). Cuddy articulates the apparent paradox as follows: 'How is it possible', he asks, 'to reconcile this normalized use of seemingly indiscriminate firepower [in Vietnam] with the concern to avoid civilian casualties exhibited by high-level U.S. political and military officials?'[99] Cuddy offers two principal explanations, one of which we have already touched upon. Disposing of conventional explanations that focus in one way or another on illegality—either the rules were sound and badly applied, which led inadvertently to illegal acts, or the rules themselves were rotten and allowed for illegal acts—Cuddy suggests we pay close attention to the law itself. When we do this, Cuddy argues, we might 'consider that violence visited upon the people and environment of Vietnam did not occur despite the international legal framework but, in part, because of it'. Such an explanation, Cuddy insists, recognises 'that much of the violence enacted in Vietnam was regularized not just in the sense of being normal, but also in the alternative sense of being rule-based'.[100] The civilian 'paradox' is squared in the first instance, then, by the concomitant routinization and juridification of violence.

Cuddy's second and related explanation helps to explain the shift in US targeting logic towards proportionality-based targeting that took place during the Vietnam War. It concerns the US attempt to convince populations at home and abroad that the US military was fighting with some measure of restraint. As I have shown, Johnson and successive administrations were adamant in portraying US involvement in Vietnam as limited, advocating a gradual (and sometimes secret) military build-up in South East Asia, and aerial campaigns so apparently gradualist that they would become a great source of frustration for Air Force planners. Cuddy's argument about the need to show restraint is doubly important and novel because he shows that as the US war in Vietnam wore on, the US expanded the scope of what it deemed a legitimate military target, both geographically and conceptually.[101] As evermore objects and places became defined as legitimate 'military targets'—a process that Cuddy describes as target 'creep' and 'drift'—conventional legal arguments about US attacks being reprisals or self-defence in response to North Vietnamese

[99] Cuddy, 'Wider War: American Force in Vietnam, International Law, and the Transformation of Armed Conflict, 1961–1977', 202.

[100] Ibid., 203.

[101] 'Over the course of the Johnson Administration [1963–1969], U.S. targets in North Vietnam tended to drift, both geographically (with target selections creeping northbound from the DMZ, up the Vietnamese panhandle, and ever-closer to the Hanoi-Haiphong region) and conceptually (with the category of "military targets" burgeoning over time).' Ibid., 166.

attacks steadily lost traction and legitimacy, even among those making such arguments:

> The insistence that the United States only struck military targets gave Washington some cover as those targets broadened in reach and type. But this steady movement upwards and outwards of American targets in North Vietnam also put targeting policies and practices increasingly out of the reach of international law—or, at least, out of the reach of State Department lawyers.[102]

Cuddy further insists that Crawford misses a key driver of the shift away from the deliberate targeting of civilians:

> [A]s much as any other reason, the prominence given to minimizing civilian casualties emerged out of a need to prove restraint in general, and limited war aims in particular. Civilian casualties became the measure of limited war—or, perhaps more accurately, they provided evidence that the United States was waging war in a measured manner.[103]

In short, the move towards civilian casualty mitigation became a proxy for US restraint and had the added advantage of distracting from the burgeoning category of (evermore difficult to justify) 'military targets'.[104]

Cuddy suggests that the move towards civilian casualty mitigation and the rise of the proportionality principle over the course of the Vietnam War constituted no less than a shift in paradigms of the 'legal geography of war'. His analysis is perceptive and the paradigm shift that he traces bears on my analysis of military lawyers in important ways, so is worth quoting at length:

> In the older paradigm both the civilian population and target area (usually the country's industrial base) were merged together. To strike the latter was also to hit the former. The failure of that paradigm—to adequately signal strategic restraint in the air war against North Vietnam, and to draw a comprehensible line around legitimate killing in the war within South Vietnam—necessitated divorcing targets from their surrounding territory. That became increasingly feasible physically with the rise of precision-guided munitions;

[102] Ibid., 173.
[103] Ibid., 193.
[104] 'If putting the spotlight on minimizing civilian casualties would allow the spotlight to come off target creep (both in terms of geography and category), then all the better'. Ibid., 190.

> it became possible conceptually with the rise of the rule of proportionality. The grammar of war then shifted from a territorially-bound vocabulary filled with rear zones, front zones, hinterlands, defended places, and open cities to a simple, deterritorialized binary: estimated civilian casualties and military objectives. Unconnected from any geographical marker and related to military value by means of a sliding scale, targets could now move freely through space.[105]

The paradigm shift is likely not as complete or totalising as this passage suggests: place-based targeting still forms an important part of US aerial warfare. But there has certainly been something of a move towards the calculative space of proportionality with its attendant thresholds and grey zones, as noted by scholars elsewhere.[106] It is not difficult to see the impact that this paradigm shift would have had on the sorts of legal questions that were being asked of targets. A paradigm of warfare in which 'oppositions are replaced by the elasticity of degrees, negotiations, proportions and balances' is a paradigm that requires an interpretational mind set and steady legal hand.[107] Strictly operational concerns could be left in the hands of commanders, but when it came to adjudicating questions about the balancing of military advantage with civilian concerns a new skill-set was required, and military lawyers had it. Reflecting on the new paradigm of proportionality that emerged during the Vietnam War, a US Air Force lawyer made precisely this point:

> [T]argets that are capable of being used for military purposes are generally conceded to be legitimate military targets. The line between possible and probable military use is one for the operations analyst in terms of cost effectiveness and for the lawyers in terms of proportionality.[108]

The increased emphasis placed on proportionality and civilian casualties that emerged during the Vietnam War was important in precipitating the later involvement of military lawyers in targeting. While military lawyers may not have been involved in Rolling Thunder and Linebacker, these bombing campaigns

[105] Ibid., 216.

[106] Henry Shue, 'Targeting Civilian Infrastructure with Smart Bombs: The New Permissiveness', *Philosophy & Public Policy Quarterly* 30, no. 3/4 (2010): 2–8; Eyal Weizman, 'Legislative Attack'. *Theory, Culture & Society* 27, no. 6 (2010).

[107] Eyal Weizman, *The Least of All Possible Evils: Humanitarian Violence from Arendt to Gaza* (London: Verso, 2012), 6;

[108] Gerald J. Adler, 'Targets in War: Legal Considerations', *Houston Law Review* 8, no. 1 (1970): 24–5, quoted in: Cuddy, 'Wider War: American Force in Vietnam, International Law, and the Transformation of Armed Conflict, 1961-1977', 216.

raised new political-legal issues that would come to require new forms of operational legal advice and input from legal specialists. But the evolution of air targeting, and the incorporation of these specialists into the kill chain was also critically determined from a rather different direction, namely atrocities on the ground in Vietnam and the establishment of the Law of War Program.

1.4 Discipline, War Crimes, and the Law of War Program

Discipline and the Uniform Code of Military Justice

Many of the resources and hours available to JAGs in Vietnam were expended on the traditional labour of military justice and, specifically, prosecuting and defending military courts martial.[109] The US courts martial system is governed by the Uniform Code of Military Justice (UCMJ), which was enacted by Congress in 1950 and became effective in 1951. If a member of the armed forces is suspected of violating the UCMJ they are subject to a court martial, a trial in a military court. The Manual for Courts-Martial is the text that implements the UCMJ and outlines the procedures that JAGs must follow in the pre-trial, trial and post-trial process.[110] JAGs serve as both trial and defence counsel. Crimes under the UCMJ run the gamut and include everything from possession of drugs to war crimes.[111] Prugh describes JAGs in Vietnam working under a 'staggering case load,' with time imposing 'unrelenting pressure' on those involved with military justice cases. All of this was compounded by the twelve-month rotation cycle, which meant that soldiers under investigation—and JAGs conducting the investigation—would often leave Vietnam half way through a trial.[112] JAGs were often assisted and were sometimes even replaced by paralegals and non-JAG officers (though still qualified lawyers) because, as

[109] Borch, *Judge Advocates in Combat*, 28.

[110] Gary D. Solis, *The Law of Armed Conflict: International Humanitarian Law in War*, 1st edition (Cambridge: Cambridge University Press, 2010), 87.

[111] As legal scholar and Lieutenant Colonel (ret.) former US Army lawyer Geoffrey S. Corn explains: 'It is the longstanding practice of the Department of Defense to charge "war crimes" as violations of the punitive articles of the Uniform Code of Military Justice (UCMJ). These articles include statutory prohibitions against murder, manslaughter, and many other "common law" criminal offenses.' Geoffrey S. Corn, 'War Crimes and the Limits of Combatant Immunity', Jurist: Legal News and Research, 28 May 2006, https://www.jurist.org/commentary/2006/05/war-crimes-and-limits-of-combatant/, accessed 7 August 2019.

[112] Prugh, *Law at War, Vietnam*, 100. If a soldier was under investigation and did not plead guilty to the offences against him or her, s/he would ordinarily be required to return to Vietnam to testify and, if found guilty, receive sentencing. Interview, Rodriguez.

a Brigade Staff Judge Advocate in 1970 noted, 'there are simply not enough JAG officers to go around'.[113]

Military justice issues varied over the course of the Vietnam War but JAGs commonly cite three major issues: illicit drugs, 'white-collar' crimes (including black-marketing and currency violations), and disciplinary problems.[114] The latter, especially, was exacerbated by racism and by insubordination between racial groups and some younger servicemen and their superiors.[115] Burke notes: 'Drug use and distribution was a significant problem in Vietnam. The drugs of choice were marijuana and heroin. Both were locally grown, inexpensive and readily available, often sold by small children on the street'.[116] JAGs frequently complained about the problem of drug use. In an exit interview at the end of his tour in Vietnam in 1971, one frustrated JAG reported: 'I have difficulty in establishing any sort of empathy with drug users. I cannot understand how, with all the information available, they still get hooked on the stuff.'[117] Drug use and other tensions only got worse, and the amount of crime greater, as troop build-up increased and by 1969 the US Army alone found itself trying some 9,922 courts-martial.[118] Military Justice issues were so commonplace that they accounted for the vast majority—and sometimes all—JAG work in Vietnam. Because they were both tedious and time consuming, military justice issues were a source of frustration among JAGs and some even felt that officers in Vietnam were using military justice as a 'substitute for good leadership'.[119]

[113] Exit interview with Captain Thomas Hokinson, Staff Judge Advocate, 199th LIB. Interview by 44th MHD, 1LT James G. Lindsay, tape recording, 11 January 1970, Vietnam Interview Tape Collection, US Army Center of Military History, Historical Research Branch, Fort McNair, DC. VNIT-557.

[114] Burke, 'Changing Times and New Challenges: The Vietnam War', 120–1. See also: exit interview conducted in 1970 with Captain David Bengston, Staff Judge Advocate, 199th Infantry Brigade. Interview by 44th MHD, Danny. P. Barrett, tape recording, 28 July 1970, Vietnam Interview Tape Collection, US Army Center of Military History, Historical Research Branch, Fort McNair, DC. VNIT-731.

[115] According to Burke: 'Distrust and misunderstanding between racial groups were problems that threatened unit cohesion and mission effectiveness. At times, racial unrest collided head-on with the military justice system. Airmen of all races were offered Article 15s and even court-martialed for offenses that had undertones of racial intolerance and ignorance': Burke, 'Changing Times and New Challenges: The Vietnam War', 124. Several JAGs mention in their end-of-tour interviews that racism was a significant issue and a constant source of tension among the troops: exit interview with Major David Norris, Brigade Adjutant General, and Captain David Kull, Staff Judge Advocate. Interview by 18th MHD, Captain Gerard J. Monaghan, tape recording, 27 February 1971, Vietnam Interview Tape Collection, US Army Center of Military History, Historical Research Branch, Fort McNair, DC. VNIT-834; exit interview conducted in 1970 with Captain David Bengston, Staff Judge Advocate, 199th Infantry Brigade. Interview by 44th MHD, Danny. P. Barrett.

[116] Burke, 'Changing Times and New Challenges: The Vietnam War', 123.

[117] Exit interview with COL Vernon Newman, Staff Judge Advocate. Interview by 16th MHD, CPT. Joel D. Meyerson, tape recording, 17 June 1971, Vietnam Interview Tape Collection, U.S. Army Center of Military History, Historical Research Branch, Fort McNair, DC. VNIT-991.

[118] Borch, *Judge Advocates in Combat*, 29.

[119] Exit interview with MAJ David Norris, Brigade Adjutant General, and CPT David Kull, Staff Judge Advocate. Interview by 18th MHD, CPT Gerard J. Monaghan.

JAG work on the ground in Vietnam is a far cry from the hands-on role that military lawyers play in aerial targeting operations on the contemporary battlefield. But the experiences I have outlined were nevertheless vital in both expanding the scope of their work and proving their competence and helpfulness to a military that faced evermore juridically complex challenges. Several of these issues went to the very heart of the US military, coalescing around a profound question: how to maintain discipline among hundreds of thousands of troops deployed to a place thousands of miles away from home, to an environment that they knew little about and were ill equipped to deal with, who among them some were high on drugs and fighting with one another, and who were called upon to fight a war that was becoming increasingly unpopular at home? (A variation of this question is crucial to all militaries and, of course, is by no means new).

They may have been imperfect (and sometimes understaffed) systems but the central involvement of JAGs in administering both the POW procedures and courts martial took some weight off commanders, whose ultimate responsibility it was to ensure proper troop discipline. In so doing they proved their value in a difficult environment. What is more, these observations would seem to support Eyal Benvenisti and Amichai Cohen's argument that the presence of legal advisers, and the laws of war more generally, help in some ways to maintain discipline (if always in an imperfect way). In turn, troop discipline is crucial to the massification of huge militaries as exemplified by US deployments to Vietnam—and around the world—because without discipline a military is greatly diminished. At least indirectly then, military lawyers in Vietnam helped institutionalize legal governance mechanisms that sought to discipline individual troops at the same time as enabling and unleashing the near-full might of the entire US military.[120]

War crimes and the law of war program

In the early morning of 16 March 1968, ninety-nine soldiers from 'Charlie' Company of the 11th Light Infantry Brigade, Americal Division, US Army, entered the hamlet of Tu Cung, in the village of Son My on the coast of central Vietnam.[121] They were on a search and destroy

[120] Eyal Benvenisti and Amichai Cohen, 'War Is Governance: Explaining the Logic of the Laws of War from a Principal-Agent Perspective', *Michigan Law Review* 112, no. 8 (2014).

[121] For a description of what happened at My Lai see: Bernd Greiner, *War Without Fronts: The USA in Vietnam* (New Haven, CA: Yale University Press, 2009) 181–238, and in particular 211–29.

mission.[122] The soldiers faced no enemy forces when entering the village, nor were they fired at: their entry was officially recorded as '"cold" or free of enemy fire'.[123] Around four hours after Charlie Company entered Son My, well over 300 civilians lay dead.[124] Most of those killed were women and children, and many were raped and sexually humiliated before being murdered.[125] A little over a mile away another unit, Bravo Company, killed close to one hundred civilians in the neighbouring hamlet of My Hoi. Those who partook in the massacres, along with their superiors, subsequently covered up their crimes.[126]

According to Nick Turse:

> There were scores of witnesses on the ground and still more overhead, American officers and helicopter crewmen perfectly capable of seeing the growing piles of civilian bodies. Yet when the military released the first news of the assault, it was portrayed as a victory over a formidable enemy force, a legitimate battle in which 128 enemy troops were killed without the loss of a single American life.[127]

It was not until mid-1969, over a year later, that what would become known in Vietnam as the Son My massacre—and in America, the My Lai massacre—would come to US and international public attention.[128] In December 1969 Life magazine published graphic colour photographs of the dead by Ronald Haeberle, the Army photographer who had accompanied Charlie Company (Figure 1.1)[129] Twenty-five years later, two JAG Corps soldiers reflected on

[122] William Raymond Peers, *Report of the Department of the Army Review of the Preliminary Investigations into the My Lai Incident: The Report of the Investigation*, vol. 1 (The Department of the Army, 1974), 5–1, http://www.loc.gov/rr/frd/Military_Law/Peers_inquiry.html, accessed 31 July 2015.

[123] Ibid., 1:5–16.

[124] Kendrick Oliver, *The My Lai Massacre in American History and Memory* (Manchester: Manchester University Press, 2006), 1. Reliable facts and statistics are still difficult to ascertain, as Bernard Greiner explains: 'As no soldier in C Company had an overview of the entire action, the Criminal Investigation Division of the Army consulted population statistics and compared these equally unreliable details with the statements of survivors and the tax registers of the provincial administrators. This yielded an overall figure of between 400 and 430 victims in Xom Lang and Bihn Tay—the villages known as My Lai': Greiner, *War without Fronts*, 212. Gary Solis puts the number at approximately 345: Solis, *The Law of Armed Conflict*, 236. Nick Turse claims, 'Over four hours, members of Charlie Company methodically slaughtered more than five hundred unarmed victims'. Turse, *Kill Anything That Moves*, 3.

[125] Greiner, *War without Fronts*, 221.

[126] Joseph Goldstein et al., *The My Lai Massacre and Its Cover-Up: Beyond the Reach of Law? The Peers Commission Report* (New York, NY: Free Press, 1976); Michael Bilton and Kevin Sim, *Four Hours in My Lai*, reprint edition (New York, NY: Penguin Books, 1993).

[127] Turse, *Kill Anything That Moves*, 3.

[128] Jeffrey F. Addicott and William A. Hudson, 'The Twenty-Fifth Anniversary of My Lai: A Time to Inculcate the Lessons', *Military Law Review* 139 (1993): 156.

[129] In 1969 Haeberle told the *The Plain Dealer*, the Cleveland Newspaper which originally published the photographs, that he did not take photographs of US soldiers in the act of killing. In 2009 he admitted that he did take such photographs but destroyed them 'I shot pictures of the shooting [. . .] But those photographs were destroyed [. . .] by me': Evelyn Theiss, 'My Lai Photographer Ron Haeberle

Figure 1.1 A soldier burning down a hut in My Lai village. The photographer, Ronald L. Haberle, was deployed with one of the units who committed the massacre. His photos of the My Lai massacre galvanized the antiwar movement in the United States.

Source: Report of Army review into My Lai incident, book 6, 14 March 1970[1], https://commons.wikimedia.org/w/index.php?curid=2461676, accessed 27 April 2020.

My Lai as 'the greatest emblem of American military shame in the twentieth century'.[130]

According to historian Bernd Greiner, the initial investigations of the My Lai massacre were a 'farce'.[131] But in November 1969, the Army appointed Lieutenant General William Peers, US Army, to 'explore the nature and scope of the original Army investigations' and to find out what happened at My Lai.[132] The so-called Peers Report, described by former JAG and international law scholar Gary Solis as the 'most comprehensive of the My Lai investigations',

Admits He Destroyed Pictures of Soldiers in the Act of Killing', *Cleveland.Com* (blog), http://blog.cleveland.com/pdextra/2009/11/post_25.html, accessed 6 August 2015.

[130] Addicott and Hudson, 'The Twenty-Fifth Anniversary of My Lai', 154.

[131] Greiner, *War without Fronts*, 283.

[132] William Raymond Peers, 'Report of the Department of the Army Review of the Preliminary Investigations into the My Lai Incident: The Report of the Investigation', vol. 1, The Department of the Army, 1974, 1-1, http://www.loc.gov/rr/frd/Military_Law/Peers_inquiry.html, accessed 31 July 2015.

was published in four volumes in March 1970. It contained over 20,000 pages of witness statements and about 10,000 pages of evidence.[133] Despite its extensive nature, the Peers Report was hampered by soldiers and senior officers who refused to testify. Moreover, the time for Peers' investigation was severely limited because of a clause in the UCMJ stipulating that offences must be set out in writing and given to the prosecuting authorities *within a maximum of two years after the event*.[134] In the Vietnam era, charges could only be brought upon those who were still in military service, effectively 'leaving ex-soldiers suspected of war crimes free of possible prosecution'.[135]

Had it been up to Peers, the My Lai tribunals would have taken place as a mass trial based on the Nuremberg model, with thirty-seven soldiers from Charlie Company sitting together in the dock, but what came to pass was a much more limited set of courts martial.[136] According to Turse, the Peers inquiry:

> [E]ventually determined thirty individuals were involved in criminal misconduct during the massacre or its cover-up. Twenty-eight of them were officers, including two generals, and the inquiry concluded they had committed a total of 224 serious offenses. But only [William] Calley was ever convicted of any wrongdoing. He was sentenced to life in prison for the premeditated murder of twenty-two civilians, but President Nixon freed him from prison and allowed him to remain under house arrest. He was eventually paroled after serving just forty months, most of it in the comfort of his own quarters.[137]

The scope of the Peers Inquiry was limited to what happened at My Lai; possible crimes committed by US troops elsewhere were not part of the Inquiry. More recently, as new archives have been opened, it has become apparent that My Lai was not an aberration; in fact, it was part of a pattern of US violence.[138] Nick Turse writes:

> Looking back, it's clear that the real aberration was the unprecedented and unparalleled investigation and exposure of My Lai. No other American

[133] Greiner, *War without Fronts*, 313.

[134] Ibid.

[135] 'In that era, court-martial jurisdiction did not survive discharge from active military duty and, in 1969, there was no U.S. domestic court with jurisdiction over foreign shore grave breaches, [...] Trial in Vietnam, the site of the crimes, was a theoretical option but a practical impossibility': Solis, *The Law of Armed Conflict*, 87–88.

[136] Greiner, *War without Fronts*, 313.

[137] Turse, *Kill Anything That Moves*, 4.

[138] Greiner, *War without Fronts*; Turse, *Kill Anything That Moves*.

> atrocity committed during the war—and there were so many—was ever afforded anything approaching the same attention. Most, of course, weren't photographed, and many were not documented in any way. The great majority were never known outside the offending unit, and most investigations that did result were closed, quashed, or abandoned. Even on the rare occasions when the allegations were seriously investigated within the military, the reports were soon buried [. . .] Whistle-blowers within the ranks or recently out of the army were threatened, intimidated, smeared, or—if they were lucky—simply marginalized and ignored.[139]

These are strong words but they are supported indirectly and anecdotally by observations made by Prugh, the MACV Staff Judge Advocate discussed at length in section 1.2:

> [D]uring the period between 1 January 1965 and 31 August 1973, there were 241 cases (excluding My Lai) which involved allegations of war crimes against United States Army troops. One hundred and sixty of these cases, upon investigation, were determined to be unsubstantiated. Substantiated allegations of war crimes violations committed in Vietnam by personnel subject to the Uniform Code of Military Justice were prosecuted under the provisions of the code. From January 1965 through August 1973, 36 cases involving war crimes allegations against Army personnel were tried by court-martial. Sixteen cases involving thirty men resulted in acquittal or dismissal after arraignment. Twenty cases involving thirty-one Army servicemen resulted in conviction.[140]

According to Peers, the crimes committed at My Lai resulted from a combination of several factors. Two are especially pertinent to the history of JAG involvement in law of war issues: the lack of proper training in the law of war and lack of leadership.[141] Stephen Myrow explains the significance of the latter:

> Because the primary responsibility for ensuring that conduct on the battlefield is kept within professional norms lies directly on the officer corps,

[139] Turse, *Kill Anything That Moves*, 5.

[140] Prugh, *Law at War, Vietnam*, 74; see also: Solis, *The Law of Armed Conflict*; Greiner, *War without Fronts*; Turse, *Kill Anything That Moves*; Borch, *Judge Advocates in Combat*, 21–2.

[141] Other factors cited by the Peers Report include: attitudes towards the Vietnamese, the nature of the enemy, organizational problems, and the lack of a grand strategy by the United States: Addicott and Hudson, 'The Twenty-Fifth Anniversary of My Lai', 164–72.

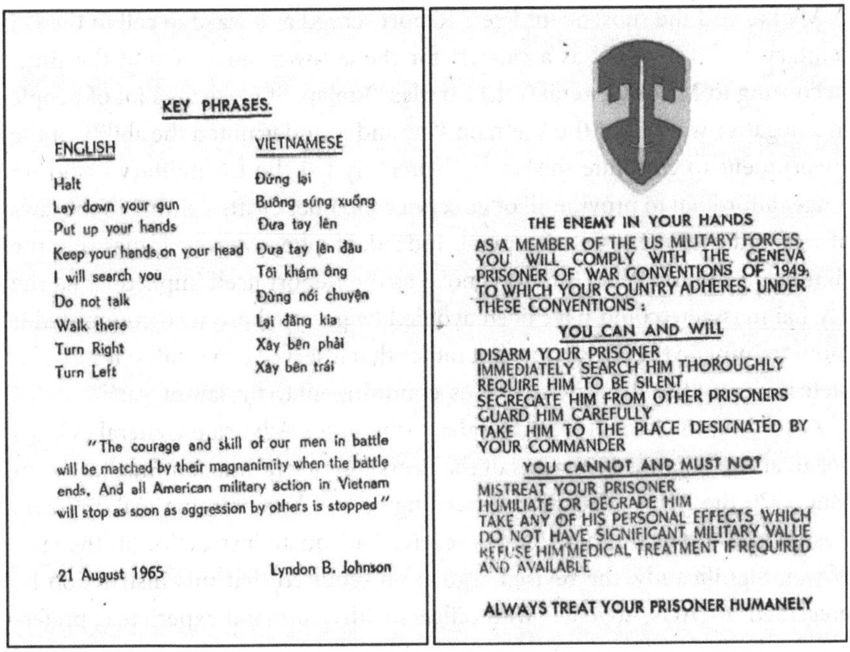

KEY PHRASES.

ENGLISH	VIETNAMESE
Halt	Đứng lại
Lay down your gun	Buông súng xuống
Put up your hands	Đưa tay lên
Keep your hands on your head	Đưa tay lên đầu
I will search you	Tôi khám ông
Do not talk	Đừng nói chuyện
Walk there	Lại đằng kia
Turn Right	Xây bên phải
Turn Left	Xây bên trái

"The courage and skill of our men in battle will be matched by their magnanimity when the battle ends. And all American military action in Vietnam will stop as soon as aggression by others is stopped"

21 August 1965 Lyndon B. Johnson

THE ENEMY IN YOUR HANDS

AS A MEMBER OF THE US MILITARY FORCES, YOU WILL COMPLY WITH THE GENEVA PRISONER OF WAR CONVENTIONS OF 1949, TO WHICH YOUR COUNTRY ADHERES. UNDER THESE CONVENTIONS:

YOU CAN AND WILL

DISARM YOUR PRISONER
IMMEDIATELY SEARCH HIM THOROUGHLY
REQUIRE HIM TO BE SILENT
SEGREGATE HIM FROM OTHER PRISONERS
GUARD HIM CAREFULLY
TAKE HIM TO THE PLACE DESIGNATED BY YOUR COMMANDER

YOU CANNOT AND MUST NOT

MISTREAT YOUR PRISONER
HUMILIATE OR DEGRADE HIM
TAKE ANY OF HIS PERSONAL EFFECTS WHICH DO NOT HAVE SIGNIFICANT MILITARY VALUE
REFUSE HIM MEDICAL TREATMENT IF REQUIRED AND AVAILABLE

ALWAYS TREAT YOUR PRISONER HUMANELY

Figure 1.2 'The Enemy in your hands'. All troops arriving in Vietnam received a 3x5 inch MACV-issued booklet on how to treat enemy prisoners. They were often considered a substitute for training.

Source: Sergeant Major Herb Friedman, US Army (ret.) personal collection: reproduced with permission.

> 'nowhere is the need for law of war training more critical than in the proper development of the military's officer corps.' Thus, a lack of leadership breeds the potential for violations of the law of war.[142]

Moreover, the Peers Report specifically found evidence indicating that, 'at best, the soldiers of TF [Task Force] Barker [which included Bravo and Charlie Company] had received only marginal training in several key legal areas prior to the Son My operation' (Figure 1.2). These areas were: (a) provisions of the Geneva Conventions; (b) handling and safeguarding of non-combatants; and (c) rules of engagement. These 'training deficiencies', the Report goes on to note, 'played a significant part in the Son My operation'.[143]

[142] Stephen. A. Myrow, 'Waging War on the Advice of Counsel: The Role of Operational Law in the Gulf War', *United States Air Force Academy Journal of Legal Studies* 7 (1996): 133, quoting: Addicott and Hudson, 'The Twenty-Fifth Anniversary of My Lai', 184.

[143] Peers, 'Report of the Department of the Army Review of the Preliminary Investigations into the My Lai Incident', 8–13.

My Lai and the subsequent Peers Report served as a wakeup call to the US military and also acted as a catalyst for the antiwar movement at the time. According to Major General (ret.) Charles Dunlap, 'it woke up a lot of people in a negative way about the Vietnam War and it undermined the ability of the government to continue the war'.[144] After My Lai the US military could no longer afford *not* to provide all of its service members with training in the laws of war and the rules of engagement. Indeed, Stephen Myrow argues that the significance of the Peers Report is not—as the Report itself implied—that the My Lai massacre could have been avoided by giving those who committed it more training in the law of war, 'but rather that it served as a catalyst for a complete review of the U.S. Armed Forces' commitment to the law of war'.[145]

According to Colonel David Graham, the Judge Advocate General's Corps began addressing the criticisms of the Peers Report '[a]lmost immediately'. In May 1970 the Army regulation governing Law of War training, AR 350-216, was revised to ensure that soldiers received adequate instruction in the laws of war. Significantly, the revised regulation required that this instruction be presented by JAGs, 'together with officers with command experience, preferably in combat'.[146] This ensured that training would be grounded in 'real world experience'.[147] The most important change would come several years later at the initiative of General George Prugh. In November 1974, the Department of Defense published Directive 5100.77, a direct descendant of the My Lai massacre, and drafted by Prugh.[148] This directive mandated the establishment of the first law of war Program of its kind, requiring every member of the armed forces to undertake law of war training:

> The Armed Forces of the United States shall comply with the law of war in the conduct of military operations and related activities in armed conflict, however such conflicts are characterized.
>
> The Armed Forces of the U.S. shall institute and implement programs to prevent violations of the law of war to include training and dissemination, as required, by the Geneva Conventions.[149]

[144] Dunlap, interview.

[145] Myrow, 'Waging War on the Advice of Counsel', 133.

[146] David Graham, 'Operational Law: A Concept Comes of Age', *Army Law* 175 (1987): 2.

[147] Ibid., 3.

[148] According to Army JAG historian Frederic Borch: 'This Department of Defense policy decision—and a subsequent and complementary Joint Chiefs of Staff directive requiring the chairman's legal counsel to review all operations plans—was a direct result of My Lai [. . .] the Defense Department recognized that preventing similar incidents required a new approach to ensuring obedience to the Law of War.': Borch, *Judge Advocates in Combat*, 319.

[149] United States Department of Defense, 'Department of Defense Directive: "DoD Law of War Program"', 10 July 1979, 2, https://apps.dtic.mil/dtic/tr/fulltext/u2/a272470.pdf, accessed 20 April 2020.

The new program placed JAGs at the centre of law of war training, even if they were not yet incorporated fully into combat and targeting operations. Other Department of Defense initiatives emanating from Vietnam created yet more new roles for military lawyers. Critics of the Vietnam War often took issue with the kind of weapons employed by the United States, arguing that, for example, the 'M-16 rifle, cluster munitions, and napalm' were illegal.[150] In response, the Department of Defense issued Instruction 5500.15, which 'established a requirement that any new weapon or munition being considered for development or acquisition by the United States must undergo a legal review to ensure its consistency with the law of war obligations of the United States'.[151] JAGs immediately became responsible for conducting this legal review. For its part (somewhat later than the Navy and Army), the Air Force created its first ever Air Force pamphlet in 1976 on the Law of Armed Conflict, which subsequently became the Air Force JAG 'bible'.[152] That same year, the Air Force published Regulation 110-32, which implemented Department of Defense Directive 5100.77: the Regulation made the Air Force JAG Corps 'primarily responsible for training and monitoring Law of Armed Conflict issues in the Air Force'.[153] The seeds of change were sown but it would be some years before these doctrinal changes were registered at the level of military practice. With time, a whole new discipline of law would come into being, and with it a new kind of military lawyer. In the next chapter, Chapter 2, we turn to explore the birth of operational law and the operational lawyer.

[150] W. Hays Parks, 'The Gulf War: A Practitioner's View', *Dickinson Journal of International Law* 10, no. 3 (1992): 397.

[151] Ibid.

[152] Until 1976 the Air Force did not have so much as even a basic statement of its law of war policy. Colonel Robert Bridge points out that this deficiency was highlighted during a Senate debate in 1972: 'Why is it that the Air Force, for example, refuses to develop a set of rules-a manual for air warfare? The Navy does. The Army does. But the Air Force refuses to do it. They refuse to give instructions to the young men who are going out there [to Vietnam]—to make them sensitive and more cautious to civilian needs.' Robert L. Bridge, 'Operations Law: An Overview', *Air Force Law Review* 37 (1994): 1.

[153] Kerns, *First 50 Years*, 2004, 137, citing Air Force Regulation 1 10–32, Judge Advocate General Training and Reporting to Ensure Compliance with the Law of Armed Conflict, 2 August 1976.

2

The Birth of 'Operational Law'

> [Judge advocates] do not fly jets and drop bombs when they are not conducting a trial; they do not control a war, but they do actively and aggressively support the wartime commander by providing him with proactive legal support before bombs start dropping, as operations unfold, and after hostilities cease.
>
> Brigadier General Charles Dunlap[1]

2.1 Putting the Laws of War to Work

After the Vietnam War, the US military instituted a series of changes that sought to instil law of war principles across its forces, introducing a cross-service Law of War Program that would teach and train soldiers and commanders in the basic principles. In Chapter 1, I explained why the US military implemented the Law of War Program, and how this was tied closely to the issue of troop conduct in Vietnam, and especially to the My Lai massacre. In this chapter I move to explore how the US military implemented the Program, focusing especially on the role that military lawyers played in creating and crafting a new legal regime that became known as 'operational law'.[2]

To operationalize something is to put it to use. So, what 'use' did operational law serve? In both practitioner-oriented and scholarly literature, operational law is generally conceived of as a feature of military training and instruction in the laws of war which helps to improve discipline and compliance.[3] But operational law is not simply or only about enhancing military governance in the sense of narrowly defined compliance-building, especially where compliance

[1] Charles Dunlap, 'It Ain't No TV Show: JAGs and Modern Military Operations', *Chicago Journal of International Law* 4, no. 2 (2003): 481.

[2] Operational law is also frequently called operations law. For consistency, I refer to operational law.

[3] W. Hays Parks, 'Teaching the Law of War', *The Army Lawyer* 174 (1987): 4–10; David E. Graham, 'My Lai and Beyond: The Evolution of Operational Law', in *The Real Lessons of the Vietnam War: Reflections Twenty-Five Years after the Fall of Saigon*, ed. John Norton Moore and Robert F. Turner (Durham, NC: Carolina Academic Press, 2002); Laura Dickinson, 'Military Lawyers on the Battlefield: An Empirical Account of International Law Compliance', *American Journal of International Law* 104, no. 1 (2010): 1–28.

The War Lawyers. Craig Jones, Oxford University Press (2020). © Craig Jones.
DOI: 10.1093/oso/9780198842927.001.0001.

is understood as limitation. I argue that the invention and development of operational law allowed the US military to *domesticate* the laws of war in two key senses—it allowed them to 'nationalise' the international laws of war (and therefore advance claims of ownership to and dominance over the laws of war), and it permitted the US military to 'tame' the laws of war, rendering them ever more pragmatic, practitioner-oriented, and military-friendly.[4]

A key strand of this domestication involved an organized, concerted, positive assertion of US military rights under the laws of war.[5] The US bid to operationalize the laws of war was never a straightforward process of translation; it involved an active reconstitution of their content. In short, operational law put the laws of war to work for the US military—not for the first time, but to a (then) unprecedented degree. The *raison d'être* of operational law is to specify that which cannot be articulated by international law, transforming the abstract and general to the specifics of what is militarily 'necessary'. The move from the laws of war to operational law is not a neutral or purely technical exercise of rescaling, but rather represents an interpretation, transformation, and 'worlding' of the laws of war. As I have argued elsewhere, this worlding is done through a specifically military register and is designed to shape and reshape the laws of war in the US image:

> Operational law [is] the tip of the international law spear, a space far away from the sites and institutes commonly associated with the treaty making of international law—the UN, ICC, or the International Committee of the Red Cross—but nonetheless working on the same project of defining and rewriting the power and purpose of law in war, albeit from a radically different direction.[6]

The United States has a long history of contributing to and helping define the laws of war. The Lieber Code of 1863 is an early example of how domestic US military law became incorporated into and informed the regulation of

[4] Kay Anderson defines domestication in part as a 'bringing in' of the 'the wild'; counterintuitively perhaps, there was a widespread perception among soldiers and commanders after the Vietnam War that the laws of war 'out there' should not be 'brought in' to wreak havoc on US military operations: Kay Anderson, 'A Walk on the Wild Side: A Critical Geography of Domestication', *Progress in Human Geography* 21, no. 4 (1997): 463.

[5] Parks, 'Teaching the Law of War'; W. Hays Parks, 'Rules of Engagement: No More Vietnams', in *The U.S. Naval Institute on Vietnam: A Retrospective*, ed. Thomas Cutler (Annapolis, MD: Naval Institute Press, 2016), 150–5.

[6] Craig Jones, 'Frames of Law: Targeting Advice and Operational Law in the Israeli Military', *Environment and Planning D: Society and Space* 33, no. 4 (2015): 691.

hostilities and laws of war treaties.[7] But the emergence of operational law in the 1970s placed a burgeoning emphasis on the laws of war and created the institutional structures to ensure that law would become—and would *remain*—a key pillar of US war. Operational law helped to 'fix' some of the governance and perception problems that emerged in Vietnam by fostering a law of war culture *internally* and projecting a culture of compliance *externally*.

The chapter is organized as follows. The next section discusses how the establishment and institutionalization of the Law of War Program in the 1970s gave birth to the new legal regime of operational law (section 2.2). I then show how operational law was 'invented' in order to overcome negative attitudes towards the laws of war (section 2.3) by making positive and proactive assertions about the potential of the laws of war to enable and facilitate military operations (section 2.4). The following section examines how operational law fostered improved relationships and mutual understanding between commanders and lawyers, a crucial ingredient in the subsequent integration of military lawyers into targeting operations (section 2.5). The chapter finishes with a brief discussion of the US invasion of Panama in 1989, the first real 'test' for operational law and the first time that military lawyers were called upon to give advice on targeting operations (section 2.6).

2.2 Going 'Operational'

In 1979 the Joint Chief of Staff (JCS) ordered that 'all operations plans, contingency plans, and rules of engagement undergo a legal review'.[8] This JCS memorandum would put military lawyers at the very centre of military operations, effectively securing their seat in the operational planning room of future military operations. The directive was expanded in 1983 and included two vital new roles for military lawyers:

1. <u>Conduct of Operations.</u> Legal advisors should be immediately available to provide advice concerning law of war compliance during joint and combined operations. Such advice on law of war compliance shall be provided in the context of the broader relationships of international

[7] John Fabian Witt, *Lincoln's Code: The Laws of War in American History* (New York, NY: Free Press, 2013).

[8] Quoted in: Parks, 'Teaching the Law of War', 8.

and U.S. and allied domestic law to military operations and, among other matters, shall address not only legal restraints upon operations but also *legal rights to employ force.*

2. **Review of Joint Documents.** All plans, rules of engagement, policies and directives shall be consistent with the DOD [Department of Defense] Law of War Program, domestic and international law, and shall include, as necessary, provisions for (1) the conduct of military operations and exercises in accordance with laws affecting such operations, including the law of war, and (2) the reporting and investigation of alleged law of war violations, whether committed by or against U.S. or allied military or civilians or their property. Such joint documents should be reviewed by the joint command legal advisor at each stage of preparation.[9]

This memorandum was entitled 'Implementation of the DOD Law of War Program,' but it went further than simply implementing structures that were already in place. By requiring legal advisers to review military practice in the planning and execution stages of war, the memorandum simultaneously expanded the then-accepted role of military lawyers into combat operations, while also helping to usher in the new legal regime of operational law. As one senior military lawyer reflected, the decision to have military lawyers review the Operation Plans (or 'OPLANS'), 'represented the first institutionally mandated involvement of military attorneys in the operational planning process', a move that would 'require that they begin to communicate directly with commanders and their staff principals throughout the course of planning for an operation.'[10]

A subsequent Forces Command (FORSCOM) Message—'Review of Operations Plans'—in October 1984 ensured that commanders could not bypass legal advice by mandating that 'JAs [judge advocates] will make direct liaison with the operations officer [. . .] to act as the operational law advisor.'[11] Thus, even if the commander in charge of an operation had not sought legal counsel prior to 1984, they would henceforth be *required* to have their operational plans reviewed by military lawyers. This would 'push' legal review and judge advocate (JAG) involvement deep into the operational planning process, juridifying plans even before they could be put 'on the shelf', let alone 'taken off' for execution. These directives and mandates were subsequently adopted

[9] Quoted in: Ibid. (emphasis added).

[10] Graham, 'My Lai and Beyond: The Evolution of Operational Law', 5.

[11] The Judge Advocate General's School, International & Operational Law Department, United States Army, 'Operational Law Handbook 1997' (Charlottesville, VA: United States Army, 1997), on file with author, 1–1.

by each of the services and they form the institutional and regulatory basis for the emergence of operational law.[12] The 1997 edition of the annual Operational Law Handbook, published by The Judge Advocate General's Legal Center & School in Charlottesville, Virginia, cites the above institutional directives as necessitating 'aggressive operational law programs'.[13]

In 1987 Army Lieutenant Colonel David E. Graham provided the first widely accepted definition of operational law, namely:

> Domestic and international law associated with the planning and execution of military operations in peacetime or hostilities. It includes, but is not limited to, Law of War, law related to security assistance, training, mobilization, predeployment preparation, deployment, overseas procurement, the conduct of military combat operations, anti-and counter-terrorist activities, status of forces agreements, operations against hostile forces, and civil affairs operations. In essence, then, OPLAW [Operational Law] is that body of law, both domestic and international, affecting legal issues associated with the deployment of U.S. forces overseas in peacetime and combat environments.[14]

In proposing this definition, Graham was at pains to point out that 'OPLAW' was a new concept and not 'simply a modified form of international law, as traditionally practiced by Army judge advocates, dressed in a battle dress uniform and given a "catchy" name.'[15] Graham was also insistent that OPLAW did not presage a move away from traditional JAG roles (e.g. military justice, administrative and civil law). Those responsibilities would remain important, but they would be joined by a new series of responsibilities that focused especially on national security law, international law and—most of all—the laws of war.

Graham's definition became the foundation of what JAGs would come to describe as their new legal discipline. In May 1992 the Center for Military Law and International Law Division (later renamed the International and Operational Law Department) began publishing an annual Operational Law Handbook.[16] The 'cargo pocket sized' Handbook—the 1997 edition was 495 pages!—was to serve as a 'how to' guide for 'the soldiers, marines, airmen, and sailors of the

[12] There is considerable overlap between the Law of War Program and operational law. During the 1970s–1980s the two converged with the latter effectively incorporating the former, and hence 'operational law' becoming the preferred term.

[13] The Judge Advocate General's School, International & Operational Law Department, United States Army, 'Operational Law Handbook 1997', 1-1.

[14] David E. Graham. 'Operational Law: A Concept Comes of Age', *Army Law* 175 (1987): 10, 9–12.

[15] Ibid., 9.

[16] Frederic Borch, email correspondence, 17 June 2015. CLAMO no longer have a copy of the 1992 Handbook. The 1997 edition is the earliest that I could locate.

service judge advocate general's corps, who serve alongside their clients in the operational context.'[17] The 1997 Handbook defined operational law as: 'That body of domestic, foreign, and international law that impacts specifically upon the activities of U.S. Forces across the entire operational spectrum.'[18] Like the definition proposed by Graham, this was purposively expansive. It was designed to capture the entirety of military operations from air, land, and sea through peacetime and war to so-called 'military operations other than war' (section 2.6).[19] The idea was to create an umbrella concept that would encompass *all* military legal specializations. As Lieutenant Colonel Marc Warren, the editor of the 1994 and 1995 OPLAW Handbook, explained:

> [O]perational law is the essence of the military legal practice. Operational law exists to provide legal support and services to commanders and soldiers in the field. It is not a specialty, nor is it a discrete area of substantive law. *It is a discipline, a collection of all of the traditional areas of the military legal practice focused on military operations* [. . .] Operational law also includes proficiency in military skills. It is the *raison d'être* of the uniformed judge advocate. Every judge advocate must be an operational lawyer.[20]

The expansive understanding of operational law has been preserved across the services since its inception and remains in place today. In 1994 Colonel Robert Bridge of the United States Air Force (USAF) noted that a 'mind-numbing array of legal specialties seems to be required of the operations lawyer'.[21] In 1996, Army JAG Marc Warren similarly noted: 'Operational lawyers must be decathletes, not boxers', and opined that 'substantive specialization' should be 'the exception rather than the rule'.[22] US military lawyers today are still for the most part generalists, even those who give legal advice on targeting (see Chapter 5). The Judge Advocate General of the US Air Force, Christopher F. Burne warns his JAGs to be ready and alert to the full spectrum of the Air Force mission:

[17] The Judge Advocate General's School, International & Operational Law Department, United States Army, 'Operational Law Handbook 1997', Preface.

[18] Ibid., 1-1.

[19] The moniker 'military operations other than war', which was popular in the 1990s, has since fallen out of fashion in favour of the euphemistic term 'stability operations'. United States Joint Chiefs of Staff, 'Stability' (Washington, DC: Joint Chief of Staff, 3 August 2016), http://www.dtic.mil/doctrine/new_pubs/jp3_07.pdf, accessed 3 January 2017; John Morrissey, 'Securitizing Instability: The US Military and Full Spectrum Operations', *Environment and Planning D: Society and Space* 33 (2015): 609–25.

[20] Marc L. Warren, 'Operational Law–A Concept Matures', *Military Law Review* 152 (1996): 27.

[21] Robert L. Bridge, 'Operations Law: An Overview', *Air Force Law Review* 37 (1994): 3.

[22] Warren, 'Operational Law–A Concept Matures', 38.

> [O]perations law presupposes that every judge advocate and paralegal fully comprehends his or her unit's mission. Do you? Can you explain your unit's mission? Are you conversant with the mission of the tenant units your legal office supports? Can you connect the dots to explain how your unit's mission supports the USAF core missions of (1) air and space superiority; (2) intelligence, surveillance and reconnaissance; (3) rapid global mobility; (4) global strike; and (5) command and control? [. . .] The old adage found on plaques and bookmarks, 'good lawyers know the law, great lawyers know the judge,' can be modified for our purposes to read, 'good JAGs know the law, great JAGs know the mission.' You, of course, must know both [. . .][23]

The advent of operational law brought about profound changes for the practising military lawyer as well as a number of new responsibilities. By 1990 JAGs were expected to:

> 1) disseminate the law of war; 2) administer the law of war through the administration of article 5, GPW [Third Geneva Convention on the Treatment of Prisoners of War], tribunals and the prisoner of war program; 3) review new weapons systems to ensure they are in compliance with international law; 4) review operations plans for compliance with the law of war; 5) determine rules of engagement; 6) determine lawful targets; and 7) provide advice and support on investigation and evaluation of information concerning war crimes.[24]

But operational law did more than expand the responsibilities of military lawyers. It also sought to transform how the US military would view the laws of war and encouraged a much more proactive approach be taken towards defining the relationship between law and military operations.

2.3 What's in a Name: the Communications Dimension

Although the working definition of operational law came from Army Lieutenant Colonel Graham, W. Hays Parks (the Marine infantry officer and

[23] United States Air Force Judge Advocate General's School, 'Air Force Operations and the Law' (Maxwell Air Force Base, AL: US Air Force, 2014), ii–iii, http://www.afjag.af.mil/Portals/77/documents/AFD-100510-059.pdf, accessed 13 February 2014.

[24] Matthew E. Winter, 'Finding the Law—The Values, Identity, and Function of the International Law Adviser', *Military Law Review* 128 (1990): 6–7 (references removed).

military lawyer who served in Vietnam and who we met in Chapter 1), claims that he originally coined the term.[25] He proposed it as a way of trying to overcome what he saw as a twofold negativity associated with the laws of war in the US military after the Vietnam War: first, the laws of war had become synonymous with military restrictions for many commanders; and second, there was a related 'general distrust of lawyers and their motives'.[26] As Parks explained: 'Lots of people came out of Vietnam thinking things were illegal when they were not.'[27] Major General William Moorman, the Judge Advocate General from 1999–2002 (i.e. the most senior JAG in the US military at the time), had similar recollections of this period: 'The senior officers on the staff having grown up in the Vietnam/post-Vietnam era had it so inculcated that there were these legal restrictions out there that they were subconsciously constraining their own range of options.'[28]

Previous poor instruction and training was partly to blame according to Parks, who laments how past schooling in the laws of war 'suffered [. . .] a heavy dose of negativism' where instructors 'tended to emphasize that which was prohibited, and were reluctant to acknowledge that anything was permitted'.[29] JAGs were seen as obstructing military operations, creating an uneasy relationship between commanders and lawyers.[30] Perhaps understandably, then, commanders did not want to be lectured by lawyers on yet more things that they were *not* able to do. Air force pilots and other air force personnel displayed a similar scepticism towards law of war training when it was rolled out in the US Air Force in the late 1970s. Colonel Bridge of the US Air Force recollected:

> Quite frankly, many of the initial efforts at training the front line personnel met with apathy—or worse. The training was hard for judge advocates to sell; not because line personnel did not want to do what was right; but rather, because they could not easily accept being told how to do their jobs by lawyers.[31]

According to legal scholar John Norton Moore, the negative attitude towards the laws of war was symptomatic of a more general scepticism towards international law within the national security community. Norton argued that in

[25] Steven Keeva, 'Lawyers in the War Room', *American Bar Association Journal* 77, no. 12 (1991): 52–59.
[26] Ibid., 56.
[27] Quoted in: Ibid.
[28] Moorman, Interview.
[29] Parks, 'Teaching the Law of War', 9.
[30] W. Hays Parks, 'The Gulf War: A Practitioner's View'. *Dickinson Journal of International Law* 10 (1992): 397.
[31] Bridge, 'Operations Law', 2 (emphasis added).

the early 1970s there were 'widespread misperceptions about the value of the legal tradition in the management of national security'.[32] He notes three particular misconceptions. First, international law is wrongly 'thought of as saying what cannot be done, solely as a system for restraining and controlling national actions'. Second, it is believed that 'a concern for international law is opposed to a concern for the national interest'. Finally, the power of 'community perceptions of legality as a base for increase or decrease in national power' is substantially underestimated.[33] Norton does not say exactly who holds these misperceptions—hence the passive voice in the preceding sentences—but he makes clear that the United States and its lawyers should actively challenge these misperceptions and harness international law in the pursuit of the national agenda.

This is precisely what operational law sought to do; one way or another it would come to challenge each of the 'misperceptions' identified by Moore. Indeed, Colonel Bridge notes how a 'revolution in thinking' took place within the Air Force in the 1980s and early 1990s. Formerly sceptical commanders became 'more than willing to take their lawyers' advice on a wide range of subjects, not the least of which is how to wage war legally'.[34] Something had changed—but what?

When W. Hays Parks and the military lawyers around him came up with the idea of renaming the laws of war training program they did more than come up with a new name; they also successfully *rebranded* the laws of war. Parks recounts exactly what happened: 'Frankly, any time I'd tell a group that I wanted to talk about the Law of War, I'd get a big groan, [. . .] So I tried changing it. I'd say, we're going to talk about law affecting military operations. From there, we shortened it to operational law.'[35] The hope was that changing the name would lead to a change in thinking and thus behaviour. The rationale was affirmative, in direct opposition to the then mainstream thinking: 'emphasis was placed on the use of the law as a planning tool that set forth the legal rights of the client [the US Department of Defense] (such as the right of self defense) as well as his responsibilities.'[36] This explicit emphasis on the right to employ force was natural, Parks insisted, because '[i]n fact, the law of war permits more than it prohibits'—and teaching and training should therefore reflect this.[37]

[32] John Norton Moore, 'Law and National Security', *Foreign Affairs* 51, no. 2 (1973): 415.
[33] Ibid., 415–17.
[34] Bridge, 'Operations Law', 2.
[35] Quoted in: Keeva, 'Lawyers in the War Room', 55–6.
[36] Parks, 'Gulf War', 398 (emphasis added).
[37] Parks, 'Teaching the Law of War', 9.

The term 'law affecting military operations' sought to institutionalize a different (if not necessarily new) way of seeing and understanding law and its relationship to military violence. In inventing operational law, the choice of name was deliberately to settle on familiar territory for the military commander. The now ubiquitous acronym—'OPLAW'—further discursively distanced the military from the laws of war, transforming them into a familiar *military* language and an abstract shorthand. Directives from Washington drove 'OPLAW'—Pentagon interpretations of the US military's legal rights and responsibilities. If this was law from Geneva, it was first filtered through the US-owned space of operational law, and thus imbued with trustworthiness. Operational law was thus an assertion of US military proprietary over the laws of war. Like the Lieber Code over a century earlier, this way of thinking about the laws of war would emphasize the contiguities between legal regulation and military violence. Indeed, operational law would all but collapse the distinction between (international) law and (domestic) military operations, challenging the notion that law and military violence need necessarily be oppositional to one another.

2.4 The Zone of Permissible Conduct and Force Multiplication

As late as the 1990s JAG Moorman tells of how he still found himself having to explain to commanders some of the more permissive aspects of the laws of war:

> Against my expectations I would have to tell them [commanders] 'you can't do this, that, or the other thing', I frequently found myself telling them 'no, the law will permit you to go to a broader range of options; you need to select what makes operational sense within that area'. *The zone of permissible conduct was generally larger than they believed.*[38]

He gave the following example:

> I confronted one or two officers who said 'well, we have to make sure that we don't have any civilian casualties' and I said 'well, that's not necessarily accurate. You have to look at the law of war and proportionality and the idea that some level of collateral damage is acceptable. And we ought to do what

[38] Moorman, Interview (emphasis added).

we can to minimize casualties but that doesn't necessarily preclude you from planning an operation that could result in civilian casualties.'[39]

What Moorman tells his commanders and officers is true: killing civilians is not absolutely prohibited but must conform to the laws of war and particularly the principles of military necessity and proportionality. But the laws of war do not specify exactly what level of civilian harm is 'acceptable'. As I argued in the Introduction, on this and other issues the laws of war are indeterminate: they both restrain and enable, permit and prohibit depending on the context. The laws of war pose a series of questions that have more than one answer. In the above account, the military lawyer becomes crucial in helping commanders and officers resolve legal indeterminacy by providing one particular answer. In this way, the law is not 'found', but *made*, and in the space of operational law the military lawyer *produces* juridical outcomes by resolving indeterminacy on a case-by-case basis. Here, the commander's caution is overcome by the lawyer's positive assertion that law *accepts* 'some level of collateral damage', carving out both an expanded permissible zone of conduct while also helping to cultivate a commander who is aware that he is entitled to operate in a zone he once though off-limits.

By furnishing the military commander with information about the full range of possible legal options and the zone of permissibility, operational law and operational lawyers would become force multipliers. I once used this term—'force multiplier'—in relation to military lawyers at an academic conference on drone warfare in Birmingham. A UK military lawyer in the audience objected and suggested its use was 'polemic'. What I perhaps should have made clear in my presentation was that I was borrowing the idea from Brigadier General Pitzul, a senior Canadian military lawyer who used the term in his opening remarks for the US Air Force Judge Advocate General School's Operations Law Course in 2001. Making a case for the future of operational law and celebrating the involvement of military lawyers in reviewing targets for the NATO aerial campaign in Kosovo two years earlier, Pitzul assured his audience of trainee US military lawyers, '[t]he law is a force multiplier for commanders'.[40] Other prominent military figures, including Major General David Petraeus, have since employed this language, describing military lawyers who served in Iraq as 'true combat multipliers'.[41] This is not to say that military lawyers always

[39] Ibid.

[40] Jerry S. T. Pitzul, 'Operational Law and the Legal Professional: A Canadian Perspective Speeches and Comments', *Air Force Law Review* 51 (2001): 321.

[41] Major General David H. Petraeus, Commander 101st Airborne Division (Air Assault) 2003–2004 quoted in: United States Joint Chiefs of Staff, 'Legal Support to Military Operations' (Washington,

and only 'multiply combat', but it is a significant part of what they do and operational law explicitly sought to institutionalize their combat credentials.

The DOD defines 'force multiplier' as: 'A capability that, when added to and employed by a combat force, significantly increases the combat potential of that force and thus enhances the probability of successful mission accomplishment.'[42] This aptly describes the world of operational law and the operational military lawyer: they help to increase combat *potential,* and increase the probability of *mission success*. Military lawyers are mandated to increase operational effectiveness, to know the mission inside out, and to help achieve it. As military lawyer Lieutenant Colonel Marc L. Warren (US Army JAG Corps) insisted: 'Every judge advocate must be an operational lawyer [and] [o]ur central focus must be to *facilitate* operations.'[43]

Operational law was invented partly to address the increasing complexity of military operations—and their attendant manifold rules—and the fundamental role of the operational lawyer was to make sense of this complexity and distil it into something clear and direct enough for a non-legal specialist (i.e. the military commander) to understand. Corn and Corn explain this necessity to transform legal complexity into something commanders can readily understand:

> [C]commanders and their staffs (including military legal advisors), as well as the soldiers, sailors, airmen, and marines that execute military missions, depend on simplified systems that make the integration of law into operational planning and execution routine. These systems—all of which must effectuate the synchronization of law and operations (sometimes referred to as 'operationalizing' the law)—transform the complex rules and principles of the LOAC into digestible, understandable, trainable, and easily applicable concepts.[44]

Simplification is not the only kind of transformation that takes place when law is operationalized, however. Corn and Corn go on to note: 'operationalizing'

DC: Joint Chiefs of Staff, 2 August 2016), II–6, https://www.jcs.mil/Portals/36/Documents/Doctrine/pubs/jp1_04.pdf, accessed 28 January 2016.

[42] United States Joint Chiefs of Staff, 'Joint Special Operations Task Force Operations' (Washington, DC: Joint Chiefs of Staff, 26 April 2007), GL-11, https://fas.org/irp/doddir/dod/jp3_05_01.pdf, accessed 24 November 2019.

[43] Warren, 'Operational Law–A Concept Matures', 37 (emphasis added).

[44] Geoffrey S. Corn and Gary P. Corn, 'The Law of Operational Targeting: Viewing the LOAC through an Operational Lens', *Texas International Law Journal* 47, no. 2 (2011): 334.

the law necessitates an understanding of the relationship between the law and the principles of military operations that the law regulates. With respect to targeting [. . .] it requires an appreciation of the targeting process, the capabilities of the assets to be employed, and the anticipated effects of employment."[45]

The key here is that operational law must consider 'military principles' and is expected in at least some ways to *defer* to these principles in the very making of law. If operational law were a recipe, it would be one-part military exigencies and one-part law. As Michael Smith has argued:

> Operational legality is fundamentally shaped by strategic considerations; in other words, the mission objectives dictate to a substantial degree what is authorized. Seen in this light, like war itself, OPLAW [operational law] is politics continued by other means, and the geopolitics of this martial legality are never far from the surface.[46]

Corn and Corn frame the operational shaping of law as imperative to those who must use it: 'Allowing the law to develop without consideration of *operational reality* will undermine its ultimate efficacy because the constituents who must embrace the law will view it as inconsistent with their *operational instincts*.'[47] To be effective, operational law must conform in part to the military 'facts on the ground' as well as with the military imaginations of those fighting the war. To 'operationalize law' implies not only that the law must be simplified for the commander but also that the commander has some say in how the law is interpretation and applied. Operational law, therefore, is informed and influenced by the very military apparatus that it is purportedly designed to regulate.

Early proponents and practitioners of operational law emphasized the specifically *military* orientation of their new practice and placed *combat* operations at its centre. As W. Hays Parks wrote in 1992, the 'heart' of operational law 'lies with the heart of military operations—the application of force on the modern battlefield and the protection of noncombatants'.[48] Lawyers who served in the Gulf War (1990–1991)—the first major combat test for operational law—referred to their new practice as 'soldiering law'. Colonel Dennis Coupe, former JAG and Director of National Security Law at the Army War

[45] Corn and Corn, 'Law of Operational Targeting', 344–5.

[46] Michael Smith, 'States That Come and Go: Mapping the Geolegalities of the Afghanistan Intervention', in *The Expanding Spaces of Law: A Timely Legal Geography*, ed. Irus Braverman et al. (Stanford, CA: Stanford Law Books, 2014), 152.

[47] Corn and Corn, 'Law of Operational Targeting', 344.

[48] Parks, 'Gulf War', 394.

College, went further in emphasizing the centrality of combat violence to operational law: 'The job of the [operational] lawyer is to get involved with all the operational stuff, with the targeting—all the stuff involved with breaking things and killing people.' Coupe also insists that JAG 'involvement' does not mean getting in the way of military operations: 'You don't want to stick your nose in where it doesn't belong.'[49] Such a remark implies that law and military lawyers belong to a sphere that is separate from, and should not intrude upon, the real business of executing military operations.

We may infer that operational law is a legal regime that helps solve military problems with juridical solutions, shifting the 'military' into the 'juridical' and vice-versa, so much so that these categories no longer hold. Perhaps these categories have never held, but what is interesting about operational law is that it is explicit and unapologetic about the use of law as a martial technology. Indeed, operational law appears to have been created with this intention and so has more than a passing resemblance to what became known in the twenty-first century as 'lawfare' (a neologism that recognized that the law can be used as a potent weapon of war—see Introduction).[50]

2.5 The Commander–Lawyer Relationship

The commander–lawyer relationship is a manifestation and a microcosm of the relationship between war and operational law. The relationship between military lawyers and commanders is a crucial interface because it is here where indeterminate legal ideas and principles are resolved and then translated into military practice—or not. I have claimed previously that the laws of war are, in part, what military lawyers say and do. But where operational law comes into contact with the commander—where the legal rubber meets the military road, so to speak—it is perhaps more accurate to say that law is what lawyers say and what commanders do.

The advent of operational law heralded important changes for the relationship between military commanders and military lawyers, particularly at

[49] Quoted in: Keeva, 'Lawyers in the War Room', 57.

[50] Charles Dunlap, 'The Revolution in Military Legal Affairs: Air Force Legal Professionals in 21st Century Conflicts', *Air Force Law Review* 51 (2001): 293. For a critical discussion of lawfare see: Neve Gordon, 'Human Rights as a Security Threat: Lawfare and the Campaign against Human Rights NGOs', *Law & Society Review* 48, no. 2 (2014): 311–44; Freya Irani, '"Lawfare", US Military Discourse, and the Colonial Constitution of Law and War', *European Journal of International Security* 3, no. 1 (2018): 113–33; Craig Jones, 'Lawfare and the Juridification of Late Modern War', *Progress in Human Geography* 40, no. 2 (2016).

the higher levels of command where the strategic advantages of law and legal compliance—in fact and perception—were more easily recognized (Figure 2.1). But to understand the success of operational law and the general acceptance of military lawyers into combat-facing military communities, I argue that we must also understand a cultural shift that took place in the US military from the late 1970s to the First Gulf War. I have already detailed the lawyers' part of the bargain: to explain to commanders that the law can *facilitate* military operations (section 2.4). But in return, the military lawyer had to learn the business of the military commander and had to come to terms with the

Figure 2.1 Publications such as this one, now in its fifteenth edition, once heralded a new synergy between commanders and military lawyers.

Source: The Judge Advocate General's School, United States Air Force, 'The Military Commander and the Law', Maxwell Air Force Base, AL: United States Air Force (2019).

military-operational world. Lawyers learning the art of war; commanders learning the art of law.

This shift recast the lawyer from an 'outsider' to an 'insider'. Lawyers were no longer seen as strangers espousing laws made in Europe but as real operators who understood the needs of their American 'client' (i.e. the commander). The 2019 edition of The Military Commander and the Law makes clear just how successful the recasting of military lawyers as 'insiders' has been:

> Operations law attorneys are mission-focused and provide commanders with options and recommendations to enable mission accomplishment. Operations law is a mindset as much as an area of practice.[51]

Major General Charles Dunlap (ret.), the former two-star Air Force Deputy Judge Advocate General generally agrees with this framing, though he points out that that the acceptance of military lawyers into the 'community' has not been not universal. He told me:

> Commanders haven't fallen in love with [military] lawyers [. . .] But they do understand the critical importance of adherence to the law and to the rules of engagement, especially at the more senior levels. I think as you get down to some mid-level officers you'll get resistance in the sense of [. . .] they think that they know more than they do. But as you get to the more senior level, people who have been around the Horn, so to speak, they understand the strategic importance of adherence to the law in both fact and perception.[52]

According to W. Hays Parks, the next initiative after the change of nomenclature (from laws of war to operational law) was to create forums where 'the client and his lawyer' could 'come together to discuss issues of mutual interest—even if the client was unaware of their mutual interest'.[53] As part of this, military lawyers would learn to speak the language of commanders and would take it upon themselves to learn the technicalities of military operations, however idiosyncratic, difficult, or unfamiliar they were. As former Director of Legal Services of the British Army, G.I.A.D Draper put it in 1978:

[51] The Judge Advocate General's School, United States Air Force, 'The Military Commander and the Law', 15th edition (Maxwell Air Force Base, AL: United States Air Force, 2019), 444, https://media.defense.gov/2019/Apr/11/2002115350/-1/-1/0/B_0159_JAG_MILITARY_COMMANDER_AND_THE_LAW_.PDF, accessed 1 March 2020.

[52] Dunlap, interview.

[53] Parks, 'Gulf War', 398.

> If one considers the nature of modern weaponry, the changing technology of weapons systems, the development and sophistication of electronic devices in weaponry and communications systems, it is apparent that if the legal adviser is going to be competent to give a field commander useful advice [. . .] he will also require a highly technical, non-legal training.[54]

While Draper frames such military training as 'non-legal', it is more accurate to think about the many ways in which the newfound expertise in military practices would become part of the field of operational law. Military exigencies might be subject to operational law, but operational law is not an external force to such exigencies. Indeed, following Leander and Alberts we might say that military operations and legal expertise give shape to one another in co-constitutive 'processes of mutual, simultaneous, and ongoing creation and production'.[55]

Dunlap explains why learning the language of the military and understanding operational processes is so vital: 'In the high-stakes environment of combat operations, a JAG must have credibility with the operator, which comes more easily if the lawyer is a fellow military member and if he or she has a working fluency in the language of the operator's system.'[56] He also notes how:

> This can be a daunting challenge for a new JAG, especially one assigned to a smaller base without robust flying operations. Not only must a JAG learn weapon systems, but he or she must also learn a new vocabulary related to deploying troops, designing operational missions, and integrating everything into the planning process.[57]

My interviews with JAGs who served in an operational law capacity since 1980 reveal the extent to which military lawyers have succeeded in learning the language of their 'client'. The JAGs that I interviewed all spoke about military operations with fluency and ease. Often, and especially early in the research process, I was confounded by the military jargon that they used. Complex acronyms about abstract targeting processes rolled off the tongue as though they were second nature—because they were: 'the JTAC [joint terminal attack

[54] G. I. A. D. Draper, 'Role of Legal Advisers in Armed Forces', *International Review of the Red Cross (1961–1997)* 18, no. 202 (February 1978): 12.

[55] Anna Leander and Tanja Aalbert, 'Introduction: The Co-Constitution of Legal Expertise and International Security'. *Leiden Journal of International Law* 26, no. 4 (2013): 9.

[56] Dunlap, 'It Ain't no TV Show', 484–5.

[57] Ibid., 485

controller] calls back to the AOC [air operations center] to request A10 assistance [a fighter jet aircraft] for a TST [time sensitive target] or CAS [close air support], with an anticipated CDE [collateral damage estimate] of five CIVCAS [civilian casualties].' The heavy use of acronyms and technical language to a non-specialist reveals something of a social disconnect between the 'inside' and 'outside' world, revealing that an internal culture has saturated the consciousness of JAGs—so much so that many seem completely unaware that others (outsiders) do not speak, or are not fully conversant with, their military-legal language.

So internalized and normalized have military operations become for JAGs that even specialists might mistake them for actual military operators. JAGs interact a lot with operators—be they pilots, weaponeers, intelligence analysts or front-line soldiers, and sometimes share living and sleeping quarters with them.[58] These JAGs are not simply 'talking the talk' though; they understand operators and commanders world and worldview, and they sympathize with the daily dilemmas that US military personnel face. JAGs do not stand apart from military culture or military operations; they are part of them and they form part of what Amichai Cohen (following Peter Hass) has called an 'epistemic community'.[59] In turn, operators have become legally savvy and have learnt much of the law related to targeting. For example, an interviewee, Lieutenant General (ret.) David Deptula, former US Air Force Deputy Chief of Staff for Intelligence, Surveillance and Reconnaissance (ISR) and principal architect of the First Gulf War air campaign (see Chapter 3) explained that he 'internalized' much of the law of targeting, so much so that he often felt like he did not need to be told certain things by military lawyers: 'Is it a proper military target? Have we taken proper action to minimize collateral damage and civilian casualties? In the war plan you do those things inherently. I don't have to have a lawyer come and tell me that.'[60] If nothing else, this is testimony to just how successful operational law has been.

This cross-culturalization between the lawyer and the commander has been an integral part of operational law since its inception. Two forums were particularly important in the formative days of operational law. The first was the US signing of the Additional Protocols in 1977. As I detailed in the

[58] Stefano (pseudonym), interview; Brown, interview.

[59] Amichai Cohen, 'Legal Operational Advice in the Israeli Defense Forces: The International Law Department and the Changing Nature of International Humanitarian Law', *Connecticut Journal of International Law* 26, no. 2 (2011): 367–413. Peter M. Haas, 'Introduction: Epistemic Communities and International Policy Coordination', *International Organization* 46, no. 1 (1992): 1–35.

[60] Deptula, Interview (emphasis added).

Introduction, the Protocols gave rights to those fighting for independence in internal (or 'non-international') armed conflicts, something that the United States was very cautious of. The US signature was contingent on a full 'political-military review' of the Protocols. According to Parks, during this review 'there was ample interaction between the lawyer and client [the US military]' and through this process the military realized 'the important role of lawyers with respect to the law of war and warfighting'.[61] The United States subsequently ratified Protocol II but, after more than a decade of review, refused to ratify Protocol I partly on the basis that it gave too much power to national liberation movements and afforded too many protections to combatants of 'irregular forces'. In his letter of Transmittal to the US Senate on 29 January 1987, President Ronald Reagan wrote:

> Protocol I is fundamentally and irreconcilably flawed. It contains provisions that would undermine humanitarian law and endanger civilians in war. One of its provisions, for example, would automatically treat as an international conflict any so-called 'war of national liberation.' Whether such wars are international or non-international should turn exclusively on objective reality, not on one's view of the moral qualities of each conflict. To rest on such subjective distinctions based on a war's alleged purposes would politicize humanitarian law and eliminate the distinction between international and non-international conflicts. It would give special status to 'wars of national liberation,' an ill-defined concept expressed in vague, subjective, politicized terminology. Another provision would grant combatant status to irregular forces even if they do not satisfy the traditional requirements to distinguish themselves from the civilian population and otherwise comply with the laws of war. This would endanger civilians among whom terrorists and other irregulars attempt to conceal themselves. These problems are so fundamental in character that they cannot be remedied through reservations [. . .][62]

A number of its provisions were also deemed 'militarily unacceptable'; again, the JAGs were there to ensure that the military did not tie its own hands.[63] These legal reservations continue to animate US war policy in the 9/11 era, thus

[61] Parks, 'Gulf War', 338–9.

[62] Ronald Reagan, 'Agora: The U.S. Decision Not to Ratify Protocol I to the Geneva Conventions on the Protection of War Victims', *American Journal of International Law* 81, no. 4 (1987): 911.

[63] Ibid. The US Supreme Court has since held that at least some articles of Additional Protocol I have gained the status of customary international law. See, e.g. Supreme Court of the United States, *Hamdan v. Rumsfeld* 548 US 557 (2006), (stating that Art. 75 'Fundamental guarantees' is 'indisputably part of the customary international law').

showing the staying-power that legal advice can have.[64] The value of the presence of JAGs is not difficult to understand. By bringing the military's needs and interests to the table, the JAG is able to ensure that high-level policy makers do not bind the average military commander to laws that unnecessarily obstruct or restrict military operations. This is not some marginal view. In an influential lecture (and subsequent article) entitled 'Terrorism, the Law and the National Defense', Judge Abraham Soafer, then Legal Adviser to the State Department, urged lawyers 'to identify and to revise or reject unjustifiable legal restrictions on our nation's capacity to protect its security'.[65]

The second forum was the Military Operations and Law Symposium, the first of which took place at The Judge Advocate General's School, United States Army, in 1982. The symposium was attended by military lawyers and operational planners from every major US command and was held annually into the 1990s when it was renamed and reconfigured. These—and similar venues like it—have been important sites where lawyers and commanders come together outside the theatre of operations to understand past and emergent problems in a shared professional setting. Symposiums and conferences such as the John Fugh Annual Symposium on Law and Military Operations and the YANKEE Operational Law Symposium remain important venues for commanders and lawyers to discuss contemporary problems and more than ever these meetings today attract a wide range of international participants, including military lawyers from Israel, the UK, Canada, and elsewhere.[66]

Parks claims these initiatives were a great success and implies that they provided a corrective to the hostile relationship between commander and lawyer that emerged out of the Vietnam War. This is probably an over-simplification. In fact, and as Parks shows, it was never the case that all commanders distrusted all lawyers after Vietnam, but it is equally true that even after the invention and development of operational law and up to the present day, there remains some scepticism amongst commanders towards legal advisers, even if the general attitude towards them has warmed significantly. Take for example what a highly experienced Air Force JAG told me after more than ten deployments to the Combined Air Operations Center (CAOC) in al Udeid, Qatar (Chapters 5

[64] Yuval Shany, 'The Israeli Unlawful Combatants Law: Old Wine in a New Bottle?', *The Hebrew University of Jerusalem Faculty of Law Research Paper* No. 03-12 (2012), 1–23; Nathaniel Berman, 'Privileging Combat—Contemporary Conflict and the Legal Construction of War', *Columbia Journal of Transnational Law* 43, no. 1 (2004): 1–72; Frédéric Mégret, 'From "savages" to "Unlawful Combatants": A Postcolonial Look at International Humanitarian Law's Other', in *International Law and Its Others*, ed. Anne Orford (Cambridge: Cambridge University Press, 2006), 265–317.

[65] Abraham D. Sofaer, 'The Sixth Annual Waldemar A. Solf Lecture in International Law: Terrorism, the Law, and the National Defense', *Military Law Review* 126 (1989): 91.

[66] Email correspondence, Frederic Borch, 16 June 2015.

and 6): 'There is a lot of initial anti-lawyerish kind of attitudes going on' even if these are 'quickly overcome'.[67] It is 'with majors and captains on the operations floor itself [lower-rank commanders in the CAOC] where the JAGs have to prove their worth.'[68] The historical relationship between commanders and military lawyers is therefore more complex than initial scepticism followed by loving embrace. Indeed, contra Parks, Army JAG Historian Frederic Borch argues that the pace of change in the 1980s was 'slow'. He also characterizes the steps taken by the Army JAGC to integrate itself into military operations as 'fragmented'.[69] Not to put too fine a point on it, but all the JAGs that I interviewed said that personalities matter, and that the commander–lawyer relationship, like any relationship, is negotiated on a case-by-case basis. Indeed, at an After-Action Conference following the First Gulf War it was noted that 'personalities will still play an important part in getting the Judge Advocate into the operations center'.[70]

Alongside the JAG-led efforts outlined by Parks, Stephen Myrow identifies three factors that motivated commanders not only to accept but also to seek out legal advice. First, commanders 'want to believe that their destructive actions are nevertheless morally right, and complying with the established legal norms for combat is one way to reinforce this belief'.[71] This aligning of law and morality is highly contingent and subjective, and on the face of it, law would seem unlikely to be able to satisfactorily settle what is 'morally right'. Yet, with the juridical turn in late modern war, the last couple of decades have also witnessed a concomitant turn towards military ethics.[72] Military ethics and military law are not reducible to one another. One thing they do have in common, though, is their complex relationship to violence, for as James Eastwood has suggested, 'ethics has become increasingly bound up with militarism, and [. . .] there are therefore clear limits to its capacity to constrain the violence of war'.[73] Neither military ethics nor operational law seek to prevent violence;

[67] Stefano (pseudonym), interview. These kinds of attitudes are hardly unique to the military; they are apparent across many areas of law.

[68] Stefano (pseudonym), interview.

[69] Frederic L. Borch, *Judge Advocates in Combat: Army Lawyers in Military Operations from Vietnam to Haiti* (Washington, DC: Government Printing Office, 2001), 320.

[70] Quoted in: Stephen A. Myrow, 'Waging War on the Advice of Counsel: The Role of Operational Law in the Gulf War', *United States Air Force Academy Journal of Legal Studies* 7 (1996): 136.

[71] Ibid., 134. Myrow is drawing on interviews with Army and Air Force officers who served in the First Gulf War.

[72] Martin L. Cook and Henrik Syse, 'What Should We Mean by "Military Ethics"?', *Journal of Military Ethics* 9, no. 2 (2010): 119–22.

[73] James Eastwood, '"Meaningful Service": Pedagogy at Israeli Pre-Military Academies and the Ethics of Militarism', *European Journal of International Relations* 22, no. 3 (2016): 671. See also: James Eastwood, 'Ethics in the Service of Violence in Israel/Palestine', *The Disorder of Things* (blog), 23

at best, they seek to curb 'unnecessary' violence, where possible. Given that militaries are, after all, in the business of injuring and killing, ethics and law can sometimes enable, legitimize, and even extend military operations and make it easier—psychologically—on those who execute violence (as I will show in Chapters 4–6).

The second factor motivating commanders was that obtaining 'approval' prior to an operation was a way of protecting themselves from personal legal ramifications.[74] Strictly speaking, JAGs are supposed to offer legal advice, rather than legal approval, and legal advice entails more than merely giving an operation a rubber stamp. In reality, advice and approval operate in a grey zone, and if commanders understand that they are receiving approval—rather than advice—this could influence their decision-making process. Both JAGs who served in the First Gulf War and others who served in the Israeli military reported that commanders did indeed seek legal advice in order to gain approval for their actions (Chapters 3 and 4). This is a contentious issue, not least because the notion of 'approval' suggests a blurring of the line between the decision maker (doctrinally, the commander) and those who advise him/her (doctrinally, the JAG and others on the command staff). My reading of this issue, which I will return to in the Conclusion, is that these 'decisions' (if we can call them that) are taken and produced collectively.

The third reason that commanders came to increasingly rely on JAGs in the late 1980s and early 1990s was to protect the reputation of their military unit.[75] This speaks to the idea of law as a strategic imperative in the age of lawfare (Conclusion), where abiding by law—in fact and perception—has become vital to mission success. Recall Moore's third and final warning that people tend to underestimate the legitimizing and delegitimizing power of law. In this period, and particularly after the Vietnam War—the 'first to be televised'—there was an increasing realization among senior commanders and military lawyers that breaches of law—and even the perception of legal breaches—could have a significant detrimental effect on military operations.[76] But how would it all

October 2015, https://thedisorderofthings.com/2015/10/23/ethics-in-the-service-of-violence-in-israelpalestine/, accessed 4 January 2017.

[74] Myrow, 'Waging War on the Advice of Counsel', 134.

[75] Ibid.

[76] Conventional histories of the Vietnam War suggest that the US defeat was linked in no small way to the extensive daily TV coverage of the war. Historians have since questioned the causal link between the specific medium of TV and the loss of the war, but the idea that public attitudes shape the conduct and outcome of war is particularly powerful. As Michael Mandelbaum has argued: 'The United States lost the war in Vietnam because the American public was not willing to pay the cost of winning, or avoiding losing. The people's decision that the war was not worth these costs had nothing to do with the fact that

work when, as one military lawyer put it, 'the chips are down and the bullets are flying?[77]

2.6 Testing Grounds

In 1983 the United States invaded Grenada, a Caribbean island off the coast of Venezuela. Operation Urgent Fury, as it was called, should have been the first real test of operational law's mettle but instead it was a 'wake-up call' for the JAG Corps.[78] The pace of change since Vietnam had not been fast enough and despite doctrinal change, JAGs in Grenada were not equipped to provide the kind of operational legal advice that had become essential to mission success. According to Borch: 'Grenada served as a watershed in the evolution of a formal recognition by the leadership of the Judge Advocate General's Corps that Army lawyers could no longer focus on performing traditional peacetime legal functions in what had become a contingency-oriented Army.'[79] Grenada therefore deserves a small mention in the history of operational law because it was the last military operation where operational law was *not* practised, and also because it acted as a catalyst for its emergence in subsequent military operations.

On 20 December 1989 the United States invaded Panama, in what was the largest US so-called 'military operation other than war' (or 'MOOTW') since the Second World War.[80] According to the US military, MOOTWs 'encompass the use of military capabilities across the range of military operations short of war', a definition which does little to clarify what these operations involve.[81] The line between what counts as 'war' and what counts as a military operation 'short of war' is far from clear, and where force is used it seems primarily

they learned about it from television.' Michael Mandelbaum, 'Vietnam: The Television War', *Daedalus* 111, no. 4 (1982): 167.

[77] Benjamin, interview.

[78] Borch, *Judge Advocates in Combat*, 58.

[79] Ibid., 81. 'Contingency' is defined as "an emergency caused by natural disasters, terrorists, subversives, or other unexpected events and involving military forces'. A. Timothy Warnock, ed. *Short of War: Major USAF Contingency Operations, 1947-1997* (Maxwell Air Force Base, AL: Air University, 1983), xi.

[80] Operation Just Cause was the culmination of several operations during 1989 to fulfil President H. W. Bush's policy towards Panama. William J. Allen, 'Intervention in Panama: Operation Just Cause', ed. A. Timothy Warnock (Maxwell Air Force Base, AL: Air University, 1983), 167–78.

[81] United States Joint Chief of Staff, 'Joint Doctrine for Military Operations Other Than War' (Washington, DC: Joint Chiefs of Staff, 16 June 1995), I-1, http://www.bits.de/NRANEU/others/jp-doctrine/jp3_07.pdf, accessed 3 January 2017.

rhetorical. The designation of the Panama operation as 'other than war' appears somewhat Orwellian given its aims, the number of US forces involved, and the resulting casualties. The aims of 'Operation Just Cause', as it was called, were to depose Manual Noriega, the de facto leader of Panama, to neutralize the Panamanian Defense Forces, and to instil a new pro-US government while also protecting US lives and interests in Panama.[82] An internal Army memo estimated that there were one thousand Panamanian civilian casualties alone.[83] Over 20,000 service personnel, including 3,400 Air Force members were deployed. They were joined by JAGs, who deployed to seven different locations across Panama.[84]

The invasion of Panamax was the first true test for operational law and operational lawyers.[85] More importantly, it was the proving ground for the First Gulf War and the invasion of Iraq eight months later (Chapter 3). Unlike in Operation Urgent Fury, the US military had been planning the invasion of Panama almost a year and a half in advance. This meant that, as per the DOD Law of War Directives (section 2.2), JAGs were able to insert themselves into the *planning* stages of the operation, which in turn secured their continued involvement when it came to the *execution* of combat operations. Moorman explains just how crucial this was:

> Late legal advice is no legal advice. If you're in the execution phase and you haven't written into the plan the things that people need to know and you haven't done the advanced training then you're giving *ad hoc* advice to people who are really focused elsewhere [i.e. on executing the mission]. So, we built more robust training and more robust involvement by JAGs in every phase of operations.[86]

JAGs in Panama performed two vital new roles that would set important precedents for the practice of operational law. When planning for Operation Just Cause JAGs assisted in the formulation of the rules of engagement (ROE) that

[82] Anon, 'Operation Just Cause', n.d., http://www.globalsecurity.org/military/ops/just_cause.htm, accessed 7 July 2015.

[83] John Lindsay-Poland, *Emperors in the Jungle: The Hidden History of the U.S. in Panama* (Durham, NC: Duke University Press, 2003), 118.

[84] Borch, *Judge Advocates in Combat*, 92–3.

[85] Patricia A. Kerns, *First 50 Years: U.S. Air Force Judge Advocate General's Department* (Washington DC: US Air Force Judge Advocate General's Department, 2004), 138; Terrie. M. Gent, 'The Role of Judge Advocates in a Joint Air Operations Center: A Counterpoint of Doctrine, Strategy, and Law', *Airpower Journal* 13, no. 1 (1999): 40–55; Charles Dunlap, 'The Revolution in Military Legal Affairs: Air Force Legal Professionals in 21st Century Conflicts', *Air Force Law Review* 51 (2001): 296; Borch, *Judge Advocates in Combat*, 95.

[86] Moorman, Interview.

would apply when the US invaded Panama. Importantly, this involved helping to write both peacetime and combat ROE, that is, the rules that would apply before, during, and after the period of combat. JAGs approached the combat ROE with two particular propositions in mind. First, soldiers should always exercise their right of self-defence, regardless of any restrictions on the use of force that might exist in the ROE.[87] The ROE in both Vietnam and Grenada had been criticized for impinging on the self-defence of US troops and JAGs were mindful of this while drafting the ROE for Panama. The second rule that JAGs sought to make explicit was that the ROE would adhere strictly to the law of war and that 'particular emphasis would be placed on minimizing collateral damage and casualties'.[88]

The involvement of military lawyers in drafting the ROE raises the important issue of who is responsible for them. Traditionally understood, operational commanders are responsible for the ROE as it is they—and their troops—who live and die by them. As Grunawalt explains:

> The development, maintenance and implementation of ROE are the province of the operational directorate—not the staff judge advocate, not the intelligence officer, not the planner, and not the logistician. All of the latter have important roles to play in this process, but it is imperative that both the operational commander and the judge advocate (or other staff specialists) understand that ROE are properly within the responsibility of the operations directorate.[89]

But in recent decades the responsibilities have become blurred. In some instances, commanders and their staff default on their responsibility, 'leaving ROE formation to their military lawyer alone'.[90] W. Hays Parks recounts a particularly extreme case of commanders refusing even to read, let alone engage proactively with the ROE:

> [A] judge advocate tried repeatedly without success to get his commander and the staff to review his draft ROEs. In desperation, he inserted clearly ridiculous rules, such as 'if an individual stays in a telephone booth for more

[87] Borch, *Judge Advocates in Combat*, 96.

[88] Ibid.

[89] Richard J. Grunawalt, 'JCS Standing Rules of Engagement: A Judge Advocate's Primer, The', *Air Force Law Review* 42 (1997): 248.

[90] Gary D. Solis, *The Law of Armed Conflict: International Humanitarian Law in War*, 1st edition (Cambridge: Cambridge University Press, 2010), 499. See also: W. Hays Parks, 'Deadly Force Is Authorized', *U.S. Naval Institute Proceedings* 127, no. 1 (2001): 32.

> than three minutes, nuclear weapons are authorized.' Members of the staff cleared the ROEs, making it apparent they had not read them.[91]

Some JAGs expressed concerns about this apathy toward the ROE: 'The commander and the mission will not be well served [. . .] if unwarranted deference is made to the special ROE expertise that we expect of the operational lawyer.'[92] Others have been happy to take on the responsibility and have frequently found themselves writing the ROE with only minimal input from commanders.[93] The first instance of JAGs writing the ROE was in preparation for the peacetime phase of the Grenada operation, but since then there has been a broad 'integration of legal vocabularies, legal expertise, and legal institutional mechanisms' that Kristin Bergtora Sandvic argues has created a 'juridification of ROE.'[94] There is much debate as to whether or not this juridification is a move in the right direction. Major Mark S. Martins, an Army JAG, argues that it is not, stating that: 'A legislative approach to land force ROE can create danger when the time comes for living, breathing, sweating soldiers to translate the texts into results on the ground.'[95] This is why some soldiers have dismissed JAG-drafted ROE as '"ivory tower" nonsense.'[96] Others disagree and believe that juridifying the ROE may both enhance the legitimacy of the armed forces and provide civilians affected by those armed forces with a stronger basis for accountability.[97] Regardless of where those involved stand on these issues, the broader point here is that through these 'small wars', military lawyers gained an important foothold in crafting the ROE and have been extensively involved in shaping them ever since.

The involvement of JAGs in drafting the ROE for Operation Just Cause led to a second and related new role for JAGs in Panama. As mentioned, the ROE stipulated that special attention be paid to 'collateral damage' and civilian casualties. A concrete example of this was the weapons release authority requirement that 'an officer of the grade of at least lieutenant colonel approve all artillery fire that impacted in any populated area.'[98] Rules like this, which seek to regulate conduct by imposing rank-related restrictions on who is authorized

[91] Parks, 'Deadly Force Is Authorized.'

[92] Grunawalt, 'JCS Standing Rules of Engagement', 248.

[93] Borch, *Judge Advocates in Combat*, 73.

[94] Kristin Bergtora Sandvik, 'Regulating War in the Shadow of Law: Toward a Re-Articulation of ROE.' *Journal of Military Ethics* 13, no. 2 (2014): 120.

[95] Mark S. Martins, 'Rules of Engagement for Land Forces: A Matter of Training, Not Lawyering', *Military Law Review* 143 (1994): 55.

[96] Ibid., 20.

[97] Sandvik, 'Regulating War in the Shadow of Law', 131.

[98] Solis, *The Law of Armed Conflict*, 495.

to use force are common components of ROE but they are based on something more fundamental: the idea that a specific act (in this case, artillery fire) has to be proportional to the military advantage gained by taking said action. In other words, an attack on a 'populated area', which is likely to result in civilian casualties, must be weighed against the concrete military advantage and objective (reason) for the attack. In this formulation we have both military considerations (a reason to attack a populated area) and legal considerations (the principle of proportionality). The former is the province of the military commander but in order to assess the latter the commander requires both training in the law of war and legal advice from a JAG. In Panama, for the first time, JAGS became 'deeply involved' in planning a major operation and provided real time legal advice during its execution, including, among other matters, advice on the legality of targeting operations.[99]

Operation Just Cause was the first time that JAGs had given advice on targeting operations, and they had done so both in the planning and execution stages. For their part, US commanders had twenty-four-hour access to professional legal advice (another first) and could turn to their JAGs for a whole range of issues from the lawfulness of proposed targets to the prosecution of service personnel for petty misconduct. To say that Operation Just Cause was hugely significant in US warfare would be an exaggeration, but as far as the history of operational law is concerned, it was certainly a turning point. Terrie M. Gent describes the new operational involvement of JAGs in the targeting process:

> Col William A. Moorman, staff judge advocate for Twelfth Air Force, established a close liaison not only with his counterparts at Headquarters Tactical Air Command and USSOUTHCOM [United States Southern Command] but also with Col John R. Bozeman, staff judge advocate for XVIII Airborne Corps, and Col Michael Nye, an Air Force judge advocate assigned to the CJCS legal staff.[43] To ensure that the command had continuous access to legal counsel, Colonel Moorman joined the battle staff, put four operations lawyers on 12-hour shifts, and assigned Maj Mary Boone to review all applicable 'off-the-shelf" war plans.[100]

Twenty-five years later, I was in Tel Aviv interviewing Daniel Reisner, the Israeli JAG who claims to have first introduced the concept of providing legal advice

[99] Gent, 'The Role of Judge Advocates in a Joint Air Operations Center'.
[100] Ibid.

on targeting operations to the Israeli military (see Preface and Introduction). His inspiration? The US invasion of Panama:

> The question of a legitimate or unlawful target was not a question in which a lawyer was involved in the IDF [Israel Defense Force] targeting process [until 2000] and I decided to change that on the basis of the US experience in Panama. [. . .] They fielded lawyers with the units in Panama in [19]89 and I understood why. I mean it was a crazy situation. It was a drug dealer [Manual Noreiga] who was a president of a country with his army defending him [. . .] so the question of *who* is the enemy is a complicated one, and so rules of engagement were very complicated so they decided to field lawyers with combat units to help them decide these issues.[101]

As I will show in Chapter 3, some of the JAGs who participated in the Panama operation were involved shortly after in the preparation and execution of the First Gulf War. They would be joined by hundreds more JAGs deployed to the Gulf to fight what one military lawyer claimed was 'the most legalistic war that we've [the US] ever fought'.[102] To the so-called 'lawyers war' we now turn.[103]

[101] Reisner, interview.
[102] Keeva, 'Lawyers in the War Room', 52.
[103] Ibid.

3
'The Lawyers' War'
Slow Violence in Iraq

> The emotional sanitation of war involves, in entangled ways, technological, geographical, temporal, and linguistic strategies for distancing. Particularly in our age of slow-acting 'precision' weapons delivered from afar, we're readily distracted from the violence of deferred effects—those causal chains stretched thin by time.
>
> Rob Nixon, Slow Violence and the Environmentalism of the Poor[1]

3.1 Lawyers Inside, Destruction Outside

On 2 August 1990, Iraq invaded and occupied Kuwait. Within a week the United States launched Operation Desert Shield, a full-scale military build-up for war against Iraq. In January of the following year a US-led coalition unleashed Operation Desert Storm—the combat phase—and for forty-two consecutive days and nights, the coalition forces subjected Iraq to one of the most intensive air bombardments in military history.

The First Gulf War is widely remembered as one of the cleanest, most precise, and most legal wars; a report to Congress in 1992 characterized it as the 'most discriminate air campaign in history'.[2] It was a war in which 'air power and aerial bombardment was to almost exclusively decide the outcome' according to Danielle Infeld, and 'it was also the first war in which precision-guided munitions (PGMs) would prove their capabilities'.[3] Much was made of the 'precise' and 'surgical' nature of the bombing campaign, which could be

[1] Rob Nixon, *Slow Violence and the Environmentalism of the Poor* (Cambridge, Mass: Harvard University Press, 2011), 220.

[2] United States Department of Defense, *Conduct of the Persian Gulf War: Final Report to Congress* (Washington DC: United States Department of Defence, 1992), 612, https://apps.dtic.mil/dtic/tr/fulltext/u2/a249270.pdf.mil%2Fdtic%2Ftr%2Ffulltext%2Fu2%2Fa249445.pdf&usg=AOvVaw19zIQ0RXtrfYzfu9yAIOA4, accessed 28 June 2020.

[3] Danielle L. Infeld, 'Precision-Guided Munitions Demonstrated Their Pinpoint Accuracy in Desert Storm; but Is a Country Obligated to Use Precision Technology to Minimize Collateral Civilian Injury and Damage', *George Washington Journal of International Law and Economics* 26, no. 1 (1992): 109.

The War Lawyers. Craig Jones, Oxford University Press (2020). © Craig Jones.
DOI: 10.1093/oso/9780198842927.001.0001.

followed to the point of impact by viewers at home. As one impressed commentator noted: 'Films of laser-guided bombs speeding unerringly through ventilation shafts and doorways provided stunning images of the effectiveness of precision-guided bombs.'[4] A new era of warfare was said to have arrived, and it had a human face.[5]

Contrary to these representations, the First Gulf War was devastating for Iraq and Iraqis. The bombing proved to be but 'an early moment in a far longer story' of what Rob Nixon has called the 'slow violence' of the war's aftermath.[6] The pain inflicted by the war, combined with the punishing sanctions regime and re-invasion of Iraq in 2003 and its subsequent occupation by US-led coalition forces, is still being felt today.[7] Criticism of the war has unfortunately centred around a vastly inflated figure of estimated child mortality.[8] A United Nations Children's Fund (UNICEF) study conducted in 1999 wrongly estimated the number of premature child deaths at approximately 500,000. This figure has since been discredited, in part because the data that informed the study was manipulated by Saddam Hussein's Government.[9] The fact that one measure has been discredited should not, however, take away from other multiple and cascading forms of destruction and ruin that were visited upon Iraq. Compared to other US wars, relatively few Iraqi civilians were killed during the 'hot' phase of operations—around 3,000—but the bombing destroyed critical infrastructures in Iraq that led to thousands more deaths, widespread suffering, and a health crisis of epic proportions.[10] A demographer with the U.S. Census Bureau estimated that 111,000 Iraqi civilians had died from war-related health effects by the end of 1991.[11]

[4] Ibid., 110.

[5] Chris Jochnick and Roger Normand, 'The Legitimation of Violence: A Critical History of the Laws of War (1994)', *Harvard International Law Journal* 35, no. 1 (1994): 49–95.

[6] Nixon, *Slow Violence and the Environmentalism of the Poor*, 216.

[7] Gordon, *Invisible War*.

[8] Henry Shue, eds., 'Force Protection, Military Advantage, and "Constant Care" for Civilians', in *The American Way of Bombing: Changing Ethical and Legal Norms, from Flying Fortresses to Drones* (Ithaca; London: Cornell University Press, 2014), 147.

[9] Tim Dyson, 'Child Mortality in Iraq since 1990', *Economic and Political Weekly* 41, no. 42 (2006): 4487–96; Tim Dyson, 'New Evidence on Child Mortality in Iraq', *Economic and Political Weekly* 44, no. 2 (2009): 56–59; Joy Gordon, *Invisible War: The United States and the Iraq Sanctions* (Cambridge, MA: Harvard University Press, 2010), 255–7, fn 82. A Harvard Study Team completed the first comprehensive survey of public health in post-war Iraq in May 1991 and it projected that 'at least 170,000 children under five years of age will die in the coming years from the delayed effects of the Gulf Crisis', a figure that represented a doubling in infant and child mortality compared to pre-war levels: Harvard Study Team, 'The Effect of the Gulf Crisis on the Children of Iraq' (Boston, MA: Harvard School of Public Health, 1991), 1, on file with author; accessed via Harvard Library Inter-Library Loan from Newcastle University.

[10] Neta C. Crawford, 'Targeting Civilians and U.S. Strategic Bombing Norms', in *The American Way of Bombing: Changing Ethical and Legal Norms, from Flying Fortresses to Drones*, ed. Matthew Evangelista (Ithaca, NY; London: Cornell University Press, 2014), 76.

[11] Ibid.

In 1993 the US Air Force commissioned a five-volume, several thousand-page report to document and analyse its performance during the Gulf War. The so-called Gulf War Air Power Survey famously concluded that the systematic destruction of Iraq's electric power grid was achieved with 'remarkably little collateral damage'.[12] In one sense this is true—the immediate damage was *relatively* contained—but it is also a patently dishonest appraisal because it fails to account for the longer-term effects and slow violence that would inevitably follow the bombing. In March 1991 Martti Ahtisaari, Under-Secretary-General for Administration and Management, led a UN delegation to Iraq. His report makes for sobering reading:

> The recent conflict has wrought near-apocalyptic results upon the economic infrastructure of what had been, until January 1991, a rather highly urbanized and mechanized society. Most means of modern life support have been destroyed or rendered tenuous. Iraq has, for some time to come, been relegated to a pre-industrial age, but with all the disabilities of post-industrial dependency on an intensive use of energy and technology.[13]

Ahtisaari went to some effort to describe the cascading collateral effects of the bombing, detailing how Iraq's power plants, oil refineries, main oil storage facilities, water-related chemical plants, and all electrically operated installations had ceased to function, effectively turning off Iraq's society and economy. Without electricity, he noted how:

> Food that is imported cannot be preserved and distributed; water cannot be purified; sewage cannot be pumped away and cleansed; crops cannot be irrigated; medicaments cannot be conveyed where they are required; needs cannot even be effectively assessed. It is unmistakable that the Iraqi people may soon face a further imminent catastrophe, which could include epidemic and famine, if massive life-supporting needs are not rapidly met.[14]

Electricity is so important to modern societies that many people believe attacks with the potential for such severe effects on a civilian population should be

[12] Quoted in: J. W. Crawford, 'The Law of Noncombatant Immunity and the Targeting of National Electric Power Systems', *The Fletcher Forum of World Affairs* 21, no. 2 (1997): 110.

[13] Martti Ahtisaari, 'Report to the Secretary-General on Humanitarian Needs in Kuwait and Iraq in the Immediate Post-Crisis Environment' (United Nations UN Doc. S/22366, 30 March 1991), 5.

[14] Ibid., 13.

prohibited.[15] Legal scholar Judith Gardam, for example, has forcefully argued: 'If the total destruction of the infrastructure of an industrialized state with the predictable impact on civilians is not contrary to international law, then the rules are totally ineffective and need urgent revision.'[16] All of this prompted J. W. Crawford at the United States Naval War College to observe a perverse sort of paradox in which civilians were spared in the initial bombing only to experience a delayed, extended, slow, and simmering violence afterwards. 'Never before has there been so much devastation visited upon a civilian population as a result of accurately placed munitions', Crawford writes, '[c]ivilian harm was *exacerbated* by the fact that noncombatants were otherwise spared the direct effects of urban aerial assault by the use of Precision Guided Munitions (PGMs) and other highly efficient techniques which eliminated the life support systems.'[17] In this sense, Crawford argues that the Gulf War was a 'real world laboratory' within which the reality of collateral damage and collateral casualties can be examined.[18]

It is perhaps more accurate then to speak about the 'calibration' rather than 'mitigation' of civilian suffering in the First Gulf War because, as I will show in this chapter, much of the destruction of Iraqi life-worlds was meticulously planned and evaluated in advance. This was destruction by design, and the laws of war and operational law played no small part in the patterning of violence.

* * *

Ten months after the bombs stopped falling, the American Bar Association journal published an article entitled 'Lawyers in the War Room' by Steven Keeva.[19] The article documented for the first time the extent to which judge advocates (JAGs) were involved in the conduct of the First Gulf War. Keeva interviewed several of the JAGs who had served in the Gulf and they told a similar story: 'Desert Storm was the most legalistic war we've ever fought', reported Colonel Raymond Ruppert, US Army, the Central Command (CENTCOM) Staff Judge Advocate, and General Schwarzkopf's legal adviser during the Gulf

[15] William Arkin, 'The Environmental Threat of Military Operations', in *Protection of the Environment During Armed Conflict*, ed. Richard J. Grunawalt, John E. King, and Ronald S. McClain, vol. 69 (Newport, RI: Naval War College, 1996), 123.

[16] Judith G. Gardam, 'Noncombatant Immunity and the Gulf Conflict', *Virginia Journal of International Law* 32, no. 4 (1992): 828.

[17] Crawford, 'The Law of Noncombatant Immunity and the Targeting of National Electric Power Systems', 110 (emphasis added).

[18] Ibid.

[19] S. Keeva, 'Lawyers in the War Room', *American Bar Association Journal* 77, no. 12 (1991): 52.

War.[20] (General Schwarzkopf was the Commander of CENTCOM, the man in charge of executing the entire war.) Twenty-five years later I spoke to Colonel (ret.) Ruppert and he stood by his claim: 'Commanders sought out legal advice, they listened to it and they generally followed it.'[21] Another senior-level JAG, who worked at the Pentagon during the Gulf War, told of how he had 'heard Gen. Schwarzkopf, Gen. [Colin] Powell and just about any other general officer who I run into, say that they consider the lawyer to be absolutely indispensable to military operations.'[22] Keeva used these and other statements to make some fairly lofty claims about the role that JAGs played in the Gulf 'war room'. 'Lawyers were everywhere during the Gulf War', he wrote, 'the Persian Gulf War was a lawyers' war'.[23]

Lawyers were not quite 'everywhere' as Keeva claimed, but more than 350 US JAGs were deployed to at least twenty-two different locations in the theatre of operations, including Saudi Arabia, United Arab Emirates, Bahrain, Qatar, and Egypt.[24] Of these, approximately 280 were Army JAGs.[25] As in Vietnam, the vast majority of deployed JAGs were accounted for by the Army because it deployed more personnel of all kinds than other services, and because it liked to 'put the lawyer as far forward a[s] possible'.[26] Forty-nine Air Force JAGs were deployed to the Gulf, accompanied by nearly as many Air Force paralegals, serving at thirty different locations across the area of operations and in Europe and elsewhere.[27] JAGs also did important work from the United States.[28] Those who served in the First Gulf War performed a myriad of tasks, some of them more traditional and others at the cutting edge of operational law. In particular, JAGs were involved in unprecedented ways with the targeting process and they had input at multiple points in the chain of command.

[20] Ibid., 52.

[21] Ruppert (Raymond), interview.

[22] Keeva, 'Lawyers in the War Room', 59. See also: W. Hays Parks, 'The Gulf War: A Practitioner's View', *Dickinson Journal of International Law* 10, no. 3 (1992): 393–423.

[23] Keeva, 'Lawyers in the War Room', 52.

[24] Leonard Broseker, 'Sword in the Sand', *The Reporter* 26, Special History edition (1999): 140. Other JAGs put the total number of legal office locations in the theatre of operations at thirty-two: Kansala, Interview.

[25] Stephen A. Myrow, 'Waging War on the Advice of Counsel: The Role of Operational Law in the Gulf War', *United States Air Force Academy Journal of Legal Studies* 7 (1996): 136.

[26] Colonel Ruppert, quoted in: Ibid., 147. This means putting lawyers in or close to areas of combat. In contrast, the furthest 'forward' an Air Force JAG commonly serves is at the 'Wing level', an air base in the theatre of operations but not necessarily close to active areas of combat.

[27] Scott L. Silliman, 'JAG Goes to War: The Desert Shield Deployment', *Air Force Law Review* 37 (1994): 91. There were forty-six paralegals.

[28] Harry L. Heintzelman and Edmund S. Bloom, 'A Planning Primer: How to Provide Effective Legal Input into the War Planning and Combat Execution Process', *Air Force Law Review* 37 (1994): 6. Green, interview.

What is a 'lawyers' war'? What are the implications of lawyers being 'everywhere' during the conduct of war? And how are we to make sense of an image of war in which lawyers sit inside war rooms while 'outside' Iraq is being destroyed? Jochnick and Normand have argued that in the Gulf War, 'the laws of war have facilitated rather than restrained wartime violence. Through law, violence has been legitimated.'[29] So long as the destruction was a second, or third order effect and not immediate or direct this legitimation process seems to have been very powerful. While the targeting of infrastructure was not new,[30] unprecedented use of legal advisers makes the Gulf War an important theatre in which to examine what we might call the juridification of infrastructural destruction.

3.2 Legally Conditioning the Battlefield

Military lawyers were involved from the outset in formulating the response to the Iraqi invasion of Kuwait and in investigating the options for the use of force available to the United States.[31] The Department of State, with assistance from its legal counsel, worked with the UN to condemn the Iraqi invasion.[32] In November 1990 the UN Security Council passed Resolution 678 threatening the use of force against Iraq unless it withdrew its forces from Kuwait.[33] Onerous sanctions were imposed to urge Iraq to withdraw. Meanwhile, US and coalition forces began moving vast quantities of military assets, weapons, supplies, and personnel to the region—to Saudi Arabia and the Persian Gulf in particular—both to deter Iraq from invading Saudi Arabia and in preparation for an offensive war against Iraq.[34]

Making war and amassing troops requires all sorts of work, including work of a legal nature. One of the more complicated legal issues during this time was whether President George H. W. Bush should ask for explicit authorization from Congress to use force against Iraq. A team of lawyers informally called the 'War Powers Group of Executive Lawyers', which included military lawyer

[29] Jochnick and Normand, 'The Legitimation of Violence', 50.

[30] Stephen Graham, *Cities, War, and Terrorism: Towards an Urban Geopolitics* (Malden, MA: Blackwell publishing, 2004); Jeannie L. Sowers, Erika Weinthal, and Neda Zawahri, 'Targeting Environmental Infrastructures, International Law, and Civilians in the New Middle Eastern Wars', *Security Dialogue* 48, no. 5 (2017): 410–30.

[31] Green, interview.

[32] Parks, 'Gulf War', 403.

[33] United Nations Security Council, 'Resolution 679' (30 November 1990), https://digitallibrary.un.org/record/102678?ln=en, accessed 28 June 2020.

[34] Parks, 'Gulf War', 404.

Colonel Fred Green, discussed the matter and concluded that the President did not require Congressional approval; the President could use force against Iraq by exercising his right as Commander-in-Chief and as Chief Executive.[35] Some of these lawyers nevertheless thought that Congressional authorization would be politically prudent as it would guarantee a broader base of support for the use of force. Colin Powell, the Chairman of the Joint Chief of Staff agreed, but the Secretary of Defense, Dick Cheney, did not want to give Congress a vote because he believed that the United States would have to use force with or without Congressional support. A 'no' vote could damage the case for going to war.[36]

With the UN deadline for Iraq's withdrawal approaching, Powell did not want to be seen to be disagreeing with Cheney. Rather than meeting with Cheney face-to-face, Powell sent his lawyer, Colonel Fred Green, to the critical White House meeting where these matters were discussed. Acting on Green's advice, President George H. W. Bush decided to write to Congress to ask for authorization: 'Check it over and give it [. . .] the last scrub', Bush reportedly told his team of lawyers.[37] Having given it a final look over, Colonel Green replied: 'We've got to change one word in here. We've got to go from "authorize" to "support"'.[38] The lawyers reasoned that by asking for authorization Bush might set a precedent and negate his own right to use force as Executive and Commander-in-Chief. By asking for 'support' only, the president would have a free hand whichever way the vote went. In the event, Congress passed a joint resolution in January 1991 to 'authorize the use of United States Armed Forces pursuant to United Nations Security Council Resolution 678'.[39] This was the best possible outcome as far as the lawyers were concerned for it combined formal legality with Congressional legitimacy, thereby securing a broad base of support for the war. Operation Desert Storm began five days later.

To conduct an offensive campaign against Iraq, the United States first had to build its troop and military strength in the region, a mission that was named Operation Desert Shield. The Pentagon estimated seventeen weeks for the necessary forces to be deployed, and immediately began work on securing an 'invitation' from Saudi Arabia.[40] JAGs assisted in Operation Desert Shield in

[35] Green Fred, USARMY. Oral History—Colonel (R) Fred K. Green. Interview by Kate Gowel and John Gowel. Transcript, 4 December 2010. Green's personal collection; on file with author (with permission from Fred Green).

[36] Ibid., 436.

[37] Ibid., 437.

[38] Ibid.

[39] United Nations Security Council, Resolution 679.

[40] United States Department of Defence, *Conduct of the Persian Gulf War*, 32–3. 'They have invited us! They want us to come!', Secretary of Defense Paul Wolfowitz would later tell Chuck Horner, the leader of air campaign, quoted in: Diane T. Putney, *Airpower Advantage: Planning the Gulf Air Campaign, 1989-1991* (Honolulu: University Press of the Pacific, 2006), 28.

a number of ways and at a number of levels.[41] Because it was not a combat operation, their main role was in providing assistance to the command and to troops as they transitioned from the United States to the theatre of operations.[42] Colonel Raymond Ruppert describes his office as addressing 'an entire spectrum of legal issues ranging from contract law, legal assistance, tax questions, standards of conduct, [and] criminal law matters'.[43] Dennis Kansala, the Central Command Air Force (CENTAF) Staff Judge Advocate who was based in Riyadh, recalls a similarly extensive workload that included even the most idiosyncratic and seemingly minor legal issues such as helping troops to pay their bills at home while they were deployed abroad.[44]

Troops cannot be deployed in a third-party state (in this case, Saudi Arabia) without prior consent and so 'status of forces agreements' (SOFAs) must be negotiated and signed before battle commences.[45] The SOFA between the United States and Saudi Arabia was co-drafted by a JAG. One of the principal concerns was obtaining legal immunity from prosecution under Saudi law for US troops while in the country.[46] In turn, Saudi Arabia wanted guarantees that US troops would obey local customs. Most importantly, perhaps, was that the SOFA also established the legal guarantee whereby US forces could move from a defensive posture to an offensive one. The agreement, negotiated directly between Prince Bandar, Saudi Arabia's ambassador to the United States, and Dick Cheney and Colin Powell is still classified. Significantly, this was the first permanent US ground presence in Saudi Arabia. As one of the drafters of the SOFA explained in quite extraordinary terms, one of its primary purposes was to 'preserve the illusion of Saudi Arabia as a sovereign state'.[47]

3.3 'Instant Thunder'

Planning for an offensive operation against Iraq had begun the day after Iraq invaded Kuwait, that is, over five months before the United States launched its

[41] For a detailed account see: Parks, 'Gulf War', 403–14.
[42] Ruppert (Mark), interview.
[43] Ruppert (Raymond), interview.
[44] Kansala, interview.
[45] A SOFA is 'an agreement that defines the legal position of a visiting military force deployed in the territory of a friendly state': John Morrissey, 'Liberal Lawfare and Biopolitics: US Juridical Warfare in the War on Terror', *Geopolitics* 16, no. 2 (2011): 293.
[46] Katia Snukal and Emily Gilbert, 'War, Law, Jurisdiction, and Juridical Othering: Private Military Security Contractors and the Nisour Square Massacre', *Environment and Planning D: Society and Space* 33, no. 4 (2015): 660–75.
[47] Green, interview.

opening salvo on 17 January 1991.[48] Colonel John Warden III, the Air Staff's deputy director for Warfighting Concepts (who headed a sub-division in the Pentagon called Checkmate),[49] drew up the air campaign plan with the assistance of Lieutenant Colonel David Deptula.[50] Originally, Warden was requested to consider a defensive air plan but he and Deptula turned it into a fully fledged strategic air campaign and 'sold it to Schwarzkopf'[51] as the 'Punishment ATO [Air Tasking Order]', a reference to the aggressive targeting schedule they had planned.[52] Warden called the air campaign plan 'Instant Thunder'. Warden, who had served as a pilot in the Vietnam War, chose the name as a direct contrast to the ill-fated Operation Rolling Thunder, which had mandated a gradualist approach to targeting and had been micromanaged by political leaders (Chapter 1). 'This is not your Rolling Thunder', he told the Checkmate planners: 'This is real war, and one of the things we want to emphasize right from the beginning is that this is not Vietnam! This is doing it right! This is using air power!'[53] As its name implied, Instant Thunder was to employ 'a massive application of airpower as rapidly as possible'.[54] The initial plan was to destroy eighty-four targets in Iraq in a single week, but the target list soon expanded to 237 (Figure 3.1). According to Deptula, CENTCOM Commander Schwarzkopf 'understood the value of using airpower up front like a thunderstorm and not like a rain shower'.[55]

Instant Thunder had four aims:

(1) to force Iraqi withdrawal from Kuwait;
(2) to degrade Iraq's offensive capability;
(3) to secure oil facilities; and
(4) to render Saddam ineffective as a leader.[56]

[48] United States Department of Defence, *Conduct of the Persian Gulf War*, 1991.

[49] Checkmate is a unique directorate in Air Force Plans known for encouraging independent thinking and analysis on important combat-employment issues: Richard T. Reynolds, *Heart of the Storm, The Genesis of the Air Campaign Against Iraq* (Maxwell Air Force Base, AL: Air University Press, 1995), 16, https://apps.dtic.mil/dtic/tr/fulltext/u2/a292091.pdf, accessed 28 June 2020.

[50] Mark David Mandeles, Thomas Hone, and Sanford S. Terry, *Managing 'Command and Control' in the Persian Gulf War* (Westport, CT: Praeger, 1996), 10. For a full account of Warden's Instant Thunder plan, see: Reynolds, 'Heart of the Storm, The Genesis of the Air Campaign Against Iraq'.

[51] Putney, *Airpower Advantage*, vi.

[52] Sebastian Cox and Peter Gray, *Air Power History: Turning Points from Kitty Hawk to Kosovo* (Abingdon, Oxon: Routledge, 2013), 251.

[53] Reynolds, 'Heart of the Storm, The Genesis of the Air Campaign Against Iraq', 29.

[54] Deptula, interview.

[55] Ibid.

[56] Alexander Cochran et al., 'Gulf War: Air Power Survey: Volume 1, Planning, Command & Control' (Washington, DC: United States Air Force, 1993), 109, http://www.dtic.mil/dtic/tr/fulltext/u2/a279741.pdf, accessed 13 July 2015.

Target Sets (symbols used by the Special Planning Group and their explanations)	21 August	20 December
SAD (strategic air defense)	10	27
C (chemical, nuclear, and biological facilities)	8	20
L (leadership)	5	27
CCC (command, control and communication sites)	19	30
E (electric power)	10	16
0 (oil facilities)	6	8
RR (railroads and bridges)	3	21
A (airfields)	7	25
N (naval ports and facilities)	1	4
MS (military support facilities	15	46
SC (Scud facilities)	N/A	13
RG (Republican Guards)	N/A	0
Totals	84	237

Noles; Highway bridges were added to the category that was originally railroads alone; Scud facilities were counted as part of the chemical, nuclear, and biological category in August; the Republican Guard was a new target set; specific targets added at a later date.

Figure 3.1 Growth of targets in Operation Desert Storm planning (1990).
Source: Thomas A. Keaney and Eliot A. Cohen, *Revolution in Warfare?: Air Power in the Persian Gulf* (Annapolis, ML: Naval Institute Press, 1995), 35.

The fourth objective was the centrepiece. In his book, *The Air Campaign: Planning for Combat*, Warden had suggested that command (leadership) was a 'center of gravity' to be attacked, but had cautioned that a senior leader would be difficult to target and that his staff might be able to carry on without him.[57] Warden developed a targeting concept illustrated by five

[57] John Warden, *The Air Campaign: Planning for Combat* (Washington, DC: National Defense University Press, 1988). Warden was right to worry, especially as many of the enemies that the United States has come to fight are non-state groups and organizations who adopt a radically decentralized *modus operandi*. Al Qaeda, the Taliban, and Al Shabab illustrate the point, while the Islamic State may have been an exception. Colonel Pietrucha argues that Warden's theories are equally invalid even when applied to war against another state: 'Modern governments, even totalitarian ones, have their control measures well spread out or the state cannot function, making strategic paralysis unlikely.' Mike Pietrucha, 'The Five-Ring Circus: How Airpower Enthusiasts Forgot About Interdiction', *War on the*

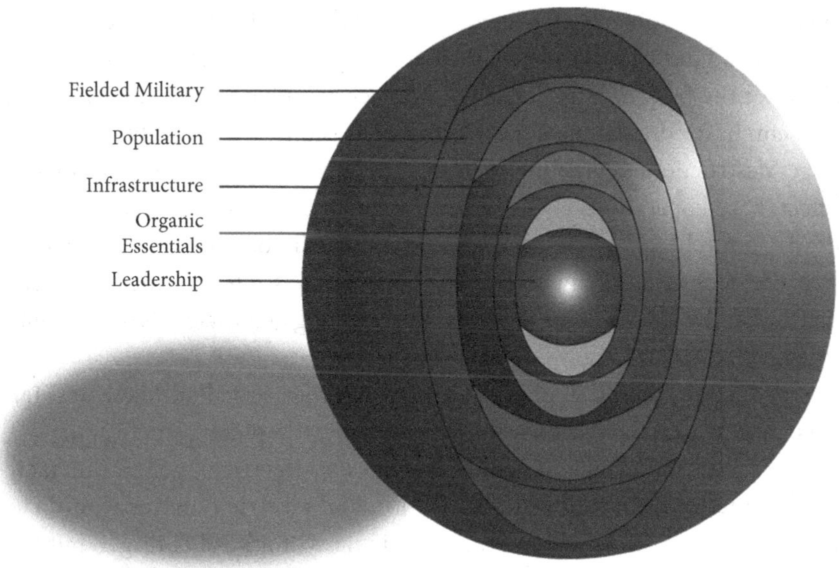

Figure 3.2 Warden's five-ring system theory of targeting diagram.
Source: Graphic by Gary Noel, reproduced in Pietrucha, Mike. 'The Five-Ring Circus: How Airpower Enthusiasts Forgot About Interdiction'. *War on the Rocks* (blog), 29 September 2015. https://warontherocks.com/2015/09/the-five-ring-circus-how-airpower-enthusiasts-forgot-about-interdiction/, accessed 5 January 2017. Reproduced with permission from War on The Rocks.

concentric rings (Figure 3.2). According to the authors of the Gulf Air Power Survey: 'The central ring in his theory of target importance was leadership. He planned attacks on the other four rings (key production, infrastructure, population, and fielded forces on the outer rim) in terms of their potential effect on leadership.'[58] Targeting the Iraqi military leadership could lead to a direct military advantage because without command and control a military would be unable to function in a coherent and organized manner, at least in theory.[59]

Rocks (blog), 29 September 2015, https://warontherocks.com/2015/09/the-five-ring-circus-how-airpower-enthusiasts-forgot-about-interdiction/, accessed 5 January 2017.

[58] Cochran et al., 'Gulf War: Air Power Survey: Volume 1, Planning, Command & Control', 111. See also: Gordon Nathaniel Lederman, *Reorganizing the Joint Chiefs of Staff: The Goldwater-Nichols Act of 1986* (Westport, CT: Greenwood Publishing Group, 1999), 98.

[59] Warden's theory and the emphasis he placed on leadership (the central ring) prefigured what is today called high value targeting (against specific, small, and frequently mobile and highly protected targets). These 'personality strikes' have been achieved through countless mistakes, with varying degrees of accuracy and at a high cost to civilians: Spencer Ackerman, '41 Men Targeted but 1,147 People Killed: US Drone Strikes—the Facts on the Ground', *The Guardian*, 24 November 2014, sec. US, https://www.theguardian.com/us-news/2014/nov/24/-sp-us-drone-strikes-kill-1147, accessed 3 April 2015; Reprieve US, 'You Never Die Twice: Multiple Kills in the US Drone Program' (New York, NY: Reprieve,

With Warden leading, the Checkmate planners devised a plan to sever Saddam Hussein and the leadership from their combat forces in an attempt to instigate chaos for the Iraqi military. I use the word 'chaos' advisedly because Warden's plan emphasized 'creating and exploiting confusion'[60] over and above absolute target destruction, a targeting philosophy that would later become known as 'effects based operations'.[61] Today, the US Air Force boasts that it can 'put warheads on foreheads', a reference to the putative pinpoint accuracy of modern targeting technologies but also a claim that demonstrates the increasing emphasis that the US Air Force places on the targeting of individuals (or so-called 'personality strikes').[62]

The Instant Thunder plan involved bombing so called 'dual use' targets: targets that have both a military and a civilian component, purpose, or use; for example, telephone lines, bridges, or electricity generating facilities. Sometimes lines of communication and electricity wires would run under bridges, which made them a particularly 'high value target' but one that would have devastating consequences for Iraqi civilians, as Barton Gellman explains: 'The worst civilian suffering [. . .] has resulted not from bombs that went astray but from precision-guided weapons that hit exactly where they were aimed—at electrical plants, oil refineries and transportation networks.'[63] According to Janina Dill, 'the intent behind many of the air strikes on dual use infrastructure in Iraq was at least in part to influence Saddam Hussein, his regime and ultimately also the Iraqi people'.[64] In short, the plan involved 'morale bombing'—an attempt to destroy the resolve of the enemy population so that they concede the fight. David Deptula confirmed that bombing key infrastructures like the electricity grid was motivated partly to punish the civilian population. As he told me several years later:

24 November 2014), https://reprieve.org/uploads2633263381312014_11_24_pub_you_never_die_twice_-_multiple_kills_in_the_us_drone_program-pdf/, accessed 8 September 2019.

[60] Putney, *Airpower Advantage*, 121.

[61] EBO is 'based upon achieving specific effects, not absolute destruction of target lists', David A. Deptula, 'Effects Based Operations: Change in the Nature of Warfare' (Arlington, VA: Aerospace Education Foundation, 2001), 3, https://secure.afa.org/Mitchell/reports/0901ebo.pdf, accessed 28 June 2020.

[62] Anna Mulrine, 'Warheads on Foreheads', *Air Force Magazine*, 2008, 44.

[63] Barton Gellman, 'Allied Air War Struck Broadly in Iraq: Officials Acknowledge Strategy Went beyond Purely Military Targets', *Washington Post*, 23 June 1991, reproduced at: https://www.globalpolicy.org/component/content/article/169/36375.html, accessed 1 March 2020.

[64] Janina Dill, *Legitimate Targets?: Social Construction, International Law and US Bombing* (Cambridge: Cambridge University Press, 2014).

> Part of the plan was [. . .] now you let the people know 'alright help us help you, you overthrow Saddam, we will be in rapidly to reconstruct your electricity as soon as possible'. So there's a psychological component here as well. So, of course you understand that there's an impact on the civilian side. That's a consequence of their allowing this guy to stay in position in government.[65]

The air campaign would try to avoid *direct* civilian casualties but 'Warden was not being cautious'.[66] One JAG who served in the Gulf War explained that civilians were not immune from attack: 'The psychological effect of the depletion of electrical power on the part of the Iraqi people was a valid consideration in that particular targeting decision.'[67] Lieutenant General Charles Horner, who would be responsible for the execution of the air combat plan (section 3.4), later confirmed that many middle of the night bombings 'were intended to remind the Iraqis that they were at war'.[68] Unfortunately for Iraqis, that 'reminder' would reverberate long afterwards. Many post-war deaths, injuries, and diseases were attributable to the bombing of Iraq's electricity producing infrastructure which caused serious 'adverse health effects' for large parts of the population.[69]

Diane T. Putney claims that the Instant Thunder planners 'followed international law (codified in the laws of armed conflict) and its strictures about discrimination, although nowhere in Instant Thunder did they mention the legal code'.[70] It is difficult to verify the extent to which Instant Thunder planners were guided by international law but according to both John Warden and David Deptula—its main planners—JAGs did not participate in Instant Thunder. Warden recollects: 'I do not believe we had any JAG participation in IT [Instant Thunder]. A number of people [later] challenged the plan to attack Saddam Hussein on legal grounds, but the answer seemed simple: no issue as he was commander-in-chief of Iraq armed forces.'[71] This is a surprising admission given that Joint Chief of Staff guidance from as early as the late 1970s and early 1980s *required* a full legal review for all operations plans (Chapter 2).

Horner's Instant Thunder plan would be executed the following January, and many of the specific targets proposed by him and the Checkmate planners

[65] Deptula, interview.
[66] Cochran et al., 'Gulf War: Air Power Survey: Volume 1, Planning, Command & Control', 111.
[67] Ariane L. DeSaussure, 'The Role of the Law of Armed Conflict During the Persian Gulf War: An Overview", *Air Force Law Review* 37 (1994): 63.
[68] Ibid.
[69] Jochnick and Normand, 'The Legitimation of Violence', 50.
[70] Putney, *Airpower Advantage*, 51.
[71] Email correspondence between John Warden and David Deptula, forwarded to the author.

would eventually be struck.[72] In the words of Colin Powell, Instant Thunder 'remained the heart of the Desert Storm air war'.[73] The absence of JAGs and the lack of legal questions therefore suggest that law of war considerations did not drive the generation of the target list from the outset, as would happen years later when the US launched Operation Iraqi Freedom (Chapter 5). However, making for some complexity were two parallel and largely separate air planning cells in two different locations: in addition to Washington was Riyadh. Later in the war these plans would merge but tracing the origins of the target lists is crucial in figuring out how, when, and where JAGs were involved in giving legal advice on targeting operations.

3.4 Into the Black Hole: the Rules of Engagement

Before Warden's Instant Thunder plans were finished, a separate and highly secretive planning cell that became known as the Black Hole was established in the basement of the Royal Saudi Air Force headquarters in Riyadh. It is easy to get lost in the detail of these various plans, but importantly they laid the foundations for the later execution of the air war. Military lawyers may have been largely absent during Instant Thunder planning process but as we shall see they played an important—if relatively hands-off—role in the Black Hole.

On 19 August 1990 Warden was flown out to Saudi Arabia to brief key members of the CENTCOM and CENTAF staff on the Instant Thunder plan. General Charles ('Chuck') Horner, the Supreme Air Commander and the man who would go on to lead the Gulf air campaign, was dissatisfied with the plan, in part because it originated in Washington. It reminded him too much of the Vietnam War and of the micromanagement of the Johnson administration (Chapter 1).[74] As Horner recollected:

> Remember our great President saying, 'They don't bomb a shit house in North Vietnam if I don't approve it.' Well, I was the guy bombing the shit houses, and I was never going to let that happen if I ever got in charge, because it is not right. If you want to know whether war is going to be successful or not, just ask where the targets are being picked. If they say, 'We picked them in

[72] Mandeles, Hone, and Terry, *Managing 'Command and Control' in the Persian Gulf War*, 13.
[73] Putney, *Airpower Advantage*, vi.
[74] Lederman, *Reorganizing the Joint Chiefs of Staff*, 99.

Washington,' get out of the country. Go to Canada until the war is over because it is a loser.[75]

Horner wanted to 'reject the plan and the planners' and after a series of meetings he sent Warden back to Washington.[76] In his place Horner appointed Brigadeer General Buster Glosson to head up a new planning cell composed of joint and allied officers but with very few US Air Force personnel. A single JAG, Major Harry Heintzelman, was on the staff.

Horner liked to 'hop in a fighter [jet] and buzz the desert to get the feel of the terrain over which his pilots would be risking their lives'.[77] Glosson, another Vietnam vet, was 'known for his fiery temper and fighter-pilot get-it-done attitude'.[78] In an interview after the war was over, Glosson recalled: 'Chuck [Horner] and I remember flying in Vietnam with less than a full load of weapons [. . .] You can bet we were not going to let that happen again'. According to Lieutenant Colonel John Humphries, a US Air Force JAG, they got what they wanted: 'Horner and his staff had exceptionally broad latitude in determining the course of the air campaign [. . .] not once did Pentagon officials reverse decisions from the Black Hole about what weapons to use, what targets to strike, and how and when to attack them.'[79]

Horner and Glosson personally selected members of the planning cell[80] and drew on informal networks to get the people and intelligence they needed.[81] They circumvented the normal channels—such as the Joint Targeting Coordination Board, created and vetted their own target lists, and developed their own Air Tasking Orders––the air attack plan that matches targets to available resources (e.g. fighter jets and weapons) in a clearly executable and prioritized order (Figure 3.3).[82] They began with four target lists, which included Warden's Instant Thunder plan (eighty-four targets), and 200 additional targets from CENTCOM. Instead of adding these lists together to create a centralized compound database, each target was re-evaluated, some deleted, and others added. By the end of the initial review process, the number of targets

[75] Charles Horner, quoted in: Putney, *Airpower Advantage*, 5.

[76] Ibid., 125.

[77] Tom Mathews, 'The Secret History of the War', *Newsweek* 117, no. 11 (18 March 1991).

[78] Reynolds, 'Heart of the Storm, The Genesis of the Air Campaign Against Iraq', 133.

[79] John G. Humphries, 'Operations Law and the Rules of Engagement in Operation Desert Shield and Desert Storm', *Airpower Journal* 6, no. 3 (1992). Matthews claims: 'Bombing targets, except in a few rare instances, were selected and approved in Riyadh, not in Washington.' Dennis Kansala supports these observations. Kansala, interview. There was one exception, however, which I discuss below.

[80] Mandeles, Hone, and Terry, *Managing "Command and Control" in the Persian Gulf War*, 11.

[81] Ibid., 19.

[82] Ibid., 15. The Air Tasking Order was historically known as the 'fragmentary order' or 'frag order'.

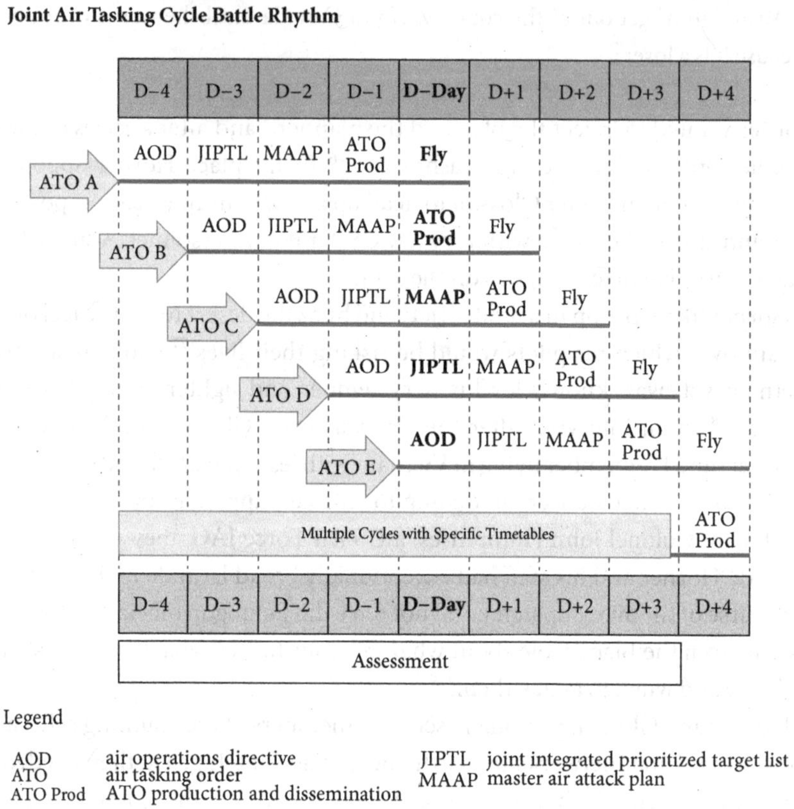

Figure 3.3 The Joint Air Tasking Cycle Battle Rhythm.
Source: United States Joint Chiefs of Staff, 'Joint Targeting', Joint Publication 3-60 (Washington, DC, 31 January 2013), C-5.

had grown substantially to 712.[83] When Glosson moved into the basement room of the Saudi Air Force headquarters—the Black Hole—he had a large sign hung on one wall.[84] It read: 'THE WAY HOME IS THROUGH BAGHDAD'.[85] Deptula, who was also in the Black Hole, explained that 'Baghdad' was a reference to the importance of Iraqi leadership in the targeting plan. Only once the leadership was defeated could the war be won and Americans return home.[86]

[83] Ibid., 13. See also: DeSaussure, 'The Role of the Law of Armed Conflict During the Persian Gulf War', 62.
[84] Mandeles, Hone, and Terry, *Managing 'Command and Control' in the Persian Gulf War*, 28.
[85] Mathews, 'The Secret History of the War'.
[86] Deptula, interview. Deptula never got his man, Saddam Hussein. A decade later, Deptula served as the Director of the Combined Air Operations Center (CAOC) for Operation Enduring Freedom (OEF) where he orchestrated the air campaign against targets in Afghanistan and searched, again without success, for Osama bin Laden (Chapter 5).

The team was sworn to secrecy and worked on laptop computers on a secure system that could not be tapped into by anyone else, however high ranking, in the allied Central Command.[87] The Air Tasking Order was printed after normal working hours and carried by hand along with the 'Master Attack Plan' to one or two 'trusted agents' in each of the 'wings' at airbases in Saudi Arabia (a wing is a US Air Force unit). The first Air Tasking Order was classified top secret. It and the Master Attack Plan were destroyed as they were superseded by new ones. So meticulous was the destruction that copies of the earliest version of the first Air Tasking Order no longer exist.[88] The need for secrecy was twofold. First, the group wanted to avoid complicating or terminating diplomatic efforts between the US and the Saudis by making it known that, contrary to what had been agreed, the US was planning *offensive*—and not just defensive—strikes against Iraq. Second, they wanted to ensure their attack plans would take the enemy by surprise.[89] According to a CENTAF planner, the cell was dubbed the Black Hole 'because we would send people in, and they would never come out. We would never see them again because they would just stay there'.[90]

The plan drawn up by the Black Hole team would eventually become the blueprint for the air war in January 1991. The most important operational law contributions made by JAGs were in the areas of rules of engagement (ROE) and targeting.

Writing the rules

As I detailed in Chapter 2, US military doctrine requires that operators—military staff responsible for planning and coordinating operations—write the ROE and submit them to a JAG for legal review. In the Gulf War, the US relied on two different sets of ROE, one for Operation Desert Shield, the build-up phase, and one for Operation Desert Storm, the combat phase. CENTCOM issued ROE to its component commands (Air Force, Army, Navy, Marines) that were very broad in scope and established the general guidelines for military operations at the theatre level.[91] Once the component-specific ROE were

[87] Mathews, 'The Secret History of the War'.

[88] Mandeles, Hone, and Terry, *Managing 'Command and Control' in the Persian Gulf War*, 14.

[89] Deptula, interview.

[90] Lieutenant Colonel Sam Baptiste, quoted in: Edward C. Mann, 'Thunder and Lightning: Desert Storm and the Airpower Debates, Volume 2' (DTIC Document, 1995), 46, https://apps.dtic.mil/docs/citations/ADA421939, accessed 29 June 2020.

[91] It was then each component command's responsibility to draft ROE with more specific guidance for their particular operation. These component-specific ROE were then reviewed by CENTCOM to

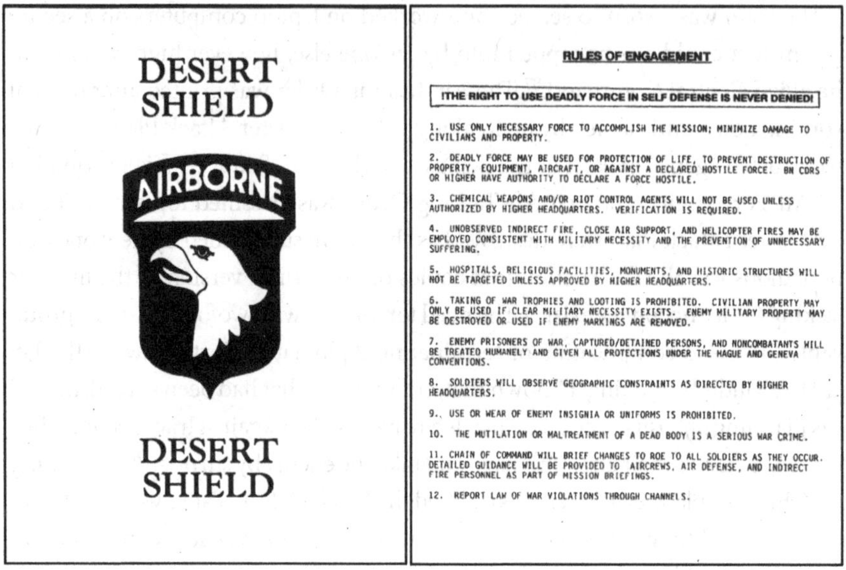

RULES OF ENGAGEMENT

!THE RIGHT TO USE DEADLY FORCE IN SELF DEFENSE IS NEVER DENIED!

1. USE ONLY NECESSARY FORCE TO ACCOMPLISH THE MISSION; MINIMIZE DAMAGE TO CIVILIANS AND PROPERTY.

2. DEADLY FORCE MAY BE USED FOR PROTECTION OF LIFE, TO PREVENT DESTRUCTION OF PROPERTY, EQUIPMENT, AIRCRAFT, OR AGAINST A DECLARED HOSTILE FORCE. BN CDRS OR HIGHER HAVE AUTHORITY TO DECLARE A FORCE HOSTILE.

3. CHEMICAL WEAPONS AND/OR RIOT CONTROL AGENTS WILL NOT BE USED UNLESS AUTHORIZED BY HIGHER HEADQUARTERS. VERIFICATION IS REQUIRED.

4. UNOBSERVED INDIRECT FIRE, CLOSE AIR SUPPORT, AND HELICOPTER FIRES MAY BE EMPLOYED CONSISTENT WITH MILITARY NECESSITY AND THE PREVENTION OF UNNECESSARY SUFFERING.

5. HOSPITALS, RELIGIOUS FACILITIES, MONUMENTS, AND HISTORIC STRUCTURES WILL NOT BE TARGETED UNLESS APPROVED BY HIGHER HEADQUARTERS.

6. TAKING OF WAR TROPHIES AND LOOTING IS PROHIBITED. CIVILIAN PROPERTY MAY ONLY BE USED IF CLEAR MILITARY NECESSITY EXISTS. ENEMY MILITARY PROPERTY MAY BE DESTROYED OR USED IF ENEMY MARKINGS ARE REMOVED.

7. ENEMY PRISONERS OF WAR, CAPTURED/DETAINED PERSONS, AND NONCOMBATANTS WILL BE TREATED HUMANELY AND GIVEN ALL PROTECTIONS UNDER THE HAGUE AND GENEVA CONVENTIONS.

8. SOLDIERS WILL OBSERVE GEOGRAPHIC CONSTRAINTS AS DIRECTED BY HIGHER HEADQUARTERS.

9. USE OR WEAR OF ENEMY INSIGNIA OR UNIFORMS IS PROHIBITED.

10. THE MUTILATION OR MALTREATMENT OF A DEAD BODY IS A SERIOUS WAR CRIME.

11. CHAIN OF COMMAND WILL BRIEF CHANGES TO ROE TO ALL SOLDIERS AS THEY OCCUR. DETAILED GUIDANCE WILL BE PROVIDED TO AIRCREWS, AIR DEFENSE, AND INDIRECT FIRE PERSONNEL AS PART OF MISSION BRIEFINGS.

12. REPORT LAW OF WAR VIOLATIONS THROUGH CHANNELS.

Figure 3.4 A portion of the rules of engagement for Operation Desert Storm, 101st Airborne.

Source: Sergeant Major Herb Friedman, personal collection, reproduced with permission.

approved, individual combat units adopted them and subsequently made their own (often minor) adjustments (Figure 3.4).

The Legal Annex to Desert Storm published by CENTCOM Headquarters in Riyadh on 16 December 1990 clarifies the role of the JAG vis-à-vis the ROE: 'All ROE shall be reviewed by command/supporting command judge advocates for clarity, consistency, and harmony with international law'[92] In reality, however, JAGs at CENTCOM actually wrote the aforementioned overarching wartime ROE, and JAGs at CENTAF wrote the component-specific ROE for the air operation, albeit with input from the operators.[93]

Why did CENTCOM depart from its own doctrine and have JAGs write the ROE? I put this question to Colonel (ret.) Raymond Ruppert, CENTCOM's

ensure consistency with the operational intent of CENTCOM's ROE and were then forwarded to the Joint Chief of Staff for final approval: Raymond Ruppert, email correspondence, 29 July 2015.

[92] Raymond Ruppert personal collection files, E, pp 4–5, on file with author (used with permission).

[93] Lieutenant-commander Walt Jacobsen, a JAG at CENTCOM headquarters, initially drafted the CENTCOM ROE for Desert Storm which were subsequently reviewed, edited, and approved by Raymond Ruppert, the CENTCOM SJA: Raymond Ruppert, email correspondence, 27 July 2015. The CENTAF ROE were drafted by Major Harry Heintzelman, who was located in the Black Hole, and subsequently reviewed, edited and approved by the CENTAF Staff Judge Advocate, Dennis Kansala.

most senior JAG during the Gulf War and General Schwarzkopf's chief legal adviser. Ruppert had previously worked with Schwarzkopf during Operation Earnest Will, where the United States deployed ships to the Persian Gulf to protect US interests. According to Ruppert, their prior relationship fed into the decision to allow lawyers to write the ROE. As he explained:

> It was very clear to me that General Schwarzkopf looked to us – the lawyers—to do the rules of engagement [. . .] Schwarzkopf was a brilliant man in terms of tactics and strategy: he realized very early on that the US would be watched very very closely by the rest of the world and particularly by the media. [. . .] When you take that fact and add it to the fact that he, like just about every senior commander, whether they served at CENTCOM or at CENTAF, were Vietnam veterans and knew the impact of negative publicity. In order to hopefully minimize bad publicity he turned to people on his staff that were good writers and—if practicing their skills correctly, their *profession* correctly—could write in clear and concise language.[94]

The fact that Schwarzkopf sought out assistance from his JAG in writing the ROE is both a symbol and a result of the institutional and cultural change in the US military that took place throughout the 1970s and 1980s (Chapter 2). Schwarzkopf understood that JAGs were not there to impede military operations and thus trusted them with a significant task. In turn, JAGs better understood the business of their client and went to great lengths to become experts in all matter of military subjects. By the time the Gulf War began in 1990, close working relationships like that between Ruppert and Schwarzkopf had become so institutionalized that some have characterized the role played by JAGs in the Gulf War as 'natural and expected'.[95] Yet much of what JAGs did in the Gulf War, including the writing of the ROE, was nonetheless a radical departure from previous major wars and especially from the Vietnam War (Chapter 1).

A second factor is also crucial in explaining how and why JAGs came to write the ROE for Operation Desert Storm. Conventionally understood, ROE are informed by the laws of war and are designed so that no part of them contravenes the laws of war (or more accurately *national interpretations* of the laws of war.) In addition to the laws of war, ROE are also informed by political and military considerations, be these sensitivities about civilian casualties, not wanting to offend the 'host' state (in this case Saudi Arabia), or certain restrictions on

[94] Ruppert, interview.
[95] Kansala, interview.

when, where, and what type of weapons should be used. In principle, therefore, the zone of permissible conduct imagined by ROE should be no wider than that understood to be the zone of conduct permissible under the laws of war—but it can be substantially narrower. In an ideal form ROE can be more restrictive but not more permissive than the laws of war. According to Lieutenant Colonel (ret.) John Humphries, the ROE 'were about as broad as they could be [and] extended, in the main, to the bounds of the law of armed conflict'.[96] In claiming this, Humphries is employing the conventional understanding that the laws of war *contain* ROE. He is also making both an empirical and normative claim: The ROE were as broad as they could be (empirical claim), and this is a good thing because it allowed the US military to execute the air war without additional constraints (normative claim).

Schwarzkopf, Horner, and other senior commanders wanted broad latitude when executing the Gulf War and Washington ultimately granted it to them.[97] More than anybody else on the military staff, JAGs understand the content of the laws of war and in this sense if broad ROE that do not contravene the laws of war are what military planners want, then who better to write the ROE than the JAGs themselves? JAGs were entrusted with writing the ROE, then, because they can enable military operations without jeopardizing their legality and legitimacy—crucial components in winning (or at least not losing) wars on the late modern battlefield.

But this conventional understanding assumes that the laws of war are static and have fixed boundaries. In reality, the laws of war are a developing and flexible legal regime with enough elasticity to allow for a variety of interpretations and a variety of ROE (Introduction). In addition to being subject-matter experts in the laws of war, military lawyers are also 'authorized interpreters'[98] well placed to exploit the 'polysemy or the ambiguity of legal formularies'[99] in the creation and development of ROE. The laws of war do not only contain and constrain ROE (though this is what Humphries is suggesting): the laws of war are *constituted* by ROE and standard operating procedures—that is, customary practice—constantly give new meaning and shape to 'operationalized' versions of the laws of war. In fact, Humphries goes on to claim that JAGs who served in the Gulf War sought to change the negative or restraining view of

[96] Humphries, 'Operations Law and the Rules of Engagement in Operation Desert Shield and Desert Storm', no page.

[97] Ibid., Deptula, interview.

[98] Pierre Bourdieu, 'The Force of Law: Toward a Sociology of the Juridical Field', *Hastings Law Journal* 38, no. 5 (1987): 818.

[99] Ibid., 287.

ROE by emphasizing that the latter 'should not unduly impede the effective use of force'.[100]

For veterans now in positions of leadership this proactive approach was partly about applying the lessons of the Vietnam War and correcting for the possibility of repeating its mistakes. Many of the pilots who served in Vietnam had 'misunderstood' the function of ROE and laws of war, according to Colonel (ret.) Dennis Kansala, and they tended to 'over apply' the rules. Colonel Kansala was the CENTAF Staff Judge Advocate and he claims that the airmen seemed more aware of their responsibilities than of their rights under the ROE. He gave the example of a pilot asking him during Desert Storm: 'If we had fired we would have been over Saudi territory by then and that would have been a violation, right?' His answer: 'no'. In short, for Kansala airmen were by now 'more conservative' than the JAGs, and they had to be trained and briefed so that they didn't get the 'wrong impression' about ROE and laws of war.[101]

Kansala's recollections are supported by other accounts. According to Steven Keeva, the memory of restrictive ROE in Vietnam resulted in JAGs in Operation Desert Storm having to 'tell commanders that it was okay to do something the commanders had assumed was illegal'.[102] One JAG gives the example of commanders who assumed that 'a particular type of bomb was required to hit a designated target, a bomb that would limit the possibility of so-called collateral damage, but would require the pilot to fly low over the target'. The JAG's response was that this would have made pilots 'unnecessarily vulnerable' and that he 'had to tell them that they [could] take a more liberal approach'.[103]

With these considerations in mind, the JAGs who wrote and reviewed the ROE for the Gulf War sought to emphasize the right of self-defence. 'THE RIGHT TO USE FORCE IN SELF DEFENSE IS NEVER DENIED!' read the opening line of the 101st Airborne Division ROE (Figure 3.4). The concept of self-defence was by no means new and such clauses are the uncontroversial cornerstone of many military ROE. What was new, seemingly, was the degree of emphasis placed on self-defence and the proactive training given to soldiers that emphasized permissibility of the use of force.

The CENTAF JAGs who wrote the wartime ROE for the air operations 'ensured that the rules were not more restrictive of coalition operations than was

[100] Humphries, 'Operations Law and the Rules of Engagement in Operation Desert Shield and Desert Storm', no page.

[101] Kansala, interview.

[102] Keeva, 'Lawyers in the War Room', 57.

[103] Ibid.

required by the law of armed conflict and collateral limitations'.[104] Major Harry Heintzelman, who was one of two lawyers working in the Black Hole targeting cell, wrote the first version of the CENTAF ROE.[105] According to Kansala (Heintzelman's boss), the first draft of the ROE was eighteen pages long. Typed on 8x8-inch paper, they read like 'a paper for a publication in a journal' and were 'written as though you were going to teach a class on the subject, using examples from bombing chapels in World War Two'. They were impractical and 'way too formalized'. Kansala, as the more senior of the two JAGs but also the one with less expertise in international and operational law ideally wanted 'something that a pilot could put in plastic and maybe tape to his leg when he was flying' but he knew that this was unrealistic. Heintzelman and Kansala went through the first draft of the ROE together and cut them down to four pages.[106] Using shorthand and deleting the examples that were used in the first draft achieved many of the cuts, and using this method, the spirit of the original was left intact 'but just condensed tremendously'.[107] All of this made the ROE much more practical for the aircrews flying missions. Once they were happy with the ROE Kansala forwarded them on to CENTCOM for review. CENTCOM's Staff Judge Advocate Colonel Raymond Ruppert does not recall making any changes to the CENTAF ROE.[108]

Perhaps one of the most telling aspects of the Desert Storm ROE is the short shrift given to the concern for civilian casualties. Drawing on the work of W. Hays Parks (Chapter 2), John Humphries argues that prior to the Gulf War: 'superfluous language in rules of engagement has illogically and without legal foundation elevated the concern for civilian casualties above the desire for mission success and aircrew safety.'[109] Following the Gulf War Humphries reviewed the full ROE files. Contrary to the purportedly heavy restrictions found in the Vietnam War and elsewhere,[110] he found that the 'rules in the Persian Gulf [War] contained none of these cautionary statements' concerning civilian

[104] Humphries, 'Operations Law and the Rules of Engagement in Operation Desert Shield and Desert Storm'.

[105] Heintzelman, interview; Kansala, interview.

[106] Kansala remembered the first draft of the ROE to be around twelve pages, and subsequently shortened to one or two. These recollections are slightly different from the number of pages given by John Humphries (eighteen pages condensed to four), which are likely the more accurate of the two given that Humphries' reading is based on documents from the Air Force Judge Advocate General's Operation Desert Shield/Desert Storm After Action Workshop that took place in Maxwell AFB, Alabama, in June 1991.

[107] Kansala, interview.

[108] Raymond Ruppert, email correspondence, 29 July 2015

[109] Humphries, 'Operations Law and the Rules of Engagement in Operation Desert Shield and Desert Storm'.

[110] W. Hays Parks, 'Rules of Engagement: No More Vietnams', in *The U.S. Naval Institute on Vietnam: A Retrospective*, ed. Thomas Cutler (Annapolis, MD: Naval Institute Press, 2016), 150–5.

casualties. This pleased him immensely because '[t]his kind of language implied that avoiding collateral noncombatant casualties and incidental damage to civilian objects is a *sine qua non* to a lawful air campaign'. In his opinion, however, it was and is not.[111] The fact that the ROE were written in such a way that avoided 'cautionary language'[112] had an impact on the calculations of those who planned and executed the air campaign. As Deptula recalls: 'there were no constraints on targeting other than the one that you internalize: is it a proper military target? Have we taken proper action to minimize collateral damage and civilian casualties?'[113]

As has already been noted, none of this means that the air campaign planners simply disregarded civilian suffering. According to David Deptula, civilian casualties were an 'inherent concern', and the air operation was designed to 'minimize damage and to minimize civilian casualties'.[114] As the chief air campaign planner for Desert Storm Deptula would say that, of course, but it is more accurate to say that the air campaign plan distributed damage and civilian suffering in a bid to compel Iraqis to reject Saddam Hussein's leadership. These 'effects-based operations' may not have aimed at the absolute destruction of a target, but their *raison d'être*, to use Deptula's own words, was to 'spread out the impact across the entire country', and by definition this necessarily entailed the kinds of mass civilian suffering detailed in section 3.1.

3.5 Targeting and the Execution of the Air War

By September 1990, the Black Hole had become the centre of the air campaign targeting process. It was here, in the basement of the Royal Saudi Air Force, where Buster Glosson and David Deptula put together the targeting plan and where the twelve target sets proposed would form the basis of the air campaign (Figure 3.1). Major Harry Heintzelman, a US Air Force JAG with international and operational law experience was on the staff and I interviewed him about his role in the targeting process.

As the single JAG on site, Heintzelman was responsible for reviewing all targeting work and methodology. Prior to the Gulf War Heintzelman had been the head of Horner's international law staff and had participated in training

111 Humphries, 'Operations Law and the Rules of Engagement in Operation Desert Shield and Desert Storm'.
112 Ibid.
113 Deptula, interview.
114 Ibid.

exercises with him in the Middle East. Originally Horner had been sent a different JAG—Lieutenant Colonel William Smith—but apparently their personalities clashed; Smith 'pissed Horner off' and was promptly sent home.[115] We do not have the details as to exactly what happened, but if Horner sent the JAG home because he did not like him or the advice he was giving, this was not a legitimate reason to do so and in breach of protocols. If nothing else, the episode shows just how much personalities matter when it comes to giving legal advice in the midst of combat. As it turned out, Heintzelman and Horner trusted one another, and they worked closely together. Heintzelman did not have a permanent office in the Black Hole because he was also working with Dennis Kansala reviewing CENTCOM targets in another building nearby. Nevertheless, Heintzelman would go to the Black Hole basement every day and would personally inspect the target folders and identify possible legal issues. He was considered a key member of the targeting board meetings in the Black Hole and in addition to his formal duties he would also meet with senior ranking officers to discuss particular targets and 'resolve issues'.

Heintzelman claims that there was a high sensitivity toward collateral damage, especially when dealing with targets that were thought to be—or might contain—weapons of mass destruction. To help minimize collateral damage Heintzelman requested—and frequently received—highly sensitive data and intelligence before he was willing to sign off on a target. It was not unusual for JAGs to have some information about potential targets but Heintzelman won greater access both for himself and his fellow JAGs at 9th and 5th Air Force, the units responsible for 'maintaining' CENTCOM target sets.[116] Today, JAGs enjoy extensive access to classified information on targets (Chapter 5).

After Heintzelman had given the targets what he called the first legal 'scrub' he would carry the list of targets that were planned for execution the following day over to his boss, Dennis Kansala, for a second 'scrub'. Because the targets were already pre-assembled into 'target sets', Kansala describes those targets he reviewed as 'very routine'. The process looked something like this:

> Harry [Heintzelman] would come over and give me the list and I would start at the top. It didn't take me very long to learn what the terminology was and so I had a good grip of what the targets were and that kind of thing. Certainly, if there was anything unusual Harry would say 'this means this' and 'this is why, and here's the reasons why, this is the munitions they'll be using' [. . .]

[115] Heintzelman, interview.
[116] Ibid.

> That went on every day that they flew missions. Of course, we worked 7 days a week so saw them all [the targets] [. . .] I distinctly remember making the note to myself that I wanted to do them all; *no JAG had ever done it that way.* [. . .] *I had an awareness that we might be setting a precedent.*[117]

Occasionally, Kansala would raise questions about a target and would seek clarification from Heintzelman and another JAG on his staff, Bill Smith. Kansala recalls one particular target that was labelled a 'dam' on the targeting sheet, which raised alarm bells for him because of the possible collateral damage that would result downstream: 'What's this? Bombing a dam?', he remembers thinking. After looking into it, Kansala realized that it was not a dam but an irrigation structure over which was a road that was being used to carry arms: he deemed it a legal target, it was struck and there was 'no downstream disaster or flooding to worry about'. On other occasions, important legal questions would come to Kansala's desk in the middle of the night.

In one incident Kansala recalls General Glosson coming to him in person: 'Hey judge, here's what we got: I need to know if this is legal.' Glosson had intelligence on a convoy thought to be carrying Saddam Hussein himself. There were 'a couple parts to that question', Kansala recalls, 'one: can we kill Saddam Hussein? Two: how good does the intelligence have to be?' Everything from the intelligence people on that night was 'good evidence'; the intelligence had been 'reasonably interpreted', and according to Kansala 'a reasonable commander would conclude that it was a lawful target', so Kansala said 'yes'. But Glosson wanted legal cover for his plans and so asked Kansala to put his opinion in writing. Kansala did so and months later he received a note from Glosson to the effect: 'I'm returning your letter. Thank you very much.' Kansala laughs when he tells the story, but it demonstrates the considerable extent to which targeting decisions depended on JAG input. The fact that Glosson wanted the legal opinion in writing shows how potentially controversial the decision to target Saddam Hussein was (or could have been). Glosson is imagining himself being subject to scrutiny after the fact and thus seeks tangible reassurance—a 'get out of jail' card should things go wrong—from Kansala. The convoy never did show up, but if it had, and had the operation gone to plan, the CENTAF Staff Judge Advocate, Dennis Kansala would have played a not insignificant role in killing Saddam Hussein in 1991.[118]

[117] Kansala, interview (emphasis added).
[118] Kansala, interview.

The operators that Kansala and Heintzelman advised confirm their description of the role played by JAGs in the targeting process. Deptula recounts that he saw JAGs as 'an integral part of the process', adding that his 'perspective toward Judge Advocates involved in overseeing and interacting in the targeting process was as *facilitators* and their views and perspectives were always welcome'.[119] The targeting process in the Black Hole was very fluid (as well as highly stressful) and the legal review was kept informal and collegial.[120] As Deptula recalls, their work was integrated with the work of the operators and was woven into the fabric of the targeting process. For example, Heintzelman would often proactively seek and obtain his own intelligence and information, which he then passed on to commanders 'for use in making decisions about what to hit'. He would then ask them, 'Did you know such and such, and will that affect your targeting decision?'[121] As this shows, legal expertise should not be thought of as outside of or separate to military operations or vice versa: legal expertise is contingent on military expertise, and targeting outcomes are produced by a certain symbiosis of juridical-military knowledge and expertise.[122]

Heintzelman and Kansala did not, in fact, look at every target. War planners Horner and Glosson carved Kuwait and south-eastern Iraq into grid squares called 'kill boxes'. Kill boxes are 'three-dimensional cubes of space on a battlefield in which members and allies of the United States military are completely free to open fire'.[123] Kill boxes date back to the Vietnam War (where they were called 'target boxes') but they were formalized in the First Gulf War.[124] Quadrants roughly 350 cubic miles in size were designated by specific coordinates and regularly patrolled.[125] When so-called 'killer scouts' spotted a potential target within the 'kill box' they would direct in strike flights from attack aircraft such as the heavily armed A-10 or F-16; these were called the 'killer bees'.[126] According to Heintzelman, the 'killer bees' did not need to 'call

[119] Deptula, interview (emphasis added).

[120] 'They [JAGs] would review the targeting, but there wasn't any formal meeting': Deptula, interview. 'Our [JAGs] involvement was very unstructured': Kansala, interview,

[121] Keeva, 'Lawyers in the War Room', 58.

[122] Anna Leander and Tanja Aalberts, 'Introduction: The Co-Constitution of Legal Expertise and International Security', *Leiden Journal of International Law* 26, no. 4 (2013): 783–92.

[123] Scott Beauchamp, 'The Moral Cost of the Kill Box', *The Atlantic*, 28 February 2016, https://www.theatlantic.com/politics/archive/2016/02/the-cost-of-the-kill-box/470751/, accessed 9 September 2019.

[124] Derek Gregory, 'Theory of the Drone 3: Killing Grounds', *Geographical Imaginations* (blog), 30 July 2013, https://geographicalimaginations.com/2013/07/29/theory-of-the-drone-3-killing-grounds/, accessed 9 September 2019.

[125] Beauchamp, 'The Moral Cost of the Kill Box'.

[126] Rick Atkinson, *Crusade: The Untold Story of the Persian Gulf War* (Boston, MA: Houghton Mifflin Harcourt, 1993), 218; Richard Hallion, *Storm Over Iraq: Air Power and the Gulf War* (Washington, DC: Smithsonian Institution, 1992).

home' to CENTCOM or CENTAF; they had their own rules and did not need legal permission from Heintzelman or anyone else before they released their weapons.[127] This shows that the same level of juridical review was not given to every target. But this does not mean that kill boxes were somehow devoid or empty of law. Scott Beauchamp argues that kill boxes require a 'sophisticated web of logistical, bureaucratic, and technological expertise to implement', and perhaps more than anything else kill boxes are a *juridical* space for prioritizing the use of lethal force. The kill box acquires its novelty precisely because the normal regulations for the use of force do not apply. Heintzleman and Kansala did not have to review targets in the kill box because force against all targets in the kill box was *a priori* legally sanctioned by the designation of a particular space (and anyone or anything in this space) as a 'kill box'.

3.6 Exceptional Intervention

Try as they might, the planners and executors of the air war could not locate Saddam Hussein. In December 1990 intelligence officers at CENTCOM suggested strikes against two targets in Baghdad: the Victory Arch, an arch of Saddam Hussein's hands holding crossed swords, and a 40-foot statue of Saddam Hussein.[128] The Saddam statue was the same one that US troops famously toppled in the 2003 reinvasion of Iraq. Unlike Saddam Hussein, who was a top priority on the target list because of his centrality to the 'command and control' target set, the statues were on the list for 'psychological warfare purposes'.[129] When Deptula first heard of these target nominations 'he scoffed because of the large number of military targets to hit'[130] but by the end of the war he had changed his mind and wanted to hit the statues in order 'to show that they [the Iraqi leadership] no longer had control of the population, that they had lost control over Baghdad'.[131] Glosson was convinced by Deptula's rationale and so the statues were added to the strike list for the coming days. The story about these statues is important because it represents the only instance that I have been able to unearth where JAG input directly and completely changed the course of a planned targeting operation. What happened with the

[127] Heintzelman, interview.
[128] Putney, *Airpower Advantage*, 298.
[129] Deptula, interview.
[130] Putney, *Airpower Advantage*, 298.
[131] Deptula, interview.

statues was an exceptional intervention—one that many planners and commanders did not at all appreciate.

The statues were nominated by CENTCOM from Washington, which meant that Dennis Kansala, the Staff Judge Advocate at CENTAF who was 'scrubbing' all the Black Hole targets in Riyadh—*but not the CENTCOM targets*—had not seen them.[132] As a courtesy CENTCOM had routinely shared the seventy-two-hour Air Tasking Order and mission planning information with Tactical Air Command (TAC) in Langley. There, the TAC Staff Judge Advocate Scott Silliman, 'looked at the target graphic in the battle staff at Langley prior to the mission being flown' and told his superior, General Mike Ryan, that he, 'wanted to make sure that, even though it was a "category 17" psy-op [psychological operations] target, that someone either in the Pentagon or in Riyadh had screened it [. . .] against the 1954 convention and language in 1907 Hague law about protection of cultural monuments'.[133]

Silliman never suggested that the target was illegal, only that 'it deserved a close look by the lawyers'. He then called Kansala in Riyadh to share his concerns and check whether it had been screened by a JAG in theatre. Kansala had not seen it, nor had Heintzelman so they went over to CENTCOM headquarters to discuss the issue with Ray Ruppert, the CENTCOM Staff Judge Advocate. This was the first that Ruppert had seen or heard of the target, which suggests that the JAGs at CENTCOM were not providing a legal review for all of their targets (as CENTAF were). Ruppert looked at the target 'packet' and also had reservations, though his concerns were different to the issues raised by Silliman back in Langley. The issue for Ruppert was not that the targets were cultural or historical monuments (and therefore protected under the laws of war) but that attacking them appeared to yield no clear military advantage. Ruppert 'did not see any military value or necessity to the target' and so expressed his reservations about it to General Schwarzkopf at a staff meeting.[134] Schwarzkopf still wanted to strike the targets (Ruppert recounts that 'it would be an understatement to say that Schwarzkopf did not like being told he shouldn't do something'),[135] so he called General Horner demanding: '[S]ave me one bomb for the Saddam Hussein statue. I intend to make a personal request to the President.'[136]

132 Silliman, email correspondence, 24 July 2015.

133 Ibid., 24 July 2015.

134 Ruppert, email correspondence, 30 July 2015

135 Schwarzkopf was so displeased with Ruppert's opinion that one general officer who was present at the staff meeting told him as they were walking out that Ruppert 'had more guts than brains': Ruppert, email correspondence, 30 July 2015.

136 H. Norman Schwarzkopf, *It Doesn't Take a Hero: General H. Norman Schwarzkopf, the Autobiography* (New York, NY: Bantam Books, 1992), 68.

Aware of the fact that Schwarzkopf would likely ignore his advice and seek permission from Washington, Ruppert called Colin Powell's office at the Joint Chief of Staff to speak with the chief legal counsel, Colonel Fred Green: 'Fred, we've got this problem. He wants to take down these two statues.'[137] Green agreed with Ruppert's reservations and also added some of his own:

> The possibility of collateral damage is way too high. They're right in the middle of the city. If we did kill a lot of civilians, we'll get beat up on that and it's no longer militarily necessary to take those targets out anyway. You've got the collateral damage argument; you've got the militarily necessary analysis; military necessity no longer plays in; and as an aside, the media and much of the world will certainly challenge us as to whether these are cultural monuments which should be protected. We don't need that kind of a sideshow, so let's not do it.[138]

Green assured Ruppert that he would talk to Colin Powell about the issue. As Green recalls:

> I had a copy of the Hague Regulation in my hand and also the Geneva Cultural Convention. I went in and told General Powell what had gone down that morning and that Norm [Schwarzkopf] still wanted to target those monuments and was not taking his SJA's [Staff Judge Advocate] advice. General Powell started questioning me about the reasoning, 'Why can't we? Why can't we do that?' He really wanted to do it, too, I think. I explained, 'Well, several reasons. It's no longer militarily necessary,' and then I said, 'And we don't need the media hassle we'll get for blowing away these so-called cultural objects.' Then he asked 'You mean to tell me these things might have the same value as the Washington Monument or the Jefferson Monument over here?" and I replied, 'No, that's exactly what I'm telling you, they don't have that kind of significance.' He said, 'Okay. But people would argue that?' I said, 'Yes, but we just need to make that problem go away and not do it,' and then I dropped the collateral damage argument on him and he capitulated. He said, 'Okay, yeah, you're right. I'll go tell [Dick] Cheney.'[139]

[137] Green, 'Oral History', 424.
[138] Ibid.
[139] Ibid., 425–6.

Powell wrote about the episode in his autobiography. He embellished the story a little: 'Colonel Fred Green, my legal advisor, came to see me with a battery of lawyers [. . .] "Sorry, General", Fred said, "you can't touch them." '[140] In Green's version he did not use such strong terms; instead, he remembers *advising* Powell that the whole thing was a bad idea. Nevertheless, it is interesting to note how Powell reports he interpreted such 'advice'; in his mind, Green was showing him the red flag. Perhaps Powell is attempting to give the impression that he and his soldiers were more deferential to law than they really were, or perhaps this is an example of a JAG's advice being interpreted instead as a decision (despite Colin Powell having had the *formal* decision-making power). On either interpretation, the episode illustrates the new-found role of JAGs in targeting operations and the increased power of the appeal to law.

This chain of events reveals something of a chaotic legal geography with varied legal input from multiple locations. But the extended and dispersed geographies of legal advice, together with the negative reaction of some of the commanders involved, also suggest how provisional and precarious legal lines of communication could be. Events which had begun in Langley (with JAG Silliman's initial reservations) and came to a head in Riyadh (the disagreement between Schwarzkopf and JAG Ruppert), eventually reached a conclusion in Washington (involving Powell and JAG Green). The arch and the statue were taken off the target list. Deptula thought it was 'a stupid call. Cultural targets? Really? I mean they were put there by Saddam Hussein [. . .] give me a break'.[141] Glosson was so angry that he called up Silliman's boss, Mike Ryan, in Langley and told him 'he resented the TAC staff getting into CENTAF's business'. Ryan subsequently 'chewed [Silliman] out royally'. In retribution Glosson then 'punished' the TAC battle staff by cutting them out of the loop for seventy-two hours on mission planning information.[142] This adverse reaction by those in charge of executing the air war suggests that they did not like being told that they could not do something by JAGs, and neither were they used to it. That is not all. When Powell explained what had happened to Cheney, the Secretary of Defense, he allegedly shook his head and muttered, 'Lawyers running a war?'[143]

[140] Colin L. Powell and Joseph E. Persico, *My American Journey*, 1st edition (New York, NY: Ballantine Books, 2003), 482.

[141] Deptula, interview.

[142] Silliman, email correspondence, 24 July 2015.

[143] Powell and Persico, *My American Journey*, 483.

3.7 'Routine' Targets

Whatever we make of those exchanges, the most crucial thing to say about the JAGs' intervention here is that it was indeed the exception and not the norm. As Deptula recalls, referring to the statue and the arch, 'that was the only instance that I recall of lawyers being involved in turning something off, otherwise they were much more part of the solution than they were part of the problem'.[144] Deptula's language is troublesome as it implies that military lawyers are part of the solution only when they adopt a permissive stance. In some ways this is not surprising because this is how operational law is designed to work. Operational law and operational lawyers are most effective when they are integrated into the very inception of military operations and are embedded early in the planning process (Chapter 2). In this way, JAGs can influence targeting with legal input without proposing a drastic change later in the process (and given the reaction of the generals and commanders to being told they could not target the statues, it is not difficult to see why JAGs try to involve themselves as early as possible in the targeting process). As Colonel Ruppert put it, 'very few targeting issues arose out of the war [. . .] because for the first time lawyers were inserted in significant numbers into operational planning and execution'.[145]

The analysis so far, however, has shown that military lawyers were *not* involved in the planning of the Instant Thunder target list. It has also shown that very few JAGs were involved in the Black Hole targeting planning process—and one JAG was sent home for reasons that are not entirely clear. The involvement of military lawyers in the planning process cannot be the only reason why, to use Ruppert's words, 'very few targeting issues arose' because they were not especially involved in the planning process. Something else was also at play—something tied to the way in which the overwhelming majority of targets became thought of as legally 'routine', with very few targets perceived as exceptional and therefore worthy of in-depth legal review. As Ruppert reminded me, the statues were 'one target out of literally thousands'.[146] Yet it is remarkable that 'few targeting issue arose' in such a vast and complex war.

In circular fashion the statues came to be understood as exceptional targets because they raised a particular series of legal issues which subsequently required additional levels of legal scrutiny. By intervening in only the exceptional

[144] Deptula, interview.

[145] Ruppert, email correspondence, 30 July 2015. Another plausible explanation could be that for reasons of confidentiality or deference to the chain of command JAGs did not want to disclose information about targeting issues.

[146] Ruppert, email correspondence, 30 July 2015.

cases, military lawyers also helped to produce the threshold between exception and norm. The norm would become legally and operationally routine, more an exercise in bureaucratic green-lighting than critical interventionism. This was war on legal autopilot, where JAGs were called upon only when the commander seemed to be navigating far from the capaciously defined 'flight path'. To further understand how the vast majority of targets became legally and operationally routine, and to unpack some of the consequences this routinization, we now turn to two examples: the bombing of an air raid shelter and the bombing of dual use infrastructures.

One of the more controversial targeting decisions of the Gulf War was the bombing of the Amiriyah air-raid shelter on 13 February 1991. According to Human Rights Watch, the bombing killed between 200 and 300 civilians.[147] The Black Hole had put it on the target list because they had received faulty information that the Iraqi Intelligence service, the Mukhabarat, had relocated to the bunker. Deptula, who did the targeting for the bunker, recalls: 'it turned out to be family members of the secret police who were in there. If we had known that we wouldn't have struck it.'[148] The target had received a double legal 'scrub', the first by Heintzelman in the Black Hole and the second by Kansala at CENTAF Headquarters in Riyadh. They raised no questions about the target. Kansala, who confirms that the team did not know there were civilians inside, considered it a 'legitimate target'. This example raises questions about what constitutes, in legal terms, reasonable interpretation of intelligence and the reliability of intelligence. When we think about lawyers 'scrubbing' targets in the Black Hole we are not talking about judges who are furnished with evidence that is interpreted with 'reasonable certainty' and making decisions in the calm of a courtroom. This is simply not the way that legal advice in the military works in the middle of a combat operation, especially when it comes to targeting, nor could or should it be. Nevertheless, the devastating case of the Amiriyah shelter shows that the involvement of JAGs in targeting augments the ever-present danger in war that untold numbers of civilians could, at any time, be killed. I am not implying that the JAGs who looked at this target did anything wrong procedurally; to the contrary, they approached this target as they would any other. But it seems that this is part of a wider problem. For Kansala, most targets were 'very routine' and so required little in the way of his

[147] Human Rights Watch, 'Needless Deaths in the Gulf War: Civilian Casualties During the Air Campaign and Violations of the Laws of War' (New York, NY, 1991), https://www.hrw.org/reports/1991/gulfwar/index.htm#TopOfPage, accessed 26 June 2017.

[148] Deptula, interview.

intervention. Ruppert too only saw targets that raised particularly important issues and according to him, most did not.[149]

The 'routine' cases may appear seemingly straightforward from a legal perspective but the routinization of legal review, and targeting protocols more broadly, contributes to and is part of the normalization of military violence. That targets come to be understood as routine and as raising no particular legal issue is itself a routinization of violence. The routine target receives a routine legal review; law and target mutually defining one another. It is not the responsibility of the military lawyer to *intervene* in such violence (they are not there to 'turn off' military operations, in Deptula's words); rather, military lawyers participate and are involved in the calibration of what Eyal Weizman has called 'legislative violence', in this case the (accidental) death of hundreds of civilians.[150] This is not a critique of any particular military lawyer; it is a critique of the juridical field of targeting and the violence that is inherent to it. Or perhaps more accurately it is a critique of what Bourdieu identifies as the 'collective work of sublimation' designed to attest that legal interpretations and decisions 'express not the will or the world-view of the judge but the will or the law or the legislature'.[151] This is violence rationed and rationalized by law.

If the Amiriyah shelter was one of the more controversial and accidental episodes during Operation Desert Storm, the bombing of key 'dual use' infrastructures, and especially the disruption of the entire electrical grid, proved to be the most controversial once the bombing had ceased. Part of the reason it was so controversial, in fact, was because it was deliberate. 'Dual use' targets are a deeply contentious and legally fraught issue when it comes to the laws of targeting.[152] Yet, as far as I have been able to discern through an extensive review of the literature and through interviews with several (though admittedly not all) of the military lawyers and operators involved in the execution of the Gulf air war, no serious legal objections were raised by JAGs or operators about targeting Iraq's vital infrastructures.

To be clear: the US military had a valid military reason to attack dual use infrastructures such as electricity production facilities and water treatment facilities and they considered—and in many cases anticipated—at least some of

[149] Ruppert, interview.

[150] Eyal Weizman. 'Legislative Attack'. *Theory, Culture & Society* 27, no. 6 (2010): 11–32.

[151] Bourdieu, 'The Force of Law', 828.

[152] Thomas W. Smith, 'The New Law of War: Legitimizing Hi-Tech and Infrastructural Violence', *International Studies Quarterly* 46, no. 3 (2002): 355–74; Shue, 'Targeting Civilian Infrastructure with Smart Bombs'; Michael N. Schmitt, 'Wired Warfare: Computer Network Attack and Jus in Bello', *International Review of the Red Cross* 84, no. 846 (2002): 365–99.

the civilian cost of doing so.[153] But these are fraught calculations that involve manifold second and third order effects (section 3.1).[154] As Judith Gardam has argued: 'The majority of civilian casualties appear to be the result of targeting objectives which, although apparently serving a military purpose, and thus a legitimate military objective, were also directed at facilities integral to the survival of the civilian population.'[155] One would expect such complex proportionality calculations to raise any number of potential legal questions, especially with regards to anticipated civilian suffering. Proportionality calculations were part of the targeting process, but the crucial questions that remain are around how the perceived military advantage was weighed in relation to anticipated civilian harm and which, and how many, reverberating effects were part of the calculations. The military lawyers and operators that I interviewed talked about these sorts of questions but were quick to point out that they also saw them as posing no particular difficulties in terms of determining the legality of the decisions to target dual use infrastructures.[156] The targeting of dual use infrastructures, though certainly not novel in the First Gulf War, nevertheless became part of an operational and legal routine.

Several scholars have argued that the disruption of Iraq's electric grid served a military purpose but did not honour a reasonable interpretation of the laws of war.[157] Henry Shue claims that the attacks constituted a 'a clear violation' of the First Additional Protocol, Art. 57(3), which reads: 'When a choice is possible between several military objectives for obtaining a similar military advantage, the objective to be selected shall be that the attack on which may be expected to cause the least danger to civilian lives and to civilian objects.'[158] For Shue and others the attack was not proportional because the objective selected was *not* that 'which may be expected to cause the least danger to civilian lives and civilian objects'. This conclusion stems in part from a legal and operational interpretation that suggests either (or both) that the indirect effects of an attack

[153] Gordon, *Invisible War*, 89–90; Crawford, 'Targeting Civilians and U.S. Strategic Bombing Norms', 75–8.

[154] Crawford, 'The Law of Noncombatant Immunity and the Targeting of National Electric Power Systems'; Schmitt, 'Wired Warfare'. Schmitt defines knock-on effects as 'those effects not directly and immediately caused by the attack, but nevertheless the product thereof—it is the problem of the effects caused by the effects of an attack': Ibid., 392.

[155] Gardam, 'Noncombatant Immunity and the Gulf Conflict', 832.

[156] Interviews with Deptula, Kansala, Heintzleman, and Ruppert (Ray).

[157] Matthew Evangelista and Henry Shue, eds., *The American Way of Bombing: Changing Ethical and Legal Norms, from Flying Fortresses to Drones* (Ithaca, NY; London: Cornell University Press, 2014); Gardam, 'Noncombatant Immunity and the Gulf Conflict'; Jochnick and Normand, 'The Legitimation of Violence'.

[158] Henry Shue, 'Force Protection, Military Advantage, and "Constant Care" for Civilians', in *The American Way of Bombing: Changing Ethical and Legal Norms, from Flying Fortresses to Drones*, ed. Matthew Evangelista and Henry Shue (Ithaca, NY; London: Cornell University Press, 2014), 153.

were not fully considered (or were given less weight than direct effects), or that broadly conceived 'war sustaining' efforts were a fair-game military objective. Both seem to have been in play in the decision to disrupt Iraq's electricity.

First, the lack of weight given to indirect effects. In his thoughtful evaluation on the bombing of Iraq's electrical grid, J. W. Crawford suggests that the United States could have used greater restraint and that the extensive damage inflicted upon the civilian population resulted in part from a failure to give due weight to the indirect reverberating effects of the bombing.[159] He criticizes those who claim that the Gulf War was clean and discriminate because they fail to take into account what happened in the weeks, months, and years after the bombing had ceased.[160]

The unwillingness of the United States to consider such long-term effects, Rob Nixon argues, marks a major gap in how we think about war casualties. He takes aim at US practice in the First Gulf War and in particular the extensive and frequently downplayed use of 'depleted' uranium weapons:[161]

> [W]e have an ethical obligation to challenge the military body counts that consistently underestimate (in advance and in retrospect) the true toll of waging high-tech wars. Who is counting the staggered deaths that civilians and soldiers suffer from depleted uranium ingested or blown across the desert? [. . .] Who is counting deaths from chemical residues left behind by so-called pinpoint bombing, residues that turn into foreign insurgents, infiltrating native rivers and poisoning the food chain? [Environmental casualties . . .] may suffer slow, invisible deaths that don't fit the news cycle at CNN or Fox, but they are war casualties nonetheless.[162]

Since the First Gulf War there have been some developments towards institutionalizing the calculation of indirect effects within the US military.[163] After

[159] Crawford, 'The Law of Noncombatant Immunity and the Targeting of National Electric Power Systems'.

[160] 'Targeting considerations must extend beyond direct effects. Collateral damage, by legal definition, must include a requirement to examine the reverberative effects of military action. Every target set is different, but some targets (like electricity), due to the potential for long-term effects, demand that collateral damage be considered with a significantly broader view.' Ibid., 114, quoted in: Shue, 'Force Protection, Military Advantage, and "Constant Care" for Civilians', 154–5.

[161] As Nixon insists 'depleted' is a euphemism for a substance possessing 60 per cent of natural uranium's radioactivity: 'Depleted uranium (DU) possesses a durability beyond our comprehension: it had a radioactive half-life of 4.51 billion years. When it enters the environment, DU effectively does so for all time, with consequences that are resistant to military metrics, consequences that we are incompetent to judge.' Nixon, *Slow Violence and the Environmentalism of the Poor*, 201.

[162] Ibid.

[163] Henry Shue provides a useful overview of some of these developments: Shue, 'Force Protection, Military Advantage, and "Constant Care" for Civilians', 155–6.

all, As Henry Shue has pithily argued: 'To ignore reverberative effects is to deny a big chunk of reality.'[164] But such realities were, if not entirely ignored, certainly insufficiently acknowledged in the decision to target Iraq's electrical grid. Again, to my knowledge, JAGs raised no significant objections to the bombing of dual use infrastructures in the Gulf air war. Either the full extent of the devastation was not anticipated, or it was anticipated but not opposed.

Second, the expansion of targets to include 'war sustaining objects'. Janina Dill explains how by the late 1990s the US definition of a military object defied international consensus and particularly the understanding of a military object advanced by the First Additional Protocol Art. 52(2). Her analysis is particularly perceptive and bears on my analysis in important ways, so is worth quoting at length:

> [...] in the 1997 'Field Manual on the Joint Targeting Process' a new criterion to assess the significance of a mission emerged: 'war-sustaining.' The document asks whether an attack or an operation reduces the enemy's ability to 'sustain the war effort.' The Joint Doctrine for Targeting of 2002 draws on the term war-sustaining to explain the definition of military objectives. The term then forms part of this definition in Military Commission Instruction No. 2 of 2003. Military objectives are therein defined as objects that 'effectively contribute to the opposing force's war-fighting or war-sustaining capability,' as opposed to the Protocol's criterion of 'an effective contribution to military action.' This new formulation suggests that a direct link to the competition between two militaries is not the only way an object can become a military objective. Another way is to contribute to an enemy's 'war-sustaining capability.' The military advantage that may ultimately arise has only an indirect connection to such attacks.[165]

This logic of 'war-sustaining' objects was explicitly used by Air Force planners to justify the attacks on Iraq's infrastructure, but as we saw in section 3.1, the definition also seemed to encompass the Iraqi population at large. Recall Deptula's claim that Iraqi suffering was a consequence of their 'allowing' Saddam Hussein, a dictator, to stay in power. But the evidence also suggests

[164] Ibid., 156.

[165] Janina Dill, 'The American Way of Bombing and International Law: Two Logics of Warfare in Tension', in *The American Way of Bombing: Changing Ethical and Legal Norms, from Flying Fortresses to Drones*, ed. Matthew Evangelista and Henry Shue (Ithaca, NY; London: Cornell University Press, 2014), 135–6. Henry Shue traces similar developments in US military doctrine and draws parallels with US strategic and morale bombing in the 1950s: Shue, 'Targeting Civilian Infrastructure with Smart Bombs'.

that there was a deliberate blurring of civilian and military worlds in order to justify attacks that had devastating impacts on the former. As one anonymous Air Force officer told the *Washington Post* shortly after the war was over: 'The definition of innocents gets to be a little bit unclear', noting that many Iraqis supported the invasion of Kuwait: 'They do live there, and ultimately the people have some control over what goes on in their country.' Another officer insisted how strategic bombing permits strikes against 'all those things that allow a nation to sustain itself'.[166]

I recount these two legal-operational interpretations—the lack of weight given to indirect effects and the expansive definition of a military object—because they were crucial in providing a legal justification and rationalization for the bombing of 'dual use' infrastructures. In describing some of the literature that criticizes the complete disruption of Iraq's electrical grid, and in particular detailing how some scholars argue that the bombing was in contravention of the laws of war, I hope to have shown (a) that another interpretation was possible; and (b) that the law proved malleable enough to allow for both (seemingly contradictory) legal interpretations. The military lawyers who served in the First Gulf War performed vital interpretive work that made a particular type of targeting possible. They provided a legal review of many—if not all—targets, they informed commanders of what they could and could not strike from a legal point of view, and they intervened in the exceptional case where the statue targets appeared too politically and legally risky.

But generally speaking, JAG input and legal advice did not typically intervene in the pattern of violence; it was instead a constitutive part of it. When JAGs were part of the problem rather than the solution (in Deptula's words), the generals and commanders who they advised were less than happy. Indeed, according to one source, Glosson 'even considered having a judge advocate transferred out of the Black Hole' because he did not 'consider the attorney to be a credible staff officer'.[167] This is in addition to the JAG that Horner sent home because of a 'clash of personality' (section 3.6).

The JAG Corps made huge inroads into the operational world during the Gulf War. As we have seen, they were far better equipped to deal with an unprecedented range of legal issues than they had been in previous wars. JAGs prepared national level policy statements and advised on the overarching strategic legalities that would define the US reaction to the Iraqi invasion of Kuwait

[166] Anonymous Air Force officers, quoted in: Gellman, 'Allied Air War Struck Broadly in Iraq: Officials Acknowledge Strategy Went beyond Purely Military Targets'.

[167] Myrow, 'Waging War on the Advice of Counsel', 153.

and, ultimately, the direction of the Gulf War. As for operational law, JAGs were instrumental in drafting and reviewing the ROE and, for the first time ever, at least as far as CENTAF were concerned, JAGs 'scrubbed' every single target before it was struck.

Some of the very JAGs who did these things look back not on a 'lawyer's war', as Keeva would have it, but one in which lawyers played roles of modest and varying significance. Colonel Fred Green, Colin Powell's legal adviser, saw much of what has been made of the lawyers' contribution as hyperbole, or what he calls 'lawyer puffery'. 'This is lawyers beating their own drum', he told me. Other JAGs corroborated Green's observations. Kansala 'didn't find anything profound or unique that we [JAGs] did that impacted on the effort'. Instead, he 'viewed it as an opportunity to show how good the American armed forces could be in setting up a mission, planning a deployment and execution a mission as flawlessly as possible'. He 'sure as hell did not want a bunch of lawyers getting in the way of what [he] felt was a great opportunity to do good'.[168]

Colonel Ruppert expressed a similar sentiment in terms of the modest contribution made by JAGs: 'I can't represent to you what I did as changing the course of operations' but he also viewed the main contribution of JAGs in somewhat more normative and philosophical terms:

> War is an inherent ugly business, an obscene business and by having lawyers involved what we were able to do was to keep it within some degree of bounds. [. . .] What lawyers did was advise the commanders what the rules were. I'm talking not just targeting but across the board. When you do that, by God, I think it helps. [. . .] [it] helps the US to obtain, in this particular case, the high moral ground. [. . .] When you don't follow the rules, you pay a tremendous price. You pay a tremendous price within the unit that is not following the rules, you pay a tremendous price on the national level and you pay a tremendous price on the international level and that is what I think the lawyers were able to do in the Gulf War, is to ensure that to the best of everyone's ability, the rules were followed and at the end of that, you not only had a victory but you had a clean victory.[169]

There is a palpable slippage between law and morality in both Kansala's and Ruppert's account, one that I encountered regularly in my conversations with US and Israeli military lawyers (Chapters 4–6). The slippage equates the law (or

[168] Kansala, interview.
[169] Ruppert, interview.

here, projection of US military power) with the good and rule-based conduct with morality. Legal rules are supposed to lay a path to higher moral ground. Yet holding the higher moral (and legal) ground is a geopolitical and military posture: here, 'paying a price' is scripted in strategic terms. When the rules are not followed it is the United States that loses ground; the loss of legitimacy on domestic and international fronts rather than the populations who have been killed and injured. If the United States is inherently a force for good then, when the United States loses ground, so does 'doing good'.

But given what I have argued in this chapter, it is not easy to discern the link between US action in the Gulf War and the 'high moral ground' that Ruppert sees the United States as occupying. There is plenty within the laws of war that would strike many of us as deeply immoral. The bombing of the electrical grid is a prime example of how law and morality might become detached or how both might be put to belligerent ends.[170] Giving targets a legal 'scrub'—in the Gulf War and elsewhere—routinizes the legality of targeting; it also cleanses modes of warfare that might otherwise appear, to use Colonel Ruppert's words, a little more 'ugly' and 'obscene'.

[170] On the weaponization of ethics, see: Eastwood, *Ethics as a Weapon of War*; Maja Zehfuss, *War and the Politics of Ethics* (Oxford: Oxford University Press, 2018).

4

Targeting Gaza

The Israeli Military and the Expansion of the Target

4.1 Targeted Killing and Legal Advice

This chapter examines how Israeli military lawyers came to play an important role in targeting operations and in particular the emergence of what has become known as 'targeted killing' policy. As part of a proactive juridical approach to the Second Intifada, Israeli military lawyers became instrumental in devising new legal concepts and categories designed to expand the definition of who and what constitutes a lawful military target. As I pointed out in the Introduction, targeted killing focuses exclusively on the killing of *individuals* (as distinct from both objects and the more generalized form of the 'enemy', who are a collective).[1] The advent of targeted killing in the early 2000s helped to create a new paradigm of Israeli warfare, and it played no small part in paving the way for legal input from lawyers on targeting in the Israeli military.

As we saw at the close of Chapter 2, these developments drew, in part, from US operational law, and in particular the invasion of Panama (according to Daniel Reisner). As we shall see, influences have also run in the return direction: the putative 'legal right to kill' as asserted by Israel was subsequently adopted, and later expanded, by the United States. The targeting of Iranian Major General Qassem Soleimani, killed in a US drone strike in Baghdad in January 2020, represented a particularly bold assertion of this legal right to kill but the United States has targeted and killed thousands of others using the same rationale over the last nearly two decades.[2]

* * *

[1] Nils Melzer defines targeted killing as 'the use of lethal force attributable to a subject of international law with the intent, premeditation and deliberation to kill *individually selected persons* who are not in the physical custody of those targeting them'. Nils Melzer, *Targeted Killing in International Law* (Oxford; New York, NY: Oxford University Press, 2009), 5 (emphasis added). There are important nuances to this definition but the crucial point is that targeted killing is a specific kind of targeting.

[2] The Bureau of Investigative Journalism, 'Drone Warfare'; Lawfare Blog, 'Civilian Casualties & Collateral Damage', Lawfare Blog, 28 January 2013, https://www.lawfareblog.com/civilian-casualties-collateral-damage, accessed 4 March 2020.

The War Lawyers. Craig Jones, Oxford University Press (2020). © Craig Jones.
DOI: 10.1093/oso/9780198842927.001.0001.

On the morning of 9 November 2000, Israeli Air Force helicopters could be heard above the Palestinian village of Beit Sahour, near Bethlehem. Then came the explosion. Sitting in his unarmoured Jeep, Hussein Abiyat, a senior member of the Palestinian political party Fatah, was torn to pieces. The anti-tank missile that killed Abiyat also killed two elderly women who happened to be nearby. Later that day, the Israeli military publicly assumed responsibility for the strike: 'During an operation initiated by the IDF [Israel Defense Force], near the village of Beit Sahour, missiles were launched from Air Force helicopters towards the vehicle of a senior activist of the Fatah Tanzim. The pilots reported an accurate hit. The activist was killed and his deputy, who was with him, was injured.'[3] No mention was made of the elderly women. Aside from this omission, the announcement is significant because it marked the beginning of Israel's *official* assassination policy, what would become known as targeted killing. Paramilitary Jewish groups had carried out political assassinations during the British mandate period (1939–1947), and state-sponsored assassination continued with remarkable frequency under the structure of the Israeli state from 1948 through to the 1990s.[4] What was different about the assassination of Hussein Abiyat was that the Israeli military admitted responsibility.

By carrying out the attack openly on Abiyat the Israeli military was also asserting that it had the legal right to kill Palestinian leaders and individuals: it was authorizing assassination and attempting to bring it within the law. According to military lawyers involved in these legal manoeuvres, these attacks were something different. Their contention was that Israel was now engaged in what they called an 'armed conflict short of war'—a legal term of art—and the military was now therefore legally entitled to target and kill enemy individuals.[5] This assertion would henceforth involve military lawyers in providing legal advice on Israel's targeting operations on a full-time basis.

[3] Public Committee Against Torture in Israel (PCATI) and LAW—Society for the Protection of Human Rights and the Environment, Assassination Policy Petition (BGZ/02 2002).

[4] Nachman Ben-Yehuda, *Political Assassinations by Jews a Rhetorical Device for Justice* (Albany, NY: State University of New York Press, 1993); Ronen Bergman, *Rise and Kill First: The Secret History of Israel's Targeted Assassinations* (London: John Murray, 2018); Markus Gunneflo, *Targeted Killing: A Legal and Political History* (Cambridge: Cambridge University Press, 2016); Yossi Melman, 'Targeted Killings—a Retro Fashion Very Much in Vogue—Features', *Haaretz.Com*, 24 March 2004, http://www.haaretz.com/print-edition/features/targeted-killings-a-retro-fashion-very-much-in-vogue-1.117714, accessed 2 October 2014; Dan Raviv and Yossi Melman, *Every Spy a Prince: The Complete History of Israel's Intelligence Community* (Boston, MA: Houghton Mifflin, 1990).

[5] George Mitchell et al., 'Sharm El-Sheikh Fact-Finding Committee' (Washington, DC: US Department of State, 30 April 2001), http://2001-2009.state.gov/p/nea/rls/rpt/3060.htm, accessed 29 September 2015.

Israeli military lawyers were involved in providing ad hoc legal advice on targeting operations prior to 2000 but these were covert and classified operations—'they never took place'—and lawyers' involvement was the exception, not the rule. Military lawyers in Israel were understandably reluctant to provide details, but one recalled:

> As part of my career in the army I encountered several different incidents where suddenly I was called in for an operational meeting to give advice on the rules of engagement. But it was always a special operation. So, for example, I will never forget . . . I think in the late 1980s, the Palestinians [. . .] came up with this PR idea of bringing in a ship with deported Palestinian terrorists back to the Promised Land; it was full of media coverage. It was called 'The Ship of the Deported', and they planned to sail to Israel and then come aboard with all the journalists of the world. CNN had just come on air in [19]88 so it was a new idea to do a public media stunt world-wide. And there was a planning committee. The IDF wanted to do a response to this. I won't go into the operational details. [. . .] 'And what do you do in areas A,B,C, and D?'[6] was a legal question, but no one knew the answer, so they said 'let's bring in a lawyer for this one'. [. . .] At the end of the day the ship never sailed because it had a mishap. A bomb exploded in its engine compartment in Cyprus, and it sank. I wonder how that happened [laughter] [. . .] without anyone on board, by the way. But the bottom line was that that was the first time that I encountered the reality that in really complicated situations the army doesn't have a clue.[7]

Once the targeted killing policy was in place, the ad hoc amateurishness referred to here was overcome. The Israeli military were prepared to publicly and openly assassinate individuals, backed up with day-to-day legal advice.

4.2 Institutional Context: Law and Occupation

Military lawyers in Israel are not new. The modern Military Advocate General's Corps (MAG Corps) developed from the legal service of the *Haganah*, a Jewish paramilitary organization in what was then the British Mandate of Palestine (1920–1948).[8] In 1948, under the auspices of the State of Emergency

[6] This is not a reference to the administrative areas of the West Bank under the Oslo II Accords.

[7] Anonymous Israeli military lawyer #1, interview.

[8] 'The Haganah, aiming to operate as an army, tried cases of alleged unlawful conduct in courts, with its members serving as prosecutors and defenders': Maayan Geva, 'Military Lawyers Making Law: Israel's Governance of the West Bank and Gaza', *Law & Social Inquiry* 44, no. 3 (2019): 708.

Regulations, the *Haganah* legal services were formalized into the Israeli military, becoming known as the Legal Services Corps.[9] With the passing of the Military Justice Act in 1956 the Legal Services Corps was renamed the MAG Corps. Its goal, in partnership with military commanders, remains to 'promote justice and the integration of the rule of law within the army; and with determination that stems from striving for excellence in order to bring the IDF to full success on the legal front'.[10] Such 'success' requires MAG lawyers—who today number around 300[11]—to perform a number of tasks pertaining to four primary functions: (1) The enforcement of military justice and disciplinary issues; (2) the provision of legal advice 'to the Chief of Staff and all divisions of the military in areas relating to military, domestic and international law'; (3) the writing of military legislation and policy, including the drafting and promulgation of the military orders that govern Gaza and 'Judea and Samaria' (i.e. the Occupied Palestinian Territories); and (4) Legal education and training, which includes the Israel Defense Force School of Military Law.[12]

The simultaneous disciplinary and advisory roles of the MAG are problematic because they lead to a conflict of interest and lack of independence, or what one Israeli military lawyer refers to as 'double hatting'.[13] Israeli human rights organization B'Tselem raised concerns about the model during the investigation of suspected Israeli violations of the laws of war in the 2014 assault on Gaza, so-called 'Operation Protective Edge':

> On one hand, the MAG gives legal counsel to the military before and during combat; on the other hand, he is responsible for deciding whether to open criminal investigations into soldiers' conduct. This dual role creates an inherent conflict of interests in cases where orders and commands given following the MAG's counsel raise suspicion that the law was breached. In these situations, *the MAG— who was responsible for legally authorizing measures suspected of being unlawful—is charged with retrospectively deciding whether to initiate a criminal investigation into his own conduct and that of his subordinates.*[14]

[9] Military Advocate General of the Israel Defense Force, 'The MAG Corps—History', n.d. Source with similar information available at: https://www.idf.il/en/minisites/military-advocate-generals-corps/about-the-mag-corps/, accessed 30 June 2020.

[10] Military Advocate General of the Israel Defense Force, 'The MAG Corps— Mission', n.d.

[11] Mandelblit, interview.

[12] Military Advocate General of the Israel Defense Force, 'The MAG Corps—Mission'.

[13] Liron A. Libman, 'Legal Advice in the Conduct of Operations in the Israel Defense Forces', *Military Law and Law of War Review* 50, nos. 1–2 (2011): 68.

[14] B'Tselem, 'Investigation of Incidents That Took Place during Recent Military Action in Gaza: July-August 2014', 4 September 2014, https://www.btselem.org/download/201400904_15390_letter_to_

Accordingly, leading Israeli human rights organizations refused in 2014 to provide information to the MAG concerning incidents in which Israeli war crimes may have been committed.[15]

The advice branch of the MAG is split into three departments: The Advice and Legislation Department, legal adviser for Judea and Samaria,[16] and the International Law Department. My focus in this chapter is on the legal advice aspect of MAG work and the provision of legal advice in targeting operations, specifically through the International Law Department. As the Department has grown, its lawyers have become more influential and more widely respected; the International Law Department now holds a 'very important place in key military decision making'.[17]

This is not to suggest that legal advice and operational law are the only mechanisms through which lives in the Occupied Palestinian Territories are—in Judith Butler's phrase—'rendered killable':[18] broader ideological and policy factors are clearly at work. (In March 2017 the United Nations Economic and Social Commission for Western Asia reported, 'available evidence establishes beyond a reasonable doubt that Israel is guilty of policies and practices that constitute the crime of apartheid as legally defined in instruments of international law.'[19]) By the same token, nor are legal advice and the juridification of the kill chain the sole means of rendering military operations more effective and legitimate. Targeting advice in the Israeli military should be understood as working in concert with a series of legitimacy-producing discourses and technologies that include, *inter alia*, the permissive doctrines written and developed by Asa Kasher (military ethicist and 'moral conscience' of the Israeli military) and former Air Force General Amos Yadlin. Strikingly, the Israeli military claim to be 'the most moral army in the world' but not 'the most legal army in the world'.[20] Thus for James Eastwood:

mag_corps_regarding_protective_edge_investiations_eng.pdf, accessed 2 October 2014 (emphasis added).

[15] Ibid.

[16] Judea and Samaria are biblical terms for the occupied West Bank. This is a Zionist assertion that these lands belong to the Jewish people and thus to the Israeli state.

[17] Benjamin, interview. The International Law Department has existed in its present form since the early 1990s when it consisted of only a handful of lawyers. Today, the International Law Department has grown into a unit of about thirty–thirty-five lawyers, plus support staff and around thirty reservists (who are drafted during the planning, execution, and investigation phases of larger operations).

[18] Judith Butler, *Precarious Life: The Powers of Mourning and Violence* (London: Verso, 2006).

[19] United Nations Economic and Social Commission for Western Asia, 'Israeli Practices towards the Palestinian People and the Question of Apartheid' (Beirut: United Nations, 2017), 1, https://www.unescwa.org/news/escwa-launches-report-israeli-practices-towards-palestinian-people-and-question-apartheid, accessed 26 June 2017.

[20] Asa Kasher and Amos Yadlin, 'Military Ethics of Fighting Terror: An Israeli Perspective', *Journal of Military Ethics* 4, no. 1 (2005): 3–32; Avishai Margalit and Michael Walzer, 'Israel: Civilians &

> Rather than providing a means for the restraint of military violence, ethics has become part of an arrangement which makes violence easier for the military to commit. [. . .] ethics can in fact offer powerful support to militarism at a number of levels. Indeed, under certain conditions, ethics can function as a weapon of war.[21]

The turn to 'precision weapons' and 'surgical strikes'—which is at once both substantive and rhetorical—enables advanced militaries like Israel's to claim that weapons technologies are improving at such a rate that they can measurably reduce the scope of 'collateral damage' and thus minimize civilian casualties.[22] To this should be added Israel's court systems—both civilian and military;[23] as I will show, the Israel Supreme Court in its capacity as the High Court of Justice lent great weight to the legality of targeted killing in its controversial decision on the matter in 2006. The obvious yet crucial point is that law and operational legal advice have been one of the many ways that Israel has

Combatants', *The New York Review of Books*, 14 May 2009, http://www.nybooks.com/articles/archives/2009/may/14/israel-civilians-combatants/, accessed 11 February 2014; James Eastwood, '"Meaningful Service": Pedagogy at Israeli Pre-Military Academies and the Ethics of Militarism', *European Journal of International Relations* 22, no. 3 (2016): 671–95; James Eastwood, 'Ethics in the Service of Violence in Israel/Palestine', *The Disorder Of Things* (blog), 23 October 2015, https://thedisorderofthings.com/2015/10/23/ethics-in-the-service-of-violence-in-israelpalestine/, accessed 4 January 2017.

[21] James Eastwood, *Ethics as a Weapon of War: Militarism and Morality in Israel* (Cambridge: Cambridge University Press, 2017), 3

[22] In an article published on the blog of the Israel military entitled 'State of the art technology helps minimize harm to civilians', Noam Witman quotes a retired Major General: 'From operation to operation the IDF succeeds in significantly decreasing harm to civilians, something which is allowed for by evolving technology and measures that we did not have in the past': Noam Witman, 'State of the Art Technology Helps Minimize Harm to Civilians', *Israel Defense Force* (blog), 2 June 2013. For a critique of this position see: Marc Herold, 'The "Unworthy" Afgan Bodies: "Smarter" U.S. Weapons Kill More Innocents', in *Inventing Collateral Damage: Civilian Casualties, War, and Empire*, ed. Stephen J. Rockel and Rick Halpern (Toronto: Between the Lines, 2009), 303–28; Maja Zehfuss, 'Targeting: Precision and the Production of Ethics', *European Journal of International Relations* 17, no. 3 (2011): 543–66.

[23] In his study of the jurisprudence of the Israel Supreme Court, David Kretzmer argues, 'the main function of the Court has been to legitimize government actions in the Territories. By clothing acts of military authorities in a cloak of legality, the Court justifies and rationalizes these acts': David Kretzmer, *The Occupation of Justice: The Supreme Court of Israel and the Occupied Territories* (Albany, NY: State University of New York Press, 2002), 2. See also: Orna Ben-Naftali and Noam Zamir, 'Whose "Conduct Unbecoming"? The Shooting of a Handcuffed, Blindfolded Palestinian Demonstrator', *Journal of International Criminal Justice* 7, no. 1 (2009): 155–75; Orna Ben-Naftali, Aeyal Gross, and Keren Michaeli, 'The Illegality of the Occupation Regime: The Fabric of Law in the Occupied Palestinian Territory', in *The Power of Inclusive Exclusion: Anatomy of Israeli Rule in the Occupied Palestinian Territories*, ed. Adi Ophir, Michal Givoni, and Sari Hanafi (New York, NY: Zone Books, 2009), 31–88; Aeyal M. Gross, 'The Construction of a Wall between the Hague and Jerusalem: The Enforcement and Limits of Humanitarian Law and the Structure of Occupation', *Leiden Journal of International Law* 19, no. 2 (2006): 393–440; Lisa Hajjar, *Courting Conflict: The Israeli Military Court System in the West Bank and Gaza* (Berkeley, CA: University of California Press, 2005); David Kretzmer, 'The Law of Belligerent Occupation in the Supreme Court of Israel', *International Review of the Red Cross* 94, no. 885 (2012): 207–236.

lent legitimacy to the occupation and, more recently, its assassination policy as well. Only by taking this comprehensive view can we adequately weigh claims such as Colonel Liron Libman's (former head of the International Law Department): 'If you look at it simply, the lawyer is the stick in the wheel, stopping the machine [. . .] the person who slows things down.'[24]

* * *

Orna Ben-Naftali and her colleagues write that the story of occupation in Palestine 'had been framed by law even before it became a fact of power' in 1967. They claim that, 'already in the early 1960s, the then military advocate-general—and eventually chief justice of the Israeli Supreme Court—Meir Shamgar, had designed the legal framework within which the Israeli Defense Forces (IDF) were to exercise their power as an occupier'.[25] The preparations for the still-ongoing occupation were not made in a vacuum, and Israel was no stranger to military government when it seized the West Bank and Gaza in 1967, having imposed it over Palestinians from October 1948 to December 1967 and having also occupied Gaza from 1956 to 1957. Zertal and Eldar point out that:

> [D]espite the differences in the nature of control in the two instances [1948–1967 and post 1967], Israel could transfer to the newly conquered territories the experience and know-how that had been accumulated during the eighteen years of military rule in Israel, including the large systems of control and intelligence that were shaped in its framework; but most important the culture and mentality of military occupation of a civilian population.[26]

By 1967 scores of officers had been trained by the MAG's office in the laws of war and occupation; the 'simulation games' in which they honed their skills created what Shamgar called 'a trained reservoir of forces from within which it was possible to organise the units for action during times of war'.[27] In addition:

[24] Libman, interview.

[25] Ben-Naftali, Gross, and Michaeli, 'The Illegality of the Occupation Regime: The Fabric of Law in the Occupied Palestinian Territory', 44.

[26] Idith Zertal and Akiva Eldar, *Lords of the Land: The War over Israel's Settlements in the Occupied Territories, 1967-2007* (New York, NY: Nation Books, 2007), 432. See also: Nur Masalha, 'The 1956-57 Occupation of the Gaza Strip: Israeli Proposals to Resettle the Palestinian Refugees', *British Journal of Middle Eastern Studies* 23, no. 1 (1996): 55–68.

[27] Zertal and Eldar, *Lords of the Land*, 432.

> Specific officers were designated by name for key posts in the establishment of military occupation in the territories, and emergency boxes were prepared for the MAG units that included basic volumes on military occupation theory, among them Shamgar's own book, *The Military Guide for the Member of the Military Prosecution in Military Government*.[28]

All of this was done before any bullets were fired. This is noteworthy because it shows a level of preparedness by the MAG that in many ways pre-empted the realities on the ground at the time. As Azoulay and Ophir point out, the early deployment of an administrative and legal apparatus also calls into question the 'commonly held narrative presenting the Occupation as an event that took Israel by surprise'.[29]

According to Zertal and Eldar, squads from the military prosecution accompanied the Israeli forces in the war of 1967: 'These teams set up courts; gave legal advice; and issued notices, orders, and announcements that had been prepared in advance to calm the conquered territory and take control of it.'[30] One of these notices, a 'general staff ordinance', decreed that Israel would observe the provisions of the Fourth Geneva Convention of 1949 relating to civilian populations during wartime, but this was soon rescinded and replaced by a claim that the convention does not apply.[31] The basis for the claim was that the Territories were not formally occupied but rather 'administered', a radical legal (re)interpretation not least because the Fourth Convention effectively bans colonization and asserts the inalienable right to sovereignty and self-determination of colonized peoples and establishes their right to resist. This was therefore a way for Israel to relieve itself of the humanitarian obligations conferred by occupation while also maintaining effective military control of the Territories. This legal blueprint—military control without full legal responsibility—is still implemented today, even though its precise contours have changed, and the legal position has never been accepted internationally. Nevertheless, the legal preparation for 1967 and the early execution of military

[28] Ibid.

[29] Ariella Azoulay and Adi Ophir, *The One-State Condition: Occupation and Democracy in Israel/Palestine* (Stanford, CA: Stanford University Press, 2012), 4.

[30] Zertal and Eldar, *Lords of the Land*, 433. In the war of 1967, Israel seized control of the Gaza Strip and the Sinai Peninsula from Egypt, the West Bank, and East Jerusalem from Jordan, and the Golan Heights from Syria. The Sinai was returned in 1982—and the Golan effectively annexed—but Gaza, the West Bank, and East Jerusalem remain occupied.

[31] The Supreme Court has applied the humanitarian principles of the Geneva Conventions on the basis of the 'willingness of the state—rather than its legal obligation—to abide by these provisions'. Such a position is designed to elicit legitimacy without the formal legal obligations and constraints: Ben-Naftali, Gross, and Michaeli, 'The Illegality of the Occupation Regime: The Fabric of Law in the Occupied Palestinian Territory', 44.

proclamations in the Occupied Palestinian Territories is celebrated today on the MAG Corps website as its 'finest hour'.[32]

A second decision, taken in 1968 by Meir Shamgar in his new capacity as Attorney General, mandated that the Israel Supreme Court be given power to review the actions of military authorities in the West Bank and Gaza. This meant that all military procedures, as well as legal opinions written by the MAG, became subject to judicial review; more importantly, it constituted an annexation of those territories taken in 1967. The annexation also granted the populations under Israeli control the legal right to appeal to the highest judicial authority in Israel, but those rights came at the expense of the *imposition of Israeli rule*.[33] The MAG made no opposition to judicial oversight of the military.[34] Even after thirty years of occupation, which brought untold violence with it, Shamgar looked back on the decision to allow Palestinian petitions in Israeli courts as an international innovation that 'even enlightened countries like the United States and Britain' did not follow.[35]

Far from guaranteeing the rights of Palestinians, however, the court has rejected over 99 per cent of Palestinian petitions and the main function of the court has been to legitimize military activities in the Occupied Palestinian Territories.[36] Nimer Sultany writes:

> Under the all-seeing eye of the judicial review exercised by the ISC [Israel Supreme Court] [. . .] a sophisticated system of oppression has developed in the Occupied Palestinian Territories. Confiscation of land and colonization (allowing the population of the occupier to settle in the occupied territory);

[32] Military Advocate General of the Israel Defense Force, 'The MAG Corps—History'.

[33] There is debate as to whether Palestinian legal advocacy and petitions to Israeli courts legitimizes the occupation or challenges it. See: George E. Bisharat, 'Courting Justice? Legitimation in Lawyering under Israeli Occupation', *Law & Social Inquiry* 20, no. 2 (1995): 349–405; Hassan Jabareen, 'Transnational Lawyering and Legal Resistance in National Courts: Palestinian Cases Before the Israeli Supreme Court', *Yale Human Rights and Development Journal* 13, no. 1 (2010): 239–80; Nimer Sultany, 'The Legacy of Justice Aharon Barak: A Critical Review', *Harvard International Law Journal Online* 48 (2007): 83–92.

[34] Amichai Cohen, 'Legal Operational Advice in the Israeli Defense Forces: The International Law Department and the Changing Nature of International Humanitarian Law', *Connecticut Journal of International Law* 26, no. 2 (2011): 367–413. The MAG would later celebrate the judicial oversight of the military as a triumph of legal liberalism: '[J]udicial review by Israel's highest Court has not only provided a form of redress for the grievances of Area inhabitants and a safeguard for their rights; it has also provided a powerful symbol and reminder to the officials of the Military Government and Civil Administration of the supremacy of law and legal institutions and of the omnipresence of the Rule of Law wherever Israeli officials' writ may run': MAG, quoted in: Kretzmer, *The Occupation of Justice*, 2.

[35] Quoted in: Zertal and Eldar, *Lords of the Land*, 344.

[36] Ben-Naftali, Gross, and Michaeli, 'The Illegality of the Occupation Regime: The Fabric of Law in the Occupied Palestinian Territory', 44. See also: Ronen Shamir, '"Landmark Cases" and the Reproduction of Legitimacy: The Case of Israel's High Court of Justice', *Law & Society Review* 24, no. 3 (1990): 781–806; Kretzmer, *The Occupation of Justice*.

> two different systems of law applying to two populations within the same territory (the Palestinians on the one hand and the privileged Israeli settlers on the other hand); a military court system virtually immune from the ISC's intervention; a widespread and long-standing policy of house demolition; extrajudicial executions; a hostile family unification policy; arbitrary manned and unmanned checkpoints and roadblocks preventing ordinary life; the separation wall; detention—including administrative detention—of large numbers of Palestinians and inhumane conditions of incarceration and torture; expulsion and deportation; curfews and closures; and killings with impunity are the highlights of this system [. . .][37]

Nevertheless, the increased volume of petitions from Palestinians invariably meant that at least some of the military's decisions would end up being challenged in court. It was this, Cohen claims, that 'contributed to the realization of commanders that they needed legal advice as to the performance of their tasks, lest their decisions be overturned'.[38] Recent events confirm this observation. Following the 2014 war Tzipi Livni, former Foreign and Vice Prime Minister of Israel, wrote that Israel had, 'acted decisively, using our understanding of the law to its full extent, so that IDF soldiers would be able to protect Israeli citizens while being *furnished with a legal flak jacket and with a legal Iron Dome over their heads*'.[39] Legal advice in the Israeli military is thus not only a way for the military to ensure that individual military actions cohere with established MAG protocols but also serves as something of a defence mechanism against external—and purportedly independent—judicial oversight. The latter is doubly important, Kretzmer claims, because it helps to create and maintain a sense of legitimacy both among the Israeli public and for foreign observers sympathetic to Israel's position.[40]

In summary, the MAG helped to devise and develop the rules of occupation outlined by Sultany. It oversaw the seizing of land, the destruction of homes, and the construction of settlements using an old Ottoman law called *muwat* (or 'dead land') and they have been partly responsible for the creation and perpetuation of a two-tiered legal system ever since.[41] This brief sketch of the history

[37] Sultany, 'The Legacy of Justice Aharon Barak', 84–5 (footnotes removed).

[38] Cohen, 'Legal Operational Advice in the Israeli Defense Forces', 373.

[39] This message appeared in Hebrew on Livni's Facebook wall on 10 September 2014 (emphasis added). Translation provided by Sol Salbe.

[40] Kretzmer, *The Occupation of Justice*.

[41] Oren Yiftachel, 'Indigenous Challenge to Legal Doctrine: Bedouin Land Rights in Israel/Palestine' (Association of American Geographers Annual Meeting, New York, 26 February 2012); Oren Yiftachel, *Ethnocracy: Land and Identity Politics in Israel/Palestine* (Philadelphia, PA: University of Pennsylvania Press, 2006); Shira Robinson, *Citizen Strangers: Palestinians and the Birth of Israel's Liberal Settler State*

of MAG legal advice goes some way to explaining why, more recently, legal advisers have been invited into the operations room to give advice on targeting operations. So long as we refuse Liron Libman's instruction to look at things 'simply', it is possible to trace a historical line of permissiveness in the approach of military lawyers in Israel. They have always been force-multipliers, invested in 'military success' not so much at the expense of the 'rule of law' but rather in the pursuit of military success *through* law. As one military lawyer explained to *Haaretz* following the 2008–2009 war ('Operation Cast Lead'): the MAG's job 'was not to fetter the army, but to give it the tools to win in a lawful manner'.[42]

4.3 'Armed Conflict Short of War'

To fully understand how military lawyers came to play such an important role in targeting operations it is first necessary to consider the shift in political and legal paradigms that took place in Israel in 2000. The Second Intifada was triggered by Ariel Sharon's provocative visit to Jerusalem's Haram al Sharif on 28 September 2000 (albeit the foundations were laid long before, in what Tanya Reinhart calls the 'false expectations' of the Oslo Peace Process).[43] Riots erupted when, with his entourage of police, Israeli Prime Minister Ariel Sharon tried to make his way into the protected Muslim religious site. Within three days thirty Palestinians and two Israelis were killed.[44] The violence spread quickly through the month of October as the Israeli military replaced rubber bullets with live ammunition. Meanwhile, helicopter gunships—like the one that killed Hussein Abiyat and the two elderly women (section 4.1)—took to the skies against mostly unarmed Palestinians.

On the street and amid the growing death toll the rules of the game had seemingly changed. On 15 November 2000 the Israel Ministry of Foreign Affairs released a press briefing describing new military regulations. The speaker who conducted the briefing was Colonel Daniel Reisner of the International Law Department, who was introduced in the Preface. He announced:

(Stanford, CA: Stanford University Press, 2013); Ilan Pappé, *The Forgotten Palestinians: A History of the Palestinians in Israel* (New Haven, CT: Yale University Press, 2011).

[42] Quoted in: Yotam Feldman and Uri Blau, 'Consent and Advice', *Haaretz*, 29 January 2009, http://www.haaretz.com/cmlink/consent-and-advise-1.269127, accessed 26 May 2013.

[43] Tanya Reinhart, *Israel/Palestine: How to End the War of 1948, Second Edition*, 2nd edition (New York, NY: Seven Stories Press, 2004), 13.

[44] Ibid., 94.

> The rules of engagement for the IDF in the West Bank and Gaza Strip have been modified in accordance with the change in the situation. Prior to the violent events, 'police rules of engagement' were applied. [. . .] the situation has now changed. The Palestinians are using violence and terrorism on a regular basis. They are using live ammunition at every opportunity. As a result, Israeli soldiers no longer are required to wait until they are actually shot at before they respond.[45]

Here we witness the transfer of risk away from Israeli soldiers (who used to be able to fire only in self-defence but who henceforth could fire pre-emptively and unprovoked) to the Palestinian population, a trend that was later incorporated into Israeli military doctrine and written into the Israeli military's 'code of ethics'.[46] These new procedures were prepared in advance by MAG lawyers, in much the same way as their predecessors had foreseen and prepared for the occupation in 1967. Sometime shortly after the start of the Intifada the Israeli military Chief of Staff, Shaul Mofaz, placed a telephone call to the office of the MAG asking Commander General Menachem Finklestein (the head of the MAG) and Reisner (head of the International Law Department): 'Am I allowed, if I identify a terrorist leader on the other side, am I allowed to kill him—*publicly*, not using clandestine "007" techniques? Can I kill him, and if so under what conditions?'[47] Reisner's response to Mofaz shows how law can privilege, authorise, and channel violence, rather than prevent it: '[W]e came up with a legal opinion which [said] that on the basis of our understanding of the law [. . .] we think that you can target an enemy terrorist, intentionally target an enemy terrorist if you fill five conditions.'[48] (According to media sources there were in fact six conditions, as I detail in section 4.4.)

This was a foundational, creative, and novel legal opinion that would have far-reaching consequences. The legal contention was that Israel had entered what MAG lawyers termed an 'armed conflict short of war'.[49] Daniel Reisner recounted how he—and by extension the MAG—arrived at this new terminology:

[45] Israel Ministry of Foreign Affairs, 'Press Briefing by Colonel Daniel Reisner', IMFA, 15 November 2000, http://www.mfa.gov.il/MFA/MFAArchive/2000_2009/2000/11/Press+Briefing+by+Colonel+Daniel+Reisner-+Head+of.htm?DisplayMode=print, accessed 12 June 2020.

[46] Eastwood, *Ethics as a Weapon of War*.

[47] Reisner, interview (emphasis in original).

[48] Reisner, interview.

[49] Mitchell et al., 'Sharm El-Sheikh Fact-Finding Committee Final Report'; Reisner, interview.

> What we said is we have a new form of combat which is . . . I coined the term 'armed conflict short of war'. And I could have used something else, later I changed it to 'state vs. non-state armed conflict', but it doesn't matter. And that was the origin of the term. I just sat in my office one night and decided I need a new name for this.[50]

'Armed conflict' is a legal label for war. Therefore, if we substitute one term for the other, we are left with 'a war short of a war' or 'an armed conflict short of an armed conflict'. It did not seem to matter to Reisner or the MAG that the term made little sense; its purpose was to create a third category that was neither international armed conflict nor non-international armed conflict. As Reisner explained: 'armed conflict is a term of art in international law for war. War is a term of art in international law for armed conflict between armies of states and we are fighting non-state actors and there is no word for that.'[51]

The category may have been a late-night semantic invention by a single military lawyer, but it would have profound implications on the rules of engagement and the permissibility of the use of force by Israel. 'Armed conflict short of war' relates directly to the legal permissibility of the war paradigm discussed in the Introduction and, in particular, the combatant's privilege to kill once a situation of war is established. The rationale was that placing the Intifada in the context of war—rather than civil unrest or police operations—would pre-empt and deny the applicability of other, more restrictive legal regimes.[52] International Human Rights Law or traditional law-enforcement paradigms, unlike the laws of war, prohibit targeted killing in all but the most exceptional of circumstances—they place far greater restrictions on the use of lethal force.[53] In the context of the 'war on terror', to substitute one whole paradigm for another speaks to what Mariana Valverde calls the 'games of jurisdiction', *the rules that govern which rules will apply*.[54] As a way of pre-conditioning the battlefield, it later travelled from Israel to the United States, where the logic

[50] Reisner, interview.

[51] Ibid.

[52] This position is deeply controversial. Nils Melzer points out the applicability of one legal regime—the *lex specialis* (in this case, International Humanitarian Law (IHL))—does not preclude the applicability of another legal regime—the *lex generalis* (e.g., International Human Rights Law (IHRL)): Melzer, *Targeted Killing in International Law*.

[53] Ibid.; Philip Alston, 'Report of the Special Rapporteur on Extrajudicial, Summary or Arbitrary Executions', *United Nations Human Rights Council*, 2010, https://ap.ohchr.org/documents/dpage_e.aspx?si=A/HRC/14/24, accessed 30 June 2020.

[54] Mariana Valverde, 'Jurisdiction and Scale: Legal "Technicalities" as Resources for Theory', *Social & Legal Studies* 18, no. 2 (2009): 139–57.

of targeted killing has been used not only in Iraq and Afghanistan but also in Yemen, Pakistan, and Somalia (section 4.6).

In the weeks that followed the assassination of Hussein Abiyat, the Israeli government denied that an assassination policy existed. Then, in a meeting of the Foreign Affairs and Defence Committee on 9 January 2001, Shaul Mofaz confirmed the existence of an assassination policy but insisted that it was used as an 'exceptional method whose goal is to save human life in the absence of any other alternative'.[55] Later that year, the then Attorney General Elyakim Rubinstein made the case that the various terms used to describe Israel's assassination policy—'liquidations', 'extra-judicial killings' etc.—were politically damaging and proposed new sanitizing terms instead: in Hebrew they would be called סיכול ממוקד (*sikul memukad*), which translates as 'focused prevention' or 'focused foiling'. In English, assassinations would be referred to as 'targeted killings'[56] but there is evidence to suggest that the euphemistic term has been successful in normalizing them.[57]

At the centre of this new mode of governance—what Neve Gordon calls the 'separation principle' and what Eyal Weizman calls the 'airborne occupation'—is the assertion of control from a distance, a process that was already underway in the mid-to-late 1990s.[58] Gordon explains:

> [B]y the turn of the new millennium, Israel had almost totally abandoned forms of control whose goal was to manage the lives of the Palestinian inhabitants residing in the West Bank and Gaza Strip, and was also reluctant to allow the PA [Palestinian Authority] to continue administering the occupied population.[59]

[55] Gideon Alon, 'Mofaz: IDF Jurist Approves Killings', *Haaretz*, 11 January 2001, https://lists.capalon.com/pipermail/imra/2014-January/024543.html, accessed 30 September 2014.

[56] Ibid.; Gideon Alon, 'Rubinstein Backs IDF's Policy of 'targeted Killings'', Haaretz.com, 2 December 2001, http://www.haaretz.com/print-edition/news/rubinstein-backs-idf-s-policy-of-targeted-killings-1.76289, accessed 6 July 2012; Leonard Small, 'Roundtable on Targeted Killing: Lawyering and Targeted Killing', *Jadaliyya*, 7 March 2012, http://www.jadaliyya.com/pages/index/4567/roundtable-on-targeted-killing_lawyering-and-targeted-killing, accessed 3 May 2012.

[57] B'Tselem's Yael Stein writes: 'The use of clean language to describe this policy may conveniently allow the perpetrators to persist in its implementation and believe it is legal': Yael Stein, 'By Any Name Illegal and Immoral', *Ethics & International Affairs* 17, no. 1 (2003): 128. Yet as Neve Gordon has argued, together with popular media representations of targeted killing as morally and rationally legitimate, clean language apparently has a tremendous legitimizing power not only for those within the military apparatus but also on the broader Israeli public: Neve Gordon, 'Rationalising Extra-Judicial Executions: The Israeli Press and the Legitimisation of Abuse', *The International Journal of Human Rights* 8, no. 3 (2004): 305–24.

[58] Neve Gordon, *Israel's Occupation* (Berkeley: University of California Press, 2008); Eyal Weizman, *Hollow Land: Israel's Architecture of Occupation* (London; New York, NY: Verso, 2007).

[59] Gordon, *Israel's Occupation*, 199.

To further facilitate what Adi Ophir has called the 'catastrophization' of Gaza, in August/September 2005 Israel withdrew its troops and dismantled its settlements there.[60] A statement in which Israel declared it was no longer responsible for the functioning of Gaza accompanied the 'disengagement'. From this point on Israel claimed that Gaza was not occupied.[61] The legal rationale depended on a controversial definition of occupation as requiring a permanent 'ground troop presence' in Gaza.[62] Although Israel had indeed withdrawn its troops from the ground—at least for the meantime[63]—the military maintained (and still maintains) full security control of Gaza's territorial waters and seaports, its air space, its borders, and even its subterranean and digital/cellular resources.[64] 'In this way', Helga Tawil-Souri writes, 'Gaza is not a sealed-off territory, but a space through which and inside which the Israeli military apparatus continuously operates'.[65] Two years later, in 2007, Israel's security cabinet labelled Gaza a 'hostile entity', thus solidifying a political-juridical process of formally designating Gaza as a threat that must be 'contained' only by piercing it with the use of lethal juridical force.[66] And wherever lethal force would be used, henceforth the advice of military lawyers would be vital to the pursuit of what was deemed militarily 'necessary'.

The political-juridical shift away from direct occupation and the management of Palestinian lives towards remote occupation, abandonment, and new forms of 'necropolitical' governance was important because it in turn laid the foundations for the destruction of an ever-expanding scope of targets and—eventually—the *mass* bombing of Gaza.[67] The casualty

[60] Adi Ophir, 'The Politics of Catastrophization', 7 October 2014, http://humanities1.tau.ac.il/segel/adiophir/files/2015/08/Ophir-The-Politics-of-Catastrophizaton.pdf, accessed 30 June 2020.

[61] Gordon argues: 'Sharon's redeployment from Gaza has proven ultimately to be about Israel's entrenchment of colonial control rather than its abandonment': Neve Gordon, 'How Israel's Occupation Shifted From a Politics of Life to a Politics of Death', *The Nation*, 5 June 2017, https://www.thenation.com/article/israels-occupation-shifted-politics-life-politics-death/, accessed 18 December 2019.

[62] See: Ben-Naftali, Gross, and Michaeli, 'The Illegality of the Occupation Regime: The Fabric of Law in the Occupied Palestinian Territory'.

[63] The ground troops did not stay out of Gaza for long. On 28 June 2006 (i.e. approximately nine months after the 'disengagement' was complete) troops once again entered Gaza in so-called 'Operation Summer Rain'. Summer soon turned into 'Operation Autumn Clouds', which involved yet another invasion by Israeli ground troops.

[64] Weizman, *Hollow Land*; Helga Tawil-Souri, 'Digital Occupation: Gaza's High-Tech Enclosure', *Journal of Palestine Studies* 41, no. 2 (2012): 27–43; Helga Tawil-Souri, 'The Technological End Between the "Inside" of Gaza and the "Outside" of Gaza', 7iber حبر - شو قصتك؟, 29 September 2014, http://www.7iber.com/2014/09/the-technological-end-between-the-inside-of-gaza-and-the-outside-of-gaza, accessed 9 November 2014.

[65] Tawil-Souri, 'The Technological End Between the "Inside" of Gaza and the "Outside" of Gaza'.

[66] Lisa Bhungalia, 'A Liminal Territory: Gaza, Executive Discretion, and Sanctions Turned Humanitarian', *GeoJournal* 75, no. 4 (2010): 347–57.

[67] Achille Mbembe defines sovereignty as '*the generalized instrumentalization of human existence and the material destruction of human bodies and populations*': Achille Mbembe, *Necropolitics* (Durham, NC: Duke University Press Books, 2019), 68 (emphasis in original).

counts from recent wars on Gaza bear witness to Israel's increasing willingness to use lethal force.[68] During the three-week assault of December 2008 to January 2009 (so-called 'Operation Cast Lead') Israeli forces killed 1,398 Palestinians. Of these 764, or 55 per cent, were civilians, including 345, or 25 per cent, children.[69] The one-week attack in November 2012 ('Operation Pillar of Defense') saw Israeli military violence kill a further 168 Palestinians, of whom 101, or 60 per cent, are believed to be civilians, including thirty-three children.[70] The most recent round of war, fifty days of 'Operation Protective Edge' in July and August 2014, was the most destructive yet (Figure 4.1): 2,251 Palestinians were killed and 18,000 homes destroyed or damaged. Of these, 1,462, or 65 per cent, were civilians, including 551 children.[71] The United Nations Human Rights Council noted that in the wake of the war, 'the scale of the devastation was unprecedented'.[72]

Neve Gordon has written that the 'most striking characteristic of the Second Intifada is the extensive suspension of the law'.[73] In contrast, I argue the paradigm of war, the rules of engagement for the Second Intifada, and the integration of Israeli military lawyers into the kill chain were made possible not by abandoning or suspending the law but by (re)interpreting and applying it. This was not so much an 'assault on international law' to borrow from Jens David Ohlin; rather, it was an assault *through* international law.[74] The Second Intifada brought with it new levels of flagrant lethality but contrary to what Gordan has argued, we will now see how such lethality was realized *through* law and legal advice.

[68] Jasbir Puar has argued that in recent years Israel has also employed less than lethal force in order to deliberately maim and injure Palestinians, especially since the Great March of Return (the Gaza border protests) that began in March 2018: Jasbir K. Puar, *The Right to Maim: Debility, Capacity, Disability* (Durham: Duke University Press, 2017).

[69] B'Tselem, 'Fatalities during Operation Cast Lead', B'Tselem, n.d., https://www.btselem.org/statistics/fatalities/during-cast-lead/by-date-of-event, accessed 19 November 2019.

[70] United Nations Human Rights Council, 'Concerns Related to Adherence to International Human Rights and International Humanitarian Law in the Context of the Escalation between the State of Israel, the de Facto Authorities in Gaza and Palestinian Armed Groups in Gaza That Occurred from 14 to 21 November 2012', 4.

[71] United Nations Human Rights Council, 'Report of the Detailed Findings of the Independent Commission of Inquiry Established Pursuant to Human Rights Council Resolution S-21/1', 153.

[72] Ibid.

[73] Gordon, *Israel's Occupation*, 21.

[74] Jens David Ohlin, *The Assault on International Law* (New York, NY: Oxford University Press, 2015).

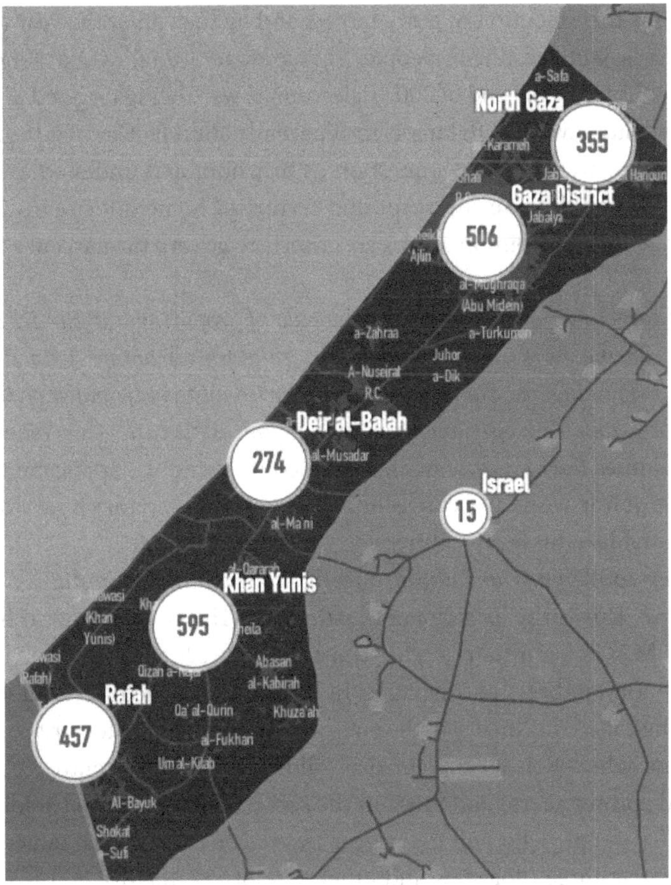

Figure 4.1 Fatalities in Gaza during the 2014 military campaign.

Source: B'Tselem, '50 Days: More than 500 Children—Facts and Figures on Fatalities in Gaza, Summer 2014', http://www.btselem.org/2014_gaza_conflict/en, accessed 27 June 2017, reproduced with permission.

4.4 Layers of Law

Criteria for killing

While the paradigm of war and the language of the laws of war proved a powerful juridical regime through which targeted killing could be justified at the strategic policy level, it still required a *modus operandi* to ensure that it functioned on a daily, operational basis. After assassinating Hussein Abiyat in November 2000, the General Security Services (also known as Shin Bet) began pushing for the execution of more targets and by the end of the year the military had assassinated fifteen people. This grew to a total of sixty-one by the end of 2001 and by the end of 2003 Palestinians were being targeted at a rate of one every four days.[75] With targets in apparently abundant supply, the military needed an answer to Mofaz's question as to whom and under what circumstances they could 'prosecute' suspected 'terrorists'. Sometime in early 2001 the MAG issued a legal opinion setting six criteria to govern the nascent policy:[76]

(1) *All targeting must comply with the rule of proportionality under the laws of war, meaning that the anticipated 'military advantage' gained by conducting a targeted killing must be proportional to anticipated civilian casualties and the destruction of civilian infrastructure.* This requirement presumes the existence of an armed conflict and the applicability of the laws of war, while also concealing the careful preparatory legal work done to establish this legal reality;
(2) *Only combatants and those 'directly participating in hostilities' are targeted.* This is the 'principle of distinction'. The crucial proviso here was the MAG's definition of what constitutes 'direct participation'. The legal opinion on direct participation in hostilities was defined around something called the 'theory of the circles of involvement in terrorist organizations', which Reisner explained as follows: those in the centre (the leaders and commanders) and those in the second circle (the 'foot soldiers', 'the actual people who pull the trigger') were considered legal targets. Those in circle three ('logistics and other supporters, the driver, the guy who provides ammunition etc.') *could* be construed as legal but because the question of what constitutes 'support' was especially difficult, the MAG advised the military to focus on circles one and two because they deemed them 'undisputedly combatants'. The final, outer circle (those 'who support the organization politically, or religiously') was not considered legal to target, at least not for the time being;
(3) *Arrest rather than kill a suspected 'terrorist' if possible. A killing can be enacted only after: a) appeals to the Palestinian Authority calling for the arrest of the 'terrorist' and have failed or, b) the Israeli military has attempted and failed to arrest the suspect.* This and the fourth requirement are unlike the others because their source is International Human Rights Law and

[75] B'Tselem, 'Statistics', http://www.btselem.org/statistics, accessed 18 February 2012.

[76] Reisner, interview; Gideon Alon and Amos Harel, 'IDF Lawyers Set "conditions" for Assassination Policy', *Haaretz.Com*, 4 February 2002, http://www.haaretz.com/print-edition/news/idf-lawyers-set-conditions-for-assassination-policy-1.53911, accessed 21 February 2012.

not the laws of war; the key difference being that the latter has no provision that militaries should seek to arrest the enemy before killing the targeted person. For the MAG, this provision sought to avoid a 'slippery slope' whereby 'if you give them [the military] the right to kill anyone, then there is no limitation'.[77] But it was also a tacit admission that, alone, the armed conflict/laws of war model that the MAG itself had so recently devised did not provide sufficient safeguards against abuses of the nascent assassination policy. The critical concept here was what constitutes a 'feasible arrest opportunity', hence condition four;

(4) *'Terrorists' under Israeli security control cannot be targeted because in these areas there is a feasible arrest opportunity.* If the target is located in areas *outside* of Israel's security control (as defined by Israeli security), however, 'a viable arrest opportunity is much more difficult' and therefore the target can be struck. This requirement explains why the Israeli 'withdrawal' from Gaza in 2005 was so crucial (section 4.3): from this point on Israel claimed that it no longer had security control over Gaza. It is no surprise that around this time the geography of targeting changed radically from the West Bank to Gaza, and by 2007 all targeted killings were conducted in the latter;[78]

(5) *Ministerial level approval from the Defense Minister or Prime Minister must be sought prior to a planned attack.* This was introduced as a 'bureaucratic way of keeping the numbers down', according to Reisner. Whether this worked in practice is a matter of perspective: Between 29 September 2000 and 7 July 2014, 543 Palestinians were killed in targeted killing operations; 191, or 35 per cent, of them were civilians (these statistics exclude thousands of Palestinians killed by other means);[79]

(6) *Assassination is not to be carried out in retribution for past events. It must be aimed at 'terrorists' who plan to carry out a terror attack in the 'near future'.*[80] The key concept here is the notion of imminence and by refusing

[77] Reisner, interview.

[78] B'Tselem, 'Statistics'.

[79] Ibid. B'Tselem archives Israeli targeted killings into three time periods: (1) fatalities since the outbreak of the Second Intifada (29 September 2000) to the start of Operation Cast Lead (26 December 2008); (2) the duration of Operation Cast Lead (26 December 2008–18 January 2009); and (3) post-Operation Cast Lead to 8 July 2014. The statistics quoted use an aggregate of these three periods and represent the total of targeted killings from 29 September 2000 to 8 July 2014. A further sixty-two Palestinians were killed in 'declared targeted killings' during the course of Operation Protective Edge (8 July 2014– 26 August 2014): B'Tselem, '50 Days: More than 500 Children—Facts and Figures on Fatalities in Gaza, Summer 2014', 2014, https://www.btselem.org/2014_gaza_conflict/en/il/, accessed 27 June 2017.

[80] Gideon Alon and Amos Harel, 'IDF Lawyers Set "conditions" for Assassination Policy', *Haaretz.Com*, 4 February 2002, http://www.haaretz.com/print-edition/news/idf-lawyers-set-conditions-for-assassination-policy-1.53911, accessed 21 February 2012.

to delimit what constitutes the 'near future', the legal opinion granted the military wide interpretational power.

As an ensemble, these rules are an interesting and often confusing mix—an intentional blurring—of the laws of war, human rights law, and the concept of self-defence. These requirements served as the primary legal guideline of the assassination policy for its first six years (i.e. until the Supreme Court ruling on targeted killing in 2006). In 2001 the Attorney General approved the MAG legal opinion on targeted killing.[81] The Chief of Staff, Shaul Mofaz also accepted the opinion but found that the military was not ready to implement it: 'We need to *interpret* it. When is an 'arrest viability' not viable? What does proportionality mean? All these things are good questions. [But] we want them [military lawyers] in the room with us when we make these decisions.'[82] Following this request, which came from the highest quarters in the Israeli military, there was a debate between the MAG (a military office) and the Attorney General (a civilian office) as to whether a military lawyer should be present at operational meetings. The Attorney General's office believed that they should *not* and opined that the role of the lawyer should be to provide legal opinions in *advance* of operations and not *during* them. The MAG, however, felt differently: 'If my clients say[s] to me that they want to make sure that they comply [with the law], therefore they want me to be in the room to help them make the right decisions, how dare I say no?'[83]

The debate was ultimately resolved in favour of involving military lawyers in live operations, but the approach continues to attract criticism. In 2008 a government-appointed investigatory committee published its findings into Israel's military shortcomings in the 2006 Lebanon War. In that war, commanders had been given a generous range of *planned* targets—150 of them, according to Antony Cordesman[84]—but what worried the Winograd Commission was the involvement of lawyers *during* operations: 'We fear that the extended reliance on legal advice during military operations might cause the transference of responsibility from elected officials and commanders to

[81] Gideon Alon, 'Rubinstein Backs IDF's Policy of "targeted Killings"'. *Haaretz.Com*, 2 December 2001, http://www.haaretz.com/print-edition/news/rubinstein-backs-idf-s-policy-of-targeted-killings-1.76289, accessed 6 July 2012. Gideon Alon, 'Mofaz: IDF Jurist Approves Killings'. *Haaretz*, 11 January 2001. https://lists.capalon.com/pipermail/imra/2014-January/024543.html, accessed 30 September 2014.

[82] Reisner, interview, paraphrasing Mofaz (emphasis in original).

[83] Ibid.

[84] Anthony H. Cordesman, 'The "Gaza War"' (Washington, DC: Center for Strategic and International Studies (CSIS), 2 February 2009), 20, https://www.csis.org/analysis/gaza-war, accessed 1 July 2020.

advisors [. . .]'.[85] Similar sentiments were expressed following the 2014 war when a number of anonymous senior officers issued a statement that the MAG had 'prevented a greater [military] success [. . .] because of the *limitations* it placed on the army in conducting certain missions.'[86]

My findings confirm that military lawyers have come to have a shared responsibility in making targeting decisions, but they do not support the Commission's conclusion that this hindered the 'quality of the decisions and the operational activity'.[87] To the contrary, live legal input *enhances* operational activities and it does so by channelling especially rapid and ostensibly arbitrary forms of violence through legal process (however rushed or short-circuited those processes may be) towards more legitimate and legally sanctioned outcomes. Indeed, arguing in defence of legal input during military operations, legal scholar Emanuel Gross has argued: 'The thankless role of the Military Advocate General Corps, which helps commanders understands which targets are legitimate under international law, *testifies to the strength of a country in an asymmetric war*.'[88] Legal input is operationally enabling but is also central to the projection of Israel as a higher and more moral military power, or as Gross puts it, the MAG 'allows the state to *show* it is a state of law'.[89]

Refusing the International Criminal Court

In the early 2000s, Israeli commanders were becoming increasingly aware of the threat of universal jurisdiction[90] and the growing use of transnational legal activism scrutinizing military activity.[91] In 2002 the International Criminal

[85] Quoted in: Cohen, 'Legal Operational Advice in the Israeli Defense Forces', 268.

[86] Emanuel Gross, 'The Watchdog of the IDF—Opinion', *Haaretz.Com*, 18 September 2014, http://www.haaretz.com/opinion/.premium-1.616349, accessed 19 September 2014.

[87] Quoted in: Cohen, 'Legal Operational Advice in the Israeli Defense Forces', 268.

[88] Gross, 'The Watchdog of the IDF—Opinion' (emphasis added).

[89] Ibid. (emphasis added).

[90] According to Lisa Hajjar, universal jurisdiction is 'a distinct method and model of accountability: it permits individuals accused of gross human rights violations and grave breaches of the Geneva Conventions to be prosecuted in foreign national legal systems with no connection to the crime': Lisa Hajjar, 'Universal Jurisdiction as Praxis', in *When Governments Break the Law: The Rule of Law and the Prosecution of the Bush Administration*, ed. Austin Sarat and Nasser Hussain (New York, NY: New York University Press, 2010), 88.

[91] Lori Allen, *The Rise and Fall of Human Rights Cynicism and Politics in Occupied Palestine* (Stanford: Stanford University Press, 2013); Charles Dunlap, 'Law and Military Interventions: Preserving Humanitarian Values in 21st Century Conflicts', in *Conference on Humanitarian Challenges in Military Intervention* (Online), Washington, DC: Carr Center for Human Rights Policy, Kennedy School of Government, Harvard University. November, 29: 4–43, Washington, DC, 2001; Neve Gordon, 'Human Rights as a Security Threat: Lawfare and the Campaign against Human Rights NGOs', *Law & Society Review* 48, no. 2 (2014): 311–44.

Court (ICC) was established, thus providing a formal avenue for human rights groups and other non-state actors to pursue claims against Israeli politicians and military personnel. Alongside the United States, Russia, and Sudan, Israel signed the Rome Statute of the ICC, but has since declared that it no longer intends to ratify the treaty.[92] Israel expressed 'deep sympathy with the goals of the court' but the Office of the Legal Adviser to the Ministry of Foreign Affairs objected to ratifying the Rome Statute of the ICC because it was concerned that the court 'will be subjected to political pressures and its impartiality will be compromised'. Among other objections Israel singled out the following reason for reneging on its signature:

> The list of crimes included in the court's statute is highly selective. Offenses such as terrorism and drug-trafficking are not included, because of political disputes over their definition and scope. The paradoxical result is that a state acting against acts of terrorism may find itself under the scrutiny of the court for the way it exercises its right of self-defense, while the terrorists themselves are outside the court's jurisdiction.[93]

In recent years Israel has fought vociferously against organizations—especially Israeli organizations—that collect evidence that could be used in proceedings against Israeli citizens.[94] Despite these efforts, in 2001 a Belgian court indicted Ariel Sharon, the then Foreign Minister, for crimes committed in the Sabra and Shatila refugee camps in Beirut in 1982, and since then it is reported that over 1,000 lawsuits alleging war crimes by Israeli ministers and military personnel have been filed around the world.[95] The Israeli Government and the MAG's anxieties about universal jurisdiction have been heightened since the publication of the Goldstone Report in 2009 (the UN investigation into crimes committed by Israel and Hamas in the 2008–2009 war), which was very critical of Israel's targeting policies, characterizing them as 'disproportionate' and 'indiscriminate'. War crimes charges brought abroad against Israeli soldiers and

[92] A signature is non-binding whereas ratification indicates a state's formal consent to be bound to a treaty.

[93] Office of the Legal Adviser to the Ministry of Foreign Affairs, 'Israel and the International Criminal Court', 30 June 2002, https://mfa.gov.il/MFA/MFA-Archive/2002/Pages/Israel%20and%20the%20International%20Criminal%20Court.aspx, accessed 18 December 2019.

[94] Gordon, 'Human Rights as a Security Threat'.

[95] David Sapsted, 'Hundreds of War Crimes Lawsuits Filed against Israelis', *The National*, 11 October 2009, http://www.thenational.ae/news/world/middle-east/hundreds-of-war-crimes-lawsuits-filed-against-israelis, accessed 9 November 2014; Human Rights Watch, 'Universal Jurisdiction in Europe: The State of the Art', 28 June 2006, http://www.hrw.org/node/11298, accessed 12 October 2014.

officers involved in Operation Cast Lead were characterized as 'legal terrorism' by Colonel Liron Libman.[96]

Cables leaked by Wikileaks show how, shortly after the publication of the Goldstone Report, the MAG Avichai Mandelblit met with US Ambassador James B. Cunningham and even advised him that the Palestinian Authority's 'pursuit of Israel through the ICC would be viewed as war by the GOI [Government of Israel]'.[97] It is difficult to see how such a belligerent response to judicial remedy would ever be justified (let alone proportional), especially because Israel already considers itself at war with Palestinian groups. No Israeli has been prosecuted under universal jurisdiction but if this were a 'merely fanciful debating point for cocktail party conversations', Israel (like the United States) would not have devoted significant resources and political capital to counter efforts to bring officials to justice abroad. [98] Against this background, it is hardly surprising that commanders would want legal cover for their actions. As Reisner pointed out, '[t]he commanders hear about this [accusations of criminality] and say, "I might find myself in that court; where is my lawyer?"'[99]

The High Court of Justice

In 2001 Siham Thabet—the wife of the assassinated Palestinian Authority leader Thabet Thabet—filed the first petition challenging the targeted killing policy to the High Court of Justice. Israeli Knesset member Muhammad Barakeh filed a second petition for an *order nisi* and an interim injunction.[100] The High Court of Justice dismissed these claims, declaring that targeted killing is a 'non-justiciable' political question.[101] In 2003 the Court eventually

[96] Tomer Zarchin, 'IDF: War Crime Charges Over Gaza Offensive Are "Legal Terror"', *Haaretz.Com*, 19 February 2009, https://www.haaretz.com/1.5077434, accessed 18 December 2019.

[97] Wikileaks, 'IDF MAG Mandelblit on IDF Investigations into Operation Cast Lead', Telegram (cable) (American Embassy Tel Aviv to Secretary of State, Washington, DC, 23 February 2010), https://wikileaks.org/plusd/cables/10TELAVIV417_a.html, accessed 7 January 2017; Lisa Hajjar, 'Lawfare and Armed Conflict: Comparing Israeli and US Targeted Killing Policies and Challenges against Them' (Beirut: American University of Beirut, January 2013), https://www.daleel-madani.org/ar/civil-society-directory/issam-fares-institute-public-policy-and-international-affairs/resources/lawfare-and-armed-conflict-comparing-israeli-and-us-targeted-killing-policies-and-challenges-against, accessed 1 July 2020.

[98] Hajjar, 'Universal Jurisdiction as Praxis', 87.

[99] Quoted in: George E. Bisharat, 'Violence's Law', *Journal of Palestine Studies* 42, no. 3 (2013): 75.

[100] Hajjar, 'Lawfare and Armed Conflict'. An order nisi is a court order that does not have any force unless a particular condition is met

[101] The US courts have refused to hear any cases relating to targeted killing in part using the same reasoning. For an important discussion of non-justicability and the rules which govern what counts as a 'legal' question see: Melinda Benson, 'Rules of Engagement: The Spatiality of Judicial Review', in *The Expanding Spaces of Law: A Timely Legal Geography*, ed. Irus Braverman et al. (Stanford, California: Stanford Law Books, 2014), 215–38.

accepted a petition filed by the Public Committee against Torture in Israel and LAW: The Palestinian Society for the Protection of Human Rights and the Environment. The Court decision handed down by Justice Aharon Barak in 2006 accepted without question that Israel was at war with Palestine. Crucially, it also affirmed the legality of the targeted killing policy, stating 'we cannot determine that a preventative strike is always legal, just as we cannot determine that it is always illegal'.[102] To this end, the Court set the following criteria to ensure the legality of targeted killing operations: (1) precaution must be taken to harm only combatants and civilians who are directly participating in hostilities (the principle of distinction); (2) lethal force should not be used if 'less harmful means can be employed' (e.g. arrest and trial); (3) excessive harm is prohibited (the proportionality principle); (4) in cases where excessive harm is believed to have been caused they should be investigated.

The conditions set by the Court were remarkably similar to those laid out in the MAG legal opinion outlined earlier in this section. This is perhaps unsurprising given that 240 Palestinians had already been assassinated by the time the Court had reached its judgment, providing it with a great deal of precedent (and an equal measure of very serious and senior criminal prosecutions to attend to if it found aspects of the policy illegal).[103] For Lisa Hajjar this demonstrates 'another instance in which international law is interpreted by the state and endorsed by the HCJ [High Court of Justice] to frame existing state practices as compatible with the law itself'.[104] Yet it is again perhaps unsurprising that the Court should so closely adopt the legal principles laid out in the MAG legal opinion given Kretzmer's important finding that, 'in almost all of its judgments relating to the Occupied Territories, especially those dealing with questions of principle, the Court has decided in favor of the authorities, *often on the basis of dubious legal arguments*'.[105]

In one key instance, however, the High Court of Justice went further than the MAG opinion. The Israeli State, with advice from the MAG Office and Attorney General, requested the Court to help them create a third category between civilian and combatant called an 'unlawful combatant'.[106] This controversial

[102] Israel Supreme Court, *Public Committee Against Torture in Israel v. Government of Israel*, HCJ 769/02 (Israel Supreme Court, 11 December 2006).

[103] B'Tselem, 'Statistics'.

[104] Hajjar, 'Lawfare and Armed Conflict', 18.

[105] Kretzmer, *The Occupation of Justice*, 2–3 (emphasis added).

[106] Israel Supreme Court, *Public Committee Against Torture in Israel v. Government of Israel*, ¶27. In 2002 the Knesset enacted the Incarceration of Unlawful Combatants Law, which held that Israel can incarcerate anyone who the Chief of General Staff has 'reasonable cause' to believe is 'an unlawful combatant and that his release will harm State security': Israel Knesset, 'Incarceration of Unlawful Combatants Law', 5762-2002 § (2002), 1, https://ihl-databases.icrc.org/applic/ihl/ihl-nat.nsf/0/7A09C457F76A452BC12575C30049A7BD, accessed 27 June 2017. According to Human Rights Watch: 'Israel

designation had already been employed by the United States in the 'war on terror' (and would later be challenged by the US Supreme Court).[107] This new category of person could be killed (based on their status as a combatant) but would not be afforded the rights accorded to combatants (such as prisoner of war protection). The Court rejected the legal basis for recognizing this third category.[108] More accurately, it found a creative way to operationally achieve what the state was asking without having to adopt the controversial 'unlawful combatant' category. Instead, the Court embraced a doubly expansive interpretation of direct participation in hostilities. The first extension concerned the definition of 'direct participation'. The MAG had opined that only circles one and two could be legally targeted, but the Court expanded the scope of legality to the third circle, to those who provide logistical and other support to 'terrorists'.[109] Even more controversially, the Court also said that the homes of 'terrorists' and those who allowed 'terrorists' to use their home would also be considered as taking a direct part in hostilities and could therefore be targeted accordingly (as so-called 'collective punishment').

I use the word 'controversial' advisedly: one of the very lawyers who helped write the MAG legal opinion justifying assassination thought that the Court went too far in its definition of who and what constitutes a legal target. He confides:

> Barak, in his ruling came up with a crazy definition of DPH [Direct Participation in Hostilities]. He said that the famous issue, for example, if someone allows a terrorist to use his house [. . .] Now in my world that person is a civilian who may be tacitly or passively supporting the terrorist but he is not a legitimate target in and of himself. He could be collateral damage in an attack against a legitimate target—could be depending on proportionality. But he [Barak] specifically writes that this person is a legitimate target in and

has detained 18 Palestinian residents of Gaza under the Internment of Unlawful Combatants Law since its 2005 disengagement with the Gaza Strip':Human Rights Watch, 'Gaza: "Unlawful Combatants Law" Violates Rights', 1 March 2017, https://www.hrw.org/news/2017/03/01/gaza-unlawful-combatants-law-violates-rights, accessed 27 June 2017.

[107] Curtis Bradley, 'The United States, Israel, and Unlawful Combatants', *Green Bag* 12 (2009): 399.

[108] '[T]he State asked us to recognize a third category of persons, that of unlawful combatants. [. . .]. In our opinion, as far as existing law goes, the data before us are not sufficient to recognize this third category': Israel Supreme Court, *Public Committee Against Torture in Israel v. Government of Israel*, ¶35. Reisner laid out the nature of the request and the nature of the Court response thus: 'He [Justice Barak] said, look I would love to do this but I don't have enough legal precedent to base my decision on. I was asking him, actually, to help me invent new law. And he didn't want to. He preferred the very wide interpretation of existing law': Reisner, interview.

[109] Ibid.

> of himself because he is providing direct support to him. I disagree. I think he went way too far. I think he went way too far because he refused to accept [our] unlawful combatant [opinion]; he wanted to compensate.[110]

The second expansion concerned the element of time that is built into the concept of direct participation in hostilities. According to Additional Protocol One (which the Court recognized as customary law, thereby reaffirming that Israel is bound to it), 'all persons who are not members of State armed forces or organized armed groups of a party to the conflict are civilians and, therefore, entitled to protection against direct attack unless and *for such time* as they take a direct part in hostilities'.[111] This provision was designed to protect civilians, and this right to protection would extend even to those civilians who are *planning* to take or who had *previously taken* a 'direct part in hostilities'. The Court rejected this rule, however, stating:

> [A] civilian who has joined a terrorist organization which has become his 'home', and in the framework of his role in that organization he commits a chain of hostilities, with short periods of rest between them, loses his immunity from attack 'for such time' as he is committing the chain of acts. Indeed, regarding such a civilian, the rest between hostilities is nothing other than preparation for the next hostility.[112]

By inventing the category of a 'chain of hostilities' and by claiming that 'rest' amounts to 'preparation' (thus constituting participation) the Court effectively transformed a temporary action into a permanent combatant status. With it, the Court radically expanded the definition of a lawful target.

What was an audacious legal thesis only six years earlier became a standard practice endorsed by the highest court in Israel in 2006. But what is more, in pushing the definition of direct participation in hostilities beyond that imagined by the MAG, the Court expanded yet again the definition of who and what constitutes a permissible target. In part, this legalized actions that had already become standard operating procedure. But in expanding the definition of direct participation in hostilities the Court also set a precedent for and gave strength to *future* MAG legal opinions; legal advice and rules of engagement

[110] Anonymous Israeli military lawyer #1, interview.

[111] International Committee of the Red Cross, 'Interpretive Guidance on the Notion of Direct Participation in Hostilities under International Humanitarian Law', *International Review of the Red Cross* 90, no. 872 (2008): 991–1047.

[112] Israel Supreme Court, *Public Committee Against Torture in Israel v. Government of Israel*, ¶39.

(ROE) that would, when the operational circumstances required it, push the envelope on permissible targets even more.[113] To these operations we now turn.

4.5 Legal Advice and Planned Targeting

For planned operations military lawyers provide 'legal advice to the IDF on a range of issues including with regards to the formulation of ROE and legal assessment of potential targets'.[114] Target lists are drawn up by the General Security Services and are then prioritized before being viewed by a special committee comprised of senior ranking military officers (drawn from, *inter alia*, intelligence; imagery analysis; munitions; and operations branches) and at least one military lawyer with the rank of General or above. The committee is then responsible for the vetting of individual 'target folders' in the 'target bank'. Each operation has what is called an 'operational order', the legal section of which governs 'the legal principles with regard to particular targets', including the stipulation of prohibitions.[115] In planning meetings, which can involve up to twenty people and typically run for sixty to ninety minutes, the lawyer is expected to speak quickly (anywhere between two and five minutes) and to put the 'bottom line up front', to necessitate quick decision making (even in deliberative targeting operations, time is of the essence).[116] There is a special page inside each target folder—these folders contain a mix of printed and electronic files—where the legal adviser writes her/his opinion on the operation, often only a line or two. Sometimes this will be straightforward, and the target receives legal approval. Other times the lawyer will set conditions and only when these conditions are met will an operation be considered legal.

Unlike the legal criteria outlined in section 4.4, these are what are known as 'operational orders' or ROE and provide a more detailed and individualized operational instruction. ROE are dynamic documents, as Demarest explains: 'a

[113] A concrete example of this is the MAG legal analysis of 'Operation Pillar of Defense'. It cites the section of the HCJ ruling dealing with the definition of direct participation in hostilities and from this concludes: 'Thus, sites that were once purely civilian buildings can be transformed into legitimate military objectives due to the tactics and strategy of the opposing force': Military Advocate General of the Israel Defense Force, 'Operation "Pillar of Defense" 14–21 November 2012' (MAG: International Law Department, 19 December 2012), 7, https://www.legal-tools.org/doc/84f408/pdf/, accessed 1 July 2020. The Israel Ministry of Foreign Affairs 'factual and legal' analysis of Operation Cast Lead also cites the same section of the HCJ decision in order to justify the killing of civilians: Israel Ministry of Foreign Affairs, 'The Operation in Gaza—Factual and Legal Aspects', 37 (IMFA, 2010, p. 37).

[114] Military Advocate General of the Israel Defense Force, 'Operation "Pillar of Defense" 14–21 November 2012'.

[115] Israel Ministry of Foreign Affairs, 'The Operation in Gaza—Factual and Legal Aspects', 83.

[116] Libman, interview.

mission may require multiple ROE instructions to correspond with varying phases of a deployment, different geographic locations and even different levels of classification.'[117] Although the exact details are classified, the following are typical provisions for targeted operations: a specific day or specific time of day is designated (e.g. if it is during school hours, children are presumed to be at school); a target may be struck only when 'x' number of civilians or fewer are present (this calculation depends on the value and priority of the target).[118] Target folders may be incomplete or might have out-of-date intelligence that requires updating before it can be given proper legal consideration. In such cases, the legal department would say 'well, this isn't good enough [. . .] go back and get some more [intelligence]',[119] which is fine *if* there is time to collect more intelligence. Where time is limited, responsibility is delegated to commanders in the field, a point I return to in Chapter 6.[120]

A common rule is that a target may be hit only after warnings are given for civilians to evacuate.[121] This practice, reflected in the First Additional Protocol (Art. 57(2)(c) was not universally applied in the 2014 war when the MAG took the view Israel did not have a legal obligation to provide early warning about attacks to civilians and that such warnings would undermine the purpose of an attack.)[122] This interpretation of the laws of war led directly to civilian casualties. A MAG investigation into six separate 'Exceptional Incidents' where civilians received no warning found that they led to a total of ninety-seven

[117] Geoffrey Demerest, 'The Strategic Implications of Operational Law', *US Army*, April 1995, https://community.apan.org/wg/tradoc-g2/fmso/m/fmso-monographs/252318, accessed 1 July 2020.

[118] See: Eyal Weizman, *Lesser Evils: Scenes of Humanitarian Violence from Arendt to Gaza* (London: Verso, 2011), 12–14.

[119] Benjamin, interview.

[120] '[P]ursuant to IDF standing orders, commanders in the field are expected to carefully assess both the expected military gain and the potential of collateral injury to civilians and civilian property in the area. In making this determination, the commander considers numerous factors. [. . .] In assessing possible collateral damage, the commander will consider the number of civilians near the target; whether they are exposed or protected; the expected radius of the strike's lethal effects; and whether or not the attack can be delayed or carried out effectively with a more precise or less powerful weapon in the prevailing circumstances: Israel Ministry of Foreign Affairs, 'The Operation in Gaza—Factual and Legal Aspects', 96–7.

[121] Janina Dill, 'Israel's Use of Law and Warnings in Gaza', *Opinio Juris* (blog), 30 July 2014, http://opiniojuris.org/2014/07/30/guest-post-israels-use-law-warnings-gaza/#more-30943, accessed 8 October 2014; Eyal Weizman, 'Gaza Attacks: Lethal Warnings', *Al Jazeera*, 14 July 2014, http://www.aljazeera.com/indepth/opinion/2014/07/gaza-attacks-lethal-warnings-2014713162312604305.html, accessed 11 October 2014; Eyal Weizman, 'Legislative Attack', *Theory, Culture & Society* 27, no. 6 (2010): 11–32.

[122] Cohen and Shany write: 'We fear that this approach will lead the exception to the rule—no advanced warning in extreme circumstances—to become the norm, and that attacks will be sanctioned even when it is apparent that the IDF acts with partial or unconfirmed information on the number of civilians located inside targeted buildings': Amichai Cohen and Yuval Shany, 'Israel's Military Advocate General Terminates "Black Friday" and Other Investigations: Initial Observations', *Lawfare* (blog), 27 August 2018, https://www.lawfareblog.com/israels-military-advocate-general-terminates-black-friday-and-other-investigations-initial, accessed 20 December 2019.

civilian casualties.[123] Civilians in Gaza are frequently killed even when warnings are issued,[124] but what is remarkable about the MAG's approach is the juridical flexibility it affords: sometimes warnings are appropriate, other times not. Palestinian civilians are left guessing whether or not they will receive a warning, and either way the results are often fatal.

Military lawyers rarely find themselves in a position where they are required to say a straightforward 'no' to a commander for a planned targeting operation. This is partly because commanders are operationally aware of prevailing legal advice and do not want to waste time and energy proposing targets that likely will not be approved.[125] Occasionally this does happen: 'they [the commanders] would sometimes try and, you know, get it through. But we'd [the lawyers] say no that's not good enough'. There is also a sense in which military lawyers do not want to be the 'stick in the wheel, stopping the machine', to use Colonel Libman's phrase, once an operation is in the advanced planning stages, so lawyers try to avoid these situations by involving themselves in the early planning stages of operations. All commanders receive some training in the laws of war and there is little doubt that there has been a growing institutional acceptance of law of war principles in the Israeli military.[126] But accepting the laws of war principles is not the same thing as accepting the more *restrictive* principles of that legal regime, which is why the MAG and International Law Department refer not to International *Humanitarian* law (IHL) but rather the Law of Armed Conflict (LOAC), semantically emphasizing the *armed conflict* over and above the humanitarian obligations conferred by that legal regime.

Another explanation for why legal advisers rarely say 'no' could be that they have taken a generally permissive approach to targeting.[127] Linked to this is the obvious fact that legal advisers belong to the same military institute as their client; their ability to actually say 'no' is therefore culturally conditioned. Evidence of this lies in the wake of every planned target because military lawyers purportedly vet all targets that are 'withdrawn' from the 'target bank' before execution. But legal approval has been given even to starkly indiscriminate 'targeted' operations. On 22 July 2002 the Israeli Air Force dropped a one-tonne bomb on the house of Saleh Shehade, the leader of Hamas's military wing. In

[123] Military Advocate General, 'Decisions of the IDF Military Advocate General Regarding Exceptional Incidents That Allegedly Occurred During Operation "Protective Edge"', 15 August 2018, https://www.idf.il/en/minisites/military-advocate-generals-corps/releases-idf-military-advocate-general/mag-corps-press-release-update-6/, accessed 20 December 2019.

[124] Weizman, 'Gaza Attacks'.

[125] Libman, interview.

[126] Cohen, 'Legal Operational Advice in the Israeli Defense Forces'. Guiora, interview.

[127] Feldman and Blau, 'Consent and Advice'.

addition to Shehadeh and his guard, thirteen civilians, including eight children were killed and dozens more injured. The strike proved so controversial that Israel set up a special investigatory committee to find out why so many civilians had been killed. Nearly a decade later, the Israel Ministry of Foreign Affairs published its report, which included this immensely important passage:

> [A] gap arose between what was expected and what actually occurred. The central reason for this gap was incomplete, unfocused and inconsistent intelligence information with regard to the presence of civilians in the structures adjacent to the Shehadeh house (the garage and huts), where most of the civilians died. This gap stemmed from incorrect assessments and mistaken judgment based on an intelligence failure in the collection and transfer of information to the various echelons involved in the points of contact between the different agencies involved.[128]

The Israel Ministry of Foreign Affairs excused all those involved of any wrongdoing—including the military lawyers and Defense Minister who authorized the strike—because the disproportionate killing was 'unintended, undesired and unforeseen'.[129] Paradoxically, the strike was legalized precisely because proper procedures were *not* followed and because it resulted from an *incompetent* planning process through which civilians could not be identified or seen.

From targeted killing to wholesale targeting

The role played by military lawyers in individual targeted killing operations such as the one that killed Saleh Shehade and his family later paved the way for their wholesale involvement in large-scale targeting decisions during major military campaigns. Arguably, it is in the planning stages of major military operations—rather than individual targeted killing operations—that military lawyers have proved most potent in extending the scope of legal violence.

In 2002, the Israeli military laid the foundations for the attacking of civilian and government infrastructure. During that war, dubbed 'Operation Defensive

[128] Israel Ministry of Foreign Affairs, 'Salah Shehadeh - Special Investigatory Commission' (http://www.mfa.gov.il, 27 February 2011), ¶12, http://www.mfa.gov.il/MFA/Government/Law/Legal+Issues+and+Rulings/Salah_Shehadeh-Special_Investigatory_Commission_27-Feb-2011, accessed 6 July 2012.

[129] Ibid., ¶10.

Shield', the Israeli Air Force struck a variety of targets including the Ministry of Education; the Ministry of Civil Affairs; the Palestinian Legislative Council; the Central Bureau of Statistics; and the al-Bireh Municipal library.[130] A MAG legal memo (which remains classified) defined these as legitimate targets. In 2006, in Lebanon, the Israeli military demonstrated that the targeting of the civilian population and civilian infrastructure was not an anomaly but would henceforth become a policy. Not unlike what the US had done in its 1991 invasion of Iraq (Chapter 3), the logic was to bomb the civilian population into rejecting Hezbollah and in turn deter Hezbollah fighters from taking up arms against Israel; that is, morale bombing. Two years later—and making a promise for future violence of this kind—the Commanding Officer of Northern Command, Major General Gadi Eisenkott, unveiled what became known as the 'Dahiya Doctrine':

> In the Second Lebanon War we used a great deal of bombs. How else were 120,000 houses destroyed? [. . .] What happened in the Dahiya Quarter of Beirut in 2006, will happen in every village from which shots are fired on Israel. We will use disproportionate force against it and we will cause immense damage and destruction. From our point of view these are not civilian villages but military bases. [. . .] This is not a recommendation, this is the plan, and it has already been authorized.[131]

This is not a legitimate interpretation of the laws of war; disproportionate force is by definition illegal as it constitutes a violation of the principle of proportionality. Yet just two months before the outbreak of 'Operation Cast Lead' in December 2008 the Institute for National Security Studies, a think-tank at the Tel Aviv University which reflects mainstream military thinking, published an article by Dr Gabriel Siboni, a Colonel reservist who claimed that '[t]his approach is applicable to the Gaza Strip as well'.[132]

The planning for 'Operation Cast Lead' began six months in advance and military lawyer David Benjamin boasted that military lawyers were 'intimately

[130] Jessica Montell, 'Operation Defensive Shield', *Tikkun* 17, no. 4 (2002): 33–41; B'Tselem, 'Operation Defensive Shield' (Jerusalem, July 2002), http://www.btselem.org/download/200207_defensive_shield_eng.pdf, accessed 28 October 2014.

[131] Quoted in: Public Committee Against Torture in Israel (PCATI), 'No Second Thoughts: The Changes in the Israeli Defense Forces' Combat Doctrine in Light of "Operation Cast Lead"' (Jerusalem: PCATI, November 2009), 20, http://stoptorture.org.il/wp-content/uploads/2015/10/no-second-thoughts_ENG_WEB-2009.pdf, accessed 1 July 2020.

[132] Quoted in: Ibid., 21.

involved [in the] approval of targets'.[133] On the opening day of the assault the Israeli Air Force bombed a police cadet graduation ceremony, killing nearly fifty police personnel. By the end of the three-week assault, the Israeli military had killed a total of 248 civilian police officers who were not directly participating in hostilities. An *ex post facto* investigation by the Israel Ministry of Foreign Affairs revealed that the MAG had approved the targeting of police on the basis that the 'police are part of the armed forces' of Hamas.[134]

This gives a sense of the power of pre-defining targets through legal categories and it is not difficult to see how a *single* legal opinion—'the police now constitute a military target'—conditions and sets in motion not one but *several* targeting decisions. Two weeks into the operation Israeli military spokesman Captain Benjamin Rutland confirmed that the 'theory of the circles of involvement in terrorist organizations' had been revised and expanded to include the third and possibly also the fourth circles that had once been considered illegal targets by the MAG (section 4.4). Rutland told the BBC: 'our definition is that anyone who is involved with terrorism within Hamas is a valid target. This ranges from strictly military institutions and includes the political institutions that provide the logistical funding and human resources for the terrorist arm.'[135]

As documented by the Goldstone Report, the expansion of the definition of what constitutes a legitimate target led to mass destruction and death of persons and objects that should have been immune from attack, including, *inter alia*, civilians attempting to evacuate their houses; whole families who were in no way directly participating in hostilities; homes and whole residential areas; food and energy production facilities; medical facilities and medical vehicles; and UN buildings and mosques.[136] To justify each of these strikes the MAG offered two legal innovations: first, it defined civilian infrastructure as 'dual use', meaning that when a given facility or building is also used for military purposes it loses its protected status thus rendering it a 'legitimate target' (Chapter 3).[137] The same principle was later used to restrict imports into

[133] Quoted in: Gwen Ackerman, 'Israel Deploys Lawyers to Head Off War-Crimes Charges', *Bloomberg.Com*, 22 January 2009, http://www.bloomberg.com/apps/news?pid=newsarchive&sid=aMvUB8w9xphM&refer=home, accessed 10 October 2014. See also: Barak Ravid, 'IAF Strike Followed Months of Planning', *Haaretz.Com*, 28 December 2008, http://www.haaretz.com/print-edition/news/iaf-strike-followed-months-of-planning-1.260363, accessed 15 October 2014.

[134] Israel Ministry of Foreign Affairs, 'The Operation in Gaza—Factual and Legal Aspects', 89.

[135] Quoted in: Bisharat, 'Violence's Law', 77.

[136] United Nations Human Rights Council, 'Report of the United Nations Fact Finding Mission on the Gaza Conflict', 2009, 199–217, http://www2.ohchr.org/english/bodies/hrcouncil/docs/12session/A-HRC-12-48.pdf, accessed 10 September 2013.

[137] Israel Ministry of Foreign Affairs, 'The Operation in Gaza—Factual and Legal Aspects', 55.

Gaza: materials that could be used for military purposes—which includes supplies like concrete that are vital to everyday life and reconstruction after military bombardment—were prohibited or severely limited from entering Gaza from 2006 onwards. Many of these restrictions remain in place today. Second, and as documented by Eyal Weizman, the Israeli military made extensive use of 'technologies of warning', which were used as a *carte blanche* to target civilian areas after they had received warnings to evacuate.[138]

Despite the Israeli military's refusal to accept the findings of the Goldstone Report there is some evidence to suggest that the legal onslaught faced by Israel following Operation Cast Lead—and especially following the publication of the Goldstone Report in September 2009—impacted the conduct of the following operation in November 2012. A month after 'Operation Pillar of Defense' came to an end, former air force General and now director of The Institute for National Security Studies Amos Yadlin confirmed, 'the ghost of the Goldstone Report was hovering in the rooms where the list of targets was approved'.[139] Operation Pillar of Defense did result in far fewer Palestinian casualties than Operation Cast Lead: 168[140] compared to 1,398.[141]

However, the lower casualty count is more likely due to the twin facts that, unlike Operation Cast Lead, Operation Pillar of Defense did not have a ground invasion component and lasted eight days in comparison to three weeks. In stark contrast to the official Israeli narrative, a report issued by Israeli human rights organization B'Tselem, 'challenges the common perception in the Israeli public and media that the operation was "surgical" and caused practically no fatalities among uninvolved Palestinian civilians'.[142] Furthermore, in a letter to *The New York Times*, Israeli military spokesperson Lieutenant Colonel Avital Liebovitch outlined the legal justification for striking media and communications facilities and killing Palestinian and foreign journalists:

[138] Weizman, *Lesser Evils*; Weizman, 'Gaza Attacks'.

[139] Amos Yadlin, 'Conclusion' in *In the Aftermath of Operation Pillar of Defense: The Gaza Strip November 2012*, ed. Shlomo Brom (Tel Aviv: The Institute for National Security Studies (INSS), December 2012), Memorandum No. 124, 93, https://www.inss.org.il/publication/in-the-aftermath-of-operation-pillar-of-defense-the-gaza-strip-november-2012/, accessed 16 October 2014.

[140] United Nations Human Rights Council, 'Concerns Related to Adherence to International Human Rights and International Humanitarian Law in the Context of the Escalation between the State of Israel, the de Facto Authorities in Gaza and Palestinian Armed Groups in Gaza That Occurred from 14 to 21 November 2012', 4.

[141] B'Tselem, 'Fatalities during Operation Cast Lead'.

[142] B'Tselem, 'Harm to Civilians Significantly Higher in Second Half of Operation Pillar of Defense', 8 May 2013, http://www.btselem.org/press_releases/20130509_pillar_of_defense_report, accessed 16 October 2014. See also: Human Rights Watch, 'Unlawful Israeli Attacks on Palestinian Media', 20 December 2012, http://www.hrw.org/news/2012/12/20/israelgaza-unlawful-israeli-attacks-palestinian-media, accessed 30 September 2014.

> [W]hen terrorist organizations exploit reporters, either by posing as them or by hiding behind them, they are the immediate threat to freedom of the press. Such terrorists, who hold cameras and notebooks in their hands, are no different from their colleagues who fire rockets aimed at Israeli cities and cannot enjoy the rights and protection afforded to legitimate journalists.[143]

If any lessons were learnt from Operation Cast Lead they were in any case forgotten by the summer of 2014. When UN Secretary General Ban Ki-moon visited Gaza nearly two months after the end of 'Operation Protective Edge' he could not find words for the destruction he witnessed, saying that it was 'beyond description'.[144] The Israeli military struck some 5,266 targets in Gaza and the air force also carried out 840 strikes in support of troops on the ground.[145] According to a bomb disposal expert in the Gaza Ministry of Interior this amounted to over 20,000 tonnes of explosives, the equivalent of six nuclear bombs in as many weeks.[146]

Reports from human rights organizations suggest that the overly permissive approach adopted by legal advisers in Operation Cast Lead were re-adopted and even extended in preparation for Operation Protective Edge, giving rise to what Laleh Khalili has called a 'habit of destruction'.[147] Medical facilities and medical workers were targeted,[148] as were UN shelters and schools;[149] acts that were condemned by the White House as 'totally unacceptable' and 'totally indefensible'.[150] In a letter to the MAG, B'Tselem suggested that legal and military

[143] Quoted in: Bisharat, 'Violence's Law', 77.

[144] Peter Beaumont and Hazem Balousha, 'Ban Ki-Moon: Gaza Is a Source of Shame to the International Community', *The Guardian*, 14 October 2014, sec. World, http://www.theguardian.com/world/2014/oct/14/ban-ki-moon-visits-gaza-views-destruction-of-un-school, accessed 16 October 2014.

[145] Ben Hartman, '50 Days of Israel's Gaza Operation, Protective Edge—by the Numbers', *The Jerusalem Post*, 28 August 2014, http://www.jpost.com/Operation-Protective-Edge/50-days-of-Israels-Gaza-operation-Protective-Edge-by-the-numbers-372574, accessed 16 October 2014.

[146] Ma'an News, 'Police: Israel Dropped "equivalent of 6 Nuclear Bombs" on Gaza', *Maan News Agency*, 22 August 2014, http://group194.net/english/article/36928, accessed 1 July 2020.

[147] Laleh Khalili, 'A Habit of Destruction', *Society and Space—Environment and Planning D* (blog), 2014, http://societyandspace.com/material/commentaries/laleh-khalili-a-habit-of-destruction/, accessed 9 November 2014.

[148] Amnesty International, 'Evidence of Medical Workers and Facilities Being Targeted by Israeli Forces in Gaza', 7 August 2014, http://www.amnesty.org/en/library/asset/MDE15/023/2014/en/c931e37b-a3c2-414f-b3a6-a00986896a09/mde150232014en.pdf, accessed 16 October 2014; Derek Gregory, 'Destructive Edge', *Geographical Imaginations* (blog), 8 August 2014, http://geographicalimaginations.com/2014/08/08/destructive-edge/, accessed 16 October 2014; Derek Gregory, 'Gaza 101', *Geographical Imaginations* (blog), 21 July 2014, https://geographicalimaginations.com/2014/07/21/gaza-101/, accessed 7 January 2017.

[149] Human Rights Watch, 'Israel/Gaza'.

[150] Paul Lewis and Ian Black, 'Gaza Conflict: US Says Israeli Attack on UN School Was "Totally Unacceptable"', *The Guardian*, 31 July 2014, http://www.theguardian.com/world/2014/jul/31/gaza-conflict-us-israeli-attack-un-school, accessed 16 October 2014.

directives had been given 'to attack the homes of operatives in Hamas and other organizations as though they were legitimate military targets'.[151] B'Tselem's investigations also found a 'proliferation of incidents in which many civilians were killed in a single incident—more than in previous operations—in terms of both the number of casualties in each incident and the overall number of such instances'.[152]

Since September 2014 the Israeli military has been conducting investigations into what the MAG call 'Exceptional Incidents' that occurred during Operation Protective Edge. So far, the MAG has received 'around 500 complaints and reports' and have reviewed some 360 'incidents'.[153] So far, twenty-four cases have been referred for criminal investigation, which has led to the conviction of three soldiers for the crime of looting. An additional 220 incidents were referred to a fact-finding team, which resulted in seven further criminal investigations (five did not result in criminal charges and two are ongoing at the time of writing). The MAG has published periodic updates about its decision to continue or close investigations (the vast majority of investigations have been closed without being referred for criminal investigation) and in August 2018 it announced that it was closing investigations into several high-profile and controversial targeting decisions.

In one aerial strike, the Israeli military targeted a residential building in order to kill a senior Hamas commander. The intelligence assessment found that 'no civilians were present in the structure', and that the 'entire structure' (rather than a particular part of it) must be struck in order to attack the commander. After issuing no warnings, thirty-five civilians were killed and a further twenty-seven were injured.[154] In another strike, a family home in Al-Bureij was hit because it was allegedly being used as an active Hamas command and control centre. This time the intelligence assessment showed that civilians were 'likely to be present in the building' but the anticipated 'collateral damage' was not expected to be 'excessive'. Again, no warnings were issued because this may have 'frustrated the objective of the attack'. The strike killed nineteen or twenty civilians (no data on the injured), a figure that the MAG concedes is 'substantially higher' than had been anticipated by the intelligence assessment.[155] In yet

[151] B'Tselem, 'Investigation of Incidents That Took Place during Recent Military Action in Gaza: July–August 2014', 4 September 2014, 2.

[152] Ibid., 3.

[153] Military Advocate General, 'Decisions of the IDF Military Advocate General Regarding Exceptional Incidents That Allegedly Occurred During Operation "Protective Edge" '. The discrepancy between the number of complaints received and the number of reviews undertaken is explained by the fact that some incidents received multiple complaints.

[154] Ibid., 24–6.

[155] Ibid., 26–8.

another attack on a 'structure' that allegedly served as a Hamas weapons depot in Khan Younis, military intelligence again assessed that 'no civilians would be harmed'. The planning of the strike neglected to reveal the fact that the 'structure' contained a café and the strike killed a further nine civilians (again, no data on the injured).

In each of these cases—and many more—the MAG took no disciplinary or criminal proceedings on the basis that the actions reviewed 'accorded with Israeli domestic law and international law requirements' (a phrase repeated more than thirty times in the MAG investigation updates). Key law of war principles are summoned in order to defend Israeli military action: the attacks were against *military* targets; civilian casualties were *proportionate* (and often unforeseen); steps were taken to *minimize* civilian casualties; and though strikes often led to 'difficult and regrettable' results, civilian harm 'does not affect the legality of the attack[s] *ex post facto*'.[156]

It is difficult to meaningfully engage with, let alone dispute, these conclusions because the relevant information is not in the public domain and remains classified. Even if we were to accept at face value the MAG's assertions that Israeli aerial action in 'Protective Edge' was overwhelmingly lawful (*qua* procedurally compliant), serious doubts remain about the quality of intelligence and the standards required in order to authorize a strike. For Cohen and Shany there are:

> [D]ifficult questions regarding the amount and quality of intelligence a military commander should gather prior to ordering an attack, particularly against buildings used by enemy combatants that might contain civilians. [. . .] the MAG suggests that, at least in relation to criminal law, the burden on military commanders to gather substantial amounts of quality intelligence is low."[157]

But more to the point, military lawyers 'were constantly present and available to commanders [. . .] to provide ongoing operational legal advice' during 'Protective Edge'.[158] Even the most lethal and large-scale violence went through legal review. Much like in the First Gulf War, successive Israeli military

[156] Ibid., 26.
[157] Cohen and Shany, 'Israel's Military Advocate General Terminates "Black Friday" and Other Investigations'.
[158] Military Advocate General of the Israel Defense Force, 'Operation "Pillar of Defense" 14–21 November 2012', 5.

operations in Gaza over the last decade have witnessed widespread infrastructural and human destruction by legal design (Chapter 3).

4.6 Violence Legislates

Though it may now seem difficult to believe, the European Union and the United States condemned the 2000 attack on Hussein Abiyat, and rejected Israel's legal justification for targeting individuals. British Foreign Secretary Jack Straw claimed that the assassinations were 'unlawful, unjustified and self-defeating'.[159] The European Union insisted that the policy amounted to 'extra-judicial killings', while the United States State Department spokesman Richard Boucher said such action was 'heavy-handed'. The US government made it repeatedly clear that it opposed targeted killings.[160] An international fact-finding mission, established by President Clinton and led by former US Senator George Mitchell, refused to accept the Israeli view that the threshold of 'armed conflict' had been crossed. As far as Mitchell was concerned, the Second Intifada constituted civil unrest—a domestic *police* issue—and not war. The Mitchell Report dismissed the idea of war as being 'overly broad' and noted that the 'IDF should adopt crowd-control tactics that minimize the potential for deaths and casualties', further urging that 'an effort should be made to differentiate between terrorism and protests'.[161] The message was clear: terrorism could not legitimately be dealt with via recourse to war, and Israel should revert back to the law enforcement approach, a legal regime that places far greater restrictions on the use of lethal force than the laws of war does.[162]

Daniel Reisner recalls that the United States and the United Kingdom 'aggressively attacked' the legal opinions of the International Law Department and the MAG. That was in late 2000 and early 2001. Then 9/11 happened. He

[159] House of Commons, 'Oral Answers to Questions: Foreign and Commonwealth Affairs' (available from the Palestinian Centre for Human Rights, 30 March 2004), http://pchrgaza.org/files/campaigns/english/almog/jack.pdf, accessed 19 July 2012.

[160] Craig Jones, 'Travelling Law: Targeted Killing, Lawfare and the Deconstruction of the Battlefield', in *American Studies Encounters the Middle East* (Chapel Hill: University of North Carolina Press, 2016), 207–40. General Counsel to the Department of Defence Jeh Charles Johnson rejected the label of assassination for his administration's drone-led killing operation, calling it 'one of the most repugnant in our vocabulary': Jeh Charles Johnson, 'National Security Law, Lawyers, and Lawyering in the Obama Administration-Dean's Lecture at Yale Law School, February 22, 2012', *Yale Law and Policy Review* 31, no. 1 (2012): 147.

[161] Mitchell et al., 'Sharm El-Sheikh Fact-Finding Committee Final Report': no page.

[162] Ibid. See also: Daniel Reisner, 'International Law and Military Operations in Practice —III—Jerusalem Center For Public Affairs', Jerusalem Center For Public Affairs, 18 June 2013, http://jcpa.org/article/international-law-and-military-operations-in-practice-iii/, accessed 11 November 2013.

drily pointed out 'it took four months and four aircraft to change the mind of the US government'.[163] Early in 2001, the United States had sent delegations to Israel to try to persuade the Israeli military to stop the targeted killings. After the attacks on New York and Washington DC they returned with a different mission: they wanted to learn from Israel and to study how Israel had developed and justified its targeted killing policy.[164] The exact nature of those meetings is classified but news sources at the time reported:

> The Bush administration has been seeking Israel's counsel on creating a legal justification for the assassination of terrorism suspects [. . .] Legal experts from the United States and Israel have met in recent months to discuss the issue, and are considering widening the consultation circle to include representatives of America's closest allies in the war against terrorism [. . .] American representatives were anxious to learn details of the legal work that Israeli government jurists have done during the last two years to tackle possible challenges—both domestic and international—to its policy of 'targeted killings' of terrorist suspects.[165]

Needless to say, the results are opaque. But several advocates of a more permissive approach to the US targeted killing policy have been inspired by or have drawn upon the Israeli experience. Former UN Special Rapporteur on extrajudicial, summary, or arbitrary executions Philip Alston has usefully catalogued some of the most vocal of these opinions:

> [Amos] Guiora [. . .] argues that, 'international laws explicitly providing for active self-defense should be formed out of what has been learned from Israel's struggle with terrorism.' The tendency to extrapolate from Israel's experience in order to arrive at policy prescriptions for the United States is well illustrated by the title and subtitle of a later article by the same author: 'License to Kill: When I advised the Israel Defense Forces, here's how we decided if targeted kills were legal—or not.' [. . .] Similarly, Michael Gross criticises the inflexibility of international humanitarian lawyers who are not prepared to 'reconsider the merits' of targeted killings, chemical warfare, and attacks on

[163] Reisner, 'International Law and Military Operations in Practice—III—Jerusalem Center for Public Affairs', 63.

[164] Reisner, interview.

[165] Ori Nir, 'Bush Seeks Israeli Advice on "Targeted Killings"', *The Electronic Intifada/The Forward*, 7 February 2003, http://electronicintifada.net/content/bush-seeks-israeli-advice-targeted-killings/4391, accessed 5 November 2013.

> currently protected groups of civilians. [. . .] almost all of the factual information and case studies are drawn from Israel's policies. [. . .] other commentators [Gabriella Blum and Phillip Heyman] suggest that there is already an identity of interest and indeed even a degree of symmetry in terms of both law and policy between Israeli and American approaches.[166]

The US criticism of the Israeli targeted killing policy was indeed short-lived. By 2000, the Central Intelligence Agency (CIA) was flying Predator drones over Afghanistan in search of Osama bin Laden, but they were still unarmed when Israel announced its targeted killing campaign. In late 2000 the head of the CIA's Counter Terrorism Center, Cofer Black, decided to arm the Predator even though the head of the CIA, George Tenet, still had 'serious questions about the new killing technology and the ethics and legality behind its use'.[167] Shortly after the 9/11 terror attacks, George W. Bush approved a presidential finding that sanctioned CIA strikes on Al Qaeda as a 'defensive' measure in the then nascent 'global war on terror'.

The first lethal drone missions were conducted in Afghanistan in late 2001. Only a year later armed drones were introduced into Yemen, a fact that demonstrated the malleability of the 'war on terror' concept while also radically expanding its geographies. On 3 November 2002 CIA operatives fired a Hellfire missile from a Predator drone, killing Qaed Salim Sinan al Harethi who was allegedly responsible for organizing the suicide bombing attack on the USS Cole (a US Navy destroyer) in October 2000. Two days after killing al Harethi, Deputy Defense Secretary Paul Wolfowitz openly confirmed it was a US strike and called it a 'very successful tactical operation'.[168] The first strike by an armed drone outside of Afghanistan—and thus outside any defined battlefield—this resembled and yet also exceeded Israel's attempt to justify assassination by further expanding the definition of war. Both the United States and Israel have defied the international consensus on assassination, and in this sense, we may read the invention, development, and legal conditioning of Israel's 'targeted

[166] Philip Alston, 'The CIA and Targeted Killings beyond Borders', *Harvard National Security Journal* 2, no. 1 (2011): 408–9. The works cited by Alston in order are: Amos N. Guiora, 'License to Kill', *Foreign Policy*, 14 July 2009, http://www.foreignpolicy.com/articles/2009/07/13/licence_to_kill#sthash.zCjE83OL.dpbs, accessed 14 December 2014; Michael L. Gross, *Moral Dilemmas of Modern War: Torture, Assassination, and Blackmail in an Age of Asymmetric Conflict* (Cambridge; New York, NY: Cambridge University Press, 2010); Gabriella Blum and Philip Heymann, 'Law and Policy of Targeted Killing', *Harvard National Security Journal* 1 (2010): 167, 169.

[167] Quoted in: Brian Glyn Williams, 'The CIA's Covert Predator Drone War in Pakistan, 2004–2010: The History of an Assassination Campaign', *Studies in Conflict & Terrorism* 33, no. 10 (2010): 873.

[168] Quoted in: Jeremy Scahill, 'The Dangerous US Game in Yemen', *The Nation*, 30 March 2011, http://www.thenation.com/article/dangerous-us-game-yemen/, accessed 29 September 2015.

killing' policy as the origins of a radical and potentially global assassination programme.

Military lawyers in Israel have been central to this monumental reinterpretation of the laws of war and their applicability to targeted killing. Their lawyerly practices at many different levels—from military policy to tactical arrangements—and daily involvement in targeting issues constitute important interpretive acts that are no less than law making in character. Walter Benjamin once famously wrote that military violence has a 'lawmaking character'—it establishes new social and legal orders—but clearly some forms of military violence are more likely to legislate than others.[169] Targeted killing proved convenient beyond Israel's borders and has been taken up by the United States and other states as a hyper and legally rationalized form of warfare. In this chapter I have shown that the involvement of military lawyers in targeting and specifically in the development of Israel's targeted killing policy have helped legalize certain forms of (once prohibited) violence. But perhaps more fundamentally I have also exposed the legislative nature of a specifically and deliberately *juridically conditioned* violence. For violence may indeed legislate,[170] but *juridically conditioned* violence is far more alluring and persuasive than arbitrary forms of military violence untouched by law.

[169] Walter Benjamin, 'Critique of Violence', in *Walter Benjamin: Selected Writings, Volume 1: 1913-1926*, ed. Marcus Bullock and Michael W. Jennings, 1st edition (Cambridge, MA: Belknap Press, 1996), 236–52.

[170] Weizman, 'Legislative Attack'.

5

The Kill Chain (I)

Deliberate Targeting

5.1 Groundhog Day in the 'CAOC'

'Was there such a thing as a day in the life of the CAOC?', I asked Colonel Gary Brown, who served as the senior legal adviser at the US Combined Air Operations Center (CAOC) in Qatar in 2008 and 2009.[1] 'Sure there was', replied Brown, 'the guys called it Groundhog Day'. 'The guys' were the men and women who worked with Brown in the CAOC, whose collective job it was to put the right weapons on the right targets in Afghanistan and Iraq.

His typical day, he explained, would look something like this. He would wake up at around 06.00, have 'chow' (breakfast), and then attend the intelligence briefing given by the Chief of Intelligence at around 06.30. The morning brief where the most senior commander in the CAOC, the Combined Forces Air Component Commander, or his deputy, would get everyone up to speed on the Air Tasking Order (ATO) and the operational priorities for that day was at 07.00. The ATO is a planning document that maps out the sorties and targeting missions to be flown within a specified timeframe, normally twenty-four hours. After that was yet another briefing, this time from the 'operations floor'—those in charge of conducting aerial operations in real time. Brown would then begin to settle into what is known doctrinally as the 'battle rhythm' (see Chapter 3, Figure 3.3).[2] He would locate the other Judge Advocates (JAGs) to find out what had happened overnight and then, usually in the mid-morning, the handover from night shift to day shift would take place. There was no downtime when he and his three subordinate JAGs were working (on rotation), and their duties ranged from revising sophisticated flow charts to

[1] Colonel Brown retired from military service in 2012 and went to work for the International Committee of the Red Cross (ICRC). He is now a Professor of Cyber Security at Marine Corps University, Quantico, Virginia.

[2] Several ATO's are stitched together to make a 'battle rhythm' and 'planning cycle' of seventy-two to ninety-six hours: United States Joint Chiefs of Staff, 'Joint Air Operations' (Washington, DC: Joint Chiefs of Staff, 25 July 2019), xvii, https://www.jcs.mil/Portals/36/Documents/Doctrine/pubs/jp3_30.pdf, accessed 5 February 2020.

The War Lawyers. Craig Jones, Oxford University Press (2020). © Craig Jones.
DOI: 10.1093/oso/9780198842927.001.0001.

making sure that everyone understood the ROE (because they were constantly changing) to providing advice on ongoing targeting operations. 'We spent hours talking about how the chart could best portray the ROE [rules of engagement] so people could quickly look at it and give an answer', Brown recalled. If there were strikes being planned, Brown would go to the intelligence building and talk to the 'intelligence guys'; he would find the weaponeers and the targeteers or talk to the pilots and 'go over some ATO things'.

The daily battle rhythm in 2008 and 2009 was driven by events in Afghanistan, but both the Afghan and Iraqi theatres required a considerable amount of Intelligence, Surveillance and Reconnaissance (ISR), which Brown and everyone else in the CAOC relied upon for maintaining 'situational awareness'.[3] Predator and Reaper drone feeds were always up on the big display screens on the wall. For the rest of the day, Brown would immerse himself in targeting operations. He was stationed in the 'battle cab' overlooking the operations floor; this is where the senior commanders—the decision makers—are located. Brown would sit with them and answer any questions they had. He would also ask questions to others in the kill chain—intelligence analysts, pilots, weaponeers, and planning staff—both to check what they were doing and to improve his own situational awareness.[4] He would also check intelligence and assess its reliability. But most importantly he would *advise*.

Brown was not always able to provide legal advice or perform a legal review of every single target; some were struck without him—or other lawyers at the CAOC—seeing them. Every time there was a deliberate strike, Brown was called, even if it was in the middle of the night. The CAOC never sleeps, not when there are literally hundreds of sorties to fly in a twenty-four-hour period.[5] But when the CAOC received a request to provide close air support (CAS) to troops in contact (TIC) they often left Brown in bed. When troops are in contact with the enemy a quick response is paramount. 'TICs' happen on a

[3] The first month of Operation Iraqi Freedom (OIF) alone generated 42,000 images and 3,200 hours of full motion video: Michael T. Moseley, 'Operation Iraqi Freedom: By the Numbers', Assessment and Analysis Division, US Air Force Central Command (AFCENT), 30 April 2003, 3 (on file with author).

[4] 'JAGs and paralegals should maintain situational awareness to identify legal issues resulting from the execution of planned or time-sensitive operations.' United States Air Force, 'Air Force Doctrine Document 1-04, Legal Support to Operations' (US Air Force LeMay Center for Doctrine Development, 4 March 2012), 10, https://fas.org/irp/doddir/usaf/afdd1-04.pdf, accessed 28 January 2016.

[5] The number of sorties flown in any given period is dictated by the battle rhythm and intensity of the conflict. According to David Deptula: 'In the campaign against the Islamic State, we are averaging 12 strike sorties per day. During Operation Desert Storm in Iraq and Kuwait in 1991, the average was 1,241; in Operation Allied Force in Kosovo in 1999, it was 298; in the first 30 days of Operation Iraqi Freedom in 2003, 691; during Operation Enduring Freedom in Afghanistan in 2001, 86.' David A. Deptula, 'How to Defeat the Islamic State', *The Washington Post*, 5 June 2015, https://www.washingtonpost.com/opinions/how-to-defeat-the-islamic-state/2015/06/05/50ff6fca-0af7-11e5-a7ad-b430fc1d3f5c_story.html?utm_term=.2052f6469bda, accessed 28 October 2016.

'very regular basis', according to Brown, and it was not possible to provide legal advice on them all. Air Force doctrine maintains that the procedures for deliberate (planned) and dynamic (unplanned, including TIC) targeting are very similar, but Brown's account of being woken for the former and sometimes left in bed for the latter—suggests otherwise. (The two types of targeting are the subject of the current and subsequent chapter, respectively.)

Brown would not stop at giving only legal advice. A good kill chain lawyer gives a commander a wide spectrum of advice that considers the full range of issues: not only 'is this legal?' but also, 'is this smart?' or, 'how will this look on CNN?' So important was the twenty-four-hour news cycle and the issue of public perception that 'dead center in the middle of the command center data wall was a massive television projection of CNN'.[6] This not only enabled the CAOC staff to see how their targeting operations were being reported in the media but also allowed JAGs to 'get in front of the CNN news cycle', preempting situations that 'could turn into a public relations nightmare'.[7]

Good kill chain lawyers leave their desks a lot. They are proactive and make themselves known to others in the kill chain. They take it upon themselves to learn as much as they can about the various technical aspects of aerial targeting so that they are better able to situate their legal advice and speak in a language that commanders understand. Lawyers in the CAOC eat and breathe the targeting process.[8] Brown was one such lawyer and well-liked among commanders. He joked around with them, knowing that 'the military is sort of famous for its dark and cutting humour'. 'Comedy is where I got where I am', he told me. The serious point is that the commander–lawyer relationship is personality driven and it cannot work unless there is mutual respect between the two parties.[9] Key members and senior staff in the kill chain lived within the CAOC compound so that they were always near the operations floor where all the action took place. Brown slept just a 'one-minute walk away . . . two minutes from my bed to my desk'. He shared close quarters in a trailer with two other colonels, including the CAOC deputy director, about fifteen feet from the CAOC. 'We three colonels lived together, shared a bathroom, had a little tight living area so we got to know each other really well [. . .].'[10]

[6] William Arkin, 'Air Heads', *Armed Forces Journal*, 1 June 2006, http://armedforcesjournal.com/air-heads/, accessed 12 December 2016.

[7] Landreneau, interview, 24 March 2015.

[8] 'Commanders should fully integrate JAGs and paralegals into combat operations processes': United States Air Force, 'Air Force Doctrine Document 1-04, Legal Support to Operations', 10.

[9] Prescott, interview; Landreneau, interview; Meyer, interview.

[10] The CAOC has since moved to the provision of private quarters: Brown, interview.

Brown's last scheduled briefing was at 18.00, followed by dinner. Brown went to bed early and would then do it all over again, seven days a week. The six-month rotations could be quiet or busy depending on the shift and much of the work was monotonous. On quieter Sundays—a rarity—Brown would take the afternoon off or go into work a little later. There were a gym and a couple of bars on the base, but the bars generally imposed a three-drink maximum rule. There was not much else to do.

Brown's day is a partial snapshot of a particular time and place, but it is also a fairly typical snapshot, at least among those who worked in the CAOC that I interviewed. His account speaks to the deep and often intimate involvement of kill chain lawyers in the very bureaucratic yet also fundamentally social structures of targeting and everyday life in the CAOC: battle rhythms that mix with sleeping rhythms; the sharing of close quarters; the importance of humour as well as a wide appreciation of military sub-specializations, languages and—of course—acronyms. Kill chain lawyers are not outside the CAOC (as they were once outside of the Vietnam War's equivalent—Chapter 1), or even on its periphery: they are part of its very fabric.

This homogeneity of experience across time ('Groundhog Day'), and within and across specializations—one might even call it inter-operability of experience—is critical for how we think about the role of law in structuring targeting operations. This is because now more than ever the later modern kill chain and its legalities are co-produced. In the CAOC and at other locations in the kill chain, technical registers mix with and animate law and legal advice, and vice versa, in a co-constitutive, iterative process.[11] Military necessity produces and is produced by 'PID' (Positive Identification (of the target)), which produces and is produced by FMV (Full Motion Video), enabling a 'visual chain of custody' over the target, supplemented by (legal) interpretations over the reliability of 'HUMINT', 'SIGINT', 'GEOINT', 'CYBINT' (human, signals, geographic, and cyber intelligence) assessments, and so much more. Proportionality produces and is produced by 'CDEM' (Collateral Damage Estimation Methodology), 'NCV' (Non-Combatant cut-off Value), considerations around 'CIVCAS' (Civilian Casualties), and calculations of CEP (Circular Error Probable), which are produced by and produce techno-legal questions like: what type and size of munition should we use? What angle should we fire the weapon at? Delayed fuse or not? Is that building—where

[11] '[L]egal expertise and their objects generate each other': Anna Leander and Tanja Aalberts, 'Introduction: The Co-Constitution of Legal Expertise and International Security', *Leiden Journal of International Law* 26, no. 4 (2013): 784.

the target is thought to be located—made of concrete or wood, and what is the likely blast radius and 'frag' (fragmentation) pattern? What about the structure next door—is that a shop, a house, or something else? And having answered all those questions, another: have we done enough to satisfy proportionality requirements and the ROE given the military objective at hand, or should we run the CDE (Collateral Damage Estimate) again now the target is on the move? As I shall show in this and the following chapter (Chapter 6), the war lawyer has gained operational expertise and, meanwhile, operators have internalized what war lawyers have taught them.

Brown's account is also important because the monotony of the CAOC's routines arguably facilitate killing by rendering it banal and unremarkable, precluding external points of reference through which one might ordinarily be sensitized. To borrow from Zygmunt Bauman and Elke Schwarz, the kill chain writ large, and the role of the war lawyer within it, contribute to the *adiaphorization* of killing.[12] Adiaphorization is an ecclesiastical term that describes the process by which certain forms of action come to be excluded from moral judgement. As Elke Schwarz puts it, adiaphorization 'is the product of organized modern societies that enables people 'to silence their moral misgivings in order to get certain jobs done' ".[13] I will return to this idea and explore its consequences in more depth in the Conclusion, but suffice it to say for now, the banality of the kill chain and its routinization of procedures contributes in no small part to the normalization and neutralization of aerial violence. In the later modern kill chain, more than ever, ethical horizons are eclipsed by technical effectiveness and procedural legality.

* * *

The CAOC is located on Al Udeid Air Base in Doha, Qatar, and since 2003 it has been the command and control centre for US-led aerial targeting operations not only in Afghanistan and Iraq but also Syria and '17 other nations'.[14]

[12] Zygmunt Bauman, 'Ethics of Individuals', *The Canadian Journal of Sociology/Cahiers Canadiens de Sociologie* 25, no. 1 (2000): 83–96; Elke Schwarz, 'Prescription Drones: On the Techno-Biopolitical Regimes of Contemporary "Ethical Killing"', *Security Dialogue* 47, no. 1 (2016): 59–75.

[13] Schwarz, 'Prescription Drones', 70. Quoting: Michael Hviid Jacobsen and Poul Poder, *The Sociology of Zygmunt Bauman: Challenges and Critique* (Aldershot; Burlington, VT: Ashgate, 2008), 81.

[14] United States Air Forces Central Command, 'Combined Air Operations Center (CAOC)', 6 February 2011, http://www.afcent.af.mil/About/FactSheets/Display/tabid/4822/Article/217803/combined-air-operations-center-caoc.aspx, accessed 15 December 2016. (A subsequent version of this URL removed all references to these seventeen other nations.) The initial phase of the Afghan air war was conducted from the US Central Command CAOC at Prince Sultan Air Base in Saudi Arabia, but from late 2002 operations began to migrate to Al Udeid: Benjamin S. Lambeth, *The Unseen War: Allied Air Power and the Takedown of Saddam Hussein* (Annapolis, MD: Naval Institute Press, 2013), xvi. The US arrangement with Qatar allowed 'a wider range of military operations' than were permitted

Figure 5.1 The Combined Air Operations Center (CAOC) at Al Udeid Air Base, Qatar. The CAOC provides command and control of air power throughout Iraq, Syria, Afghanistan, and seventeen other nations.
Source: US Air Force photo by Tech. Sergeant Joshua Strang, https://www.robins.af.mil/News/Article-Display/Article/1246724/airmen-given-direct-access-to-aoc-development-process/, accessed 13 July 2017.

The CAOC at Al Udeid is the largest US military base in the Middle East and in 2015 it was home to some 10,000 US troops.[15] Built from scratch at the cost of US$60 million, the value of the CAOC to the US Air Force is difficult to overstate.[16] General (ret.) Ron Keys, the former Air Force Deputy Chief of Staff, claimed that without the CAOC, the US Air Force would 'amount to little more than an expensive flying club'.[17]

With its advanced ISR capabilities and multitude of display screens, the US Air Force claims that the CAOC 'resembles the set of a futuristic movie' (Figure 5.1).[18] Advances in ISR have transformed the role of JAGs in aerial targeting

by the US agreement with Saudi Arabia and prior to the opening of the CAOC the Qataris 'indicated they would not place limits on rules of engagement': Global Security, 'Al Udeid Air Base', accessed 15 December 2016, http://www.globalsecurity.org/military/facility/udeid.htm, accessed 15 December 2016. See also: Lambeth, *The Unseen War*, 35–36.

[15] Global Security, 'Al Udeid Air Base'.
[16] United States Air Forces Central Command, 'Combined Air Operations Center (CAOC)'.
[17] Quoted in: Lambeth, *The Unseen War*, 218.
[18] United States Air Forces Central Command, 'Combined Air Operations Center (CAOC)'.

operations, providing a stream of what Issacharoff and Pildes call 'adjudicative facts' about potential enemy targets.[19] As Colonel James Bitzes, an Air Force lawyer with CAOC experience, recalled: 'When I was sitting at my desk I could call up a picture that showed me exactly where all the planes are in Afghanistan, I could look at imagery on my own if I wasn't satisfied with the imagery that was presented to me for a target, or I wanted to see more about what the surrounding area looked like.'[20] Maintaining what the US Air Force call a 'visual chain of custody'[21] over potential targets allows for precision in targeting-legalities, according to Colonel Brown:

> It's airborne ISR that gives us the ability to actually apply [laws of war] principles (with almost mathematical precision) [. . .] we most often have photos of the target and often have FMV [full motion video] of the target area before, during and after the strike, so we can know with near certainty what collateral casualties or damage we are likely to cause.[22]

Former US military lawyer Jack M. Beard similarly praises what he calls 'virtual weapons systems' for their ability to provide 'unprecedented quantities and types of ISR data for targeting', which in turn enables 'an extraordinary level of legal review for an air strike in progress.'[23] He too insists that advances in ISR allow for ever more precise legal adjudication of the target:

> [T]he availability of new types of information can change the meaning of what constitutes an appropriate legal review. In place of the limited, sporadic information issued by satellites and manned aircraft, virtual technologies can supply lawyers and planners with data that encompass all visible activities around a target on a continuous basis. The same 'unblinking eye' that enables persistent surveillance of a target long before an attack can thus capture [. . .] the presence at that site of civilians that would be endangered by any planned attack.[24]

[19] Samuel Issacharoff and Richard H. Pildes, 'Drones and the Dilemma of Modern Warfare', *NYU School of Law, Public Law Research Paper No. 13-34*, 1 June 2013, 6, http://papers.ssrn.com/abstract=2268596, accessed 4 November 2013.

[20] James Bitzes, 'Role of an Air Operations Center Legal Advisor in Targeting' (Drones, targeting and the promise of law conference, Washington, DC, 24 February 2011, notes on file with author).

[21] Dana Priest and William M. Arkin, *Top Secret America: The Rise of the New American Security State* (New York, NY; Boston, MA; London: Little, Brown and Company, 2011), 213.

[22] Quoted in: Charles Dunlap, 'Come the Revolution: A Legal Perspective on Air Operations in Iraq since 2003', *International Law Studies. US Naval War College* 86 (2010): 146.

[23] Jack M. Beard, 'Law and War in the Virtual Era', *American Journal of International Law* 103, no. 3 (2009): 413, 410.

[24] Ibid., 419.

Yet as much as ISR and virtual technologies enable operators, commanders, and lawyers to identify, track, and ultimately 'prosecute' targets, they do not provide an omniscient view of the battlespace, and neither do they render it transparent—far from it. The kill chain is replete with blind spots and biases—technological, legal, and cultural—and its planning and execution is not nearly as clean and surgical in practice as doctrine and protocols suggest. Access to ISR is provisional and not everybody in the kill chain has access to drone and FMV feeds. Moreover, the images they produce can be extremely low-quality.[25] Even high-quality images require extensive interpretive work (is that a 'VBIED'—Vehicle-Borne Improvised Explosive Device—or has that family car just broken down at the side of the road?). The clearest drone feeds do not—could not—provide those in the kill chain with an omniscient or neutral vantage point from which to divine the legality of a potential strike. Rather, militarized ways of knowing and seeing—engendered by the mundane yet powerful norms and rhythms of the kill chain—proactively shape the 'prosecution' of the target (Introduction).[26]

What Beard calls the 'extraordinary level of legal review' enabled by ISR is, in fact, extraordinarily conditional. As revealed by Brown's daily routine, military lawyers do not sign off on every single target and many are struck without any legal input, let alone precise legal adjudication. Sometimes the possibility and extent of legal review are determined as much by whether a JAG happens to be sleeping or is present on the CAOC 'operations floor' as by protocols set out in lengthy military manuals.[27] Time-sensitivity is a key variable. Specifically, deliberate (planned) targeting operations receive more extensive and in-depth legal input than dynamic (unplanned) operations (Chapter 6) do. In sum, JAG involvement in aerial targeting operations is today far more extensive than it ever has been—but the nature and extent of JAG input is conditioned by the everyday materialities and messiness of military operations.

[25] 'The drone's optics may well be dazzling but they are far from crystal-clear [. . .] The quality of the images is highly variable in time and space, depending on atmospheric conditions, bandwidth compression, and the sensor that is used': Derek Gregory, 'The Territory of the Screen', *MediaTropes* 6, no. 2 (2017): 144.

[26] Derek Gregory, 'Kunduz and "Seeing like a Military"', *Geographical Imaginations* (blog), 2 January 2014, https://geographicalimaginations.com/2014/01/02/kunduz-and-seeing-like-a-military/, accessed 24 January 2017.

[27] e.g. United States Joint Chiefs of Staff, 'Legal Support to Military Operations' (Washington, DC: Joint Chiefs of Staff, 2 August 2016), https://www.jcs.mil/Portals/36/Documents/Doctrine/pubs/jp1_04.pdf, accessed 28 January 2016.

5.2 Unblinking Eyes? The Scale of Lawyer Deployment

Around 2,200 JAGs, 350 civilian attorneys, and 1,400 paralegals accompanied US troops into Iraq in 2003.[28] All of the services experienced a 'rush of JAG applicants' after 9/11.[29] Most of these JAGs, at least in the early years of the wars in Iraq and Afghanistan, were occupied with detainee operations.[30] The US military arrested and detained thousands of people in Afghanistan and Iraq, creating vast amounts of legal work as military lawyers struggled to process detainees and fulfil their duty of care under the Geneva Conventions.[31] One JAG describes the extent of detainee operations in a single city in 2003: 'By the time we got in there [An-Nasiriyah], we were facing three Iraqi Brigades and 1,000 Fedayeen.... They would show up in civilian clothes, acting like tourists..First day, we ended up taking about 2,000 males between the ages of 18-40 years as detainees.'[32] (Against the will of the JAG community, many detainees ended up in 'black sites' like Guantanamo Bay, Abu Ghraib, and the Afghan Salt Pit where they were mistreated and tortured in violation of the Geneva Conventions.[33])

[28] Janina Dill, *Legitimate Targets?: Social Construction, International Law and US Bombing* (Cambridge: Cambridge University Press, 2014), 149.

[29] Charles Dunlap, 'It Ain't No TV Show: JAGs and Modern Military Operations', *Chicago Journal of International Law* 4, no. 2 (2003): 490.

[30] 'Detainee operations occupied JAs in OEF and OIF more than any other ILAW [international law] issue', The Judge Advocate General's Legal Center & School, Center for Law and Military Operations (CLAMO), United States Army, 'Legal Lessons Learned From Afghanistan and Iraq Volume I Major Combat Operations (11 September 2001–1 May 2003)', 40 (Charlottesville, VA: United States Army, 1 August 2004), https://fas.org/irp/doddir/army/clamo-v1.pdf, accessed 15 December 2016. For a firsthand account of how JAGs are involved in prosecuting 'high-threat detainees' see: Miguel Acosta, 'Prosecuting High-Threat Detainees', *The Florida Bar News*, 15 September 2009, http://www.floridabar.org/DIVCOM/JN/JNNews01.nsf/8c9f13012b96736985256aa900624829/3a9be3daf196c64e852576250069d73b!OpenDocument, accessed 12 December 2016.

[31] The Judge Advocate General's Legal Center & School, Center for Law and Military Operations (CLAMO), United States Army, 'Legal Lessons Learned From Afghanistan and Iraq Volume I Major Combat Operations (11 September 2001–1 May 2003)', 41. See also: Richard Nisa, 'Capturing Humanitarian War: The Collusion of Violence and Care in US-Managed Military Detention', *Environment and Planning A* 47, no. 11 (2015): 2276–91.

[32] Quoted in The Judge Advocate General's Legal Center & School, Center for Law and Military Operations (CLAMO), United States Army, 'Legal Lessons Learned From Afghanistan and Iraq Volume I Major Combat Operations (11 September 2001–1 May 2003)', 41.

[33] United States Department of Defense General Counsel Working Group, 'Working Group Report—Detainee Interrogations in the Global War on Terrorism: Assessment of Legal, Historical, Policy, and Operational Considerations', 4 April 2003, https://en.wikisource.org/wiki/Working_Group_Report_on_Detainee_Interrogations, accessed 5 June 2015; Spencer Ackerman, 'Island Mentality', *New Republic*, 22 August 2005, https://newrepublic.com/article/68370/island-mentality-1, accessed 22 March 2017; Human Rights Watch, 'Getting Away with Torture', 12 July 2011, https://www.hrw.org/report/2011/07/12/getting-away-torture/bush-administration-and-mistreatment-detainees, accessed 22 March 2017. Cf.: Lisa Hajjar, *Torture: A Sociology of Violence and Human Rights* (New York, NY: Routledge, 2013); Derek Gregory, 'The Black Flag: Guantánamo Bay and the Space of Exception', *Geografiska Annaler: Series B, Human Geography* 88, no. 4 (2006): 405–27.

In 2004 Charles Dunlap reported that around 50–100 Air Force JAGs and paralegals were deployed to the Middle East, serving in sixteen locations. The number of deployed JAGs varies, 'depending on the tempo of operations and the number of Air Force personnel present in the region' (in 2004 there were around 14,000 US Air Force personnel deployed).[34] Not all deployed JAGs are involved in targeting, however. In fact, even at the height of Operation Iraqi Freedom (OIF) in 2003 only sixteen JAGs and paralegals were assigned to the Al Udeid CAOC, and this included four JAGs from the United Kingdom and Australia. [35] This was during a major combat operation, but since then the numbers have dwindled and in recent years there have been only three or four JAGs at the CAOC at any one time.[36]

The intensity of combat operations in Iraq and Afghanistan has varied tremendously over the last nearly two decades. Airpower statistics, published by US Air Forces Central Command, give us some idea of the intensity of various components of aerial targeting, including the numbers of sorties flown and the number of weapons released.[37] Figure 5.2 shows airpower statistics for OIF and Operation Enduring Freedom (OEF) from 2004 to 2011. Among other things, these statistics demonstrate the importance of close air support (CAS) sorties and 'kinetic' strikes in the wars in both Iraq and Afghanistan. Between 2004 and 2008 Iraq saw in the order of 15,000 to 20,000 CAS sorties each year. Afghanistan saw a staggering 20,000 to 30,000 such sorties each year between 2008 and 2011. These sorties resulted in nearly 15,000 operations between 2004 and 2011 in these two theatres—with the vast majority (12,038) in Afghanistan.

[34] Charles Dunlap, '. . . With Helmet and Flak Vest: Practicing International Law in War Zones', *US Air Force, Judge Advocate General*, 4 December 2004, http://scholarship.law.duke.edu/faculty_scholarship/3476/, accessed 4 July 2015. A 2001 Air Force Instruction elaborates: 'The size and nature of the air, space, and cyberspace operations, the tempo, and the number of processes in use by the AOC will assist in determining the number of JAs assigned to support an AOC.' United States Air Force, 'United States Air Force Instruction 13-1AOC, Volume 3: Operational Procedures—Air Operations Center' (United States Air Force, 2 November 2011), 93, http://static.e-publishing.af.mil/production/1/af_a3_5/publication/afi13-1aocv3/afi13-1aocv3.pdf, accessed 17 December 2016.

[35] Dunlap, '. . . With Helmet and Flak Vest'. 'Some of these people focused on Air Force support issues, but most were used to directly advise commanders and others on the conduct of operations': Dunlap, 'Come the Revolution', 149–50.

[36] Brown, interview; Landreneau, interview.

[37] For many years the US military claimed that airpower statistics included data on the use of airpower across all military services. However, an investigation by the *Military Times* in February 2017 revealed that the data does not include airstrikes carried out by attack helicopters and armed drones operated by the US Army. The investigation found that the US military, 'failed to publicly disclose potentially thousands of lethal airstrikes conducted over several years in Iraq, Syria and Afghanistan [. . .] The enormous data gap raises serious doubts about transparency in reported progress against the Islamic State, al-Qaida and the Taliban, and calls into question the accuracy of other Defense Department disclosures documenting everything from costs to casualty counts': Andrew deGrandpre and Shawn Snow, 'The U.S. Military's Stats on Deadly Airstrikes Are Wrong. Thousands Have Gone Unreported', *Military Times*, 5 February 2017, http://www.militarytimes.com/articles/airstrikes-unreported-syria-iraq-afghanistan-islamic-state-al-qaeda-taliban, accessed 13 March 2017.

2004-2011 Combined Forces Air Component Commander Airpower Statistics								
	2004	2005	2006	2007	2008	2009	2010	2011
Tanker								
Sorties	12,465	12,391	12,787	15,875	18,361	17,465	17,845	19,431
Fuel Offload	740	778	871	946	1,106	1,076	1,072	1,170
Receive rs	N/A	N/A	42,083	79,798	86,288	82,095	84,674	90,616
ISR								
Sorties	7,400	6,615	7,832	11,202	16,193	18,898	28,365	38,340
Airlift {US only)								
Sorties	47,450	54,727	55,264	56,179	51,945	52,905	64,826	57,510
Ca rgo	150,580	113,359	205,816	270,007	251,738	264,839	262,160	230,630
Passengers	702,000	933,806	1,075,583	1,177,533	1,269,710	1,301,740	1,289,407	1,218,339
Close Air Support								
OIF Sorties	14,292	16,924	15,676	19,542	18,422	8,061	6,238	5,433
OEF Sorties	6,495	7,421	10,519	13,962	19,092	26,474	17,816	29,265
OIF Kinetic	285	404	229	1,447	334	35	1	5
OEF Kinetic	86	176	1,770	3,572	1,378	1,462	1,816	1,778

Figure 5.2 Airpower statistics for Iraq and Afghanistan, 2004–2011.
Source: United States Air Force, Air Force Central Command Combined Forces Air Component Commander Airpower Statistics, archived by Alex O'Brien, https://alexaobrien.com/afcent-cfacc-airpower-summaries-and-statistics, accessed 16 June 2020.

This confirms Brown's observation that CAS operations were so frequent that it was difficult for JAGs in the CAOC to be involved in them all (recall that in 2007–2008 Brown served the CAOC alongside only three other JAGs).

Fast forward to 2016, and the US Air Force was flying over 5,000 CAS sorties in Afghanistan (Figure 5.3) and an additional 21,181 sorties in Iraq and Syria under the banner of Operation Inherent Resolve (OIR) (Figure 5.4). That year, over half of the CAS sorties flown in OIR—11,825—released at least one weapon. This amounted to a total of over 30,000 weapons being fired in 2016 in OIR alone. In 2017 this figure increased to nearly 40,000; in the first nine months of that year weapons were being fired at a rate well in excess of 100 per day (Figure 5.4). Yet despite the significant increase in the number of sorties flown and weapons fired, the number of JAGs in the CAOC between 2008 and 2016 remained consistent, at around three or four individuals.[38]

[38] Stefano (pseudonym), interview. The US Air Force JAG Corps were unable to provide full data on how many JAGs have been deployed to the CAOC over the last decade and a half. Nevertheless, my interviews with military lawyers who served at the CAOC over the course of several years consistently

United States Air Forces Central Command
Combined Air Operations Center

UNCLASSIFIED

As of Dec 31, 2019

Combined Forces Air Component Commander
2013–2019 Airpower Statistics

Afghanistan

OPERATION FREEDOM'S SENTINEL/RESOLUTE SUPPORT MISSION

Strike Aircraft (manned)

Sorties	
2013	21,900
2014	12,978
2015	5,774
2016	5,162
2017	4,603
2018	8,196
2019	8,773

Sorties with at least one weapon release	
2013	1,408
2014	1,136
2015	411
2016	615
2017	1,248
2018	966
2019	2,434

Number of Weapons Released (Manned & RPA strike assets)

	Jan	Feb	Mar	Apr	May	Jun	Jul	Aug	Sep	Oct	Nov	Dec	Total
2013	193	297	250	284	368	337	256	158	232	189	118	76	2,758
2014	92	114	95	115	164	272	205	437	441	217	87	126	2,365
2015	40	30	47	31	41	109	79	156	111	203	69	31	947
2016	127	115	58	62	89	94	160	108	162	205	92	65	1,337
2017	54	200	203	460	328	389	350	503	414	653	352	455	4,361
2018	378	469	339	562	591	572	746	715	841	769	841	539	7,362
2019	463	327	673	548	635	441	613	783	948	777	519	696	7,423

Statistics provided includes numbers of sorties (not strikes) and munitions expended by aircraft under CFACC control

	2013	2014	2015	2016	2017	2018	2019
Intel, Surveillance and Recon Sorties	31,049	32,999	21,634	19,681	15,404	12,716	17,723
Airlift and Airdrop Sorties	32,000	17,040	6,900	10,300	11,166	12,783	10,926
Airlift Cargo (Short Tons)	201,000	158,400	50,000	69,200	84,208	89,584	79,705
Airlift Passengers	506,000	202,700	78,000	111,100	120,554	150,330	141,294
Supplies Airdropped (Pounds)	10,883,000	28,000	0	0	33,423	667,880	606,600
Tanker Sorties	12,319	9,085	5,323	4,910	5,714	4,673	2,637
Fuel Offloaded (Millions of Pounds)	723	636	201	150	170	189	99
Aircraft Refuelings	53,266	46,793	26,162	18,137	17,989	19,214	12,877

- Some figures may have changed due to data re-calculation and re-verification
- Assets under CFACC control include a compilation of aircraft from all U.S. military branches of service, as well as Coalition aircraft; however, not all aircraft flying in the AOR fall under CFACC control.

POC: AFCENT (CAOC) Public Affairs–afcent.pa@afcent.af.mil

Figure 5.3 Airpower statistics for Afghanistan, 2013–2019. From 2001 to 2014 the US government called the war in Afghanistan Operation Enduring Freedom but renamed it Operation Freedom Sentinel/Resolute Support Mission in 2015.
Source: United States Air Force, Airpower Summaries, 31 December 2019, https://www.afcent.af.mil/About/Airpower-Summaries/, accessed 16 June 2020.

The number of Air Force JAGs ready to 'plug in and play' in the CAOC environment is very small—as low as twenty to twenty-five, according to one JAG with extensive CAOC experience.[39] Another JAG explained why the Air Force JAG Corps has so few military lawyers with the requisite targeting experience:

> If you're going to send someone to deploy to Iraq do you want to send someone who has never gone, or do you want to send someone who has done two or three other deployments? Logically, I want to pick the person who has done it before [. . .] You don't necessarily go with someone new because it's

suggest that there are ordinarily approximately three or four military lawyers in the CAOC at any one time.

[39] Landreneau, interview, 8 August 2013.

United States Air Forces Central Command
Combined Air Operations Center

Iraq & Syria

Combined Forces Air Component Commander
2015–2019 Airpower Statistics

UNCLASSIFIED

As of Dec 31, 2019

OPERATION INHERENT RESOLVE

Strike Aircraft (manned)

Sorties	
2015	21,116
2016	21,181
2017	19,680
2018	16,056
2019	13,694

Sorties with at least one weapon release	
2015	9,912
2016	11,825
2017	9,944
2018	1,591
2019	976

Number of Weapons Released (Manned & RPA strike assets)

	Jan	Feb	Mar	Apr	May	Jun	Jul	Aug	Sep	Oct	Nov	Dec	Total
2015	2,426	1,853	1,685	1,862	2,145	1,683	2,823	2,758	2,380	2,694	3,242	3,145	28,696
2016	2,718	2,090	2,052	2,582	2,341	3,160	2,439	2,244	2,427	3,038	2,709	2,943	30,743
2017	3,600	3,439	3,878	3,274	4,374	4,848	4,313	5,075	3,550	1,642	1,000	584	39,577
2018	780	747	294	254	431	356	241	338	758	876	1,424	2,214	8,713
2019	2,005	607	900	90	54	135	105	218	137	166	153	159	4,729

Statistics provided includes numbers of sorties (not strikes) and munitions expended by aircraft under CFACC control

	2015	2016	2017	2018	2019
Intel, Surveillance and Recon Sorties	9,514	12,270	14,015	7,782	13,377
Airlift and Airdrop Sorties	10,050	8,400	9,448	8,450	7,382
Airlift Cargo (Short Tons)	78,500	72,800	68,537	43,566	35,520
Airlift Passengers	47,200	46,900	76,802	76,369	64,525
Supplies Airdropped (Pounds)	111,200	822,171	641,746	605,670	930,700
Tanker Sorties	14,737	13,064	13,243	8,697	7,049
Fuel Offloaded (Millions of Pounds)	912	804	778	620	487
Aircraft Refuelings	84,381	80,912	70,536	52,061	44,994

- Some figures may have changed due to data re-calculation and re-verification
- Assets under CFACC control include a compilation of aircraft from all U.S. military branches of service, as well as Coalition aircraft; however, not all aircraft flying in the AOR fall under CFACC control

POC: AFCENT (CAOC) Public Affairs–afcent.pa@afcent.af.mil

Figure 5.4 Airpower statistics for Iraq and Syria, 2015–2019. Data for Operation Iraqi Freedom (2003–2010) and its successor Operation New Dawn (2010–2011) are not included.

Source: United States Air Force, Airpower Summaries, 31 December 2019, https://www.afcent.af.mil/About/Airpower-Summaries/, accessed 16 June 2020.

> tough [. . .] in the middle of a deployment to say 'hey let's learn something'. You want someone who can hit the ground and know exactly what they're doing.[40]

It is only recently that JAGs began to receive specific training in targeting. JAGs assigned to an Air Operations Center (AOC)[41] undertake a four-week AOC training course at the 505th Command and Control Wing at Hurlburt Field in Okaloosa County, Florida.[42] The course is designed to orient personnel (not

[40] Meyer, interview.

[41] In addition to the CAOC at Al Udeid, the US military has a number of other AOCs located around the world in places such as South Korea and Germany, but most AOCs are located in the United States.

[42] This is one of a number of AOC-related courses conducted by the 505th Training Squadron. See 505th Command and Control Wing, United States Air Force, '505th Training Squadron', 17 April 2013, http://www.505ccw.acc.af.mil/AboutUs/FactSheets/Display/tabid/6713/Article/376112/505th-training-squadron.aspx, accessed 16 December 2016.

just JAGs) to working in the AOC environment and covers 'doctrine, AOC organization and processes, air battle plan development, air tasking order production and execution, operational assessment, and more'.[43] One JAG who formerly taught part of the course reported that students learn 'the systems and the roles and responsibilities of the different players in an AOC'.[44] The course is supposed to be standard for all AOC personnel.[45] However, when the United States invaded Iraq in March 2003 only 43 per cent of those deployed to the Al Udeid CAOC received the training.[46]

A contingent in the Air Force JAG Corps believes that while vital, and even to the extent it is made available, the training is insufficient. There are very few formal requirements that JAGs must meet before they are deployed to the CAOC. This has led to a situation in which there is extensive training for some JAG assignments like military justice, but far less for those involving lethal targeting operations. The irony is not lost on one JAG who is particularly vocal about the lack of CAOC-specific training:

> We certify Judge Advocates in the Air Force to . . . you can't go into a court room [. . .] until you've been certified by your boss, your peers and a couple of judges. You have to have this JAG Corps certification to go into a courtroom. And I always say, 'what certifications do we have for telling JAGs that they can advise commanders whether they can kill somebody or not?'[47]

The relatively low number of JAGs actively involved in targeting in the CAOC, combined with the fact that very few JAGs receive AOC-specific training, suggests that legal oversight of targeting is not quite as 'unblinking' as some suggest. The CAOC is not the only location where JAGs provide legal advice on targets. Nevertheless, when viewed against the intensity of operations, as discussed, legal input across the various kill chain nodes and locations is necessarily partial and provisional, especially when it comes to CAS and dynamic targeting.

* * *

43 Dunlap, 'Come the Revolution', 148.
44 Landreneau, interview.
45 Dunlap, 'Come the Revolution', 148.
46 Moseley, 'Operation Iraqi Freedom: By the Numbers', 3.
47 Stefano (pseudonym), interview.

Deliberate targeting consists of six idealized phases that link to make the kill chain—or what the US Air Force refer to colloquially as the 'doughnut of death' (the chart representing the 'Joint Targeting Cycle' is shaped like a doughnut-ring: Figure 5.5). The kill chain is idealized in the sense that its phases are not as discrete and sequential as doctrine suggests; in reality phases bleed into one another and are often operationalized simultaneously. Its intended pattern of execution is persistently interrupted by messy military realities that do not conform to the bloodless, neat, and adiaphorized doctrine. JAGs provide input throughout the kill chain and, *ideally*, each phase requires bespoke legal interpretation and advice, though these processes, too, are often less straightforward than military-legal doctrine would have us believe. In what remains of this chapter I trace the six phases in order to show how at each and every phase: (a) the laws of war and rules of engagement (ROE) are found to have elastic limits; (b) law and war lawyers produce the violence that they also help to regulate; and (c) through interpretation and application, rules and laws are (re)made. Thus, legal procedures channel (rather than prevent) the violence of aerial targeting operations even in these, the most pre-planned and deliberate cases.

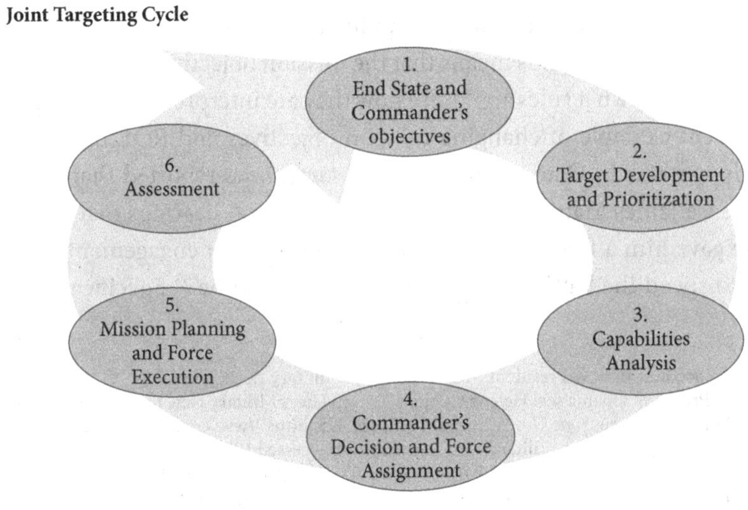

Figure 5.5 The 'ideal' deliberate targeting cycle—known colloquially as the 'kill chain' and 'doughnut of death'.

Source: United States Joint Chiefs of Staff, 'Joint Targeting', Joint Publication 3-60 (Washington, DC, 31 January 2013), II-4.

5.3 Mission Objectives/Trump's New Rules of Engagement

In the idealized sequence, the kill chain begins with senior military commanders setting mission objectives. Overall 'campaign' objectives and parameters are dictated from the highest levels of the US military, including the President (as Commander-in-Chief) and the Secretary of Defense.[48] According to US Air Force doctrine, the role of JAGs in this phase is to ensure that all proposed strategy and plans comply with international law, including the laws of war, domestic law and ROE, as well as orders from superior headquarters.[49] Military lawyers are key personnel in the Strategy Division[50] and also typically sit on the Joint Targeting Coordination Board (JTCB),[51] which maintains a macro-level view of target sets and their compliance with command intent. Military lawyers are also responsible for reviewing the Joint Air Operations Plan (JAOP) and the daily Air Operations Directive, which are the planning components of what will later determine the targets to be struck.[52]

In practice, mission objectives and the rules that govern them are co-produced in an evolving dialectical relationship that military (and civilian) lawyers facilitate. Contrary to what the doctrine suggests of this phase, military lawyers do not so much ensure compliance as help *to establish the rules and conditions of compliance itself*. That is, military lawyers are actively involved in shaping mission objectives and creating the ROE. As shown in the Introduction, ROE are informed by political and military considerations as well as legal restraints; this means that the mission objective itself has a significant bearing on what rules apply and how they are interpreted.

A recent example of changing mission objectives and ROE demonstrates what is at stake. In October 2017 the *Military Times* reported that Secretary of Defense James Mattis 'told a pair of congressional hearings that the White House gave him a free hand to reconsider the rules of engagement and alter them to speed the battle against the Taliban if need be'.[53] Specifically, Mattis

[48] For an account of how President Trump delegates military decision making to the Pentagon in contrast to President Obama see: Helene Cooper, 'Trump Gives Military New Freedom. But With That Comes Danger', *The New York Times*, 5 April 2017, sec. US, https://www.nytimes.com/2017/04/05/us/politics/rules-of-engagement-military-force-mattis.html, accessed 10 February 2020.

[49] United States Air Force Judge Advocate General's School, 'Air Force Operations and the Law' (Maxwell Air Force Base, AL: US Air Force, 2014), 280, http://www.afjag.af.mil/Portals/77/documents/AFD-100510-059.pdf, accessed 13 February 2014.

[50] United States Air Force, 'Air Force Doctrine Document 1-04, Legal Support to Operations', 9.

[51] United States Joint Chiefs of Staff, 'Legal Support to Military Operations', III–3.

[52] United States Air Force Judge Advocate General's School, 'Air Force Operations and the Law', 280.

[53] Aaron Mehta, 'Mattis Reveals New Rules of Engagement', *Military Times*, 5 October 2017, https://www.militarytimes.com/flashpoints/2017/10/03/mattis-reveals-new-rules-of-engagement/, accessed 29 January 2020.

announced that US forces would henceforth be permitted to launch airstrikes without a requirement that the intended objects of attack be 'proximate' to US forces or US advised Afghan Forces. Reflecting on the change in ROE Mattis noted: 'It used to be we have to basically be in contact with that enemy.' Under the new ROE, he said: 'That is no longer the case [. . .] So these kind of restrictions that did not allow us to employ the air power fully have been removed.' Rather than 'proximity' or 'contact' (as in 'troops in contact') the new rules place greater emphasis on target identification: 'Wherever we find them, anyone who is trying to throw the NATO plan off, trying to attack the Afghan government, then we can go after them', Mattis said.[54]

Mattis did not go into detail on the origins of the proximity requirement but former JAG Lieutenant Colonel (ret.) Geoffrey S. Corn points out, 'it almost certainly emerged from the U.S. effort to minimize Afghan civilian casualties resulting from both collateral damage and from mistakes'.[55] Many of those measures were put in place under President Obama and under pressure from President Hamid Karzai because of the unacceptable levels of civilian casualties resulting from US airstrikes in Afghanistan.[56] Specifically, an International Security Assistance Force (ISAF) Directive issued by General Stanley McChrystal in July 2009 placed a series of restrictions on the use of CAS designed to reduce civilian casualties (Chapter 6).[57] The specifics of Mattis' new ROE are classified but they appear to undo some of the previous restrictions on the use of airstrikes. Certainly, they reflect mission objectives that place greater emphasis on the military 'necessity' of employing US airstrikes more fully in the battle against the Taliban. This shows the malleability of the concept of necessity, and thus also the malleability of operational legalities. It is important to remember that mission objectives and ROE are military *directives* in the most active sense; they *direct* military activities and have a real and tangible impact on who and what can be targeted, and under what circumstances. Colonel (ret.) Corn reflects on how this particular iteration of the ROE might manifest itself on the ground in Afghanistan:

[54] Ibid.

[55] Geoffrey S Corn, 'The Newly Relaxed Rules of Engagement in Afghanistan and Civilian Casualties', *Just Security*, 6 October 2017, https://www.justsecurity.org/45680/newly-relaxed-rules-engagement-afghanistan-civilian-casualties/, accessed 10 January 2020.

[56] Neta C. Crawford, *Accountability for Killing: Moral Responsibility for Collateral Damage in America's Post-9/11 Wars* (New York, NY: Oxford University Press, 2013), 101–16; Alissa J. Rubin, 'Karzai to Ban His Forces to Request Foreign Airstrikes', *The New York Times*, 16 February 2013, http://www.nytimes.com/2013/02/17/world/asia/karzai-to-forbid-his-forces-from-requesting-foreign-airstrikes.html, accessed 3 April 2017.

[57] Crawford, *Accountability for Killing*, 102–3.

> Will civilians face increased risk of accidental distinction errors or incidental injury and collateral damage as the result of this change? Perhaps [. . .] But consistent with the LOAC [Laws of Armed Conflict], that is a risk that commanders are entrusted to weigh and to accept when *justified by the dictates of mission accomplishment*. Whatever else may evolve in our ongoing Afghan mission, it seems that maximizing the effect of superior U.S. combat power will be an increased priority.[58]

Corn's assessment does more than assert the compliance and compatibly of the ROE with the laws of war; it also reveals the extent to which the rules governing the use of force—and in particular the use of airstrikes—are in fact *produced* by evolving mission objectives (or what he calls 'dictates of mission accomplishment'). Mission priorities shape mission legalities, telescoping the zone of permissible conduct so that it aligns with what has been made militarily 'necessary'. As Corn further insists: 'ROE must be inherently mission responsive.'[59] This means that the mission itself dictates in no small part the form and content of the rules that govern it.

Just weeks before Mattis made public these changes in the ROE, President Trump promised that his new Afghanistan strategy would 'lift restrictions' and 'expand authorities for American armed forces to target the terrorists and criminal networks that sow violence and chaos throughout Afghanistan'.[60] Because ROE are classified, JAGs and other military personnel will not discuss them. But the JAGs I interviewed reported that they were extensively involved in developing the ROE at all levels, including the strategic levels which produced Mattis' revised ROE on 'no contact' airstrikes.[61] In this phase and others, military lawyers are not checking compliance with rules; instead, they are helping to establish the mission objectives and the rules that will govern them. [62] In this sense, military lawyers are engaged in a dialectical *war-making* and *law-making* enterprise—the realization of the mission *through* law. As such, the kill

[58] Corn, 'The Newly Relaxed Rules of Engagement in Afghanistan and Civilian Casualties' (emphasis added).

[59] Ibid.

[60] Aaron Mehta and Tara Copp, 'Trump Afghanistan Strategy Calls for More Troops, Regional Pressure', *Defense News*, 21 August 2017, https://www.militarytimes.com/news/2017/08/22/trump-afghanistan-strategy-calls-for-more-troops-regional-pressure/, accessed 10 February 2020.

[61] Air Force doctrine mandates: 'Early involvement ensures legal issues are identified and legally acceptable courses of action and supporting ROE are developed consistent with the commander's intent': United States Air Force, 'Air Force Doctrine Document 1-04, Legal Support to Operations', 26 (emphasis added).

[62] Dickinson, 'Military Lawyers on the Battlefield'.

chain becomes the *juridical* kill chain, and law and killing remake one another in a reciprocal and evolving relationship.

5.4 Production of the Target

Once mission objectives and overarching ROE have been produced, the next step is to produce specific targets and target sets (the US military call this the 'target development' phase).[63] Target production begins before combat commences and continues during combat[64] with targets developed and nominated to Central Command (CENTCOM) databases from several different locations in 'theatre' and in 'CONUS' (Continental United States).[65] The timeframes for 'executing' deliberate targets can vary greatly and are highly dependent on context, including the physical location of the target and which part of the kill chain is involved in its development. According to one source, deliberate target development 'normally begins 36–40 hours before the effective time of the ATO [Air Tasking Order]'.[66] Another source, Colonel Stevenson, Commander of the 63rd Intelligence Surveillance and Reconnaissance Wing at Joint Base Langley-Eutis, Virginia, reported that it takes thirty to forty-five days for his nominated targets to 'make it to the finish line'.[67]

A target set may be something like electricity production facilities (Chapter 3) or enemy air defences, but increasingly it is a list of individuals known as High-Value Individuals ('HVIs'). The full target sets for the air wars in Iraq and Afghanistan have not been published, but we know that in the initial stages of the Iraq war they included among others 'terrorists', 'leadership', and 'weapons of mass destruction' (the latter, of course, turned out not to exist).[68] 'Leadership', whether this be Taliban, Al Qaeda, or its 'associated

[63] Target development is the 'analysis, assessment, and documentation processes to identify and characterize potential targets that, when successfully engaged, support the achievement of the commander's objectives': United States Joint Chiefs of Staff, 'Joint Targeting', Joint Publication 3-60 (Washington, DC, 31 January 2013), II–5, cfr.org/.../Joint_Chiefs_of_Staff-Joint_Targeting_31_January_2013.pdf, accessed 24 January 2017.

[64] 'Much of peacetime targeting readiness is geared toward target development. [. . .] the US often enters contingencies without established deliberate planning products, or those that exist require extensive modification when an actual contingency arises. Obviously, it is impossible to have a plan for every conceivable contingency, but waiting to conduct target development until a contingency develops will put planners at a huge disadvantage.': United States Air Force, 'Air Force Doctrine Document 3-60, Targeting' (US Air Force LeMay Center for Doctrine Development, 8 June 2006), 70–1, https://fas.org/irp/doddir/usaf/afdd3-60.pdf, accessed 13 December 2016.

[65] Deptula, interview.

[66] United States Air Force Judge Advocate General's School, 'Air Force Operations and the Law', 280.

[67] Stevenson, interview.

[68] Moseley, 'Operation Iraqi Freedom: By the Numbers'.

forces', or key members of the Ba'ath regime, like Saddam Hussein, quickly became an increasingly important part of targeting operations in Iraq and Afghanistan.[69] The infamous 'Personality Identification Playing Cards' issued to US troops when Iraq was invaded in 2003 were an early example of a leadership target set in the then nascent 'war on terror'.[70] But that set was dwarfed by the Joint Prioritized Effects List (JPEL), which began with the leaders of the Taliban and Al Qaeda and soon grew to more than 2,000 people as the insurgency in Afghanistan widened in the mid to late 2000s.[71]

Military lawyers play an important role in this phase. A military lawyer is assigned as a member to the Combat Plans Division (CPD) and works closely with the Intelligence, Surveillance and Reconnaissance Targeting Effects Team and the Master Air Attack Plan cell as they develop specific targets.[72] The JAGs' role within these targeting cells and working groups is to vet and validate targets as they are being developed. This involves a legal review of 'ALL proposed targets'[73], that is, against the information in their respective target folders. Target folders may be hard copy or electronic,[74] but are increasingly the latter.[75] Target folders contain 'imagery from various sources, maps, and intelligence information about the target, including its military purpose and importance, and information regarding any nearby facilities such as churches, museums, or schools'.[76] According to a targeting training manual, the folders contain a 'mass of detail' that 'may very quickly overwhelm' anybody looking at them, so targeteers are encouraged to condense the material into target briefs, which provide a summary of the contents of the target folder.[77]

[69] 'For several years now U.S. military and intelligence operations have relied on a concept of "associated forces" of al-Qaeda to add militant groups to the list of who can be killed or captured as potential threats to the nation': Ryan Goodman, 'Associated Forces: Why the Differences between ISIL and al-Qaeda Matter', *Just Security*, 30 March 2015, https://www.justsecurity.org/21621/forces-differences-isil-al-qaeda-matter/, accessed 13 December 2016.

[70] Ben Tuft, 'Iraq's "most-Wanted" Playing Cards Go on Display at the Pentagon', *The Independent*, 18 October 2014, http://www.independent.co.uk/news/world/americas/iraqs-most-wanted-playing-cards-go-on-display-at-the-pentagon-9803525.html, accessed 13 December 2016.

[71] Jeremy Scahill, *Dirty Wars: The World Is A Battlefield* (London: Serpent's Tail, 2013), 167. See also: Spiegel Staff, 'Obama's Lists: A Dubious History of Targeted Killings in Afghanistan', Der Spiegel, 28 December 2014, http://www.spiegel.de/international/world/secret-docs-reveal-dubious-details-of-targeted-killings-in-afghanistan-a-1010358.html, accessed 13 December 2016.

[72] United States Air Force Judge Advocate General's School, 'Air Force Operations and the Law', 280.

[73] United States Air Force, Twelfth Air Force, 'Chapter 9 Judge Advocate' (Air Operations Center (AOC) Standard Operating Procedure (SOP) Twelfth Air Force (12AF) Air Force Forces (AFFOR), n.d.), document no longer available online (on file with author, capitalization in original).

[74] United States Air Force Judge Advocate General's School, 'Air Force Operations and the Law', 280.

[75] Stevenson, interview.

[76] United States Air Force Judge Advocate General's School, 'Air Force Operations and the Law', 281.

[77] United States Joint Targeting School, 'Joint Fires and Targeting Student Guide' (Suffolk, Virginia & Dam Neck, VA: Joint Doctrine Analysis Division/Joint Targeting School, 5 March 2014), III–68, https://docplayer.net/47603976-Joint-fires-and-targeting-student-guide-5-march-2014.html, accessed 24 June 2020.

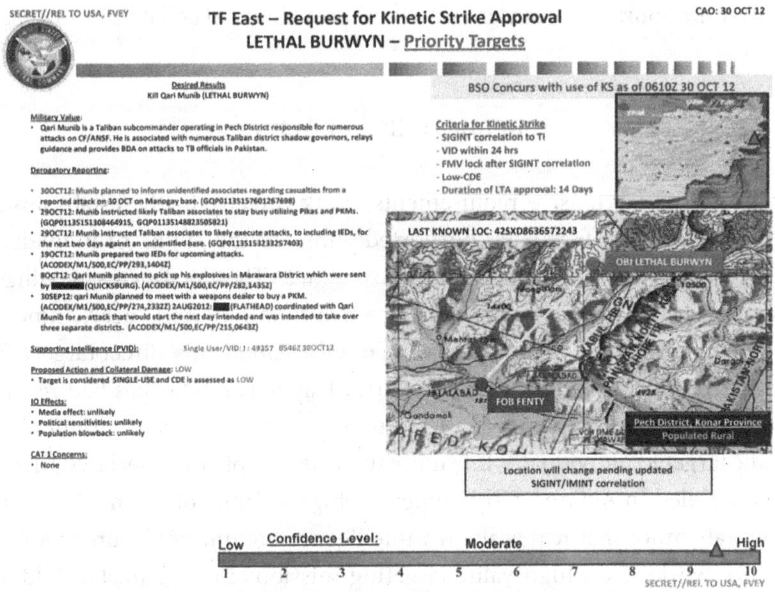

Figure 5.6 A 2012 US military request for an airstrike targeting Qari Munib, an alleged Taliban sub-commander operating in north-eastern Afghanistan.
Source: Intelligence Community Documents, obtained by The Intercept: Ryan Devereaux, 'Manhunting in the Hindu Kush', *The Intercept*, 18 October 2015, https://theintercept.com/drone-papers/manhunting-in-the-hindu-kush/, accessed 13 December 2016.

But what does this look like in practice? Figure 5.6 shows a US military request for a lethal strike against Taliban sub-commander Qari Munib (mission name: 'LETHAL BURWYN)'. The strike was approved, and he was killed on 8 November 2012 as part of Operation Haymaker, a Special Forces operation designed to destroy the Taliban and Al Qaeda forces that remained in the valleys of the Hindu Kush (along Afghanistan's northeastern border with Pakistan). According to documents released to the online news publication *The Intercept*, Munib was targeted because he allegedly exercised command and control over a specific portion of the Taliban and was responsible for numerous attacks on both coalition and Afghan security forces.[78] Certain ROE criteria had to be met for the strike to go ahead: the operation would 'require a signals intelligence

[78] Ryan Devereaux, 'Manhunting in the Hindu Kush', *The Intercept*, 18 October 2015, https://theintercept.com/drone-papers/manhunting-in-the-hindu-kush/, accessed 13 December 2016.

"correlation", followed by a full motion video lock, visual identification within twenty-four hours of the strike, and a 'low' probability of collateral damage'.[79]

'Enemies killed in Action'

These lofty and extensive requirements speak directly to the establishment of the 'adjudicative facts' that purportedly inform the killing of individuals, but which prove worryingly fallible in practice. The documents relating to Operation Haymaker show that during a five-month period, 'nearly nine out of 10 people who died in airstrikes were not the Americans' direct targets'. *The Intercept* reveals how, '[b]y February 2013, Haymaker airstrikes had resulted in no more than 35 "jackpots," a term used to signal the 'neutralization' of a specific targeted individual, while more than 200 people were declared EKIA—"Enemy Killed In Action"'.[80] This appears a high number of enemy deaths, but it conceals more that it reveals. An intelligence community source with experience working on high-value targeting missions in Afghanistan told *The Intercept*: 'If there is no evidence that proves a person killed in a strike was either not a MAM [military aged male], or was a MAM but not an unlawful enemy combatant, then there is no question [. . .] They label them EKIA.'[81] What this means is that those killed were automatically considered enemies *en masse* unless specific evidence (not always easy to come by in a warzone) provided otherwise. The notion of a 'MAM' constitutes what Nick Turse has called 'lethal profiling',[82] and Afghanistan is not the first or the only place where the US military has employed this highly dubious method of determining combatancy.[83] As much as anything else, 'MAM' is a juridical descriptor with juridical consequences; designating a body as 'MAM' *signifies* that body as enemy—or 'EKIA'. The implication, of course, is that a 'MAM' is not a civilian; he is an enemy about to be, or already, killed in action—legally and legitimately.

[79] Ibid.

[80] Ibid.

[81] Anonymous intelligence source quoted in: Ibid.

[82] Nick Turse, 'America's Lethal Profiling of Afghan Men', *The Nation*, 18 September 2013, https://www.thenation.com/article/archive/americas-lethal-profiling-afghan-men/, accessed 11 February 2020.

[83] 'The Military-Aged Male category is not synonymous with "combatant," but marks boys and men for differentiated treatment in conflict zones, to the point where male bodies are used as a shorthand for "combatant" when assessing the collateral damage count:' Sarah Shoker, 'Military-Age Males in U.S. Counterinsurgency and Drone Warfare', PhD thesis, Hamilton, Ontaio, McMaster University, 2018, https://macsphere.mcmaster.ca/handle/11375/24294, accessed 11 February 2020.

These are not so much 'adjudicative facts', then, as adjudicative *assumptions* and the kill chain, necessarily, is full of them.[84]

Adjudicative assumptions can easily be *magnified* (rather than minimized) as the target 'travels' through the various phases of the kill chain, as the next example shows. The first and most important thing that JAGs must establish is that each proposed target has been positively identified (PID) as a legitimate military objective. PID is defined as the 'reasonable certainty that a functionally and geospatially defined object of attack is a legitimate military target in accordance with the Law of War and applicable Rules of Engagement.'[85] In the absence of PID there is no military objective (and thus no legal and legitimate target). PID involves steps taken to ensure that the target is what or who the intelligence claims it is.[86] The ROE will determine the 'quantity, quality, timeliness, and duration of the intelligence necessary to establish' PID.[87] Specifically, intelligence analysts who have contributed to a target folder should try to 'distinguish between what is known with confidence based on the facts' and 'what are untested assumptions', and should numerically indicate their confidence level from low to high or on a scale of one to ten.[88] (The confidence level on the LETHAL BURWYN target was between nine and ten, i.e. 'high' certainty: Figure 5.6.)

In reality, determining PID can be extremely difficult. One JAG attests: 'While on its face [PID] appears to be a simple requirement, this was truly the most difficult aspect of [our] participation in Operation Enduring Freedom from an ROE perspective.'[89] In its two-volume retrospective on legal lessons learned from Afghanistan and Iraq, the Center for Law and Military Operations (CLAMO) makes a similar admission:

[84] One military lawyer I interviewed described the difficulties of providing legal advice in an environment where there are so many assumptions. Some lawyers, he told me, 'don't feel comfortable' giving advice when they have 'about 80 per cent facts, and about 20 per cent assumption [. . .].' Landreneau, interview.

[85] 505th Command and Control Wing, United States Air Force, 'The Air and Space Operations Center: The Judge Advocate's Role' (505th Command and Control Wing, Hurlburt Field, Florida, 2013), presentation on file with author, slide 22.

[86] Ibid., slide 23.

[87] James A. Burkart, 'Deadly Advice: Judge Advocates and Joint Targeting', *The Army Lawyer*, no. 6 (2016): 16.

[88] United States Joint Chiefs of Staff, 'Joint Intelligence' (Washington, DC: Joint Chiefs of Staff, 22 October 2013), A-1, https://www.jcs.mil/Portals/36/Documents/Doctrine/pubs/jp2_0.pdf, accessed 14 December 2015.

[89] Major Ian D. Brasure, Staff Judge Advocate, 26th Marine Expeditionary Unit (Special Operations Capable), After Action Report: Operation Enduring Freedom/Operation Swift Freedom, para. (3) (b) (22 March 2002) (on file with CLAMO), quoted in: The Judge Advocate General's Legal Center & School, Center for Law and Military Operations (CLAMO), United States Army, 'Legal Lessons Learned From Afghanistan and Iraq Volume I Major Combat Operations (11 September 2001–1 May 2003)', 98.

> [I]t was difficult to determine who exactly was a hostile force in Afghanistan. The Taliban was an amorphously defined group comprised of the Taliban regime itself as well as their armed units, various members of which were not committed to any cause and willingly switched allegiances. Al Qaeda members similarly were difficult to define.[90]

The legal lessons learned also revealed significant disagreements over the meaning of even foundational terms like 'PID'. Lieutenant Colonel Thomas Ayres reported that the ROE cards issued to soldiers in Afghanistan were 'confusing' and 'not written with the 18 year old E-1 [junior officer] in mind'. He gave the example of how PID was 'the first element on the card and it states that if PID is not established to call higher for guidance' but Ayres then points out how hopelessly impractical this guidance was: 'how in fact would a soldier in contact, or near it, do that?'[91]

The 'No-Strike List'

The No-Strike List (NSL) is a list of 'objects or entities characterized as protected from the effects of military operations under international law and/or rules of engagement'.[92] Attacking something on the list 'may violate the laws of war [. . .] or interfere with friendly relations with other nations, indigenous populations, or governments'.[93] The NSL is so extensive that, regarding Operation Enduring Freedom, one JAG stated: 'if we're striking a structure, a building or whatever, there's a pretty good chance that, there's a 100% chance I guess I could say, that that target is on a no-strike list'.[94] Examples of objects and entities that might appear on the NSL can be seen in Figure 5.7.

As may seem obvious to the layperson, the NSL is *not* a target list because the entities on the NSL are not targets.[95] However, while entities on the NSL should not be targeted there is a process whereby they can be taken off the list and subsequently targeted. As a 2009 military instruction notes:

[90] Ibid., 101.
[91] Email from Lieutenant Colonel Thomas E. Ayres, Staff Judge Advocate, 82d Airborne Division, to Colonel Karl M. Goetzke, Staff Judge Advocate, Coalition Forces Land Component Command (29 April 2003) (on file with CLAMO), quoted in: Ibid., 93–94.
[92] United States Joint Chiefs of Staff, 'Joint Targeting', GL-7.
[93] Ibid., II-12.
[94] Landreneau, 20 April 2016.
[95] United States Joint Chiefs of Staff, 'Joint Targeting', II-12.

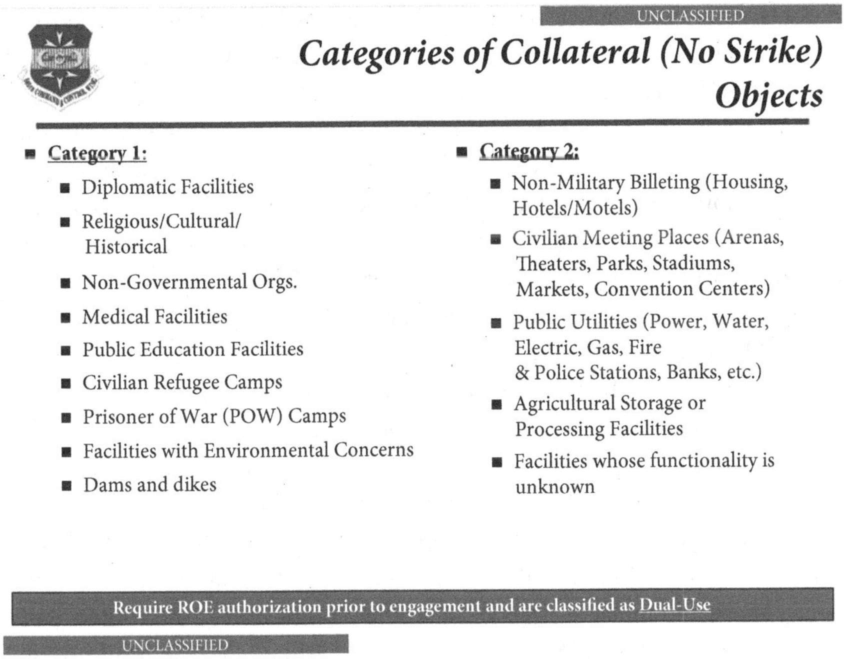

Figure 5.7 The 'No Strike List'.
Source: Anon, presentation on the role of the judge advocate in the air operations center, on file with author.

> [I]f a hospital or a place of worship is used for a purpose that is inconsistent with its protected status, such as storing weapons, housing combatants or unlawful belligerents, or functioning as an observation post, the facility loses immunity from attack under the LOW [laws of war] and is subject to attack.[96]

Military lawyers working in the kill chain must be familiar with the NSL and with another list known as the Restricted Target List (RTL). The RTL consists of targets that have been nominated but which 'have specific restrictions imposed upon them'.[97] However, as the former Director of Intelligence for Air

[96] United States Joint Chiefs of Staff, 'Chairman of the Joint Chiefs of Staff Instruction 3160.01A No Strike Collateral Damage Method', 13 February 2009, Appendix B, Enclosure C-4, https://www.aclu.org/files/dronefoia/dod/drone_dod_3160_01.pdf, accessed 14 December 2016.

[97] United States Air Force, 'Air Force Doctrine Document 3-60, Targeting', 38. The Joint Chiefs of Staff Instruction 'No-strike and the collateral damage estimation methodology' provides a more elaborate definition: 'Restricted targets are those valid military targets which support the attainment of operational objectives, but have been restricted from specified means of effects or engagement for operational, political, intelligence gain/loss, environmental, collateral damage, and/or ROE considerations': United States Joint Chiefs of Staff, 'Chairman of the Joint Chiefs of Staff Instruction 3160.01A No Strike Collateral Damage Method', C–2.

Force Central Command (AFCENT) disclosed, the RTL is 'not as restrictive as it sounds' and might include ROE provisions such as obtaining approval from the Iraqi or Afghani governments before a target can be struck.[98] The role of the JAG vis-à-vis these lists is, ideally, twofold. First, they ensure that due diligence has been carried out in removing an entity from the NSL and ensure that the provisions for striking a target on the RTL have been met. Second, they cross-reference targets that have been nominated for 'execution' (and which sit in a database called the Joint Integrated Prioritized Targeting List or 'JIPTL') 'to make sure something that is on a NSL [or RTL] is not going to be affected by a strike'. Extra caution is taken when a target is located near a place or facility that is on the NSL or RTL because the collateral damage concerns will likely be greater and will require a higher level of approval.[99]

But despite all these lists, and their various restrictions and requirements pored over and calibrated by JAGs, 'no strike' procedures can and do go badly wrong. In October 2016 a US AC-130 gunship fired 211 shells at the Médicines Sans Frontièrs (MSF) hospital in Kunduz, Afghanistan, killing at least thirty-one civilians and injuring twenty-eight others (Figure 5.8). The United States military headquarters at Bagram knew the coordinates of the MSF hospital and the hospital was on the NSL. However, an internal US Army investigation found that key commanders, including Afghan military forces and the AC-130 gunship crew, did not have access to the NSL.[100] The crew might have presumed the hospital was protected—as indeed it was—but the problem was that they did not *know* they were firing at the MSF hospital. Their intelligence told them they were firing at a building that had been designated as 'hostile'. In the eyes of the attackers, therefore, the building had lost its protected status. The investigation concluded that the strike was the result of both human and intelligence failures, but the tragic episode demonstrates two crucial issues. First, in practice—again—US targeting operations are not nearly as clean and precise as Air Force doctrine maintains they are. Second, no legal review or input from military lawyers on the NSL was ever going to be sufficient to prevent the MSF hospital from being attacked, if that guidance did not reach all relevant forces within range of it.

[98] Murray, interview.

[99] Landreneau, interview.

[100] Derek Gregory, 'Fighting over Kunduz', *Geographical Imaginations* (blog), 17 November 2016, https://geographicalimaginations.com/2016/11/17/fighting-over-kunduz/, accessed 16 January 2017; Al Jazeera, 'Bombed MSF Kunduz Hospital Was on US No-Strike List before Attack', 25 November 2015, http://america.aljazeera.com/articles/2015/11/25/afghan-hospital-said-to-be-misidentified-before-being-bombed.html, accessed 23 January 2017; May Jeong, 'Searching for Ground Truth in the Kunduz Hospital Bombing', *The Intercept*, 28 April 2016, https://theintercept.com/2016/04/28/searching-for-ground-truth-in-the-kunduz-hospital-bombing/, accessed 23 January 2017.

Figure 5.8 The Médecins Sans Frontières trauma center, Kunduz, Afghanistan, after it was attacked by the US military on 3 October 2015.
Source: Médecins Sans Frontières, reproduced with permission.

The messiness and contingencies of everyday military operations trump even the most meticulously planned elements of lethal targeting operations. In this instance, the fact that the AC-130 gunship crew took off without the coordinates of the MSF hospital loaded onto their onboard computer system proved the decisive operational factor. Blind spots like this in turn shape the legality of the attack; because this was ultimately a mistake, and the gunship crew thought they were attacking a 'hostile entity' (rather than a no-strike entity), there was no legal foul play as far as the US military were concerned. The attack on the MSF hospital was legal not in spite of the human and technical intelligence failures but precisely because of them. In this way, law and legal procedures condition targeting operations even when military lawyers may not have direct legal input in a specific attack or strike.

5.5 The Calibration of Force

If phases one and two of the deliberate kill chain are largely about establishing military objectives and PID, the third phase is ultimately about the calibration of force so as to operationalize (in theory) the principle of proportionality.

What the US military call 'capability analysis and weaponeering'[101] involves a series of calculations about the 'efficient' and 'feasible' use of military force.[102] Considerations include: the availability of weapons and the forces necessary to deploy them; risk to forces and to mission objectives; the quantity and type of lethal and non-lethal weapons; and weaponeering options designed to limit civilian casualties and collateral damage.[103] In this phase, perhaps more than any other, operational legalities are profoundly shaped by military capacities and efficiencies. Specifically, proportionality calculations are not divined from above or outside but are forged in and through the constraints of the kill chain.

Military lawyers play a crucial role in this phase of the targeting cycle. Their efforts can be understood with respect to two related tasks: weaponeering and collateral damage estimation (CDE). Every weapon in the US inventory undergoes a legal review before US forces can employ it.[104] The question facing military lawyers is therefore not about the legality of a weapon per se but rather *how* the weapon is to be used. Each target is weaponeered to include a wide range of technical calculations and projections.[105] During this process JAGs interact closely with weaponeers; they sit and talk with them and answer any questions that they may have about the ROE and the laws of war. One JAG described the process:

> I would actually sit with the weaponeers, the targeteers, and everybody else. I was so intimately familiar with the operation that there were no questions by the end. They were just looking for somebody, right before they get the go ahead, they're just looking for the JAG to say 'yes, I concur, this meets ROE'.

[101] Weaponeering is the 'process of determining the quantity of a specific type of lethal or nonlethal means required to create a desired effect on a given target': United States Joint Chiefs of Staff, 'Department of Defense Dictionary of Military and Associated Terms' (Washington, DC: Joint Chiefs of Staff, 16 February 2016), 258, http://www.dtic.mil/doctrine/new_pubs/jp1_02.pdf, accessed 11 January 2017.

[102] 'The primary purpose of capabilities analysis is to maximize the employment efficiency of forces through application of enough force to create the desired effects while minimizing collateral damage and waste of resources': United States Joint Chiefs of Staff, 'Joint Targeting', II–13.

[103] United States Air Force, 'Air Force Doctrine Document 3-60, Targeting', 38–9.

[104] 'Armed service regulations require that every weapon employed by the United States is reviewed for compliance with the law of armed conflict before it is fielded. All major powers conduct similar review programs': Gary D. Solis quoted in: Scott Horton, 'The Law of Armed Conflict: Six Questions for Gary Solis', *The Stream—Harper's Magazine Blog* (blog), 20 April 2010, http://harpers.org/blog/2010/04/_the-law-of-armed-conflict_-six-questions-for-gary-solis/, accessed 16 January 2016. See also: Gary, D Solis, *The Law of Armed Conflict: International Humanitarian Law in War*, 1st edition (Cambridge: Cambridge University Press, 2010), 271; Kathleen Lawand, 'Reviewing the Legality of New Weapons, Means and Methods of Warfare', *International Review of the Red Cross* 88, no. 864 (2006): 925–30; Kathleen Lawand, Robin M. Coupland, and Herby Peter, *A Guide to the Legal Review of New Weapons, Means and Methods of Warfare: Measures to Implement Article 36 of Additional Protocol I of 1977* (Geneva: International Committee of the Red Cross, 2006).

[105] United States Air Force, 'Air Force Doctrine Document 3-60, Targeting', 39.

> So they're just looking for the final check for you to say . . . for you to 'go green', say 'yep, I'm good with the strike'.[106]

ROE can raise particular concerns when it comes to deploying weapons. Specific weapons, or the use of a weapon in a particular way or in a particular place, may require permissions from a 'higher release authority'—a commander further up the chain of command. JAGs help to develop and must be fully conversant with these rules, and they work to ensure that, where relevant, the use of a particular weapon has been cleared by the correct release authority.[107]

The proportionality principle underlies an increasingly important part of calibrating the destructiveness of US Air Force targeting operations. The US military uses a process called the collateral damage methodology (CDM) in order to estimate the possible harm done to civilians and civilian objects. The CDM asks commanders '5 basic questions' that should be answered before striking any target (Figure 5.9).

Operators and JAGs insist that the methodology and casualty assessments are 'very scientific' and involve 'a lot of math' but as military lawyers Corn, Dapper, and Williams admit 'the CDM has limits'.[108] A Joint Chiefs of Staff Instruction makes this seem like an understatement when it concedes:

> [T]he casualty assessment is not an exact science. No precise means exists to predict noncombatant demographics and this effort is limited to the knowledge of the unique characteristics and cultural behaviors of the region and country as well as the population distributions, customs, and cultural practices, as well as particular habits unique to a region.[109]

Additionally, the CDM does not account for a number of variables, including 'weapon malfunctions, operational delivery errors, or altered delivery tactics based on operator judgment'.[110] It also does not apply to certain weapons due to 'operational practicality'.[111] Furthermore, the CDM:

[106] Brown, interview.

[107] Landreneau, interview.

[108] Geoffrey Corn, James Dapper, and Winston Williams, 'Targeting and the Law of Armed Conflict', in *U.S. Military Operations: Law, Policy, and Practice*, eds Geoffrey S. Corn, Rachel E. VanLandingham, and Shane R. Reeves (Oxford; New York, NY: Oxford University Press, 2015), 196.

[109] United States Joint Chiefs of Staff, 'Chairman of the Joint Chiefs of Staff Instruction 3160.01A No Strike Collateral Damage Method', Enclosure D, A-30.

[110] Ibid., Enclosure D-4.

[111] This includes, 'surface-to-surface direct fire weapon systems (e.g., 120mm cannon on M1 Main Battle Tank, 25mm Bushmaster, M-2 .50 Caliber Machinegun), rotary wing or fixed-wing air-to-surface

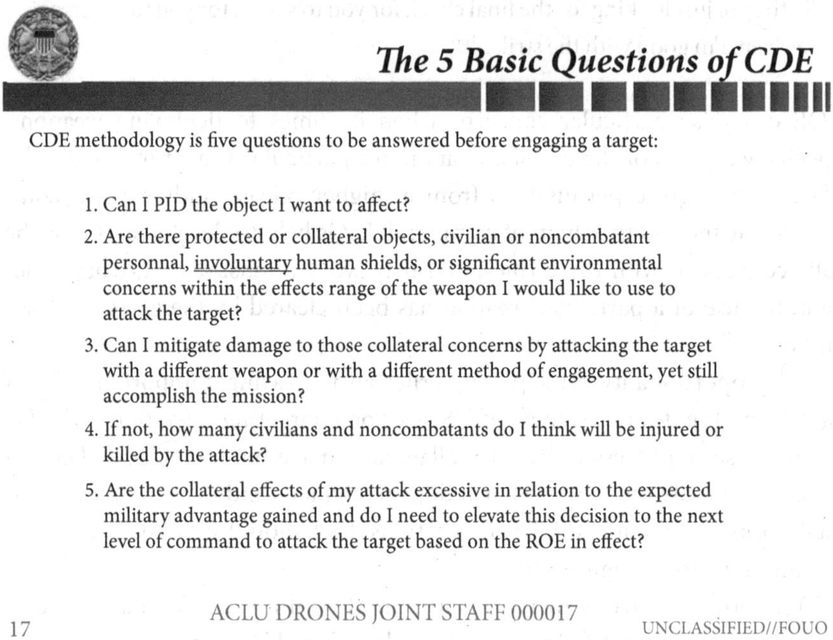

Figure 5.9 The Collateral Damage Estimation Methodology. Five questions that should be answered before engaging any target.

Source: United States Joint Chiefs of Staff/American Civil Liberties Union, Joint Targeting Cycle and Collateral Damage Estimation Methodology (CDEM), presentation briefing (Washington, DC, 10 November 2009), 17, https://www.aclu.org/files/dronefoia/dod/drone_dod_ACLU_DRONES_JOINT_STAFF_SLIDES_1-47.pdf, accessed 15 June 2020.

> [D]oes not account for unknown transient civilian or noncombatant personnel and/or equipment in the vicinity of a target area. This includes cars passing on roads, people walking down the street, or other noncombatant entities whose presence in the target area cannot be predicted to reasonable certainty within the capabilities and limitations of intelligence collection means.[112]

The CDM aims not to eliminate the risk of causing civilian casualties but to 'minimize' them, that is, within a particular range. Accidents happen, and the

direct fire weapon systems less than 105mm (e.g., 2.75in rockets, M2A1 40mm Bofors, GAU-8 30mm Gatling gun, and GAU-4 20mm Gatling gun)': Ibid.

[112] Ibid.

most advanced CDM in the world cannot prevent civilian casualties (though as Patricia Owens suggests, we should question how 'accidents' involving civilian deaths have been normalized in the post 9/11 era).[113] But in addition to accidental civilian casualties the CDM tolerates even *foreseeable* civilian casualties.

In fact, the US military has developed an elaborate set of procedures for dealing with anticipated civilian casualties. The CDM's fifth 'level' of civilian casualty estimation, for instance, has a special annex known as the non-combatant cut-off value or 'NCV'. The NCV is 'a threshold above which the United States will hesitate to strike because there is a likelihood that too many civilians will be killed or injured' and it works something like as follows.[114] A casualty estimate is made, and commanders are warned by the Chairman of the Joint Chiefs of Staff—in bold typeface—that they are '**assuming significant risk of collateral damage when engaging a target assessed under CDE Level 5**'.[115] If the casualty estimate is *below the current NCV value*, the commander would be permitted to proceed with the strike. For example, if the NCV is ten and it is anticipated that a strike will cause eight civilian casualties, the strike would, from a proportionality perspective, be permitted. If, however, the casualty estimate *exceeds* the NCV (say, fifteen anticipated civilian casualties) then the target must be forwarded for consideration and approval at a higher (and often very high) command level.[116]

The calibration of acceptable levels of civilian harm through both the CDM and the NCV is derived in no small part from the very exigencies of military operations that these tools also regulate. Operational legalities and the CDM and NCV are, thus, co-constitutive. The NCV is established by the President or the Secretary of Defense and is written into the relevant ROE governing a particular military operation.[117] Ali Watkins characterizes the process as somewhat chaotic: 'Determining an NCV requires a cocktail of military strategy,

[113] Patricia Owens, 'Accidents Don't Just Happen: The Liberal Politics of High-Technology "Humanitarian' War", *Millennium—Journal of International Studies* 32, no. 3 (2003): 595–616.

[114] Neta C. Crawford, 'Death Toll: Will The U.S. Tolerate More Civilian Casualties In Its Bid To Vanquish ISIS?', 21 January 2016, http://www.wbur.org/cognoscenti/2016/01/21/civilian-casualties-iraq-syria-us-war-on-isis-neta-c-crawford, accessed 11 April 2018.

[115] United States Joint Chiefs of Staff, 'Chairman of the Joint Chiefs of Staff Instruction 3160.01A No Strike Collateral Damage Method', Enclosure D, A-30 (bold in original).

[116] This is called the Sensitive Target Approval and Review Process (STAR), and STAR targets require approval by either the President or the Secretary of Defense. The STAR process is used for targets whose engagement present 'the potential for damage and/or injury to non-combatant property and persons; potential political consequences; or other significant effects estimated to exceed predetermined situation-specific criteria', thus presenting an 'unacceptable strategic risk'. ACLU slides, 38.

[117] Gregory S. McNeal, 'Targeted Killing and Accountability', *The Georgetown Law Journal* 102, no. 3 (2014): 751.

legality, proportionality, and subjective assessments by soldiers on the ground, lawyers in the Pentagon, and higher-ups in the executive branch.'[118] A former military lawyer told Watkins: 'There's no benchmark. And there's nothing in the law or doctrine, like a table you could open up . . . [that says] a tank is worth two civilian casualties, or a command post is worth five civilian casualties', meaning that most of the 'science' behind an NCV 'is left up to commanders' subjective analysis'.[119]

In other words, the NCV is not a stable number; it is operationally, geographically, and temporally changeable. The tolerance for civilian casualties has waxed and waned in both Iraq and Afghanistan over the last nearly two decades and is reflected in the NCV's changing values. At the height of the 'shock and awe' bombing of Baghdad in 2003, 'the magic number was 30', according to Marc Garlasco, the Pentagon's chief of high-value targeting at the start of the Iraq war. This meant, 'if you hit 30 as the anticipated number of civilians killed, the airstrike had to go to Rumsfeld or Bush personally to sign off'. If the expected number of civilian deaths was less than thirty, neither the President nor the Secretary of Defense needed to know and a strike could proceed without their input.[120] There were reportedly around 300 deliberate targets that were considered 'high collateral damage' in 2003 when the target 'packages' were finalized, and all but two of them were ultimately approved. (The two that were not approved were buildings housing foreign journalists.[121]) During the surge in Iraq beginning in 2007, the NCV was 'as high as 26'.[122] In 2008 the NCV in Afghanistan was thirty-five.[123]

This relatively high tolerance for civilian casualties could not last as strategy shifted towards counterinsurgency and 'winning hearts and minds'. As mentioned, in July 2009 ISAF Commander General Stanley McChrystal issued a Tactical Directive placing greater emphasis on the avoidance of civilian

[118] Ali Watkins, 'This Is How The U.S. Decides How Many People It Can Kill In Syria', BuzzFeed, 28 February 2016, http://www.buzzfeed.com/alimwatkins/syria-civilian-casualties-policy, accessed 19 December 2016.

[119] Geoffrey Corn quoted in: Ibid.

[120] Marc Garlasco, quoted in: Mark Benjamin, 'When Is an Accidental Civilian Death Not an Accident?', *Salon*, 30 July 2007, http://www.salon.com/2007/07/30/collateral_damage/, accessed 19 June 2016.

[121] Ibid.

[122] Tom Vanden Brook, 'New Rules Allow More Civilian Casualties in Air War against ISIL', *USA TODAY*, 19 April 2016, http://www.usatoday.com/story/news/politics/2016/04/19/new-rules-allow-more-civilian-casualties-air-war-against-isil/83190812/, accessed 7 November 2016.

[123] 'An estimate that more than thirty-five civilians might be killed also triggered the external approval process, which included almost any strike within an urban area. While the rules for Iraq were that all strikes (except STAR targets) could be approved by commanders on the ground, for Afghanistan, the Central Command in Tampa acted as the approval authority': Priest and Arkin, *Top Secret America*, 214.

casualties. According to some sources, in 2009 'forces employed an NCV of 1' for planned operations in Afghanistan.[124] During the surge in Afghanistan in 2010, however, the NCV had increased to nine.[125] In Operation Inherent Resolve (OIR)—the war against ISIS—the NCV in mid-2015 was purportedly zero as Obama redoubled efforts to reduce civilian casualties. According to one operator, the targeting restrictions in the target folder required operators to verify: 'If this target is struck, there is a reasonable degree of certainty that no civilians will be killed.'[126] Again in 2015, the *New York Times* reported that US intelligence had identified the main ISIS headquarters in downtown Raqqa, but the Air Force had not been allowed to target the seven buildings 'out of fear that the attacks will accidentally kill civilians'.[127]

There are voices within the US Air Force—and the US military more generally—who believe that the NCV has become *too* restrictive, especially in the war against ISIS. First, they claim, a restrictive NCV compromises the ability to administer a quick and decisive defeat. According to retired US Air Force General David Deptula, a key planner of the First Gulf War air campaign (Chapter 3): 'Complicating the effort to defeat the Islamic State is an excessive focus on the avoidance of collateral damage and casualties.' He argued that to defeat ISIS, 'air power has to be applied like a thunderstorm, not a drizzle'. Interestingly, Deptula believes that the laws of war should have been the US Air Force's guide in the war against ISIS. The rules, he argued 'far exceed accepted "Law of War" standards'.[128] He told me 'you cannot conduct lethal operations without some collateral damage or, as reprehensible as they are, unintentional civilian casualties. In fact [. . .] the laws of armed conflict recognize it'.[129] Deptula is correct in this, and the argument that the laws of war are more permissive than prevailing ROE is not new; it was employed by proponents of a more aggressive approach to air warfare both during and after the Vietnam War (Chapters 1 and 2).

Deptula is not alone in noting the discrepancy between what the law allows and the rules that have been 'self-imposed' on the US military. A JAG reported: 'The ROE is so restrictive. We're always trying to minimize collateral damage far beyond what LOAC requires.'[130] This raises a second risk: that these

[124] McNeal, 'Targeted Killing and Accountability', 752–3. McNeal derives this finding from a series of statements by NATO spokesmen reported in the media at the time.

[125] Vanden Brook, 'New Rules Allow More Civilian Casualties in Air War against ISIL'.

[126] Murray, interview.

[127] Eric Schmitt, 'U.S. Caution in Strikes Gives ISIS an Edge, Many Iraqis Say', *The New York Times*, 26 May 2015, http://www.nytimes.com/2015/05/27/world/middleeast/with-isis-in-crosshairs-us-holds-back-to-protect-civilians.html, accessed 19 December 2016.

[128] Deptula, 'How to Defeat the Islamic State'.

[129] Deptula, interview.

[130] Landreneau, interview.

restrictions, which begin as political and operational *choices*, will become *law* through precedent-setting practice. As one intelligence analyst rhetorically asked: 'because we can be precise, are we morally obligated now going forward because of the ability we've demonstrated to be precise? [. . .] it's fast becoming a moral obligation to conduct warfare at that level'.[131] Morals are one thing, but the real concern from some quarters seems to be about these restrictions becoming *law* and the implications this has for lawfare. As former military lawyer and now legal scholar Jack Beard cautions, 'less developed states can argue that richer countries with extensive, widely deployed and sophisticated virtual surveillance [and] once-unimaginable levels of ISR information, are subject to a higher standard of care in verifying targets as military objectives and taking other precautionary measures'.[132]

Beyond their particular content, arguments such as these underscore the fundamental malleability of targeting restrictions like the NCV (and at the same time, the stability of a much older idea, that of pressing military advantage). The laws of war are sufficiently flexible to allow for expansions and contractions in the NCV, another example of how rules are telescoped to allow for adjustments in military 'necessities'. The job of the military lawyer in this phase is not to impose an objective legal standard but instead to assist in the calibration of force within the broad parameters carved out by shifting objectives, emergent military necessities, and changeable political directives. By late 2015 Deptula's logic had begun to win favour in the fight against ISIS in Syria and Iraq, and the US relaxed the ROE to allow for an NCV of five.[133] By April 2016, '[p]ockets of Ramadi and other areas of intense fighting [. . .] had non-combatant values of 10 or more'.[134] As Nick McDonell of the *Los Angeles Times* explained: 'In Iraq and Syria, the calculus is different [to Afghanistan]. The Pentagon believes Islamic State is a greater threat than the Taliban; the Iraqis have been requesting more aggressive support; the fighting is more urban.'[135] In one noteworthy airstrike in January

[131] Murray, interview. See also: Scott F. Murray, 'The Moral and Ethical Implications of Precision-Guided Munitions' (DTIC Document, 2007), http://uploads.worldlibrary.net/uploads/pdf/20121012233256moral_and_ethical_implications_pdf.pdf, accessed 1 July 2020.

[132] Beard, 'Law and War in the Virtual Era', 445.

[133] Dustin Wong, 'Fears of civilian casualties grow as Ramadi push nears', *The Hill*, 24 December 2015, http://thehill.com/policy/defense/264159-us-warns-civilians-ahead-of-major-isis-battle, accessed 19 December 2016.

[134] Vanden Brook, 'New Rules Allow More Civilian Casualties in Air War against ISIL'. See also: Watkins, 'This Is How The U.S. Decides How Many People It Can Kill In Syria' (citing a soldier as saying 'As long as it's under 10 [. . .] we're good to take the shot'.)

[135] Nick McDonell, 'Civilian Casualties Are Not Inevitable. The Military Sets an Acceptable Number in Advance', *Los Angeles Times*, 31 March 2017, https://www.latimes.com/opinion/op-ed/la-oe-mcdonell-civilian-casualties-ncv-20170331-story.html, accessed 13 February 2020.

2016, the US Air Force dropped two 2,000-pound bombs on a building in a civilian area of central Mosul. The building contained 'huge amounts of cash' that ISIS was using for its operations. But while much attention was paid to that aspect of the strike, reporting from CNN revealed something very important about the NCV: 'U.S. commanders had been willing to consider up to *50 civilian casualties* from the airstrike due to the importance of the target. But the initial post-attack assessment indicated that perhaps five to seven people were killed.'[136] Examples like this show just how much mission objectives (section 5.3) can impact operational outcomes and legalities: everything from zero to fifty foreseeable civilian casualties have been considered the appropriate cut-off for a single strike.

5.6 'ATO' Time

Once targets have been weaponeered and assessed for possible collateral damage, they are presented to the commander for final approval at the Joint Targeting Coordination Board (JTCB).[137] During this phase (phase four—'Commander's Decision and Force Assignment') approved targets are mapped onto the Air Tasking Order (ATO), which dictates which targets will be hit, in what order, and when. A JAG who regularly oversaw the production of the ATO in the CAOC describes what is involved:

> I would not even pretend to understand any of the magic that went into building the Air Tasking Order. Those guys, senior captains, majors and lieutenant colonels in charge of it, they were grizzled veterans of air power. They were brilliant. They knew where to put tankers, when to put tankers, where to put the bombers and fighters, they were just great and it's this finely orchestrated dance.[138]

JAGs do not sit on the periphery of the operations floor and merely admire the ATO 'dance', however. Before targets become part of the ATO they are

[136] Barbara Starr, 'First on CNN: US Bombs "millions" in ISIS Currency Stock—CNNPolitics', *CNN*, 13 January 2016, sec. Politics, https://edition.cnn.com/2016/01/11/politics/us-bombs-millions-isis-currency-supply/, accessed 13 February 2020 (emphasis added).

[137] The intensity of combat operations dictates the frequency of the JTCB. In Operation Desert Storm (1991), the Targeting Board would meet daily. In Operation Inherent Resolve, in 2016, the Targeting Board would meet three days a week: Murray, interview.

[138] Brown, interview.

re-reviewed by the Combat Plans Division JAG to ensure that that the intelligence is up to date and the target has received prior legal review. As one JAG explained:

> [T]he JAGs in the plans division do a review of all of the targets that are going to be nominated to be struck on a particular ATO day. [. . .] The first thing a JAG is going to do is pull up all the targets that are nominated for a particular day and do a search and see which ones haven't been reviewed by legal, then he can pull up all the ones that have been reviewed by legal, and then kind of sort them by when their last review date was. So you set the priority based off of that: not reviewed versus more attenuated review versus most current review, and they'll start going down the list and reviewing the reviewer in a lot of cases.[139]

The Combat Plans Division JAG or the senior CAOC JAG attends the Targeting Board meeting and must be ready to answer any legal questions that the joint or component forces commander has about the targets on the list.[140] The Targeting Board meeting is not the first occasion a JAG can see a particular target. As Marine JAG Major James Burkart, points out: 'by actively participating in the prior phases of the targeting process, including conducting a formal legal review of the entire target package, the judge advocate can identify and address legal issues prior to the target being briefed at the board.'[141] By the time a target is being reviewed at the Board, it will likely have been through more than one, and possibly several, rounds of legal review. One JAG described the ISAF targets in Afghanistan as passing through a 'pre-targeting board' review for an initial 'scrub' (review).[142]

An operator responsible for nominating target packages out of Shaw Air Force base for subsequent review by the CJTF-OIR (Combined Joint Task Force Commander for Operation Inherent Resolve) in Kuwait told me that many of his nominated targets were being rejected in late 2014 and early 2015. The reason was that the target packages did not meet the standard of 'reasonable certainty' that zero civilians would be killed as a result of engaging the

139 Landreneau, interview.

140 United States Air Force Judge Advocate General's School, 'Air Force Operations and the Law', 281. See also: Michael F. Lohr and Steve Gallotta, 'Legal Support in War: The Role of Military Lawyers', *Chicago Journal of International Law* 4, no. 2 (2003): 478 (noting, 'The fact that the legal advisor brings the principles of war to the planning cell, or the Targeting Board, is an important part of the US commitment to comply with the LOW').

141 Burkart, 'Deadly Advice', 18.

142 Prescott, interview.

target (that is, an NCV of zero—see section 5.5). In order to meet this criterion, the operator approached his Staff Judge Advocate and said:

> 'Hey, I need a full-time JAG in the targeting development cell' [. . .] he agreed and the rest is history. We actually bring in lawyers to Shaw who spend six months here at a time and that's all they do; they don't have any other legal responsibilities other than to be part of the target cell.[143]

This operator went on to describe how his deputy sat on his right and his JAG on his left in the targeting cell, demonstrating how important legal advice had become at this stage of the target development process. 'I didn't even entertain [a] target going anywhere outside of my organization until I as the leader and my co-workers to my right and my left agreed that this target was worthy of being sent to the Joint Task Forces', he told me.[144] Having a JAG involved in this initial vetting process 'naturally slowed the process down' according to the operator. But where previously more targets 'were rejected earlier because of a lack of JAG review [. . .] with the JAG in the process, the vast majority of them were approved'.[145]

This example shows how extensive JAG involvement in the targeting review process is not limited to the space of the CAOC. Targets often receive a 'double scrub', or when combat operations are slow (as they frequently have been in OIR), they get what one JAG described as 'entirely too much scrubbing'.[146] The example also shows how JAGs facilitate the decision-making and targeting-approval processes. Filtering out targets that would not get approval further down the line may be slower in some respects, but it leads to a higher rate of targets being approved, saving time and resources later on. The operator was grateful for the assistance and assured me that the JAGs 'weren't there to stop the process; they were there actually to enable it'.[147]

[143] Murray, interview.

[144] Ibid.

[145] Ibid.

[146] Stefano (pseudonym), interview. 'In my experience when they don't have that many deliberate targets they get entirely too much scrubbing. Idle hand syndrome kicks in and you got a tonne of lawyers, a tonne of operators and they're all looking at targets because that's the only show in town, there's only 5 targets being struck tomorrow, on tomorrow's ATO so they do a "gnats-ass" analysis, I mean the level of detail is phenomenal. What I was trying to tell the JAGS is that "its fine for you to do that now but in a major combat operation you can't expect to have that level of fidelity and intensity on the target because you'll never get anything done." The current fight allows for that and so human nature will sort of gravitate toward that, which is fine, I just try to remind them . . . if we were in Korea and this was going on, you would not be able to do that analysis for each target. You just don't have the personnel or the intel [. . .] Just remember that perfection is the enemy when you have 800 of these things coming at you everyday.'

[147] Murray, interview.

5.7 Execute, Assess, Repeat

In phase five the kill chain moves from planning to execution, and those targets on the ATO are struck. The execution phase is extremely fluid, and scheduled targets are often shuffled or delayed to make way for emergent and more time-sensitive targets (Chapter 6, section 6.4). As one JAG put it, 'even deliberately planned missions are dynamically executed'.[148] Demonstrating just how much plans can change, one pilot recalls that during the 2009–2010 surge in Afghanistan 'it was common for aircrew to brief a set of missions, *but execute none of them*. Instead, they would be re-tasked multiple times while in a briefing, while stepping to the aircraft, during takeoff, and even enroute [sic].'[149]

JAGs are part of the Combat Operations Division and they support the execution phase from the CAOC 'operations floor'. As previously noted, JAGs at the CAOC work shifts so that at least one of them (of typically three or four in total) is available on or near the operations floor. A senior-ranking military lawyer is part of the 'battle cab' staff (overlooking the operations floor), which places him or her at the very heart of the force execution process. The battle cab is home to the weapons release authorities (the commanders who have authority to release weapons),[150] who work closely with JAGs to resolve last-minute legal issues—such as the unanticipated presence of civilians near a target. Both the JAG on the operations floor and the JAG in the 'battle cab' are responsible for monitoring operations in real time to facilitate and produce compliance with prevailing US interpretations of the laws of war, the current ROE, and other stipulations such as commander's directives.

JAGs also monitor communications between the CAOC and other locations in the kill chain, both in 'theatre' (i.e. on the ground in Afghanistan and Iraq) and in the United States.[151] They are looking for any changes in circumstances that may alter their legal and ROE calculations. Preventing fratricide is of utmost concern and fire support coordination measures are put in place to help ensure that friendly forces are not in the air or on the ground close to a target.[152] Planners may adopt means to mitigate certain last-minute risks, for

[148] Burkart, 'Deadly Advice', 19.

[149] Mike Benitez, 'How Afghanistan Distorted Close Air Support and Why It Matters', War on the Rocks, 29 June 2016, http://warontherocks.com/2016/06/how-afghanistan-distorted-close-air-support-and-why-it-matters/ , accessed 12 December 2016 (emphasis added).

[150] In the CAOC there are several weapons release authorities because each state that is part of the coalition in either Afghanistan or Iraq has its own authority. These commanders are sometimes also called the 'red card holders' because they hold the authority to approve or deny a target based upon national caveats. Each weapons release authority/red card holder has access to a military lawyer.

[151] United States Air Force Judge Advocate General's School, 'Air Force Operations and the Law', 280.

[152] United States Joint Chiefs of Staff, 'Joint Targeting', III–1.

example, warning civilians by dropping leaflets prior to attack or performing a 'show of force', a common tactic in Afghanistan where an aircraft will fly over a target at low altitude in the hope of persuading the enemy to retreat.[153] However, such precautions are taken 'only when circumstances permit', and in dynamic targeting operations the circumstances often do not.[154] As the moment approaches for a target to be struck—deliberate or dynamic—the area of the target is reassessed to see if there are any concerns that warrant suspension or cancellation of the attack.[155]

After the target has been struck the next and last phase is to assess whether: (a) the 'desired effects' have been achieved; and (b) any fratricide or collateral damage has been caused.[156] The assessment performs an intelligence function as well as being the first step in a possible investigation. A 'battle damage assessment' helps to determine whether a target should be 'reengaged', and the information garnered should also be factored into future targeting decisions.[157]

According to Air Force doctrine, JAGs have 'limited involvement' in the assessment phase unless a specific issue has arisen such as 'a friendly fire incident, target misidentification, or allegations of LOAC violations'.[158] In such cases JAGs perform a number of tasks: perhaps most importantly they are involved in providing legal advice to the investigation team.[159] They also help to gather and preserve evidence—usually communications—that were generated by the CAOC and elements of the Tactical Air Control; they may assist in gathering weapon system videos for the strike aircraft as well as data from other assets, including ISR assets.[160] JAGs are also responsible for reviewing reports that are generated by pilots and operators following a mission; these are known as mission reports (MISREPS).[161] JAGs also help to capture 'lessons learned'

153 Beth Van Schaack, 'Targeting Tankers Under the Law of War (Part 1)', *Just Security*, 2 December 2015, https://www.justsecurity.org/28064/targeting-tankers-law-war-part-1/, accessed 16 November 2016; David Wood, 'Holding Fire Over Afghanistan', *Air Force Magazine*, 1 January 2010, https://www.airforcemag.com/article/0110afghanistan/, accessed 24 January 2017.

154 United States Joint Chiefs of Staff, 'Joint Targeting', A-5.

155 'Target intelligence may be found to be faulty before an attack is started or completed. If it becomes apparent that a target is no longer a lawful military objective, the attack must be cancelled or suspended': Ibid.

156 John P. Abizaid and Rosa Brooks, 'Recommendations and Report of the Task Force on US Drone Policy' (Washington, DC: Stimson, April 2015), https://www.stimson.org/2014/recommendations-and-report-stimson-task-force-us-drone-policy-0/, accessed 13 February 2020.

157 United States Air Force, 'Air Force Doctrine Annex 3-60 Targeting' (US Air Force LeMay Center for Doctrine Development, 10 January 2014), 12, https://doctrine.af.mil/DTM/dtmtargeting.htm, accessed 17 December 2016.

158 United States Air Force Judge Advocate General's School, 'Air Force Operations and the Law', 282.

159 Oler, interview.

160 United States Air Force Judge Advocate General's School, 'Air Force Operations and the Law', 282.

161 Landreneau, interview.

and write after action reports,[162] which are stored on a classified database made available to all JAG Corps military members so that they may research the database ahead of future deployments.[163]

In recent years the United States has placed greater emphasis on its responsibility to investigate allegations of civilian casualties; several different components of the military have conducted a number of high-profile investigations into strikes that have killed civilians.[164] A 2011 ISAF/US Forces-Afghanistan Tactical Directive ordered the conduct of 'ground battle damage assessments in all situations where there is a potential loss of life or injury to insurgents or Afghan civilians, except when an assessment would put ISAF personnel at greater risk'.[165] The Directive also ordered the investigation of 'every allegation of civilian casualties', its author John R. Allen adding: '[w]here engagements appear to have breached any aspect of this Directive, whether or not they resulted in civilian casualties, I expect commanders to investigate. We are in a better position tactically, operationally and strategically when we are first with the truth.'[166]

Neta C. Crawford, scholar and Co-Director of the Costs of War project at Brown University, details the extensive mechanisms that the United States has put in place for the investigation of civilian casualties.[167] But not all allegations are looked into; in fact, the overwhelming majority are deemed not credible by US Central Command and are therefore not investigated.[168] According to Larry

[162] 'A Lesson Learned is an insight gained that, when validated and resolved, results in an improvement in military operations or activities at the strategic, operational, or tactical level and results in long-term, internalized change to an individual or an organization. An After Action Report (AAR) is a report that includes observations which result in improvements in military operations': United States Air Force, 'United States Air Force Instruction 51-108: The Judge Advocate General's Corps Structure, Deployment, and Operational Support' (United States Air Force, 9 October 2014), 19, http://static.e-publishing.af.mil/production/1/af_ja/publication/afi51-108/afi51-108.pdf, accessed 15 December 2016.

[163] Ibid.

[164] See e.g. Derek Gregory's in-depth analysis of the US mechanisms of investigation: Derek Gregory, 'Angry Eyes (1)', *Geographical Imaginations* (blog), 1 October 2015, https://geographicalimaginations.com/2015/10/01/angry-eyes-1/, accessed 16 January 2017; ibid.; Derek Gregory, 'Watching the Detectives', *Geographical Imaginations* (blog), 8 October 2015, https://geographicalimaginations.com/2015/10/08/watching-the-detectives/, accessed 16 January 2017; Derek Gregory, 'Killing over Kunduz', *Geographical Imaginations* (blog), 3 October 2016, https://geographicalimaginations.com/2016/10/03/killing-over-kunduz/, accessed 16 January 2017; Gregory, 'Fighting over Kunduz'.

[165] John Allen, 'Headquarters, International Security Assistance Force (ISAF) Tactical Directive', Unclassified, ISAF, NATO, 30 November 2011, http://www.rs.nato.int/images/docs/20111105%20nuc%20tactical%20directive%20revision%204%20(releaseable%20version)%20r.pdf, accessed 16 January 2017.

[166] Ibid.

[167] Crawford, *Accountability for Killing*.

[168] Terry Moon Cronk, 'Centcom Releases Civilian Casualty Assessments', US Department of Defense, http://www.defense.gov/News/Article/Article/741155/centcom-releases-civilian-casualty-assessments, accessed 16 January 2017.

Lewis, who in 2010 co-wrote an important—and still classified—Joint Civilian Casualty Study (JCCS),[169] much of the data that the US military uses is unreliable and unevenly collected. He told *The Nation*: 'There are some commanders that, any time a civilian casualty is suspected, they'll do an investigation to try to get to the bottom of it [. . .] Others, they'd only do it if they thought there could be neglect or actual criminality. So there are a lot of different criteria.'[170] Many civilian casualties are not recorded or reported, which is why official US estimates are often much lower than estimates by independent groups like the United Nations Assistance Mission to Afghanistan (UNAMA) and Airwars.[171]

Airwars is a UK-based independent organization that monitors and assesses civilian harm from airpower-dominated international military actions. Because of its rigorous and multi-source counting methodology,[172] Airwars has become an important source of data relating to civilian casualties and more and more news media rely on it in their reporting of ongoing US wars.[173] There is a vast discrepancy between Airwars' data on estimated civilian casualties and the US's own official data. For example, the US-led Coalition's estimate of civilian harm in OIR—Iraq and Syria combined—is at least 1,370 civilians killed since 2014 in 340 separate incidents. In comparison, Airwars estimates that 8,251 to 13,159 civilians have likely been killed by the Coalition since 2014 in 1,481 incidents.[174] Overall, local communities have alleged up to 29,535 noncombatant deaths across 2,919 incidents from US-led actions, but Airwars does not include these in its estimates because they are considered either 'weak' or 'contested' claims.[175]

How are we to make sense of the discrepancies—in this case, five to tenfold—between what the US military self-reports and what organizations

[169] General Petraeus described the study as 'the first comprehensive assessment of the problem of civilian protection'. Center for Naval Analysis, 'Our Expert: Larry Lewis', n. d., https://www.cna.org/experts/Lewis_L, accessed 7 March 2020.

[170] Bob Dreyfuss and Nick Turse, 'America's Afghan Victims', 18 September 2013, https://www.thenation.com/article/archive/americas-afghan-victims/, accessed 2 March 2020.

[171] Crawford, *Accountability for Killing*, 105.

[172] See: Airwars, 'Methodology', n.d., https://airwars.org/about/methodology/, accessed 7 March 2020.

[173] e.g. Azmat Khan and Anand Gopal, 'The Uncounted—The New York Times', *The New York Times*, 16 November 2017, https://www.nytimes.com/interactive/2017/11/16/magazine/uncounted-civilian-casualties-iraq-airstrikes.html, accessed 28 November 2019; Nick Turse, 'New Data Shows the U.S. Military Is Severely Undercounting Civilian Casualties in Somalia', *The Intercept* (blog), 25 February 2020, https://theintercept.com/2020/02/25/africom-airstrikes-somalia/, accessed 7 March 2020; Jared Szuba, 'Slow Admissions of Civilian Harm in Somalia Raise Questions about US Transparency', *The Defense Post*, 24 February 2020, sec. Africa, https://thedefensepost.com/2020/02/24/somalia-us-africom-civilian-casualty-reports/, accessed 7 March 2020.

[174] Airwars, 'US-Led Coalition in Iraq & Syria', 7 March 2020, https://airwars.org/conflict/coalition-in-iraq-and-syria/, accessed 7 March 2020.

[175] Ibid.

like Airwars report? I put this question to Chris Woods, Founder and Director of Airwars,[176] and he suggested several explanations:

(a) Even where the Coalition admits casualties, the public estimate may be higher based on local community reporting.
(b) The US-led Coalition has a bias towards finding 'credible' only those events where it has visible evidence, usually from ISR. However, the great majority of civilians killed in the war died in unobservable urban spaces.
(c) Even where there is compelling local evidence, the Coalition has too often deemed events 'non credible'—meaning that the experiences of local communities are ignored.
(d) While the US military now routinely engages with external NGOs and agencies like Airwars and Amnesty, its close allies generally do not. The United Kingdom and France—responsible for perhaps one in seven of all air and artillery strikes between them during the war—have admitted just one death between them. By contrast, the Americans have declared around one death for every forty of their own actions.[177]

While all are important, points (b) and (c) above are interesting for our purposes because they refer once again to the techno-cultural apparatus of military 'seeing' via ISR (I return to point (d) in the Conclusion). Despite constant interruptions (Chapter 6, section 6.4), the United States and other later modern militaries are driven by an ideology of precision, perfection, and omniscience.[178] As authors at the Intelligence Geospatial Forum magazine claim: intelligence, surveillance and reconnaissance (ISR) needs to be 'persistent, pervasive and timely [. . .] Gathering intelligence on fast, fleeting, hidden and unpredictable adversaries requires knowledge of *everyone, everywhere, all the time*.'[179] (See Chapter 6, section 6.1.) Such dreams of 'technological

[176] Before founding Air Wars, Chris Woods was a senior reporter at the Bureau of Investigative Journalism and a Senior producer at the BBC. He is also the author of a book on drone warfare that has been widely acclaimed across the political spectrum and by top military thinkers and commanders in both the United States and the United Kingdom. See: Christopher Woods, *Sudden Justice: America's Secret Drone Wars* (New York, NY: Oxford University Press, 2015).

[177] Email correspondence with Chris Woods. 14 February 2020 (on file with author).

[178] For a critique of these ideologies see: Maja Zehfuss, 'Targeting: Precision and the Production of Ethics', *European Journal of International Relations* 17, no. 3 (2011): 543–66; Maja Zehfuss, *War and the Politics of Ethics* (Oxford: Oxford University Press, 2018); Derek Gregory, 'War and Peace', *Transactions of the Institute of British Geographers* 35, no. 2 (2010): 154–86; Derek Gregory, 'From a View to a Kill Drones and Late Modern War', *Theory, Culture & Society* 28, no. 7–8 (2011): 188–215; Derek Gregory, 'Lines of Descent'. *OpenDemocracy.Net*, 8 November 2011, http://www.opendemocracy.net/derek-gregory/lines-of-descent, accessed 16 February 2012.

[179] This quote, slightly modified, is taken from: Gregory, 'From a View to a Kill Drones and Late Modern War', 193 (emphasis added). US Army Major David Pendall explains the game-changing

omniscience'[180] are not new but rather form the backdrop to other later modern fantasies about what US Colonel Mackubin Owens has called, 'the immaculate conception of warfare'.[181] (Immaculately conceived, that is, war produces no civilian casualties.) If Woods is correct in having identified a bias in civilian incident (non)reporting, then the obverse of this ideology is that if something was *not* seen (by the military, and in recordable form), then for all intents and purposes, it did not happen. But as noted in the Introduction, there is every reason to expect non-observable deaths, especially in urban spaces.[182]

Of course, not everyone agrees with Airwars' data[183] but the US military itself relies extensively on external reporting from Airwars (and other organizations) and, moreover, recent declassified documents confirm significant parts of Woods' account. A secret US military Civilian Casualty (CIVCAS) Review commissioned by the Joint Chiefs of Staff and published in April 2018 (declassified in February 2019) not only used Airwars data,[184] but also made a series of startling admissions about its own inadequate procedures in an attempt to understand 'the gap between CIVCAS figures reported by the US military and NGOs' (Airwars is cited several times in the Review).[185] Two related issues in particular are worth highlighting: (a) the Review concedes the possibility that

advances made in intelligence, surveillance, and reconnaissance (ISR) technologies in much the same way: 'the targeted entity will be unable to move, hide, disperse, deceive, or otherwise break contact with the focused intelligence system. Once achieved, persistent ISR coverage will, in theory, deny the adversary sanctuary, enabling coherent decisionmaking [sic] and action with reduced risk': David W. Pendall, 'Persistent Surveillance and Its Implications for the Common Operating Picture', *Military Review* 85, no. 6 (2005): 41.

[180] Stephen Graham, *Cities Under Siege: The New Military Urbanism* (London; New York, NY: Verso, 2011), xii.

[181] Quoted in: Marc Herold, 'The "Unworthy" Afgan Bodies: "Smarter" U.S. Weapons Kill More Innocents', in *Inventing Collateral Damage: Civilian Casualties, War, and Empire*, ed. Stephen J. Rockel and Rick Halpern (Toronto: Between the Lines, 2009), 303.

[182] In effect, local complainants are adjuncts to a *self-regulatory and self-referential* process; whatever the undoubted strengths of kill chain technologies these are outstripped by the claims made for them, claims which are force-multiplying once cashed out as juridical assumptions. To make availability of ISR evidence the arbiter of the 'credible' is tantamount to holding victims and bystanders to a high standard of visual access to the battlespace—higher than even the US military can achieve.

[183] Charles Dunlap, 'The (Un)Accountable? Why Critics Need to Be Scrutinized as Much as the Military', *Lawfire* (blog), 11 December 2017, https://sites.duke.edu/lawfire/2017/12/11/the-unaccountable-why-critics-need-to-be-scrutinized-as-much-as-the-military/, accessed 7 March 2020; Stephen J. Townsend, 'Reports of Civilian Casualties in the War Against ISIS Are Vastly Inflated', *Foreign Policy* (blog), 15 September 2017, https://foreignpolicy.com/2017/09/15/reports-of-civilian-casualties-from-coalition-strikes-on-isis-are-vastly-inflated-lt-gen-townsend-cjtf-oir/, accessed 7 March 2020.

[184] United States Joint Chiefs of Staff and National Defense University, 'Executive Summary: Civilian Casualty (CIVCAS) Review', 17 April 2018, 11, https://www.justsecurity.org/wp-content/uploads/2019/02/Civ-Cas-Study-Redacted-just-security.pdf, accessed 7 March 2020, stating: 'The study team used Airwars data because it was the only NGO that provided consistent reporting on the number of CIVCAS for Iraq and Syria within the study period.'

[185] Ibid., 1.

the US military undercounts civilian casualties;[186] and (b) two (unnamed) dissenting members of the Review 'study team' suggest that the investigation mechanisms are *systematically deficient*. Focusing particularly on the issue of PID (section 5.4) they claim that their own methodology 'will tend not to detect PID problems, because military personnel are generally unaware of misidentifications when they occur'.[187] This, they say, has profound implications for the very possibility of investigations, let alone their execution:

> Investigations and CCARs [Credibility Assessment Reports] are the best way to detect potential CIVCAS; however, because of the combination of the lack of a robust US presence on the ground and a sometimes overly restrictive process for evaluating external reports, it is reasonable to expect a systematic undercounting of misidentifications in US military reports in the context of OIR [Operation Inherent Resolve]. This may be particularly true given the more complex nature of the Mosul and Raqqa operations.[188]

A JAG confirmed that the Air Force does not have an 'institutionalized process for conducting civilian casualty investigations with a view towards accountability. It's always done ad hoc and after the fact.' He compared this to Air Force accident investigations (e.g. into a helicopter or airplane crash), which have a permanent designated investigation board:

> The accident board investigation is something that is done with a view toward accountability and releasability and they are mandated and most accidents above a certain threshold [are investigated] when there's an aircraft accident. But you don't have that kind of equivalent during armed conflict; it's really a 'commander discretion' kind of thing.[189]

The patchiness of investigation procedures might strike some readers as surprising, but it is entirely in keeping with the targeting cycle more broadly. Investigation procedures have their own blind spots and biases not dissimilar to those in each phase of the deliberate kill chain, and highlighted throughout this chapter. The ad hoc and reluctant nature of investigatory mechanisms tell

[186] 'A considerable number of external allegations are disregarded due to insufficient information. The US military's verification process has also led to a backlog of pending external allegations, which, if eventually deemed credible would narrow this gap [between US and Airwars estimates] but not close it': Ibid., 11.

[187] Ibid., 6.

[188] Ibid.

[189] Dunlap, interview.

us something important about military priorities. For all that foreign policy also proceeds though bureaucracies of aid and trade (and civilian and military contractors significantly overlap) this is not, after all, an investigatory, compensatory, or postwar reconstruction 'doughnut'; it is a doughnut of *death*. This is not to say that the US military or any of its components are indifferent to civilian casualties—they certainly are not—but the kill chain is first and foremost a necropolitical bureaucracy: one aimed at allocating and distributing death among a disenfranchised 'targeted class'[190] wherever—and whomsoever—its members are deemed to be at the time.

That the targeting cycle is a killing machine is an obvious point, (which in some ways makes it all the more important).[191] That the kill chain allocates and distributes death and does so through a series of calibrations—legal, technical, and otherwise—is perhaps also unsurprising: later modern war is all about the 'smart' application of force and the minimization of unnecessary violence, and these require careful and extensive 'calibrative' work. Besides, what is the alternative: *not* to calibrate force? To employ *more* than minimal force? In responding to questions like these, something perhaps less obvious comes into view: the often unseen and silent work that law and war lawyers do. It is all very well to calibrate force, but the ethico-legal question that follows must be: *to what end?*

* * *

The legal frameworks that are brought to bear on and through the kill chain do not provide objective standards from which the legality of a particular targeting operation can be divined, let alone a set of ethical principles for the adjudication and distribution of death. Instead, the legal frameworks are born in battle: they are *of* war, not outside of it. It is thus not within the remit of law or war lawyers to meaningfully disrupt the kill chain. The frameworks themselves are malleable and provide scope for a wide range of possible interpretations; those interpretations meet the materialities of war, producing new military realities and new legal interpretations in a never-ending cycle. As

[190] Parks, Lisa, 'Drones, Vertical Mediation, and the Targeted Class', *Feminist Studies* 42, no. 1 (2016): 227–35.

[191] I am reminded of Elaine Scarry's injunction to interrogate those things in war that have become so obvious that commentators seem to forget to say them. Scarry reminds us: 'The main purpose and outcome of war is injuring. Though this fact is too self-evident and massive ever to be directly contested, it can be indirectly contested by many means and can disappear from view along many separate paths. It may disappear from view simply by being omitted': Elaine Scarry, 'Injury and the Structure of War', *Representations* 10, Spring (1985): 1.

I have shown, the process is messier and far bloodier in practice than military doctrine (or the infrequency of incident investigations) would suggest. The malleability of targeting law means that its constraining function often loses out to its enabling function, and this has real-world consequences for who and what is targeted. Such is a day in the life of a kill chain lawyer, and as days turn into weeks, weeks into months and months into years, still the cycle continues. Even 'interruptions' to the planned battle rhythm are routine, and tend to increase lethality rather than temper it, as Chapter 6 will now explain.

6

The Kill Chain (II)

Dynamic Targeting

6.1 Emergent Events and Mobile Targets

The deliberate targeting cycle can take anywhere from one or two days to several weeks—or even months—from the first identification of a target to its being struck (Chapter 5). This often-painstaking mode of targeting lacks the speed and responsiveness required for the overwhelming majority of US aerial targeting operations today. The deliberate kill chain is well suited to identifying and destroying static military structures and objects such as an enemy air base or a weapons production facility. These are difficult and slow for the enemy to relocate, so once identified they can sit in the target 'bank' for as long as necessary and be targeted whenever it makes most military sense. But the deliberate kill chain is less well suited to tracking mobile targets, like an enemy leader on the move or a vehicle being used to transport combatants. The window of opportunity to strike fleeting targets such as these can be extremely narrow. Furthermore, if troops come into contact with enemy forces on the ground, they may require air support as soon as possible. In responding to battle *events* as they emerge in real time, every minute counts. A kill chain that expends precious time in deliberation cannot deliver support that was needed moments ago (and counting).

For these reasons, over the last fifty years, the US Air Force has developed and refined a more time-sensitive and responsive mode of targeting, namely *dynamic* targeting. The US Air Force is extremely proud of what it calls the 'compression of the kill-chain' as compared with the traditional targeting cycle.[1] Dynamic targeting allows it to respond to unfolding events in real time, but also to 'put warheads on foreheads',[2] that is, target with high precision, even to the extent of eliminating particular enemy individuals—or so the claim goes. An Air Force pilot explains that with 'precision' has come additional targeting

[1] Adam J. Hebert, 'Compressing the Kill Chain', *Air Force Magazine* 86, no. 3 (2003): 50–5.
[2] Anna Mulrine, 'Warheads on Foreheads', *Air Force Magazine* 91, no. 10 (2008): 44.

The War Lawyers. Craig Jones, Oxford University Press (2020). © Craig Jones.
DOI: 10.1093/oso/9780198842927.001.0001.

pressures: 'We [. . .] operate in an environment where "precise" does not mean what it once did. Hitting the right *building* used to be enough. We now have to hit the right *person*'.[3] People, unlike buildings, will not sit still, and this has presented challenges and opportunities for an expanding targeting apparatus.

Dynamic targeting's ontology of violence has three key characteristics. First, dynamic targeting is oriented towards *the event*. As I observed in the Introduction (and following Derek Gregory), militaries like the United States and Israel have moved away from an *object*-ontology of fixed and static targets, to an *event*-ontology characterized by emergence, mobilities, and the future-present.[4] Objects—and infrastructures—remain vital in this targeting ontology but their 'criticality' to the military mission is increasingly understood through the lens of the event. The destruction of an object (fixed or mobile) or infrastructural node has ripple effects that enable or foreclose a series of events (so-called 'effects based operations'): the truck that can no longer deliver its weapons; the night spent without access to electricity, and other vital amenities because the city has been 'switched off' (Chapter 3).[5]

Second, and related, dynamic targeting is increasingly concerned with *emergent* threats. It operates largely, though not exclusively, in a pre-emptive register that involves the tracking of potential targets in real time. As Graham has argued, targeting is focused increasingly on: 'the task of identifying insurgents, terrorists and an extensive range of ambient threats [. . .] whether in the queues of Heathrow, the tube stations of London or the streets of Kabul and Baghdad, the latest doctrine stresses that ways must be found to identify such people and threats *before their deadly potential is realized*'.[6] This time-sensitive mode of targeting involves what media theorist Jordan Crandall calls 'anticipatory seeing'[7]—a 'gradual colonization of the now, a now always slightly ahead of itself'.[8] For this reason, dynamic targeting is particularly resource-heavy and

[3] Derek O'Malley and Andrew Hill, 'The A-10, the F-35, and the Future of Close Air Support', War on the Rocks, 27 May 2015, http://warontherocks.com/2015/05/the-a-10-the-f-35-and-the-future-of-close-air-support-part-i/, accessed 9 June 2015 (emphasis in original).

[4] For a discussion of event-ontologies see: Derek Gregory, 'Seeing Red: Baghdad and the Event-Ful City', *Political Geography* 29, no. 5 (2010): 266.

[5] 'Although terrorists have chosen to target urban infrastructures in an attempt to disrupt modern urban life', Stephen Graham 'suggests that the greater threat to metropolitan existence comes from systematic attempts by traditional powers, such as the United States, to disrupt urban networks, thereby effectively "switching cities off"': Stephen Graham, 'Switching Cities Off', *City* 9, no. 2 (2005): 169. See also: Stephen Graham, ed., *Disrupted Cities: When Infrastructure Fails* (New York, NY: Routledge, 2009).

[6] Stephen Graham, *Cities Under Siege: The New Military Urbanism* (London; New York, NY: Verso, 2011) xii (emphasis added).

[7] Jordan Crandall, 'Envisioning the Homefront: Militarization, Tracking and Security Culture (Jordan Crandall in Conversation with John Armitage)', *Journal of Visual Culture* 4, no. 1 (2005): 20.

[8] Jordan Crandall, 'Anything That Moves: Armed Vision', *CTheory* (1999), http://ctheory.net/ctheory_wp/anything-that-moves-armed-vision/, accessed 6 March 2020, cited in: Graham, *Cities Under Siege*, 66.

involves a vast intelligence apparatus. By way of illustration, in 2009 alone US Air Force drones collected the equivalent of twenty-four years worth of video footage. In 2014 the US Air Force introduced DARPA's Argus system to its Reaper drone (DARPA is a US military research agency): the system uses hundreds of cell phone cameras and can generate eight years' worth of continuous video each day.[9]

Third, and as a corollary of the previous, dynamic targeting focuses military attention on *mobile* targets and involves the tracking of both people and objects in and through space. Key here is the notion of the 'battlespace' for as Graham argues, unlike the battlefield: 'Nothing lies outside battlespace, temporally or geographically. Battlespace has no front and no back, no start nor end.'[10] Because the battlespace is understood in such expansive terms, anything and everything—almost everyone—is a potential target. Targeting attempts to sort through objects and populations in a continual bid to tell friend from foe; what *dynamic* targeting allows is the tracking of mobilities as a key space and medium of sorting. But because there is no sure and reliable way of distinguishing between insurgent mobilities and the rest of the population, dynamic targeting increasingly chases after social life in its entirety.[11] Inevitably, of course, it cannot catch up—as US military doctrine laments, 'not all targets can be tracked constantly due to limited resources.'[12]

In sum, the fluid and emergent characteristics of later modern war encourage those who work in the kill chain to 'prosecute' war in an ever-unfolding

[9] Stephen Graham, *Vertical: The City from Satellites to Bunkers* (London; New York, NY: Verso Books, 2016), 78. See also: Arthur Holla Michel, *Eyes in the Sky: The Secret Rise of Gorgon Stare and How It Will Watch Us All* (Boston, MA: Houghton Mifflin Harcourt USA, 2019); Zygmunt Bauman et al., 'After Snowden: Rethinking the Impact of Surveillance', *International Political Sociology* 8, no. 2 (2014): 121–44; Glenn Greenwald, *No Place to Hide: Edward Snowden, the NSA, and the U.S. Surveillance State* (New York, NY: Metropolitan Books, 2014); Edward Snowden, *Permanent Record*, Main Market edition (London: Macmillan, 2019).

[10] Graham, *Cities Under Siege*, 31.

[11] Gaston Gordillo, following Derek Gregory, makes a similar point in relation to the militarized vision of the drone: 'The gaze guiding the drones', Gordillo shows, 'follows a binary logic that seeks to distinguish 'normal' from 'abnormal activity' from amid an extremely heterogeneous and complex spatial universe: Gastón Gordillo, 'Space and Politics: Opaque Zones of Empire', *Space and Politics* (blog), 25 June 2013, http://spaceandpolitics.blogspot.com/2013/06/opaque-zones-of-empire_25.html, accessed 6 March 2020, quoted in: Graham, *Vertical*, 80.

[12] United States Joint Chiefs of Staff, 'Joint Doctrine for Targeting' (Washington, DC: Joint Chiefs of Staff, 17 January 2002), C-3, https://www.bits.de/NRANEU/others/jp-doctrine/jp3_60%2802%29.pdf, accessed 24 June 2020, cited in: Astrid H. M. Nordin and Dan Öberg, 'Targeting the Ontology of War: From Clausewitz to Baudrillard': *Millennium* 43, no. 2 (2014): 405. The US military's increasing reliance on vast amounts of data prompted former Army intelligence analyst William Arkin to comment: 'the Data Machine has become the supreme authority and influential silent partner in all that has unfolded. [. . .] American involvement [in Afghanistan, Iraq, and elsewhere] would be given over completely to "intelligence, surveillance, and reconnaissance" ': William M. Arkin, *Unmanned: Drones, Data, and the Illusion of Perfect Warfare* (New York, NY: Little, Brown and Company, 2015), 276.

'instantaneous present'[13] where targets could, in principle, emerge anywhere at any time.[14] Whether it is 'rational' in broad terms for highly resourced states to so construe their security interests at home and abroad, notwithstanding the constraints mentioned, is a matter for separate discussion.[15]

In this chapter I focus instead on how, for legal purposes, there is both more and less in this transition from deliberate to dynamic targeting (which is far from universal and complete) than US military doctrine suggests. *More*, because dynamic targeting is not simply a sped-up form of deliberate targeting; it involves a series of different procedures that can and do produce radically different results. To see why, we must leave the relative safety of the Combined Air Operations Centre (CAOC) to hear from judge advocates (JAGs) and operators at other locations. These sites and perspectives reveal the radically dispersed geographies of the dynamic kill chain and, crucially, they also show how the pressures of rapid response change both the calculation of operational legalities and the type and extent of JAG involvement. *Less*, because as with deliberate targeting, the vaunted precision, omniscient visuality and rules-based characteristics of dynamic targeting are greatly exaggerated. Indeed, by comparison with deliberate targeting it even cuts some corners as regards legal 'oversight'—which once again confronts us with a timeless feature of armed conflict: its extreme violence and destructiveness is not fully controlled or predictable.

* * *

Just two days into Operation Enduring Freedom (OEF) Donald Rumsfeld bluntly informed the press that Afghanistan was 'running out of targets'. He was referring to *deliberate* targets and went on to clarify that other targets 'are emerging as we continue', promising that constantly evolving intelligence would enable the United States 'to seize targets of opportunity, and that means you have to wait until they emerge'.[16] Emerge they did, so much so that one

[13] Nordin and Öberg, 'Targeting the Ontology of War', 405.

[14] '[O]ne of the characteristics of late modern war is the emergent, "event-ful" quality of military, paramilitary and terrorist violence that can, in principle, occur anywhere': Derek Gregory, 'The Everywhere War', *The Geographical Journal* 177, no. 3 (2011): 238.

[15] Thomas Gregory has powerfully argued of US checkpoint killings in Iraq: 'the decision to use lethal force is often a peculiar mix of conscious and unconscious thought, where feelings, intuitions and affects combine with reason, logic and sense': Thomas Gregory, 'Dangerous Feelings: Checkpoints and the Perception of Hostile Intent', *Security Dialogue* 50, no. 2 (2019): 137.

[16] The Washington Post, 'Pentagon Briefing on Latest Military Strikes', *The Washington Post*, 9 October 2001, http://www.washingtonpost.com/wp-srv/nation/specials/attacked/transcripts/rumsfeld_100901.html, accessed 22 December 2016.

year into the war in Afghanistan, Rebecca Grant reported that '80 percent of the targets struck by US airpower were "flex targets"—those given to pilots *en route*'.[17] Afghanistan was not the only theatre where dynamic targeting was predominant.

In the first month of Operation Iraqi Freedom (OIF) the US Air Force executed 156 'Time-Sensitive Targets' (TSTs—see Introduction, Figure 0.1).[18] During the same period an additional 686 dynamic targets were struck.[19] US airpower statistics published by the Air Force for both Afghanistan and Iraq do not allow for direct comparison between deliberate and dynamic targeting operations but they do reveal the extent to which both theatres relied heavily on one particular form of dynamic targeting—close air support (CAS) (see section 5.2 and Figure 5.2, Chapter 5). Moreover, since Operation Inherent Resolve (OIR) was launched in 2014, approximately 85 per cent of targets have been dynamic.[20] These numbers offer a simplified and partial overview of what are often interwoven targeting processes (involving both deliberate and dynamic modes), but the fact is that the vast majority of targeting operations carried out by the US Air Force are dynamic—or at the very least have dynamic and time-sensitive components. As we shall see, these proportions have an important bearing on the involvement of military lawyers and on the targeting process itself.

The US Air Force first encountered the need to perform dynamic targeting during its bombing campaigns in Vietnam, Laos, and Cambodia in the 1960s and early 1970s. There, much like in Afghanistan and Iraq over the last two decades, the aim was to support US and local counter-insurgency forces on the ground. These efforts required a responsive mode of targeting 'in which cruising aircraft are directed to (usually fleeting) targets of opportunity that emerge in flight, and often involves providing close air support to ground troops suddenly finding themselves in contact with the enemy'.[21] The response

[17] Rebecca Grant, 'An Air War Like No Other', *Air Force Magazine*, 1 November 2002, https://www.airforcemag.com/article/1102airwar/, accessed 21 December 2016. She elaborates: 'For airmen, the war shifted rapidly from strikes against preplanned targets to a combination of preplanned and flexible targets. "After the first week, the pilots didn't know what targets they'd be striking when they launched," said Vice Adm. John B. Nathman, then commander, Naval Air Force, Pacific Fleet'. According to Spedro, OEF marked 'the definitive establishment of TST as a viable and vital mission, with many of the targets being classified as high value and possessing a fleeting engagement vulnerability window:' Paul C. Spedero, 'Time Sensitive Targeting—The Operational Commander's Role' (Naval War College, 2004), 8, https://apps.dtic.mil/sti/pdfs/ADA422747.pdf, accessed 12 January 2017.

[18] These included targets under three broad categories: terrorist, leadership, and so-called 'weapons of mass destruction': Michael T. Moseley, 'Operation Iraqi Freedom: By the Numbers', Assessment and Analysis Division, US Air Force Central Command (AFCENT), 30 April 2003 (on file with author), 9

[19] Ibid., 3.

[20] Deptula, email correspondence.

[21] Derek Gregory, 'Lines of Descent', in *From Above: War, Violence, and Verticality*, eds Peter Adey, Mark Whitehead, and Alison Williams (New York, NY: Oxford University Press, 2014), 51

was sluggish compared to today. At the start of the Vietnam War it took on average 100 minutes for strike aircraft to respond to a request for assistance,[22] a delay that must have felt like an eternity for those troops waiting on the ground in harm's way. In the 1960s and 1970s the US Air Force also had immense difficulty in locating, tracking, and hitting mobile targets. Air Force Historian Dick Anderegg describes how limited this particular form of time-sensitive targeting was during the Vietnam War:

> Their [airborne Forward Air Controllers' (FAC)] mission was to find targets along the stretch of dirt highway known as Route 7 [. . .] Once they found a target, typically a truck or two, or perhaps a poorly hidden supply cache, they would rendezvous with other fighters, mark it with a white phosphorous smoke rocket, and then direct the other fighters' bombs onto the target. The scheme of fast FACs directing flights of other fighters onto small targets was the predominant interdiction tactic used in Laos along the Ho Chi Minh Trail, but it was very ineffective. Even the fast FAC familiar with his area had a difficult time finding targets, because he had to fly fast enough to survive antiaircraft artillery and he had to fly high enough to stay out of the small arms fire [. . .] Even when the fast FAC did find a target, the fighters had a difficult time hitting it because their ordnance and delivery systems were ineffective [. . .][23]

From 1968 to 1973 the US Air Force attempted to automate dynamic targeting by constructing a networked system of ground sensors and strike aircraft along the Ho Chi Minh Trail, a key military supply route running from North Vietnam through Laos and Cambodia to South Vietnam. Derek Gregory shows that the objective of 'Igloo White', as the system was called, was 'not so much to damage the Trail network—which was readily repaired or altered—but to strike traffic moving along it, and since the targets were fleeting, the interval between sensor and shooter had to be minimised'.[24] There were no JAGs involved (Chapter 1), and these early attempts to garner intelligence from the 'electronic battlefield' for dynamic targeting were both slow and inaccurate.[25]

22 Ibid., 58.

23 Quoted in: Robert P. Haffa and Jasper Welch, *Command and Control Arrangements for the Attack of Time-Sensitive Targets* (Los Angeles: Northrup Grumman, 2005), 8.

24 Gregory, 'Lines of Descent', 52.

25 Andrew Cockburn, *Kill Chain: The Rise of the High-Tech Assassins* (New York, NY: Henry Holt and Co., 2015); Gregory, 'Lines of Descent'.

Not much progress was made on time-sensitive targeting between the wars in Southeast Asia and the First Gulf War in 1990–1991. Lack of progress was highlighted by the inability of the Air Force to target Saddam Hussein's mobile Scud missile launchers as they roamed the vast Iraqi desert, and which fired several missiles towards Israel. Although the Air Force devoted a vast number of its most valuable Intelligence, Surveillance and Reconnaissance (ISR) assets to the 'Scud hunt', they were unable to destroy a single one. US Air Force Lieutenant Colonel John M. Fyfe explains the problem:

> Because the Iraqi tactic was to shoot and relocate, often a Scud launcher would be five miles away from its launch site within 10 minutes after launching a missile. The result was that unless there were assets practically overhead the site at missile launch, it was very unlikely that a launcher would ever be found near a detected launch site.[26]

The futility of the task frustrated Air Force planners immensely. Shortly after Operation Desert Storm was over, Lieutenant General Chuck Horner commented: 'If you want to learn lessons from warfare, look to failures, and our inability to stop the Iraqis from launching ballistic missiles certainly could be considered a failure. That is a lesson that's not going to be lost on other people.'[27]

In 2000 General John P. Jumper, Commander of Air Combat Command challenged the US Air Force to respond to emerging targets in 'single digit-minutes'.[28] The key innovation was to combine and integrate the 'sensor' and 'shooter' functions into a single platform so, for example, the aircraft that locates the target would also be capable of striking it.[29] The drone—or Unmanned Aerial Vehicle (UAV) as the US Air Force prefers to call it—was the solution to this problem. When the Predator drone was first armed in 2001, it allowed for the integration of hunter and killer into a single platform, making it possible to 'find, fix, and finish' targets near-instantaneously: a radical compression of the kill chain.

Another component of dynamic targeting honed during the war in Afghanistan has been the use of intelligence gathered by an older technology: ground troops. As Fyfe explains: 'Because of the widely dispersed

[26] John Fyfe, 'Evolution of Time Sensitive Targeting: Operation Iraqi Freedom Results and Lessons', Maxwell Air Force Base, Alabama: Air University, College of Aerospace Doctrine, Research and Education, 2005, 5

[27] Quoted in: Ibid., 1.

[28] Quoted in: Hebert, 'Compressing the Kill Chain'.

[29] See Derek Gregory, 'From a View to a Kill Drones and Late Modern War', *Theory, Culture & Society* 28, no. 7–8 (2011): 188–215; Gregory, 'Lines of Descent'.

nature of the Taliban and elements of al Qaida, the air war in Afghanistan was largely fought with Special Operations Forces supporting the air component effort to detect and identify enemy emerging targets.'[30] Benjamin Lambeth, writing for the RAND Corporation, provides further insight into the process:

> The successful insertion of a small number of U.S. SOF [Special Operations Force] teams into Afghanistan [. . .] signaled the onset of a new use of air power in joint warfare, in which Air Force terminal attack controllers working with SOF spotters positioned forward within line of sight of enemy force concentrations directed precision air attacks against enemy ground troops who were not in direct contact with friendly forces.[31]

Known as air interdiction, this tactic has been a staple of the war, where there has been a dearth of deliberate targets from very early on. Air interdiction is very similar to CAS.[32] It involves ground troops actively seeking out enemies and enemy positions in order for them to be targeted from the air and, like CAS, it has a strong offensive component.[33] Air interdiction and CAS thus signify the first of several important moves between the aerial views of the CAOC and the grounded views of those closer to the fighting (section 6.3).

In 2003 Alex Koven, the Time-Sensitive Targeting Command and Control Operations Director at the CAOC at Al Udeid reported: 'We've had instances where (special operations forces) teams needed immediate support. We were able to provide that support within *two to three minutes*.'[34] By the time of the 2003 Iraq war, time-sensitive targeting was given a much higher priority even

[30] Fyfe, 'Evolution of Time Sensitive Targeting: Operation Iraqi Freedom Results and Lessons', 11.

[31] Benjamin S. Lambeth, *Air Power Against Terror: America's Conduct of Operation Enduring Freedom*, 2nd edition (Santa Monica, CA: RAND Corporation, 2006), xvii.

[32] Colonel John Warden III writes: 'Close air support can look like interdiction, and vice versa. To help reduce the confusion, finding common areas of agreement and disagreement is useful. An air attack on enemy forces crossing the wire 50 yards from friendly troops, and controlled at least indirectly by the concerned ground commander, certainly is close air support. Just about everyone will agree that air attack on enemy troops within rifle range of friendly forces also is considered close air support. Similarly, just about everyone would agree that air attack on a tank factory is not. Clearly, substantial room is left between these two extremes': John A. Warden, *The Air Campaign: Planning for Combat* (Lincoln, NE: ToExcel Press, iUniverse, 2000), 86.

[33] Dynamic targeting carried out in collaboration with ground forces takes both defensive and offensive forms. According to Army Lawyer Major Eric C. Husby: 'In recent conflicts, self-defense and TIC scenarios involving U.S. Forces have often been quasi-offensive in nature. For example, some patrol missions in Afghanistan have been designed to draw out adversaries [. . .] Further, the U.S. definition of self-defense includes pursuit doctrine, which could otherwise be characterized as a hasty conduct-based offensive operation': Eric C. Husby, 'A Balancing Act: In Pursuit of Proportionality in Self-Defense for On-Scene Commanders, A', *Army Law*, May 2012, 11.

[34] Brian Orbarn, 'Time-Sensitive Targeting Adds Combat Flexibility', US Air Force, 18 April 2003, http://www.af.mil/News/ArticleDisplay/tabid/223/Article/139411/time-sensitive-targeting-adds-combat-flexibility.aspx, accessed 13 January 2017.

than in Afghanistan. At the start of the Iraq war, Central Command updated its targeting doctrine to prioritize the various categories of dynamic targets and established a twenty-five-member team to respond to time-sensitive targets (the equivalent targeting cell for the war in Afghanistan was only five strong).[35] Today, the US Air Force doctrine echoes Koven's point: 'targets can actually be struck in minutes from when information is made available in the dynamic targeting process.'[36] Speed, rather than deliberation, has been the hallmark of these quite remarkable transformations in aerial targeting—changes that have themselves moved at a rapid pace.

6.2 The Same, but Different

Dynamic targets often require 'near-immediate' prosecution if they are to be targeted at all.[37] Like the deliberate targeting cycle, the dynamic targeting cycle is extremely fluid. Unlike the deliberate cycle, however, the various steps of the dynamic cycle are often completed near-simultaneously. According to a US Air Force JAG School manual:

> If a target is detected by the aircraft or system that will engage it (for example, by a missile-armed Predator, or a battle management command and control platform such as the joint surveillance target attack radar system (JSTARS)), this may result in the find and fix phases being completed near-simultaneously, without the need for traditional intelligence input.[38]

Despite the significant ontological and technical transformations outlined in the previous section, US Air Force doctrine and military practitioners suggest that dynamic targeting is not that different from its deliberate counterpart. In this they are partially correct. Dynamic targeting has its own rhythms and phases and is handled through a specialized targeting sub-process known as the 'Find, Fix, Track, Target, Engage and Assess' (F2T2EA) cycle (Figure 6.1). Like the deliberate targeting cycle, the F2T2EA is also a kill chain and it too

[35] Fyfe, 'Evolution of Time Sensitive Targeting: Operation Iraqi Freedom Results and Lessons', 20.

[36] United States Air Force, 'Air Force Doctrine Document 3-60, Targeting' (US Air Force LeMay Center for Doctrine Development, 8 June 2006 [updated 28 July 2011]), 25, https://fas.org/irp/doddir/usaf/afdd3-60.pdf, accessed 13 December 2016.

[37] United States Air Force Judge Advocate General's School, 'Air Force Operations and the Law' (Maxwell Air Force Base, AL: US Air Force, 2014), 282, http://www.afjag.af.mil/Portals/77/documents/AFD-100510-059.pdf, accessed 13 February 2014.

[38] Ibid., 285.

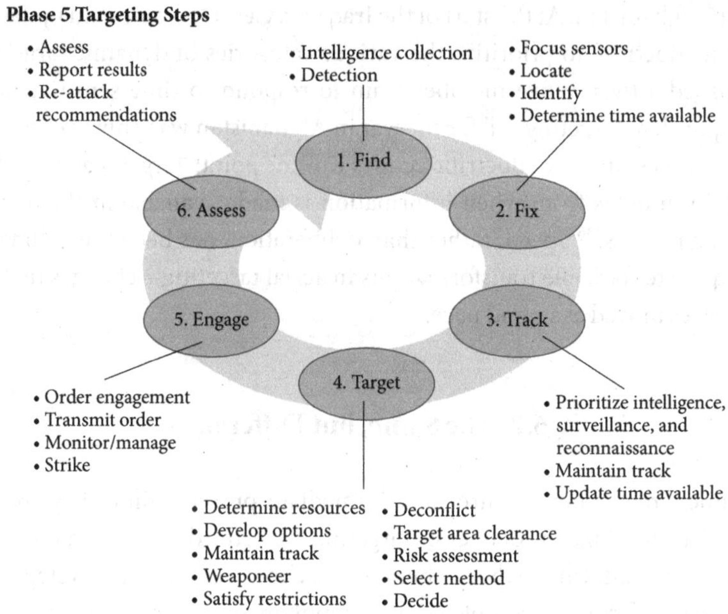

Figure 6.1 The dynamic targeting cycle, more commonly known in the US Air Force as the 'F2T2EA'—Find, Fix, Track, Target, Engage and Assess.
Source: United States Joint Chiefs of Staff, 'Joint Targeting', Joint Publication 3-60 (Washington, DC, 31 January 2013), II-23.

resembles a doughnut, albeit one produced with different 'ingredients' (compare Chapter 5, Figure 5.5 and Figure 6.1. According to the US Air Force:

> Dynamic targeting is different from deliberate targeting in terms of the timing of the steps in the process, *but not different in the substance of the steps.* Ultimately, 'dynamic' targets are targets—as such, their nomination, development, execution, and assessment still take place within the larger framework of the [deliberate] targeting and tasking cycles.[39]

The Air Force also assert that the laws of war and rules of engagement (ROE) apply in full and equal measure to both forms of targeting.[40] Department of Defense General Counsel Jennifer O'Connor claims that the only difference is that the 'urgency associated with dynamic targeting means the process often

[39] United States Air Force, 'Air Force Doctrine Annex 3-60 Targeting' (US Air Force LeMay Center for Doctrine Development, 10 January 2014), 40 (emphasis added), https://doctrine.af.mil/DTM/dtmtargeting.htm, accessed 17 December 2016.
[40] Ibid.

plays out much faster'.[41] US Air Force lawyers similarly insist that their role in deliberate and dynamic targeting operations is very similar. According to JAG James Burkart: 'Dynamic targeting applies the same operational and legal principles' as deliberate targeting.[42] Colonel James Bitzes, another JAG, claims:

> We do deliberate target reviews. Those are the ones where you have the luxury to sit back and spend a lot more time thinking about *but we essentially do the same thing real-time for dynamic and time-sensitive targets* [. . .] the only difference is that we do it a heck of a lot quicker when it's time-sensitive.[43]

These accounts suggest that there is little difference between deliberate and dynamic targeting: the procedures are the same, the laws and rules are the same, and they are they are both subject to legal review. The only difference, apparently, is the time it takes to perform them. Dynamic targeting is carried out much faster than deliberate targeting; but, again, as Colonel Bitzes insists, 'just because it's happening dynamically' it does not mean that the US Air Force 'cut procedures short'.[44]

However, in practice, and contrary to what the above accounts suggest, dynamic targeting creates its own unique military 'necessities', operational ground truths, and legalities. (Perceived) shortage of time means that decisions must often be made without double checking the intelligence, or seeking second and third opinions. Delaying a strike and waiting for more favourable circumstances is often not an option in time-sensitive targeting operations; the target may be fleeting or else might be perceived as posing an immediate threat to friendly forces on the ground. But time is also a central consideration when adjudicating the *legality* of striking a target. Whereas a fixed, deliberate target may pose no immediate or proximate threat, when troops are in contact with enemy forces greater levels of risk and uncertainty in the decision to strike are commonly allowed because of the 'necessity'

[41] Jennifer O'Connor, 'Applying the Law of Targeting to the Modern Battlefield' (New York University School of Law, 28 November 2016), https://dod.defense.gov/Portals/1/Documents/pubs/Applying-the-Law-of-Targeting-to-the-Modern-Battlefield.pdf, accessed 14 December 2016.

[42] James A Burkart, 'Deadly Advice: Judge Advocates and Joint Targeting', *The Army Lawyer*, no. 6 (2016): 19.

[43] James Bitzes, 'Role of an Air Operations Center Legal Advisor in Targeting', presented at the Drones, targeting and the promise of law conference, Washington, DC, 24 February 2011 (notes on file with author, emphasis added).

[44] James Bitzes, quoted in: David Kurle, 'Lawyers Provide Operational Advice to CAOC Commanders', Air Force Central Command Public Affairs, 4 March 2010, http://www.afcent.af.mil/News/Features/Display/tabid/4819/Article/223901/lawyers-provide-operational-advice-to-caoc-commanders.aspx, accessed 17 December 2016.

of near-immediate response. ROE are also necessarily less restrictive when acting in self-defence.[45] The increased risk applies to both civilians and 'friendly forces' on the ground (including fratricide), and potentially to the pilots flying the missions. This is factored into the decision to strike a dynamic target: 'Particular targets may be determined to be such a threat to the force or to mission accomplishment that the CFACC [Combined Forces Air Component Commander] is willing to accept a *higher level of risk* in order to attack the target immediately upon detection.'[46]

Against a backdrop of technological change, then, legal principles and ingredients that govern aerial targeting cannot simply be taken 'off the shelf' to replicate a neat fit (if, indeed, there ever was one). Deliberate and dynamic targeting demand that different weight be placed on certain ingredients, but the tempo of the operation—not to mention its 'temperature'—is absolutely crucial in shaping operational legalities. Thus, it is only in the most general of senses that the laws of war and the ROE are 'equally applicable' to deliberate and dynamic targeting. It is perhaps more accurate to say that while the ROE and laws of war apply, deliberate and dynamic targeting demand quite different *interpretations* of the laws of war and the ROE, depending on the nature of the operations.

Deliberate and dynamic targeting can often produce radically different results. Significantly, particular forms of dynamic targeting have been associated with causing more civilian casualties than deliberate targeting (section 6.5). The US Air Force concedes that the compression of the kill chain involves compression of the *decision cycle*, and this in turn produces 'increased risk due to insufficient time for the more detailed coordination and deconfliction that takes place during deliberate targeting'.[47] But as we have seen, rather than halting dynamic targeting operations *per se* (see section 6.6 for what was a temporary exception), the greater risk simply *changes* the legal and operational calculation for striking a particular target.

That calculation—to strike or not to strike—is contingent on many factors including, *inter alia*, the exigent geographies of the kill chain. We thus now turn to consider the question: by whom (and where) are life and death decisions being made in dynamic targeting operations?

[45] McDonnell, interview.

[46] United States Air Force, 'Air Force Doctrine Document 3-60, Targeting', 54 (emphasis added).

[47] Ibid., 53–4.

6.3 Beyond the 'CAOC'

Although the CAOC is central to the conduct of deliberate targeting operations, its role in dynamic targeting is not always as important; and in both cases, the CAOC is only one site in a vast and geographically dispersed targeting network. Moving outside of the CAOC to what are known as Forward Operating Bases (FOBs), and places like Kandahar or Bagram Airfield in Afghanistan, helps us to gain a different perspective on dynamic targeting. Military lawyers *can* be involved in dynamic targeting operations at these sites, but their role is less well-defined and arguably more provisional than that of their CAOC counterparts.

The CAOC's role in dynamic targeting operations itself is provisional. Sometimes it is involved, other times not, and the type and extent of 'involvement' is conditioned by a series of operational contingencies, as I will show. The US Air Force is organized according to a doctrine of what it calls 'centralized control, decentralized execution'. This means that the CAOC (and other key sites in the United States such as Central Command Headquarters at MacDill Air Force Base in Tampa, Florida) oversee the broad and strategic level of aerial targeting operations while particular targeting missions, especially at the tactical and local levels, are often delegated to the FOBs and other 'in theatre' locations.[48] This organizational logic is partly a product of the US Air Force's experience in Vietnam, which saw something close to 'centralized control and centralized execution' (Chapter 1). The aim today, and especially since the First Gulf War (Chapter 3), is to delegate at least some decision-making authority to those who are in theatre and on the ground, (a) because they are closer to the action, and (b) because, crucially, they might be in harm's way.[49] With decentralized execution comes a more complex and geographically fragmented dynamic kill chain. As target nominations increasingly come from US forces (and US advised forces) on the *ground*, it increasingly involves a range of actors beyond the CAOC and beyond the US Air Force itself. Specifically, the FOBs and

[48] In practice, this typology is far more chaotic and complex. Various actors at several locations around the world have input on live targeting operations and visualities are dispersed between a suite of pilots, sensors, and operators, some flying drones from the United States, others flying helicopters or gunships in theatre—each with their own screen and with variable and often interrupted access to vast amounts of information, including live audio and online chat feeds. Derek Gregory provides an extensive analysis of the various technologies and personnel involved in dynamic targeting operations: Derek Gregory, 'Angry Eyes (1)', *Geographical Imaginations* (blog), 1 October 2015, https://geographicalimaginations.com/2015/10/01/angry-eyes-1/, accessed 16 January 2017; Derek Gregory, 'Angry Eyes (2)', *Geographical Imaginations* (blog), 7 October 2015, https://geographicalimaginations.com/2015/10/07/angry-eyes-2/, accessed 16 January 2017.

[49] McDowell, interview.

operational centres in theatre are predominantly staffed by Army personnel and Army JAGs; only a very small minority of forward deployed JAGs are Air Force.[50]

Because the CAOC's role in dynamic targeting is provisional, so too is the role of its JAGs. Recall Colonel Brown's day in the life of a CAOC JAG from Chapter 5, where Brown explained that one type of dynamic targeting—troops in contact (TIC)—was so frequent that, if he was sleeping, commanders would often not wake him to ask for legal advice. Colonel Todd McDowell, another Air Force JAG, explains why it is not possible—and often not preferable—to have input from JAGs at the CAOC/strategic level when executing targets at the tactical level. He explained that the CAOC is most often 'aware' that a dynamic strike is taking place and JAGs there frequently monitor communications between ground force commanders and whatever platform is providing fire support, but the CAOC does not *control* these strikes. There is an important difference between being aware of (or monitoring) a strike and controlling a strike. In many tactical dynamic targeting situations, it is not the job of the CAOC to second guess the commander whose troops are taking fire. As Colonel McDowell explains:

> The CAOC is aware that fire support has been requested but it's not necessarily going to be the CAOC that is making the approval or authorization. Again, it's the commander on the ground who requires fire support. [. . .] in a self defence response it's going to be the ground force commander who is going to be in the best position [to make a decision]. [. . .] The commander who is asking for that TIC is the one who 'buys the bomb'. They're telling me they're in contact, we've cleared the target and we're going to engage. [. . .] if they have a question they can reach back [to the CAOC], but not always and for good reason.[51]

Colonel McDowell further explains that the involvement of the CAOC can be very limited and even when CAOC JAGs are involved it can be 'a fairly basic analysis, not one that would require a lot of nuance or complexity and certainly

[50] Ibid.; McKee, email correspondence 20 March, 2017; The Judge Advocate General's Legal Center & School, Center for Law and Military Operations (CLAMO), United States Army, 'Legal Lessons Learned From Afghanistan and Iraq Volume I Major Combat Operations (11 September 2001–1 May 2003)' (Charlottesville, VA: United States Army, 1 August 2004), 102, https://fas.org/irp/doddir/army/clamo-v1.pdf, accessed 15 December 2016 (citing an After Action Report recommending that 'an Air Force JA [Judge Advocate] be staffed within the Army corps-level Air Support Operations Center (ASOC) to help resolve joint interoperability issues'.)

[51] McDowell, interview.

it wouldn't be one where you would be trumping the assessment of the ground forces commander who is saying "I'm taking fire, I need support"'.[52]

The extent to which the CAOC—and CAOC JAGs—are involved in dynamic targeting depends on whether or not the CAOC 'owns' and operates the 'asset' (e.g. a Predator drone or F-15 strike aircraft) that is being used. The above account assumes that the asset is controlled by the CAOC. But this is not always the case. Colonel McDowell, again:

> If it is a platform owned and operated by the CAOC then they're certainly going to be involved in that decision [. . .] [however] there are certain scenarios where certain platforms would not necessarily be controlled by the CAOC because they're not part of that daily tasking order process.[53]

The picture becomes even more complicated when ground force commanders and/or Special Operations units operating in theatre have their own 'organic' assets, meaning that they own and control these assets. Given what we learnt above about the central role of air interdiction and the extensive role played by Special Operations Forces in both Iraq and Afghanistan, this is no small number of assets and operations that are controlled largely outside of the CAOC's purview. Special Operations Forces:

> [O]perate with their own organic air support and that air support could be both transportation as well as attack. It could be helicopters or it could be the AC-130 gunship—they're predominantly a Special Operations air asset. You'd have a Combined Joint Special Operations Air Component (or CJSOAC) and that CJSOAC would be responsible for the Special Operations Forces. They'd certainly be in coordination with the overall Joint Forces Air Component Command (JFACC) [in the CAOC or situated elsewhere at the strategic-level] but they're going to be a separate element because of the specialized mission that the Special Operations Forces are doing.[54]

If all of this sounds quite messy, that is because it is. The CAOC attempts to impose a coherent visualization of the battlespace—which itself is a conceit—but as we move outside, the kill chain becomes even more contingent on the messy and grounded realities of military operations. It is not simply that the CAOC

[52] Ibid.
[53] Ibid.
[54] Ibid.

does not 'see' everything but that even those who have the more granular perspective at the tactical level and in the FOBs do not—cannot—see everything. Different people within the kill chain see different things depending on where they are and what technology is available to them, as well as who they are—and are not—in communications with (assuming, of course, that the communications are working properly). The views and visualities afforded by the various sites and spaces of the kill chain cannot be added up or stitched together to produce a somehow 'whole' or 'perfect' image. The CAOC is not a panopticon and neither can the multiple sites of the kill chain be. Instead, the picture produced is a shifting mosaic, one that is necessarily incomplete.

The counter-argument, one which is built into the *modus operandi* of so-called 'precision warfare' is this: with technological improvement and technical tweaking, what is logically impossible might nevertheless become a 'line of best fit', an 'as-good-as' reality. We may not be quite there yet, the conceit goes, but 'full spectrum dominance' is within our grasp. However, much like the temporalities chased after by dynamic targeting, the notion of near-complete control in anything resembling armed conflict is forever over the horizon, temptingly close and always out of reach. The obstacles are both practical and ontological, and there is no infallible technical or technological solution to them.

Practically, telling friend from foe is difficult, especially in a battlespace of shifting identities and allegiances, and among cultures that are poorly understood. In a landscape of threat, attacking forces struggle to make sense of the populations in front of them—both on the screen and on the street. As suggested in the Introduction, and further emphasized in section 6.5, these difficulties are acute when it comes to urban warfare; cities are especially stubborn battlespaces and do not reveal their military infrastructures without significant cost to civilian inhabitants.

Ontologically, the problem runs even deeper. Rather than asking the technical question of *how* militaries can distinguish between civilians and combatants and their infrastructures, militaries find themselves ruminating on such questions as: *what is* a combatant and *what is* a civilian?[55] Such definitional questions can only be resolved according to a standard of what is meaningful

[55] As Derek Gregory has argued, 'it is formidably, constitutively difficult to distinguish between combatants and civilians'. For Gregory this is a 'central, existential problem' and as he insists it, 'would remain *even if the battlespace could be made fully transparent*. It may be mitigated by the persistent presence of UAVs and their enhanced ISR capability, and in some measure by the 'pattern of life' analysis this makes possible, but it cannot be erased': Gregory, 'From a View to a Kill Drones and Late Modern War', 200 (emphasis in original).

(useful) in a particular context for particular purposes. Maintenance of military superiority—and with very low tolerance for casualties on one's own side—is an open-ended project that demands continual change in techno-cultural practices. Given this context and purpose, then, the neatness and finality of any definitional solutions is likely to prove short-lived or even illusory (in the absence of rules *qua* genuine, substantive constraints). In the following section I examine yet another feature of the kill chain where conceptual clarity, and with it the possibility of juridical coherence, gives way to permissive utilization of air power: in this case, when strikes are called in by colleagues on the ground.

6.4 Troops in 'Contact' and 'Close' Air Support

There is a certain type of dynamic targeting operation that almost ceaselessly interrupts Air Force planning and the 'deliberate targeting cycle' (Chapter 5):

> Every night, the airmen of the CAOC come up with a grand blueprint of how they're going to spread planes around Afghanistan and Iraq the next day—where all the bomb-droppers and surveillance drones and cargo haulers will go. Back in the day, when air campaigns were pre-scripted, the CAOC would've made sure that plan was executed. Now, if the plan lasts an hour intact, it's a miracle. There's a TIC, invariably.[56]

When Army and Special Forces counterparts call 'troops in Contact'—'TIC'—what they need more than anything is for the Air Force—or any military component with air power—to provide them with close air support (CAS). The US military defines CAS as 'air action by fixed-wing (FW) and rotary-wing (RW) aircraft against hostile targets that are *in close proximity to* friendly forces and *requires detailed integration* of each air mission with the fire and movement of those forces'.[57] The definition of closeness and proximity is flexible: 'CAS can be conducted at any place and time friendly forces are in close proximity to

[56] Noah Shachtman, 'The Phrase That's Screwing Up the Afghan Air War', *Wired*, 9 December 2009, https://www.wired.com/2009/12/the-phrase-thats-screwing-up-the-afghan-air-war/, accessed 29 February 2020.

[57] United States Joint Chiefs of Staff, 'Close Air Support', Joint Publication 3-09.3 (Washington, DC: Joint Chiefs of Staff, 25 November 2014), I–1, http://fas.org/irp/doddir/dod/jp3_09_3.pdf, accessed 10 November 2014 (emphasis in original).

enemy forces. The word "close" does not imply a specific distance; rather, it is situational.'[58]

TICs and CAS are not military sideshows; in the last nearly two decades, and especially since the surge in Afghanistan in 2009–2010, they have dominated US aerial operations and have also been a crucial tool in the fighting of the ground wars.[59] Pilots frequently refer to CAS as 'doing the Lord's work', a sentiment that 'reflects their deep commitment to protecting ground forces'.[60] Rapid—and therefore *close*—support is crucial as lives could be on the line and 'a few minutes can make all the difference for ground forces in a firefight'.[61] An Army infantry officer explains how crucial it is for CAS to respond quickly: 'Look, I don't care how you do it, or what you do it with—I just need you to find the bad guys that are shooting at me, kill them quickly, don't hurt or kill me, and help me find more bad guys before they shoot at me!'[62]

As this quote also shows, CAS is delicate work and it presents dangers for all involved. As one commentator points out: 'the difference between the catastrophe of friendly-fire casualties and wiping out the enemy can be measured in metres or fractions of seconds. Close air support [. . .] is among the most delicate, dangerous and difficult aspects of modern warfare.'[63] Other accounts suggest that CAS has become more perilous in the last two decades, especially in Afghanistan. According to Major Mike Benitez, who has taken part in over 250 combat missions and has deployed to Afghanistan six times:

> Prior to 2001, CAS evoked images of air support to conventional force-on-force ground campaigns and armored battles—linear operations that are proactive and offensive in nature. Fast-forward through 15 years of conflict in Afghanistan. The premise of non-linear operations used in counterinsurgency strategy dictates that all of the conventional coordination lines on the

[58] Ibid., I–2. See also: Mike Benitez, 'How Afghanistan Distorted Close Air Support and Why It Matters', War on the Rocks, 29 June 2016, http://warontherocks.com/2016/06/how-afghanistan-distorted-close-air-support-and-why-it-matters/, accessed 12 December 2016.

[59] 'The US and NATO are using airstrikes in an "economy of force" battle against insurgents. Instead of having a large ground footprint, they use a relatively small number of ground forces supplemented with airpower': Human Rights Watch, '"Troops in Contact": Airstrikes and Civilian Deaths in Afghanistan', September 2008, 12, http://www.hrw.org/sites/default/files/reports/afghanistan0908webwcover_0.pdf, accessed 9 November 2014

[60] O'Malley, Derek, and Andrew Hill, 'The A-10, the F-35, and the Future of Close Air Support', War on the Rocks, 27 May 2015, http://warontherocks.com/2015/05/the-a-10-the-f-35-and-the-future-of-close-air-support-part-i/, accessed 9 June 2015.

[61] Ibid.

[62] Quoted in: Ibid.

[63] Paul Koring, 'Handling the Perilous Job of Close Air Support', *The Globe and Mail*, 5 September 2006, http://www.theglobeandmail.com/news/world/handling-the-perilous-job-of-close-air-support/article18172321/, accessed 8 January 2017.

map be erased. During the 2010 surge, there were over 400 coalition operating bases and 100,000 U.S. troops spread across Afghanistan and among the enemy."[64]

The dangers and difficulties associated with CAS multiply exponentially when entering the urban environment. As a RAND Corporation report notes:

> From Stalingrad to Grozny, close air support has compiled a mixed record of achievement in urban operations. Historically, aerospace power has performed best when supporting defensively organized ground troops, pitted against easily identifiable opposition forces, in fairly open terrain on the outskirts of small, isolated towns. Close air support has generally been less effective in offensive operations conducted within densely built urban metropolises, where adversary forces have been dispersed in well-fortified defensive positions or intermixed with local civilians.[65]

The report goes on to note several technological developments that have led to improvements in the ability of the US military to provide CAS but ultimately concedes, 'factors such as restrictive rules of engagement (ROE), poor visibility, inadequate air-ground cooperation, insufficient intelligence, potent adversary air defenses, and the opposition's clever use of urban terrain and non combatants have degraded the effectiveness of CAS'.[66] Despite these shortcomings, commentators insist that CAS must be made available not just in any city but also in some of the world's largest megacities.[67] For some, the answer to urban complexities is more technology and data in the hands of US troops. As one account promises: 'Department of Defense research programs and industry partnerships are working with drone swarm technology, drone delivery to reduce logistics chains, increased electronic jamming of enemy sensors and networks, and pulling data from every corner of the battlefield into a digestible form.'[68] For others, the technical fix is not so promising. Bing West, former Assistant

[64] Benitez, 'How Afghanistan Distorted Close Air Support and Why It Matters'.

[65] Alan J. Vick et al., 'Aerospace Operations in Urban Environments: Exploring New Concepts', Monograph Reports (RAND Corporation, 2002), 218, https://www.rand.org/pubs/monograph_reports/MR1187.html, accessed 7 March 2020.

[66] Ibid.

[67] 'CAS platforms also must be prepared to operate in megacities': O'Malley and Hill, 'The A-10, the F-35, and the Future of Close Air Support'. See also: Todd South, 'The Future Battlefield: Army, Marines Prepare for "Massive" Fight in Megacities', Military Times, 8 March 2018, https://www.militarytimes.com/news/your-army/2018/03/06/the-future-battlefield-army-marines-prepare-for-massive-fight-in-megacities/, accessed 5 March 2020.

[68] Todd South, 'The Future Battlefield'.

Secretary of Defense and combat Marine cautions: 'No technology can accurately detect and count humans inside buildings and tunnels.'[69] Making a seemingly unlikely comparison between the battle of Hue in 1968 (one of the longest and bloodiest urban battles of the Vietnam War)[70] and the 2016–2017 war on the Islamic State in Mosul, West points out stubborn continuities. 'Urban warfare remains characterized by slow, massive destruction', he argues, and despite 50 years of 'progress': 'Urban battle will remain a slugfest, with the basic ingredient remaining heavy doses of high explosives.'[71]

The return of Mosul resident Ayman Hashem to his home in July 2017 bore this out, with the smell of death hanging over the Old City. 'All that's left is rubble and the bodies of families trapped underneath', he told *Military Times*.[72] Nearly a third of the Old City—more than 5,000 buildings—was damaged or destroyed in the final three weeks of bombardment, according to a survey by UN Habitat using satellite imagery. Across the city, 10,000 buildings were damaged over the course of the war, the large majority in western Mosul, the scene of the most intense artillery, airstrikes, and fighting.[73] When it was only half done, a Pentagon spokesman would call the fighting in Mosul 'the most significant urban combat since WWII'.[74]

Air interdiction and CAS-style strikes played no small part in the devastation. According to a firsthand account by journalist James Verini, the Iraqi Counter Terrorism Service (CST) set up a forward air command 'center' on a terrace in Eastern Mosul led by an Iraqi colonel who served as the Joint Terminal Attack Controller (JTAC), calling in coalition strikes on the west of the city.[75] According to another account, Iraqi soldiers were '[h]esitant to risk casualties among their own troops' and so 'relied on airpower and artillery to clear neighborhoods'.[76] Despite objections from the UN and human rights groups, 'the U.S.-led coalition repeatedly approved the use of 500- and 2,000-pound bombs inside the densely populated district'.[77]

[69] Bing West, 'Urban Warfare, Then and Now', The Atlantic, 30 June 2017, https://www.theatlantic.com/international/archive/2017/06/urban-warfare-hue-mosul/532173/, accessed 5 March 2020.

[70] Mark Bowden, *Hue 1968: A Turning Point of the American War in Vietnam* (New York, NY: Atlantic Monthly Press, 2017).

[71] West, 'The Battle for Mosul'.

[72] Susannah George and Associated Press, 'Liberation from Militants Leaves Devastation in Mosul', Military Times, 8 August 2017, https://www.militarytimes.com/flashpoints/2017/07/15/liberation-from-militants-leaves-devastation-in-mosul/, accessed 5 March 2020.

[73] Ibid.

[74] Quoted in: James Verini, 'How the Battle of Mosul Was Waged on WhatsApp', *The Guardian*, 28 September 2019, sec. World, https://www.theguardian.com/world/2019/sep/28/battle-of-mosul-waged-on-whatsapp-james-verini, accessed 7 March 2020.

[75] Ibid.

[76] George and Associated Press, 'Liberation from Militants Leaves Devastation in Mosul'.

[77] Ibid.

What constitutes contact?

'Closeness' and 'proximity' are not the only terms lacking stable definition. At several levels across the US military there is some confusion around what constitutes 'contact' with regard to troops in contact scenarios. Journalist Noah Shachtman has witnessed the unfolding of many TIC situations as part of his extensive coverage of US air warfare. For Shachtman, TIC, which 'started as a cry for help has now come to mean [. . .] almost anything'.[78] He cites a senior Air Force officer as saying, 'The most abused thing in this war [Afghanistan] is declaring a TIC'.[79]

The Air Force and Army often see things differently when it comes to TIC and CAS, particularly the issue of command and control.[80] One Air Force JAG who served in the CAOC recalled instances when Army commanders requested air support and the CAOC staff would say 'that doesn't meet the definition of a TIC'. He also recalled 'serious disagreement' and 'exchanged harsh words on many occasions' with his Army colleagues in Afghanistan. He explained that in his view:

> [T]he Army, when they're conducting operations on the ground they just want the bomb off the rails. They seemed much less concerned about what would be the ultimate result of the bomb, whereas the Air Force we're more deliberate because we're up above. We have the luxury of time. Army troops [. . .] now if they're under fire, if they're *truly* under fire there is no question. Nobody is going to question. But if it was a matter of defining troops in contact as something which is imminent or using some other standard then sometimes the Air Force would be like 'we need more time to think about this, we don't have to do that, that's not the right call'.[81]

Army JAGs and troops on the ground would likely have a different view of all of this, but what is interesting in this account is that the Army and the Air Force not only see things differently when it comes to troops in contact and close air support; they also literally see different things. The Army view is a horizontal plane of the battlefield they find themselves immersed in, whereas the Air Force view is—as the JAG notes—from above. It is a conceit to say that the Air Force can see *more* merely because they see from above; even the

78 Shachtman, 'The Phrase That's Screwing Up the Afghan Air War'.
79 Ibid.
80 Benitez, 'How Afghanistan Distorted Close Air Support and Why It Matters'.
81 Brown, interview.

vaunted drone provides a 'soda straw' view of the battlefield and their pilots can 'lack the wider field of vision that would help them contextualize what they are seeing'.[82] Those in the CAOC and other locations may have the 'luxury of time' and so may the troops on the ground, but the crucial question here is perceived threat to life, and to whose. From the safety of the COAC the battlespace looks and also looks relatively relaxed. The view on the front lines, in the sweat and heat of battle, does not feel so safe as the following account by Shachtman demonstrates:

> Anibal Paz, Eric Meador and their squad of 15 Marines are crouched behind the crumbling mud walls of a small Afghan compound taking fire from three directions. They are in a small farming community, called Mian Poshteh, roughly 100 miles from the border of Pakistan's Balochistan province. The mission is to monitor suspected Taliban movements, but instead they have been ambushed. Meador, the company commander asks air controller Josh Faucett to review the standoff. 'This is where the friendlies are,' Faucett says, pointing to the screen. 'This is where we think the sniper is.' It's a building in the northern compound, next to the main east-west road.
>
> The next step seems obvious: Call in the F-15s and have them reduce the Taliban's positions to rubble. That's how the Marines took out insurgents in Fallujah in 2004. It's how they went after the Taliban in August 2008. But it's August 2009, and today Meador is not sure.
>
> Faucett stares at an aerial view of the village, Moba Khan, on his tablet computer. He sees a problem: The building Paz has identified as the sniper's perch is next to several farmhouses. 'Man, the target house is right on the edge of that village,' Meador says. If he orders a strike that hits a farmer's kid instead of a sniper, the Taliban will have some angry new allies, and the brass will be apoplectic. Meador tells Faucett to wave off the F-15s—and hopes he hasn't made a serious mistake.
>
> For the next three days the Marines battle with the Taliban. Overwhelmed by fire they try to call again for air support but this time the radio is broke. They eventually fix the radio and call for artillery (rather than air) support: It's fairly easy to call in mortars, artillery, and attack helicopters—even though those are less precise than strikes from a fighter jet. The difference, of course, is the size of the blast. The shells hit the ground and send shock waves through

[82] Paul Scharre, Jacquelyn Schneider, and Julia Macdonald, 'Why Drones Are Still the Future of War', 15 February 2018, https://www.foreignaffairs.com/articles/united-states/2018-02-15/why-drones-are-still-future-war, accessed 1 March 2020.

> the Marines' chests. Then more mortars. Then artillery again. But every time, the pattern is the same: a brief pause, followed by more sniper shots. What they need is a 500-pound bomb. Eventually air support is approved but only one bomb—by now the Harrier jets are low on fuel and need to return to base.
>
> A plume of smoke shoots from the compound. Direct hit. Moba Khan goes quiet. 'Receiving no more fire,' Paz radios Meador. Seventeen minutes pass. Then the gunfire, including sniper, open up again. Did they miss? Is this a second sniper? Nobody knows. There won't be a second aerial run, so Meador calls in more mortars, artillery, and helicopters.[83]

In short, how threatening the enemy may appear constitutes the appropriate military response and its attendant legalities. The soldier's definition of what constitutes 'contact' and 'imminent threat' is not the same as the operators' or JAGs' who are out of harm's way. But the lack of agreement cannot be chalked up to inter-service differences and rivalries alone. As the Center for Law and Military Operations (CLAMO) concedes, there are fundamental differences as to the very definition of 'contact':

> [Some] commanders advocated a broad reading of the term, arguing that given the definition of contact, the situation of troops in contact existed if friendly forces were within weapons range of enemy forces. USCENTCOM [US Central Command] held that this reading was flawed in a number of ways not the least of which it failed to follow the plain reading under the field manual which requires a physical engagement of the enemy [. . .][84]

As may seem obvious to the layperson, there is a significant difference between being within range of enemy fire and actually receiving it. Much of the problem is the differential perception not only of the threat itself (i.e. the threat of contact) but also how *immediate* the threat is perceived to be. These are fundamental and crucial determinations because they carry with them different weights of military necessity and proportionality: taking fire is a situation of dire military necessity, whereas possible enemy combatants a few kilometres away are potentially important but do not pose an immediate risk.

[83] Adapted from: Noah Shachtman, 'How the Afghanistan Air War Got Stuck in the Sky,' *Wired*, 8 December 2009, https://www.wired.com/2009/12/ff-end-air-war/, accessed 2 March 2020.

[84] The Judge Advocate General's Legal Center & School, Center for Law and Military Operations (CLAMO), United States Army, 'Legal Lessons Learned From Afghanistan and Iraq Volume II Full Spectrum Operations (2 May 2003–30 June 2004)' (Charlottesville, VA: United States Army, 1 August 2004), 136, https://fas.org/irp/doddir/army/clamo-v2.pdf, accessed 22 March 2017.

We might expect that this is precisely where lawyers prove their military worth and provide some legal clarity amidst operational confusion. Either it is a TIC or not, and it surely cannot be both, so surely the military lawyer could act as arbiter to resolve the issue? But there are at least two major problems. First, military lawyers are not always 'in the loop' for TIC and CAS operations and so may be unable to take part in these fraught discussions let alone resolve them. Second, military lawyers themselves are not always clear on which definition of TIC to use.

In a well-documented airstrike involving a major CAS component that took place in the Uruzgan district of Afghanistan in 2010, US forces killed at least fifteen to sixteen civilians and injured another twelve. (I recount the wider details of the strike in section 6.6.[85]) The US Army launched an investigation, which included interviews with two military lawyers; an unnamed Army Major serving at the Combined Joint Special Operations Task Force—Afghanistan base at Bagram Airfield and Army Captain Brad Cowan serving at Special Operations Task Force—South at Kandahar Airfield. A short transcript from the interview with the Major reveals the operational messiness of how TIC is defined and can easily be (mis)understood:

COL: What is TIC?

MAJ: Troops in contact, that is a free flowing doctrinal term it is used differently here, CAOC uses a different term, I think everywhere throughout the CJOA [Combined/Joint Operations Area] everyone uses it differently.

COL: Let's forget the CSOTF [Combined Special Operations Task Force] definition; tell me what you believe the CAOC definition to be and the ISAF [International Security Assistance Force] definition to be.

MAJ: Facing imminent threat.

COL: Whose definition is that?

MAJ: I want to say the OEF [Operation Enduring Freedom—i.e. the US rather than ISAF definition]

COL: I want to share with you that it is not. The one in the joint publication that the CAOC uses means that lead is being shot at you. The ISAF does use the word imminent but not from the same meaning as [US defined] imminent threat but they refine it to mean immediate.[86]

[85] David S. Cloud, 'Anatomy of an Afghan War Tragedy', *Los Angeles Times*, 10 April 2011, http://articles.latimes.com/2011/apr/10/world/la-fg-afghanistan-drone-20110410, accessed 19 July 2013.

[86] United States Central Command (CENTCOM), 'AR 15-6 Investigation, 21 February 2010 U.S. Air-to-Ground Engagement in the Vicinity of Shahidi Hassas, Uruzgan District, Afghanistan' (Kabul, Afghanistan: United States Forces—Afghanistan, 21 May 2010), 690, https://archive.org/details/dod_centcom_drone_uruzgan_foia/page/n3, accessed 20 January 2020.

As this exchange shows, there are multiple definitions of TIC and different military operations (e.g. OEF or ISAF) and different service components within those operations (e.g. the CAOC or CSOTF) work on different understandings. The Colonel's final remark, correcting the JAG, is crucially important because it shows: (a) that the JAG involved in the strike was not clear about which definition should have applied; and (b) that there are crucial differences between the US military definition of imminent threat (which includes *non*-immediate threats[87]), the CAOC definition ('lead being shot') and the ISAF definition (which means *immediate*). These are all legally plausible definitions that might yield reasonably consistent results. But while a 'TIC' might be declared during battle as if it were a concrete fact, in *practice* TIC is a subjective determination that requires multiple levels of interpretive work. The issue here goes beyond finding the 'right' definition or identifying who is working with which. The issue is that legal interpretational work and the latitude given to it has material consequences, especially significant in TIC and CAS, and not only for the troops on the ground.[88]

6.5 Contact Casualties

CAS provided to TIC is one of the most common but also the riskiest kind of targeting. CAS targeting can be risky to the pilot because traditionally missions are flown at low altitude to allow them to visually identify the target, and 'getting closer to the target means flying in the threat environment'.[89] However, advances in weapons technologies increasingly allow for 'standoff' CAS, allowing missions 'to be carried out from aircraft flying higher and faster'.[90] Drones like

[87] Department of Justice White Paper, 'Lawfulness of a Lethal Operation Directed Against A U.S. Citizen Who Is a Senior Operational Leader of Al-Qa'ida or an Associated Force', 8 November 2011, https://fas.org/irp/eprint/doj-lethal.pdf, accessed 1 July 2020; Luca Trenta, 'The Obama Administration's Conceptual Change: Imminence and the Legitimation of Targeted Killings', *European Journal of International Security* 3, no. 1 (2018): 69–93.

[88] The very existence of definitional vagueness or disagreement within and between structures—which are, after all, highly trained and resourced teams, answering to a unified command—is perhaps indicative of military priorities *in common*, if only in a diffuse and functional way, as well as priorities that *differ* further down the chain of command.

[89] Leon E. Elsarelli, 'From Desert Storm to 2025: Close Air Support in the 21st Century' (Maxwell Air Force Base, Alabama, Air Command and Staff College, Air University, 1998), 8, https://fas.org/man/dod-101/sys/ac/docs/98-086.pdf, accessed 21 December 2016.

[90] Amy Butler, 'USAF Eyes New Era of Close Air Support', 30 March 2015, http://aviationweek.com/defense/usaf-eyes-new-era-close-air-support, accessed 12 December 2016. There is considerable debate about whether standoff close air support missions are as effective as low-altitude close air support. As Member of Congress and former US Air Force A-10 pilot Martha McSally explained in a letter to President Obama and Secretary of Defense Ash Carter (attempting to persuade them not to retire the A-10 'Warthog' aircraft): 'There are times, and there will be future times, where you must provide very close air support to the troops on the ground who are often on the run or unable to provide coordinates.

the Reaper and Predator have been providing ISR support to CAS missions flown by conventional strike aircraft for many years now, but recently they have been used to employ weapons in a direct CAS role, effectively putting the pilot out of harm's way.[91] CAS missions also pose a threat to the friendly forces who are relying on the air support because they are often extremely close to the target. Selecting too large a weapon or missing by metres can mean life or death for 'friendlies', which is why these missions are called 'danger close'.[92] When we hear about 'friendly fire' incidents on the news, they very often refer to CAS missions gone wrong.[93]

But CAS poses most risk to civilians. When friendly forces are under fire it is not always possible to run a lengthy collateral damage estimate, and when acting in self-defence the proportionality calculation strongly favours those under fire, even if their actions lead to collateral damage and civilian casualties. In fact, as JAGs Corn, Dapper, and Williams note:

> Differing views exist on the importance of collateral damage when force is used in unit self-defense. Some nations take the view that, even in self-defense, the LOAC [Laws of Armed Conflict] principle of proportionality must have a moderating effect. Other nations oppose this view, positing that in matters of unit self-defense, all necessary means may be employed without regard to collateral damage and/or proportionality.[94]

I have flown CAS missions in these conditions where the pilot must visually identify friendly forces and enemy combatants to hit the target and avoid fratricide. You cannot stand off in all CAS scenarios, even in the future': Martha McSally, 'Letter to the President and the Honorable Ash Carter', 28 January 2016, reproduced at: https://nationalinterest.org/blog/the-buzz/mcsallys-case-lethal-next-gen-10-warthog-15064, accessed 1 July 2020. See also: Benitez, 'How Afghanistan Distorted Close Air Support and Why It Matters'; Mike Benitez and Peter Garretson, 'Offsetting Air Superiority with Air Force Special Operations', War on the Rocks, 3 November 2016, http://warontherocks.com/2016/11/offsetting-air-superiority-with-air-force-special-operations/, accessed 12 December 2016; Bruce R. Pirnie, Alan Vick, Adam Grissom, Karl P. Mueller, and David T. Orletsky, *Beyond Close Air Support: Forging a New Air Ground Partnership* (Santa Monica, CA: Rand Publishing, 2005).

[91] 'While not doctrinally executed or described as Close Air Support, the RQ-1 Predator has already employed weapons in direct support of troops on the ground, and the U.S. Marine Corps has used its RQ-2B Pioneer to make artillery calls for fire and to coordinate air strikes on targets it has detected. There seems little doubt that future unmanned systems will have the capability for these operations and much more.' Jay Stout, 'Close Air Support Using Armed UAVs?', *The Naval Institute: Proceedings*, http://www.military.com/NewContent/1,13190,NI_0705_Air-P1,00.html, 18 January 2017.

[92] Butler, 'USAF Eyes New Era of Close Air Support'.

[93] For a list of US and coalition friendly fire incidents see: Close Air Solutions, 'Close Air Support Fratricide Incidents—Friendly Fire!', Close Air Solutions—FAC and JTAC Training Services, http://www.closeairsolutions.com/close-air-support-fratricide-incidents/, accessed 18 January 2017.

[94] Geoffrey Corn, James Dapper, and Winston Williams, 'Targeting and the Law of Armed Conflict', in *U.S. Military Operations: Law, Policy, and Practice*, eds Geoffrey S. Corn, Rachel E. VanLandingham, and Shane R. Reeves (Oxford; New York, NY: Oxford University Press, 2015), 200.

These JAGs are careful not to point the finger at particular states, but when they refer to certain liberties being taken with respect to the principle of proportionality they likely have the United States in their sights; the US military operates with more aggressive and anticipatory ROE for self-defence than ISAF forces do.[95] Another US JAG praises the steps that the US military has taken in recent years to avoid civilian casualties caused by CAS but he concedes that even today, 'there exists a continued gap in training of, and application by, on-scene commanders of related obligations under international humanitarian law'.[96] Still more startling, Husby further suggests that 'the training gap may result from *confusion among judge advocates* about the applicability of the proportionality balancing test to defensive operations, whether deliberate or hasty'.[97] The fact that there is a debate about whether—and how much—the proportionality principle applies (and to whom) suggests that there is a good deal of flexibility and variation in practice. Again, one may ask what purposes and priorities that flexibility serves.

A 2008 investigation by Human Rights Watch found:

> The combination of light ground forces and overwhelming airpower has become the dominant doctrine of war for the US in Afghanistan. The result has been large numbers of civilian casualties, controversy over the continued use of airpower in Afghanistan, and intense criticism of US and NATO forces by Afghan political leaders and the general public.[98]

The report, *Troops In Contact: Airstrikes and Civilian Deaths in Afghanistan* claims: 'Whether civilian casualties result from aerial bombing in Afghanistan seems to depend more than anything else on whether the airstrike was planned

[95] '[C]ritics have noted that the definition used in the [US] SROE [standing rules of engagement] is much more expansive than the one used by other coalition allies, which created its own set of problems when it came to planning joint operations. In contrast to the SROE, which suggested that imminent does not necessarily mean immediate or instantaneous, NATO rules of engagement stated that a threat must be "manifest, instant and overwhelming"': Gregory, 'Dangerous Feelings'. A Human Right Watch report highlights key differences between US and NATO air strike ROE: 'NATO and the US both require "hostile intent" for aerial munitions to be employed to defend their forces. NATO defines "hostile intent" as "manifest and overwhelming force." The US ROE defines hostile intent as "the threat of the imminent use of force," a much lower threshold than NATO for employing airstrikes, permitting anticipatory self-defense': Human Rights Watch, '"Troops in Contact": Airstrikes and Civilian Deaths in Afghanistan', 31 (footnotes removed). See also: Harvard Law School International Human Rights Clinic, 'Tackling Tough Calls: Lessons from Recent Conflicts on Hostile Intent and Civilian Protection', March 2016, https://www.justsecurity.org/wp-content/uploads/2016/03/Tackling-Tough-Choices-Hostile-Intent-HLSIHRC-2016.pdf, accessed 1 March 2020.

[96] Husby, 'Balancing Act', 6.

[97] Ibid. (emphasis added).

[98] Human Rights Watch, '"Troops in Contact": Airstrikes and Civilian Deaths in Afghanistan', 2.

or was an unplanned strike.'[99] Human Rights Watch draws a sharp distinction between deliberate and dynamic targeting, suggesting that when 'aerial bombing is planned, mostly against suspected Taliban targets, US and NATO forces in Afghanistan have had a very good record of minimizing harm to civilians. In 2008, no planned airstrikes appear to have resulted in civilian casualties.'[100] The NGO attributes the low collateral damage to the fact that planned attacks allow the United States and NATO to use 'civilian risk mitigation procedures', including formal Collateral Damage Estimate (CDE), and pattern of life (POL) analysis 'which looks for civilians in the area for hours or days before an attack.' This results in a 'far more detailed intelligence' picture of 'who is and is not in the target area.'[101] As we saw in Chapter 5, even these time-consuming procedures provide no guarantee against civilian casualties. But according to Human Rights Watch, unplanned strikes by US and NATO forces 'have been far more likely to cause civilian casualties [. . .] normally when ground troops call in airstrikes as tactical support when under attack from insurgent forces, or to target insurgent forces on the move.'[102] The report further notes that: '[. . .] high civilian loss of life during airstrikes has almost always occurred during the fluid, rapid-response strikes often carried out in support of ground troops after they came under insurgent attack.'[103]

The Human Rights Watch investigation provides insight into several cases where TIC and CAS operations resulted in civilian casualties. The following excerpts from two CAS operations are typical and establish a common pattern of TIC-associated violence:

(a) On March 4, 2007, nine civilians—five women, three children, and an elderly man— were killed when their mud house in Kapisa province, just north of Kabul, was hit by two 2,000 pound bombs dropped by US aircraft. A survivor of the airstrike, Mujib, age 7, told a journalist, 'I saw my mom, my sisters, and my brother and my grandfather were dead. And our house was destroyed.' US forces said they were targeting two insurgents seen entering the house after they had fired a rocket at a US military outpost.[104]

(b) At least 21 Afghan civilians were killed in OEF airstrikes in Sangin district, Helman province, on the night of May 8, 2007. Twenty-one bodies were

[99] Ibid., 29.
[100] Ibid.
[101] Ibid.
[102] Ibid.
[103] Ibid., 4.
[104] Ibid., 15.

> presented for examination, most of which were women and children. 23 residents disputed the reported number and claimed upwards of 80 dead. [. . .]
>
> General Dan McNeil, commander of NATO forces at the time, told the media that the airstrikes were called in after US special forces were ambushed by what he called 'a far superior force.' He said, 'It does appear there were civilian casualties—exactly what caused them, we're working our way through all that.'
>
> Abdul Nasir, a resident of the bombed village, told The New York Times: 'It was around 4 p.m. when the foreign vehicles came through on the main road. The Taliban shot at them and they turned back. Then airplanes came and bombed the village at 10 p.m.' He said that Taliban forces were in the village during the day, but not at the time of the air raid. [. . .]
>
> According to the Pajhwok Afghan News agency, a US military commander made apologies to the families of 19 Afghan civilians killed and 50 wounded and offered payments of about US$2000 for each death. Coalition forces also reported that they would conduct a joint investigation into the incident.[105]

These are not the findings of a fringe group unversed in the complexity of such operations. The author of the report, Marc Garlasco, formerly worked for the US military as the chief of high-value targeting at the start of the Iraq war. The investigation involved extensive field research in Afghanistan, interviews with US, NATO, and Afghan officials, and the creation of a detailed database of every reported airstrike in Afghanistan between November 2005 and July 2008. Significantly, many JAGs agree with the report's findings and one JAG I interviewed even used the report for teaching purposes.[106] All of this confers weight and legitimacy, but the findings are also corroborated by other accounts. A US Air Force Weapons Systems Officer concedes that: 'Almost every airstrike civilian casualty and fratricide report from the war [in Afghanistan] shares common themes: Air support was un-briefed prior to the mission, reactive in nature, and was not integrated in detail sufficient to prevent tragedy.'[107]

[105] Ibid., 18–21.

[106] 'There is a really good report titled Troops in Contact and its by Human Rights Watch. I think they did it in [20]08 and I used to teach some of the stuff; I thought it was a pretty balanced report. They were critical of some of the things that happened during TICs [troops in contact] but they got the part right about deliberate strikes and they were complementary about the way we did deliberate strikes. I think they got it right. I think that when mistakes were made, they were made typically during quote unquote "TIC"': Brown, interview. Also: Deptula, interview; Mckee, interview.

[107] Benitez, 'How Afghanistan Distorted Close Air Support and Why It Matters'.

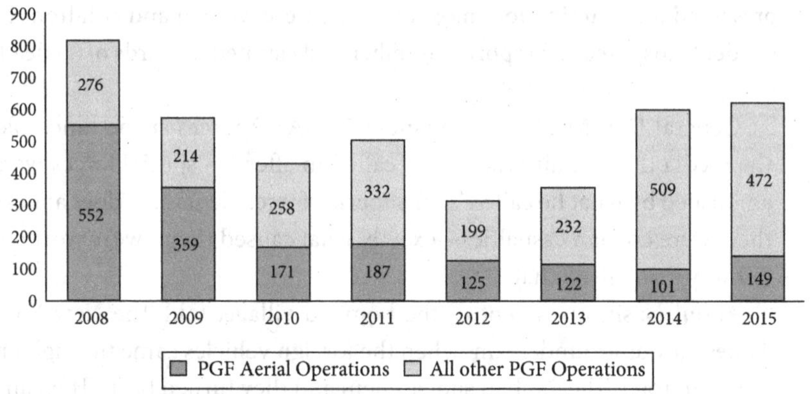

Figure 6.2 Civilian deaths in Afghanistan (2008–2015).
Source: Neta C. Crawford, 'Update on the Human Costs of War for Afghanistan and Pakistan, 2001 to Mid-2016' (Providence, RI: Costs of War, Brown University, August 2016), 5, http://watson.brown.edu/costsofwar/files/cow/imce/papers/2016/War%20in%20Afghanistan%20and%20Pakistan%20UPDATE_FINAL_corrected%20date.pdf, accessed 24 January 2017.

In 2015 the United Nations Assistant Mission to Afghanistan (UNAMA) found that 'the conflict in Afghanistan continued to cause extreme harm to the civilian population, with the highest number of total civilian casualties recorded by UNAMA since 2009'[108] It is important to note that the overwhelming majority of these casualties were caused not by ISAF or 'pro-government forces' (17 per cent) but by 'anti-government elements' (62 per cent), including the Taliban. Nevertheless, in 2015 UNAMA documented 1,854 civilian casualties (621 deaths and 1,233 injured) caused by pro-government forces, a 28 per cent increase compared to 2014.[109] Looking further back, UNAMA attributed 1,766 civilian deaths to aerial operations out of a total of 4,258 deaths attributed to pro-government forces from 2008 to 2015 (Figure 6.2).[110] 'Pro-government forces' refers to both ISAF and the Afghan security forces and UNAMA attribute the increase in civilian casualties to the significant growth of operations conducted by the latter (Afghans having assumed primary responsibility for

[108] United Nations Assistance Mission in Afghanistan, 'Afghanistan: Protection of Civilians in Armed Conflict, Annual Report 2015' (United Nations, February 2016), 1, https://unama.unmissions.org/sites/default/files/poc_annual_report_2015_final_14_feb_2016.pdf, accessed 24 January 2017.

[109] Ibid., 4.

[110] Crawford points out: 'Some of the increase in civilian death in 2015 may be due to the fact that Afghans are now flying more of their own missions, and may be using less stringent rules of engagement and more "dumb", unguided, gravity bombs': Crawford, 'Update on the Human Costs of War for Afghanistan and Pakistan, 2001 to Mid-2016', 5; See also:Neta C. Crawford, *Accountability for Killing: Moral Responsibility for Collateral Damage in America's Post-9/11 Wars* (New York, NY: Oxford University Press, 2013).

security throughout their own country).[111] Moreover, the leading cause of civilian casualties in Afghanistan in 2015 was ground engagements, not aerial operations. Nevertheless, despite attempts to mitigate collateral damage and civilian casualties, US and ISAF airstrikes—deliberate and especially dynamic—still kill civilians.

6.6 Time to Ask the JAG?

As mentioned, the involvement of JAGs in dynamic targeting, and TIC/CAS in particular is operationally contingent. Sometimes JAGs at the tactical level supporting Ground Force Commanders will have 'eyes on a target', be it a brief 'verbal thumbs up' or a more involved analysis.[112] Serving at multiple locations throughout Afghanistan and Iraq, commonly attached to a Joint Special Operations Task Force (JSOTF), these are predominantly Army JAGs overseeing ground operations—but where required they are joined by Air Force and Marine JAGs.[113] Special Operations are by definition classified, and the JAGs I spoke to were unable to go into much detail about their role in dynamic targeting operations in support. Significantly, they were unable to disclose where and in what specific unit they served, other than to say that they deployed to 'locations in Iraq and Afghanistan'.[114] Nevertheless, the JAGs interviewed were able to shed some light on when they are—and are not—involved in dynamic targeting more generally.

One individual who served in Afghanistan reported that at the tactical level, JAG participation in time-sensitive targeting is a function of several factors: (a) what level of command is asking for the strike; (b) who has the weapons-release authority in any given situation; and (c) how much training and experience the battle captain or battle major in the headquarters (i.e. 'the commander') has. He explains how these factors play out in relation to a TIC scenario:

> If we had a TIC requiring a weapon with a higher-level release authority, the initial HQ [Headquarters] involved would typically be a battalion-level command. For the most part, those commands do not have judge advocates. If

[111] United Nations Assistance Mission in Afghanistan, 'Afghanistan: Protection of Civilians in Armed Conflict, Annual Report 2015', 4–5.
[112] McKee, interview.
[113] McDowell, interview.
[114] Ibid.

> that command has the asset and the release authority, *you could see a TIC engagement with no JAG involvement*. However, an effective Brigade Judge Advocate [the JAG above the battalion level] would have a relationship with the battle captains at each battalion and would be accessible remotely for legal advice if the battle captain believes the situation is a close enough call to request advice. For easy situations the battle captain could simply direct the release of the weapon system.[115]

He provides a hypothetical example:

> The ROE sets release authority for 120mm mortars at the O-5 (battalion command) level. The battalion commander has a section of 120mm mortars under his operational control. A platoon gets into a firefight in an open field at night and calls for mortar support. The battalion battle captain, exercising delegated authority from the battalion commander, authorizes the mortars to fire. A well trained and experienced battle captain with good situational awareness of the terrain and platoon's operation may be confident enough to authorize the mortars without calling to the brigade HQ to talk with a JA [Judge Advocate]. On the other hand, a new battle captain who has at least been well trained may make a call higher just to make sure.[116]

As this account confirms, JAG involvement in dynamic targeting depends, among other things, on the confidence, training, and experience of those involved. So far as my research on these matters has been able to reveal, there are no protocols that determine exactly when a JAG must be called. Ultimately, it comes down to whether or not a commander believes he or she requires legal input, and that there is time for it. If there is doubt about the validity of the target, then the battalion battle captain should refer up to the JAG at the higher headquarters (in this case at the brigade level). Similarly, if a JAG at a lower headquarters has concerns about a target—perhaps s/he is worried that striking the target will result in civilian casualties—s/he should refer up to a JAG at higher headquarters. But military 'necessities' may prompt divergences from these procedures, as discussed.

115 McKee, email correspondence.
116 Ibid.

'Hey, we just struck something'

In the early morning of 21 February 2010, a dozen US Special Forces were dropped near the village of Khod in central Afghanistan.[117] Accompanied by Afghan army and police forces, their mission was to search the compounds in and around the village for a suspected improvised explosive device (IED) factory and to disrupt 'insurgent infrastructure'. Another US special operations unit had been attacked in the district a year earlier and a soldier had been killed. This time, an AC-130 gunship, a Predator drone (flown from Creech Air Force Base in Nevada) and two Kiowa attack helicopters were in the area to protect the Special Forces team.

At 5.00am the AC-130 crew saw a pickup truck and a sports utility vehicle converge from different directions. At 5.08, they saw one of the drivers flash his headlights in the darkness, the first of several actions that were interpreted as suspicious by US Forces. The AC-130 radioed the Predator crew in Nevada: 'It appears the two vehicles are flashing lights, signalling.' The AC-130 crew then asked the Special Forces team what it wanted to do about the suspicious vehicles. As *Los Angeles Times* journalist David S. Cloud reports:

> 'Roger, ground force commander's intent is to destroy the vehicles and the personnel,' came the unit's reply.
>
> To use deadly force, the commander would first have to make a 'positive identification' that the adversary was carrying weapons and posed an 'imminent threat.'
>
> For the next four and a half hours, the Predator crew and the screeners scrutinized the convoy's every move, looking for evidence to support such a decision.
>
> 'We all had it in our head, "Hey, why do you have 20 military age males at 5 a.m. collecting each other?"' an Army officer would say later recall. 'There can be only one reason, and that's because we've put [U.S. troops] in the area.'[118]

This would come to be one of the most extensively documented and discussed civilian casualty incidents in Afghanistan. This was no convoy, and these were not Taliban. 'They were men, women and children going about their business, unaware that a unit of U.S. soldiers was just a few miles away, and that teams of

[117] This section draws from the extensive accounts of the Uruzgan strike provided by David S. Cloud and Derek Gregory: Cloud, 'Anatomy of an Afghan War Tragedy'; Gregory, 'Angry Eyes (1)'; Gregory, 'Angry Eyes (2)'.

[118] Cloud, 'Anatomy of an Afghan War Tragedy'.

U.S. military pilots, camera operators and video screeners had taken them for a group of Taliban fighters.'[119] At the end of the mission at least fifteen to sixteen civilians lay dead and a further twelve were injured.

Commentators have offered various diagnoses of the strike, each highlighting serious and systemic shortcomings in its handling by US forces and especially the predator crew. Derek Gregory offers a far-ranging and forensic analysis that shows how the strike went ahead *despite various dissenting voices* in the kill chain that raised crucial operational and legal questions. According to Gregory:

> Throughout the night and into the morning the crew of the Predator interpreted more or less everything they saw on their screens as indicative of hostile intent: the trucks were a 'convoy' (at one stage they were referred to as 'technical trucks'); the occupants were 'Military Aged Males' ('12–13 years old with a weapon is just as dangerous'); when they stopped to pray at dawn this was seen as a Taliban signifier ('I mean, seriously, that's what they do'); and when the trucks swung west, away from the direct route to Khod, this was interpreted as 'tactical manoeuvring' or 'flanking'.[120]

An Army investigation led by Major General Timothy McHale found the Predator crew—and others—at fault, but it also demonstrated the patchy and provisional involvement of military lawyers. Ostensibly, there were two military lawyers involved: Captain Bradley Cowan, the Special Operations Task Force JAG at Kandahar Airfield and his superior (name redacted), the Combined Joint Special Operations Task Force JAG at Bagram Airfield. The senior JAG is the same one who experienced some confusion over the definition of TIC (section 6.4), and they[121] were not really involved in the strike because Captain Cowan thought this unnecessary. As part of the Army investigation an (unnamed) Lieutenant Commander asks the superior: 'Any idea why they didn't call you in on this target?' They respond: 'No. The first time I talked to anyone from the JOC [Joint Operations Center] is when I was leaving church and MAJ [redacted] said "hey we just struck something." '[122]

[119] Ibid.

[120] Gregory, 'Angry Eyes (1)'. Gregory explains the preconception of these civilians as suspected targets by reference to militarized ways of seeing, combined with the radically dispersed and chaotic geographies of the kill chain.

[121] 'They' is used here because the gender is unknown; it does not denote the plural.

[122] Timothy McHale and US Forces Afghanistan, AR 15-6 investigation, 21 February 2010 US Air-to-Ground Engagement in the Vicinity of Shahidi Hassas, Uruzgan District, Afghanistan, 21 May 2010, 698.

The only JAG *actually* involved in the strike was, therefore, Major Cowan. Major Cowan told the Army investigation that during the course of the operation, he made his legal recommendation 'crystal clear', advising the battalion commander *not* to go ahead with the strike because of the presence of children and on the basis that they had not properly established positive identification (PID) of the target.[123] For reasons that are not entirely clear from the transcript his advice did not get through to the Combined Joint Special Operations Commander (CJSOC) who made the decision to launch the attack. Cowan recalls in an interview with the investigation team that the CJSOC—who was in close contact with the battalion commander that Cowan was advising—'*wanted* to strike the convoy'.[124] At no point in the lead up to the attack did any JAG have direct contact with the CJSOC who ordered the attack.

This example raises all sorts of questions about who has access to legal advice and under what conditions (in this case, the JAG's advice seems to have been disregarded or not heard). But more than anything, it speaks to the broader issue highlighted throughout this chapter: legal advice in dynamic targeting operations is provisional and patchy at best. JAGs do not see every target and even when they do, there is no guarantee that their advice will make it to the places where the final decisions are made. According to Cowan, JAGs are frequently not involved in TIC strikes and if they are sleeping they are often left in bed. In certain circumstances, Cowan would be woken up, for example when there were 'civilian casualties, death of a US Service Member or ANSF [Afghan National Security Forces], serious property, vehicle or issue on the ROE and Escalation of Force'. But he was not called to give advice on a TIC strike unless there was 'some question about the ROE'.[125] Cowan's senior, the Major at Bagram, similarly noted how it 'is impossible to be present for the full TIC process', adding 'I am not always brought in for a TIC. It depends on the situation. If we have a casualty I am notified, if we are in a high collateral area I am notified, If I am walking around I have a pager [. . .]'.[126]

A JAG who served as an attachment to a Special Operations Task Force in Afghanistan tells a similar story:

> I would say I participated directly in 80% of our TST/TIC strikes. When I did, I walked through my analysis verbally with the battle captain and then we reviewed the action afterwards to make improvements. The remaining 20%

[123] Ibid., 604.
[124] Ibid., 608 (emphasis added).
[125] Ibid., 601.
[126] Ibid., 690.

> were almost entirely late in the deployment when the battle captains were confident enough to make these calls without my presence. I almost always received an immediate back-brief from the battle captains when I returned (I was at the Brigade level, and I did not have enough personnel to keep an officer in the ops [operations] center at all times. We had someone in the ops center approximately 75% of the time, and I did a late gym/shower cycle from midnight until 0300 so I could be easily located and coherent during night ops—the runner came and got me from the gym, shower, or my quarters on numerous occasions).[127]

In sum, whether and how JAGs are involved in TIC and CAS operations is dependent on a series of operational contingencies, including (but not limited to): (a) Who is requesting fire support and who are they requesting it from?; (b) Who owns the asset (e.g. helicopter, fighter jet, or drone) that will provide the fire support?; (c) Does the commander who makes the final call have access to a JAG and is the JAG physically present or available via reach back (e.g. on a secure telephone line)?; (d) Who has the authority to release the particular weapon(s) that will be used?; (e) How urgent is fire support needed (i.e. is the threat to troops on the ground immediate or is there time to coordinate a response, check accuracy of intelligence, and identify possible fratricide and civilian casualties)?; and (f) since the pilot or operator will often not have a direct line of communication with a JAG, how good are the communications between those who fire the weapon and the commander who authorizes the strike and the JAG that may be advising the commander?[128]

***

The US military has slowly come to recognize that TIC and CAS operations are causing civilian casualties and that this could at times have a negative strategic impact. As noted in Chapter 5, ISAF Commander General Stanley McChrystal issued a Tactical Directive in July 2009 that placed greater emphasis on the avoidance of civilian casualties. McChrystal insisted: 'We must avoid the trap of winning tactical victories—but suffering strategic defeats—by causing civilian

[127] McKee, email correspondence.

[128] This composite set of questions is produced from interviews and email correspondence with both Army and Air Force JAGs.

casualties or excessive damage thus alienating the people'.[129] Much of the content and purpose of the Directive was oriented towards CAS specifically:

> I expect leaders at all levels to scrutinize and limit the use of force like close air support (CAS) against residential compounds and other locations likely to produce civilian casualties [. . .] Commanders must weigh the gain of using CAS against the cost of civilian casualties, which in the long run make mission success more difficult and turn the Afghan people against us. [. . .] The use of air-to-ground munitions and indirect fires against residential compounds is only authorized under very limited and prescribed conditions [. . .][130]

The specific conditions were deleted from the Directive for security reasons, but whatever they were, they seem to have worked—temporarily. In 2008 ISAF established the Civilian Casualty Tracking Cell, which became the Civilian Casualty Mitigation Team in 2011. The data provided by ISAF suggests that ISAF was successful at reducing civilian casualties in close air support operations, at least initially. Civilian deaths reportedly dropped by 87 per cent in the eight weeks after the Directive came into effect.[131] But in 2007, when the war began to intensify, the Human Rights arm of UNAMA began to keep its own record of casualties in Afghanistan. Their data shows that the success in mitigating civilian casualties after the Directive was issued in July 2009 was more modest. In fact, in 2009 the UN recorded *five times* more civilian deaths due to air power than the ISAF CIVCAS tracking cell, a significant difference.[132]

According to Neta C. Crawford, the ISAF tracking cell regularly underreports incidents that result in civilian casualties. She provides the particularly salient example of a US airstrike ordered by a German Officer, Colonel George Klein, on two fuel tankers in Kunduz, Afghanistan in September 2009—just months after McChrystal issued his Directive. ISAF initially reported that all those killed in the blast, up to 130 people, were Taliban fighters. After a series of investigations, ISAF forces eventually acknowledged that most of those killed were civilians.[133] Crawford notes that the ISAF CIVCAS database does not record any civilian deaths due to close air support for September 2009 in northern

[129] Stanley McChrystal, 'Tactical Directive', International Security Assistance Force (ISAF), NATO, 6 July 2009, http://www.nato.int/isaf/docu/official_texts/Tactical_Directive_090706.pdf, accessed 15 December 2016.

[130] Ibid.

[131] Shachtman, 'How the Afghanistan Air War Got Stuck in the Sky'.

[132] Crawford, *Accountability for Killing*, 105.

[133] Ibid., 107; Derek Gregory, 'Kunduz and "Seeing like a Military"', *Geographical Imaginations* (blog), 2 January 2014, https://geographicalimaginations.com/2014/01/02/kunduz-and-seeing-like-a-military/, accessed 24 January 2017.

Afghanistan, and only eight deaths in the South West 'despite the fact that this is one of the most well-known incidents of civilian killing by ISAF forces in the war'.[134] The critical point, though, is that the gains made in curtailing injury and death in the immediate weeks and months following McChrystal's Directive, have not been maintained. The counter-insurgency doctrine did not last long in Afghanistan, has been all but abandoned by the United States and its allies in Iraq, and was never applied in Syria.[135]

Ironically, just as later modern war reaches its stride and decides that it is time to 'ask the JAG', there is often just not enough time to ask. Away from the pressures of battle, a perhaps more important question presents itself: are the risks posed by TIC/CAS acceptable, taken as a whole *class* of operations? As we have seen, the current state of play is that as a share of all aerial targeting operations, these modes of air power are only increasing.

[134] Crawford, *Accountability for Killing*, 107.

[135] Michelsen Institute, 'Protection of Civilians: Why They Die in US Strikes' (Bergen, Norway: CMI CHR. Michelsen Institute, 10 November 2015), https://www.cmi.no/news/1615-protection-of-civilians, accessed 2 March 2020.

Conclusion. Juridical Warfare: Limits and Possibilities

> The puzzle is how so much struggle fades from view as experts embody the voice of reason and outcomes are assimilated as facts rather than contestable choices. [. . .] [E]xperts forget their struggles and their role in distribution to celebrate their knowledge as universal, their world as ordered, their path forward aligned with progress. Modern expertise knows and it forgets—or refuses to know—its powers and its limits. When they forget—and we forget—it becomes all the more difficult to understand how this world, with all its injustice and suffering, has been made and reproduced. [. . .] The result of continuous struggle is an eerie stability it is hard to imagine challenging or changing.
>
> David Kennedy, A World of Struggle[1]

Juridical Warfare

The War Lawyers set out to explain how and why war lawyers became kill chain lawyers. The analysis has been governed by two central challenges. First, this book has sought to explain the material and discursive effects that kill chain lawyers and the laws of war have today: on aerial targeting specifically, and the way that we understand war more generally. Second, and in so doing, this book has sought to explain how we got here: exactly when and why war lawyers became involved in the provision of legal advice in aerial targeting operations. As should by now be clear, these challenges are two sides of the same coin. Considered on their own terms, the material and discursive effects that war lawyers have had on targeting and war over the last fifty years (i.e. since the Vietnam War) have been a self-reinforcing 'success story', contributing in no

[1] David Kennedy, *A World of Struggle: How Power, Law, and Expertise Shape Global Political Economy* (Princeton, NJ; Oxford: Princeton University Press, 2018), 5.

The War Lawyers. Craig Jones, Oxford University Press (2020). © Craig Jones.
DOI: 10.1093/oso/9780198842927.001.0001.

small part to law's prominence and integration into the kill chain over the last thirty years (i.e. since the First Gulf War).

In answering the question, *why did war lawyers become involved in the provision of legal advice in aerial targeting operations?*, the historical answer of this book has rested in large part on how the US military interpreted the successes and failures of its actions in the Vietnam War (Chapter 1) and, in particular, how veterans who came to be in leadership positions after the Vietnam War took a more proactive view of how the laws of war and the rules of engagement (ROE) could and should operate. In Chapter 2 I traced the origins of operational law and showed how, through careful interpretive work, war lawyers put the laws of war to work for the US military, proving their operational worth and setting the stage for their involvement in aerial targeting operations in the early 1990s. War lawyers were deployed to provide direct legal advice on aerial targeting operations for the first time in the First Gulf War (Chapter 3). The Israeli military looked to and borrowed from the US approach in incorporating war lawyers into its kill chain but, as we saw in Chapter 4, Israeli war lawyers gained their experience from their extensive involvement in administering the occupation of the Palestinian Territories from 1968 onward. The year 2000 was a catalyst for the incorporation of Israeli war lawyers into the kill chain and the Israel military used the Second Intifada as an opportunity to legally rationalize a new 'targeted killing' policy. Targeted killing has since become a mainstay of both US and Israeli warfare—a strategy thrown into the global spotlight in January 2020 when the United States assassinated Iranian General Qassem Soleimani near Baghdad International Airport, together with several of his entourage.

By the time of the invasions of Afghanistan (2001) and Iraq (2003) US war lawyers were already well integrated into the kill chain, but these continually evolving conflicts have seen 'mission creep', too, in the expectations placed upon these specialists. Overall, their centrality to 'mission success' has become more fully appreciated over time (Chapters 5). Nevertheless, there are limits to the extent of war lawyers' involvement in aerial targeting and, as we saw in Chapter 6, the fast-paced exigencies of dynamic targeting often curtail how much input war lawyers have.

In terms of law and lawyers' material and discursive effects, this book has advanced the following argument. First, the laws of war are *indeterminate*. In the period under discussion the laws of war have become much more important to the conduct of war, and the battlespace has become more juridically complex (we return to these issues below). While this indeterminacy and complexity prove difficult for commanders to navigate alone, the United States and Israel have leveraged both for their own tactical and strategic purposes. Because they require extensive interpretive work the laws of war are a terrain of struggle. Lawyers have proven to their military employers that, carefully navigated, the laws of war can contribute to favourable outcomes and, ultimately, 'mission success'. Putting the laws of war to work in the service of military operations means that the laws of war not only constrain military action but can also permit, enable, and legitimize it.

The second claim, therefore, is that the laws of war, with help from war lawyers, are *productive of military violence*. I have provided many examples throughout this work, be it the designating of vast parts of Iraq's infrastructure as 'dual use', the gradual legalization of targeted killing, the production targets for the kill chain, or even the paradigms of war that make the kill chain possible. As these and other examples show, the laws of war are not a static legal regime; they change with the warp and weft of war itself. The malleability of the laws of war can be a blessing and a curse for militaries as different actors—foreign and domestic, allies and antagonists—vie to make the laws of war in their own image. Hence the third argument: that when war lawyers render legal advice to commanders, they are actively *making* law. In sum, war lawyers work to determine the law in an ongoing process of bounded interpretation: they provide answers and options for harried decision makers, but in negotiation with the broader indeterminacy, constraints, and permissibility of the law.

* * *

In tracing all this, I have adopted the terminology of 'later modern war' and, for the process that it has undergone, 'juridification'. As I pointed out in the Introduction, juridification is not about rendering this war or that method of combat legal; it is not about—or is not only about—how war and methods of combat have become more lawful in the sense of compliance with a legal rule. Rather, it is about how war has become more *law-full*—full of law—in the sense that it is increasingly conducted and understood in relation to law, legal discourse, and legal debates.

As Blichner and Molander have pointed out, juridification 'is an ambiguous concept'.[2] In their useful essay *Mapping Juridification* they propose a definition

[2] Lars Chr. Blichner and Anders Molander, 'Mapping Juridification', *European Law Journal* 14, no. 1 (2008): 36. Much the same could—and has—been said about the concept of 'legalization'. See: Kenneth W. Abbott et al., 'The Concept of Legalization', *International Organization* 54, no. 03 (2000): 401–19. Legalization is a narrower concept than juridification: it focuses more on formal legal process and procedures and less on the idea of law as a social and political practice, which is why I adopt the term juridification.

that delineates five dimensions of juridification, each of which are pertinent in one way or another to later modern war:

> First, constitutive juridification is a process where norms constitutive for a political order are established or changed to the effect of adding to the competencies of the legal system. Second, juridification is a process through which law comes to regulate an increasing number of different activities. Third, juridification is a process whereby conflicts increasingly are being solved by or with reference to law. Fourth, juridification is a process by which the legal system and the legal profession get more power as contrasted with formal authority. Finally, juridification as legal framing is the process by which people increasingly tend to think of themselves and others as legal subjects.[3]

Adapting this framework, the juridification of later modern war—or juridical warfare—might be thought of as:

(a) *The set of norms and technologies that constitute the sphere of war, and which enable the partial or total suspension of peace.* This includes the creation of the paradigm of war and the collapsing of the distinction between the norm and the exception[4] and a delegation of 'petty sovereignties'[5] in the making of decisions about life and death. It also includes the technological and strategic evolution of military actors who respond to and precipitate changes in the way that war is fought and understood;

(b) *The process through which law has come to regulate war.* The process of juridification is uneven across time and space; the histories and geographies of how law has—and importantly *has not*—come to regulate war should therefore be of primary concern. Regulation is to be understood broadly and can have a wide series of effects, both bifurcated and otherwise;

(c) *The process by which military, domestic and international legal systems and their associated legal professions obtain an increasing amount of power both institutionally and in shaping policy and public discourse.* These processes are open to contest and are sites of ongoing historical struggle but often run up against unequal power relations and must therefore be negotiated

[3] Blichner and Molander, 'Mapping Juridification', 38–9.

[4] Giorgio Agamben, *State of Exception*, trans. Kevin Attell, 1st edition (Chicago, IL: University of Chicago Press, 2005).

[5] On the concept of petty sovereignty, see: Judith Butler, *Precarious Life: The Powers of Mourning and Violence* (London; New York, NY: Verso, 2006).

reflexively and likely in conjunction with 'non-legal' frameworks.[6] Law does not necessarily 'solve' issues, but re-casts them in a new light; it also produces (new) issues;

(d) *The process by which people involved in war—as victim, perpetrator, bystander, or witness—tend to think of themselves (and possibly others) as legal subjects or subjects without legal rights and legal protections.* This process can both be inclusionary and exclusionary, depending on the context of the subject and whether legal rights are being invoked or denied. Juridification is not about the triumph of human rights or the applicability of legal protections to everyone, everywhere; it concerns the constitution of legal subjects but also their unmaking—that is, the subjectification and desubjectification of legal subjects—and might pay special attention to how, where, and upon who the exception is made;

(e) *The institutional apparatus by which militaries and para-military organizations seek to position themselves in relation to law (or not).* This apparatus tends to display reflexively about how its actions are perceived by complex and multiple audiences; representation and alignment of behaviour in relation to law and lawfulness become vital to the conduct of legitimate war. Juridification should not be viewed as an inevitable one-way process. Significant questions remain as to how important law may or may not remain to the conduct of war and it may therefore also be important to think about processes of de-juridification or counter-juridification.

All of this to say that law has become an increasingly important part of later modern war—for now—and the discursive terrain for both those who support and oppose war has shifted evermore into the juridical domain. Over the period examined in this book—from the Vietnam War (1955–1975) to the ongoing wars in Gaza, Afghanistan, Iraq, (and Syria)—the legal and geopolitical landscape has of course changed in other ways, too. The fortunes of legal multilateralism or supranationalism more generally—since the post-Cold War, war on terror, or global financial crisis, for example—have been beyond the scope of this book. As explained in the Introduction, for various reasons the primary interview material has been largely confined to just two states' militaries. In this closing chapter I will make some (necessarily tentative) remarks about

[6] For an account of how the 'non-legal' and the 'legal' constitute one another, see: Fleur Johns, *Non-Legality in International Law: Unruly Law* (Cambridge; New York, NY: Cambridge University Press, 2013).

other states that form the wider international context, before reflecting on juridification's possible future.

Beyond the United States and Israel

The United States and Israel are not the only states that employ war lawyers in aerial targeting operations, still less the only states to have pursued expansive interpretations of what constitutes a legitimate military target. Some NATO member states have made particularly proactive use of war lawyers in targeting operations. But both the available literature and my interviews (including interviews with Australian and UK war lawyers) suggest that there are some crucial differences between the US and Israeli approach, and that of other (non-US) NATO states. There are altogether different and perhaps greater differences between the United States and Israel and *non*-NATO states. But comparisons with and within NATO are instructive, not least because, as we have seen, the alliance has been heavily involved in Iraq and Afghanistan (and, more recently, in Syria as well).

First, the United States and Israel employ and deploy a greater number of military lawyers in targeting operations than the average NATO state. Many of the most prominent members of the various coalitions that have fought in Iraq, Afghanistan, Libya, and Syria over the last decade or so have deployed only a small number of legal advisers to key positions (places like the Combined Air Operations Center (CAOC) in Qatar—see Chapter 5).[7] According to two senior US military lawyers with extensive experience of working in Qatar, only the United States keeps a permanent legal presence on the CAOC 'operational floor'. Other states, notably the United Kingdom, Australia, and Canada deploy military lawyers to the CAOC, but they do not have a permanent physical presence there.[8] These are US-led coalitions, and deployed US forces and military assets greatly outnumber those of coalition partners, so it is not surprising that the United States would have greater legal representation when it comes to targeting.

Second, the US and Israel tend to have more permissive rules of engagement for targeting than non-US NATO members. Differences in how the United

[7] Ian Henderson, 'Legal Officers in the Australian Defence Force: Functions by Rank and Competency Level, along with a Case-Study on Operations', *Military Law and Law of War Review* 50, nos. 1–2 (2011): 37–66; Michael F. Lohr and Steve Gallotta, 'Legal Support in War: The Role of Military Lawyers', *Chicago Journal of International Law* 4, no. 2 (2003): 465.

[8] Interview, Stefano (pseudonym); Brown, interview.

States, the United Kingdom, and other NATO members interpret their rights and obligations under the laws of war come to the surface in multinational coalition operations.[9] A coalition will set rules of engagement for all multinational forces, but each state retains the right to refuse to contribute to a particular mission—or sometimes even to veto it—if they believe the mission would contravene their national interpretation of their legal responsibilities.[10] US military lawyers I interviewed provided many examples of how predominantly continental European allies would raise their national 'red flag' and withdraw their personnel and assets (e.g. fighter jets) from certain targeting missions. Crucial differences opened up between what one US military lawyer called 'NATO' versus 'NATO-lite' members, the former being the United States, the United Kingdom, Canada, and Australia, with France, Holland, Italy, and other continental European states cast as 'NATO-lite'.[11] Differences concerned core issues such as what (and who) constitutes a permissible military target, under what conditions, and what constitutes a lawful use of force in situations of self-defence.

The mechanics and machinations of what is known as coalition 'interoperability'—that is, how different states negotiate working together on military operations—is an area that requires much more research. But the existing literature shows that the United States has taken a more liberal approach than most other NATO members with the laws of war when it comes to targeting. For example, reflecting on the different approaches among states of the International Security Assistance Force (ISAF) in Afghanistan from 2002 onwards, UK Royal Navy Commander Alan Cole suggested:

> Different nations took different views of whom they were engaged with in an armed conflict, so coalition targeting arrangements had to ensure that the nation that owned the assets likely to be allocated to the particular target was satisfied that the individuals they were likely to kill were within its own national understanding of who was a combatant. It is fair to say that the United States took a wider view of whom might legitimately be targeted than some of its European allies. The US approach reflected the widespread political and

[9] Jody Prescott, 'Tactical Implementation of Rules of Engagement in a Multinational Force Reality', in *U.S. Military Operations: Law, Policy, and Practice*, ed. Geoffrey S. Corn, Rachel E. VanLandingham, and Shane R. Reeves (Oxford: Oxford University Press, 2015), 249–74.

[10] Richard C. Gross and Ian Henderson, 'Multinational Operations', in *U.S. Military Operations: Law, Policy, and Practice*, ed. Geoffrey S. Corn, Rachel E. VanLandingham, and Shane R. Reeves (Oxford: Oxford University Press, 2015), 364.

[11] Stefano (pseudonym), interview.

public support at home, while the European position reflected their more cautious national positions.[12]

Brigadier General Kenneth Watkin, Canada's most senior military lawyer from 2006–2010, similarly suggests that a more restrictive human rights legal regime holds sway in Europe as compared with North America. 'My experience', Watkins writes, 'has been that European nations are more directly impacted by the human rights framework associated with decisions of the European Court of Human Rights than non-European countries, such as Canada and the United States.'[13] Drilling down to some of the particulars, Cole details how ISAF-contributing states differed on their interpretation of the principle of proportionality:

> NATO developed its own position on what was an acceptable level of collateral damage for the air campaign in Afghanistan but some nations took a more restrictive view than NATO. Not only did that mean that assets of those nations would not conduct the mission, but officers of those nations embedded in the targeting process might be barred from contributing to its success.[14]

Cole does not explicitly signal which states took a more restrictive view of proportionality, but my interviews suggest that continental European states consistently walk a more restrictive path than their non-continental European counterparts, and especially the United States and the United Kingdom. The same US military lawyer who spoke of 'NATO-lite' saw it as follows:

> [I]ts never an issue with the UK for the most part, if I can speak frankly here. [. . .] Four Eyes— Canada, UK, Australia [and the US]—that's different than if we start bringing in the Dutch or the French because they'll have more restrictive ROE [. . .] The prospect of civilian prosecution, it makes them more reluctant to jump in with both feet like a lot of the Four Eyes normally do. Interoperability is a frustrating thing a lot of times in planning because US forces, UK in particular, will hit the ground running and start planning and

[12] Alan Cole, 'Legal Issues in Forming the Coalition', *International Law Studies, U.S. Naval War College* 85, no. 1 (2009): 146–7.

[13] Kenneth W. Watkin, 'Coalition Operations: A Canadian Perspective'. *International Law Studies* 84, no. 1 (2008): 254.

[14] Cole, 'Legal Issues in Forming the Coalition', 147.

> then all of a sudden, all these other coalition partners start signing up to the operation.[15]

The United Kingdom merits special attention in thinking about the generalizability of the US–Israel approach to targeting because there are some further crucial similarities. In 2015 the United Kingdom followed the US and Israeli practice of targeted killing when it killed Reyyad Khan and Ruhul Amin in Raqqa, Syria by means of a drone strike. Khan and Amin were UK citizens; they were targeted because they were members of Islamic State. (UK drone crews operate from RAF Waddington in Lincolnshire and, significantly, from Creech Air Force base in Nevada.) Days afterwards, and with intelligence assistance from the United Kingdom, the US targeted and killed a third UK citizen, Junaid Hussein. Reflecting on the operation, *The Guardian's* Ewan MacAskill noted: 'It was a momentous decision on various levels: to kill a British citizen, to do this using a drone and to do it in Syria, a country with which the UK is not at war.'[16] The UK 'kill list'[17] is likely nowhere near as extensive as the US and Israel's, but the episode is a significant indication that the United Kingdom may be borrowing from the US and Israeli playbook on 'extra-judicial executions' (to use increasingly outmoded terminology).

In the legal rationalization for the strike on Khan, the UK Attorney General Jeremy Wright went to great efforts to emphasize the similarities between UK and US approaches to targeted killing. He detailed how the UK's understanding of imminent threat, the legal linchpin of targeted killing, has been used and endorsed by the United States, and that the United States and the United Kingdom share diplomatic correspondence on the issue of imminence going back to the 1830s.[18] But in many ways the UK's legal position on targeted killing reflects a tension at the heart of its approach to targeting, and perhaps

[15] Stefano (pseudonym), interview. Five eyes is an Anglophone intelligence alliance comprising Australia, Canada, New Zealand, the United Kingdom, and the United States. The interviewee was not referring to New Zealand in making these observations, hence four rather than five eyes.

[16] Ewen MacAskill and Richard Norton-Taylor, 'How UK Government Decided to Kill Reyaad Khan', *The Guardian*, 8 September 2015, sec. World, https://www.theguardian.com/world/2015/sep/08/how-did-britain-decide-to-assassinate-uk-isis-fighter-reyaad-khan-drone-strike, accessed 6 November 2019.

[17] Nicholas Watt, 'Ministers Drew up "kill" List of British Jihadis Fighting with Isis in Syria', *The Guardian*, 8 September 2015, sec. UK, https://www.theguardian.com/uk-news/2015/sep/08/ministers-list-several-british-jihadis-targets, accessed 6 November 2019.

[18] Attorney General's Office and Jeremy Wright, 'Attorney General's Speech at the International Institute for Strategic Studies', GOV.UK, 11 January 2017, https://www.gov.uk/government/speeches/attorney-generals-speech-at-the-international-institute-for-strategic-studies, accessed 6 November 2019.

foreign policy more broadly.[19] On the one hand, the United Kingdom wants to be a 'big player' in shaping the future of international law, hence Wright's insistence that the country is 'a world leader in promoting, defending and shaping international law'.[20] On the other hand, and especially since the invasion of Iraq in 2003, the United Kingdom is not comfortable with blindly following US policy, hence Wright also insisting, in the same speech, that the United Kingdom was not adopting the US 'Global War on Terror paradigm'.[21]

For these and other reasons, the United Kingdom would have been an especially interesting third case study for this book, and when I began planning this research in the early 2010s I envisioned—and hoped—that an analysis of Royal Air Force (RAF) targeting and legal advice would form a substantial part of this work. I tried for more than two years to gain access to the RAF Legal Branch and made several requests for interviews, which were roundly rejected.[22] As one UK RAF lawyer informed me: 'We have concerns regarding security and have no obligation to discuss our practices with civilians.'[23] RAF Legal Branch eventually agreed to consider five questions over email: their response contained some generic details about the involvement of RAF lawyers in UK targeting operations, including assurances that RAF or Ministry of Defence Legal Officers are available throughout the targeting process for both pre-planned and time-sensitive targeting. The response from Legal Branch repeatedly insisted '*the detailed process is Official Sensitive*' and the documentation I received was marked, 'Handling Instruction: Legal—Not to be Disclosed'. For these reasons, I cannot say much more about the role of UK legal advisers in targeting operations other than to say it is an area that requires much more research.

* * *

While President Assad of the Syrian Arab Republic may make the occasional gesture to international law and the laws of war, it is hard to imagine Syrian

[19] Simon Tate, *A Special Relationship?: British Foreign Policy in the Era of American Hegemony* (Manchester: Manchester University Press, 2012).

[20] Attorney General's Office and Jeremy Wright, 'Attorney General's Speech at the International Institute for Strategic Studies', 2.

[21] Ibid., 17. For a forensic account of how the United States and the United Kingdom are furthering the war on terror through international law see: Victor Kattan, 'Furthering the "War on Terrorism" through International Law: How the United States and the United Kingdom Resurrected the Bush Doctrine on Using Preventive Military Force to Combat Terrorism', *Journal on the Use of Force and International Law* 5, no. 1 (2017): 97–144.

[22] The Legal Branch is also commonly referred to as the Directorate of Legal Services.

[23] Email correspondence with Air Commadore Alison Mardell, 9 June 2014.

war lawyers carefully sifting through target folders and signing off on airstrikes before the Syrian Air Forces unleash barrel bombs, missiles, and chemical weapons over residential areas in Syrian cities. I say this is hard to imagine because so much of the killing and destruction seems to have been wilfully indiscriminate,[24] and also because if the Syrian Air Force were closely guided by war lawyers then we might reasonably expect to have heard something about their legal advice in the defence of Syrian military actions—but we have not. It is striking that the Syrian regime has done so little to frame its war efforts in the language of international law. Syria signed but did not ratify the Rome Statute, which means that the International Criminal Court (ICC) has no independent authority to investigate or prosecute crimes that take place within Syrian territory. That is not to say that Syria's is an entirely lawless war; technically there is no such thing. The UN Security Council does have power to refer jurisdiction to the ICC but, as Ben Taub puts it, 'international criminal justice is a relatively new and fragile endeavor, and, to a disturbing extent, its application is contingent on geopolitics'.[25] In 2014, when a measure to give the ICC jurisdiction in Syria came before the council, Russia and China blocked it.

Bilateral Apologetics

Beyond the tentative comparisons drawn above I am reluctant to make any observations about the generalizability of the US–Israel approach and the extent to which law and war lawyers may or may not guide targeting by other militaries or in other locations. In an international context where war is generally becoming more juridical, not all states—and certainly not non-state actors—are going to the same efforts to ensure that their methods and means of aerial warfare are subject to legal review. There is much legal space between the extremes of the US–Israeli approach, which involves careful consideration and crafting of the laws of war, and a Syrian approach which seemingly disregards

[24] According to Ben Taub: '[S]ince 2011, not a minute has passed in which the Syrian government has not been committing multiple, simultaneous, widespread war crimes and crimes against humanity. The body of court-ready evidence against top officials within the Syrian government is more complete and damning than any that has ever previously been collected during an active conflict. [. . .] The most incriminating evidence was produced by the regime's own immense bureaucracy. Military police officers have systematically processed and photographed the emaciated corpses of thousands of detainees who were tortured to death by security and intelligence agents; more than fifty thousand of these images are currently in the possession of international lawyers and forensic investigators.' Ben Taub, 'Does Anyone in Syria Fear International Law?', *The New Yorker*, 31 August 2016, https://www.newyorker.com/news/news-desk/does-anyone-in-syria-fear-international-law, accessed 7 September 2017.

[25] Ibid.

them altogether. I suspect it is somewhere between these extremes that most actors in contemporary aerial warfare actors choose to operate.

What we can say with some confidence is that with the retreat of multilaterlism (or at least its promise) new generations of partnerships spanning law-governed, authoritarian and hybrid regimes have emerged[26] and, just as during the Cold War and post-Cold War (see Chapter 3 on Gulf War forces' rules of engagement in Saudi Arabia) this will continue to condition and sometimes complicate the juridification process. Two illustrative examples are offered: Russia's involvement in Syria and Saudi Arabia's war in Yemen.

Russia as patron, which has been providing extensive military support—and predominantly air power—to Assad's forces since September 2015, presents a slightly more complicated picture than its client. Russia has insisted that its actions in Syria comport with international law and, moreover, that their rationale for its intense airstrikes in Syria is 'basically the same' as US rationale.[27] Russia initially claimed to be targeting Islamic State targets (hence the similarity to US involvement in Syria) but it soon became clear that rebel-held areas of Syria were its main focus. In addition to tracking US-led coalition airstrikes in Iraq and Syria, Airwars (an NGO, see section 5.7) also monitors Russian airstrikes in Syria. Airwars reports that more than 39,000 airstrikes took place in the first three years of fighting and estimates that Russian military action has caused between 3,736 and 5,510 civilian deaths.[28] Russia, however, maintains that no civilians have been harmed in its strikes.[29] While clearly implausible, Russia's unwillingness to consider or acknowledge the civilian impact of its airstrikes in Syria parallels claims made by the United Kingdom and France about the extremely low levels of civilian casualties resulting from their own operations. As part of the Operation Inherent Resolve (OIR) coalition war in Syria and Iraq, the United Kingdom and France—'responsible for perhaps one in seven of all air and artillery strikes between them during the war' according to Chris Woods of Airwars, 'have admitted just one death between them' (see Chapter 5).[30]

In October 2019 a *New York Times* investigation found that the Russian Air Force 'has repeatedly bombed hospitals in Syria in order to crush the last pockets

[26] We need not of course commit ourselves to cut-and-dried definitions along this spectrum (unlike some of the literature that cheered on globalism in the post-Cold War).

[27] Somini Sengupta, 'Russian Foreign Minister Defends Airstrikes in Syria', *The New York Times*, 1 October 2015, sec. World, https://www.nytimes.com/2015/10/02/world/europe/russia-airstrikes-syria-assad.html, accessed 11 March 2020.

[28] Estimates to 28 February 2018: Airwars, 'Russian Military in Syria', 11 March 2020, https://airwars.org/conflict/russian-military-in-syria/, accessed 11 March 2020.

[29] Ibid.

[30] Email correspondence with Chris Woods, 14 February 2020 (on file with author).

of resistance' to the Syrian regime.[31] In response, a Foreign Ministry spokesman pointed to previous statements made by the Russian government that the Russian Air Force carries out precision strikes only on 'accurately researched targets'.[32] Days later President Vladimir Putin ordered Russia's withdrawal from Additional Protocol 1 to the Geneva Conventions: the protocol related to the protection of victims of international armed conflicts and an associated commission set up to investigate potential war crimes against civilians. 'In the current international environment, the risks of abuse of the commission's powers for political purposes on the part of unscrupulous states are increasing significantly', Putin said at the time.[33] Nevertheless, in March 2020 a United Nations Independent International Commission of Inquiry found that the Russian Air Force was responsible for 'the war crime of launching indiscriminate attacks in civilian areas' in the Idlib region of north-western Syria.[34] Slowly but surely, Russia's involvement in Syria has become framed perhaps not so much by the intimate forms of legal advice that US and Israeli war lawyers provide but by broad geolegal moves designed to shift the debate away from accusations of illegality and into familiar post-Cold War geopolitical tropes. It is perhaps little wonder then that Russia has responded to international allegations partly also by making its own allegations against 'indiscriminate' US airstrikes in Syria.[35]

* * *

In March 2015, a multinational coalition led by Saudi Arabia and backed by support from the United States and the United Kingdom launched 'Operation Decisive Storm' on the territory of the Republic of Yemen.[36] The bombing

[31] Evan Hill and Christiaan Triebert, '12 Hours. 4 Syrian Hospitals Bombed. One Culprit: Russia', *The New York Times*, 13 October 2019, sec. World, https://www.nytimes.com/2019/10/13/world/middleeast/russia-bombing-syrian-hospitals.html, accessed 11 March 2020.

[32] Quoted in: Ibid.

[33] Quoted in: Henry Foy and Chloe Cornish, 'Russia Guilty of War Crimes against Civilians in Syria', 2 March 2020, https://www.ft.com/content/085e94b0-5cac-11ea-8033-fa40a0d65a98, accessed 11 March 2020.

[34] Quoted in: Nick Cumming-Bruce, 'U.N. Panel Says Russia Bombed Syrian Civilian Targets, a War Crime', *The New York Times*, 2 March 2020, sec. World. https://www.nytimes.com/2020/03/02/world/middleeast/united-nations-syria-idlib-russia.html, accessed 1 July 2020.

[35] Al Jazeera, 'Russia Slams US for "indiscriminate" Attack in Syria's Idlib', *Al Jazeera News*, 1 September 2019, https://www.aljazeera.com/news/2019/09/russia-slams-indiscriminate-attack-syria-idlib-190901111704884.html, accessed 11 March 2020.

[36] Arron Merat, '"The Saudis Couldn't Do It without Us": The UK's True Role in Yemen's Deadly War', *The Guardian*, 18 June 2019, sec. World, https://www.theguardian.com/world/2019/jun/18/the-saudis-couldnt-do-it-without-us-the-uks-true-role-in-yemens-deadly-war, accessed 7 November 2019; Samuel Oakford, 'The U.S. Military Can't Keep Track of Which Missions It's Fueling in Yemen War', *The Intercept*, 18 September 2017, https://theintercept.com/2017/09/18/the-u-s-military-cant-keep-track-of-which-missions-its-fueling-in-yemen-war/, accessed 7 November 2019; Declan Walsh, 'Saudi

continues today and at the time of writing (March 2020) the coalition has launched over 20,000 air raids, killing nearly 9,000 civilians and injuring nearly 10,000 more.[37] In January 2016, the UK Ministry of Defence (MOD) confirmed that British forces were in Saudi Arabia to provide training and advice 'on best practice targeting techniques to help ensure continued compliance with international humanitarian law', but said they did not have an 'operational role'.[38] Adel al-Jubeir, Saudi Arabia's Foreign Minister, added that a host of foreign officials are routinely posted to the airbase at Khamis Mushayt, Saudi Arabia's 'CAOC'. 'We have British officials and American officials and officials from other countries in our command and control centre. They know what the target list is and they have a sense of what it is that we are doing and what we are not doing', he told journalists in London after meeting British ministers and US Secretary of State John Kerry.[39]

Much of the attention on the Saudi relationship with the United States and the United Kingdom has focused on the questionable lawfulness of supplying the Kingdom with US and British made weapons, and for good reason. *The Guardian's* Arron Merat has pointed out: 'The Saudis couldn't do it without us'. [40] The United Kingdom has defended its arms sales to Saudi Arabia by citing 'extensive UK training' provided by the MOD to the Royal Saudi Air Force, 'including training on targeting and IHL [International Humanitarian Law] compliance'.[41] But as we saw in Chapters 5 and 6, aerial warfare increasingly relies not just on weapons but weapons *systems*, that is, not just on the missiles and bombs, but the vast technological, cultural, and legal apparatus that makes using them possible. The United States and the United Kingdom not only sell weapons to Saudi Arabia, they also sell the very social relations, objects, and assemblages that surround the preparation and conclusion of each warhead: spare parts, knowledge, expertise, training, loading equipment, bomb

Warplanes, Most Made in America, Still Bomb Civilians in Yemen', *The New York Times*, 22 May 2019, sec. World, https://www.nytimes.com/2019/05/22/world/middleeast/saudi-yemen-airstrikes-civilians.html, accessed 7 November 2019.

[37] Yemen Data Project, 'Yemen Data Project', 29 February 2020, https://www.yemendataproject.org/, accessed 29 February 2020.

[38] MOD spokeswoman, quoted in: Emma Graham-Harrison, 'British and US Military "in Command Room" for Saudi Strikes on Yemen', *The Guardian*, 15 January 2016, sec. World, https://www.theguardian.com/world/2016/jan/15/british-us-military-in-command-room-saudi-strikes-yemen, accessed 7 November 2019.

[39] Quoted in: Ibid.

[40] Merat, '"The Saudis Couldn't Do It without Us"'.

[41] MOD spokeswoman, quoted in: Graham-Harrison, 'British and US Military "in Command Room" for Saudi Strikes on Yemen'.

damage assessment methodologies, thousands of engineers, technicians, and other specialists. Merat explains:

> Once these weapons arrive in Saudi Arabia, Britain's involvement is far from over. The Saudi military lacks the expertise to use these weapons to fight a sustained air war—so BAE [British Aerospace Engineering], under another contract to the UK government, provides what are known as 'in-country' services. In practice, this means that around 6,300 British contractors are stationed at forward operating bases in Saudi Arabia. There, they train Saudi pilots and conduct essential maintenance night and day on planes worn out from flying thousands of miles across the Saudi desert to their targets in Yemen. They also supervise Saudi soldiers to load bombs on to planes and set their fuses for their intended targets.[42]

Around eighty serving RAF personnel work inside Saudi Arabia. Sometimes they work for BAE to assist in maintaining and preparing aircraft. At other times they work as auditors to ensure that BAE is fulfilling its Ministry of Defence contracts. Additional RAF 'liaison officers' work inside the command and control centre, from where targets in Yemen are selected.[43]

Less commented on are the mechanisms through which the UK Government supposedly ensures that the weapons it sells are used by Saudi in accordance with the laws of war. This became the key issue in a legal challenge launched against the UK Government by the group Campaign Against Arms Trade (CAAT) in 2016. In his open witness statement defendant Peter Watkins, Director General Security Policy at the Ministry of Defence, disclosed that the United Kingdom had been assisting Saudi with laws of war training and legal compliance, in part by involving UK military lawyers:

> The Saudis have always been receptive to UK offers to provide training and advice to help them improve their processes and they have changed their approach. Examples include: sending more personnel on targeting training; being more transparent with NGOs and hosting visits; establishing the investigations committee using UK-provided advice on standards; and preparing investigation reports with the intent of publicly identifying lessons. *They have accepted offers to help train their legal advisors and allowed legal advisors to visit from the UK.* They have allowed UK liaison officers access to their

42 Merat, '"The Saudis Couldn't Do It without Us"'.
43 Ibid.

> systems from the start of the campaign, reflecting the confidence developed through our longstanding relationship.[44]
>
> The UK has provided training to the Royal Saudi Air Force both in the UK and in Saudi Arabia. In the context of their air operations this has included training in the use of specific precision guided munitions, such as Paveway IV and Storm Shadow, and aircraft. In addition, the RAF have provided four International Targeting courses for Royal Saudi Air Force pilots, analysts and other personnel involved in targeting, to improve their targeting processes and support IHL compliance. The three-week long courses included introductions to Targeting, the Law of Armed Conflict, Collateral Damage Estimation, Battle Damage Assessment (BDA) and exercises to test their learning. [. . .] And the RAF have arranged training for Saudi legal advisors and for the membership of the CIAC [Coalition Incident Assessment Committee].[45]

But these assurances did little to satisfy the UK Court of Appeal which ruled in June 2019 that British arms sales to Saudi were unlawful. The ruling found that Boris Johnson, Jeremy Hunt, Liam Fox, and other key ministers had illegally signed off on arms exports without properly assessing the risk to civilians. Sir Terence Etherton, the Master of the Rolls, said that ministers had 'made no concluded assessments of whether the Saudi-led coalition had committed violations of international humanitarian law in the past, during the Yemen conflict, and made no attempt to do so'.[46]

Whatever the legality of the Saudi-led coalition air war in Yemen, the above account shows that Saudi Arabia is becoming increasingly attentive to the laws of war. To this end, they are receiving training in the laws of war involving legal advisers from the United Kingdom. We have very little sense of what it all looks like in practice because Saudi Arabia, like the United Kingdom and many NATO members are even less transparent than the United States and Israel on matters of targeting. Nevertheless, the Saudi approach to targeting is serving as a sort of extension to the US–Israel–UK approach, strengthening it in some areas and perhaps undermining it in others. We might not be able to make

[44] Campaign Against Arms Trade and The Secretary of State for International Trade. Judicial review. Witness Statement of Peter Watkins on Behalf of the Defendant', Pub. L. No. Claim No: C0/1306/2016, 1 (2016), ¶79, https://www.caat.org.uk/resources/countries/saudi-arabia/legal-2016/watkins-statement-1.pdf, accessed 7 November 2019 (emphasis added).

[45] Ibid., ¶34.

[46] Quoted in: Dan Sabbagh and Bethan McKernan, 'UK Arms Sales to Saudi Arabia Unlawful, Court of Appeal Declares', *The Guardian*, 20 June 2019, sec. Law, https://www.theguardian.com/law/2019/jun/20/uk-arms-sales-to-saudi-arabia-for-use-in-yemen-declared-unlawful, accessed 7 November 2019.

generalizations far beyond the United States and Israel, but it seems that some of their key allies will continue to turn towards law and lawyers both to justify and to govern their lethal air operations.

Lawfare

Having tentatively sketched out of some of the broader international context, I want to return to the United States and Israel and spend the rest of this closing chapter reflecting on juridification's 'high-water mark', as it were: lawfare. I want to suggest that prevailing accounts of what has been called 'lawfare' assert rather than explain the juridical turn in later modern war and in so doing, have become overly reactive and even hostile to invocations of law that in any way diverge from US and Israeli interpretations. The argument has three parts. First, I show how discourses of lawfare work to marginalize both human rights and other 'enemy' invocations of law. Second, I show how lawfare works to expunge violence from 'Western' military invocations of law, thus legitimizing the use of lawfare by the United States, Israel, and their allies. Third, I suggest that although lawfare signals the loss of the monopoly of the 'right' of state militaries to dominate legal interpretations of permissible violence, for anyone who chooses to speak in the vernacular of international law it poses obstacles as well as opportunities.

From criticism to co-option

Two months after the fateful events of 9/11, Major General Charles Dunlap, the two-star US Air Force JAG whose presence has flickered in and out of the preceding pages, delivered a presentation in Washington, DC sponsored by Harvard's Carr Center for Human Rights. In this presentation, which was subsequently published online, Dunlap used the word 'lawfare' to describe 'a method of warfare where law is used as a means of realizing a military objective'.[47] The term had been used before, coined by two Chinese People's Liberation Army officers just two years earlier. But Dunlap popularized the term and expanded it into a language that was instantly understood by hawkish

[47] Charles Dunlap, 'Law and Military Interventions: Preserving Humanitarian Values in 21st Century Conflicts', in *Conference on Humanitarian Challenges in Military Intervention* (online), Washington, DC: Carr Center for Human Rights Policy, Kennedy School of Government, Harvard University, November, 29: 11. Washington, DC, 2001.

policy makers, legal scholars, and right-wing activists in the United States and Israel.[48]

Initially for Dunlap, lawfare was simply 'the use of law as a weapon of war',[49] imbued with negative connotations and attributed to the United States' enemies. Lawfare, he said, was the 'cynical manipulation of the rule of law' by 'U.S. opponents'.[50] He warned that in the era of lawfare:

> Rather than seeking battlefield victories, *per se*, challengers try to destroy the will to fight by undermining the public support that is indispensable when democracies like the U.S. conduct military interventions. A principle way of bringing about that end is to make it appear that the U.S. is waging war in violation of the letter or spirit of LOAC [the laws of armed conflict].[51]

Dunlap's Clausewitzian gloss of 'lawfare' spread quickly, and within a few years there was a burgeoning literature on the subject.[52] Subsequent commentators adopted Dunlap's negative characterization of lawfare and began to enumerate the subterfuge legal tactics used by US enemies.[53] For example, according to more than one commentator, the 'real' legal abuses that took place at Guantanamo Bay were not US practices of extradition, torture, and indefinite detention (which to their credit, the war lawyer community opposed) but instead the defence by human rights lawyers of the 'detainees' imprisoned there.[54] As practices of US detention gave way to a rapidly expanding US (and Israeli) targeted killing policy, the charge of lawfare was increasingly levied against

[48] Qiao Liang and Wang Xiangsui, *Unrestricted Warfare* (Beijing: PLA Literature and Arts Publishing House, 1999). Two decades later the literature and on lawfare remains overwhelmingly dominated by US and Israeli commentators, though more critical accounts from outside these places began to emerge in the early 2010s. For an overview, see: Craig Jones, 'Lawfare and the Juridification of Late Modern War', *Progress in Human Geography* 40, no. 2 (2016): 221–39.

[49] Dunlap, 'Law and Military Interventions', 5.

[50] Ibid., 11.

[51] Ibid.

[52] Dunlap's concept of lawfare is Clausewitzian in the sense that the military theorist Carl von Clausewitz insisted that war is fought over a wide terrain of activities not immediately and obviously associated with the conduct of war.

[53] For a discussion of these early complaints, see: Neve Gordon, 'Human Rights as a Security Threat: Lawfare and the Campaign against Human Rights NGOs', *Law & Society Review* 48, no. 2 (2014): 311–44.

[54] In this formulation, human rights lawyers and the human rights community at large are equated with the tactics of terror. To defend a detainee or to insist that detainees are given certain rights is seen as taking sides with the enemy. Lebowitz argues that detainees at Guantanamo constructed a 'mistreatment narrative' that they used 'as ammunition for waging tactical law-fare': Michael J. Lebowitz, 'The Value of Claiming Torture: An Analysis of Al-Qaeda's Tactical Lawfare Strategy and Efforts to Fight Back', *Case Western Reserve Journal of International Law* 43, no. 1 (2010): 361. For a critical account of how US government policies have made it more difficult for lawyers to provide legal representation to Guantanamo prisoners see: David Luban, 'Lawfare and Legal Ethics in Guantanamo', *Stanford Law Review* 60, no. 6 (2008): 1981–2026.

those seeking to challenge the policy's legality (which, plaintiffs said, amount to 'extrajudicial assassination').[55] These attempts to achieve legal remedy—and perhaps some measure of justice—for an increasing number of victims of drone warfare were dismissed as an illegitimate use of law in general and an unwelcome appeal to the norms and language of International Human Rights Law (IHRL) specifically.[56] By 2005, following several legal challenges emanating in one way or another from the 'war on terror', the annual US National Defense Strategy expressed grave concern over the use of courts and other legal instruments against the United States, asserting in no uncertain terms: 'our strength as a nation will continue to be challenged by those who employ a strategy of the weak using international fora, judicial processes, and terrorism.'[57]

As lawfare gained currency in the 2000s it became useful to those wishing to defend Israel's increasingly belligerent policies towards Palestine and, especially, the aerial assaults on Gaza (Chapter 4).[58] Perhaps most prominently, commentators focused on the UN investigation into war crimes committed by Israel and Hamas during the 2008–2009 'Operation Cast-Lead'. Dubbed the 'Goldstone Report', after its author Richard Goldstone (a former prosecutor at the UN International Criminal Tribunal for the former Yugoslavia and Rwanda), it was a damning condemnation of both Israeli *and* Hamas actions during the three-week war. But for some legal scholars, among others, Goldstone became a powerful symbol of what they characterized as illegitimate lawfare and the dangers it represented to states like Israel.[59] Legal scholar Orde Kittrie goes so far as to describe Palestine-Israel as 'the closest thing the world has to a lawfare laboratory'.[60] This tendency reached fever pitch in 2010 when,

[55] Both the US and Israeli targeted killing policies have had several legal petitions against them. See: Lisa Hajjar, 'Lawfare and Armed Conflict: A Comparative Analysis of Israeli and U.S. Targeted Killing Policies and Legal Challenges against Them', in *Life in the Age of Drone Warfare*, ed. Lisa Parks and Caren Kaplan (Durham, NC: Duke University Press Books, 2017), 59–88.

[56] e.g. Michael A. Newton, 'Illustrating Illegitimate Lawfare', *Case Western Reserve Journal of International Law* 43, no. 1 (2010): 255–78; Daniel Reisner, 'Reflections on the UN Commission of Inquiry Gaza Report, Part III: The Clash Between Human Rights and Law of War Specialists', *Lawfare* (blog), 1 September 2015, https://www.lawfareblog.com/reflections-un-commission-inquiry-gaza-report-part-iii-clash-between-human-rights-and-law-war, accessed 24 September 2016.

[57] United States Department of Defense. 'The National Defense Strategy of the United States of America' (Washington, DC: United States Department of Defense, 2005), 5, https://history.defense.gov/Historical-Sources/National-Defense-Strategy/, accessed 30 December 2013.

[58] e.g. William A. Schabas, 'Gaza, Goldstone, and Lawfare', *Case Western Reserve Journal of International Law* 43, no. 1 (2010): 307–12; Newton, 'Illustrating Illegitimate Lawfare'.

[59] Laurie R. Blank, 'A New Twist on an Old Story: Lawfare and the Mixing of Proportionalities', *Case Western Reserve Journal of International Law* 43, no. 3 (2011): 707–38; Laurie R. Blank, 'Finding Facts But Missing the Law: The Goldstone Report, Gaza and Lawfare', *Case Western Reserve Journal of International Law* 43, no. 1 (2011): 279–305; Laurie R. Blank, 'The Application of IHL in the Goldstone Report: A Critical Commentary', *Yearbook of International Humanitarian Law* 12 (2009): 347–402; Newton, 'Illustrating Illegitimate Lawfare'.

[60] Orde F. Kittrie, *Lawfare: Law as a Weapon of War* (New York, NY: Oxford University Press, 2015), 197.

as I noted in Chapter 4, Israeli Military Advocate General Avichai Mandelblit met with US Ambassador James B. Cunningham and advised him that the Palestinian Authority's 'pursuit of Israel through the ICC [International Criminal Court] would be viewed as war by the GOI [Government of Israel]'.[61] In that same year Prime Minister Binyamin Netanyahu told the press that Goldstone is a 'code word for an attempt to delegitimize Israel's right to self-defense'.[62] Echoing the sentiment of the 2005 US National Defense Strategy, Netanyahu listed Goldstone as 'one of Israel's most serious security challenges', alongside Iran's nuclear program and Hamas rocket fire.[63]

In recent years several neo-conservative think tanks have painted a similar picture of lawfare-as-threat.[64] The Lawfare Project, for example, acts as a 'safeguard against the abuse of the law as a weapon of war', according to its website. It defines lawfare as 'the abuse of Western laws and judicial systems to achieve strategic military or political ends'. The qualification of lawfare as something that is done to '*Western*' legal systems is highly significant and, as The Lawfare Project insists, lawfare: '[M]ust be defined as a negative phenomenon to have any real meaning. Otherwise, we risk diluting the threat and feeding the inability to distinguish between that which is the correct application of the law, on the one hand, and that which is lawfare, on the other.'[65]

Lawfare was nearly condemned entirely to the space of enemy territory but then came a new twist on an old story. Dunlap came to the realization that Western militaries, too, could 'do' lawfare. In 2009 he re-evaluated his initial position: 'lawfare is more than just something adversaries seek to use against law-abiding societies; it is a resource that democratic militaries can—and should—employ affirmatively'.[66] In this new formulation lawfare loses its once pejorative and partisan meaning, and the threat is turned into an opportunity for 'democratic militaries'. Others soon joined Dunlap in his reassessment. Kittre argued that the United States should embrace lawfare because it would

[61] Wikileaks. 'IDF MAG Mandelblit on IDF Investigations into Operation Cast Lead', Telegram (cable), American Embassy Tel Aviv to Secretary of State, Washington, DC, 23 February 2010, https://wikileaks.org/plusd/cables/10TELAVIV417_a.html, accessed 7 January 2017.

[62] Quoted in: Nelson, 'Goldstone Report Keeps Israel on Tenterhooks—The National', *The National*, 29 January 2010, http://www.thenational.ae/news/world/middle-east/goldstone-report-keeps-israel-on-tenterhooks, accessed 4 September 2013.

[63] Quoted in: ibid.

[64] See: Gordon, 'Human Rights as a Security Threat'.

[65] An updated version of the website uses slightly different wording: 'Lawfare is inherently negative. It is not a good thing. It is the opposite of pursuing justice. It is filing frivolous lawsuits and misusing legal processes to intimidate and frustrate opponents in the theatre of war': The Lawfare Project, 'What Is Lawfare?', *The Lawfare Project* (blog), n.d., http://thelawfareproject.org/lawfare/what-is-lawfare-1/, accessed 22 September 2016.

[66] Charles Dunlap, 'Lawfare: A Decisive Element of 21st Century Conflicts?', *Joint Forces Quarterly* 54, no. 3 (2009): 34–9.

help achieve 'some U.S. national security objectives with less or no kinetic warfare, thereby saving [. . .] some U.S. and foreign lives'.[67] Shane Bilsborough praised Dunlap's new 'austere' definition of lawfare, which he believed promised 'a wider and more flexible scope than definitions which construct "lawfare" as a purely insurgent strategy'. Crucially for Bilsborough, this wider definition 'allows for the possibility of state actors developing effective lawfare strategies of their own'.[68] '[R]ather than abandoning the legal battlespace to asymmetric opponents' he goes on, 'modern militaries should seek to map the contours of international law (particularly the law of armed conflict) and structure their operations accordingly'.[69]

Lawfare as an alternative to violence

These 'positive' invocations of lawfare came with a crucial set of differences to the lawfare allegedly practised by the enemy Other. Usefully summarizing a burgeoning literature, Freya Irani has pointed out 'non-Western invocations of law are represented as violent martial technologies' whereas what she calls 'liberal' invocations of law are mobilized as an *alternative* to violence. [70] I would add that it is not only 'non-Western' invocations of law that are represented as violent but also those of human rights groups who defend victims of armed conflict or otherwise oppose 'Western' military operations using juridical tools.[71] The crucial point, though, is that those who now advocate for lawfare from this liberal (*qua* 'Western', 'modern', 'democratic') position see law not as *intrinsically* violent but as potentially violent when 'misused' by the Other—be that actual insurgents or defenders of human rights. Irani succinctly captures the discursive strategies at play:

> For Western states [. . .] law is cast as the preference, precisely because it allows for the avoidance or reduction of violence. For non-Westerners, on the other hand, violence is cast as the preference: law is a second-choice, brought on by the necessity of perceived inferiority in conventional warfare. It should

[67] Kittrie, *Lawfare*, 343.

[68] Shane Bilsborough, 'Counterlawfare in Counterinsurgency', Small Wars Journal, 14 December 2011, http://smallwarsjournal.com/jrnl/art/counterlawfare-in-counterinsurgency, accessed 10 September 2013.

[69] Ibid.

[70] Freya Irani, '"Lawfare", US Military Discourse, and the Colonial Constitution of Law and War'. *European Journal of International Security* 3, no. 1 (2018): 118.

[71] Gordon, 'Human Rights as a Security Threat'.

be noted, however, that in both cases, lawful and violent or forceful means are cast as distinct, as alternatives.[72]

At the heart of these conceptualizations of lawfare are a series of value-laden claims about the distinctions between law and politics and law and violence, and between those who have the right to use law and inhabit juridical space and those who do not. Above all else, as Irani insists, these are civilizational tropes that draw a line between 'us', democratic states and Western militaries, and 'them', the various enemies who dare to confront 'our' military power. These discourses are, of course, hardly new. Postcolonial scholars have powerfully shown that international law in general, and the laws of war specifically have their roots in the colonial encounter and are fundamentally structured by civilizational discourses.[73] As Helen M. Kinsella has argued, '[W]e have yet to reject the fundamental distinction of barbarism and civilization that informs the laws of war and still takes its referent from Europe.'[74] In what could easily be a riposte to military conceptions to lawfare today Kinsella further points out: '[T]he empire constructs the laws of war [. . .] and the barbarians are held to be (always already) in violation, regardless of actual practice.'[75]

As will by now be clear, this book has offered its own riposte to military conceptions of lawfare. I have refused the distinction between law and politics, and law and violence, and instead gathered and evaluated testimony from the coalface of law–violence–politics: the kill chain as actually practiced. Indeed, one of my central claims has been that 'our' use of law—from policy and national-level interpretations of our rights and obligations under international law, to their operationalization, to rules of engagement—does not generally proffer an *alternative* to military violence. In fact, the prosecution of US and Israeli warfare especially over the last thirty years suggests that the law is also a *medium* of violence and that a certain form of judicial violence has played no small part in enabling, legitimizing, and in some cases, even extending military violence.

[72] Irani, '"Lawfare", US Military Discourse, and the Colonial Constitution of Law and War', 128.

[73] Antony Anghie, *Imperialism, Sovereignty and the Making of International Law* (Cambridge: Cambridge University Press, 2007); Tarak Barkawi, 'Decolonising War', *European Journal of International Security* 1, no. 2 (2016): 199–214; Helen M. Kinsella, *The Image Before the Weapon: A Critical History of the Distinction Between Combatant and Civilian* (Ithaca, NY: Cornell University Press, 2011); Frédéric Mégret, 'From "Savages" to "Unlawful Combatants": A Postcolonial Look at International Humanitarian Law's Other', in *International Law and Its Others*, ed. Anne Orford (Cambridge: Cambridge University Press, 2006), 265–317; Anne Orford, *International Law and Its Others* (Cambridge: Cambridge University Press, 2006).

[74] Kinsella, *The Image Before the Weapon*, 110.

[75] Ibid., 107.

Lawfare's lost monopolies

Others are more optimistic. From human rights organizations to legal scholars, a wide-range of actors have welcomed the advent of lawfare as the apotheosis of a decades-long struggle to have *their* voices heard and *their* interpretations of international law become part of global conversations about right and wrong in war. For this camp of opinion, lawfare is proof that states and their militaries have lost their monopoly on the 'right' to determine the legal regimes that govern war and, crucially, which legal regimes apply. More directly, for others, lawfare is a key means to challenge state illegalities through litigation and other formal legal avenues.[76] The rise of global human rights discourse is a salient theme across these perspectives; with the unassailable new prominence of International Human Rights Law and International Criminal Law (ICL) in the international arena being celebrated in particular.

In 2000, Theodor Meron, a luminary figure in the field of international law, published a landmark paper titled *The Humanization of Humanitarian Law.*[77] In it, he argued that in the late twentieth century International Humanitarian Law (IHL) acquired a 'more humane face' driven to a large extent by 'human rights and the principles of humanity'.[78] Meron provided a wide-ranging and compelling account of the several and significant ways in which humanitarian law has become more virtuous, shifting the balance of war's violence away from indiscriminate attacks, arbitrary killings, reprisals, and crimes against humanity, towards individual and inalienable rights, repatriation (of prisoners of war), protection, and reciprocity.[79] These arguments help to take stock of what humanitarian principles have achieved and, in some cases, how

[76] Lisa Hajjar, 'In Defense of Lawfare: The Value of Litigation in Challenging Torture', in *Confronting Torture: Essays on the Ethics, Legality, History, and Psychology of Torture Today*, ed. Scott Anderson and Martha Nussbaum (Chicago; London: University of Chicago Press, 2018), 319. (Arguing: 'Ultimately, lawfare has aimed to close the gap between "law in the books" and "law in action" by pressing for law enforcement through litigation.')

[77] Meron, 'The Humanization of Humanitarian Law', 239. In addition to being a leading scholar in the field of international law Meron was also Judge of the Appeals Chambers of the International Criminal Tribunal for the Former Yugoslavia (ICTY) and the International Criminal Tribunal for Rwanda (ICTR) and also served four terms as President of the ICTY.

[78] Meron is careful to signal that human rights and the principles of humanity are not the only—or even the predominant—factor driving the humanization of the laws of war: 'By focusing on developments driven by human rights and principles of humanity, I do not suggest that these principles are other than a part of the many factors that interact and compete in the formation of legal norms. Humanitarian concerns have played an important role in triggering the negotiation of treaties prohibiting the use of certain weapons, as well as arms control treaties, but strategic considerations—such as fear of proliferation, the need or lack of need for specific weapons, and the difficulty of effective defense—have played the primary role': Ibid.

[79] Ibid., 242–73. Meron later expanded his arguments into a monograph: Theodor Meron, *The Humanization of International Law* (Boston, MA: Martinus Nijhoff, 2006).

far international humanitarian law progressed from the dark days of the World Wars. Meron was realistic about what he called the 'inherent limitations to the process of humanization'[80] but, importantly, he saw non-compliance (with humanitarian law rules) as the greatest threat to progress.[81] This is significant because in focusing on the issue of non-compliance, Meron shifts attention away from the rules and the power relations that make such rules possible. Debate is telescoped and tamed into a series of conversations about who does and who does not—who, *structurally*, can and cannot—observe the rules. This is problematic because it assumes those rules are static, determinate, and universally agreed upon and as a result (in concert with enlightened self-interest), a universal force for good. In providing counter-examples for each of these assumptions, the foregoing chapters have argued something approaching the opposite.

Meron is not alone in celebrating the rising tide of humanitarian law and human rights. Legal scholar Amanda Alexander has argued that a 'truly international humanitarian law, a law in which considerations of humanity trumped military necessity' began to emerge in the 1970s (with the signing of the Additional Protocols to the Geneva Conventions in 1977) but came fully into its own in the 1990s.[82] The hallmark of this humanization, according to Alexander, is the general acceptance by states and militaries of the more humanitarian principles inscribed in the laws of war. On this theory, the 1990s marks the passing of a historic shift away from military necessity and the exigencies of armed conflict towards a more benign legal regime of war where considerations of humanity and the responsibility to protect civilians are given precedence.[83] As an example, Alexander cites the Kosovo intervention in 1998–1999, where military necessity was 'barely mentioned,' and claims that the Gulf War was fought with 'respect and optimism towards international humanitarian law,' citing as proof the fact that '[w]hen civilians were killed, their deaths were not blamed on the inadequacy of the law but, rather, on the failure of NATO to apply the law properly'.[84] Again, the limits to humanization are framed as an issue of compliance.

[80] Meron, 'The Humanization of Humanitarian Law', 275.

[81] 'More immediate and serious is the decline in observance of the rules. The normative progress in humanization brings into sharp relief the contrast between the normative framework and the harsh, often barbaric reality of the battlefield." Ibid., 276.

[82] Amanda Alexander, 'A Short History of International Humanitarian Law', *European Journal of International Law 26*, no. 1 (2015): 135.

[83] Meron offers a slightly different reading of how humanity is balanced with military necessity. In his account humanity does not trump military necessity but is one of the 'many factors that interact and compete in the formation of legal norms'. He argues that this 'tension' between military necessity and restraint is the 'hallmark' of the laws of war: Meron, 'The Humanization of Humanitarian Law', 239, 243.

[84] Alexander, 'A Short History of International Humanitarian Law', 135.

In another example of how humanity is purportedly winning the battle to define the limits of war, Kenneth Roth (Executive Director of Human Rights Watch) looks back to the early 1980s when humanitarian organizations began to seize legal territory from exclusively military control:

> [U]ntil the time that human rights groups began taking on IHL, militaries loved the fact that this was a special domain. There were only a handful of people in the world who had any idea what this specialized body of law meant and it was very comfortable for militaries because military lawyers interpret IHL in a way that is deferential to the military. [. . .] The military hated this intervention by human rights groups because suddenly they had lost their monopoly over the interpretation of humanitarian law. The military now had to deal with groups that had developed quite a bit of military expertise and which they used through the press to convince the public that the nice comfortable definitions propounded by the military lawyers were not justified. As a result, we now have a much more pluralistic environment in which these terms are interpreted. And that's all to the good in terms of defending human rights in warfare.[85]

The idea of such lost monopolies is a powerful one. Roth speaks of these developments as forms of soft-power whereby once idiosyncratic legal debates now play out among publics and the media too. There is something to this. At the very least it suggests that lawfare commentators are incorrect to dismiss such debates as a politicization of the law; the law is always and already political. For Political Scientist Tanisha Fazal, these developments coincide with hard empirical facts: she has analysed the historical record of the major legal treaties of the laws of war since the mid nineteenth century (including the Hague Conventions, Geneva Conventions and Additional Protocols) and has found that representation of militaries in these law-making efforts have declined while representation from human rights groups have increased.[86] By this view, state militaries have measurably lost out to their non-state counterparts in their bid to shape the laws of war.

[85] Kenneth Roth, quoted in adapted form from: Page Wilson, 'The Myth of International Humanitarian Law', *International Affairs* 93, no. 3 (2017): 575,.

[86] 'The earliest conferences included a fair number of representatives from the military; over time, however, this balance has shifted away from the military—those who must comply with the law, or the "law-takers"—and toward lawyers and representatives of NGOs': Tanisha, M. Fazal, *Wars of Law: Unintended Consequences in the Regulation of Armed Conflict* (Ithaca, NY: Cornell University Press, 2018), 24.

Those who prefer the language of Law of Armed Conflict (to International Humanitarian Law) have sometimes concurred with the 'lost monopolies' idea in order to bemoan it. I have already detailed how dominant framings of lawfare struggled to come to terms with the fact that the enemy Other was apparently wielding law against 'democratic militaries'. One account is particularly striking in its exasperation: that of preeminent Israeli legal scholar Yoram Dinstein in his closing remarks to the US Naval War College conference in 2011 (Dunlap was in the audience). Using all manner of allusions to summon a Manichean world (including private property and corporate governance) Dinstein warned:

> The clear and present danger of the barbarians in front remains unabated. But, in the meantime, another menace has evolved in the back. This menace comes from the human rights zealots and do-goodniks, whom I shall call 'human rights–niks' for short. Far be it from me to suggest that every human rights scholar or activist necessarily comes under this rubric. [. . .] But all too often today we encounter the unpleasant phenomenon of human rights–niks who, hoisting the banner of human rights law, are attempting to bring about a hostile takeover of LOAC. This is an encroachment that we must stoutly resist. [. . .] the danger that the human rights–niks pose is equally acute, since they threaten to pull the legal rug from under our feet. They thus aid and abet the lawfare of the enemy by leaving the civil society with the impression that we are acting (or reacting) in a manner that is incompatible with the loftier aspirations of the law.[87]

Dinstein further instructed his audience to: 'Keep up the good work on the application and interpretation of LOAC' and '[k]eep poachers off the grass'.[88]

Dinstein and others who speak the language of LOAC and military necessity have clearly indicated that they are willing to put up a fight to hold onto a majority-share of the conversation, even if they cannot own it outright.[89]

[87] Yoram Dinstein, 'Concluding Remarks: LOAC and Attempts to Abuse or Subvert It', *International Law Studies* 87, no. 1 (2011): 487.

[88] Ibid., 493.

[89] Kenneth Anderson complains that human rights groups are 'wedded far too much to a procedural preference for the international over the national. [. . . This] agenda increasingly amounts to internationalism for its own sake, and its specific purpose is to constrain American sovereignty.' Kenneth Anderson, 'Who Owns the Rules of War?', *The New York Times*, 13 April 2003, sec. Magazine, https://www.nytimes.com/2003/04/13/magazine/who-owns-the-rules-of-war.html, accessed 22 January 2019. Page Wilson claims: 'IHL is better understood not as a subfield of international law, but as a political project by and for international humanitarian and human rights organizations in support of their own political objectives. It has very little to do with the actually existing legal obligations of individual combatants during hostilities. For that, we still have LOAC/LoW.' Wilson, 'The Myth of International Humanitarian Law', 579.

Militaries have hardly rolled over to humanitarians, and while there are many reasons to celebrate the rise of human rights and concomitant 'humanization' of humanitarian law (as Meron has argued), there are also reasons to think carefully about what is at stake in this transformation—if transformation it is. What has been the real impact upon the conduct of war? On the basis of my own research, I see little reason to expect an 'inevitable' 'humanization' of the laws of war in the future.[90] Far from being the panacea that some humanitarians think it is, a supposed humanization of the laws of war has become part of the problem. This is because it holds out the prospect of 'humanizing' war itself, a project that is fundamentally misconceived.

The Rehabilitation of War—and Antiwar?

For David Kennedy, quoted at the start of this chapter, the principal issue is that as humanitarians and militaries have began to share vocabularies, any sense of responsibility among them has been lost: 'The greatest threat posed by the merger of law and war is loss of the human experience of moral jeopardy in the face of death, mutilation, and all the other horrors of warfare.'[91] Further suggesting that 'modern law has built an elaborate discourse of evasion', he lays the blame on both sides.[92] 'The problem for military professionals', he insists 'is no longer a lack of humanitarian commitment' but, rather, the 'loss of the human experience of responsible freedom and free decision—of discretion to kill and let live'.[93] The way out for them, he suggests is to renew 'a reinvigorated sense of command responsibility, and [refusal] to lighten the decision to kill'.[94] Casting his sights on humanitarians, he suggest that their problem is similarly 'an unwillingness to [advocate] *responsibly*'.[95] Moving forward for them will 'require abandoning the ethical self-confidence of normative denunciation' as well as 'facing squarely the dark sides, risks and costs of what they propose'.[96]

There are at least three problems with Kennedy's 'responsibilization' proposal. First, it is unclear what the source of these new-found ethics and responsibilities would be. Kennedy calls on humanitarian and militaries alike

[90] Vijay M. Padmanabhan, 'Legacy of 9/11: Continuing the Humanization of Humanitarian Law', *Yearbook of International Humanitarian Law* 14 (2011): 429.

[91] David Kennedy, *A World of Struggle: How Power, Law, and Expertise Shape Global Political Economy*, reprint edition (Princeton, NJ; Oxford: Princeton University Press, 2018), 275.

[92] David Kennedy, *Of War and Law* (Princeton, NJ: Princeton University Press, 2006), 169.

[93] Ibid., 170.

[94] Ibid.

[95] Ibid., 169.

[96] Ibid., 169–70.

to 'inhabit our expertise as fighting faith and experience politics as our vocation [. . .] with passion, with proportion, and with responsibility in an irrational world that cannot be known or predicted'.[97] But this is precisely how many actors *already* see themselves, as the interview material informing this book confirms. Second, Kennedy fails to convincingly apportion responsibility (ironically enough) for having reached the current situation. Humanitarians bear perhaps a sizeable responsibility, but it is governments who send their militaries to war and who are the primary duty bearers in many of our available schemes of rights (and it makes little sense to speak of one without the other). If responsibility is to be a new ground for ethics in the age of juridical warfare, that project should begin with the state, and specifically state-sanctioned violence (a point I will return to below).[98]

To his credit, Kennedy is aware that at the global level, states and militaries are in the process of off-loading responsibility onto others. But the third problem with his proposal is that he does not say enough about to whom and what responsibility is being displaced. These might reasonable include but are not limited to: national populations who are asked to fight, once Western troops withdraw (e.g. so-called 'Iraqification'); private corporations;[99] and emergent technologies such drones[100] and algorithms.[101]

Coming closer to the subject of this book, I have demonstrated that the kill chain increasingly displaces responsibility onto the enemy at two key junctures. First, the enemy *collective*—in the sense that civilian casualties are so often chalked up to the fact that enemies use civilians and civilian places as 'human shields' (see Introduction).[102] And, second, it displaces responsibility on to enemy *individuals*

[97] Kennedy, *A World of Struggle*, 278.

[98] Austin Sarat and Nasser Hussain, *When Governments Break the Law* (New York, NY: New York University Press, 2010).

[99] P. W. Singer, *Corporate Warriors: The Rise of the Privatized Military Industry*, Cornell paperbacks edition (Ithaca, NY: Cornell University Press, 2004); Katia Snukal and Emily Gilbert, 'War, Law, Jurisdiction, and Juridical Othering: Private Military Security Contractors and the Nisour Square Massacre', *Environment and Planning D: Society and Space* 33, no. 4 (2015): 660–75.

[100] Grégoire Chamayou, *Drone Theory* (London: Penguin, 2015); Derek Gregory, 'Drone Geographies', *Radical Philosophy* 183 (2014): 7–19; Anna Leander, 'Technological Agency in the Co-Constitution of Legal Expertise and the US Drone Program', *Leiden Journal of International Law* 26, no. 4 (2013): 811–31.

[101] Louise Amoore, 'Algorithmic War: Everyday Geographies of the War on Terror', *Antipode* 41, no. 1 (2009): 49–69; Lauren Wilcox, 'Embodying Algorithmic War: Gender, Race, and the Posthuman in Drone Warfare', *Security Dialogue* 48, no. 1 (2017): 11–28.

[102] For a critique of how militaries use human shielding and even 'hospital shielding' as a pretext for killing civilians and destroying civilian environs, see: Neve Gordon and Nicola Perugini, 'The Politics of Human Shielding: On the Resignification of Space and the Constitution of Civilians as Shields in Liberal Wars', *Environment and Planning D: Society and Space* 34, no. 1 (2016): 168–87; Neve Gordon and Nicola Perugini, *Human Shields: A History of People in the Line of Fire* (Oakland, CA: University of California Press, 2020); Neve Gordon and Nicola Perugini, '"Hospital Shields" and the Limits of International Law', *European Journal of International Law* 30, no. 2 (22 July 2019): 439–63.

in something resembling a criminal paradigm but without even the trappings of due process, *habeas corpus*, or justice. Enemy individuals are held responsible for their participation in hostilities—often defined expansively—and if they can be 'found' they will be 'fixed' and, if necessary, 'finished' in what George W. Bush once called an act of 'sudden justice'[103] (see Chapter 6).

The kill chain also *disperses* responsibility by means of a division of labour—necessary for any functioning bureaucracy—but it does so over an unimaginably large and complicated geography using routinized, numerical shorthands for the weightiest ethical decisions. As I detailed in Chapters 5 and 6 in particular, and borrowing from Zygmunt Bauman and Elke Schwarz, the professionalism and rigour involved is entirely compatible with the *adiaphorization* of killing.[104] This is nothing other than what Kennedy called 'lightening the decision to kill'. (It is not inconceivable that the legal 'scrubbing' of targets could soon go the way of piloting warplanes and many other skilled but routinized specialisms—automation through artificial intelligence—making decisions still more dispersed, still lighter.[105]) As a former US Air Force military lawyer explained:

> '[T]hat legal advice is being used by military forces and their commanders helps reinforce in the mind of the combatants that what they are doing is the right thing. I do think that has a psychological [impact]. [It is] one of the many psychological factors that needs to be taken into account when commanders are in the complex process of getting human beings prepared to, frankly, kill other human beings in the name of the state.[106]

Another told me:

> '[S]ometimes I feel more like chaplain than a JAG because the questions that commanders are asking us aren't necessarily legal questions: they're looking more for absolution than for legal advice a lot of times.[107]

[103] Christopher Woods, *Sudden Justice: America's Secret Drone Wars* (New York, NY: Oxford University Press, 2015).

[104] Zygmunt Bauman, 'Ethics of Individuals', *The Canadian Journal of Sociology / Cahiers Canadiens de Sociologie* 25, no. 1 (2000): 83–96; Elke Schwarz, 'Prescription Drones: On the Techno-Biopolitical Regimes of Contemporary "Ethical Killing"', *Security Dialogue* 47, no. 1 (2016): 59–75.

[105] '[W]ith the development of AI-infused systems, the military is now on the verge of fielding machines capable of going on the offensive, picking out targets and taking lethal action without direct human input': Zachary Fryer-Biggs, 'Coming Soon to a Battlefield: Robots That Can Kill', *The Atlantic*, 3 September 2019, https://www.theatlantic.com/technology/archive/2019/09/killer-robots-and-new-era-machine-driven-warfare/597130/, accessed 16 March 2020. See also: Arthur Holland Michel, 'The Killer Algorithms Nobody's Talking About', *Foreign Policy* (blog), 20 January 2020, https://foreignpolicy.com/2020/01/20/ai-autonomous-weapons-artificial-intelligence-the-killer-algorithms-nobodys-talking-about/, accessed 16 March 2020.

[106] Dunlap, interview.

[107] Stefano (pseudonym), interview.

Any objections?

I have more sympathy with the thought (if not Kennedy's version of it) that there is some ethical confusion in the ways that military actions are critiqued, both from within and without, and that this confusion is a legacy of juridification. Between the Vietnam War and the period following 9/11 the United States witnessed a significant shift in the way that activists voice their criticisms of war. The legal scholar and historian Samuel Moyn describes this as a shift from what he calls 'antiwar politics to antitorture politics'.[108] What he means by this is that rather than seeking to question and delegitimize war in its entirety, today's campaign movements increasingly focus on opposing specific tactics of war. Comparing Vietnam with the post 9/11 landscape, which witnessed the legalization of torture at the highest levels of the US government, Moyn explains:

> [M]ost attempts to legalize the war in the Vietnam era were focused on its *jus ad bellum* justification in international law rather than the *jus in bello* validity of its means and methods. [. . .] Rules governing the military conflict once it has begun were indeed almost entirely peripheral [. . .][109]
>
> After the Vietnam war, a morally introspective America first turned to human rights; after the Cold War finally ended, it went even further in defining itself in terms of the humanitarian values of international law [. . .][110] Like the culture of human rights as a whole, the post-9/11 focus, which organized moral sentiments and intellectual dissent around the laws of war in general and international law governing the conduct of war in particular, is not a cultural or legal necessity, but a choice made in the face of perceived constraints. Of these, perhaps the most obvious is the disappearance of social mobilization—or its migration from left to right.[111]

Key to the Vietnam antiwar movement was that it was truly antiwar: a 'crystalline moment of insight, in which concerns about how America fought were explicitly linked to what justification it had to fight at all', Moyn writes.[112]

[108] Samuel Moyn, 'From Antiwar Politics to Antitorture Politics', in *Law and War*, ed. Austin Sarat, Lawrence Douglas, and Martha Merrill Umphrey, *The Amherst Series in Law, Jurisprudence, and Social* Thought (Stanford, CA: Stanford University Press, 2014), 154.

[109] Ibid., 156.

[110] Ibid., 183.

[111] Ibid., 157.

[112] Ibid., 155.

Crucially, and again in stark contrast to today: 'Opposition to the war, or moral outrage about its conduct, came in the first instance *not from lawyers or in terms of law* but in ethical frameworks and not infrequently linked to visions of domestic and international transformation.'[113] Legal activism against the Vietnam war did exist,[114] of course, and it coalesced especially around the My Lai massacre (Chapter 1) but as Moyn insists, the activism 'was never separate from explicit concern about the politics of the war itself'.[115] In contrast to the Vietnam War generally and My Lai specifically, Moyn shows how 'Abu Ghraib and Guantanamo became prominent because of their centrality to a mode of attention and dissent that targeted not the *war* itself but *the illegal means of fighting it*'.[116]

Another instance of these political foreclosures is the anti-drone movement, which claims for several reasons that military drones should be outlawed.[117] Groups like the Campaign to Stop Killer Robots do not appear to be against war per se or even against other forms of more conventional aerial violence, at least not explicitly. The unstated assumption is that killing with drones is somehow morally worse than killing with conventional aircraft, for example. But what is particularly offensive about the drone? If the critique is that it enables warfare at a distance (which, of course, it does), then one might well respond: at what killing distance is tolerable—a pilot above the target, within artillery range, or perhaps gunfire or hand-to-hand combat?'[118] How do these judgements relate to the permissibility of other weapons, including nuclear weapons? There may well be particular materialities of the drone that are worthy of critique,[119] but a piecemeal approach to justification (and its refusal) would appear to be an unstable stopping point, for any progressive ethical framework.

* * *

[113] Ibid., 156 (emphasis added).

[114] 'Anti-war activists availed themselves of the discursive and performative elements of the legal in their efforts to intervene in war, or, failing that, in the workings of legal consciousness vis-à-vis strategies of de-legitimation': David Delaney, 'What Is Law (Good) For? Tactical Maneuvers of the Legal War at Home', *Law, Culture and the Humanities* 5, no. 3 (2009): 350.

[115] Moyn, 'From Antiwar Politics to Antitorture Politics', 156.

[116] Ibid., 155.

[117] For a critical overview of these debates, see: Frédéric Mégret, 'The Humanitarian Problem with Drones', *Utah Law Review* 2013, no. 5 (2013): 1283–1319.

[118] Gregory, 'Drone Geographies'; Dave Grossman, *On Killing: The Psychological Cost of Learning to Kill in War and Society*, revised edition (New York, NY: Back Bay Books, 2009).

[119] Leander, 'Technological Agency in the Co-Constitution of Legal Expertise and the US Drone Program'.

Here we are then, inheritors of regimes of war that march increasingly towards juridical terrain. This terrain shapes military outcomes in global battlespace but it also muddies our ethics and politics of war. We have turned to war lawyers, and with professional expertise and as co-commanders of the battlespace, they have responded. Their response came in earnest during a post-Cold War period in which globalized law and (legal) expertise was part of a turbocharged neoliberal project; in warfare, legalism became part of 'humanitarian' interventions (or as some would prefer, neoconservative or neocolonial ones) and the United Nations doctrine that 'sovereignty is not a shield'. Today, by contrast, multilateral security arrangements—as with trade rounds through the General Agreements on Tariff and Trade (GATT) and then the World Trade Organization (WTO), not to speak of European Union reforms—have been stalled for many years. Consensus even within NATO is not assured, let alone among the Security Council or the Quartet of powers that were supposedly to resuscitate the peace process in the Middle East. Instead, from Europe to North and South America, from South Asia to the Pacific Rim, populist styles of politics are on the rise. Their foreign policy correlate appears to be unilateralism and a refusal—in presentation or in substance—to act 'responsibly' within the parameters of international consensus. Part of the 'populist turn' has been a devaluation of technocracy and expertise in all manner of fields (again, outwardly at least) from central banking to public health, from intergovernmental bureaucracies to environmental science and yes, even judiciaries and their independence from executives. Military expertise, however, has generally been spared this withdrawal of approval. Whether or not the state militaries that have been the subject of this book, and indeed many others, will remain committed to juridification—with all that that entails—remains to be seen.

For now, though, this is what later modern war and 'precision' targeting look like—what 'our' war has become. How do we feel about this? What questions do we have? Are there any objections, and, if so, what (other) forms might they take?

Bibliography

505th Command and Control Wing, United States Air Force, '505th Training Squadron', 17 April 2013, http://www.505ccw.acc.af.mil/AboutUs/FactSheets/Display/tabid/6713/Article/376112/505th-training-squadron.aspx, accessed 16 December 2016.

505th Command and Control Wing, United States Air Force, 'The Air and Space Operations Center: The Judge Advocate's Role', 505th Command and Control Wing, Hurlburt Field, Florida, 2013 (presentation on file with author).

Abbott, Kenneth W et al., 'The Concept of Legalization', *International Organization* 54, no. 3 (2000): 401–19.

Abizaid, John P. and Rosa Brooks, 'Recommendations and Report of the Task Force on US Drone Policy', Washington, DC: Stimson, April 2015, https://www.stimson.org/2014/recommendations-and-report-stimson-task-force-us-drone-policy-0/, accessed 13 February 2020.

Ackerman, Gwen. 'Israel Deploys Lawyers to Head Off War-Crimes Charges', *Bloomberg.Com*, 22 January 2009, http://www.bloomberg.com/apps/news?pid=newsarchive&sid=aMvUB8w9xphM&refer=home, accessed 10 October 2014.

Ackerman, Spencer, '41 Men Targeted but 1,147 People Killed: US Drone Strikes – the Facts on the Ground', *The Guardian*, 24 November 2014, sec. US, https://www.theguardian.com/us-news/2014/nov/24/-sp-us-drone-strikes-kill-1147, accessed 3 April 2015.

Ackerman, Spencer, 'Island Mentality', *New Republic*, 22 August 2005, https://newrepublic.com/article/68370/island-mentality-1, accessed 22 March 2017.

Acosta, Miguel, 'Prosecuting High-Threat Detainees', *The Florida Bar News*, 15 September 2009, http://www.floridabar.org/DIVCOM/JN/JNNews01.nsf/8c9f13012b96736985256aa900624829/3a9be3daf196c64e852576250069d73b!OpenDocument, accessed 12 December 2016.

Addicott, Jeffrey F. and William A. Hudson, 'The Twenty-Fifth Anniversary of My Lai: A Time to Inculcate the Lessons', *Military Law Review* 139 (1993): 153–85.

Adler, Gerald J., 'Targets in War: Legal Considerations', *Houston Law Review* 8, no. 1 (1970): 1–46.

Agamben, Giorgio, *State of Exception*, trans. Kevin Attell, 1st edition (Chicago, IL: University of Chicago Press, 2005).

Agence France-Presse, 'Second Round of Deadly Israeli Strikes Hit Syria', France 24, 3 June 2019, https://www.france24.com/en/20190603-syria-israel-second-deadly-strikes-hit, accessed 19 November 2019.

Ahtisaari, Martti, 'Report to the Secretary-General on Humanitarian Needs in Kuwait and Iraq in the Immediate Post-Crisis Environment', United Nations UN Doc. S/22366, 30 March 1991.

Airwars, 'Methodology', n.d., https://airwars.org/about/methodology/, accessed 7 March 2020.

Airwars, 'US-Led Coalition in Iraq & Syria', 18 November 2019, https://airwars.org/conflict/coalition-in-iraq-and-syria/, accessed 18 November 2019.

Airwars, 'US-Led Coalition in Iraq & Syria', 7 March 2020. https://airwars.org/conflict/coalition-in-iraq-and-syria/, accessed 7 March 2020.

Airwars, 'Russian Military in Syria', 11 March 2020, https://airwars.org/conflict/russian-military-in-syria/, accessed 11 March 2020.

Akande, Dapo, 'Clearing the Fog of War? The ICRC's Interpretive Guidance on Direct Participation in Hostilities', *EJIL: Talk!* (blog), 4 June 2009, https://www.ejiltalk.org/clearing-the-fog-of-war-the-icrcs-interpretive-guidance-on-direct-participation-in-hostilities/, accessed 7 July 2017.

Al Jazeera, 'Bombed MSF Kunduz Hospital Was on US No-Strike List before Attack', 25 November 2015, http://america.aljazeera.com/articles/2015/11/25/afghan-hospital-said-to-be-misidentified-before-being-bombed.html, accessed 23 January 2017.

Al Jazeera, 'Russia Slams US for "indiscriminate" Attack in Syria's Idlib'. *Al Jazeera News*, 1 September 2019, https://www.aljazeera.com/news/2019/09/russia-slams-indiscriminate-attack-syria-idlib-190901111704884.html, accessed 11 March 2020.

Alexander, Amanda, 'A Short History of International Humanitarian Law', *European Journal of International Law* 26, no. 1 (2015): 109–38.

Allen, John, 'Headquarters, International Security Assistance Force (ISAF) Tactical Directive', Unclassified, ISAF, NATO, 30 November 2011, http://www.rs.nato.int/images/docs/20111105%20nuc%20tactical%20directive%20revision%204%20(releaseable%20version)%20r.pdf, accessed 16 January 2017.

Allen, Lori, *The Rise and Fall of Human Rights Cynicism and Politics in Occupied Palestine* (Stanford, CA: Stanford University Press, 2013).

Allen, Lori A., 'Martyr Bodies in the Media: Human Rights, Aesthetics, and the Politics of Immediation in the Palestinian Intifada', *American Ethnologist* 36, no. 1 (2009): 161–80.

Allen, William J. 'Intervention in Panama: Operation Just Cause', ed. A. Timothy Warnock (Maxwell Air Force Base, AL: Air University, 1983).

Alon, Gideon, 'Mofaz: IDF Jurist Approves Killings'. *Haaretz*, 11 January 2001, https://lists.capalon.com/pipermail/imra/2014-January/024543.html, accessed 30 September 2014.

Alon, Gideon, 'Rubinstein Backs IDF's Policy of "targeted Killings"', *Haaretz*, 2 December 2001, http://www.haaretz.com/print-edition/news/rubinstein-backs-idf-s-policy-of-targeted-killings-1.76289, accessed 6 July 2012.

Alon, Gideon and Amos Harel, 'IDF Lawyers Set "Conditions" for Assassination Policy'. *Haaretz*, 4 February 2002, http://www.haaretz.com/print-edition/news/idf-lawyers-set-conditions-for-assassination-policy-1.53911, accessed 21 February 2012.

Alston, Philip, 'Report of the Special Rapporteur on Extrajudicial, Summary or Arbitrary Executions', *United Nations Human Rights Council*, 2010, https://ap.ohchr.org/documents/dpage_e.aspx?si=A/HRC/14/24, accessed 30 June 2020.

Alston, Philip, 'The CIA and Targeted Killings beyond Borders', *Harvard National Security Journal* 2, no. 1 (2011): 283–446.

Amnesty International, 'Evidence of Medical Workers and Facilities Being Targeted by Israeli Forces in Gaza', 7 August 2014, http://www.amnesty.org/en/library/asset/MDE15/023/2014/en/c931e37b-a3c2-414f-b3a6-a00986896a09/mde150232014en.pdf, accessed 16 October 2014.

Amoore, Louise, 'Algorithmic War: Everyday Geographies of the War on Terror', *Antipode* 41, no. 1 (2009): 49–69.

Anderson, Kay, 'A Walk on the Wild Side: A Critical Geography of Domestication', *Progress in Human Geography* 21, no. 4 (1997): 463–85.

Anderson, Kenneth, 'Who Owns the Rules of War?' *The New York Times*, 13 April 2003, sec. Magazine, https://www.nytimes.com/2003/04/13/magazine/who-owns-the-rules-of-war.html, accessed 22 January 2019.

Andrade, Dale, *Ashes to Ashes: The Phoenix Program and the Vietnam War* (Lexington, MA: Lexington Books, 1990).

Anghie, Antony, *Imperialism, Sovereignty and the Making of International Law* (Cambridge: Cambridge University Press, 2007).

Anon, 'Operation Just Cause', n.d, http://www.globalsecurity.org/military/ops/just_cause.htm, accessed 7 July 2015.

Anon, 'Travelin' Judge'. *The Reporter* (originally published in *LOADSTAR*, an American University magazine 20, Winter 1967) 26, Special History edition (1999): 130–1.

Arkin, William M., 'Air Heads', Armed Forces Journal, 1 June 2006, http://armedforcesjournal.com/air-heads/, accessed 12 December 2016.

Arkin, William M., *Divining Victory: Airpower in the 2006 Israel-Hezbollah War* (Maxwell Air Force Base, AL: Air University Press, 2007).

Arkin, William M., *Unmanned: Drones, Data, and the Illusion of Perfect Warfare* (New York, NY: Little, Brown and Company, 2015).

Arnove, Anthony, ed, *Iraq Under Siege, Updated Edition: The Deadly Impact of Sanctions and War*, 2nd revised edition (Cambridge, MA: South End Press, 2003).

Atkinson, Rick, *Crusade: The Untold Story of the Persian Gulf War* (Boston, MA: Houghton Mifflin Harcourt, 1993).

Attorney General's Office and Jeremy Wright, 'Attorney General's Speech at the International Institute for Strategic Studies', GOV.UK, 11 January 2017. https://www.gov.uk/government/speeches/attorney-generals-speech-at-the-international-institute-for-strategic-studies, accessed 6 November 2019.

Azoulay, Ariella and Adi Ophir, *The One-State Condition: Occupation and Democracy in Israel/Palestine* (Stanford, CA: Stanford University Press, 2012).

Barkawi, Tarak, 'Decolonising War', *European Journal of International Security* 1, no. 2 (2016): 199–214.

Barrett, David M., 'Doing "Tuesday Lunch" at Lyndon Johnson's White House: New Archival Evidence on Vietnam Decision Making', *PS: Political Science and Politics* 24, no. 4 (1991): 676–9.

Bauman, Zygmunt, 'Ethics of Individuals', *The Canadian Journal of Sociology / Cahiers Canadiens de Sociologie* 25, no. 1 (2000): 83–96.

Bauman, Zygmunt, *Modernity and the Holocaust* (Ithaca, NY: Cornell University Press, 2001).

Bauman, Zygmunt et al., 'After Snowden: Rethinking the Impact of Surveillance'. *International Political Sociology* 8, no. 2 (2014): 121–44.

Beard, Jack M., 'Law and War in the Virtual Era', *American Journal of International Law* 103, no. 1 (2009): 409–45.

Beauchamp, Scott, 'The Moral Cost of the Kill Box', *The Atlantic*, 28 February 2016, https://www.theatlantic.com/politics/archive/2016/02/the-cost-of-the-kill-box/470751/, accessed 9 September 2019.

Beaumont, Peter and Hazem Balousha, 'Ban Ki-Moon: Gaza Is a Source of Shame to the International Community', *The Guardian*, 14 October 2014, sec. World, http://www.theguardian.com/world/2014/oct/14/ban-ki-moon-visits-gaza-views-destruction-of-un-school, accessed 16 October 2014.

Becker, Jo and Scott Shane, 'Secret "Kill List" Tests Obama's Principles', *The New York Times*, 29 May 2012, http://www.nytimes.com/2012/05/29/world/obamas-leadership-in-war-on-al-qaeda.html, accessed 2 June 2012.

Benac, Nancy and Associated Press, 'The Long, Unfortunate History of Friendly Fire Accidents in U.S. Conflicts', *PBS NewsHour*, 11 June 2014, https://www.pbs.org/newshour/nation/long-unfortunate-history-friendly-fire-accidents-u-s-conflicts, accessed 30 January 2020.

Benitez, Mike, 'How Afghanistan Distorted Close Air Support and Why It Matters', War on the Rocks, 29 June 2016, http://warontherocks.com/2016/06/how-afghanistan-distorted-close-air-support-and-why-it-matters/, accessed 12 December 2016.

Benitez, Mike and Peter Garretson, 'Offsetting Air Superiority with Air Force Special Operations', War on the Rocks, 3 November 2016, http://warontherocks.com/2016/11/offsetting-air-superiority-with-air-force-special-operations/, accessed 12 December 2016.

Benjamin, Mark, 'When Is an Accidental Civilian Death Not an Accident?' *Salon*, 30 July 2007, http://www.salon.com/2007/07/30/collateral_damage/, accessed 19 June 2016.

Benjamin, Walter, 'Critique of Violence', in *Walter Benjamin: Selected Writings, Volume 1: 1913-1926*, ed. Marcus Bullock and Michael W. Jennings, 1st edition (Cambridge, MA: Belknap Press, 1996), 236–52.

Ben-Naftali, Orna, Aeyal Gross, and Keren Michaeli, 'The Illegality of the Occupation Regime: The Fabric of Law in the Occupied Palestinian Territory', in *The Power of Inclusive Exclusion: Anatomy of Israeli Rule in the Occupied Palestinian Territories*, ed. Adi Ophir, Michal Givoni, and Sari Hanafi (New York, NY: Zone Books, 2009), 31–88.

Ben-Naftali, Orna and Noam Zamir, 'Whose "Conduct Unbecoming"? The Shooting of a Handcuffed, Blindfolded Palestinian Demonstrator', *Journal of International Criminal Justice* 7, no. 1 (2009): 155–75.

Benson, Melinda, 'Rules of Engagement: The Spatiality of Judicial Review', in *The Expanding Spaces of Law: A Timely Legal Geography*, ed. Irus Braverman et al. (Stanford, CA: Stanford Law Books, 2014), 215–38.

Benton, Lauren A., *A Search for Sovereignty: Law and Geography in European Empires, 1400-1900* (Cambridge; New York, NY: Cambridge University Press, 2010).

Benton, Lauren A., *Law and Colonial Cultures: Legal Regimes in World History, 1400-1900*, Studies in Comparative World History (Cambridge; New York, NY: Cambridge University Press, 2002).

Benvenisti, Eyal, 'Rethinking the Divide between Jus Ad Bellum and Jus in Bello in Warfare against Nonstate Actors Essays in Honor of W. Michael Reisman: Use of Force', *Yale Journal of International Law* 34, no. 2 (2009): 541–8.

Benvenisti, Eyal, 'The Legal Battle to Define the Law on Transnational Asymmetric Warfare', *Duke Journal of Comparative & International Law* 20, no. 3 (2010): 339–59.

Benvenisti, Eyal and Amichai Cohen, 'War Is Governance: Explaining the Logic of the Laws of War from a Principal-Agent Perspective', *Michigan Law Review* 112, no. 8 (2014).

Ben-Yehuda, Nachman, *Political Assassinations by Jews a Rhetorical Device for Justice* (Albany, NY: State University of New York Press, 1993).

Berdal, Mats, 'How "New" Are "New Wars"? Global Economic Change and the Study of Civil War', *Global Governance* 9, no. 4 (2003): 477–502.

Berdal, Mats, 'The "new Wars" Thesis Revisited', in *The Changing Character of War*, ed. Sibylle Scheipers and Hew Strachan (New York, NY: Oxford University Press, 2011), 109–33.

Bergman, Ronen, *Rise and Kill First: The Secret History of Israel's Targeted Assassinations* (London: John Murray, 2018).

Berman, Nathaniel, 'Privileging Combat - Contemporary Conflict and the Legal Construction of War', *Columbia Journal of Transnational Law* 43, no. 1 (2004): 1–72.

Bhungalia, Lisa, 'A Liminal Territory: Gaza, Executive Discretion, and Sanctions Turned Humanitarian', *GeoJournal* 75, no. 4 (2010): 347–57.

Bill, Brian J., 'The Rendulic "Rule": Military Necessity, Commander's Knowledge and Methods of Warfare', *Yearbook of International Humanitarian Law* 12 (2009): 119–55.

Bilsborough, Shane, 'Counterlawfare in Counterinsurgency', Small Wars Journal, 14 December 2011, http://smallwarsjournal.com/jrnl/art/counterlawfare-in-counterinsurgency, accessed 10 September 2013.

Bilton, Michael and Kevin Sim, *Four Hours in My Lai*, reprint edition (New York, NY: Penguin Books, 1993).

Bisharat, George E., 'Courting Justice? Legitimation in Lawyering under Israeli Occupation', *Law & Social Inquiry* 20, no. 2 (1995): 349–405.

Bisharat, George E., 'Violence's Law', *Journal of Palestine Studies* 42, no. 3 (2013): 68–84.

Bitzes, James, 'Role of an Air Operations Center Legal Advisor in Targeting', presented at the Drones, targeting and the promise of law conference, Washington, DC, 24 February 2011 (notes on file with author).

Blank, Laurie R., 'The Application of IHL in the Goldstone Report: A Critical Commentary', *Yearbook of International Humanitarian Law* 12 (2009): 347–402.

Blank, Laurie R., 'Finding Facts But Missing the Law: The Goldstone Report, Gaza and Lawfare', *Case Western Reserve Journal of International Law* 43, no. 1 (2010): 279–305.

Blank, Laurie R., 'A New Twist on an Old Story: Lawfare and the Mixing of Proportionalities', *Case Western Reserve Journal of International Law* 43, no. 3 (2011): 707–38.

Blank, Laurie R. and Amos Guiora, 'Updating the Commander's Toolbox: New Tools for Operationalizing the Laws of Armed Conflict', *PRISM* 1, no. 3 (2010): 59–78.

Blichner, Lars Chr, and Anders Molander, 'Mapping Juridification', *European Law Journal* 14, no. 1 (2008): 36–54.

Blum, Gabriella, and Philip Heymann, 'Law and Policy of Targeted Killing', *Harvard National Security Journal* 1 (2010): 145–70.

Blum, Gabriella, 'The Dispensable Lives of Soldiers', *Journal of Legal Analysis* 2, no. 1 (2010): 69–124.

Blum, Gabriella, 'The Individualization of War', in *Law and War*, ed. Austin Sarat, Lawrence Douglas, and Martha Merrill Umphrey, *The Amherst Series in Law, Jurisprudence, and Social Thought* (Stanford, CA: Stanford University Press, 2014), 48–83.

Boothby, Bill, 'And for Such Time as: The Time Dimension to Direct Participation in Hostilities', *New York University Journal of International Law and Politics* 42, no. 3 (2010): 741–68.

Borch, Frederic L., *Judge Advocates in Combat: Army Lawyers in Military Operations from Vietnam to Haiti* (Washington, DC: Government Printing Office, 2001).

Bourdieu, Pierre, 'The Force of Law: Toward a Sociology of the Juridical Field', *Hastings Law Journal* 38, no. 5 (1987): 814–53.

Bowden, Mark, *Hue 1968: A Turning Point of the American War in Vietnam* (New York, NY: Atlantic Monthly Press, 2017).

Bradley, Curtis, 'The United States, Israel, and Unlawful Combatants', *Green Bag* 12 (2009): 397–411.

Braverman, Irus et al., *The Expanding Spaces of Law: A Timely Legal Geography* (Stanford, CA: Stanford Law Books, 2014).

Bridge, Robert L., 'Operations Law: An Overview', *Air Force Law Review* 37 (1994): 1.

Broseker, Leonard, 'Sword in the Sand', *The Reporter, Office of the Judge Advocate General* 26, Special History edition (1999): 138–45.

B'Tselem, 'Fatalities during Operation Cast Lead', n.d., https://www.btselem.org/statistics/fatalities/during-cast-lead/by-date-of-event, accessed 19 November 2019.

B'Tselem, 'Operation Defensive Shield', Jerusalem, July 2002, http://www.btselem.org/download/200207_defensive_shield_eng.pdf, accessed 28 October 2014.

B'Tselem, 'Harm to Civilians Significantly Higher in Second Half of Operation Pillar of Defense', 8 May 2013, http://www.btselem.org/press_releases/20130509_pillar_of_defense_report, accessed 16 October 2014.

B'Tselem, 'Human Rights Violations during Operation Pillar of Defense', Jerusalem, May 2013, http://www.btselem.org/download/201305_pillar_of_defense_operation_eng.pdf, accessed 30 September 2014.

B'Tselem, 'Investigation of Incidents That Took Place during Recent Military Action in Gaza: July-August 2014', 4 September 2014, https://www.btselem.org/download/201400904_15390_letter_to_mag_corps_regarding_protective_edge_investiations_eng.pdf, accessed 2 October 2014.

B'Tselem, '50 Days: More than 500 Children—Facts and Figures on Fatalities in Gaza, Summer 2014', 2014, https://www.btselem.org/2014_gaza_conflict/en/il/, accessed 27 June 2017.

B'Tselem, 'Statistics', http://www.btselem.org/statistics, 18 February 2012.

Burbage, Paul, et al., *The Battle for the Skies Over North Vietnam: 1964-1972*, reprint of the 1976 edition (Washington, DC: Office of Air Force History, 1985), 150.

The Bureau of Investigative Journalism, 'Afghanistan: US Air and Drone Strikes', The Bureau of Investigative Journalism, November 2019, https://www.thebureauinvestigates.com/projects/drone-war/afghanistan, accessed 18 November 2019.

The Bureau of Investigative Journalism, 'Drone Warfare', The Bureau of Investigative Journalism, n.d., https://www.thebureauinvestigates.com/projects/drone-war, accessed 22 January 2020.

Burkart, James A., 'Deadly Advice: Judge Advocates and Joint Targeting', *The Army Lawyer*, no. 6 (2016): 10–24.

Burke, Denise, 'Changing Times and New Challenges: The Vietnam War', *The Reporter* 26, no. Special History edition (1999): 120–5.

Butler, Amy, 'USAF Eyes New Era of Close Air Support', 30 March 2015, http://aviationweek.com/defense/usaf-eyes-new-era-close-air-support, accessed 12 December 2016.

Butler, Judith, *Precarious Life: The Powers of Mourning and Violence* (London: Verso, 2006).

Butler, Judith, *Gender Trouble*, tenth anniversary edition (London; New York, NY: Routledge, 2014).

Campaign Against Arms Trade and The Secretary of State for International Trade. Judicial review. Witness Statement of Peter Watkins on Behalf of the Defendant, Pub. L. No. Claim No: C0/1306/2016, 1 (2016), https://www.caat.org.uk/resources/countries/saudi-arabia/legal-2016/watkins-statement-1.pdf, accessed 7 November 2019.

Cavallaro, James, Stephan Sonnenberg, and Sarah Knuckey, 'Living Under Drones: Death, Injury and Trauma to Civilians from US Drone Practices in Pakistan', International Human Rights and Conflict Resolution Clinic, Stanford Law School, Stanford and NYU School of Law, Global Justice Clinic, New York, 2012, https://law.stanford.edu/publications/living-under-drones-death-injury-and-trauma-to-civilians-from-us-drone-practices-in-pakistan/, accessed 19 November 2019.

Caverley, Jonathan D., 'The Myth of Military Myopia: Democracy, Small Wars, and Vietnam', *International Security* 34, no. 3 (2010): 119–57.

CBS News, 'The Afghan War's Deadliest Friendly Fire Incident for U.S. Soldiers', *CBS News*, 9 November 2017, https://www.cbsnews.com/news/the-afghan-wars-deadliest-friendly-fire-incident-involving-u-s-soldiers/, accessed 30 January 2020.

Center for Naval Analysis, 'Our Expert: Larry Lewis', n.d., https://www.cna.org/experts/Lewis_L, accessed 7 March 2020.

Chamayou, Grégoire, 'The Manhunt Doctrine', *Radical Philosophy* (blog), October 2011, https://www.radicalphilosophy.com/commentary/the-manhunt-doctrine, accessed 6 July 2017.

Chamayou, Grégoire, *Manhunts: A Philosophical History*, trans. Steven Rendall (Princeton, NJ: Princeton University Press, 2012).

Chamayou, Grégoire, *Drone Theory* (London: Penguin, 2015).

Chomsky, Noam, *The New Military Humanism: Lessons from Kosovo*, Pages Bent edition (London: Pluto Press, 1999).

Chow, Rey, *The Age of the World Target: Self-Referentiality in War, Theory, and Comparative Work* (Durham, NC: Duke University Press, 2006).

Clodfelter, Mark, *The Limits of Air Power: The American Bombing of North Vietnam* (New York, NY: The Free Press, 2006).

Close Air Solutions, 'Close Air Support Fratricide Incidents - Friendly Fire!' Close Air Solutions—FAC and JTAC Training Services, http://www.closeairsolutions.com/close-air-support-fratricide-incidents/, accessed 18 January 2017.

Cloud, David S., 'Anatomy of an Afghan War Tragedy', *Los Angeles Times*, 10 April 2011, http://articles.latimes.com/2011/apr/10/world/la-fg-afghanistan-drone-20110410, accessed 19 July 2013.

Cochran, Alexander et al., *Gulf War: Air Power Survey: Volume 1, Planning, Command & Control* (Washington, DC: United States Air Force, 1993), http://www.dtic.mil/dtic/tr/fulltext/u2/a279741.pdf, accessed 13 July 2015.

Cockburn, Andrew, *Kill Chain: The Rise of the High-Tech Assassins* (New York, NY: Henry Holt and Co., 2015).

Cohen, Amichai, 'Legal Operational Advice in the Israeli Defense Forces: The International Law Department and the Changing Nature of International Humanitarian Law', *Connecticut Journal of International Law* 26, no. 2 (2011): 367–413.

Cohen, Amichai and Yuval Shany, 'Israel's Military Advocate General Terminates "Black Friday" and Other Investigations: Initial Observations', *Lawfare* (blog), 27 August 2018, https://www.lawfareblog.com/israels-military-advocate-general-terminates-black-friday-and-other-investigations-initial, accessed 20 December 2019.

Cole, Alan, 'Legal Issues in Forming the Coalition', *International Law Studies, U.S. Naval War College* 85, no. 1 (2009): 141–53.

Conway-Lanz, Sahr, *Collateral Damage: Americans, Noncombatant Immunity, and Atrocity after World War II* (New York, NY: Routledge, 2006).

Cook, Martin L. and Henrik Syse, 'What Should We Mean by "Military Ethics"?' *Journal of Military Ethics* 9, no. 2 (2010): 119–22.

Cooper, Helene, 'Trump Gives Military New Freedom. But With That Comes Danger', *The New York Times*, 5 April 2017, sec. US, https://www.nytimes.com/2017/04/05/us/politics/rules-of-engagement-military-force-mattis.html, accessed 10 February 2020.

Cordesman, Anthony H., 'The "Gaza War"', Washington, DC: Center for Strategic and International Studies (CSIS), 2 February 2009, https://www.csis.org/analysis/gaza-war, accessed 1 July 2020.

Corn, Geoffrey S., 'War Crimes and the Limits of Combatant Immunity', *Jurist: Legal News and Research*, 28 May 2006, https://www.jurist.org/commentary/2006/05/war-crimes-and-limits-of-combatant/, accessed 7 August 2019.

Corn, Geoffrey S., 'The Newly Relaxed Rules of Engagement in Afghanistan and Civilian Casualties', *Just Security*, 6 October 2017, https://www.justsecurity.org/45680/

newly-relaxed-rules-engagement-afghanistan-civilian-casualties/, accessed 10 January 2020.

Corn, Geoffrey S. and Gary P. Corn, 'The Law of Operational Targeting: Viewing the LOAC through an Operational Lens', *Texas International Law Journal* 47, no. 2 (2011): 337–80.

Corn, Geoffrey, James Dapper, and Winston Williams, 'Targeting and the Law of Armed Conflict', in *U.S. Military Operations: Law, Policy, and Practice*, ed. Geoffrey S. Corn, Rachel E. VanLandingham, and Shane R. Reeves (Oxford; New York, NY: Oxford University Press, 2015), 167–208.

Cover, Robert M., 'Violence and the Word', *Yale Law Journal* 95, no. 8 (1986): 1601.

Cox, Sebastian and Peter Gray, *Air Power History: Turning Points from Kitty Hawk to Kosovo* (Abingdon, Oxon: Routledge, 2013).

Craig, Alan, 'Lebanon 2006 and the Front of Legitimacy', *Israel Affairs* 15, no. 4 (2009): 427–44.

Craig, Alan, 'The Struggle for Legitimacy: A Study of Military Lawyers in Israel', PhD thesis, University of Leeds, 2011, White Rose eTheses Online, http://etheses.whiterose.ac.uk/2702/, accessed 12 June 2020.

Crandall, Jordan, 'Anything That Moves: Armed Vision', *CTheory*, 1999, http://ctheory.net/ctheory_wp/anything-that-moves-armed-vision/, accessed 6 March 2020.

Crandall, Jordan, 'Envisioning the Homefront: Militarization, Tracking and Security Culture (Jordan Crandall in Conversation with John Armitage)', *Journal of Visual Culture* 4, no. 1 (2005): 17–38.

Crawford, J. W., 'The Law of Noncombatant Immunity and the Targeting of National Electric Power Systems', *The Flecture Forum of World Affairs* 21, no. 2 (1997): 101–19.

Crawford, Neta, *Accountability for Killing: Moral Responsibility for Collateral Damage in America's Post-9/11 Wars* (New York, NY: Oxford University Press, 2013).

Crawford, Neta, 'Targeting Civilians and U.S. Strategic Bombing Norms', in *The American Way of Bombing: Changing Ethical and Legal Norms, from Flying Fortresses to Drones*, ed. Matthew Evangelista (Ithaca, NY; London: Cornell University Press, 2014), 64–86

Crawford, Neta, 'Update on the Human Costs of War for Afghanistan and Pakistan, 2001 to Mid-2016', Providence, RI: Costs of War, Brown University, August 2016, http://watson.brown.edu/costsofwar/files/cow/imce/papers/2016/War%20in%20Afghanistan%20and%20Pakistan%20UPDATE_FINAL_corrected%20date.pdf, accessed 24 January 2017.

Crawford, Neta, 'Death Toll: Will The U.S. Tolerate More Civilian Casualties In Its Bid To Vanquish ISIS?', 21 January 2016, http://www.wbur.org/cognoscenti/2016/01/21/civilian-casualties-iraq-syria-us-war-on-isis-neta-c-crawford, accessed 11 April 2018.

Cronk, Terry Moon, 'Centcom Releases Civilian Casualty Assessments', US Department of Defense, http://www.defense.gov/News/Article/Article/741155/centcom-releases-civilian-casualty-assessments, accessed 16 January 2017.

Cubukcu, Ayca, *For the Love of Humanity: The World Tribunal on Iraq* (Philadelphia: University of Pennsylvania Press, Inc., 2018).

Cuddy, Brian, 'Wider War: American Force in Vietnam, International Law, and the Transformation of Armed Conflict, 1961-1977', PhD thesis, Cornell University, Ithaca, NY, 2016 (on file with author; cited with permission).

Cumming-Bruce, Nick, 'U.N. Panel Says Russia Bombed Syrian Civilian Targets, a War Crime', *The New York Times*, 2 March 2020, sec. World. https://www.nytimes.com/2020/03/02/world/middleeast/united-nations-syria-idlib-russia.html, accessed 1 July 2020.

Dalby, Simon, 'Calling 911: Geopolitics, Security and America's New War', *Geopolitics* 8, no. 3 (2003): 61–86.

Daponte, Beth Osborne, 'A Case Study in Estimating Casualties from War and Its Aftermath: The 1991 Persian Gulf War', *PSR Quarterly* 3, no. 2 (1993): 57–66.

deGrandpre, Andrew and Shawn Snow, 'The U.S. Military's Stats on Deadly Airstrikes Are Wrong. Thousands Have Gone Unreported', *Military Times*, 5 February 2017, http://www.militarytimes.com/articles/airstrikes-unreported-syria-iraq-afghanistan-islamic-state-al-qaeda-taliban, accessed 13 March 2017.

Delaney, David, 'What Is Law (Good) For? Tactical Maneuvers of the Legal War at Home', *Law, Culture and the Humanities* 5, no. 3 (2009): 337–52.

Demerest, Geoffrey, 'The Strategic Implications of Operational Law', *US Army*, April 1995, https://community.apan.org/wg/tradoc-g2/fmso/m/fmso-monographs/252318, accessed 1 July 2020.

Demmers, Jolle and Lauren Gould, 'An Assemblage Approach to Liquid Warfare: AFRICOM and the "Hunt" for Joseph Kony', *Security Dialogue* 49, no. 5: 364–81.

Department of Defence Australia, 'Report of an Inquiry Officer: Possible Civilian Casualties from Close Air Support Strike at [Redacted] Afghanistan on 28 Apr 09', Government of Australia, online: Defence Publications Commission of Inquiry, 2009, http://www.defence.gov.au/publications/coi/reports/28APR09%20CIVCAS%20report%20-%20redacted.pdf, accessed 9 January 2017.

Department of Justice White Paper, 'Lawfulness of a Lethal Operation Directed Against A U.S. Citizen Who Is a Senior Operational Leader of Al-Qa'ida or an Associated Force', 8 November 2011, https://fas.org/irp/eprint/doj-lethal.pdf, accessed 1 July 2020.

Deptula, David, A., *Effects Based Operations: Change in the Nature of Warfare* (Arlington, VA: Aerospace Education Foundation, 2001), https://secure.afa.org/Mitchell/reports/0901ebo.pdf, accessed 28 June 2020.

Deptula, David, A., 'How to Defeat the Islamic State', *The Washington Post*, 5 June 2015, https://www.washingtonpost.com/opinions/how-to-defeat-the-islamic-state/2015/06/05/50ff6fca-0af7-11e5-a7ad-b430fc1d3f5c_story.html?utm_term=.2052f6469bda, accessed 28 October 2016.

DeSaussure, Ariane L., 'The Role of the Law of Armed Conflict During the Persian Gulf War: An Overview', *Air Force Law Review* 37 (1994): 62.

Devereaux, Ryan, 'Manhunting in the Hindu Kush', *The Intercept*, 18 October 2015, https://theintercept.com/drone-papers/manhunting-in-the-hindu-kush/, accessed 13 December 2016.

Dickinson, Laura, 'Military Lawyers on the Battlefield: An Empirical Account of International Law Compliance', *American Journal of International Law* 104, no. 1 (2010): 1–28.

Dill, Janina, 'Israel's Use of Law and Warnings in Gaza', *Opinio Juris* (blog), 30 July 2014, http://opiniojuris.org/2014/07/30/guest-post-israels-use-law-warnings-gaza/#more-30943, accessed 8 October 2014.

Dill, Janina, *Legitimate Targets?: Social Construction, International Law and US Bombing* (Cambridge: Cambridge University Press, 2014).

Dill, Janina, 'The American Way of Bombing and International Law: Two Logics of Warfare in Tension', in *The American Way of Bombing: Changing Ethical and Legal Norms, from Flying Fortresses to Drones*, ed. Matthew Evangelista and Henry Shue (Ithaca, NY; London: Cornell University Press, 2014), 131–44

DiMeglio, Richard P., 'Training Army Judge Advocates to Advise Commanders as Operational Law Attorneys', *Boston College Law Review* 54, no. 3 (2013): 1185.

Dinstein, Yoram, 'Concluding Remarks: LOAC and Attempts to Abuse or Subvert It', *International Law Studies* 87 (2011): 483–94.

Dixon, Jennifer M., 'Rhetorical Adaptation and Resistance to International Norms', *Perspectives on Politics* 15, no. 1 (2017): 83–99.

Doswald-Beck, Louise, 'Implementation of International Humanitarian Law in Future Wars, *Naval War College Review* 52, no. 1 (1999): 24.

Douzinas, Costas, *Human Rights and Empire: The Political Philosophy of Cosmopolitanism* (Abingdon; New York, NY: Routledge-Cavendish, 2007).

Douzinas, Costas, 'Humanity, Military Humanism and the New Moral Order', *Economy and Society* 32, no. 2 (2003): 159–83.

Douzinas, Costas, 'The Many Faces of Humanitarianism', *Monthly Review Online*, 29 May 2009, https://mronline.org/2009/05/29/the-many-faces-of-humanitarianism/, accessed 24 February 2020.

Draper, G. I. A. D., 'Role of Legal Advisers in Armed Forces', *International Review of the Red Cross (1961 - 1997)* 18, no. 202 (1978): 6–17.

Dreyfuss, Bob and Nick Turse, 'America's Afghan Victims', 18 September 2013, https://www.thenation.com/article/archive/americas-afghan-victims/, accessed 2 March 2020.

Dunlap, Charles, 'Law and Military Interventions: Preserving Humanitarian Values in 21st Century Conflicts', in *Conference on Humanitarian Challenges in Military Intervention* (online), Washington, DC: Carr Center for Human Rights Policy, Kennedy School of Government, Harvard University, 29 November: 4–43. Washington DC, 2001.

Dunlap, Charles, 'Revolution in Military Legal Affairs: Air Force Legal Professionals in 21st Century Conflicts, The', *Air Force Law Review* 51 (2001): 293–309.

Dunlap, Charles, 'It Ain't No TV Show: JAGs and Modern Military Operations', *Chicago Journal of International Law* 4, no. 2 (2003): 379–491.

Dunlap, Charles, ' . . . With Helmet and Flak Vest: Practicing International Law in War Zones', *US Air Force, Judge Advocate General*, 4 December 2004, http://scholarship.law.duke.edu/faculty_scholarship/3476/, accessed 4 July 2015.

Dunlap, Charles, 'Come the Revolution: A Legal Perspective on Air Operations in Iraq since 2003', *International Law Studies. US Naval War College* 86 (2010): 139–54.

Dunlap, Charles, 'Lawfare: A Decisive Element of 21st Century Conflicts?', *Joint Forces Quarterly* 54, no. 3 (2009): 34–9.

Dunlap, Charles, 'The (Un)Accountable? Why Critics Need to Be Scrutinized as Much as the Military', *Lawfire* (blog), 11 December 2017, https://sites.duke.edu/lawfire/2017/12/11/the-unaccountable-why-critics-need-to-be-scrutinized-as-much-as-the-military/, accessed 7 March 2020.

Dworkin, Antony, 'Soleimani Strike Marks a Novel Shift in Targeted Killing, Dangerous to the Global Order', *Just Security* (blog), 7 January 2020, https://www.justsecurity.org/67937/soleimani-strike-marks-a-novel-shift-in-targeted-killing-dangerous-to-the-global-order/, accessed 23 February 2020.

Dyson, Tim, 'Child Mortality in Iraq since 1990', *Economic and Political Weekly* 41, no. 42 (2006): 4487–96.

Dyson, Tim, 'New Evidence on Child Mortality in Iraq', *Economic and Political Weekly* 44, no. 2 (2009): 56–59.

Eade, George, J., 'Reflections on Air Power in the Vietnam War', *Air University Review* 25, no. 1 (1973): 2–9.

Eastwood, James, *Ethics as a Weapon of War: Militarism and Morality in Israel*. (Cambridge: Cambridge University Press, 2017).

Eastwood, James, 'Ethics in the Service of Violence in Israel/Palestine', *The Disorder of Things* (blog), 23 October 2015, https://thedisorderofthings.com/2015/10/23/ethics-in-the-service-of-violence-in-israelpalestine/, accessed 4 January 2017.

Eastwood, James, '"Meaningful Service": Pedagogy at Israeli Pre-Military Academies and the Ethics of Militarism', *European Journal of International Relations* 22, no. 3 (2016): 671–95.

Elsarelli, Leon E., 'From Desert Storm to 2025: Close Air Support in the 21st Century', Air Command and Staff College, Air University, 1998, https://fas.org/man/dod-101/sys/ac/docs/98-086.pdf, accessed 21 December 2016.

Esmeir, Samera, *Juridical Humanity: A Colonial History* (Stanford, CA: Stanford University Press, 2012).

Etzioni, Amitai, 'Terrorists, Neither Soldiers Nor Criminals', *Military Review* (2009, July–August): 108–18.

Etzioni, Amitai, 'Unmanned Aircraft Systems: The Moral and Legal Case', *Joint Forces Quarterly* 57, no. 2 (2010): 66–71.

Evangelista, Matthew and Henry Shue, eds, *The American Way of Bombing: Changing Ethical and Legal Norms, from Flying Fortresses to Drones* (Ithaca, NY; London: Cornell University Press, 2014).

Exit interview with Captain David Bengston, Staff Judge Advocate, 199th Infantry Brigade. Interview by 44th MHD, Danny. P. Barrett, tape recording, 28 July 1970, Vietnam Interview Tape Collection, U.S. Army Center of Military History, Historical Research Branch, Fort McNair, DC. VNIT-731.

Exit interview with Captain Thomas Hokinson, Staff Judge Advocate, 199th LIB. Interview by 44th MHD, 1LT James G. Lindsay, tape recording, 11 January 1970, Vietnam Interview Tape Collection, US Army Center of Military History, Historical Research Branch, Fort McNair, DC. VNIT-557.

Exit interview with Colonel Vernon Newman, Staff Judge Advocate. Interview by 16th MHD, Captain Joel D. Meyerson, tape recording, 17 June 1971, Vietnam Interview Tape Collection, US Army Center of Military History, Historical Research Branch, Fort McNair, DC. VNIT-991.

Exit interview with Major David Norris, Brigade Adjutant General, and Captain David Kull, Staff Judge Advocate. Interview by 18th MHD, Captain Gerard J. Monaghan, tape recording, 27 February 1971, Vietnam Interview Tape Collection, US Army Center of Military History, Historical Research Branch, Fort McNair, DC. VNIT-834.

Fassin, Didier, *Humanitarian Reason: A Moral History of the Present* (Berkeley and Los Angeles, CA; London: University of California Press, 2012).

Fazal, Tanisha M., *Wars of Law: Unintended Consequences in the Regulation of Armed Conflict* (Ithaca, NY: Cornell University Press, 2018).

Feldman, Yotam and Uri Blau, 'Consent and Advise'. *Haaretz*, 29 January 2009, http://www.haaretz.com/cmlink/consent-and-advise-1.269127, accessed 26 May 2013.

Foy, Henry and Chloe Cornish, 'Russia Guilty of War Crimes against Civilians in Syria', 2 March 2020, https://www.ft.com/content/085e94b0-5cac-11ea-8033-fa40a0d65a98, accessed 11 March 2020.

Fryer-Biggs, Zachary, 'Coming Soon to a Battlefield: Robots That Can Kill', *The Atlantic*, 3 September 2019, https://www.theatlantic.com/technology/archive/2019/09/killer-robots-and-new-era-machine-driven-warfare/597130/, accessed 16 March 2020.

Fyfe, John, *Evolution of Time Sensitive Targeting: Operation Iraqi Freedom Results and Lessons* (Maxwell Air Force Base, Alabama: Air University, College of Aerospace Doctrine, Research and Education, 2005).

Gardam, Judith, G., 'Noncombatant Immunity and the Gulf Conflict', *Virginia Journal of International Law* 32, no. 4 (1992): 813–86.

Gellman, Barton, 'Allied Air War Struck Broadly in Iraq: Officials Acknowledge Strategy Went beyond Purely Military Targets', *Washington Post*, 23 June 1991, reproduced at: https://www.globalpolicy.org/component/content/article/169/36375.html, accessed 1 March 2020.

Gent, Terrie M., 'The Role of Judge Advocates in a Joint Air Operations Center: A Counterpoint of Doctrine, Strategy, and Law', *Airpower Journal* 13, no. 1 (1999): 40–55.

George, Susannah and Associated Press, 'Liberation from Militants Leaves Devastation in Mosul', *Military Times*, 8 August 2017, https://www.militarytimes.com/flashpoints/2017/07/15/liberation-from-militants-leaves-devastation-in-mosul/, accessed 5 March 2020.

Geva, Maayan, 'Military Lawyers Making Law: Israel's Governance of the West Bank and Gaza', *Law & Social Inquiry* 44, no. 3 (August 2019): 704–25.

Gilbert, Emily, 'The Gift of War: Cash, Counterinsurgency and "Collateral Damage"', *Security Dialogue*, 46, no. 5 (2015): 403–21.

Global Security, 'Al Udeid Air Base', http://www.globalsecurity.org/military/facility/udeid.htm, accessed 15 December 2016.

Goldstein, Joseph et al., *The My Lai Massacre and Its Cover-Up: Beyond the Reach of Law? The Peers Commission Report* (New York, NY: Free Press, 1976).

Goodman, Ryan, 'Associated Forces: Why the Differences between ISIL and al-Qaeda Matter', *Just Security*, 30 March 2015, https://www.justsecurity.org/21621/forces-differences-isil-al-qaeda-matter/, accessed 13 December 2016.

Goodman, Ryan, 'White House "1264 Notice" and Novel Legal Claims for Military Strikes Against Iran', *Just Security* (blog), 14 February 2020, https://www.justsecurity.org/68594/white-house-1264-notice-and-novel-legal-claims-for-military-action-against-iran/, accessed 23 February 2020.

Goodman, Ryan and Derek Jinks, 'The ICRC Interpretive Guidance on the Notion of Direct Participation in Hostilities under International Humanitarian Law: An Introduction to the Forum: Direct Participation in Hostilities: Perspectives on the ICRC Interpretive Guidance', *New York University Journal of International Law and Politics* 42, no. 3 (2010): 637–40.

Gordillo, Gastón, 'Space and Politics: Opaque Zones of Empire', *Space and Politics* (blog), 25 June 2013, http://spaceandpolitics.blogspot.com/2013/06/opaque-zones-of-empire_25.html, accessed 6 March 2020.

Gordon, Joy, *Invisible War: The United States and the Iraq Sanctions* (Cambridge, MA: Harvard University Press, 2010).

Gordon, Neve, 'Rationalising Extra-Judicial Executions: The Israeli Press and the Legitimisation of Abuse', *The International Journal of Human Rights* 8, no. 3 (2004): 305–24.

Gordon, Neve, *Israel's Occupation* (Berkeley: University of California Press, 2008).

Gordon, Neve, 'Human Rights as a Security Threat: Lawfare and the Campaign against Human Rights NGOs', *Law & Society Review* 48, no. 2 (2014): 311–44.

Gordon, Neve, 'How Israel's Occupation Shifted from a Politics of Life to a Politics of Death', *The Nation*, 5 June 2017, https://www.thenation.com/article/israels-occupation-shifted-politics-life-politics-death/, accessed 18 December 2019.

Gordon, Neve and Nicola Perugini, '"Hospital Shields" and the Limits of International Law', *European Journal of International Law* 30, no. 2 (2019): 439–63.

Gordon, Neve and Nicola Perugini, *Human Shields: A History of People in the Line of Fire* (Oakland, CA: University of California Press, 2020).

Gordon, Neve and Nicola Perugini, 'The Politics of Human Shielding: On the Resignification of Space and the Constitution of Civilians as Shields in Liberal Wars', *Environment and Planning D: Society and Space* 34, no. 1 (2016): 168–87.

Graham, David E., 'Operational Law: A Concept Comes of Age', *Army Law* 175 (1987): 9–12.

Graham, David, E., 'My Lai and Beyond: The Evolution of Operational Law', in *The Real Lessons of the Vietnam War: Reflections Twenty-Five Years after the Fall of Saigon*, ed. John Norton Moore and Robert F. Turner (Durham, NC: Carolina Academic Press, 2002).

Graham, Stephen, 'Cities as Battlespace: The New Military Urbanism', *City* 13, no. 4 (2009): 383–402.

Graham, Stephen, *Cities, War, and Terrorism: Towards an Urban Geopolitics* (Malden, MA: Blackwell publishing, 2004).

Graham, Stephen, 'Switching Cities Off', *City* 9, no. 2 (2005): 169–94.

Graham, Stephen, ed., *Disrupted Cities: When Infrastructure Fails* (New York, NY: Routledge, 2009).

Graham, Stephen, *Cities Under Siege: The New Military Urbanism* (London; New York, NY: Verso Books, 2011).

Graham, Stephen, *Vertical: The City from Satellites to Bunkers* (London; New York, NY: Verso Books, 2016).

Graham-Harrison, Emma, 'British and US Military "in Command Room" for Saudi Strikes on Yemen', *The Guardian*, 15 January 2016, sec. World, https://www.theguardian.com/world/2016/jan/15/british-us-military-in-command-room-saudi-strikes-yemen, accessed 7 November 2019.

Grant, Rebecca, 'An Air War Like No Other', *Air Force Magazine*, 1 November 2002, https://www.airforcemag.com/article/1102airwar/, accessed 21 December 2016.

Green, Fred, USARMY, Oral History—Colonel (R) Fred K. Green, Interview by Kate Gowel and John Gowel, Transcript, 4 December 2010 Green's personal collection; (on file with author; with permission from Fred Green).

Green, US Army, Colonel (ret), Interview with author, telephone, 14 July 2015.

Greenwald, Glenn, *No Place to Hide: Edward Snowden, the NSA, and the U.S. Surveillance State* (New York, NY: Metropolitan Books, 2014).

Gregory, Derek, *The Colonial Present: Afghanistan, Palestine, Iraq* (Malden, MA; Oxford; Carlton, Victoria: Wiley-Blackwell, 2004).

Gregory, Derek, 'The Black Flag: Guantánamo Bay and the Space of Exception', *Geografiska Annaler: Series B, Human Geography* 88, no. 4 (2006): 405–27.

Gregory, Derek, 'Seeing Red: Baghdad and the Event-Ful City', *Political Geography* 29, no. 5 (2010): 266–79.

Gregory, Derek, 'War and Peace', *Transactions of the Institute of British Geographers* 35, no. 2 (2010): 154–86.

Gregory, Derek, 'The Everywhere War', *The Geographical Journal* 177, no. 3 (2011): 238–50.

Gregory, Derek, 'Lines of Descent', *OpenDemocracy.Net*, 8 November 2011, http://www.opendemocracy.net/derek-gregory/lines-of-descent, accessed 16 February 2012.

Gregory, Derek, '"Doors into Nowhere": Dead Cities and the Natural History of Destruction', in *Cultural Memories: The Geographical Point of View*, ed. Peter Meusburger, Michael Heffernan, and Edgar Wunder (Dordrecht; Heidelberg; London; New York, NY: Springer, 2011), 249–83.

Gregory, Derek, 'From a View to a Kill Drones and Late Modern War', *Theory, Culture & Society* 28, no. 7–8 (2011): 188–215.

Gregory, Derek, 'I Don't like Tuesdays . . . ', *Geographical Imaginations* (blog), 26 October 2012, http://geographicalimaginations.com/2012/10/26/i-dont-like-tuesdays/, accessed 28 May 2015.

Gregory, Derek, 'Dis/Ordering the Orient: Scopic Regimes and Modern War', in *Orientalism and War*, ed. Tarak Barkawi and Keith Stanski (New York, NY: Columbia University Press, 2013), 151–76.

Gregory, Derek, 'Theory of the Drone 3: Killing Grounds', *Geographical Imaginations* (blog), 30 July 2013, https://geographicalimaginations.com/2013/07/29/theory-of-the-drone-3-killing-grounds/, accessed 9 September 2019.

Gregory, Derek, 'Destructive Edge', *Geographical Imaginations* (blog), 8 August 2014, http://geographicalimaginations.com/2014/08/08/destructive-edge/, accessed 16 October 2014.

Gregory, Derek, 'Drone Geographies', *Radical Philosophy* 183 (2014): 7–19.

Gregory, Derek, 'Lines of Descent', in *From Above: War, Violence, and Verticality*, ed. Peter Adey, Mark Whitehead, and Alison Williams (New York, NY: Oxford University Press, 2014), 41–70

Gregory, Derek, 'Kunduz and "Seeing like a Military"', *Geographical Imaginations* (blog), 2 January 2014, https://geographicalimaginations.com/2014/01/02/kunduz-and-seeing-like-a-military/, accessed 24 January 2017.

Gregory, Derek, 'Gaza 101', *Geographical Imaginations* (blog), 21 July 2014, https://geographicalimaginations.com/2014/07/21/gaza-101/, accessed 7 January 2017.

Gregory, Derek, 'Gabriel's Map: Cartography and Corpography in Modern War', in *Geographies of Knowledge and Power*, ed. Peter Meusburger, Derek Gregory, and Laura Suarsana, 2015 edition (New York, NY: Springer, 2015), 89–121.

Gregory, Derek, 'Angry Eyes (1)', *Geographical Imaginations* (blog), 1 October 2015, https://geographicalimaginations.com/2015/10/01/angry-eyes-1/, accessed 16 January 2017.

Gregory, Derek, 'Angry Eyes (2)', *Geographical Imaginations* (blog), 7 October 2015, https://geographicalimaginations.com/2015/10/07/angry-eyes-2/, accessed 16 January 2017.

Gregory, Derek, 'Watching the Detectives', *Geographical Imaginations* (blog), 8 October 2015, https://geographicalimaginations.com/2015/10/08/watching-the-detectives/, accessed 16 January 2017.

Gregory, Derek, 'Killing over Kunduz', *Geographical Imaginations* (blog), 3 October 2016, https://geographicalimaginations.com/2016/10/03/killing-over-kunduz/, accessed 16 January 2017.

Gregory, Derek, 'Fighting over Kunduz', *Geographical Imaginations* (blog), 17 November 2016, https://geographicalimaginations.com/2016/11/17/fighting-over-kunduz/, accessed 16 January 2017.

Gregory, Derek, 'The Natures of War', *Antipode* 48, no. 1 (2016): 3–56.

Gregory, Derek, 'Dirty Dancing and Spaces of Exception in Pakistan', in *Life in the Age of Drone Warfare*, ed. Lisa Parks and Caren Kaplan (Durham, NC: Duke University Press Books, 2017).

Gregory, Derek, 'The Territory of the Screen', *MediaTropes* 6, no. 2 (2017): 126–47.

Gregory, Thomas, 'Dangerous Feelings: Checkpoints and the Perception of Hostile Intent', *Security Dialogue* 50, no. 2 (2019): 131–47,

Greiner, Bernd, *War without Fronts: The USA in Vietnam* (New Haven, CT: Yale University Press, 2009).

Gross, Aeyal M., 'The Construction of a Wall between the Hague and Jerusalem: The Enforcement and Limits of Humanitarian Law and the Structure of Occupation', *Leiden Journal of International Law* 19, no. 2 (2006): 393–440.

Gross, Emanuel L., 'The Watchdog of the IDF—Opinion', *Haaretz*, 18 September 2014, http://www.haaretz.com/opinion/.premium-1.616349, accessed 19 September 2014.

Gross, Michael L., *Moral Dilemmas of Modern War: Torture, Assassination, and Blackmail in an Age of Asymmetric Conflict* (Cambridge; New York, NY: Cambridge University Press, 2010).

Gross, Richard C. and Ian Henderson, 'Multinational Operations', in *U.S. Military Operations: Law, Policy, and Practice*, ed. Geoffrey S. Corn, Rachel E. VanLandingham, and Shane R. Reeves (Oxford: Oxford University Press, 2015), 341–70.

Grossman, Dave, *On Killing: The Psychological Cost of Learning to Kill in War and Society*, revised edition (New York, NY: Back Bay Books, 2009).

Grunawalt, Richard J., 'The JCS Standing Rules of Engagement: A Judge Advocate's Primer', *Air Force Law Review* 42 (1997): 245.

Guiora, Amos N., 'License to Kill'. *Foreign Policy*, 14 July 2009, http://www.foreignpolicy.com/articles/2009/07/13/licence_to_kill#sthash.zCjE83OL.dpbs, accessed 14 December 2014.

Gunneflo, Markus, *Targeted Killing: A Legal and Political History* (Cambridge: Cambridge University Press, 2016).

Haas, Peter M., 'Introduction: Epistemic Communities and International Policy Coordination', *International Organization* 46, no. 1 (1992): 1–35.

Haffa, Robert P. and Jasper Welch, *Command and Control Arrangements for the Attack of Time-Sensitive Targets* (Los Angeles: Northrup Grumman, 2005).

Hajjar, Lisa, *Courting Conflict: The Israeli Military Court System in the West Bank and Gaza* (Berkeley, CA: University of California Press, 2005).

Hajjar, Lisa, 'International Humanitarian Law and "Wars on Terror": A Comparative Analysis of Israeli and American Doctrines and Policies', *Journal of Palestine Studies* 36, no. 1 (2006): 21–42.

Hajjar, Lisa, 'Universal Jurisdiction as Praxis', in *When Governments Break the Law: The Rule of Law and the Prosecution of the Bush Administration*, ed. Austin Sarat and Nasser Hussain (New York, NY: New York University Press, 2010), 87–120.

Hajjar, Lisa, 'Lawfare and Armed Conflict: Comparing Israeli and US Targeted Killing Policies and Challenges against Them', *International Affairs Research Report, American University of Beirut, January*, 2013, https://www.daleel-madani.org/ar/civil-society-directory/issam-fares-institute-public-policy-and-international-affairs/resources/lawfare-and-armed-conflict-comparing-israeli-and-us-targeted-killing-policies-and-challenges-against, accessed 1 July 2020.

Hajjar, Lisa, *Torture: A Sociology of Violence and Human Rights* (New York, NY: Routledge, 2013).

Hajjar, Lisa, 'Lawfare and Armed Conflict: A Comparative Analysis of Israeli and U.S. Targeted Killing Policies and Legal Challenges against Them', in *Life in the Age of Drone Warfare*, ed. Lisa Parks and Caren Kaplan (Durham, NC: Duke University Press Books, 2017), 59–88

Hajjar, Lisa, 'In Defense of Lawfare: The Value of Litigation in Challenging Torture', in *Confronting Torture: Essays on the Ethics, Legality, History, and Psychology of Torture Today*, ed. Scott Anderson and Martha Nussbaum (Chicago; London: University of Chicago Press, 2018), 294–319.

Hajjar, Lisa, 'The Counterterrorism War Paradigm versus International Humanitarian Law: The Legal Contradictions and Global Consequences of the US "War on Terror"', *Law & Social Inquiry* 44, no. 4 (2019): 922–56.

Hallion, Richard, *Storm Over Iraq: Air Power and the Gulf War* (Washington, DC: Smithsonian Institution, 1992).

Hampson, Françoise, 'Human Rights Law and International Humanitarian Law: Two Coins or Two Sides of the Same Coin?' *Bulletin of Human Rights* 91, no. 1 (1992): 46–54.

Haque, Adil Ahmad, 'U.S. Legal Defense of the Soleimani Strike at the United Nations: A Critical Assessment', *Just Security*, 10 January 2020, https://www.justsecurity.org/68008/

u-s-legal-defense-of-the-soleimani-strike-at-the-united-nations-a-critical-assessment/, accessed 23 February 2020.

Hartman, Ben, '50 Days of Israel's Gaza Operation, Protective Edge—by the Numbers', *The Jerusalem Post*, 28 August 2014, http://www.jpost.com/Operation-Protective-Edge/50-days-of-Israels-Gaza-operation-Protective-Edge-by-the-numbers-372574, accessed 16 October 2014.

Harvard Law School International Human Rights Clinic, 'Tackling Tough Calls: Lessons from Recent Conflicts on Hostile Intent and Civilian Protection', March 2016, https://www.justsecurity.org/wp-content/uploads/2016/03/Tackling-Tough-Choices-Hostile-Intent-HLSIHRC-2016.pdf, accessed 1 March 2020.

Harvard Study Team, 'The Effect of the Gulf Crisis on the Children of Iraq', Boston, MA: Harvard School of Public Health, 22 May 1991 (on file with author; accessed via Harvard Library Inter-Library Loan from Newcastle University).

Hebert, Adam J., 'Compressing the Kill Chain', *Air Force Magazine* 86, no. 3 (2003): 50–5.

Heintze, Hans-Joachim, 'On the Relationship between Human Rights Law Protection and International Humanitarian Law', *International Review of the Red Cross* 86, no. 856 (2004): 789–814.

Heintzelman, Harry L. and Edmund S. Bloom, 'Planning Primer: How to Provide Effective Legal Input into the War Planning and Combat Execution Process, A', *Air Force Law Review* 37 (1994): 5.

Henderson, Christian, *The Persistent Advocate and the Use of Force: The Impact of the United States upon the Jus Ad Bellum in the Post-Cold War Era* (Farnham, Surrey; Burlington, VT: Routledge, 2010).

Henderson, Ian, 'Legal Officers in the Australian Defence Force: Functions by Rank and Competency Level, along with a Case-Study on Operations', *Military Law and Law of War Review* 50, nos. 1–2 (2011): 37–66.

Herold, Marc, 'The "Unworthy" Afgan Bodies: "Smarter" U.S. Weapons Kill More Innocents', in *Inventing Collateral Damage: Civilian Casualties, War, and Empire*, ed. Stephen J. Rockel and Rick Halpern (Toronto: Between the Lines, 2009), 303–28

Hill, Evan and Christiaan Triebert, '12 Hours. 4 Syrian Hospitals Bombed. One Culprit: Russia.' *The New York Times*, 13 October 2019, sec. World, https://www.nytimes.com/2019/10/13/world/middleeast/russia-bombing-syrian-hospitals.html, accessed 11 March 2020.

Holmes, Oliver, 'UN Calls for "maximum Restraint" after Alleged Israeli Strike in Lebanon', *The Guardian*, 26 August 2019, sec. World, https://www.theguardian.com/world/2019/aug/26/israel-accused-of-targeting-iran-allies-in-lebanon-bombing, accessed 19 November 2019.

Horton, Scott, 'The Law of Armed Conflict: Six Questions for Gary Solis', *The Stream - Harper's Magazine Blog* (blog), 20 April 2010, http://harpers.org/blog/2010/04/_the-law-of-armed-conflict_-six-questions-for-gary-solis/, accessed 16 January 2016.

House of Commons, 'Oral Answers to Questions: Foreign and Commonwealth Affairs', available from the Palestinian Centre for Human Rights, 30 March 2004, http://pchrgaza.org/files/campaigns/english/almog/jack.pdf, accessed 19 July 2012.

Human Rights Watch, 'Needless Deaths in the Gulf War: Civilian Casualties During the Air Campaign and Violations of the Laws of War', New York, 1991, https://www.hrw.org/reports/1991/gulfwar/index.htm#TopOfPage, accessed 26 June 2017.

Human Rights Watch, 'Universal Jurisdiction in Europe: The State of the Art', 28 June 2006, http://www.hrw.org/node/11298, accessed 12 October 2014.

Human Rights Watch, '"Troops in Contact": Airstrikes and Civilian Deaths in Afghanistan', September 2008, http://www.hrw.org/sites/default/files/reports/afghanistan0908webwcover_0.pdf, accessed 9 November 2014.

Human Rights Watch, 'Getting Away with Torture', 12 July 2011, https://www.hrw.org/report/2011/07/12/getting-away-torture/bush-administration-and-mistreatment-detainees, accessed 22 March 2017.

Human Rights Watch, 'Unlawful Israeli Attacks on Palestinian Media', 20 December 2012, http://www.hrw.org/news/2012/12/20/israelgaza-unlawful-israeli-attacks-palestinian-media, accessed 30 September 2014.

Human Rights Watch, 'Gaza: "Unlawful Combatants Law" Violates Rights', 1 March 2017, https://www.hrw.org/news/2017/03/01/gaza-unlawful-combatants-law-violates-rights, accessed 27 June 2017.

Humphrey, David C., 'Tuesday Lunch at the Johnson White House: A Preliminary Assessment', *Diplomatic History* 8, no. 1 (1984): 81–102.

Humphries, John G., 'Operations Law and the Rules of Engagement in Operation Desert Shield and Desert Storm', *Airpower Journal* 6, no. 3 (1992).

Hurd, Ian, *How to Do Things with International Law* (Princeton, NJ: Princeton University Press, 2017).

Husby, Eric C., 'A Balancing Act: In Pursuit of Proportionality in Self-Defense for On-Scene Commanders, A', *Army Law*, May 2012, 6–14.

Infeld, Danielle L., 'Precision-Guided Munitions Demonstrated Their Pinpoint Accuracy in Desert Storm; but is a Country Obligated to Use Precision Technology to Minimize Collateral Civilian Injury and Damage', *George Washington Journal of International Law and Economics* 26, no. 1 (1992): 109–41.

International Committee of the Red Cross, 'Preamble to Convention (IV) Respecting the Laws and Customs of War on Land and Its Annex: Regulations Concerning the Laws and Customs of War on Land', The Hague, 18 October 1907, https://ihl-databases.icrc.org/applic/ihl/ihl.nsf/Article.xsp?action=openDocument&documentId=BD48EA8AD56596A3C12563CD0051653F, accessed 29 December 2016.

International Committee of the Red Cross, 'Protocol Additional to the Geneva Conventions of 12 August 1949, and Relating to the Protection of Victims of International Armed Conflicts (Protocol I)', Bern, Switzerland, 8 June 1977, https://ihl-databases.icrc.org/ihl/INTRO/470, accessed 29 December 2016.

International Committee of the Red Cross, 'Interpretive Guidance on the Notion of Direct Participation in Hostilities under International Humanitarian Law', *International Review of the Red Cross* 90, no. 872 (2008): 991–1047.

International Committee of the Red Cross, 'What Is IHL?' *International Committee of the Red Cross*, 18 September 2015, https://www.icrc.org/en/document/what-ihl?language=en, accessed 11 January 2017.

International Committee of the Red Cross, and Nils Melzer, 'Interpretive Guidance on the Notion of Direct Participation in Hostilities Under International Humanitarian Law', Geneva: International Committee of the Red Cross, 2009.

Irani, Freya, '"Lawfare", US Military Discourse, and the Colonial Constitution of Law and War', *European Journal of International Security* 3, no. 1 (2018): 113–33.

Israel Knesset, Incarceration of Unlawful Combatants Law, 5762-2002 § (2002), https://ihl-databases.icrc.org/applic/ihl/ihl-nat.nsf/0/7A09C457F76A452BC12575C30049A7BD, accessed 27 June 2017.

Israel Ministry of Foreign Affairs, 'Press Briefing by Colonel Daniel Reisner', 15 November 2000, IMFA, http://www.mfa.gov.il/MFA/MFAArchive/2000_2009/2000/11/Press+Brief

ing+by+Colonel+Daniel+Reisner-+Head+of.htm?DisplayMode=print, accessed 12 June 2020.

Israel Ministry of Foreign Affairs, 'The Operation in Gaza-Factual and Legal Aspects', www.mfa.gov.il: IMFA, 29 July 2009, http://www.mfa.gov.il/MFA/ForeignPolicy/Terrorism/Pages/Operation_in_Gaza-Factual_and_Legal_Aspects.aspx, accessed 5 November 2013.

Israel Ministry of Foreign Affairs, 'Salah Shehadeh—Special Investigatory Commission', www.mfa.gov.il, IMFA, 27 February 2011, http://www.mfa.gov.il/MFA/Government/Law/Legal+Issues+and+Rulings/Salah_Shehadeh-Special_Investigatory_Commission_27-Feb-2011, accessed 6 July 2012.

Israel Ministry of Foreign Affairs, 'The 2014 Gaza Conflict: Factual and Legal Aspects', IMFA, May 2015, http://mfa.gov.il/ProtectiveEdge/Pages/default.aspx, accessed 15 September 2016.

Issacharoff, Samuel and Richard H. Pildes, 'Drones and the Dilemma of Modern Warfare', *NYU School of Law, Public Law Research Paper No. 13-34*, 1 June 2013, http://papers.ssrn.com/abstract=2268596, accessed 4 November 2013.

Jabareen, Hassan, 'Transnational Lawyering and Legal Resistance in National Courts: Palestinian Cases Before the Israeli Supreme Court', *Yale Human Rights and Development Journal* 13, no. 1 (2010): 239–80.

Jacobsen, Michael Hviid and Poul Poder, *The Sociology of Zygmunt Bauman: Challenges and Critique* (Aldershot; Burlington, VT: Ashgate, 2008).

Jaffer, Jameel, ed. *The Drone Memos: Targeted Killing, Secrecy, and the Law* (New York, NY: The New Press, 2016).

Jeong, May, 'Searching for Ground Truth in the Kunduz Hospital Bombing', *The Intercept*, 28 April 2016, https://theintercept.com/2016/04/28/searching-for-ground-truth-in-the-kunduz-hospital-bombing/, accessed 23 January 2017.

Jeremy Bob, Yonah, 'Israel Gov't Lawyers Help NATO Fight Lawfare, Receive Awards', *The Jerusalem Post*, 2 September 2019, https://www.jpost.com/Israel-News/Israel-govt-lawyers-help-NATO-fight-lawfare-receive-awards-600346, accessed 27 November 2019.

Jochnick, Chris and Roger Normand, 'The Legitimation of Violence: A Critical History of the Laws of War', *Harvard International Law Journal* 35, no. 1 (1994): 49–95.

Johns, Fleur, 'Guantanamo Bay and the Annihilation of the Exception', *European Journal of International Law* 16, no. 4 (2005): 613–35.

Johns, Fleur, *Non-Legality in International Law: Unruly Law* (Cambridge; New York, NY: Cambridge University Press, 2013).

Johnson, Jeh Charles, 'National Security Law, Lawyers, and Lawyering in the Obama Administration-Dean's Lecture at Yale Law School, February 22, 2012', *Yale Law and Policy Review* 31, no. 1 (2012): 141–50.

Jones, Craig, 'Frames of Law: Targeting Advice and Operational Law in the Israeli Military', *Environment and Planning D: Society and Space* 33, no. 4 (2015): 676–96.

Jones, Craig, 'Lawfare and the Juridification of Late Modern War', *Progress in Human Geography* 40, no. 2 (2016): 221–39.

Jones, Craig, 'Travelling Law: Targeted Killing, Lawfare and the Deconstruction of the Battlefield', in *American Studies Encounters the Middle East* (Chapel Hill: University of North Carolina Press, 2016), 207–40.

Jones, Craig and Michael D. Smith, 'War/Law/Space Notes toward a Legal Geography of War', *Environment and Planning D: Society and Space* 33, no. 4 (2015): 581–91.

The Judge Advocate General's Legal Center & School, Center for Law and Military Operations (CLAMO), United States Army, 'Legal Lessons Learned From Afghanistan and Iraq Volume I Major Combat Operations (11 September 2001–1 May 2003)' (Charlottesville, VA: United States Army, 1 August 2004), https://fas.org/irp/doddir/army/clamo-v1.pdf, accessed 15 December 2016.

The Judge Advocate General's Legal Center & School, Center for Law and Military Operations (CLAMO), United States Army, 'Legal Lessons Learned From Afghanistan and Iraq Volume II Full Spectrum Operations (2 May 2003–30 June 2004)' (Charlottesville, VA: United States Army, 1 August 2004) https://fas.org/irp/doddir/army/clamo-v2.pdf, accessed 22 March 2017.

The Judge Advocate General's Legal Center & School, International & Operational Law Department, United States Army, 'Operational Law Handbook 2017' (Charlottesville, VA: United States Army, 2017) http://www.loc.gov/rr/frd/Military_Law/operational-law-handbooks.html, accessed 8 November 2019.

The Judge Advocate General's School, International & Operational Law Department, United States Army, 'Operational Law Handbook 1997' (Charlottesville, VA: United States Army, 1997, on file with author).

The Judge Advocate General's School, United States Air Force, 'The Military Commander and the Law', 15th edition (Maxwell Air Force Base, AL: United States Air Force, 2019), https://media.defense.gov/2019/Apr/11/2002115350/-1/-1/0/B_0159_JAG_MILITARY_COMMANDER_AND_THE_LAW_.PDF, accessed 1 March 2020.

Kahn, Paul W., 'Imagining Warfare', *European Journal of International Law* 24, no. 1 (2013): 199–226.

Kaldor, Mary, *New and Old Wars: Organized Violence in a Global Era*, 2nd edition (Stanford, CA: Stanford University Press, 2007).

Kaldor, Mary, 'In Defence of New Wars', *Stability: International Journal of Security and Development* 2, no. 1 (2013): Art. 4, 1–16.

Kamps, Charles T., 'The JCS 94-Target List: A Vietnam Myth That Still Distorts Military Thought', *Aerospace Power Journal* 15, no. 1 (2001): 67–80.

Kasher, Asa, and Amos Yadlin, 'Military Ethics of Fighting Terror: An Israeli Perspective', *Journal of Military Ethics* 4, no. 1 (2005): 3–32.

Kasher, Asa, and Amos Yadlin, 'Human Life in the War on Terrorism: A Response to "the Risk Dilemma" by Michael Walzer', *Philosophia* 44, no. 2 (2016): 295–308.

Kattan, Victor, 'Furthering the "War on Terrorism" through International Law: How the United States and the United Kingdom Resurrected the Bush Doctrine on Using Preventive Military Force to Combat Terrorism', *Journal on the Use of Force and International Law* 5, no. 1 (2017): 97–144.

Keaney, Thomas A. and Eliot A. Cohen, *Revolution in Warfare?: Air Power in the Persian Gulf* (Annapolis, MD: Naval Institute Press, 1995).

Keeva, S., 'Lawyers in the War Room', *American Bar Association Journal* 77, no. 12 (1991): 52–9.

Kennedy, David, *Of War and Law* (Princeton, NJ: Princeton University Press, 2006).

Kennedy, David, *A World of Struggle: How Power, Law, and Expertise Shape Global Political Economy* (Princeton, NJ; Oxford: Princeton University Press, 2018).

Kent, Irvin M. et al., 'A Lawyer's Day in Vietnam', *American Bar Association Journal* 54, no. 12 (1968): 1177–82.

Kerns, Patricia A., *The First 50* Years: *U.S. Air Force Judge Advocate General's Department* (Washington DC: US Air Force Judge Advocate General's Department, 2004).

Khalili, Laleh, *Time in the Shadows: Confinement in Counterinsurgencies* (Stanford, CA: Stanford University Press, 2012).

Khalili, Laleh, 'A Habit of Destruction', *Society and Space—Environment and Planning D* (blog), 2014, http://societyandspace.com/material/commentaries/laleh-khalili-a-habit-of-destruction/, accessed 9 November 2014.

Khan, Azmat and Anand Gopal, 'The Uncounted—The New York Times', *The New York Times*, 16 November 2017, https://www.nytimes.com/interactive/2017/11/16/magazine/uncounted-civilian-casualties-iraq-airstrikes.html, accessed 28 November 2019.

Khen, Hilly Moodrick-Even, 'Can We Now Tell What "Direct Participation in Hostilities" Is? HCJ 769/02 the Public Committee Against Torture in Israel v. The Government of Israel', *Israel Law Review* 40, no. 1 (2007): 213–44.

Kilcullen, David, *Out of the Mountains: The Coming Age of the Urban Guerrilla* (London: Hurst Publishers, 2013).

Kinsella, Helen M., *The Image Before the Weapon: A Critical History of the Distinction Between Combatant and Civilian* (Ithaca, NY: Cornell University Press, 2011).

Kittrie, Orde F., *Lawfare: Law as a Weapon of War* (New York, NY: Oxford University Press, 2015).

Koring, Paul, 'Handling the Perilous Job of Close Air Support', *The Globe and Mail*, 5 September 2006, http://www.theglobeandmail.com/news/world/handling-the-perilous-job-of-close-air-support/article18172321/, accessed 8 January 2017.

Koskenniemi, Martti, 'International Law and Hegemony: A Reconfiguration', *Cambridge Review of International Affairs* 17, no. 2 (2004): 197–218.

Kretzmer, David, *The Occupation of Justice: The Supreme Court of Israel and the Occupied Territories* (Albany, NY: State University of New York Press, 2002).

Kretzmer, David, 'The Law of Belligerent Occupation in the Supreme Court of Israel', *International Review of the Red Cross* 94, no. 885 (2012): 207–36.

Kurle, David, 'Lawyers Provide Operational Advice to CAOC Commanders', Air Force Central Command Public Affairs, 4 March 2010, http://www.afcent.af.mil/News/Features/Display/tabid/4819/Article/223901/lawyers-provide-operational-advice-to-caoc-commanders.aspx, accessed 17 December 2016.

Lambeth, Benjamin S., *The Transformation of American Air Power* (Ithaca, NY: Cornell University Press, 2000).

Lambeth, Benjamin S., *Air Power Against Terror: America's Conduct of Operation Enduring Freedom*, 2nd edition (Santa Monica, CA: RAND Corporation, 2006).

Lambeth, Benjamin S., *The Unseen War: Allied Air Power and the Takedown of Saddam Hussein* (Annapolis, MD: Naval Institute Press, 2013).

Lander, Heath, 'The Latency Phase - of "Terrorist Babies" and "Dead Children Strategies"', *Daily Kos* (blog), https://www.dailykos.com/story/2010/8/12/892586/-, accessed 6 July 2017.

Lauterpacht, Hersch, 'The Problem of the Revision of the Law of War', *British Year Book of International Law* 29 (1952): 360.

Lawand, Kathleen, 'Reviewing the Legality of New Weapons, Means and Methods of Warfare', *International Review of the Red Cross* 88, no. 864 (2006): 925–30.

Lawand, Kathleen, Robin M. Coupland, and Herby Peter, *A Guide to the Legal Review of New Weapons, Means and Methods of Warfare: Measures to Implement Article 36 of Additional Protocol I of 1977* (Geneva: International Committee of the Red Cross, 2006).

Lawfare Blog, 'Civilian Casualties & Collateral Damage', Lawfare Blog, 28 January 2013, https://www.lawfareblog.com/civilian-casualties-collateral-damage, accessed 4 March 2020.

Leander, Anna, 'Technological Agency in the Co-Constitution of Legal Expertise and the US Drone Program', *Leiden Journal of International Law* 26, no. 4 (2013): 811–31.

Leander, Anna and Tanja Aalberts, 'Introduction: The Co-Constitution of Legal Expertise and International Security', *Leiden Journal of International Law* 26, no. 4 (2013): 783–92.

Lebowitz, Michael J., 'The Value of Claiming Torture: An Analysis of Al-Qaeda's Tactical Lawfare Strategy and Efforts to Fight Back', *Case Western Reserve Journal of International Law* 43, no. 1 (2010): 357–92.

Lederman, Gordon Nathaniel, *Reorganizing the Joint Chiefs of Staff: The Goldwater-Nichols Act of 1986* (Westport, CT: Greenwood Publishing Group, 1999).

Lewis, Paul and Ian Black, 'Gaza Conflict: US Says Israeli Attack on UN School Was "Totally Unacceptable"', *The Guardian*, 31 July 2014, http://www.theguardian.com/world/2014/jul/31/gaza-conflict-us-israeli-attack-un-school, accessed 16 October 2014.

Liang, Qiao and Wang Xiangsui, *Unrestricted Warfare* (Beijing: PLA Literature and Arts Publishing House, 1999).

Libman, Liron A., 'Legal Advice in the Conduct of Operations in the Israel Defense Forces', *Military Law and Law of War Review* 50, nos. 1–2 (2011): 67–97.

Lindsay-Poland, John, *Emperors in the Jungle: The Hidden History of the U.S. in Panama* (Durham, NC: Duke University Press, 2003).

Lohr, Michael F. and Steve Gallotta, 'Legal Support in War: The Role of Military Lawyers', *Chicago Journal of International Law* 4, no. 2 (2003): 465–78.

Luban, David, 'Lawfare and Legal Ethics in Guantanamo', *Stanford Law Review* 60, no. 6 (2008): 1981–2026.

Luban, David, 'Military Necessity and the Cultures of Military Law', *Leiden Journal of International Law* 26, no. 2 (2013): 315–49.

Luban, David, *Torture, Power, and Law* (Cambridge: Cambridge University Press, 2014).

Ma'an News, 'Police: Israel Dropped "equivalent of 6 Nuclear Bombs" on Gaza', *Maan News Agency*, 22 August 2014, http://group194.net/english/article/36928, accessed 1 July 2020.

MacAskill, Ewen and Richard Norton-Taylor, 'How UK Government Decided to Kill Reyaad Khan', *The Guardian*, 8 September 2015, sec. World, https://www.theguardian.com/world/2015/sep/08/how-did-britain-decide-to-assassinate-uk-isis-fighter-reyaad-khan-drone-strike, accessed 6 November 2019.

Mandelbaum, Michael, 'Vietnam: The Television War', *Daedalus* 111, no. 4 (1982): 157–69.

Mandeles, Mark David, Thomas Hone, and Sanford S. Terry, *Managing 'Command and Control' in the Persian Gulf War* (Westport, CA: Praeger, 1996).

Mann, Edward C., 'Thunder and Lightning: Desert Storm and the Airpower Debates, Volume 2', DTIC Document, 1995, https://apps.dtic.mil/docs/citations/ADA421939, accessed 29 June 2020.

Margalit, Avishai and Michael Walzer, 'Israel: Civilians & Combatants', *The New York Review of Books*, 14 May 2009, http://www.nybooks.com/articles/archives/2009/may/14/israel-civilians-combatants/, accessed 11 February 2014.

Martins, Mark S., 'Rules of Engagement for Land Forces: A Matter of Training, Not Lawyering', *Military Law Review* 143 (1994): 1–160.

Masalha, Nur, 'The 1956-57 Occupation of the Gaza Strip: Israeli Proposals to Resettle the Palestinian Refugees', *British Journal of Middle Eastern Studies* 23, no. 1 (1996): 55–68.

Mathews, Tom, 'The Secret History of the War', *Newsweek* 117, no. 11 (1991).

Mbembe, Achille, 'Necropolitics', *Public Culture* 15, no. 1 (2003): 11–40.

Mbembe, Achille, *Necropolitics* (Durham, NC: Duke University Press Books, 2019).

McAllister, James, 'Who Lost Vietnam?: Soldiers, Civilians, and U.S. Military Strategy', *International Security* 35, no. 3 (2010): 95–123.

McChrystal, Stanley, 'Tactical Directive', International Security Assistance Force (ISAF), NATO, 6 July 2009, http://www.nato.int/isaf/docu/official_texts/Tactical_Directive_090706.pdf, accessed 15 December 2016.

McCue, Jason, 'Today's Wars Are Fought by Lawyers, Not Soldiers', *The Telegraph*, 25 May 2016, http://www.telegraph.co.uk/news/2016/05/25/todays-wars-are-fought-by-lawyers-not-soldiers/, accessed 14 June 2016.

McDonell, Nick, 'Civilian Casualties Are Not Inevitable. The Military Sets an Acceptable Number in Advance', *Los Angeles Times*, 31 March 2017, https://www.latimes.com/opinion/op-ed/la-oe-mcdonell-civilian-casualties-ncv-20170331-story.html, accessed 13 February 2020.

McNeal, Gregory S., 'Targeted Killing and Accountability', *The Georgetown Law Journal* 102, no. 3 (2014): 681–794.

McSally, Martha, 'Letter to the President and the Honorable Ash Carter', 28 January 2016, reproduced at: https://nationalinterest.org/blog/the-buzz/mcsallys-case-lethal-next-gen-10-warthog-15064, accessed 1 July 2020.

Mégret, Frédéric, 'From "Savages" to "Unlawful Combatants": A Postcolonial Look at International Humanitarian Law's Other', in *International Law and Its Others*, ed. Anne Orford (Cambridge: Cambridge University Press, 2006), 265–317

Mégret, Frédéric, 'The Humanitarian Problem with Drones', *Utah Law Review* 2013, no. 5 (2013): 1283–319.

Mehta, Aaron, 'Mattis Reveals New Rules of Engagement', *Military Times*, 5 October 2017, https://www.militarytimes.com/flashpoints/2017/10/03/mattis-reveals-new-rules-of-engagement/, accessed 29 January 2020.

Mehta, Aaron and Tara Copp, 'Trump Afghanistan Strategy Calls for More Troops, Regional Pressure', *Defense News*, 21 August 2017, https://www.militarytimes.com/news/2017/08/22/trump-afghanistan-strategy-calls-for-more-troops-regional-pressure/, accessed 10 February 2020.

Melman, Yossi, 'Targeted Killings—a Retro Fashion Very Much in Vogue—Features', *Haaretz*, 24 March 2004, http://www.haaretz.com/print-edition/features/targeted-killings-a-retro-fashion-very-much-in-vogue-1.117714, accessed 2 October 2014.

Melzer, Nils, 'Keeping the Balance between Military Necessity and Humanity: A Response to Four Critiques of the ICRC's Interpretive Guidance on the Notion of Direct Participation in Hostilities Forum: Direct Participation In Hostilities: Perspectives on the ICRC Interpretive Guidance', *New York University Journal of International Law and Politics* 42, no. 3 (2010): 831–916.

Melzer, Nils, *Targeted Killing in International Law* (Oxford; New York, NY: Oxford University Press, 2009).

Merat, Arron, '"The Saudis Couldn't Do It without Us": The UK's True Role in Yemen's Deadly War', *The Guardian*, 18 June 2019, sec. World, https://www.theguardian.com/world/2019/jun/18/the-saudis-couldnt-do-it-without-us-the-uks-true-role-in-yemens-deadly-war, accessed 7 November 2019.

Meron, Theodor, 'The Humanization of Humanitarian Law', *American Journal of International Law* 94, no. 2 (2000): 239–78.

Meron, Theodor, *The Humanization of International Law* (Boston, MA: Martinus Nijhoff, 2006).

Michel, Arthur Holla, *Eyes in the Sky: The Secret Rise of Gorgon Stare and How It Will Watch Us All* (Boston, MA: Houghton Mifflin Harcourt USA, 2019).

Michel, Arthur Holland, 'The Killer Algorithms Nobody's Talking About', *Foreign Policy* (blog), 20 January 2020, https://foreignpolicy.com/2020/01/20/

ai-autonomous-weapons-artificial-intelligence-the-killer-algorithms-nobodys-talking-about/, accessed 16 March 2020.

Michelsen Institute, 'Protection of Civilians: Why They Die in US Strikes', Bergen, Norway: CMI CHR, Michelsen Institute, 10 November 2015, https://www.cmi.no/news/1615-protection-of-civilians, accessed 2 March 2020.

Mieville, China, *Between Equal Rights: A Marxist Theory of International Law* (Chicago: Historical Materialism, 2006).

Military Advocate General of the Israel Defense Force, 'Decisions of the IDF Military Advocate General Regarding Exceptional Incidents That Allegedly Occurred During Operation "Protective Edge"', 15 August 2018, https://www.idf.il/en/minisites/military-advocate-generals-corps/releases-idf-military-advocate-general/mag-corps-press-release-update-6/, accessed 20 December 2019.

Military Advocate General of the Israel Defense Force, 'Operation "Pillar of Defense" 14–21 November 2012', MAG: International Law Department, 19 December 2012, https://www.legal-tools.org/doc/84f408/pdf/, accessed 1 July 2020.

Military Advocate General of the Israel Defense Force, 'The MAG Corps—History', n.d., Source with similar information available at: https://www.idf.il/en/minisites/military-advocate-generals-corps/about-the-mag-corps/, accessed 30 June 2020.

Military Advocate General of the Israel Defense Force, 'The MAG Corps—Mission', n.d.

Military Law and Law of War Review, 'Agora: The Role and Responsibilities of Legal Advisors in the Armed Forces—Evolution and Present Trends (Celebration of the Military Law and the Law of War Review's 50th Anniversary)', *Military Law and Law of War Review*, nos. 1–2 (2011): 5–617.

Mitchell, George et al., *Sharm El-Sheikh Fact-Finding Committee* (Washington, DC: US Department of State, 30 April 2001), http://2001-2009.state.gov/p/nea/rls/rpt/3060.htm, accessed 29 September 2015.

Monalisa Gharavi, Maryam and Anat Matar, 'Israeli Officer Promotes War Crimes at Harvard', *The Electronic Intifada*, 22 July 2009, https://electronicintifada.net/content/israeli-officer-promotes-war-crimes-harvard/8357, accessed 15 September 2016.

Montell, Jessica, 'Operation Defensive Shield', *Tikkun* 17, no. 4 (2002): 33–41.

Moore, John Norton, 'Law and National Security', *Foreign Affairs* 51, no. 2 (1973): 408–21.

Morehouse, David, 'A Year in Vietnam', *The Reporter* 26, Special History edition (1999): 126–29.

Morrissey, John, 'Liberal Lawfare and Biopolitics: US Juridical Warfare in the War on Terror', *Geopolitics* 16, no. 2 (2011): 280–305.

Morrissey, John, 'Securitizing Instability: The US Military and Full Spectrum Operations', *Environment and Planning D: Society and Space* 33 (2015): 609–25.

Morrissey, John, *The Long War: CENTCOM, Grand Strategy, and Global Security* (Athens, GA: University of Georgia Press, 2017).

Moseley, T. Michael, 'Operation Iraqi Freedom: By the Numbers', Assessment and Analysis Division, US Air Force Central Command (AFCENT), 30 April 2003 (on file with author).

Moyn, Samuel, 'From Antiwar Politics to Antitorture Politics', in *Law and War*, ed., Austin Sarat, Lawrence Douglas, and Martha Merrill Umphrey, *The Amherst Series in Law, Jurisprudence, and Social Thought* (Stanford, CA: Stanford University Press, 2014), 154–97.

Moyn, Samuel, *The Last Utopia: Human Rights in History* (Cambridge, MA: Belknap Press of Harvard University Press, 2010).

Mulcahy, Kevin V., 'Rethinking Groupthink: Walt Rostow and the National Security Advisory Process in the Johnson Administration', *Presidential Studies Quarterly* 25, no. 2 (1995): 237–50.

Mulrine, Anna, 'Warheads on Foreheads', *Air Force Magazine* 91, no. 10 (2008): 44–7.

Murray, Scott F., 'The Moral and Ethical Implications of Precision-Guided Munitions', DTIC Document, 2007, http://uploads.worldlibrary.net/uploads/pdf/20121012233256moral_and_ethical_implications_pdf.pdf, accessed 1 July 2020.

Myrow, Stephen A., 'Waging War on the Advice of Counsel: The Role of Operational Law in the Gulf War', *United States Air Force Academy Journal of Legal Studies* 7 (1996): 131–57.

Nelson, Craig, 'Goldstone Report Keeps Israel on Tenterhooks—The National', *The National*, 29 January 2010, http://www.thenational.ae/news/world/middle-east/goldstone-report-keeps-israel-on-tenterhooks, accessed 4 September 2013.

Newton, Michael A., 'Illustrating Illegitimate Lawfare', *Case Western Reserve Journal of International Law* 43, no. 1 (2010): 255–78.

Nir, Ori, 'Bush Seeks Israeli Advice on "Targeted Killings"', *The Electronic Intifada/The Forward*, 7 February 2003, http://electronicintifada.net/content/bush-seeks-israeli-advice-targeted-killings/4391, accessed 5 November 2013.

Nisa, Richard, 'Capturing Humanitarian War: The Collusion of Violence and Care in US-Managed Military Detention', *Environment and Planning A* 47, no. 11 (2015): 2276–91.

Nixon, Rob, *Slow Violence and the Environmentalism of the Poor* (Cambridge, MA: Harvard University Press, 2011).

Nordin, Astrid H. M. and Dan Öberg, 'Targeting the Ontology of War: From Clausewitz to Baudrillard': *Millennium*, 43, no. 2 (2014): 392–410.

North Atlantic Treaty Organisation (NATO), 'Allied Joint Doctrine for Joint Targeting', NATO Standardisation Office, April 2016, https://assets.publishing.service.gov.uk/government/uploads/system/uploads/attachment_data/file/628215/20160505-nato_targeting_ajp_3_9.pdf, accessed 24 October 2019.

North Atlantic Treaty Organization (NATO), 'Legal Gazette: Special Issue for Nato School, Oberammergau, Germany', *Nato Legal Gazette* 36 (2016): 1–167.

Oakford, Samuel, 'The U.S. Military Can't Keep Track of Which Missions It's Fueling in Yemen War', *The Intercept*, 18 September 2017, https://theintercept.com/2017/09/18/the-u-s-military-cant-keep-track-of-which-missions-its-fueling-in-yemen-war/, accessed 7 November 2019.

O'Connor, Jennifer, 'Applying the Law of Targeting to the Modern Battlefield', New York University School of Law, 28 November 2016, http://www.defense.gov/Portals/1/Documents/pubs/Applying-the-Law-of-Targeting-to-the-Modern-Battlefield.pdf, accessed 14 December 2016.

Office of the Legal Adviser to the Ministry of Foreign Affairs, 'Israel and the International Criminal Court', 30 June 2002, https://mfa.gov.il/MFA/MFA-Archive/2002/Pages/Israel%20and%20the%20International%20Criminal%20Court.aspx, accessed 18 December 2019.

Ohlin, Jens David, *The Assault on International Law* (New York, NY: Oxford University Press, 2015).

Ohlin, Jens David, Larry May, and Claire Finkelstein, eds, *Weighing Lives in War* (New York, NY; Oxford: Oxford University Press, 2017).

Oliver, Kendrick, *The My Lai Massacre in American History and Memory* (Manchester: Manchester University Press, 2006).

O'Malley, Derek, and Andrew Hill, 'The A-10, the F-35, and the Future of Close Air Support', War on the Rocks, 27 May 2015, http://warontherocks.com/2015/05/the-a-10-the-f-35-and-the-future-of-close-air-support-part-i/, accessed 9 June 2015.

Open Society Justice Initiative and Amrit Singh, 'Death by Drone: Civilian Harm Caused by U.S. Targeted Killings in Yemen', New York, NY: Open Society Justice Initiative, April 2015, http://www.opensocietyfoundations.org/reports/death-drone, accessed 15 April 2015.

Ophir, Adi, 'The Politics of Catastrophization', http://humanities1.tau.ac.il/segel/adiophir/files/2015/08/Ophir-The-Politics-of-Catastrophizaton.pdf, accessed 30 June 2020.

Orbarn, Brian, 'Time-Sensitive Targeting Adds Combat Flexibility', US Air Force, 18 April 2003, http://www.af.mil/News/ArticleDisplay/tabid/223/Article/139411/time-sensitive-targeting-adds-combat-flexibility.aspx, accessed 13 January 2017.

Orford, Anne, *International Law and Its Others* (Cambridge: Cambridge University Press, 2006).

Owens, Patricia, 'Accidents Don't Just Happen: The Liberal Politics of High-Technology "Humanitarian" War', *Millennium - Journal of International Studies* 32, no. 3 (2003): 595–616.

Padmanabhan, Vijay M., 'Legacy of 9/11: Continuing the Humanization of Humanitarian Law', *Yearbook of International Humanitarian Law* 14 (2011): 419–30.

Pappé, Ilan, *The Forgotten Palestinians: A History of the Palestinians in Israel* (New Haven, CT: Yale University Press, 2011).

Parks, W. Hays, 'The Law of War Adviser', *JAG Journal* 31, no. 1 (1980): 1–52.

Parks, W. Hays, 'Rolling Thunder and the Law of War', *Air University Review* 33, no. 2 (1982): 2–23.

Parks, W. Hays, 'Linebacker and the Law of War', *Air University Review* 34, no. 2 (1983): 2–30.

Parks, W. Hays, 'Teaching the Law of War', *The Army Lawyer* 174 (1987): 4–10.

Parks, W. Hays, 'The Gulf War: A Practitioner's View', *Dickinson Journal of International Law* 10, no. 3 (1992): 393–423.

Parks, W. Hays, 'Deadly Force is Authorized', *U.S. Naval Institute Proceedings* 127, no. 1 (2001): 32–7.

Parks, W. Hays, 'Part IX of the ICRC "Direct Participation in Hostilities" Study: No Mandate, No Expertise, and Legally Incorrect', *New York University Journal of International Law and Politics* 42, no. 3 (2010): 769–830.

Parks, W. Hays, 'Rules of Engagement: No More Vietnams', in *The U.S. Naval Institute on Vietnam: A Retrospective*, ed. Thomas Cutler (Annapolis, MD: Naval Institute Press, 2016), 150–5

Parks, Lisa, 'Drones, Vertical Mediation, and the Targeted Class', *Feminist Studies* 42, no. 1 (2016): 227–35.

Peers, William Raymond, *Report of the Department of the Army Review of the Preliminary Investigations into the My Lai Incident: The Report of the Investigation*, vol. 1, The Department of the Army, 1974, http://www.loc.gov/rr/frd/Military_Law/Peers_inquiry.html, accessed 31 July 2015.

Pendall, David W., 'Persistent Surveillance and Its Implications for the Common Operating Picture', *Military Review* 85, no. 6 (2005): 41–50.

Perugini, Nicola and Neve Gordon, *The Human Right to Dominate* (New York, NY: Oxford University Press, 2015).

Pietrucha, Mike, 'The Five-Ring Circus: How Airpower Enthusiasts Forgot About Interdiction', *War on the Rocks* (blog), 29 September 2015, https://warontherocks.com/

2015/09/the-five-ring-circus-how-airpower-enthusiasts-forgot-about-interdiction/, accessed 5 January 2017.

Pirnie, Bruce R., Alan Vick, Adam Grissom, Karl P. Mueller, and David T. Orletsky, *Beyond Close Air Support: Forging a New Air Ground Partnership* (Santa Monica, CA: Rand Publishing, 2005).

Pitzul, Jerry S. T., 'Operational Law and the Legal Professional: A Canadian Perspective Speeches and Comments', *Air Force Law Review* 51 (2001): 311–21.

Porter, Patrick, 'The Divine Victory: Hizballa, Israel and the 2006 "July War"', in *Military Orientalism: Eastern War Through Western Eyes* (New York, NY: Columbia University Press, 2009), 171–90

Powell, Colin L., and Joseph E. Persico, *My American Journey* 1st edition (New York, NY: Ballantine Books, 2003).

Prescott, Jody, 'Tactical Implementation of Rules of Engagement in a Multinational Force Reality', in *U.S. Military Operations: Law, Policy, and Practice*, ed. Geoffrey S. Corn, Rachel E. VanLandingham, and Shane R. Reeves (Oxford: Oxford University Press, 2015), 249–74.

Priest, Dana, and William M. Arkin, *Top Secret America: The Rise of the New American Security State* (New York, NY; Boston, MA; London: Little, Brown and Company, 2011).

Prugh, George Shipley, *Law at War, Vietnam: 1964-1973* (Washington, DC: Department of the Army, 1975).

Puar, Jasbir K., *The Right to Maim: Debility, Capacity, Disability* (Durham, NC: Duke University Press, 2017).

Public Committee Against Torture in Israel (PCATI), and LAW—Society for the Protection of Human Rights and the Environment. Assassination Policy Petition, No. BGZ/02 (20 January 2002), http://stoptorture.org.il/wp-content/uploads/2015/10/no-second-thoughts_ENG_WEB-2009.pdf, accessed 15 October 2014.

Public Committee Against Torture in Israel (PCATI), 'No Second Thoughts: The Changes in the Israeli Defense Forces' Combat Doctrine in Light of "Operation Cast Lead"' (Jerusalem: PCATI, November 2009), http://stoptorture.org.il/wp-content/uploads/2015/10/no-second-thoughts_ENG_WEB-2009.pdf, accessed 1 July 2020.

Putney, Diane T., *Airpower Advantage: Planning the Gulf Air Campaign, 1989-1991* (Honolulu: University Press of the Pacific, 2006).

Ravid, Barak, 'IAF Strike Followed Months of Planning', *Haaretz*, 28 December 2008, http://www.haaretz.com/print-edition/news/iaf-strike-followed-months-of-planning-1.260363, accessed 15 October 2014.

Raviv, Dan, and Yossi Melman, *Every Spy a Prince: The Complete History of Israel's Intelligence Community* (Boston, MA: Houghton Mifflin, 1990).

Reagan, Ronald, 'Agora: The U.S. Decision Not to Ratify Protocol I to the Geneva Conventions on the Protection of War Victims', *American Journal of International Law* 81, no. 4 (1987): 910–12.

Reinhart, Tanya, *Israel/Palestine: How to End the War of 1948*, 2nd edition (New York, NY: Seven Stories Press, 2004).

Reisner, Daniel, 'International Law and Military Operations in Practice—III—Jerusalem Center For Public Affairs', Jerusalem Center For Public Affairs, 18 June 2009, http://jcpa.org/article/international-law-and-military-operations-in-practice-iii/, accessed 11 November 2013.

Reisner, Daniel, 'Reflections on the UN Commission of Inquiry Gaza Report, Part III: The Clash Between Human Rights and Law of War Specialists', *Lawfare* (blog), 1 September 2015, https://www.lawfareblog.com/reflections-un-commission-inquiry-gaza-report-part-iii-clash-between-human-rights-and-law-war, accessed 24 September 2016.

Reprieve US, 'You Never Die Twice: Multiple Kills in the US Drone Program', Reprieve, 24 November 2014, https://reprieve.org/uploads2633263381312014_11_24_pub_you_never_die_twice_-_multiple_kills_in_the_us_drone_program-pdf/, accessed 8 September 2019.

Reynolds, Richard T., *Heart of the Storm, The Genesis of the Air Campaign Against Iraq* (Maxwell Air Force Base, AL: Air University Press, 1995), https://apps.dtic.mil/dtic/tr/fulltext/u2/a292091.pdf, accessed 28 June 2020.

Richards, David, *Taking Command* (London: Headline, 2014).

Robinson, Shira, *Citizen Strangers: Palestinians and the Birth of Israel's Liberal Settler State* (Stanford, CA: Stanford University Press, 2013).

Rubin, Alissa J., 'Karzai to Ban His Forces to Request Foreign Airstrikes', *The New York Times*, 16 February 2013, http://www.nytimes.com/2013/02/17/world/asia/karzai-to-forbid-his-forces-from-requesting-foreign-airstrikes.html, accessed 3 April 2017.

Ryan, Maria, *Full Spectrum Dominance: Irregular Warfare and the War on Terror* (Stanford, CA: Stanford University Press, 2019).

Sabbagh, Dan and Bethan McKernan, 'UK Arms Sales to Saudi Arabia Unlawful, Court of Appeal Declares', *The Guardian*, 20 June 2019, sec. Law, https://www.theguardian.com/law/2019/jun/20/uk-arms-sales-to-saudi-arabia-for-use-in-yemen-declared-unlawful, accessed 7 November 2019.

Sanders, Rebecca, 'Legal Frontiers: Targeted Killing at the Borders of War', *Journal of Human Rights* 13, no. 4 (2014): 512–36.

Sanders, Rebecca, *Plausible Legality: Legal Culture and Political Imperative in the Global War on Terror* (Oxford; New York, NY: Oxford University Press, 2018).

Sandvik, Kristin Bergtora, 'Regulating War in the Shadow of Law: Toward a Re-Articulation of ROE', *Journal of Military Ethics* 13, no. 2 (2014): 118–36.

Sapsted, David, 'Hundreds of War Crimes Lawsuits Filed against Israelis', *The National*, 11 October 2009, http://www.thenational.ae/news/world/middle-east/hundreds-of-war-crimes-lawsuits-filed-against-israelis, accessed 9 November 2014.

Sarat, Austin and Nasser Hussain, *When Governments Break the Law* (New York, NY: New York University Press, 2010).

Sarat, Austin and Thomas Kearns, 'A Journey Through Forgetting: Toward a Jurisprudence of Violence', in *The Fate of Law*, ed. Austin Sarat and Thomas Kearns, *The Amherst Series in Law, Jurisprudence, and Social Thought* (Ann Arbor, MI: University of Michigan Press, 1991), 209–74.

Savage, Charlie, *Power Wars: Inside Obama's Post-9/11 Presidency* (New York, NY: Little, Brown and Company, 2015).

Scahill, Jeremy, 'The Dangerous US Game in Yemen', *The Nation*, 30 March 2011, http://www.thenation.com/article/dangerous-us-game-yemen/, accessed 29 September 2015.

Scahill, Jeremy, *Dirty Wars: The World Is a Battlefield* (London: Serpent's Tail, 2013).

Scarry, Elaine, 'Injury and the Structure of War', *Representations* 10 (1985): 1–51.

Schabas, William A., 'Gaza, Goldstone, and Lawfare', *Case Western Reserve Journal of International Law* 43, no. 1 (2010): 307–12.

Scharre, Paul, Jacquelyn Schneider, and Julia Macdonald, 'Why Drones Are Still the Future of War', 15 February 2018, https://www.foreignaffairs.com/articles/united-states/2018-02-15/why-drones-are-still-future-war, accessed 1 March 2020.

Schindler, Dietrich, 'Human Rights and Humanitarian Law', *American University Law Review* 31, no. 4 (1981): 935–43.

Schmitt, Eric, 'U.S. Caution in Strikes Gives ISIS an Edge, Many Iraqis Say', *The New York Times*, 26 May 2015, http://www.nytimes.com/2015/05/27/world/middleeast/with-isis-in-crosshairs-us-holds-back-to-protect-civilians.html, accessed 19 December 2016.

Schmitt, Michael, N., 'Deconstructing Direct Participation in Hostilities: The Constitutive Elements', *New York University Journal of International Law and Politics* 42, no. 3 (2010): 697–739.

Schmitt, Michael, N., 'Wired Warfare: Computer Network Attack and Jus in Bello', *International Review of the Red Cross* 84, no. 846 (2002): 365–99.

Schmitt, Michael N., ed., *Tallinn Manual 2.0 on the International Law Applicable to Cyber Operations*, 2nd edition (Cambridge; New York, NY: Cambridge University Press, 2017).

Schrader, Stuart, 'Lyndon Johnson's Tuesday Lunch, Hold the Counterinsurgency', 31 October 2012, http://stuartschrader.com/lyndon-johnsons-tuesday-lunch-hold-counterinsurgency, accessed 2 June 2015.

Schwarz, Elke, 'Prescription Drones: On the Techno-Biopolitical Regimes of Contemporary "Ethical Killing"', *Security Dialogue* 47, no. 1 (2016): 59–75.

Schwarzkopf, H. Norman, *It Doesn't Take a Hero: General H. Norman Schwarzkopf, the Autobiography* (New York, NY: Bantam Books, 1992).

Sengupta, Somini, 'Russian Foreign Minister Defends Airstrikes in Syria', *The New York Times*, 1 October 2015, sec. World, https://www.nytimes.com/2015/10/02/world/europe/russia-airstrikes-syria-assad.html, accessed 11 March 2020.

Shachtman, Noah, 'How the Afghanistan Air War Got Stuck in the Sky', *Wired*, 8 December 2009, https://www.wired.com/2009/12/ff-end-air-war/, accessed 2 March 2020.

Shachtman, Noah, 'The Phrase That's Screwing Up the Afghan Air War', *Wired*, 9 December 2009, https://www.wired.com/2009/12/the-phrase-thats-screwing-up-the-afghan-air-war/, accessed 29 February 2020.

Shalev, Anat, 'Dershowitz: Jews Initiate Legal Terror against Israel', *Ynetnews*, 5 November 2010, http://www.ynetnews.com/articles/0,7340,L-3888025,00.html, accessed 6 July 2017.

Shamir, Ronen, '"Landmark Cases" and the Reproduction of Legitimacy: The Case of Israel's High Court of Justice', *Law & Society Review* 24, no. 3 (1990): 781–806.

Shany, Yuval, 'The Israeli Unlawful Combatants Law: Old Wine in a New Bottle?' *The Hebrew University of Jerusalem Faculty of Law Research Paper* No. 03-12 (2012), 1–23.

Shaw, Ian G. R., *Predator Empire: Drone Warfare and Full Spectrum Dominance* (Minneapolis: University of Minnesota Press, 2016).

Shaw, M., *The New Western Way of War: Risk-Transfer War and Its Crisis in Iraq* (Cambridge; Malden, MA: Polity, 2005).

Shoker, Sarah, 'Military-Age Males in U.S Counterinsurgency and Drone Warfare', PhD thesis, McMaster University, 2018, https://macsphere.mcmaster.ca/handle/11375/24294, accessed 11 February 2020.

Shue, Henry, 'Force Protection, Military Advantage, and "Constant Care" for Civilians', in *The American Way of Bombing: Changing Ethical and Legal Norms, from Flying Fortresses to Drones*, ed. Matthew Evangelista and Henry Shue (Ithaca, NY; London: Cornell University Press, 2014), 145–57.

Shue, Henry, 'Targeting Civilian Infrastructure with Smart Bombs: The New Permissiveness', *Philosophy & Public Policy Quarterly* 30, no. 3/4 (2010): 2–8.

Silliman, Scott L., 'JAG Goes to War: The Desert Shield Deployment', *Air Force Law Review* 37 (1994): 85–104.

Singer, P. W., *Corporate Warriors: The Rise of the Privatized Military Industry*, Cornell paperbacks edition (Ithaca, NY: Cornell University Press, 2004).

Small, Leonard, 'Roundtable on Targeted Killing: Lawyering and Targeted Killing', *Jadaliyya*, 7 March 2012, http://www.jadaliyya.com/pages/index/4567/roundtable-on-targeted-killing_lawyering-and-targeted-killing, accessed 3 May 2012.

Smith, Michael, 'States That Come and Go: Mapping the Geolegalities of the Afghanistan Intervention', in *The Expanding Spaces of Law: A Timely Legal Geography*, ed., Irus Braverman et al. (Stanford, CA: Stanford Law Books, 2014), 142–66.

Smith, Thomas W., 'The New Law of War: Legitimizing Hi-Tech and Infrastructural Violence', *International Studies Quarterly* 46, no. 3 (2002): 355–74.

Snowden, Edward, *Permanent Record*, Main Market edition (London: Macmillan, 2019).

Snukal, Katia and Emily Gilbert, 'War, Law, Jurisdiction, and Juridical Othering: Private Military Security Contractors and the Nisour Square Massacre', *Environment and Planning D: Society and Space* 33, no. 4 (2015): 660–75.

Sofaer, Abraham D., 'The Sixth Annual Waldemar A. Solf Lecture in International Law: Terrorism, the Law, and the National Defense', *Military Law Review* 126 (1989): 89–123.

Solis, Gary, D., *The Law of Armed Conflict: International Humanitarian Law in War*, 1st edition (Cambridge: Cambridge University Press, 2010).

South, Todd, 'The Future Battlefield: Army, Marines Prepare for "Massive" Fight in Megacities', *Military Times*, 8 March 2018, https://www.militarytimes.com/news/your-army/2018/03/06/the-future-battlefield-army-marines-prepare-for-massive-fight-in-megacities/, accessed 5 March 2020.

Sowers, Jeannie L., Erika Weinthal, and Neda Zawahri, 'Targeting Environmental Infrastructures, International Law, and Civilians in the New Middle Eastern Wars', *Security Dialogue* 48, no. 5 (2017): 410–30.

Spedero, Paul C., 'Time Sensitive Targeting-The Operational Commander's Role', Naval War College, 2004, https://apps.dtic.mil/sti/pdfs/ADA422747.pdf, accessed 12 January 2017.

Spiegel Staff, 'Obama's Lists: A Dubious History of Targeted Killings in Afghanistan', Der Spiegel, 28 December 2014, http://www.spiegel.de/international/world/secret-docs-reveal-dubious-details-of-targeted-killings-in-afghanistan-a-1010358.html, accessed 13 December 2016.

Stafford, W. A., 'How to Keep Military Personnel from Going to Jail for Doing the Right Thing: Jurisdiction, ROE & the Rules of Deadly Force', *The Army Lawyer*, November (2000): 1–25.

Starr, Barbara, 'First on CNN: US Bombs "millions" in ISIS Currency Stock—CNNPolitics', *CNN*, 13 January 2016, sec. Politics. https://edition.cnn.com/2016/01/11/politics/us-bombs-millions-isis-currency-supply/, accessed 13 February 2020.

Stein, Yael, 'By Any Name Illegal and Immoral', *Ethics & International Affairs* 17, no. 1 (2003): 127–37.

Stout, Jay, 'Close Air Support Using Armed UAVs?' *The Naval Institute: Proceedings*, http://www.military.com/NewContent/1,13190,NI_0705_Air-P1,00.html, accessed 18 January 2017.

Stratfor, 'For Israel, It's Open Skies Over Syria and Iraq', Stratfor, 14 October 2019, https://worldview.stratfor.com/article/israel-its-open-skies-over-syria-and-iraq-iran-hezbollah-airstrike, accessed 19 November 2019.

Suchman, Lucy, 'Situational Awareness: Deadly Bioconvergence at the Boundaries of Bodies and Machines', *MediaTropes* 5, no. 1 (2015): 1–24.

Sultany, Nimer, 'The Legacy of Justice Aharon Barak: A Critical Review', *Harvard International Law Journal Online* 48 (2007): 83–92, https://ssrn.com/abstract=2217060, accessed 2 October 2014.

Szuba, Jared, 'Slow Admissions of Civilian Harm in Somalia Raise Questions about US Transparency', *The Defense Post*, 24 February 2020, sec. Africa, https://thedefensepost.com/2020/02/24/somalia-us-africom-civilian-casualty-reports/, accessed 7 March 2020.

Tate, Simon, *A Special Relationship?: British Foreign Policy in the Era of American Hegemony* (Manchester: Manchester University Press, 2012).

Taub, Ben, 'Does Anyone in Syria Fear International Law?' The New Yorker, 31 August 2016, https://www.newyorker.com/news/news-desk/does-anyone-in-syria-fear-international-law, accessed 7 September 2017.

Tawil-Souri, Helga, 'Digital Occupation: Gaza's High-Tech Enclosure', *Journal of Palestine Studies* 41, no. 2 (2012): 27–43.

Tawil-Souri, Helga, 'The Technological End Between the "Inside" of Gaza and the "Outside" of Gaza', 7iber حبر - شو قصتك؟, 29 September 2014, http://www.7iber.com/2014/09/the-technological-end-between-the-inside-of-gaza-and-the-outside-of-gaza, accessed 9 November 2014.

Terdiman, Richard, trans., 'Translator's Introduction. The Force of Law: Toward a Sociology of the Juridical Field, Pierre Bourdieu', *Hastings Law Journal* 38, no. 5 (1987): 805–13.

Theiss, Evelyn, 'My Lai Photographer Ron Haeberle Admits He Destroyed Pictures of Soldiers in the Act of Killing', *Cleveland.Com* (blog), http://blog.cleveland.com/pdextra/2009/11/post_25.html, accessed 6 August 2015.

Tomuschat, Christian, 'Human Rights and International Humanitarian Law', *European Journal of International Law* 21, no. 1 (2010): 15–23.

Townsend, Stephen J., 'Reports of Civilian Casualties in the War Against ISIS Are Vastly Inflated', *Foreign Policy* (blog), 15 September 2017, https://foreignpolicy.com/2017/09/15/reports-of-civilian-casualties-from-coalition-strikes-on-isis-are-vastly-inflated-lt-gen-townsend-cjtf-oir/, accessed 7 March 2020.

Tracy, Jonathan, 'Compensating Civilian Casualties: "I Am Sorry for Your Loss and I Wish You Well in a Free Iraq"', Center for Civilians in Conflict, 30 May 2008, https://civiliansinconflict.org/publications/policy/compensating-civilian-casualties-sorry-loss-wish-well-free-iraq/, accessed 13 July 2019.

Trenta, Luca, 'The Obama Administration's Conceptual Change: Imminence and the Legitimation of Targeted Killings', *European Journal of International Security* 3, no. 1 (2018): 69–93.

Tuft, Ben, 'Iraq's "most-Wanted" Playing Cards Go on Display at the Pentagon', *The Independent*, 18 October 2014, http://www.independent.co.uk/news/world/americas/iraqs-most-wanted-playing-cards-go-on-display-at-the-pentagon-9803525.html, accessed 13 December 2016.

Turse, Nick, 'America's Lethal Profiling of Afghan Men', *The Nation*, 18 September 2013, https://www.thenation.com/article/archive/americas-lethal-profiling-afghan-men/, accessed 11 February 2020.

Turse, Nick, *Kill Anything That Moves: The Real American War in Vietnam* (New York, NY: Metropolitan Books/Henry Holt and Co., 2013).

Turse, Nick, 'New Data Shows the U.S. Military Is Severely Undercounting Civilian Casualties in Somalia', *The Intercept* (blog), 25 February 2020, https://theintercept.com/2020/02/25/africom-airstrikes-somalia/, accessed 7 March 2020.

United Nations Assistance Mission in Afghanistan, 'Afghanistan: Protection of Civilians in Armed Conflict, Annual Report 2015', United Nations, February 2016, https://unama.unmissions.org/sites/default/files/poc_annual_report_2015_final_14_feb_2016.pdf, accessed 24 January 2017.

United Nations Economic and Social Commission for Western Asia, 'Israeli Practices towards the Palestinian People and the Question of Apartheid', Beirut: United Nations, 2017, https://www.unescwa.org/news/escwa-launches-report-israeli-practices-towards-palestinian-people-and-question-apartheid, accessed 26 June 2017.

United Nations Human Rights Council, 'Concerns Related to Adherence to International Human Rights and International Humanitarian Law in the Context of the Escalation between the State of Israel, the de Facto Authorities in Gaza and Palestinian Armed Groups in Gaza That Occurred from 14 to 21 November 2012', Report of the United Nations High Commissioner for Human Rights on the Implementation of Human Rights Council Resolutions S-9/1 and S-12/1, 6 March 2013, https://www.ohchr.org/Documents/HRBodies/HRCouncil/RegularSession/Session22/A.HRC.22.35.Add.1_AV.pdf, accessed 30 December 2019.

United Nations Human Rights Council, 'Report of the Detailed Findings of the Independent Commission of Inquiry Established Pursuant to Human Rights Council Resolution S-21/1', United Nations Human Rights Council, 24 June 2015, https://www.ohchr.org/en/hrbodies/hrc/coigazaconflict/pages/reportcoigaza.aspx, accessed 30 December 2019.

United Nations Human Rights Council, 'Report of the United Nations Fact Finding Mission on the Gaza Conflict', 2009, http://www2.ohchr.org/english/bodies/hrcouncil/docs/12session/A-HRC-12-48.pdf, accessed 10 September 2013.

United Nations Security Council, Resolution 679 (30 November 1990), https://digitallibrary.un.org/record/102678?ln=en, accessed 28 June 2020.

United States Air Force, 'Air Force Doctrine Document 3-60, Targeting', US Air Force LeMay Center for Doctrine Development, 8 June 2006 [updated 28 July 2011], https://fas.org/irp/doddir/usaf/afdd3-60.pdf, accessed 13 December 2016.

United States Air Force, 'Air Force Doctrine Document 1-04, Legal Support to Operations', US Air Force LeMay Center for Doctrine Development, 4 March 2012, https://fas.org/irp/doddir/usaf/afdd1-04.pdf, accessed 28 January 2016.

United States Air Force, 'Air Force Doctrine Annex 3-60 Targeting', US Air Force LeMay Center for Doctrine Development, 10 January 2014, https://doctrine.af.mil/DTM/dtmtargeting.htm, accessed 17 December 2016.

United States Air Force, 'Airpower Summaries: 31 December 2019', https://www.afcent.af.mil/About/Airpower-Summaries/, accessed 16 June 2020.

United States Air Force, 'United States Air Force Instruction 13-1AOC, Volume 3: Operational Procedures—Air Operations Center', United States Air Force, 2 November 2011, http://static.e-publishing.af.mil/production/1/af_a3_5/publication/afi13-1aocv3/afi13-1aocv3.pdf, accessed 17 December 2016.

United States Air Force, 'United States Air Force Instruction 51-108: The Judge Advocate General's Corps Structure, Deployment, and Operational Support', United States Air Force, 9 October 2014, http://static.e-publishing.af.mil/production/1/af_ja/publication/afi51-108/afi51-108.pdf, accessed 15 December 2015.

United States Air Forces Central Command, 'Combined Air Operations Center (CAOC)', 6 February 2011, http://www.afcent.af.mil/About/FactSheets/Display/tabid/4822/Article/217803/combined-air-operations-center-caoc.aspx, accessed 15 December 2016.

United States Air Forces Central Command Public Affairs, '2004-2011 Combined Forces Air Component Commander Airpower Statistics', archived by Alexa O'Brian, https://alexaobrien.com/afcent-cfacc-airpower-summaries-and-statistics, accessed 16 June 2020.

United States Air Force Judge Advocate General's School, 'Air Force Operations and the Law', Maxwell Air Force Base, AL: US Air Force, 2014, http://www.afjag.af.mil/Portals/77/documents/AFD-100510-059.pdf, accessed 13 February 2014.

United States Air Force, Twelfth Air Force, 'Chapter 9 Judge Advocate', Air Operations Center (AOC) Standard Operating Procedure (SOP) Twelfth Air Force (12AF) Air Force Forces (AFFOR), n.d. (document no longer available online; on file with author).

United States Central Command (CENTCOM), 'AR 15-6 Investigation, 21 February 2010 U.S. Air-to-Ground Engagement in the Vicinity of Shahidi Hassas, Uruzgan District, Afghanistan', Kabul, Afghanistan: United States Forces—Afghanistan, 21 May 2010, https://archive.org/details/dod_centcom_drone_uruzgan_foia/page/n3, accessed 20 January 2020.

United States Department of Defense, 'Department of Defense Directive: "DoD Law of War Program"', 10 July 1979, http://handle.dtic.mil/100.2/ADA272470, accessed 20 April 2020.

United States Department of Defense, 'Conduct of the Persian Gulf War: Final Report to Congress' Washington, DC: United States Department of Defense, 1992, 612, https://www.google.com/url?sa=t&rct=j&q=&esrc=s&source=web&cd=&cad=rja&uact=8&ved=2ahUKEwiRy7H9_qPqAhVOTRUIHXL3BCIQFjABegQIARAB&url=https%3A%2F%2Fapps.dtic.mil%2Fdtic%2Ftr%2Ffulltext%2Fu2%2Fa249445.pdf&usg=AOvVaw19zIQ0RXtrfYzfu9yAIOA4, accessed 28 June 2020.

United States Department of Defense, 'The National Defense Strategy of the United States of America', Washington, DC: United States Department of Defense, 2005, https://history.defense.gov/Historical-Sources/National-Defense-Strategy/, accessed 30 December 2013.

United States Department of Defense General Counsel Working Group, 'Working Group Report—Detainee Interrogations in the Global War on Terrorism: Assessment of Legal, Historical, Policy, and Operational Considerations', 4 April 2003, https://en.wikisource.org/wiki/Working_Group_Report_on_Detainee_Interrogations, accessed 5 June 2015.

United States Joint Chiefs of Staff, 'Chairman of the Joint Chiefs of Staff Instruction 3160.01A No Strike Collateral Damage Method', 13 February 2009, https://www.aclu.org/files/dronefoia/dod/drone_dod_3160_01.pdf, accessed 14 December 2016.

United States Joint Chiefs of Staff, 'Joint Doctrine for Military Operations Other Than War', Washington, DC: Joint Chiefs of Staff, 16 June 1995, http://www.bits.de/NRANEU/others/jp-doctrine/jp3_07.pdf, accessed 3 January 2017.

United States Joint Chiefs of Staff, 'Joint Special Operations Task Force Operations', Washington, DC: Joint Chiefs of Staff, 26 April 2007, https://fas.org/irp/doddir/dod/jp3_05_01.pdf, accessed 24 November 2019.

United States Joint Chiefs of Staff, 'Joint Targeting', Joint Publication 3-60, Washington, DC, 31 January 2013, cfr.org/.../Joint_Chiefs_of_Staff-Joint_Targeting_31_January_2013.pdf accessed 24 January 2017.

United States Joint Chiefs of Staff, 'Joint Intelligence', Washington, DC: Joint Chiefs of Staff, 22 October 2013, https://www.jcs.mil/Portals/36/Documents/Doctrine/pubs/jp2_0.pdf, accessed 14 December 2015.

United States Joint Chiefs of Staff, 'Close Air Support', Joint Publication 3-09.3, Washington, DC: Joint Chiefs of Staff, 25 November 2014, http://fas.org/irp/doddir/dod/jp3_09_3.pdf, accessed 10 November 2014.

United States Joint Chiefs of Staff, 'Department of Defense Dictionary of Military and Associated Terms', Washington, DC: Joint Chiefs of Staff, 16 February 2016, http://www.dtic.mil/doctrine/new_pubs/jp1_02.pdf, accessed 11 January 2017.

United States Joint Chiefs of Staff, 'Legal Support to Military Operations', Washington, DC: Joint Chiefs of Staff, 2 August 2016, https://www.jcs.mil/Portals/36/Documents/Doctrine/pubs/jp1_04.pdf, accessed 28 January 2016.

United States Joint Chiefs of Staff, 'Stability', Washington, DC: Joint Chiefs of Staff, 3 August 2016, http://www.dtic.mil/doctrine/new_pubs/jp3_07.pdf, accessed 3 January 2017.

United States Joint Chiefs of Staff, 'Joint Air Operations', Washington, DC: Joint Chiefs of Staff, 25 July 2019, https://www.jcs.mil/Portals/36/Documents/Doctrine/pubs/jp3_30.pdf, accessed 5 February 2020.

United States Joint Chiefs of Staff, 'Joint Doctrine for Targeting', Washington, DC: Joint Chiefs of Staff, 17 January 2002, https://www.bits.de/NRANEU/others/jp-doctrine/jp3_60%2802%29.pdf, accessed 24 June 2020.

United States Joint Chiefs of Staff and National Defense University, 'Executive Summary: Civilian Casualty (CIVCAS) Review', 17 April 2018, https://www.justsecurity.org/wp-content/uploads/2019/02/Civ-Cas-Study-Redacted-just-security.pdf, accessed 7 March 2020.

United States Joint Targeting School, 'Joint Fires and Targeting Student Guide', Suffolk, Virginia & Dam Neck, VA: Joint Doctrine Analysis Division/Joint Targeting School, 5 March 2014, https://docplayer.net/47603976-Joint-fires-and-targeting-student-guide-5-march-2014.html, accessed 24 June 2020.

Urban, Nicole, 'Direct and Active Participation in Hostilities: The Unintended Consequences of the ICC's Decision in Lubanga', *EJIL: Talk!* (blog), 11 April 2012, https://www.ejiltalk.org/direct-and-active-participation-in-hostilities-the-unintended-consequences-of-the-iccs-decision-in-lubanga/, accessed 7 July 2017.

Valentine, Douglas, *The Phoenix Program* (New York, NY: Morrow, 1990).

Valverde, Mariana, 'Jurisdiction and Scale: Legal "Technicalities" as Resources for Theory', *Social & Legal Studies* 18, no. 2 (2009): 139–57.

Van Bergen, Jennifer and Douglas Valentine, 'The Dangerous World of Indefinite Detentions: Vietnam to Abu Ghraib', *Case Western Reserve Journal of International Law* 37, no. 2 (2006): 449–508.

Van Schaack, Beth, 'Targeting Tankers Under the Law of War (Part 1)', *Just Security*, 2 December 2015, https://www.justsecurity.org/28064/targeting-tankers-law-war-part-1/, accessed 16 November 2016.

Vanden Brook, Tom, 'New Rules Allow More Civilian Casualties in Air War against ISIL', *USA TODAY*, 19 April 2016, http://www.usatoday.com/story/news/politics/2016/04/19/new-rules-allow-more-civilian-casualties-air-war-against-isil/83190812/ accessed 7 November 2016.

Verini, James, 'How the Battle of Mosul Was Waged on WhatsApp', *The Guardian*, 28 September 2019, sec. World, https://www.theguardian.com/world/2019/sep/28/battle-of-mosul-waged-on-whatsapp-james-verini, accessed 7 March 2020.

Vick, Alan J. et al., 'Aerospace Operations in Urban Environments: Exploring New Concepts', Monograph Reports, RAND Corporation, 2002, https://www.rand.org/pubs/monograph_reports/MR1187.html, accessed 7 March 2020.

Walerstein, Jordan, 'Coping with Combat Claims: An Analysis of the Foreign Claims Act's Combat Exclusion', *Cardozo Journal Conflict Resolution* 11, no. 1 (2009): 319–51.

Walsh, Declan, 'Saudi Warplanes, Most Made in America, Still Bomb Civilians in Yemen', *The New York Times*, 22 May 2019, sec. World, https://www.nytimes.com/2019/05/22/world/middleeast/saudi-yemen-airstrikes-civilians.html, accessed 7 November 2019.

Walzer, Michael, 'The Risk Dilemma', *Philosophia* 44, no. 2 (2016): 289–93.

Warden, John A., *The Air Campaign: Planning for Combat* (Washington, DC: National Defense University Press, 1988).

Warnock, A. Timothy, *Short of War: Major USAF Contingency Operations, 1947-1997* (Maxwell Air Force Base, AL: Air University, 1983).

Warren, Marc L., 'Operational Law—A Concept Matures', *Military Law Review* 152 (1996): 33–74.

The Washington Post, 'Pentagon Briefing on Latest Military Strikes', *The Washington Post*, 9 October 2001, http://www.washingtonpost.com/wp-srv/nation/specials/attacked/transcripts/rumsfeld_100901.html, accessed 22 December 2016.

Watkin, Kenneth W., 'Coalition Operations: A Canadian Perspective', *International Law Studies* 84, no. 1 (2008): 251–62.

Watkins, Ali, 'This Is How The U.S. Decides How Many People It Can Kill In Syria', BuzzFeed, 28 February 2016, http://www.buzzfeed.com/alimwatkins/syria-civilian-casualties-policy, accessed 19 December 2016.

Watt, Nicholas, 'Ministers Drew up "kill" List of British Jihadis Fighting with Isis in Syria', *The Guardian*, 8 September 2015, sec. UK, https://www.theguardian.com/uk-news/2015/sep/08/ministers-list-several-british-jihadis-targets, accessed 6 November 2019.

Weitsman, Patricia, 'With a Little Help from Our Friends?: The Costs of Coalition Warfare', Origins: Current Events in Historical Perspective, January 2009, https://origins.osu.edu/article/little-help-our-friends-costs-coalition-warfare/page/0/0, accessed 4 November 2019.

Weizman, Eyal, *Hollow Land: Israel's Architecture of Occupation* (London; New York, NY: Verso, 2007).

Weizman, Eyal, 'Legislative Attack', *Theory, Culture & Society* 27, no. 6 (2010): 11–32.

Weizman, Eyal, *Lesser Evils: Scenes of Humanitarian Violence from Arendt to Gaza* (London: Verso, 2011).

Weizman, Eyal, *The Least of All Possible Evils: Humanitarian Violence from Arendt to Gaza* (London: Verso, 2012).

Weizman, Eyal, 'Gaza Attacks: Lethal Warnings', *Al Jazeera*, 14 July 2014, http://www.aljazeera.com/indepth/opinion/2014/07/gaza-attacks-lethal-warnings-201471316231260 4305.html, accessed 11 October 2014.

Werner, Wouter G., 'The Curious Career of Lawfare', *Case Western Reserve Journal of International Law* 43, no. 1 (2010): 61–72.

West, Bing, 'Urban Warfare, Then and Now', The Atlantic, 30 June 2017, https://www.theatlantic.com/international/archive/2017/06/urban-warfare-hue-mosul/532173/, accessed 5 March 2020.

The Lawfare Project, 'What Is Lawfare?', *The Lawfare Project* (blog), n.d., http://thelawfareproject.org/lawfare/what-is-lawfare-1/, accessed 22 September 2016.

Wikileaks, 'IDF MAG Mandelblit on IDF Investigations into Operation Cast Lead', Telegram (cable), American Embassy Tel Aviv to Secretary of State, Washington, DC, 23 February 2010, https://wikileaks.org/plusd/cables/10TELAVIV417_a.html accessed 7 January 2017.

Wilcox, Lauren, 'Embodying Algorithmic War: Gender, Race, and the Posthuman in Drone Warfare', *Security Dialogue* 48, no. 1 (2017): 11–28.

William Arkin, 'The Environmental Threat of Military Operations', in *Protection of the Environment During Armed Conflict*, ed. Richard J. Grunawalt, John E. King, and Ronald S. McClain, vol. 69 (Newport, RI: Naval War College, 1996), 116–35.

Williams, Brian Glyn, 'The CIA's Covert Predator Drone War in Pakistan, 2004–2010: The History of an Assassination Campaign', *Studies in Conflict & Terrorism* 33, no. 10 (2010): 871–92.

Wilson, Page, 'The Myth of International Humanitarian Law', *International Affairs* 93, no. 3 (2017): 563–79.

Winter, Matthew E., 'Finding the Law—The Values, Identity, and Function of the International Law Adviser', *Military Law Review* 128 (1990): 1–34.

Witman, Noam, 'State of the Art Technology Helps Minimize Harm to Civilians', *Israel Defense Force* (blog), 2 June 2013.

Witt, John Fabian, 'Form and Substance in the Law of Counterinsurgency Damages', *Loyola of Los Angeles Law Review* 41, no. 4 (2007): 1455–81.

Witt, John Fabian, *Lincoln's Code: The Laws of War in American History* (New York, NY: Free Press, 2013).

Wolfe, Major General J. P., 'More "Rolling Thunder"', *Air University Review* 33, no. 6 (1982): 82–3.

Wong, Dustin, 'Fears of civilian casualties grow as Ramadi push nears', *The Hill*, 24 December 2015, http://thehill.com/policy/defense/264159-us-warns-civilians-ahead-of-major-isis-battle, accessed 19 December 2016.

Wood, David, 'Holding Fire Over Afghanistan', *Air Force Magazine*, 1 January 2010, https://www.airforcemag.com/article/0110afghanistan/, accessed 24 January 2017.

Woods, Christopher, *Sudden Justice: America's Secret Drone Wars* (New York, NY: Oxford University Press, 2015).

Yadlin, Amos, 'Conclusion', in *In the Aftermath of Operation Pillar of Defense: The Gaza Strip November 2012*, ed. Shlomo Brom (Tel Aviv: The Institute for National Security Studies (INSS), December 2012), Memorandum No. 124, https://www.inss.org.il/publication/in-the-aftermath-of-operation-pillar-of-defense-the-gaza-strip-november-2012/, accessed 16 October 2014.

Yemen Data Project, 'Yemen Data Project', 29 February 2020, https://www.yemendataproject.org/, accessed 29 February 2020.

Yiftachel, Oren, *Ethnocracy: Land and Identity Politics in Israel/Palestine* (Philadelphia, PA: University of Pennsylvania Press, 2006).

Yiftachel, Oren, 'Indigenous Challenge to Legal Doctrine: Bedouin Land Rights in Israel/Palestine', presented at the Association of American Geographers Annual Meeting, New York, 26 February 2012.

Young, Marilyn, 'Introduction: Why Vietnam Still Matters', in *The War That Never Ends: New Perspectives on the Vietnam War*, ed. David L. Anderson and John Ernst, reprint edition (Lexington, KY: University Press of Kentucky, 2014), 1–11

Yuvaraj, Joshua, 'When Does a Child "Participate Actively in Hostilities" under the Rome Statute? Protecting Children from Use in Hostilities after Lubanga', *Utrecht Journal of International and European Law* 32, no. 83 (2016): 69–93.

Zarchin, Tomer, 'IDF: War Crime Charges Over Gaza Offensive Are "Legal Terror"', *Haaretz*, 19 February 2009, https://www.haaretz.com/1.5077434, accessed 18 December 2019.

Zehfuss, Maja, 'Targeting: Precision and the Production of Ethics', *European Journal of International Relations* 17, no. 3 (2011): 543–66.

Zehfuss, Maja, *War and the Politics of Ethics* (Oxford: Oxford University Press, 2018).

Zertal, Idith and Akiva Eldar, *Lords of the Land: The War over Israel's Settlements in the Occupied Territories, 1967-2007* (New York, NY: Nation Books, 2007).

Index

For the benefit of digital users, indexed terms that span two pages (e.g., 52–53) may, on occasion, appear on only one of those pages.

Figures are indicated by *f* following the page number

The manufacturer's authorised representative in the EU for product safety is Oxford University Press España S.A. of El Parque Empresarial San Fernando de Henares, Avenida de Castilla, 2 – 28830 Madrid (www.oup.es/en or product.safety@oup.com). OUP España S.A. also acts as importer into Spain of products made by the manufacturer.

Printed in the USA/Agawam, MA
April 9, 2026

903555.159